April 2016.

THE LION
AND THE LAMB

THE LION
AND THE LAMB

New Testament Essentials from
The Cradle, the Cross, and the Crown

ANDREAS J. KÖSTENBERGER
L. SCOTT KELLUM
CHARLES L. QUARLES

ACADEMIC
Nashville, Tennessee

ISBN: 978-1-4336-7708-3

Published by B&H Publishing Group
Nashville, Tennessee

Dewey Decimal Classification: 225.7
Subject Heading: BIBLE. N.T.—STUDY\JESUS CHRIST—HUMANITY\JESUS
CHRIST—DIVINITY

Printed in the United States of America
1 2 3 4 5 6 7 8 9 10 11 12 • 17 16 15 14 13 12
BP

Contents

Abbreviations vii
Preface xiii

PART ONE: INTRODUCTION 1
Chapter 1: The Nature and Scope of Scripture 2
Chapter 2: The Political and Religious Background of the New Testament 19

PART TWO: JESUS AND THE GOSPELS 37
Chapter 3: Introduction to Jesus and the Gospels 38
Chapter 4: The Gospel According to Matthew 53
Chapter 5: The Gospel According to Mark 76
Chapter 6: The Gospel According to Luke 87
Chapter 7: The Gospel According to John 105

PART THREE: THE EARLY CHURCH AND PAUL 121
Chapter 8: The Book of Acts 122
Chapter 9: Introduction to Paul and His Letters 138
Chapter 10: Paul's Letter to the Galatians 150
Chapter 11: Paul's Thessalonian Correspondence: 1–2 Thessalonians 162
Chapter 12: Paul's Corinthian Correspondence: 1–2 Corinthians 176
Chapter 13: Paul's Letter to the Romans 207
Chapter 14: The Prison Epistles: Philippians, Ephesians, Colossians,
    and Philemon 231
Chapter 15: The Pastoral Epistles: 1–2 Timothy, Titus 266

PART FOUR: THE GENERAL EPISTLES AND REVELATION 287
Chapter 16: The Letter to the Hebrews 288
Chapter 17: The Letter of James 309
Chapter 18: The Petrine Epistles (1–2 Peter) and the Letter of Jude 324
Chapter 19: The Johannine Epistles: 1–3 John 356
Chapter 20: The Book of Revelation 374

Glossary 397
Name Index 414
Subject Index 418
Scripture Index 422
Maps 447

Maps

Jewish Expansion Under the Hasmonean Dynasty 1

The Roman Empire in the Age of Augustus 2

The Division of Herod's Kingdom. 3

Palestine in the Time of Jesus 4

Jesus' Journeys from Galilee to Judea. 5

Herod's Temple 6

The Ministry of Jesus Beyond the Sea of Galilee 7

Jerusalem in the New Testament Period. 8

Expansion of the Early Church in Palestine. 9

The First Missionary Journey of Paul. 10

The Second Missionary Journey of Paul. 11

The Third Missionary Journey of Paul 12

Paul's Voyage to Rome. 13

Churches of the Revelation 14

The Expansion of Christianity in the Second and Third Centuries AD 15

Abbreviations

AB	Anchor Bible
AnBib	Analecta biblica
ABD	*Anchor Bible Dictionary*
ABRL	Anchor Bible Reference Library
ACCS	Ancient Christian Commentary on Scripture
AGJU	Arbeiten zur Geschichte des antiken Judentums und des Urchristentums
ANRW	*Aufstieg und Niedergang der römischen Welt*
ASNU	Acta seminarii neotestamentici upsaliensis
AUSSDDS	Andrews University Seminary Studies Doctoral Dissertation Series
AUSS	Andrews University Seminary Studies
BA	*Biblical Archaeologist*
BAR	*Biblical Archaeology Review*
BBC	Blackwell Bible Commentaries
BBR	*Bulletin for Biblical Research*
BDAG	Bauer, W., F. W. Danker, W. F. Arndt, and F. W. Gingrich, *Greek-English Lexicon of the New Testament and Other Early Christian Literature* (Chicago, 1961)
BECNT	Baker Exegetical Commentary on the New Testament
BETL	Bibliotheca ephemeridum theologicarum lovaniensium
BGBE	Beiträge zur Geschichte der biblischen Exegese
Bib	*Biblica*
BibInt	*Biblical Interpretation*
BJRL	*Bulletin of the John Rylands University Library of Manchester*
BNTC	Black's New Testament Commentaries
BR	*Biblical Research*
BSac	*Bibliotheca sacra*
BST	The Bible Speaks Today

BT	*The Bible Translator*
BTB	*Biblical Theology Bulletin*
BTNT	Biblical Theology of the New Testament
BWA(N)T	Beiträge zur Wissenschaft vom Alten (und Neuen) Testament
BZ	*Biblische Zeitschrift*
BZNW	Beihefte zur Zeitschrift für die neutestamentliche Wissenschaft
CBQ	*Catholic Biblical Quarterly*
CGTC	Cambridge Greek Testament Commentary
CJ	*Classical Journal*
ConBNT	Coniectanea biblica: New Testament Series
CRINT	Compendia rerum iudaicarum ad Novum Testamentum
CTJ	*Calvin Theological Journal*
CTR	*Criswell Theological Review*
EB	Echter Bibel
EBC	*The Expositor's Bible Commentary*
EBS	Encountering Biblical Studies
ECC	Eerdmans Critical Commentary
EDRL	*Encyclopedic Dictionary of Roman Law*
EKKNT	Evangelisch-katholischer Kommentar zum Neuen Testament
EMS	Evangelical Missiological Society
EROER	Etudes preliminaires aux religions orientales dans l'Empire romain
EstBib	*Estudios biblicos*
ET	English translation
ETL	*Ephemerides theologicae lovanienses*
EvQ	*Evangelical Quarterly*
ExpTim	*Expository Times*
FFRS	Foundations and Facets Reference Series
GCS	Die griechischen christlichen Schriftsteller der ersten [drei] Jahrhunderte
HBT	*Horizons in Biblical Theology*
HNT	Handbuch zum Neuen Testament
HNTC	Harper's New Testament Commentaries
HTKNT	Herders theologischer Kommentar zum Neuen Testament
HTR	*Harvard Theological Review*
HTS	Harvard Theological Studies
IBS	*Irish Biblical Studies*
ICC	International Critical Commentary
Int	*Interpretation*
IRT	Issues in Religion and Theology

IVPNTC	InterVarsity Press New Testament Commentary
JAAR	*Journal of the American Academy of Religion*
JBL	*Journal of Biblical Literature*
JETS	*Journal of the Evangelical Theological Society*
JQR	*Jewish Quarterly Review*
JSNT	*Journal for the Study of the New Testament*
JSNTSup	Journal for the Study of the New Testament: Supplement Series
JSOT	*Journal for the Study of the Old Testament*
JSOTSup	Journal for the Study of the Old Testament: Supplement Series
JTS	*Journal of Theological Studies*
KD	*Kerygma und Dogma*
KEK	Kritisch-exegetischer Kommentar über das Neue Testament
LEC	Library of Early Christianity
LNTS	Library of New Testament Studies
MBPS	Mellen Biblical Press Series
MNTC	Moffat New Testament Commentary
MSJ	*The Master's Seminary Journal*
NABPR	The National Association of Baptist Professors of Religion
NAC	New American Commentary
NCB	New Century Bible
NCBC	New Cambridge Bible Commentaries
Neot	*Neotestamentica*
NHMS	Nag Hammadi and Manichaean Studies
NHS	Nag Hammadi Studies
NIB	*The New Interpreter's Bible*
NIBC	New International Biblical Commentary
NIBCNT	New International Biblical Commentary on the New Testament
NICNT	New International Commentary on the New Testament
NIDNTT	*New International Dictionary of New Testament Theology*. Edited by C. Brown. 4 vols. Grand Rapids, 1986
NIGTC	New International Greek Testament Commentary
NIVAC	New International Version Application Commentary
NovT	*Novum Testamentum*
NovTSup	Supplements to Novum Testamentum
NS	New Series
NSBT	New Studies in Biblical Theology
NTD	Das Neue Testament Deutsch
NTL	New Testament Library
NTS	*New Testament Studies*

PG	Patrologia graeca [= Patrologiae cursus completus: Series graeca]. Edited by J.-P. Migne. 162 vols. Paris, 1857–1886
PL	Patrologia latina [= Patrologiae cursus completus: Series graeca]. Edited by J.-P. Migne. 217 vols. Paris, 1844–1864
PNTC	Pillar New Testament Commentaries
PTMS	Pittsburgh Theological Monograph Series
QD	Quaestiones Disputatae
ResQ	*Restoration Quarterly*
RevBib	*Revue biblique*
RHR	*Revue de l'histoire des religions*
RNT	Regensburger Neues Testament
RTR	*Reformed Theological Review*
SacPag	Sacra Pagina
SANT	Studien zum Alten und Neuen Testament
SBAB	Stuttgarter biblische Aufsatzbände
SBEV	Service Biblique Evangile et Vie
SBL	Society of Biblical Literature
SBLDS	Society of Biblical Literature Dissertation Series
SBLMS	Society of Biblical Literature Monograph Series
SBLSBS	Society of Biblical Literature Sources for Biblical Studies
SBLSP	*Society of Biblical Literature Seminar Papers*
SBLSymS	Society of Biblical Literature Symposium Series
SBT	Studies in Biblical Theology
SC	Sources chrétiennes. Paris: Cerf, 1943–
Scr	*Scripture*
SE IV, TU	*Studia evangelica IV,* Texte und Untersuchungen
SNT	Studien zum Neuen Testament
SNTSMS	Society for New Testament Studies Monograph Series
SR	*Studies in Religion*
SUNT	Studien zur Umwelt des Neuen Testaments
TANZ	Arbeiten zum neutestamentlichen Zeitalter
TBT	*The Bible Today*
TDNT	*Theological Dictionary of the New Testament.* Edited by G. Kittel and G. Friedrich. Translated by G. W. Bromiley. 10 vols. Grand Rapids, 1964–1976
Them	*Themelios*
Theol	*Theologica*
THNT	Theologischer Handkommentar zum Neuen Testament
TNTC	Tyndale New Testament Commentary
TrinJ	*Trinity Journal*

TRu	*Theologische Rundschau*
TSK	*Theologische Studien und Kritiken*
TU	Texte und Untersuchungen
TynBul	*Tyndale Bulletin*
VC	*Vigiliae christianae*
WBC	Word Biblical Commentary
WTJ	*Westminster Theological Journal*
WUNT	Wissenschaftliche Untersuchungen zum Neuen Testament
WW	*Word and World*
ZAG	*Zeitschrift für alte Geschichte*
ZAW	*Zeitschrift für die alttestamentliche Wissenschaft*
ZCS	Zondervan Church Source
ZNW	*Zeitschrift für die neutestamentliche Wissenschaft und die Kunde der älteren Kirche*
ZRGG	*Zeitschrift für Religions- und Geistesgeschichte*
ZST	*Zeitschrift für systematische Theologie*

ABBREVIATIONS OF WORKS OF THE CHURCH FATHERS AND EARLY JEWISH WRITERS

1 Apol.	*1 Apologia*, Justin
Ant.	*Jewish Antiquities*, Josephus
Apol.	*Apologeticus,* Tertullian
Apion	*Against Apion* (*Contra Apionem*), Josephus
Barn.	The Epistle of Pseudo-Barnabas
Chron.	*Chronicle,* Eusebius
Comment. Matt.	*Commentarium in evangelium Matthaei*, Origen
Dial.	*Dialogus cum Tryphone,* Justin Martyr
Eccl. Hist.	*Ecclesiastical History,* Eusebius
Eph.	*To the Ephesians,* Ignatius
Hom. Luke	*Homilies on Luke,* Origen
Hom. Matt.	*Homiliae in Matthaeum,* John Chrysostom
Legat.	*Legatio ad Gaium,* Philo
Marc.	*Against Marcion,* Tertullian
Magn.	*To the Magnesians,* Ignatius
Nat.	*Ad nationes,* Tertullian
Or.	*De oratione,* Tertullian
Paed.	*Paedagogus,* Clement of Alexandria
Pol.	*To Polycarp,* Ignatius
Praef. in Ioann.	*Preface to John,* Theophylact
Praescr.	*De praescriptione hareticorum,* Tertullian

Quis div.	*Quis dives salvetur,* Clement of Alexandria
Scorp.	*Scorpiace,* Tertullian
Trall.	*To the Trallians,* Ignatius
Vir. ill.	*De viris illustribus,* Jerome

Abbreviations of other works (e.g., apocryphal, pseudepigraphical, Mishnaic, Talmudic, classical Greek and Roman writings, etc.) conform to *The SBL Handbook of Style.*

Preface

OR BELIEVERS WHO look to Scripture as the authority for their faith and
practice, the NT, with its 27 books, presents both a wonderful, God-given treasure trove of spiritual insights and a formidable challenge for faithful, accurate
interpretation. To be sure, "All Scripture is inspired by God and is profitable for teaching,
for rebuking, for correcting, for training in righteousness, so that the man of God may
be complete, equipped for every good work" (2 Tim 3:16–17), but to be so equipped the
student of Scripture must follow Paul's exhortation to "[b]e diligent to present yourself
approved to God, a worker who doesn't need to be ashamed, correctly teaching the word
of truth" (2 Tim 2:15). This diligence required for a correct understanding of God's "word
of truth" involves a thorough acquaintance with the historical, literary, and theological
aspects of the various NT writings.

TITLE AND CONTENT OVERVIEW

Title

The Lion and the Lamb, of course, is Jesus—the one who came to die for our sins on
the cross in keeping with OT messianic prophecy (e.g., Isa 52:13–53:12) and the one who
will return in triumph to consummate God's kingdom (Revelation 19). As in the case of
its predecessor, *The Cradle, the Cross, and the Crown*, the present volume spans the NT
literature from the Gospels (where Jesus is portrayed as the Lamb of God; John 1:29,36)
to the book of Revelation (which features Jesus as the Lamb who was slain who will return
as the Lion of Judah). In a concise, yet complete format, the present volume explores the
original setting of each NT writing, engages in careful study of the respective document in
a unit-by-unit format, and closes with relevant points of application.

The Nature of Scripture

The first part of this book attempts to set the stage for the ensuing study by a discussion of the most critical foundational issues for NT interpretation: (1) the nature and

scope of Scripture (chap. 1); and (2) the political and religious background of the NT (chap. 2). It is vital for all students of Scripture to have a proper understanding of the *doctrine* of Scripture, so chapter 1 discusses the formation of the NT canon, its inspiration and inerrancy, the preservation and transmission of the Bible over the centuries, and issues pertaining to the translation of Scripture.

Unfortunately, this kind of doctrinal instruction is increasingly neglected in many publications on the topic in our day. But we judge it absolutely vital because only by understanding Scripture as divine revelation, in keeping with its own claims, will we be able to pursue our study all the way to its intended goal: the application of the "word of truth" to our personal lives and our relationships with others.[1] God has revealed himself in his inspired word, and because the Bible is the Word of God written, it is therefore inerrant, trustworthy, and authoritative, and requires obedience and personal application (Jas 1:22–25). Indeed, the purpose of Scripture is "training in righteousness, so that the man of God may be complete, equipped for every good work" (2 Tim 3:16–17).

In this regard, it is our desire that this book be more than a dry, academic compilation of various dates and facts. To be sure, the study of Scripture requires diligence—in other words, work!—but what ought to motivate our efforts is the payoff at the end of our research: a better understanding of the history, literature, and theology of the NT writings for the purpose of cultivating, in the power of the Holy Spirit, a deeper spiritual life in ourselves, our families, and our churches. This, in turn, will result in a more authentic and authoritative proclamation of the biblical message so that God's kingdom may be advanced in this world and so others may be subjected to his reign in their lives.

The Background of the New Testament

As we approach our study of the NT, we need to acquaint ourselves with the political and religious background of the NT (the contents of chap. 2). This is an ingredient not always found in standard NT introductions, an omission that when teaching NT survey courses in the past has sent us scrambling for other resources to prepare our students adequately for entering the world of the NT. In this chapter we cover the end of OT history (the exiles of Israel and Judah, the last prophets); the period between the Testaments (the Greeks, the Maccabees, and the Romans); and the political environment of Jesus' ministry (the Jewish sects, the Herodian dynasty, etc.). We also provide a survey of Second Temple literature and discuss relevant theological and philosophical issues.

History, Literature, and Theology

Once this foundation has been laid, we analyze each NT book using the same pattern, which is called a "hermeneutical triad" in Köstenberger and Patterson's *Invitation*

---

[1] See the classic article by W. A. Grudem, "Scripture's Self-Attestation and the Problem of Formulating a Doctrine of Scripture," in *Scripture and Truth*, ed. D. A. Carson and J. D. Woodbridge (Grand Rapids: Zondervan, 1983), 19–59.

to Biblical Interpretation:[2] (1) *history* (including a book's authorship, date, provenance, destination, etc.); (2) *literature* (genre, literary plan, outline, unit-by-unit discussion); and (3) *theology* (theological themes, contribution to the canon). In keeping with the three major divisions of the NT canon, the material in the body of this book is then organized into the following three parts:

- *Part Two: Jesus and the Gospels*, which features a chapter on Jesus and the relationship among the four Gospels as well as introductions to each of the four Gospels.
- *Part Three: The Early Church and Paul*, which includes chapters on the book of Acts; the ministry and message of the apostle Paul; and the 13 canonical letters of Paul in likely chronological order of writing: Galatians; 1–2 Thessalonians; 1–2 Corinthians; Romans; the Prison Epistles; and the Pastoral Epistles.
- *Part Four: The General Epistles and Revelation*, which are discussed in canonical order (except that Jude is kept with the Petrine letters because of the letter's close relationship with 2 Peter): Hebrews; James; 1–2 Peter; Jude; 1–3 John; and Revelation.

RATIONALE AND DISTINCTIVES

Rationale

It is our belief, borne out of years of teaching on both the undergraduate and the graduate levels, that the pattern of organizing the material described above best reflects the organic growth of the NT material. It allows the classroom teacher (1) to cover the foundational material, that is, the doctrine of Scripture, the NT background, and Jesus and the Gospels; and (2) to use the template provided by the book of Acts as the basis for a study of the ministry and writings of the apostle Paul and the other NT witnesses.

While the NT is a collection of writings—a body of literature—to be appreciated in the sequence in which it is given, it also reflects a historical plan. It moves from God's promise of a Messiah as described in the OT, to the coming of that Messiah as depicted in the Gospels, to the growth of the early church as narrated in the book of Acts and the NT letters, and to the consummation of human history at the return of Christ as anticipated in Revelation.[3]

To give but one example, it will be helpful for the student to understand that Paul wrote the letter to the Galatians several years prior to his letter to the Romans so that the "Judaizing controversy" surrounding circumcision (discussed in Galatians) can be seen to

---

[2] See A. J. Köstenberger and R. D. Patterson, *Invitation to Biblical Interpretation: Exploring the Hermeneutical Triad of History, Literature, and Theology* (Grand Rapids: Kregel, 2011); cf. N. T. Wright, *The New Testament and the People of God*, Christian Origins and the Question of God 1 (Minneapolis: Fortress, 1992).

[3] See the chapter, "Gospels, Acts, Epistles, and Apocalypse: The Fulfillment of the Old Testament in the New," in Köstenberger and Patterson, *Invitation to Biblical Interpretation*.

provide the backdrop to the later, more general formulation of the gospel in the book of Romans. It will also be helpful to relate both Galatians and Romans to events in the book of Acts and to other events in early Christian history and in the ministry of Paul.

Distinctives

The Lion and the Lamb represents an abridgment of *The Cradle, the Cross, and the Crown*. At almost 1,000 pages, the full NT introduction contains not only basic information but also intermediate and advanced knowledge. *The Lion and the Lamb*, by contrast, focuses on introductory-level core knowledge for each book of the NT. Typically, a chapter starts by presenting the core knowledge presented in the chapter as well as key facts and a survey of the book's contribution to the canon. This is followed by a discussion of the book's historical setting—information regarding the book's author, provenance, destination, date, occasion, and purpose. After this comes a section on the book's literary plan, including an outline and a detailed unit-by-unit discussion. Many will find this unit-by-unit discussion particularly valuable in that it gives a thorough summary of the book's contents. The final component is a survey of the major theological themes of a given NT book, followed by application points, study questions, and resources for further study.

In comparison with *The Cradle, the Cross, and the Crown*, discussions of critical challenges to a book's traditional authorship, treatments of literary rearrangement or partitioning theories, and similarly advanced types of material have been omitted. Some of the information on the original historical setting has been condensed in order to focus on the most relevant aspects of a NT book's introductory matters. The unit-by-unit discussions have been retained in their entirety, and a selection was made as to the most important theological themes. A completely new feature of *The Lion and the Lamb* is the application points, which are provided to suggest possible ways in which you may apply the teaching of a particular NT book to your life and to the life of the people in your congregation. On the whole, we have aimed to retain the best and most important information found in *The Cradle, the Cross, and the Crown* while focusing on essential core knowledge and screening out advanced discussions. That said, we have once again aimed to produce a volume with the following distinctives.

1. *User-friendly.* We have written with the teacher and the student in mind. This book is scholarly yet accessible; it is useful as a text for undergraduate NT survey classes. User-friendly features include study questions and resources for further study at the end of every chapter. A succinct glossary is found in the back of the volume.

2. *Comprehensive.* This book covers the entire NT canon, background, Jesus, the Gospels, the early church and Paul's writings in order of composition, the General Epistles, and Revelation. Studying Paul's letters in the order in which they were written helps integrate them with the historical framework of Acts.

3. *Conservative.* All three writers of this book affirm that all 27 books in the NT were written by the persons to whom they are ascribed (the four Gospels, the letters). We have included a strong defense of the apostolic authorship of Matthew and John and a rebuttal of the alleged pseudonymity of Paul's and Peter's letters, especially the Pastorals and 2 Peter.

4. *Balanced.* We have attempted to follow sound hermeneutical procedure, modeling the study of each NT book in its historical, literary, and theological context. Hence, this volume is more (though not less) than just a NT introduction dealing with the introductory issues of authorship, date, provenance, destination, and so on.

5. *Up-to-date.* This volume includes comprehensive scholarly interaction with both older and more recent scholarship, with a primary focus on English-language sources. Where appropriate we draw on recent advances in the literary study of Scripture, following a narrative or discourse analysis approach in tracing the contents of various NT books.

6. *Spiritually nurturing and application oriented.* The style of writing consistently seeks to nurture the student's spirituality and encourages application of what is learned rather than provide an arid presentation of facts to be mastered merely on a cognitive level. This is reflected especially in the unit-by-unit discussions, the theological themes sections, and the application points at the end of the chapter.

CONCLUSION

This book represents the product of collaboration between the three authors. In addition, Jason Meyer and Alan Bandy made substantial contributions by writing first serious drafts of the chapters on the Prison Epistles and the book of Revelation. Thanks are also due Grant Taylor for his help in abridging chapters 1–11. Andreas Köstenberger abridged the remaining chapters and served as general editor of the production of *The Lion and the Lamb* in its entirety. He also wrote all the application points at the end of the respective biblical chapters. As authors we are grateful to our wives and families for their support and to our students who gave feedback on portions of this book at various stages of the process. We are also grateful to Jim Baird, the publisher, for his visionary leadership and strong support and for Chris Cowan for his efforts in seeing this project through the various stages of production.

As we release this book to the public, we are well aware of the limitations associated with producing such a work. In this age of unprecedented proliferation of scholarly literature, who is adequate to such a task? Nevertheless, we believe it is a risk worth taking since the task of helping to equip another generation of Bible students with a portion of the knowledge of "the sacred Scriptures, which are able to instruct you for salvation through faith in Christ Jesus" (2 Tim 3:15) must not be left undone. On this side of heaven, our knowledge will of necessity be preliminary and incomplete: "For now we see indistinctly, as in a mirror," and long for the day when we will see Jesus "face to face" (1 Cor 13:12). In the meantime, we invite you to join us to press on to full Christian maturity (Phil 3:12–14) as we grow in the knowledge and grace of our Lord Jesus Christ (2 Pet 3:18). May God be pleased to use this volume as a small tool toward that worthy and glorious end.

Part One

INTRODUCTION

BEFORE INVESTIGATING THE Gospels and the rest of the NT in Parts Two through Four of this volume, it is appropriate to lay the groundwork for the study of the writings included in the canon of the NT by considering the nature and scope of Scripture (chap. 1) and by surveying the landscape of the political and religious background of the NT (chap. 2). This is appropriate because questions such as the extent of the NT canon, the inerrancy and inspiration of Scripture, the translation of Scripture, and its textual transmission (textual criticism) constitute important preliminary issues that have an important bearing on the interpretation of the books included in the NT.

Unless these questions are adequately addressed, NT introduction is rendered without proper foundation, resulting in a doctrinal vacuum that leaves the student in a precarious and vulnerable position when confronted with challenges to the canonicity of certain NT books or to a high view of Scripture and its authority. Also, the Gospels, Acts, the NT letters, and the book of Revelation did not appear in a vacuum. For this reason it is vital to discuss the political and religious backgrounds that form the backdrop to the study of the various NT writings. Hence, NT introduction properly commences with treatments of the nature of NT Scripture and of the relevant NT background.

Chapter 1
The Nature and Scope of Scripture

CORE KNOWLEDGE

Students should know the major issues involved in the formation of the canon, the doctrines of inerrancy and inspiration, the textual transmission of the NT, and translations of the Bible. They should have a basic grasp of the major figures and documents involved and issues addressed, including key dates.

INTRODUCTION

B. F. WESTCOTT noted long ago that a "general survey of the History of the Canon forms a necessary part of an Introduction to the writings of the New Testament."[1] For many students the discussion of the canon—the question of which books should be included in the Bible—seems moot: the canon is closed and limited to the books found in the Bible. But a study of the canon does more than merely determine the books of the OT and NT or furnish material for scholarly debate. It provides a basic orientation to how the Bible came into existence and therefore connects us more firmly to the foundations of our faith.

In this chapter we begin a journey through the NT. The very idea of a NT is traced along historical lines. As will be our practice in the case of each individual NT book later on, our discussion of the canon of the NT will proceed under the rubrics of history, literature, and theology. First, dealing with *history* we will take a look at the process of canonization in order to answer the question, Why these 27 books? Second, with regard to *literature* we will probe the reliability of the Bible and discuss the question, Is the Bible today what

---

[1] B. F. Westcott, *A General Survey of the History of the Canon of the New Testament* (London: Macmillan & Co., 1896), 1. Westcott defines *canon* as "the collection of books which constitute the original written Rule of the Christian Faith" (ibid., n1).

was originally written? Finally, the canon is bound up significantly with the church's *theology*. We will therefore close by asking, What is the nature of the canon?

THE NEW TESTAMENT CANON: WHY THESE 27 BOOKS?

Our study of the scope and extent of the NT—the NT canon—is concerned primarily with the recognition of the NT writings as Christian Scripture to the exclusion of all other possible candidates. What is a "canon"? Put succinctly, the word *canon* comes from the Greek word *kanōn*, which in turn derives from its Hebrew equivalent *kaneh* and means "rule" or "standard."[2] The term eventually came to refer to the collection of the Christian Scriptures.

The composition of the various NT writings took place starting in the late AD 40s and proceeded through the end of the first century. Subsequently, these books were copied and spread among the growing number of Christian congregations all over the Roman Empire, as is attested by the available manuscript evidence.

Generally, the main subject of debate today is not *whether* the NT canon is closed (i.e., fixed and therefore unchangeable); this is widely, though not universally, assumed. The discussion centers rather on the question of *how* and *when* the closing of the canon took place. The time frame during which this process of canonization occurred spans from the period of the early church to the ecclesiastical councils of the fourth and fifth centuries.[3]

The Witness of the New Testament

The NT canon can be viewed from both a human and a divine perspective. The traditional evangelical view affirms God's activity in the formation of the canon. From this vantage point, it can be said that, in one sense at least, the NT canon was closed the moment the last NT book was written.

God, through the agency of the Holy Spirit and the instrumentality of the NT writers, generated Holy Scripture (a phenomenon called "inspiration"); and the church's task was not the *creation* of the canon but merely the *recognition* of the Scriptures God had previously chosen to inspire. It follows that, if the church's role is primarily passive in determining the Christian canon, then it is inspired Scripture, not the church, which is in the final position of authority.

Traditionally, the second century has been viewed as the pivotal period for the canonization process of the NT writings. By the end of that century, the books of the NT were largely recognized throughout the churches. In the two subsequent centuries, all that remained was a final resolution regarding the canonicity of smaller or disputed books such as James, 2 Peter, 2–3 John, Jude, and Revelation.

That is not to say the ***idea*** of canon appears in the second century. The fact that the church's canonical consciousness appears to have left traces even in the NT itself suggests

---

[2] See L. M. McDonald, *The Biblical Canon: Its Origin, Transmission, and Authority*, 3rd ed. (Peabody: Hendrickson, 2007), 38–39; and B. M. Metzger, *The Canon of the New Testament: Its Origin, Development, and Significance* (Oxford: Clarendon, 1987), 289–93.

[3] J. Barton, *Holy Writings, Sacred Text: The Canon in Early Christianity* (Louisville: Westminster John Knox, 1997), 1.

that the NT writers were aware that God was inspiring new documents in their day. In two important NT passages, the term "Scripture,"[4] used about 50 times in the NT to refer to the OT,[5] may refer to the emerging NT writings.

The first such passage is 1 Tim 5:18: "For the Scripture says: 'You must not muzzle an ox that is threshing grain,' and, 'The laborer is worthy of his wages.'" The text uses the word "Scripture" with reference to two quotations. The first, the prohibition against muzzling an ox, is taken from Deut 25:4. The second, "The laborer is worthy of his wages," is in fact an exact verbal parallel of Luke 10:7. Whether or not Luke's Gospel was the source for this quotation, it is clear that (1) the author used a written source (demanded by the word "Scripture"); and (2) the source was considered to be authoritative on par with Deuteronomy. This demonstrates the emerging canonical consciousness in NT times.

The second relevant passage is 2 Pet 3:15–16. With reference to the apostle Paul, Peter writes that "[h]e speaks about these things in all his letters, in which there are some matters that are hard to understand. The untaught and unstable twist them to their own destruction, as they also do with *the rest of the Scriptures*" (emphasis added). From this passage we learn that Peter viewed Paul's letters as "Scripture" on par with the writings of the OT. Strikingly, therefore, 2 Peter shows that Paul's letters were accepted as Scripture even while NT writings were still being produced.

Given this kind of NT evidence, the conclusion lies close at hand that almost before the ink was dry, the earliest Christians, including leading figures in the church such as the apostles Paul and Peter, considered contemporaneous Christian documents such as the Gospels and Paul's letters as Scripture on par with the OT. From this it is not too difficult to trace the emerging canonical consciousness with regard to the formation of the NT through the writings of the early church fathers.

The Witness of the Early Church Fathers

A survey of the early patristic literature reveals that the early church fathers had no hesitancy whatsoever to quote the various NT books as Scripture. For example, the author of *1 Clement*, the first known nonbiblical Christian document (c. 96), regularly quoted Scripture organically (i.e., without introductory formulas).[6] He referred to the canonical Gospels, Acts, 1 Corinthians, Philippians, Titus, Hebrews, 1 Peter, and perhaps James much as he did to the OT. Most likely, the earliest citation of a NT passage using the term "Scripture" in the subapostolic period (the period following the apostolic era) is *2 Clem.* 2.4 (end of first cent.): "And another scripture says, 'I came not to call the righteous, but sinners'" (cf. Mark 2:17).[7]

---

[4] Greek: *graphē*.

[5] E.g., Luke 4:21; 2 Tim 3:16; 2 Pet 1:20.

[6] Generally, Clement used *graphē* to refer to the OT, except for *2 Clem.* 23.3 where he cited an unknown writing (see also *2 Clem.* 11.2–4 for the same citation). There is some connection of this unknown writing to James.

[7] M. W. Holmes, *The Apostolic Fathers*, 3rd ed. (Grand Rapids: Baker, 2007), 141: "This appears to be the earliest instance of a NT passage being quoted as *Scripture*" (emphasis original). Holmes suggested that the passage quoted is either Matt 9:13 or Mark 2:17.

It follows from these observations that most NT documents were recognized as authoritative, even Scripture, as early as at the end of the first or at least by the end of the second century of the Christian era. The four Gospels, the book of Acts, the letters of Paul, 1 Peter, and 1 John were universally recognized. With the exception of 3 John, the early church fathers cited all NT books as Scripture. Toward the end of the second century, the major contours of the NT had clearly emerged, setting the framework for the subsequent final resolution of the canonical status of several remaining smaller or disputed books.

The Witness of the Muratorian Canon and the Final Resolution of the NT Canon

Most likely in the late second century, an unknown writer composed a defense of the NT books that seems to corroborate the conclusion that most NT writings were recognized as Scripture by that time. At the very least, the writer saw the books listed as a firm canon. The Muratorian Canon, which was named for the eighteenth-century Italian historian and theologian who discovered it, lists at least 22 of the 27 books in the NT canon.[8] These works included the four Gospels, at least two of John's letters (and possibly the third), the Acts of the Apostles, Paul's 13 letters, Jude, and Revelation. Other books may very well have been included in the church's canon at the time the Muratorian Canon was written, such as Hebrews, the Petrine Letters, or the letter of James.

From the third century to the fifth century, the ultimate recognition of the rest of the General Epistles and the book of Revelation took place. During this period the remaining questions regarding the NT canon were resolved, although it cannot be said that any church council made and enforced such a ruling. It is commonly stated that the church councils selected certain works and banned others. There is no evidence for such high-handed ecclesiastical activity. Instead, certain stimuli and criteria were used by the churches to recognize canonicity.

Stimuli for Canonization and Criteria of Canonicity

Stimuli for Canonization There was likely a series of contributing factors for NT canonization. N. Geisler and W. Nix helpfully suggest the following five major stimuli for the church's determination of the NT canon.[9]

1. *The prophetic nature of the NT books.* The NT books themselves were prophetic, intrinsically valuable, and worthy of preservation.
2. *The church's need for authoritative Scriptures.* The demand for books that conformed to apostolic teaching to be read in the churches (see 1 Thess 5:27; 1 Tim 4:13) required a selection process.
3. *Heretical challenges.* Around 140, the heretic Marcion in Rome declared an edited Gospel of Luke and only 10 letters of Paul as useful while rejecting all the other

---

[8] See Metzger, *Canon*, 191–201.
[9] N. L. Geisler and W. E. Nix, *A General Introduction to the Bible*, rev. and exp. ed. (Chicago: Moody, 1986), 277–78.

apostolic works, which necessitated a response by those in the apostolic main-stream of Christianity.

4. *Missionary outreach.* Since the Bible began to be translated into Syriac and Latin as early as the first half of the second century, determining the NT canon was important for deciding which books should be translated.

5. *Persecution.* When the edict of Diocletian in 303 ordered all the sacred books of the Christians burned (a fact that may, at least in part, account for the relative scarcity of pre-AD 300 NT manuscripts), this required believers to choose which books were part of Scripture and thus most worthy of preservation.

Criteria of Canonicity   When the early church compiled the canon, it recognized which writings bore the stamp of divine inspiration. Four major criteria were used in this process.[10] The first was *apostolicity*, that is, direct or indirect association of a given work with an apostle. This criterion was met by Matthew, John, and Peter, all of whom were members of the Twelve (Matt 10:2–3 pars.), as well as Paul, an apostle commissioned by the risen Christ on the road to Damascus (Acts 9:1–9). It was also met by James and Jude, half brothers of Jesus (Matt 13:55; Mark 6:3; see Jas 1:1; Jude 1:1). Indirectly, the criterion was also satisfied by Mark, a close associate of Peter (1 Pet 5:13) and Paul (2 Tim 4:11), and Luke, a travel companion of Paul on some of his missionary journeys (see especially the "we" passages in the book of Acts).

The second criterion of canonicity was a book's *orthodoxy*, that is, whether a given writing conformed to the church's "rule of faith" (Lat. *regula fidei*). The question addressed under this rubric is whether the teaching of a given book conformed to apostolic teaching (see Acts 2:42).

The third criterion was a book's *antiquity*, that is, whether a given piece of writing was produced during the apostolic era. The fourth and final major criterion of canonicity was that of *ecclesiastical usage*, that is, whether a given document was already widely used in the early church.

Traditional evangelical opinion, then, places the closing of the canon as essentially by the late second century. All that remains is a bit of "mopping up" around the edges of the canon. However, there is reason to suggest that we should strongly consider an earlier date.

The Evidence for an Early Canon of Core NT Books

The Fourfold Gospel   It was not too long after Jesus' earthly ministry that the Synoptic Gospels were written (most likely all before the fall of Jerusalem in AD 70). Originally, the four Gospels disseminated independently of one another. Their individual status as Scripture is usually not debated. Whether the collection of Gospels should be limited to

---

[10] For helpful treatments on the formation of the Christian canon, including criteria for canonicity, see D. A. Carson and D. J. Moo, *An Introduction to the New Testament*, 2nd ed. (Grand Rapids: Zondervan, 2005), 726–43 (esp. 736–37); and L. M. McDonald, "Canon," in *Dictionary of the Later New Testament and Its Development*, ed. R. Martin and P. H. Davids (Downers Grove: InterVarsity, 1997), 134–44 (for ancient references regarding criteria for canonicity, see 135).

these four is a different matter. There are about 30 known Gospels that appeared before the year 600, but none were as popular as the canonical Gospels.[11] Only these four were recognized because, as Serapion (died 211) and others said, they were "handed down" to the church.[12] The other Gospels were rejected on the grounds that they did not agree with the commonly accepted four canonical Gospels. This implies not only antiquity but also the authority of the transmitters.[13]

While a dozen or more heretical "Gospels" may have been circulating in the second century, the manuscript evidence is telling regarding which of these Gospels the church considered canonical. First, no noncanonical Gospel appears bound with a canonical one, so there is no evidence for Matthew-Thomas or Luke-Peter, for example. This indicates that the issue of other Gospels having an equal scriptural status was a moot point among the orthodox.[14] Second, the manuscript evidence for noncanonical Gospels is amazingly thin compared with the numbers of Greek manuscripts of the canonical Gospels. For example, there is only one known full copy of the Gospel of Thomas. The evidence points to the fact that the apocryphal Gospels never had a wide hearing among the orthodox or quickly fell out of favor.

The book of Acts circulated in the manuscripts with the General Epistles. It is most likely that this was put together shortly after the 4-fold Gospel codex. Because the question naturally arises, "What do you do with Acts once you separate if from the Gospel of Luke?"

This, among other reasons, should be taken as evidence for the church's recognition that the number of the Gospels was fixed and closed by the early or at least the middle of the second century.

The Pauline Letter Collection and Revelation It is also known that Paul's letters circulated together as a collection unit. The question that arises is: How did this collection originate? Mainstream scholarship assumes that Paul's letters were a collection and (to some extent) a production of the late first century, as the letters were gradually formed into a letter collection.[15]

However, the time between the death of Paul (mid- to late 60s) and the historical references to this collection is far too short to be explained by a gradual collection. By the production of 2 Peter (mid-60s?), it is likely that there was at least a beginning collection

---

[11] The manuscript evidence alone suggests that the four canonical Gospels were far more popular than the rest. *Gospel of Thomas* has one whole manuscript (and three small fragments); the *Gospel of Peter* survives in only three small fragments; the *Egerton Gospel* in two small fragments; the *Gospel of the Hebrews* only in quotations (G. Stanton, *The Gospels and Jesus*, 2nd ed. [Oxford: Oxford Univ. Press, 2002], 122–35).

[12] See Eusebius, *Eccl. Hist.* 6.12.

[13] See especially R. Bauckham, *Jesus and the Eyewitnesses: The Gospels as Eyewitness Testimony* (Grand Rapids: Eerdmans, 2006). He stressed the eyewitness character of the Gospels and argues that the Twelve served as an "authoritative collegium" in the Gospels' preservation of eyewitness testimony regarding Jesus in the Gospels.

[14] J. K. Elliott, "Manuscripts, the Codex, and the Canon," *JSNT* 63 (1996): 107.

[15] W. G. Kümmel, P. Fein, and J. Behm, *Introduction to the New Testament* (Nashville: Abingdon, 1966), 480–81. See also Aland and Aland, *Text of the New Testament: An Introduction to the Critical Editions and to the Theory and Practice of Modern Textual Criticism,* trans. E. F. Rhodes (Grand Rapids: Eerdmans, 1987), 49.

of Paul's letters. In circa 96, Clement of Rome noted that Paul wrote "truly under the inspiration of the Spirit" (*1 Clem.* 47.3). Polycarp (c. 69–c. 155) quoted from a body of Scriptures that must have included the Pauline letter collection. Current scholarship is embracing the idea that the collection originated with Paul's retained copies of his letters, so that Paul is the ultimate source of the collection that was subsequently published.[16] Finally, it is reasonable to suspect Revelation circulated independently because the other circulation units had already been published. While it is not possible here to identify all the individuals and to pinpoint every stage of the production, the evidence thus far suggests an early recognition of the bulk of the NT canon.

The Current Order of New Testament Books The Gospels at the beginning of the NT transition from the OT quite nicely. This placement indicates their foundational nature. Virtually no arrangement of the NT starts elsewhere. The placement of Matthew first among the Gospels is most likely, at least in part, a function of the book's opening genealogy of Jesus, which provides a natural introduction to the presentation of Jesus in the four canonical Gospels as a whole. Luke's Gospel, while containing a genealogy in 3:23–37, places it immediately prior to the start of Jesus' public ministry instead of the beginning of the book.

Beyond this, there is no reason to suppose that the order of the Synoptic Gospels (Matthew-Mark-Luke) is a necessary indication of the order of their composition, just as the order of the Pauline Letters (Romans–1 Corinthians–2 Corinthians–Galatians, etc.) is manifestly not a function of the chronological sequence of their composition, as is universally recognized. Conversely, it is likely that the placement of John's Gospel last among the four canonical Gospels indicates its later composition. More importantly, the ending of John's Gospel certainly provides a fitting conclusion, not only to John's Gospel, but to the four canonical Gospels in their entirety (see 21:24–25).

Acts bridges the gap between the Gospels and the letters. As a sequel to Luke, it continues the narrative of the accomplishment of Christ (see Acts 1:1) and provides the foundation for a basic understanding of Paul and his correspondence.

As far as the order of the Pauline letters is concerned, it appears that, rather than the chronological order of writing, it was for the most part the length of the document that proved decisive in the church's placement of these letters in canonical order.[17] Regarding the order of the General Epistles, Hebrews owes its place first in this collection and in immediate proximity to Paul's letters to the traditional attribution of authorship to Paul or a member of his circle. Naturally, 1 and 2 Peter are grouped together, as are 1, 2, and 3 John. Beyond this, it is uncertain what historically led the compilers to place the writings

---

[16] See, e.g., E. R. Richards, *Paul and First-Century Letter Writing: Secretaries, Composition, and Collection* (Grand Rapids: InterVarsity, 2004), 223.

[17] "Length" may not necessarily be a function of word count but pertain to the number of lines or some other form of measurement (S. E. Porter, "When and How Was the Pauline Canon Compiled? An Assessment of Theories," in *The Pauline Canon*, ed. S. E. Porter [Boston: Brill, 2004], 115).

in the order James, 1–2 Peter, 1–3 John, and Jude. But this arrangement is consistent in the manuscripts from the beginning.

Revelation is a fitting conclusion to the whole Bible and not just the NT.[18] Not only is the subject of the return of Christ and the triumph of the Lamb over all evil appropriate as the final message of the NT, but there is a nice *inclusio* with Genesis as well. The final state, as recorded in the Apocalypse, is in many ways a return to Eden (see Rev 22:1–5). There is healing for the nations. There is no longer a curse upon the earth and its inhabitants. The tree of life is once more in plain view of humans, although there is no tree of the knowledge of good and evil. In Revelation, "Eden has not only been restored but has been elevated and expanded for the people of God in eternity."[19]

The New Testament as a Collection of New Covenant DocumentsHow is it that the early Christians so readily received new documents as Scripture—in fact, a whole new corpus of material?[20] With the new covenant having been instituted, these believers may have been expecting new covenant documents. The "Old Testament" was clearly considered to be based on covenant documents, and portions of it were called "the book of the covenant" (see Exod 24:7; Deut 29:20; 31:9,26; 2 Kgs 23:2,21; 2 Chr 34:30).

Since the establishment of the old covenant was accompanied by covenant documents, it was a reasonable expectation that there would be new covenant documents upon the institution of the new covenant. This expectation would explain not only the rapid reception of the NT writings in the churches but also the recognition that these documents were Scripture on par with the OT in virtually contemporaneous documents (1 Tim 5:18; 2 Pet 3:16). If so, the idea of a NT canon flowed organically from the establishment of a new covenant, predicted by the OT prophets and instituted in and through the Lord Jesus Christ, who thus became the very fount not only of salvation but also of the NT canon.

Conclusion

The canon of Scripture is closed. In one sense the canon was closed around 95 when the book of Revelation was written as the last book to be included in the canon of the NT. Properly conceived, the church's duty was to recognize the canon of inspired writings and to proclaim the truths they contained. This is what the church did and continues to do. Moreover, this recognition of NT canonical books came quite early, earlier than many are prepared to concede. Differences in opinion regarding individual NT books were settled through a process of deliberation until a general consensus was reached regarding the contents of the canon of the NT in the fourth century.

---

[18] See R. Bauckham, *The Theology of the Book of Revelation,* New Testament Theology (Cambridge: University Press, 1993), 144: "It is a work of Christian prophecy that understands itself to be the culmination of the whole biblical tradition."

[19] G. R. Osborne, *Revelation*, BECNT (Grand Rapids: Baker, 2002), 768.

[20] M. G. Kline, *The Structure of Biblical Authority*, 2nd ed. (Eugene: Wipf & Stock, 1997 [1987]).

THE TRANSMISSION AND TRANSLATION OF THE NEW TESTAMENT: IS THE BIBLE TODAY WHAT WAS ORIGINALLY WRITTEN?

The Bible was originally written in the languages in use at the time. The OT was written in Hebrew and Aramaic and the NT in Greek. The Bibles used today are translations from the original languages into English or other languages. Jesus most likely taught in Aramaic—though he probably also knew Hebrew and Greek—so that the Greek NT itself for the most part represents a translation of Jesus' teaching from Aramaic into Greek.

The question "Is the Bible today what was originally written?" involves two important questions. First, are the available manuscripts of the Bible accurate representations of the original manuscripts (the autographs of Scripture) of the respective books of the Bible? This is an issue of textual *transmission*. Second, are the available translations faithful renderings of the Bible in the original languages? This is an issue of *translation*.

Textual Transmission: Are the Available Manuscripts Accurate and Reliable?

With regard to the first question, no original autographs exist of any biblical text; only copies are available. The word *manuscript* is used to denote anything written by hand, rather than copies produced from the printing press.[21] Textual evidence constitutes anything written on clay tablets, stone, bone, wood, various metals, potsherds (ostraca), but most notably papyrus and parchment (animal hides, also called vellum).[22]

Most ancient books were compiled and then rolled into a scroll.[23] Since a papyrus roll rarely exceeded 35 feet in length, ancient authors divided a long literary work into several "books" (e.g., the Gospel of Luke and the Acts of the Apostles consisted of a two-volume set composed by Luke).[24] These were published by both individuals for private use and professionals for sale. In both cases the books were copied laboriously by hand.

One of the mysteries of Christian literature is the preference for the codex rather than the roll. Even when only a page of an ancient book is found, it can easily be determined if it comes from a roll or a codex: the codex has writing on both sides of the page. The roll was considered the more literary form for books. It is likely that the NT always circulated as a codex and it was most likely a Christian innovation to publish sacred books in codex form.

Books eventually succumb to the ravages of time. They either wear out or deteriorate over time. This extended also to the original writings that comprise the NT. Although the autographs are no longer available, the original texts are preserved in thousands of copies. The extant manuscript evidence instills a high degree of confidence in the text of the Bible. Both the OT and NT are attested by a large number of manuscripts in a variety of forms spanning many centuries. The NT texts remain the best-attested documents in the ancient

---

[21] N. R. Lightfoot, *How We Got the Bible*, 3rd ed. (New York: MJF, 2003), 33.

[22] B. M. Metzger and B. D. Ehrman, *The Text of the New Testament: Its Transmission, Corruption, and Restoration*, 4th ed. (New York/Oxford: Oxford Univ. Press, 2005), 4.

[23] Ibid., 5.

[24] Ibid.

world. The total tally of close to 6,000 Greek manuscripts, over 10,000 Latin Vulgate manuscripts, and more than 9,300 early versions results in over 25,000 witnesses to the text of the NT. When this is compared with other works in antiquity, no other book even comes close. Needless to say, classical scholars and historians would love to be working with books as well attested as the NT.

Table 1.1: Extant Copies of Ancient Works

Homer's *Iliad*: 643 copies
Julius Caesar's *Gallic Wars*: 10 copies, the earliest of which dates to 1,000 years after it was written
Livy wrote 142 books of Roman history, of which a mere 35 survive in only 20 manuscripts, only one of which is as old as the fourth century, and it survived only because it has a copy of the book of Hebrews written on the back!
Tacitus's *Histories* and *Annals*: 2 copies (ninth and eleventh centuries)
The *History of Thucydides*: 8 copies (tenth century)
The *History of Herodotus*: the oldest is 1,300 years later than the original
The writings of Plato: 7 copies
Chaucer's *Canterbury Tales*: 80 mss.
Beowulf: 1 copy

Translation: Are the Available Translations Faithful?

The second issue, namely that of *translation*, follows as a natural corollary once the question of *transmission* is settled. Translation theories help us consider the validity of a particular translation. Some translators maintain that accurate translation requires a word-for-word approach of formal or "essentially literal" equivalence (NKJV, NASB, ESV, HCSB). Others contend that construing a straightforward one-to-one correlation between two languages actually distorts meaning. These translators employ a phrase-for-phrase approach[25] of dynamic or functional equivalence (NRSV, NIV, CEV, NLT). The goal of all translators, no matter what translation theory they employ, is the production of an English version that is an accurate rendering of the text written in such a way that the Bible retains its literary beauty, theological grandeur, and, most importantly, its spiritual message.[26]

The good news is that there are faithful translations of the Bible in English available for a wide variety of readers. Whether a given person needs a rendition with a limited vocabulary and simple syntax or prefers an elevated style and grandeur of language, a faithful translation exists for him.

---

[25] J. R. Kohlenberger III, "Inclusive Language in Bible Translation," in *Perspectives on the TNIV from Leading Scholars and Pastors* (Grand Rapids: Zondervan, 2004), 11.

[26] G. G. Scorgie, "Introduction and Overview," in *The Challenge of Bible Translation*, ed. G. G. Scorgie, M. L. Strauss, and S. M. Voth (Grand Rapids: Zondervan, 2002), 25. See also A. J. Köstenberger and D. A. Croteau, eds., *Which Bible Translation Should I Use?* (Nashville: B&H, 2012).

As the author of Hebrews states, "Long ago God spoke to the fathers by the prophets at different times and in different ways. In these last days, He has spoken to us by His Son, whom He has appointed heir of all things and through whom He made the universe" (Heb 1:1–2). With this kind of revelation, there is no need to wait for another, greater revelation but to study, evangelize, preach, and teach the Word of God. The canon is the source of this information—inspired, illumined, and applied by the Holy Spirit. Truly, as one writer stated, the canon of Scripture is "the air we breathe."[27]

INSPIRATION AND INERRANCY: WHAT IS THE NATURE OF THE CANON?

With this we turn to the question of theology, that is, the doctrine of Scripture, and in particular the Bible's witness regarding itself. This discussion deals with Scripture's witness regarding itself in the OT; the use of and approach to OT Scripture by Jesus and the early church; NT references to Scripture as "inspired" (2 Tim 3:16) and as deriving from men "moved by the Holy Spirit" (2 Pet 1:21); and inerrancy (the doctrine that Scripture is free from error).

The Scripture's Witness Regarding Itself: The Old Testament

The God portrayed in the OT is a communicating God. He speaks to his children, and he does so through his servants the prophets (hence the prophetic "Thus says the Lord"). Because it is God who speaks to and through his servants, he demands faith and obedience to these utterances (see, for example, 2 Chr 20:20).

But what should be said about the written Word? Scripture itself contains information regarding the writing of Scripture. Exodus 17:14 states, "The LORD then said to Moses, 'Write this down on a scroll as a reminder and recite it to Joshua.'" In subsequent generations, actions were to be performed in keeping with what was written in the law of Moses (see Deut 28:58–59). Consequently, the command to Joshua was related to this book of the law: "This book of instruction must not depart from your mouth; you are to recite it day and night, so that you may carefully observe everything written in it. For then you will prosper and succeed in whatever you do" (Josh 1:8). Joshua also copied the law of Moses at its ratification (Josh 8:32). Clearly, the written law of Moses, as the Word of God, was understood as authoritative and as the path of blessing for Israel.

Significantly, after a time of religious decline in Israel, Hilkiah the priest found "the book of the law" in the temple (2 Kgs 22:8; 2 Chr 34:14). When young Josiah had the book read to him, Josiah was grieved for Israel's disobedience (2 Kgs 22:13) and instituted reforms in a movement "back to the Bible" (see also Neh 8:1).

The inclusion of the rest of the OT is related to the office of prophet that was central to the religious fidelity of Israel. The prophet's role was tied directly to the covenant relationship between Israel and God. It is best to understand their role as "covenant enforcers." What they

---

[27] S. J. Mikolaski, "Canon as the Air We Breathe," in *From Biblical Criticism to Biblical Faith: Essays In Honor of Lee Martin McDonald*, ed. W. Brackney and C. Evans (Macon: Mercer Univ. Press, 2007), 146–63.

speak is "the word of the Lord." The call of Jeremiah makes this explicit: "Then the LORD reached out His hand, touched my mouth, and told me: Look, I have filled your mouth with My words" (Jer 1:9). Just as God commanded Moses to write down his words, so many of the writing prophets were enjoined to write down God's words (see Jer 36:28; Ezek 43:11; Hab 2:2). Since God cannot lie (Num 23:19; 1 Sam 15:29; Prov 8:8; Ps 89:35), his word is truth (see Jesus' similar affirmation in John 17:17). And since God never fails (Zeph 3:5), neither can his word.

Moreover, God's word, as delivered to the prophets, was not to be edited. So Moses wrote, "You must not add anything to what I command you or take anything away from it, so that you may keep the commands of the LORD your God I am giving you" (Deut 4:2; see 12:32). As Prov 30:5–6 makes clear, the principle applies to every word of God: "Every word of God is pure; He is a shield to those who take refuge in Him. Don't add to His words, or He will rebuke you, and you will be proved a liar."

Therefore, even though the OT books span a variety of genres, feature different rhetorical forms, and represent the work of different prophets, they all share as their major common element the divine source of their words. The same is true for the NT, beginning with Jesus.

Jesus' Use of and Approach to OT Scripture

First, according to Jesus and his contemporaries, the OT Scriptures were the authority from which doctrine and practice were to derive. Thus, Jesus challenged his opponents to understand the Scriptures: "Have you never read in the Scriptures?" (Matt 21:42//Mark 12:10). Similarly, Jesus asserted that ignorance with regard to the OT Scriptures was the reason his opponents were wrong: "You are deceived, because you don't know the Scriptures or the power of God" (Matt 22:29//Mark 12:24). In John 5:39, Jesus observed that the Jews "pore over the Scriptures because you think you have eternal life in them, yet they testify about Me."[28] It is clear that Jesus and his hearers considered the OT to be the authoritative Word of God.

The Gospels also demonstrate the fulfillment of the OT with statements such as "this happened in order that the words spoken by the prophet were fulfilled," occurring especially in Matthew and John.[29] Men who spoke in the OT are described in the Gospels as God speaking. For example, Isaiah's words in Isa 7:14 are described by Matt 1:22 as "spoken by the Lord through the prophet," which reveals that Scripture in its totality was considered to be the Word of God. But this was not just a belief of the Gospel writers; it was also the view of Jesus himself (see Luke 24:27,44).

Not only were the OT Scriptures in their entirety the Word of God, but Jesus also affirmed their special nature. In John 10:35–36, Jesus affirmed that "*the Scripture cannot be*

---

[28] See many other examples: Matt 4:4; 12:5; 15:6; 22:40; 23:23; Luke 2:23–24; 4:17; 8:21; 11:28; 16:29,31; 24:25; John 7:19,23,49,51; 8:17; 10:34; 18:31; 19:7.

[29] See, e.g., Matt 1:22; 2:5,15,17,23; 3:3; 4:14; John 12:38; 13:18; 15:25; 17:12; 19:24,28,36,37; 20:9.

broken,"[30] a reminder that Scripture is the Word of God. Scripture cannot be charged with error or it would be broken—that is, rejected as the Word of God. Jesus very succinctly said something similar in John 17:17: "Your word is truth." So, in John's Gospel the word is connected with the concept of truth. Jesus, who is "the truth" (14:6), gives the "Spirit of truth" (14:17; 15:26; 16:13), who leads believers "into all the truth" (16:13).[31] And this truth is "Your [God's] word." This indicated what would serve as the foundation for new covenant documents: Jesus' words as the words of God.

One of the most striking passages related to Jesus' use of and approach to OT Scripture is found in Matt 5:18, where Jesus affirmed that he would not destroy the law: "For I assure you: Until heaven and earth pass away, not the smallest letter or one stroke of a letter will pass from the law until all things are accomplished."[32] The appeal here is to the smallest letter (*iota*, in Hebrew the *yodh*) or one stroke (*keraia*, lit. "a horn," most likely a tittle, an ornamental mark above a Hebrew letter, or a serif) being absolutely firm. Down to the minutest elements of an individual written word, Jesus affirmed the enduring authority of the OT.[33]

Jesus' stance toward Scripture was striking on two fronts. First, Jesus submitted himself to the Scriptures as any human being would. This can be seen in the account of Jesus' temptation by the devil (Matt 4:1–11; Luke 4:1–13). Second, Jesus claimed to be the fulfillment of Scripture, such as in his address at the synagogue in Nazareth (Luke 4:18–21). What was shocking to Jesus' hearers was that his interpretation was Christological in its focus. He thus became the fulfillment of God's purposes for and promises to Israel. Jesus' own use of Scripture also paves the way for the NT.

The Early Church's Use of and Approach to OT Scripture

Jesus passed on his approach to OT Scripture to his disciples.[34] Jesus himself promised his disciples that the Holy Spirit "will teach you all things and remind you of everything I have told you" (John 14:26). From John's perspective, writing in the 80s or early 90s, this promise most likely served also as an affirmation of at least his memories of Jesus' words (if not of the memories of all the apostles) recorded in the Gospel(s).

The apostles and their followers continued to use the OT Scriptures as Jesus did, namely, as their authority for life and doctrine. An OT citation helps adjudicate the issue of Gentile inclusion in the NT church at the Jerusalem Council (Acts 15:16–17). Key OT passages provide the basis for Paul's teaching in Romans regarding justification by faith (Rom 1:17; 4:3), the sinfulness of all humanity (Rom 3:10–18), and election (Rom 9:6–18). The same is true for other letters of Paul and the General Epistles.[35]

---

[30] See A. J. Köstenberger, "John," in *Commentary on the New Testament Use of the Old Testament*, ed. G. K. Beale and D. A. Carson (Grand Rapids: Baker, 2007), 464–67.

[31] A. J. Köstenberger, *John,* BECNT (Grand Rapids: Baker, 2004), 496.

[32] See Luke 16:17: "But it is easier for heaven and earth to pass away than for one stroke of a letter in the law to drop out."

[33] See L. Morris, *The Gospel According to Matthew*, PNTC (Grand Rapids: Eerdmans, 1992), 109–10.

[34] See especially R. N. Longenecker, *Biblical Exegesis in the Apostolic Period*, 2nd ed. (Grand Rapids: Eerdmans, 1999).

[35] See Gal 3:22; 4:22,27,30; Jas 2:8; 4:52; 1 Pet 1:16.

The apostles and NT writers, however, went beyond the mere affirmation and use of the OT. They continued to value the prophetic writings, but they also were deeply interested in the words of Christ. Acts 11:16 indicates that Peter confirmed direct Gentile Christian conversion because he remembered the "word of the Lord" (a reference to a saying of Jesus). The NT writers also placed their remembrances of Jesus on a par with the OT.[36] A case in point is the statement in 2 Pet 3:2 where Peter affirmed that he wrote "so that you can remember the words previously spoken by the holy prophets, and the commandment of our Lord and Savior given through your apostles."

The writer of Hebrews declared the continuity between God's revelation in the OT and the NT: "Long ago God spoke to the fathers by the prophets at different times and in different ways. In these last days, He has spoken to us by His Son, whom He has appointed heir of all things and through whom He made the universe" (Heb 1:1–2). The communication of the word of God is continued in Heb 2:3: "It was first spoken by the Lord and was confirmed to us by those who heard Him." The eyewitness nature of the apostles makes them the authoritative guarantors of the gospel message (see 1 John 1:1–5). As mentioned, 1 Tim 5:18 most likely cites Luke's Gospel as Scripture alongside Deuteronomy, and Peter referred to Paul's letters as "Scripture" on a par with the OT (2 Pet 3:16).

This puts the self-attestation of the NT on the same level as the self-attestation of the OT.[37] The basic contours of God's Word are established by Jesus' teaching. This is further extended to the apostles' teaching and the various NT writers. Beyond this, some of the NT books are recognized as Scripture elsewhere in the NT. As the Word of God, the NT, as well as the OT, is from God, and thus true, authoritative, irrevocable, and irreplaceable. What is more, there is an understanding and expectation that, accompanying the institution of the new covenant, new scriptural documents would be inspired.

Scripture as "Inspired": God the Source of Scripture (2 Tim 3:16–17)

The NT passage that addresses the issue of the inspiration of Scripture most directly is 2 Tim 3:16–17: "All Scripture is inspired by God and is profitable for teaching, for rebuking, for correcting, for training in righteousness, so that the man of God may be complete, equipped for every good work." These verses raise several important interpretive questions; only the most salient points can be noted here.[38]

1. The term "all" is singular, and it is best to think of "Scripture" in the present instance as a collective singular with Scripture being viewed in its totality.
2. The word "Scripture" in the original context refers to the OT.

---

[36] W. A. Grudem, "Scripture's Self-Attestation and the Problem of Formulating a Doctrine of Scripture," in *Scripture and Truth*, ed. D. A. Carson and J. D. Woodbridge (Grand Rapids: Zondervan, 1983), 46.

[37] Ibid., 45.

[38] See especially the helpful treatment by W. D. Mounce, *The Pastoral Epistles*, WBC (Nashville: Thomas Nelson, 2000), 565–70; cf. A. J. Köstenberger, "1–2 Timothy, Titus," in *Expositor's Bible Commentary*, rev. ed., vol. 12: *Ephesians–Philemon* (Grand Rapids: Zondervan, 2005), 591.

3. The phrase "all Scripture" in the immediate context refers to the entirety of the OT, and the logic of the verse applies by extension to the NT also (see also 1 Tim 5:18).

4. The term "inspired" (lit. "God-breathed" as in the NIV) designates the *source* of Scripture—God—rather than elaborating on the *process* of inspiration (though see below). Thus, the logic of the verse suggests that because Scripture has *God* as its source, it is true.

These observations, among other reasons, suggest that the affirmation in 2 Tim 3:16 is that "[a]ll Scripture is inspired by God and is [therefore] profitable." What this means is that Scripture has God as its source, and that it is for this reason profitable for a variety of uses to equip "the man of God . . . for every good work" (2 Tim 3:17). This fits with Paul's earlier exhortation to Timothy to be diligent to present himself approved to God as a worker who correctly teaches "the word of truth" (2 Tim 2:15).

Men "Moved by the Holy Spirit": God as Superintending the Writing of Scripture (2 Pet 1:19–21)

While the term "God-breathed" in 2 Tim 3:16 focuses on the *source* of Scripture rather than on the *mode* of inspiration, this does not mean that the NT is silent regarding the latter. Second Peter 1:19–21 states, "So we have the prophetic word strongly confirmed. . . . First of all, you should know this: no prophecy of Scripture comes from one's own interpretation, because no prophecy ever came by the will of man; instead, moved by the Holy Spirit, men spoke from God."

That the reference is to Scripture and not a spoken prophecy is clear from the designation "prophecy of Scripture." The phrase "one's own interpretation" may be better translated "from his own imagination" and be taken to refer to the reception and interpretation of a prophecy from God. The passage therefore asserts that Scripture is not merely human in origin but the product of the Holy Spirit moving human beings to speak the word of God.[39]

The description of men "moved by the Holy Spirit" suggests that the Holy Spirit took the prime initiative in the writing of Scripture while human writers freely penned the words God desired them to use. Whether the writing of Scripture involved the use of sources, the reception of a prophetic message directly from God, or some other mechanism, the final product was inspired by the Holy Spirit.

The above discussion has attempted to demonstrate that making Scripture's self-attestation primary leads inexorably to the conclusion that Scripture is inspired and inerrant. This follows both from specific scriptural references regarding the nature of Scripture as entirely trustworthy and is also required by the character of God as the ultimate source of Scripture.

When the well-known twentieth-century conservative scholar A. Schlatter was considered for a professorial appointment to the university in Berlin, he was asked by a

---

[39] See the discussion in R. Bauckham, *Jude, 2 Peter*, WBC (Waco: Word, 1983), 228–35.

churchman on the committee whether, in his academic work, he "stood on the Bible." Schlatter's reply: "No, I stand *under* the Bible!"[40] This well captures the proper stance of the biblical interpreter. Rather than elevating oneself as a supposedly neutral critic of Scripture—and claiming to be totally objective—the student of the Bible ought to take his or her place "beneath Scripture" as one who is addressed by Scripture and who seeks to be changed by "the living and effective" Word of God (Heb 4:12).

STUDY QUESTIONS

1. What is the traditional evangelical position regarding the canon?
2. Did an apocryphal Gospel ever circulate with a canonical Gospel?
3. When was the NT canon closed from a divine perspective?
4. Which NT books are called "Scripture" in the NT?
5. What is "formal equivalence"? What is "dynamic equivalence"?
6. What is an "autograph"?

FOR FURTHER STUDY

General Reference

Geisler, N. L., and W. E. Nix. *A General Introduction to the Bible.* Rev. and exp. ed. Chicago: Moody, 1986.

Patzia, A. G. *The Making of the New Testament: Origin, Collection, Text and Canon.* Downers Grove: InterVarsity, 1995.

Canon

Beckwith, R. *The Old Testament Canon of the New Testament Church.* Grand Rapids: Eerdmans, 1985.

Bruce, F. F. *The Canon of Scripture.* Downers Grove: InterVarsity, 1988.

Gamble, H. Y. *The New Testament Canon: Its Making and Meaning.* Guides to Biblical Scholarship. Philadelphia: Fortress, 1985.

Lightfoot, N. R. *How We Got the Bible.* 2nd ed. Grand Rapids: Baker, 1988.

McDonald, L. *The Biblical Canon: Its Origin, Transmission, and Authority.* 3rd ed. Peabody: Hendrickson, 2007.

McDonald, L. M., and J. A. Sanders, eds. *The Canon Debate.* 2nd ed. Peabody: Hendrickson, 2002.

Metzger, B. M. *The Canon of Scripture: Its Origin, Development, and Significance.* Oxford: Clarendon, 1987.

Westcott, B. F. *A General Survey of the History of the Canon of the New Testament.* London: Macmillan, 1896.

Inspiration and Inerrancy

Dockery, D. *Christian Scripture: An Evangelical Perspective on Inspiration, Authority, and Interpretation.* Nashville: B&H, 1995.

Geisler, N., ed. *Inerrancy.* Grand Rapids: Zondervan, 1980.

Harris, R. L. *Inspiration and Canonicity of the Scriptures.* Grand Rapids: Zondervan, 1969.

Henry, C. F. H. "The Authority and Inspiration of the Bible." In *The Expositor's Bible Commentary.* Vol. 1: *Introductory Articles.* Edited by F. E. Gaebelein. Grand Rapids: Zondervan, 1979, 1–35.

Pache, R. *The Inspiration and Authority of Scripture.* Chicago: Moody, 1969.

Warfield, B. B. *The Inspiration and Authority of the Bible.* Philadelphia: Presbyterian & Reformed, 1948.

---

[40] See W. W. Gasque, "The Promise of Adolf Schlatter," *Crux* 15/2 (June 1979): 8 (an article reprinted in *Evangelical Theological Review* 4 [1980]: 20–30).

Hermeneutics and Harmonization

Archer, G. L., Jr. *The New International Encyclopedia of Bible Difficulties.* Grand Rapids: Zondervan, 2001.

Blomberg, C. L. *The Historical Reliability of John's Gospel.* Downers Grove: InterVarsity, 2001.

_____. *The Historical Reliability of the Gospels.* 2nd ed. Downers Grove: InterVarsity, 2007.

Kaiser, W. C., Jr., ed. *Hard Sayings in the Bible.* Downers Grove: InterVarsity, 1996.

Köstenberger, A. J., and R. D. Patterson. *Invitation to Biblical Interpretation.* Grand Rapids: Kregel, 2011.

Osborne, G. R. *The Hermeneutical Spiral: A Comprehensive Introduction to Biblical Interpretation.* 2nd ed. Downers Grove: InterVarsity, 2006.

Textual Criticism

Aland, K., and B. Aland. *The Text of the New Testament: An Introduction to the Critical Editions and to the Theory and Practice of Modern Textual Criticism.* Translated by E. F. Rhodes. Grand Rapids: Eerdmans, 1987.

Gamble, H. Y. *Books and Readers in the Early Church: A History of Early Christian Texts.* New Haven: Yale Univ. Press, 1995.

Metzger, B. M., and B. D. Ehrman. *The Text of the New Testament: Its Transmission, Corruption, and Restoration.* 4th ed. New York/Oxford: Oxford Univ. Press, 2005.

Wegner, P. D. *A Student's Guide to Textual Criticism of the Bible: Its History, Methods and Results.* Downers Grove: InterVarsity, 2006.

_____. *The Journey from Texts to Translations: The Origins and Developments of the Bible.* Grand Rapids: Baker, 1999.

Bible Translation

Bruce, F. F. *The English Bible: A History of Translations.* New York: Oxford Univ. Press, 1961.

Köstenberger, A. J., and D. A. Croteau, eds. *Which Bible Translation Should I Use?* Nashville: B&H, 2012.

McGrath, A. E. *In the Beginning: The Story of the King James Bible and How It Changed a Nation, a Language, and a Culture.* New York: Doubleday, 2001.

Metzger, B. M. *The Bible in Translation.* Grand Rapids: Baker, 2001.

Ryken, L. *The Word of God in English: Criteria for Excellence in Bible Translation.* Wheaton: Crossway, 2002.

Scorgie, G. G., M. L. Strauss, and S. M. Voth, eds. *The Challenge of Bible Translation.* Grand Rapids: Zondervan, 2003.

Chapter 2

The Political and Religious Background of the New Testament

CORE KNOWLEDGE

Students should know the eight periods of control over Palestine in the Second Temple era. They should have a basic grasp of the major figures and rulers and be acquainted with other major features of this period, including key dates, names of important works, and major groups and institutions that trace their origin back to this period.

INTRODUCTION

WHEN THE OT era ended, the Persian Empire was in control of Jerusalem and Judea. When the NT era began, Rome was in charge. The following brief historical survey of this era and its literature and theology will serve as a useful background for the study of Jesus and the Gospels and the other NT writings. Since there was no prophetic voice in Israel between Malachi and the ministry of John the Baptist, the time span from approximately 400 BC to the Christian era has been called the "silent years." This rightly underscores the absence of prophet-mediated divine revelation during this period, but as the following survey will show, the time was anything but quiet.

Table 2.1: From Babylon to Rome: The Second Temple Period

Period	Time Frame
Babylonian Period	606–539 BC
Persian Period	539–331 BC
Greek Period	331–167 BC
Alexander the Great	331–320 BC
Ptolemaic Period	320–198 BC
Syrian Period	198–167 BC
Jewish Self-Rule	167–63 BC
Maccabean Period	167–135 BC
Hasmonean Period	135–63 BC
Roman Period	63 BC–AD 70

Table 2.2: The Second Temple Period: Important Events

I. End of Old Testament History: Babylonian and Persian Periods	
A. Babylonian Period (606–539 BC)	
606/5 BC	Nebuchadnezzar's conquest of Judea
587/86	Jerusalem, temple destroyed; Judah goes into exile; origin of synagogue
539 BC	Babylon falls to Cyrus the Great of Persia; exiles are allowed to return to Israel
B. Persian Period (539–331 BC)	
515 BC	Second temple dedicated (Zerubbabel, Haggai, Zechariah)
c. 400 BC	Last OT prophet Malachi: John the Baptist predicted
II. Between the Testaments: Greek Rule, Jewish Self-Rule, Roman Rule	
A. Greek Period (331–167 BC)	
1. Alexander the Great and His Conquests (331–320 BC)	
334/333 BC	Alexander defeats Persians at battles of Granicus, Issus
331 BC	Alexander defeats Darius II at Arbela, which makes him the controlling player in the Middle East (including Israel); Hellenization begins (dissemination of the Greek way of life)
323 BC	Alexander dies; kingdom divided into four parts
By 320 BC	Israel falls to Ptolemy in Egypt
2. Ptolemaic Period (320–198 BC)	
320–198 BC	Ptolemies rule Palestine from Alexandria, Egypt; Septuagint (the LXX, the Greek translation of OT) is produced

II. Between the Testaments: **Greek Rule, Jewish Self-Rule, Roman Rule (cont.)**	
198 BC	Seleucid Antiochus III defeats Ptolemy V at Paneas (near Mount Hermon) and seizes control of Palestine
3. Seleucid or Syrian Period (198–167 BC)	
198–167 BC	Seleucids, centered in Antioch of Syria, rule Palestine Two parties arise among the Jews: "the house of Onias" (pro-Egyptian) and "the house of Tobias" (pro-Syrian)
168 BC	Antiochus IV (175–163 BC): type of antichrist; replaces Jewish high priest Onias III with Onias's brother Jason, a Hellenizer; invades Jerusalem, sacrifices pig on the altar ("abomination of desolation"; Dan 9:27; 11:31; 12:11; see Matt 24:15 and parallels); priest named Mattathias in village of Modein starts Maccabean revolt
B. Jewish Self-Rule: The Maccabees and Hasmoneans (167–63 BC)	
1. The Maccabees (167–135 BC)	
165/4 BC	Temple worship restored; Feast of Dedication (see John 10:22)
164–161 BC	Judas
161–143/2 BC	Jonathan
143/2–135/4	Simon
2. The Hasmoneans (135–63 BC)	
135/4–104 BC	John Hyrcanus I
104–103 BC	Aristobulus I
103–76 BC	Alexander Janneus
76–67 BC	Salome Alexandra
67–63 BC	Aristobulus II
C. Roman Period (63 BC–AD 70)	
63 BC	General Pompey enters Jerusalem and establishes Roman rule
44 BC	Julius Caesar assassinated in Senate by Brutus and others; "Caesar" becomes title for emperors
40 BC	Herod named king of Judea by Roman Senate
37 BC	Herod repulses the Parthians to take the kingdom
31 BC	Octavian ("Augustus") prevails in Civil War against Mark Antony and Cleopatra (d. 30 BC); "Golden Age" of Rome, Roman law and order, *pax Romana* ("Roman peace"), emperor worship
c. 5 BC	Jesus is born in Bethlehem (Matt 1:18–2:12; Luke 2:1–20)*
4 BC	Herod dies, leaves kingdom to Archelaus
AD 6	Archelaus replaced by Roman prefects
AD 26	Pontius Pilate becomes governor of Judea
AD 33	Jesus is crucified*
AD 34	Conversion of Paul

* See the discussion of the chronology of Jesus' life in chap. 3.

III. Background to Jesus and the Early Church	
A. Roman Rulers	
31 BC–AD 14	Augustus: Jesus' birth; Golden Age (Luke 2:1)
14–37	Tiberius: Ministries of John the Baptist and Jesus take place during his reign (Luke 3:1–2,21)
37–41	Caligula
41–54	Claudius: Expelled Jews from Rome (Acts 18:2)
54–68	Nero: Fire of Rome (64); martyrdoms of Peter and Paul (65/66)
68–69	Galba, Otho, and Vitellius
69–79	Vespasian
81–96	Domitian: Persecution of Christians (Revelation)**
B. Jewish Revolts	
66–73	First Jewish revolt
70	Titus destroys Jerusalem, temple (cf. Matt 24:1–2 and parallels)
132–135	Bar Kokhba revolt: Jews exiled until modern times
C. The Herodian Dynasty	
40/37–4 BC	Herod the Great: Edomite vassal-ruler over Palestine Slaughter of infants in Bethlehem (Luke 2:16); three sons:
4 BC–AD 33	Herod Philip: Tetrarch of Northern provinces Iturea, Trachonitis, Gaulanitis, Auranitis, and Batanea
4 BC–AD 39	Herod Antipas: Tetrarch of Galilee and Perea: John the Baptist beheaded (Matt 14:3–12; Mark 6:17–29); Jesus called him "that fox" (Luke 13:32) and later stood trial before him (Luke 23:7–12)
4 BC–AD 6	Archelaus: Ethnarch of Judea and Samaria (banished by Augustus in AD 6); misrule caused Joseph to settle with Mary and Jesus in Nazareth after returning from Egypt (Matt 2:21–23); after AD 6, Galilee governed by Roman governors (prefects or procurators)
41–44	Herod Agrippa I: Grandson of Herod the Great; ruled as king over Judea and all Palestine; executed James the apostle and son of Zebedee and imprisoned Peter (Acts 12:1–3)
50–?	Herod Agrippa II: Great-grandson of Herod the Great; heard Paul's self-defense (Acts 25–26)

** See the discussion of the date of the book of Revelation in chap. 20.

HISTORY

The era spanning the time between the Testaments is commonly called the "Second Temple period." It ranges from the time of the building of the second temple in 515 BC by Zerubbabel until its destruction by the Romans in AD 70. From the vantage point of Israel's history, this period was a series of five eras marked by five great crises for the Jewish people.[1] For much of this time Judea was essentially a "temple state" under the immediate control of the high priests who were themselves under the authority of foreign governors or rulers. The following survey of the Second Temple Period begins with the *first great crisis*, the rule of the Babylonian King Nebuchadnezzar and his *destruction of the temple built by Solomon,* resulting in the Jews' loss of national sovereignty.

Table 2.3: The Five Major Crises of the Jews in the Second Temple Period

1. Babylonian destruction of Jerusalem and the first temple (586 BC)
2. Collapse of the Persian Empire in the wake of Alexander the Great's invasion (331 BC)
3. Persecution by Antiochus IV Epiphanes (198–167 BC)
4. Domination by Rome (63 BC–AD 70)
5. Roman destruction of the Jewish state and the second temple (AD 70)

The Babylonian Period (606–539 BC)

The account of the Babylonian occupation of Israel, which is included in the OT,[2] began in 606/5 BC with Nebuchadnezzar's conquest of Judea; the northern kingdom of Israel had already fallen to the Assyrians in 722 BC (see 2 Kgs 24:12). His conquest was completed with the siege of Jerusalem in 586 BC.[3] Nebuchadnezzar deported the higher classes in Judah (including Daniel and Ezekiel) to Babylon. The monarchy was dissolved, the central sanctuary (i.e., the temple) lost, and the Jews came to live in close proximity to Gentiles. All of this created a variety of moral and ceremonial problems.[4]

The preaching of the prophets demonstrates that the absence of the central sanctuary led Jews in the dispersion to focus on the moral dimension of God's law. Without a central place to meet and worship, the captives established the synagogue as a venue where they could gather to study and discuss the law. The synagogue was a well-established institution in NT times. While in exile, the Jews also determined permanently to renounce idolatry, the worship of gods other than Yahweh. Idolatry, in turn, had been a major cause for the exile in the first place (see 2 Kings 17).

The Persian Period (539–331 BC)

In due course Babylon came under attack from an upstart kingdom, the Persian Empire.[5] Cyrus of Persia, a former vassal of Media (from around 550 BC), achieved a rather peaceful

---

[1] See L. R. Helyer, *Exploring Jewish Literature of the Second Temple Period: A Guide for New Testament Students* (Downers Grove: InterVarsity, 2002), 18–24.

[2] See 2 Kgs 24–25; 2 Chr 36:5–21; and parts of Jeremiah, Daniel, and Ezekiel.

[3] 2 Kgs 25:3; see Jer 39:2: "In the fourth month of Zedekiah's eleventh year, on the ninth day of the month, the city was broken into" (i.e., July 18, 586 BC).

[4] J. J. Scott Jr., *Jewish Backgrounds of the New Testament* (Grand Rapids: Baker, 2000), 108–12.

[5] See L. L. Grabbe, "Jewish History: Persian Period," in *Dictionary of New Testament Background: A Compendium of Contemporary Biblical Scholarship*, ed. C. A. Evans and S. E. Porter (Downers Grove: InterVarsity, 2000), 574–76.

takeover of Babylon. On October 29, 539 BC, Cyrus entered Babylon and proclaimed himself "King of Babylon," beginning a new dynasty in the Middle East. Several OT books describe events during the Persian period, including 2 Chronicles, Ezra, Nehemiah, Esther, selected Psalms, Daniel, Haggai, Zechariah, Malachi, and Isaiah (44–45).

Cyrus's foreign policy, unlike that of Babylon, was to permit conquered peoples to maintain their local customs and religions in their homelands. Thus when Ezra petitioned Cyrus to return to Judea, he agreed (Ezra 1:1–4). Subsequently, Persia became a real superpower, with succeeding kings expanding "from India to Cush" (i.e., Ethiopia; Esth 1:1). Later, In fulfillment of biblical prophecy (Isa 44:28–45:13), Cyrus allowed the Jews to return to their homeland (Ezra 1:1–4). The captives gradually returned and with them the temple furniture and provision for the rebuilding of Jerusalem. The Persians ruled Palestine for more than 200 years, yet the empire eventually fell to the Greeks.

The Greek Period (331–167 BC)

The Greek period can be divided into three phases: (1) the conquests of Alexander the Great (331–320 BC); (2) the Ptolemaic period (320–198 BC); and (3) the Seleucid or Syrian period (198–167 BC). Beyond this, Greek influence was felt in Palestine through the pervasive impact of Greek culture called "Hellenization."

Alexander the Great and His Conquests (331–320 BC) This period officially began with Alexander the Great's conquest of Palestine.[6] Philip of Macedon (ruler of Macedonia), Alexander's father, was assassinated in 336 BC, which opened the door for Alexander's rise to the throne. After Alexander tamed the Greek city-states that did not immediately bow to his will, he turned his attention to Persia.[7] As predicted by the prophet Daniel (see Daniel 8), Alexander's conquest was brutally efficient.

Alexander's defeat of Persia, led by Darius III, was swift. Alexander won victories at the battles of Issus (near Tarsus, 333 BC) and Arbela (331 BC), then destroyed Tyre of Phoenicia[8] and Gaza on his way to Egypt. The Egyptians, who had never been fond of Persian rule, surrendered peacefully.[9] Alexander then turned northward and pursued Darius across Syria and Persia. Darius was killed after the battle of Gaugamela (331 BC). With no Persian heir to claim the throne, Alexander was declared the new world ruler.[10] Alexander sought to continue his conquest but caught fever in Persia and died at age 33, having conquered his empire in only 13 years.

The *collapse of the Persian Empire* with its lenient attitude toward self-identity and religious freedom was the *second great crisis* for the Jewish nation. The Jews would now have to deal with a series of Greek kings who believed their "superior" culture should

---

[6] Ibid., 570–74.

[7] Ibid.

[8] The port supplying the Persian navy; see R. D. Milns, "Alexander the Great," *ABD* 1.147.

[9] Milns, "Alexander," 147.

[10] A. J. Tomasino, *Judaism Before Jesus: The Events and Ideas That Shaped the New Testament World* (Downers Grove: InterVarsity, 2003), 109.

be firmly implanted in all the lands they occupied.[11] These kings arose through the inconsistent work of Alexander's four generals, who split up his empire.[12] Of the original successors to Alexander's kingdom, only Ptolemy I Soter formed a successful kingdom. Palestine thus came under the jurisdiction of the Egyptian ruler Ptolemy in about 320 BC.[13]

The Ptolemaic Period (320–198 BC)   Ptolemy set himself up as the progenitor of a ruling dynasty. Every ruler of Egypt until AD 30 bore the name "Ptolemy" regardless of actual descent. Ptolemaic rule was mainly concerned with aggressive taxation and securing the trade routes in the trans-Jordan. While the Ptolemies had gained control of Egypt, another Greek dynasty, the Seleucids, attained supremacy in Babylon. The Seleucids and the Ptolemies engaged in constant battles over Palestine. Ptolemy V lost Israel in 198 BC at Paneas to Antiochus III of Syria. Palestine would never again be ruled by Egyptian hands.

The Seleucid or Syrian Period (198–167 BC)   Although Syrian control over Palestine lasted only 31 years,[14] and was characterized by their requirement to pay tribute to Rome, it is a key period for one brutal figure. Antiochus IV, the regional ruler over Palestine, called himself "Epiphanes"—"the Glorious One"—implying he was the incarnation of Zeus on earth. His program of aggressive Hellenization outraged the Jews. His desire to spread Greek culture and the need for great amounts of money to pay Rome impacted the way in which Antiochus chose the Jewish high priest in Jerusalem, accepting bribes in exchange for awarding the office.

Antiochus eventually *attempted to ban Judaism*, which represented the *third great crisis* that affected the Jews. In instituting the ban, he prohibited possession of the Torah, circumcision, festivals, and offerings to Yahweh. Perhaps the most devastating of all of Antiochus' measures was the dedication of the Jerusalem temple to Zeus, the head of the Greek pantheon. Antiochus erected a statue of Zeus in the temple and sacrificed a pig on the altar. This abomination greatly angered the Jews and spawned a resistance movement begun by an old priest named Mattathias.

Jewish Self-Rule (167–63 BC)

The Maccabees (167–135 BC)   The Maccabean period is named for the third son of Mattathias, Judas.[15] Nicknamed "Maccabeus," "the hammer," he led a guerilla war against the Seleucids. Due to Judas Maccabeus's efforts, in 165 BC Antiochus's representative, Lysias, rescinded the ban on Judaism. The next year Judas led in a cleansing of the temple,

---

[11] Helyer, *Exploring Jewish Literature of the Second Temple Period*, 19, 75–76.

[12] See Daniel's vision where the great horn of the male goat is suddenly struck, and four lesser horns grow up in four directions (Dan 8:8).

[13] D. B. Sandy, "Ptolemies," in *Dictionary of New Testament Background*, 870–73.

[14] For a helpful introduction, see D. W. J. Gill, "Seleucids and Antiochids," in *Dictionary of New Testament Background*, 1092–93.

[15] For a selection of readings in the primary sources, see C. K. Barrett, ed., *The New Testament Background: Selected Documents* (rev. and exp. ed.; San Francisco: Harper, 1989), chap. 7.

commemorated to this day as the December Feast of Lights, an eight-day feast known as Hanukah that falls in late December. Although Judas died in battle in 160 BC at the hands of Nicanor of Syria, Judas's brothers, Jonathan and Simon, continued the resistance and achieved the benchmark of national autonomy in 142 BC. Simon was installed in the executive and religious branches of government (a departure from the biblical teachings), which began a slide into despotism for the Maccabees. After a reign characterized by economic prosperity and relative peace, Simon and two of his sons were murdered by his son-in-law Ptolemy. The surviving son, Hyrcanus, escaped and defeated Ptolemy.[16]

The Hasmoneans (135–63 BC)   Despite Simon's breakthrough, the years between 142 and 135 BC continued to be unsettled. John Hyrcanus (135/34–104 BC) was the first of the Hasmonean rulers. Hyrcanus led an expansion of Judean territories into Moab and Idumea. He forced the circumcision of the Idumeans and thus paved the way for Herod the Great in NT times. Upon the death of Hyrcanus I, his son Aristobulus I (104–103 BC) proclaimed himself king, becoming the first of the Hasmonean rulers to take that title. Upon Aristobulus's sudden death in 103 BC, his widow, Salome Alexandra, appointed Alexander Janneus, Aristobulus's older brother, as high priest and king and then promptly married him.

Alexander Janneus (103–76 BC) ruled as a Hellenistic king.[17] He expanded the country to Solomonic proportions with the use of foreign mercenaries but cared nothing for the spiritual duties of a high priest. Upon his death he gave the kingdom to his wife Salome Alexandra, who reigned relatively peacefully from 76 until 67 BC.[18] Upon her death in 67 BC, her heirs contended for the kingdom. In the meantime, Roman armies under the leadership of Pompey's representatives subdued the ever-unstable Seleucid kingdom. The independent Jewish state came to an end when Pompey walked into the holy of holies, installed Hyrcanus II as high priest but not as king, and made Judea a client kingdom under the rule of an imperial governor in Syria. Rome was now in charge of Palestine. The Jews had to deal with the *fourth great crisis* in their national identity: *life under Roman rule.*

The Roman Period (63 BC–AD 70)

Roman History and the Conquest of Palestine   According to tradition, Rome was founded in 753 BC by Romulus and Remus.[19] In the fifth century BC, Rome became a republic. Several centuries later Rome prevailed over the North African rival city Carthage (146 BC). In 63 BC, Pompey extended Roman rule to Palestine. At first, Roman rule must not have looked any different to the local populace from Syrian dominance. Several men were jockeying for power—Antigonus (the heir of Aristobulus II), Hyrcanus II, Antipater (the Idumean), and Antipater's sons Phasael and Herod.

---

[16] See Josephus, *Ant.* 20.240; *Jewish War* 1.54.

[17] Josephus called him *philellen*, that is, "Greek-lover" (*Ant.* 13.318).

[18] See Josephus, *Ant.* 13.407.

[19] For a survey of the Roman period, see L. L. Grabbe, "Jewish History: Roman Period," in *Dictionary of New Testament Background*, 576–80.

The Herodian Dynasty Herod was named "king of Judea" by the Roman Senate in 40 BC but did not actually win his kingdom until 37 BC when he deposed Antigonus with the help of Antony.[20] Herod was technically a client king under the authority of Rome; thus he was considered "a friend and ally of the Roman people." He was an able administrator, but he was cruel and paranoid. His ability is seen in the agricultural and commercial enterprises he started that brought prosperity to the region. His cruelty is seen in his murder of his own sons and wife, Mariamne (a Hasmonean princess, granddaughter of both Hyrcanus and Aristobulus), whom he suspected of plotting to take his kingdom. Although some of the particular stories of Herod in the NT (see Matthew 2) are not corroborated by external sources, the cruel and paranoid picture painted there is in keeping with what we know of Herod's character elsewhere.

Before Herod died, Herod's sons were briefly given ruling positions. Archelaus was appointed ethnarch over Judea, Samaria, and Idumea, which included Jerusalem (4 BC). Rome dismissed him in AD 6 because of his incompetence. Archelaus was not a skillful administrator like his father, but he was like him in being cruel and paranoid. Ultimately, the most significant outcome of Archelaus's rule was that Jerusalem was placed under direct Roman control.

Another of Herod's sons, and the one considered to be the most capable and astute, Herod Antipas, was made tetrarch over Galilee and Perea (4 BC). He divorced his wife (daughter of the Nabatean King Aretas IV) to marry the wife of his half brother, Herod Philip (not the Philip mentioned above), and martyred John the Baptist after his condemnation of this act (Mark 6:14–29 and parallels).

After AD 6, Judea was made a Roman province and as such was under the rule of Roman imperial governors (prefects until Claudius, later procurators). The governors lived in Caesarea and only went up to Jerusalem on feast days. However, they kept a strong military presence in Judea. The Jews were allowed to mint coins without offensive images, containing only names without ascriptions of deity. A sacrifice to Yahweh on behalf of the Roman government took the place of the required sacrifice to the gods. They also had limited autonomy through the rule of the Sanhedrin, over which the high priest presided.

The Roman Emperors and Governors of Palestine As mentioned, Rome was constituted as a republic in the fifth century BC, with the Roman Senate governing the affairs of the nation. The second and first centuries BC saw the Romans rise to world supremacy. The "Golden Age" (so called by the Roman poet Virgil) of Rome was ushered in under Augustus, who ruled from 31 BC until AD 14. This period was characterized by the rule of Roman law, providing it stability; the "Roman peace" (*pax Romana*), providing a climate conducive for the construction of roads and the unification of the empire; and general

---

[20] For helpful primary source material, see Barrett, *New Testament Background*, 148–55; cf. H. W. Hoehner, "Herodian Dynasty," in *Dictionary of New Testament Background*, 485–94 (see esp. the chart on p. 321 and further bibliographic references on pp. 325–26).

prosperity and affluence. Tiberius (14–37) succeeded Augustus and reigned during the lifetimes of John the Baptist and Jesus (Luke 3:1).[21]

The Roman governor of Palestine at the time of Christ's ministry was Pontius Pilate.[22] His tenure was characterized by bribery, insults, executions without trials, and grievous cruelty. Pilate's early career was marked by arrogance and a willingness to offend the Jews, likely facilitated by the support provided by his powerful patron in Rome, Sejanus, prefect of the praetorian guard under Tiberius. This Sejanus administered the empire for Tiberius, while the latter stayed on the Isle of Capri. According to Philo, Sejanus had a particular dislike of the Jews and the Jewish nation, and Pilate may have been implementing Sejanus's policy toward Judea.[23]

From the time of the Babylonian captivity to *the destruction of Jerusalem and the temple in the year 70* (*the fifth great crisis*), the Jewish nation was subjected to a series of occupational forces with only a brief interlude of self-rule during the Maccabean era. When Jesus was born and later began his public ministry, messianic expectations were widespread, and the Jewish hope of liberation—though construed primarily in political and nationalistic terms—was at a fever pitch.

The "Fullness of Time"

Paul stated in his letter to the Galatians that the Lord Jesus appeared "when the fullness of time came" (Gal 4:4 NASB). The expression "fullness of time," among other things, conveys the notion that Jesus came "at just the right time." But what made the time of Christ's coming "just the right time"? In the context, Paul's reference to the "fullness of time" in Gal 4:4 pertains to believers' adoption to sonship through the redemptive work of Christ (see vv. 5–7). This marked a new phase in salvation history subsequent to the period during which the law served as the primary point of reference (see Gal 3:16–26).

In addition to this salvation-historical point of reference of the phrase "fullness of time," which must remain primary, conditions were indeed ideally suited for the coming of Jesus due to factors such as the following: (1) the *pax Romana*; (2) Roman roads; (3) the Greek language; and (4) Jewish messianic expectations.

First, the 200 years of unprecedented (though militarily imposed) peace known as the *pax Romana* provided "just the right time" for Jesus' appearing.[24] This peace enabled the development of the second factor: roads. The Romans had built a network of roads throughout the empire. By common parlance, "All roads lead to Rome," providing relatively easy travel. Thus, in God's providence the roads built by the Romans paved the way

---

[21] See J. E. Bowley, "Pax Romana," in *Dictionary of New Testament Background*, 771–75.

[22] The famous "Pilate Inscription," discovered in 1961 in Caesarea, reads as follows:
TIBERIEUM ("To Tiberius")
[PON]TIUS PILATUS ("From Pontius Pilate")
[PRAEF]ECTUS IUDA[EA]E ("Governor of Judea")

[23] See P. L. Maier, "Sejanus, Pilate, and the Date of the Crucifixion," *Church History* 37 (1968): 3–13.

[24] See D. Guthrie, *Galatians*, NCBC (Grand Rapids: Eerdmans, 1974), 113.

for the spread of the gospel of Jesus Christ from Jerusalem all the way to Rome (see the book of Acts, esp. 1:8; 28:14–31).

Third, the conquests of Alexander the Great made Greek the language of commerce throughout the Roman Empire. The result was a common idiom that provided a universal vehicle for the spread of the gospel. In fact, the language became so influential that the OT was translated into Greek (the LXX) and the NT was written in Greek. Fourth, the various strands of first-century Judaism, each in its own way, sustained a vibrant, albeit diverse, hope for a Messiah. When Jesus came claiming to be the Messiah, he entered a world in which many were already expecting such a figure. Thus, from the perspective of salvation history, Jesus came indeed "at just the right time."

LITERATURE

While the production of canonical writings ceased in the intertestamental era, there is an abundance of extant literature dating from this period that sheds considerable light on the background of the NT. The following brief survey of Second Temple literature will acquaint you with the vast array of relevant source material for the study of this era. The OT itself is available in three versions: (1) in the original Hebrew; (2) in Greek translation (the Septuagint or LXX; see above); and (3) in Aramaic paraphrase (the Targums). In addition, Jewish Second Temple literature includes the following three bodies of writings: (1) the Apocrypha; (2) the Pseudepigrapha; and (3) the Qumran writings or Dead Sea Scrolls (DSS).

The Apocrypha

The Greek word *apocrypha* originally meant "things that are hidden."[25] The designation *Apocrypha* may also refer to the mysterious or esoteric nature of some of the contents of these books or to their spurious or heretical nature (or both). Roman Catholics employ the label "deutero-canonical," by which they mean that the books of the Apocrypha were added to the canon at a later time. Nevertheless, they consider the Apocrypha canonical rather than apocryphal. Protestants have traditionally distinguished between the Hebrew Scriptures as canonical and the Apocrypha as noncanonical.

The writings comprising the OT Apocrypha included in this category represent several different genres:

1. Historical writings (1 Esdras, 1–2 Maccabees)
2. Moralistic novels (Tobit, Judith, Susanna, Bel and the Dragon)
3. Wisdom or devotional literature (Wisdom of Solomon; Sirach, also called Ecclesiasticus; Prayer of Manasseh; Prayer of Azariah; Song of the Three Young Men)
4. Pseudonymous letter (Letter of Jeremiah)
5. Apocalyptic literature (2 Esdras)

---

[25] D. A. deSilva, "Apocrypha and Pseudepigrapha," in *Dictionary of New Testament Background*, 58; see the entire entry on pp. 58–64, including additional bibliographic references.

In addition, there are NT Apocrypha that emerged in the second and subsequent centuries of the Christian era, consisting of spurious Gospels, Acts, and Apocalypses. Many of these writings seek to fill in perceived gaps in Scripture, frequently resulting in false teaching. Along with the Apocrypha, the Pseudepigrapha display an imaginative "reading between the lines" that led to a body of literature lacking true divine inspiration.

Pseudepigrapha

The Pseudepigrapha (from *pseudos*, "false," and *graphein*, "write") encompass the following types of literature (selected works).

1. Apocalyptic and related literature (1–2 Enoch; 2–3 Baruch; 4 Ezra; Sibylline Oracles)
2. Testaments (Testaments of the Twelve Patriarchs)
3. Pseudonymous epistle (Letter of Aristeas)
4. Wisdom or devotional literature (Psalms of Solomon; Odes of Solomon; Psalm 151)
5. Expansions of OT material (Jubilees; Joseph and Aseneth; Jannes and Jambres; Assumption of Moses; Martyrdom and Ascension of Isaiah)
6. Religious novels and philosophical treatises (3–4 Maccabees)

Dead Sea Scrolls

The discovery of the Dead Sea Scrolls (DSS) began in 1947, constituted the major archeological find of the twentieth century, and greatly affected biblical and Jewish studies. The DSS come from a Jewish sect that most likely arose in the Maccabean era around the middle of the second century BC and continued through the first Jewish revolt in AD 66–73. The community's use of Scripture also provides an intriguing precedent for John the Baptist's self-identification as "a voice crying in the wilderness" (taken from Isa 40:3). The Dead Sea community used the same passage of Scripture with reference to itself.[26] The community and the DSS provide a helpful background for understanding the NT in general and key NT figures such as John the Baptist and Jesus.

THEOLOGY

The chapters on the various books of the NT investigate the specific background relevant for each book. At this stage it will be helpful to provide a general backdrop of the first-century Jewish and Greco-Roman world in order to convey a general sense of the environment in which Jesus and the early church lived. The following discussion presents the most significant background issues for the study of the NT: (1) paganism; (2) emperor worship; (3) mystery religions; (4) superstition and syncretism; (5) Gnosticism; (6) philosophy; and (7) Judaism.

---

[26] See A. J. Köstenberger, "John," in *Commentary on the New Testament Use of the Old Testament*, ed. G. K. Beale and D. A. Carson (Grand Rapids: Baker, 2007), 421, 425–28.

Paganism

People in the ancient world were profoundly religious whether they embraced the religion of Israel or Christianity (see Acts 14:11–13). Greek mythology featured Zeus as the head of the hierarchy of gods. Apollos, son of Zeus, was cast as one who inspired poets and prophets. Roman religion appropriated much of the Greek pantheon, identifying Roman gods with Greek ones (Jupiter = Zeus, Venus = Aphrodite, etc.). The Roman emperor himself served as high priest (*pontifex maximus*), merging the political and religious realms.

Emperor Worship

The Roman Senate instituted the emperor cult by deifying Augustus (31 BC–AD 14) and subsequent emperors after his death. Domitian (81–96) claimed the title *dominus et deus* ("lord and god"), to which John may allude in his citation of Thomas's confession of Jesus as "My Lord and my God!" (John 20:28).[27] Emperor worship provides especially important background to the book of Revelation, which in all likelihood was written during the persecution of Christians under Nero or Domitian.[28]

Mystery Religions

The ancient world in the first few centuries of the Christian era was replete with "mystery religions," various cults that conceived of the heart of religion as mystical union with the divine. There were Greek, Egyptian, and Oriental mystery religions. Secret initiatory rites involved ceremonial washings, sacred meals, intoxication, and emotional frenzies. The purpose of these rites was to enter into union with the deity.

Superstition and Syncretism

The ancient world was filled with superstition and syncretism, an eclectic mix of religious practices. These practices included magic, horoscopes, oracles, and augury (the prediction of future events by observing birds' flight patterns). The book of Acts features numerous examples of superstition and syncretism in the first-century world (see Acts 8:9–24; 13:7; 19:19; 28:3–6).

Gnosticism

Gnosticism (from Gr. *gnōsis*, "knowledge") is rooted in the Platonic dualism that sharply distinguished between the invisible world of ideas and the visible world of matter. Generally, this worldview equated matter with evil and viewed only the spirit realm as good. It is important to note that the NT era only documents a very early form of Gnosticism. Full-fledged Gnosticism did not emerge until the second century.

In a possible reference to gnostic-type thought, Paul warned Timothy to avoid "irreverent, empty speech and contradictions from the 'knowledge' [*gnōsis*] that falsely bears that name" (1 Tim 6:20). Paul also denounced false teachers who forbade marriage and

---

[27] E. Ferguson, *Backgrounds of Early Christianity*, rev. ed. (Grand Rapids: Eerdmans, 1993), 35.
[28] See the discussion of the emperor cult in chap. 20.

demanded abstinence from certain foods, maintaining that, to the contrary, everything God created was good (1 Tim 4:1–5; see 1 Tim 2:15). He also condemned the Colossian heresy that advocated false asceticism and legalism (Col 2:4–23; see 1 Tim 4:7–8), though this may have been a unique form of syncretism.

Philosophy

Greek philosophy pervaded the first-century Mediterranean world as well.[29] Three particular philosophies were most popular. (1) *Epicureanism* taught that pleasure (in the sense of happiness, not necessarily sensual pleasure) was the chief good in life. This led to an advocacy of "hedonism," the pursuit of pleasure as a matter of ethical principle: "Let us eat and drink for tomorrow we die" (1 Cor 15:32; see Isa 22:13). (2) *Stoicism* taught the dutiful acceptance of one's fate—a form of fatalism—as determined by impersonal reason ruling the universe. People were enjoined to face their destiny "stoically," that is, without emotion. Paul encountered both Epicurean and Stoic philosophers in Athens (Acts 17:18). (3) Advocates of *Cynicism* were itinerant preachers who taught that simplicity was life's supreme virtue and that people ought to cultivate it instead of popular pursuits. However, in reality superstition and syncretism largely prevailed among the masses.

Judaism

The last—and in many ways the most important—element of NT background is Judaism, which made several important contributions to early Christianity. For this reason, the following treatment of Judaism is more extensive than the previous sections. The most relevant features for our purposes are:

Monotheism   Judaism taught *monotheism*, a firm commitment to the belief in one God as taught in the OT and proclaimed in the *Shema* (Hb. "Hear"): "Hear, O Israel: The LORD our God is one LORD" (Deut 6:4 KJV).[30] The first two of the Ten Commandments (the Decalogue) forbade Israelites from worshipping other gods (Exod 20:2–6; Deut 5:6–10). This commitment distinguished Jewish religion in a polytheistic environment and was recognized by Greco-Roman historians such as Tacitus, who wrote, "The Jews conceive of one God only" (*Hist.* 5.5).

The Synagogue   The importance of the synagogue for Jewish life and for the early church is undisputed.[31] The liturgy and leadership structure of the synagogue provided the early church with a pattern for the establishment of distinct Christian liturgical practices and leadership structures. For Jesus, Paul, and the early Christian mission, the synagogue provided a natural platform for proclaiming salvation through faith in Jesus as the Messiah (Luke 4:16–30; John 6:30–59; 18:20; Acts 13:13–52).

---

[29] See J. M. Dillon, "Philosophy," in *Dictionary of New Testament Background*, 793–96.

[30] See A. J. Köstenberger and S. R. Swain, *Father, Son and Spirit: The Trinity and John's Gospel*, NSBT 24 (Downers Grove: InterVarsity, 2008), chap. 1.

[31] See B. Chilton and E. Yamauchi, "Synagogues," in *Dictionary of New Testament Background*, 1145–53.

The Temple Another important feature of Judaism was the Jerusalem temple, which served as a vital symbol of national and religious unity. The original temple built by Solomon (1 Kings 5–8) was destroyed by the Babylonians in 586 BC. After the exile a new temple was built by Zerubbabel (Ezra 3; Haggai 1–2; Zechariah 4). Surrounded by porticoes, the temple consisted of an outer court (the Court of the Gentiles) and an inner temple. The first room was the "holy place," which was separated from the outside by a heavy veil. The innermost room, the "holy of holies," was separated from the holy place by another heavy veil. The high priest entered it but once a year on the Day of Atonement.

In Jesus' day, the temple, once the glorious symbol of God's dwelling with his people, had degenerated into a place of commerce and perfunctory ritual (John 2:14–16). With the destruction of the temple in the year 70, Judaism was forced to adjust its sacrificial and liturgical practices because the central element of its entire system of worship had been removed.

The Religious Calendar The OT Jewish religious calendar provides an important backdrop for the NT account of Jesus' life and for the worship of the early church. The institution of many important holy days in the life of Israel—including the Sabbath, Passover, the Day of Atonement—is recorded in Leviticus 23, and these festivals pervade the entire OT. These festivals marked the life of Jews in the era leading up to the NT.

Rabbinic Schools In first-century Palestine, rabbis in certain schools maintained that the oral law could be traced back to Moses at Mount Sinai and that it superseded the OT itself. Jesus charged them with revoking God's word because of their tradition (Matt 15:6) and excoriated them for this (Matt 23:1–7). Understanding this background proves helpful, for example, when one reads the following question posed by the Pharisees to Jesus: "Is it lawful for a man to divorce his wife on any grounds?" (Matt 19:3).[32]

Proselytes and God-Fearers Proselytes were full converts to Judaism who observed the Sabbath, food laws, and circumcision of all males; and God-fearers were those who only accepted the moral teachings and general religious practices of Judaism without submitting to circumcision.[33] The NT, especially the Gospels and the book of Acts, makes repeated references to proselytes and God-fearers.[34] God-fearers who approached Jesus in order to have healings include a Roman centurion (Matt 8:5–13 and parallels) and a royal official (John 4:46–54). The story of God-fearing Cornelius (Acts 10:9–16) showed that Gentiles were equal with Jews in the new messianic community. This was a revolutionary concept for many first-century Jews, including many early Christians (see 1 Cor 12:13; Gal 2:11–21; 3:28).

---

[32] See A. J. Köstenberger (with D. W. Jones), *God, Marriage, and Family: Rebuilding the Biblical Foundation,* 2nd ed. (Wheaton: Crossway, 2010), chap. 11, esp. 228–29.

[33] See Ferguson, *Backgrounds of Early Christianity,* 512–17; S. McKnight, "Proselytism and Godfearers," in *Dictionary of New Testament Background,* 835–47.

[34] The word *theosebeis* ("God-fearer" or "worshipper of God") occurs in Acts 10:2,22,35; 13:6,26; the related term *sebomenoi* ("worshipper[s] of God") is found in Acts 13:43,50; 16:14; 17:4,17; 18:7.

Table 2.4: Jewish Festivals

The Jewish religious calendar began in March/April and included the following festivals:
1. Passover (Exod 12:1–14; Lev 23:5; Num 9:1–14; 28:16; Deut 16:1–7)
2. Unleavened Bread (Exod 12:15–20; 13:3–10; 23:15; 34:18; Lev 23:6–8; Num 28:17–25; Deut 16:3–4,8), both celebrated at the beginning of wheat harvest (March/April) and commemorating God's deliverance of Israel at the time of the exodus
3. The Feast of Firstfruits (Lev 23:9–14)
4. The Feast of Weeks or Pentecost (Exod 23:16; 34:22; Lev 23:15–21; Num 28:26–31; Deut 16:9–12), celebrated at the end of the wheat harvest (May/June)
5. Trumpets or *Rosh Hashanah* (Lev 23:23–25; Num 29:1–6), commemorating the beginning of the civil year (September/October)
6. The Day of Atonement or *Yom Kippur* (Lev 16; 23:26–32; Num 29:7–11), a day of national repentance (September/October; technically not a feast)
7. Tabernacles or Booths or Ingathering (Exod 23:16; 34:22; Lev 23:33–36,39–43; Num 29:12–34; Deut 16:13–15; Zech 14:16–19), commemorating the Israelites' living in tents in the wilderness after the exodus (September/October)
8. Lights or Dedication or *Hanukkah* (John 12:22), celebrating the rededication of the temple by Judas Maccabeus in 165 or 164 BC (December 25) after it had been desecrated by Antiochus Epiphanes
9. Purim (Esth 9:18–32), commemorating the deliverance of the Jews in the time of Esther (February/March).

Jewish Theology   Many Jewish beliefs are significant as NT background, including those regarding the end time, the nature of man, and the coming of the Messiah. With regard to the end time, Jews typically embraced the teaching of "two ages," whereby "the present (evil) age" preceded the "days of the Messiah" or "the Day of the Lord," inaugurating "the coming age." This is clearly seen in the Gospels.[35] Paradoxically, the Gospels indicate that, with Jesus' coming, the "age to come" has already begun. Hence Jesus taught that God's kingdom was already present (Luke 17:21), and those who believed in him already had eternal life (John 3:16; 10:10).

Messianism   One of the most important aspects of Jewish theology was messianism, that is, various beliefs regarding a coming figure called the "Messiah" or "Anointed One." Most Jews were looking for one, and in some cases several, Messiah(s). In view of Micah 5:2 some believed that the Messiah was to be born in Bethlehem (Matt 2:5–6; see John 7:41–42); others held that the Messiah's origins would be mysterious (John 7:27; see Dan 7:13). Few (if any) expected that the Messiah would have to suffer (though this is clearly taught in Isa 52:13–53:12; see Matt 16:21–23; John 12:34). Most thought of the Messiah in nationalistic terms, expecting him to establish an earthly rule with Israel at its center and delivering the Jews from their foreign oppressors (see John 1:49; 6:14; 12:12–13).

---

[35] See G. E. Ladd, *A Theology of the New Testament*, rev. ed. (Grand Rapids: Eerdmans, 1993), 54–67.

Jewish Sects and Other Groups of People Several prominent Jewish sects appear in the Gospels.[36]

The *Pharisees* were Jesus' primary antagonists and practiced a form of righteousness that observed a complex system of oral traditions in an effort to flesh out the implications of scriptural commands for everyday life. Unlike the Sadducees, the Pharisees believed in the resurrection and in angels (Acts 23:8).

The *Sadducees*[37] held a majority on the Sanhedrin, the Jewish ruling council, accepted only the Pentateuch as Scripture, denied the future resurrection and did not believe in angels (Acts 23:8). The Sadducees allied with the Pharisees to crucify Jesus, providing the maxim that politics makes strange bedfellows.

The *Zealots*[38] were fiercely loyal to Jewish traditions and opposed to any foreign influence in Palestine. One of Jesus' followers appears to have been a Zealot (Simon the Zealot; Matt 10:4).

The common people of Palestine are at times referred to in the Gospels as the "people of the land." They were scorned by the religious leaders. Typical is the Pharisees' attitude conveyed by the statement in John's Gospel: "But this crowd, which doesn't know the law, is accursed!" (7:49).

There was also a large number of Jews in the Diaspora outside Palestine (see John 7:35) who worshipped in their synagogues and attracted a considerable number of proselytes and God-fearers.

The Sanhedrin The *Sanhedrin*, variously called "Council," "the rulers," "chief priests, elders, and scribes," or a combination thereof in the NT, was the Jewish supreme council in all religious and political matters and was convened by the high priest.[39] Ideally, it consisted of 70 members on the precedent set by Moses in Exodus 18, though this may not always have been their actual number.

CONCLUSION

In this chapter we laid the foundation for our study of the NT in the rest of this book. While Palestine was ruled by the Roman governor who reported to the emperor in Rome, the Jews enjoyed a considerable degree of religious and political autonomy in Jesus' day. By acquiring a basic understanding of historical and political developments and theological views prior to the NT period, you will be well equipped for understanding the historical context of each of the writings of the NT.

---

[36] On their origin in the period of the Maccabees, see "History" above; cf. S. Mason, "Theologies and Sects, Jewish," in *Dictionary of New Testament Background*, 1221–30.

[37] See G. G. Porton, "Sadducees," in *Dictionary of New Testament Background*, 1050–52.

[38] See Josephus, *Jewish War* 2.598–606.

[39] For a detailed discussion of Jewish high priests appointed by Herod the Great and his successors, see E. Schürer, *The History of the Jewish People in the Age of Jesus Christ (175 BC–AD 135)*, rev. and ed. G. Vermes, E. Millar, and M. Black, vol. 3 (Edinburgh: T&T Clark, 1973, 1979, 1986, 1987), 2:229–36.

STUDY QUESTIONS

1. What is the significance of the following events or books for the NT?
    a. The Assyrian exile of Israel (the northern kingdom)
    b. The Babylonian exile of Judah (the southern kingdom)
    c. The conquests of Alexander the Great
2. What was the name of the Greek ruler who erected a statue of Zeus in the Jerusalem temple, and when did this event take place?
3. What are the years of rule for the following Roman emperors?
    a. Augustus
    b. Tiberius
    c. Nero
    d. Domitian
4. When did the Romans destroy the Jerusalem temple?
5. What were the three major Jewish sects active in first-century Judaism?
6. What was the name of the Jewish ruling council?

FOR FURTHER STUDY

Barrett, C. K., ed. *The New Testament Background: Selected Documents.* San Francisco: Harper, 1989.

Bruce, F. F. *New Testament History.* Garden City, NY: Doubleday, 1980.

Burge, G. M., L. H. Cohick, and G. L. Green. *The New Testament in Antiquity: A Survey of the New Testament Within Its Cultural Contexts.* Grand Rapids: Zondervan, 2009.

Chapman, D. W., and A. J. Köstenberger. "Jewish Intertestamental and Early Rabbinic Literature: An Annotated Bibliographic Resource Updated." *Journal of the Evangelical Theological Society* 55 (2012).

Charlesworth, J. H., ed. *The Old Testament Pseudepigrapha.* 2 vols. Garden City, NY: Doubleday, 1983, 1985.

DeSilva, D. A. *Introducing the Apocrypha: Message, Context, and Significance.* Grand Rapids: Baker, 2002.

Evans, C. A., and S. E. Porter, eds. *Dictionary of New Testament Background: A Compendium of Contemporary Biblical Scholarship.* Downers Grove, IL: InterVarsity, 2000.

Evans, C. A. *Ancient Texts for New Testament Studies.* Peabody, MA: Hendrickson, 2005.

Ferguson, E. *Backgrounds of Early Christianity.* Rev. ed. Grand Rapids: Eerdmans, 1993.

Gowan, D. E. *Bridge Between the Testaments: A Reappraisal of Judaism from the Exile to the Birth of Christianity.* 3rd ed. Allison Park, PA: Pickwick, 1986.

Helyer, L. R. *Exploring Jewish Literature of the Second Temple Period: A Guide for New Testament Students.* Downers Grove, IL: InterVarsity, 2002.

Nickelsburg, G. W. E. *Jewish Literature Between the Bible and the Mishnah.* Philadelphia: Fortress, 1981.

Schürer, E. *The History of the Jewish People in the Age of Jesus Christ (175 BC–AD 135).* Rev. and ed. G. Vermes, F. Millar, and M. Black. 3 vols. in 4. Edinburgh: T&T Clark, 1973, 1979, 1986, 1987.

Scott, J. J., Jr. *Jewish Backgrounds of the New Testament.* Grand Rapids: Baker, 2000.

———. *Customs and Controversies: Intertestamental Jewish Backgrounds of the New Testament.* Grand Rapids: Baker, 1995.

Strack, H. L., and G. Stemberger. *Introduction to the Talmud and Midrash.* Translated by M. Bockmuehl. Minneapolis: Fortress, 1992.

Witherington, B., III. *New Testament History: A Narrative Account.* Grand Rapids: Baker, 2001.

Part Two

JESUS AND THE GOSPELS

PART 1 SOUGHT to lay a proper foundation for this introduction to the NT by discussing the nature and scope of Scripture (chap. 1) and surveying the political and religious background of the NT (chap. 2). Part 2 provides an introduction to Jesus and the Gospels (chap. 3) as well as treatments of the history, literature, and theology of each of the four Gospels: Matthew, Mark, Luke, and John, in canonical order (chaps. 4–7).

This chapter will examine the historical evidence that supports the portrayal of Jesus in the Gospels, the historical reliability of the Gospels, and the relationship of the Gospels to each other. The chapters on the individual Gospels consider each of these Gospels in their own right, discussing the standard introductory matters for each as well as their literary plan, outline, and theological themes. While most likely written after Paul's earlier letters, it is appropriate to treat the Gospels first due to their placement first in the NT canon and due to their foundational nature as presentations of Jesus as the Messiah, Savior, and Lord.

Chapter 3

Introduction to Jesus and the Gospels

CORE KNOWLEDGE

Students should be able to identify key references to Jesus in Jewish and Roman extra-biblical materials and know major data in Jesus' life, including the date of his birth, the length of his ministry, and the date of the crucifixion. They should also be familiar with the basic similarities and differences among the Synoptic Gospels.

INTRODUCTION

FOR THE CHRISTIAN, no study can be more important than that of Jesus and the Gospels. Jesus of Nazareth is the focus of the Christian faith. It is no accident that the earliest Christian councils were convened and creeds were written to address questions surrounding Jesus' nature and identity. The early church recognized that an understanding of Jesus' identity is essential to genuine Christianity and a prerequisite for experiencing salvation and enjoying a relationship with God.

While the OT predicted the coming of Jesus, and later portions of the NT frequently refer to Jesus, the most thorough descriptions of Jesus' life and teachings are in the four canonical Gospels. The early titles (e.g., "The Gospel According to Matthew") capture the important fact that while there are four canonical Gospels, there is only one gospel of Jesus Christ. The four Gospels, then, can be understood as four complementary perspectives or versions of the one gospel of Jesus Christ.

REFERENCES TO JESUS OUTSIDE THE GOSPELS

Non-Christians sometimes challenge the Christian faith by claiming that Jesus never existed. They often incorrectly assert that no ancient texts outside of the NT even refer to Jesus. Even if no texts outside of the NT mentioned Jesus, this would not be reasonable grounds for denying his existence. The NT should not be regarded as a single source since it is actually composed of 27 books by at least eight different authors. The NT thus provides multiple independent attestations to Jesus' existence, life, teachings, miracles, death, and resurrection. Other early Christian writings by the apostolic and early church fathers offer further evidence regarding Jesus' existence.[1] In addition, several non-Christian extrabiblical texts, both Jewish and pagan, mention Jesus of Nazareth and offer brief descriptions of him.

The first-century Jewish historian Josephus wrote of Jesus as a historical figure. Josephus briefly referred to Jesus in a discussion of the identity of his brother James (*Ant.* 20.9.1 §§200–203):

> He [Ananus the high priest] seated the judges of the Sanhedrin Council and after he led to them the brother of Jesus who was called Messiah, the man whose name was James, and certain others, and accused them of having transgressed the Law, he handed them over to be stoned.

The passage attests to the existence of Jesus of Nazareth as a historical person and to his relationship to James. It also confirms that some of Jesus' contemporaries recognized him as the Messiah. Josephus also is thought to have written more specifically of Jesus (*Ant.* 18.3.3 §§63–64):

> At this time there was a wise man who was called Jesus. And his conduct was good, and he was known to be virtuous. And many people from among the Jews and the other nations became his disciples. Pilate condemned him to be crucified and to die. And those who have become his disciples did not abandon his discipleship. They reported that he had appeared to them three days after his crucifixion and that he was alive; accordingly he was perhaps the Messiah concerning whom the prophets have recounted wonders.[2]

Although Josephus's work is not to be regarded as inspired, it is for the most part reliable history written during the first century AD. The testimony of Josephus constitutes the most important early testimony about Jesus of Nazareth outside of the Bible.

In addition to Jewish writings, references to Jesus are found in Roman sources. One key example is the work of the Roman historian Tacitus (c. 56–after 113) who wrote his *Annals* in the early second century. Tacitus covered the great fire of Rome that Nero blamed on the Christians to divert attention from his own involvement in the arson.

---

[1] "Apostolic Fathers" is a technical label for the following writings: *1 and 2 Clement*; *The Letters of Ignatius*; *The Letter of Polycarp to the Philippians*; *The Martyrdom of Polycarp*; *The Didache*; *The Epistle of Barnabas*; *The Shepherd of Hermas*; *The Epistle to Diognetus*; the *Fragment of Quadratus*; and *Fragments of Papias*. See M. W. Holmes, *The Apostolic Fathers: Greek Texts and English Translations*, 3rd ed. (Grand Rapids: Baker, 2007), esp. pp. 5–6. Beyond this, other writings of early church fathers are gathered in various other collections.

[2] S. Pines, *An Arabic Version of the Testimonium Flavianum and Its Implications* (Jerusalem: Academy of Sciences and Humanities, 1971), 16.

Tacitus wrote, "Therefore, to squelch the rumor, Nero created scapegoats and subjected to the most refined tortures those whom the common people called 'Christians,' [a group] hated for their abominable crimes. Their name comes from Christ, who, during the reign of Tiberius, had been executed by the procurator Pontius Pilate" (*Annals* 15.44).

Jesus was a historical figure, and the references above provide important corroboration of this fact. While these early non-Christian references to Jesus should generally be regarded as testimony about Jesus from hostile witnesses, they nonetheless demonstrate the historical reliability of the Gospels.

CHRONOLOGY OF JESUS' MINISTRY

Introduction

Westerners obsessed with making and keeping appointments may be disappointed to find few references to precise dates in the NT. They may be shocked to discover that Jesus was not born on December 25, AD 1, and that modern scholars are not certain of the day, month, or even year of his birth. However, the lack of concern for precise chronology or frequent references to times and dates is to be expected from people from first-century agrarian societies. In general, early Christians were far more concerned with the events of Jesus' life and their theological significance than issues of chronology. Modern believers could learn from the priorities of the early Christians.

Nevertheless, developing a chronology of Jesus' life is a worthy exercise as it helps us understand the historical nature of the Gospels and the relationship between the Gospels. We therefore briefly investigate the date for Jesus' birth, beginning and duration of his ministry, and his death.

The Birth of Jesus

Beginning students may assume that Jesus was born in AD 1. Yet, as will shortly be evident, matters are not quite so straightforward. Matthew 2:1 and Luke 1:5 indicate that Jesus was born in the later years of the reign of Herod the Great. Josephus stated that an eclipse of the moon occurred shortly before Herod's death.[3] This eclipse may be dated from astronomical data to precisely March 12/13 in 4 BC.[4] Moreover, Herod died before Passover that same year. The Passover celebration in 4 BC began on April 11. Herod thus died between March 12 and April 11 in the year 4 BC. The date of Herod's death establishes the latest possible date (*terminus ad quem*) for Jesus' birth.

Luke stated that Jesus' birth occurred during the period of the Roman census ordered by Caesar Augustus. He further pinpointed the time of the census by associating it with Quirinius's governorship over Syria (Luke 2:1–2). Unfortunately, no ancient historian refers to this particular census or to Quirinius's role in Syria during the reign of Herod the Great.

---

[3] Josephus, *Ant.* 17.6.5–6 and 17.8.1 §§ 167–81, 188–92.

[4] H. Hoehner, "Chronology," *Dictionary of Jesus and the Gospels*, ed. J. B. Green, S. McKnight, and I. H. Marshall (Downers Grove: InterVarsity, 1992), 118–22.

Good historical reasons exist for affirming the accuracy of Luke's description of a census under Quirinius. However, without extrabiblical references to the census or to Quirinius's term of office, the census does not really assist in determining the date of Jesus' birth.

Matthew 2:16 implies that Jesus may have been up to two years old at the time Herod ordered the slaughter of the innocents. This suggests that Jesus was born by at least early 6 BC. However, it is possible that Herod extended the age of the children he slew in Bethlehem to two even though the star appeared more recently than two years before to make sure that the Messiah did not escape his sword. Thus Jesus may have been born any time between late 7 BC and early 4 BC.

Both the Western Church (December 25) and the Eastern Church (January 6) celebrate the birth of Jesus in the winter. None of the NT data is inconsistent with a mid-winter date. If the traditional dates approximate the actual date of Jesus' birth, Jesus was probably born in the winter of either 7–6 BC, 6–5 BC, or 5–4 BC, with a 5 BC date for Jesus' birth being perhaps the most likely.[5]

The Beginning of the Ministry of John the Baptist and Jesus

Luke 3:1–2 dates the beginning of the ministry of John the Baptist with greater precision than any other event in the Gospels: "In the fifteenth year of the reign of Tiberius Caesar, while Pontius Pilate was governor of Judea, Herod was tetrarch of Galilee, his brother Philip tetrarch of the region of Iturea and Trachonitis, and Lysanias tetrarch of Abilene, during the high priesthood of Annas and Caiaphas, God's word came to John the son of Zechariah in the wilderness."

Although Luke could have counted the fifteenth year of Tiberius's reign from the beginning of an alleged coregency with Augustus, this is unlikely. None of the ancient sources—including Josephus, Appian, Plutarch, Tacitus, Suetonius, and Dio Cassius—adopted such a system. More likely, Luke counted from either the death of Augustus (August 19, AD 14), the vote of the Roman senate to approve Tiberius as Caesar (September AD 14), or the beginning of the first full calendar year of Tiberius's reign (AD 15).[6] This year may have begun on January 1 (Roman system), Nissan 1 (March or April; Jewish system), or even October 1 (Syro-Macedonian system).

Although it is impossible to be certain, the most probable views are (1) that Luke either began his calculation on the date of Augustus's death, in which case Tiberius's first year extended from August 19, AD 14, to August 18, AD 15; or (2) that Luke calculated using an ascension year system and reckoned time in accordance with the newly devised Julian calendar in which the year began on January 1, in which case Tiberius's first year

---

[5] This is affirmed by, among others, P. L. Maier, "The Date of the Nativity and the Chronology of Jesus' Life," in *Chronos, Kairos, Christos: Nativity and Chronological Studies Presented in Jack Finegan*, ed. J. Vardaman and E. Yamauchi (Winona Lake: Eisenbrauns, 1989), 113–30.

[6] For bibliographic references, see A. J. Köstenberger, *John*, BECNT (Grand Rapids: Baker, 2004), 55–56n2. Ancient sources regarding the date of Augustus's death are listed in H. W. Hoehner, *Chronological Aspects of the Life of Christ* (Grand Rapids: Zondervan, 1978), 32n13.

of reign extended from January 1, AD 15, to December 31, AD 15.[7] Consequently, the fifteenth year of Tiberius's reign likely fell within dates ranging from August 19, AD 28, to December 31, AD 29. John the Baptist's ministry began sometime during this period.

Jesus' ministry likely began only a few months after John's. Hoehner noted that if Jesus were born in the winter of 5/4 BC as suggested above and if he were baptized in the summer of the year 29, he would have been 32 years old at the time he began his public ministry.[8] This comports with the statement in Luke 3:23 that Jesus was "about" 30 years old when he began his public ministry.

This chronology fits nicely with another important clue that appears in John 2:20. During Jesus' first Passover in Jerusalem after the beginning of his ministry, Jesus' Jewish opponents provided an important reference that is helpful for establishing dates for Jesus' ministry by mentioning the construction of Herod's temple. Unfortunately, most of the major English translations of the Bible probably misconstrue the actual meaning of the Greek text. The translations of John 2:20 in the NIV, HCSB, and NRSV imply that the conversation took place 46 years after the construction of the temple *began* and that the temple was still under construction. However, the Greek grammar and extrabiblical references to the construction of the temple seem to imply that the conversation took place 46 years after construction on the temple *had been completed*. Hence the translation "This sanctuary was built 46 years ago" (ESV footnote) may be superior to the translation "This sanctuary took 46 years to build" (HCSB). Although the construction of the entire temple complex (*hieron*) would continue until AD 64, Josephus noted that the inner sanctuary (*naos*) of the temple was completed by the priests in only 18 months. Thus when the Jews referred to the temple (*naos*) in John 2:20, they were speaking of the inner sanctuary that had been completed in 18/17 BC. The Passover 46 years after the completion of the sanctuary would fall in the spring of AD 30. This date would confirm that Jesus began his ministry in the summer or fall of AD 29.

The Duration of Jesus' Ministry

The Synoptic Gospels refer to Jesus' visiting Jerusalem only once during his entire ministry. But the Gospel of John refers to Jesus' visiting Jerusalem three times for the Passover, in addition to visits related to other Jewish feasts.[9] Most scholars today affirm the accuracy of John's Gospel at this point. This does not mean that the Synoptic Gospels are in error. Although they mention only one Passover visit to Jerusalem, they do not deny that other Passover visits occurred during Jesus' ministry. In general, it appears that John was even more concerned with the chronology of Jesus' ministry than the Synoptic writers were. Moreover, John has a demonstrable interest in showing that Jesus fulfilled the symbolism

---

[7] For an excellent introduction to the various chronological options, see J. Finegan, *Handbook of Biblical Chronology*, rev. ed. (Peabody: Hendrickson, 1998), 329–44; cf. Hoehner, *Chronological Aspects*, 29–38.

[8] Hoehner, *Chronological Aspects*, 38.

[9] See the chart on the chronology of Jesus' ministry in John's Gospel in Köstenberger, *John*, 11–13.

underlying various Jewish festivals and thus narrates Jesus' visits to Jerusalem on the occasion of religious feasts including Passover.

Jesus' first Passover visit to Jerusalem during his ministry occurs in John 2:13,23; a later Passover visit takes place in John 6:4; and a final Passover visit is recorded in John 11:55; 12:1; 13:1; 18:28,39; and 19:14. However, John did not necessarily record every single Passover visit during Jesus' ministry. He may have omitted references to a particular Passover just as the Synoptic writers did. H. Hoehner has argued that a comparison of the Synoptics with John suggests that another Passover occurred between the Passover in John 2:13,23 and the one in John 6:4.[10] An extra year of ministry between these two Passovers may be necessary to accommodate Jesus' ministry in Judea, Galilee, and Samaria during this period and to allow for the various seasons described in the Gospel accounts.[11]

If one affirms that Jesus' ministry included only three Passovers, his ministry lasted approximately two and a half years.[12] If one allows for another Passover between the first and second Passovers explicitly mentioned by John, Jesus' ministry lasted approximately three and a half years, the latter being more likely.[13]

The Death of Jesus

Scholars typically date Jesus' death to either AD 30 or 33, and either date is possible. However, the preponderance of evidence examined above suggests that Jesus was crucified in AD 33.

Jesus was crucified on a Friday and rose on a Sunday. The Gospels explicitly state that Jesus was executed on Friday, the day of preparation for the Sabbath (Matt 27:62; Mark 15:42; Luke 23:54; John 19:14,31,42). Because Jesus clearly rose from the dead on Sunday and because Matt 12:40 stated that the Son of Man would be in the heart of the earth "three days and three nights," some interpreters have argued that Jesus was crucified on a Wednesday or Thursday. However, several OT texts suggest that "three days and three nights" (which occurs only in Matt 12:30) might function as an idiom for any portion of a day plus an entire day plus any portion of a day (Gen 42:17–18; 1 Sam 30:12–13; 2 Chr 10:5,12; Esth 4:16–5:1). This method of reckoning time was also affirmed in rabbinic literature.[14] Jesus apparently used the expression "three days and three nights" in a similar fashion. This is confirmed by the frequent references to his resurrection occurring "on the third day" (see Matt 16:21; 17:23; 20:19; 27:64).

---

[10] Hoehner, *Chronological Aspects*, 56–63.

[11] See the discussion of the possible chronological significance of Mark 2:23; 6:39 and John 6:4,10 in J. P. Meier, *A Marginal Jew*, 3 vols. (New York: Doubleday, 1991, 1994, 2001), 1:413–14; cf. the chronological chart in Köstenberger, *John*, 11–12.

[12] See D. A. Carson and D. J. Moo, *An Introduction to the New Testament*, 2nd ed. (Grand Rapids: Zondervan, 2005), 125–26, esp. n129 (with further bibliographic references).

[13] Some suggest that John's account of Jesus' clearing of the temple at the beginning of his ministry is unhistorical, which would potentially reduce the span of Jesus' ministry according to John by one year. But see the discussion in Köstenberger, *John*, 111.

[14] See *TDNT* 2:949–50.

The Gospels make clear that Jesus ate the Last Supper on the day before his crucifixion (Matt 26:20; Mark 14:17; Luke 22:14; John 13:2), and this is confirmed by Paul (1 Cor 11:23). The Gospels also portray the Last Supper as shared in conjunction with the Passover meal.

Some scholars have argued that John's Gospel does not portray the Last Supper as a Passover meal but instead presents Jesus' crucifixion as occurring at the time of the Passover in order to portray Jesus' death as the sacrifice of the Passover lamb. However, the most natural reading of the reference to the "preparation day for the Passover" refers to the day of preparation for the Sabbath during Passover week, the Friday of the Passover celebration.[15] The word translated "day of preparation" (*paraskeuē*) was the normal word for Friday. This interpretation is confirmed by John 19:31: "Since it was the preparation day, the Jews did not want the bodies to remain on the cross on the Sabbath (for that Sabbath was a special day)." Both the Synoptics and John present the Last Supper as a Passover meal and show that Jesus was executed on the Friday of Passover week.[16] Thus no real conflict between the accounts exists at all.

The Passover meal was eaten by the Jews on Nissan 14. Thus the year of Jesus' execution must be a year in which Nissan 14 fell on a Thursday. This possibly occurred in AD 30 and definitely occurred in the year 33.[17] Since AD 30 would not allow for sufficient time between Jesus' baptism and death for his extensive public ministry unless one posits that Josephus or Luke used unusual methods of reckoning time or that Jesus' ministry lasted only one or two years, the most likely year of Jesus' death is AD 33.

Table 3.1: Chronology of Jesus' Life

Date	Event	Major Data for Dating Event
c. 5 BC	Birth of Jesus	Death of Herod the Great (4 BC) (Matt 2:13–20)
28–29	Beginning of John the Baptist's ministry	15th year of Tiberius's rule (Luke 3:1)
29	Beginning of Jesus' ministry	46 years since completion of renovation of temple (John 2:20)
33	Death of Jesus	Occurrence of Nissan 14 on a Thursday

Conclusion

Jesus was probably born between 6 and 4 BC (5 BC being the most likely date) and began his public ministry around AD 29. His ministry apparently lasted about three and

---

[15] See the original NIV rendering of John 19:14: "It was the day of Preparation of Passover Week."

[16] See Andreas J. Köstenberger, "Was the Last Supper a Passover Meal?" in *The Lord's Supper: Remembering and Proclaiming Christ Until He Comes*, ed. Thomas R. Schreiner and Matthew R. Crawford, NAC Studies in Bible & Theology (Nashville: B&H Academic, 2010), 6–30.

[17] C. J. Humphreys and W. G. Waddington, "Dating the Crucifixion," *Nature* 306 (1983): 743–46.

a half years and included three or four Passover celebrations. His crucifixion probably occurred in AD 33.

THE RELATIONSHIPS BETWEEN THE GOSPELS

Scholars often refer to Matthew, Mark, and Luke as the Synoptic Gospels. The term *synoptic* means "to see together, to have the same view or outlook," so the first three Gospels are "synoptic" because they offer similar presentations of the life and teachings of Jesus. Despite remarkable similarities, differences between these Gospels exist as well. Today scholars generally refer to questions regarding this puzzling combination of differences and similarities between these three Gospels as the Synoptic Problem. This terminology is less than ideal. It seems to presuppose that there is a "problem" needing to be solved rather than an opportunity to view Jesus from a variety of complementary perspectives that enrich rather than contradict one another.

This section explores the similarities between the Gospels and surveys various explanations that scholars have offered to account for those similarities. It also highlights the strengths and weaknesses of the various ways in which the relationship between the Synoptic Gospels has been construed.

Similarities Between the Gospels

Scholars seek to identify the similarities and differences between the Gospels by using a tool called a Gospels Synopsis.[18] This tool places similar accounts in the various Gospels side by side in parallel columns so scholars can compare them more easily. The quest to determine the literary relationships between the Gospels is called "source criticism." Comparisons of the Synoptic Gospels highlight three major similarities: (1) in wording; (2) in order; and (3) in parenthetical and explanatory material.

Similarities in Wording Some of the wording of the Synoptic Gospels, especially the wording of Jesus' sayings, is identical or almost identical, as seen in the following comparison of Jesus' first prediction of his sufferings (Matt 16:21–23; Mark 8:31–33; Luke 9:22).

In the example on the next page, the HCSB translation has been slightly adapted to show agreements that exist in the Greek texts of the Gospels. Small caps indicate agreements in all three Synoptics; italics indicate exact agreements between Mark and Luke; bold italics indicate exact agreements between Matthew and Mark; underlines indicate exact agreements between Matthew and Luke. An examination of the parallels shows that the three Synoptics agree on the essence of Jesus' saying.

The only clear conclusion to be derived from these parallels is the special connection of Mark to Matthew and Luke. But this special connection may be explained in two different ways: (1) Mark wrote his Gospel first, and Matthew and Luke used Mark in writing

---

[18] See K. Aland, ed., *Synopsis of the Four Gospels* (New York: United Bible Societies, 1982; repr. Peabody: Hendrickson, 2006); id., *Synopsis Quattuor Evangeliorum*, 3rd ed. (New York: American Bible Society, 1988).

their own Gospels; (2) Matthew and Luke wrote first, and Mark used both of these earlier Gospels in writing his Gospel. These two possible interpretations of the parallels constitute the two major solutions to the Synoptic Problem. The view that Mark wrote first and was used by the other two synoptic writers is called "Markan priority." The view that Matthew and Luke wrote first, and Mark used both of these earlier Gospels is called the "Griesbach (or Two Gospel) hypothesis."

Table 3.2: Synoptic Comparison of Jesus' First Passion Prediction

Matt 16:21–23	Mark 8:31–33	Luke 9:21–22
From then on Jesus **began** to point out to His disciples that He must go to Jerusalem and SUFFER MANY THINGS FROM THE ELDERS, CHIEF PRIESTS, AND SCRIBES, BE KILLED, AND be raised the third day. **And Peter took Him aside and began to rebuke Him,** "Oh no, Lord! This will never happen to You!" **But the One turning** told Peter, "**Get behind Me, Satan**! You are an offense to Me **because you're not thinking about God's concerns, but man's.**"	Then He **began** to teach them THAT *the Son of Man* must SUFFER MANY THINGS, *and be rejected* by THE ELDERS, THE CHIEF PRIESTS, and the SCRIBES, BE KILLED, AND rise after three days. He was openly talking about this. **And Peter took Him aside and began to rebuke Him.** **But the One** turning around and looking at His disciples, rebuked Peter and said, "**Get behind Me, Satan, because you are not thinking about God's concerns, but man's.**"	But he strictly warned and instructed them to tell this to no one, saying that *the Son of Man* MUST SUFFER MANY THINGS *and be rejected* by THE ELDERS, CHIEF PRIESTS, AND SCRIBES, BE KILLED, AND be raised the third day.

Similarities in Order   The Gospels contain numerous pericopes, self-contained units of narrative such as the account of Jesus' healing of the leper in Mark 1:40–45. Although these pericopes could be arranged in a number of different ways in the individual Gospels—topically, chronologically, or geographically (based on the locations in which they occurred)—the Gospels share a remarkable similarity in the order of the pericopes. The following chart shows how the Synoptic Gospels order pericopes describing the early ministry of Jesus. In this table, italics indicate pericopes Matthew or Luke place in an order different from Mark.[19]

The shared order of the pericopes suggests a literary relationship between the Synoptic Gospels. But the similarities and differences in order can be explained according to either of the major theories of Gospel composition: Markan priority or the Griesbach (Two-Gospel) hypothesis. Analysis of the order of pericopes by itself cannot prove one theory over the other but must be used in conjunction with the study of other types of similarities and differences.

---

[19] This table was adapted from R. Stein, *The Synoptic Problem: An Introduction* (Grand Rapids: Baker, 1987), 35.

Table 3.3: Synoptic Comparison of Early Ministry of Jesus

Pericopes (arranged in Markan order)	Matthew	Mark	Luke
1. Jesus' teaching in Capernaum synagogue		1:21–22	4:31–32
2. Healing of demoniac in Capernaum		1:23–28	4:33–37
3. Jesus' healing of Peter's mother-in-law	8:14–15	1:29–31	4:38–39
4. Jesus' healing in the evening	8:16–17	1:32–34	4:40–41
5. Jesus leaves Capernaum		1:35–38	4:42–43
6. Jesus' preaching in Galilee	4:23	1:39	4:44
7. Miraculous catch of fish			5:1–11
8. Jesus' healing of the leper	8:1–4	1:40–45	5:12–16
9. Jesus' healing of the paralytic	9:1–8	2:1–12	5:17–26
10. Calling of Levi	9:9–13	2:13–17	5:27–32
11. Controversy over fasting	9:14–17	2:18–22	5:33–39
12. Controversy over plucking grain	12:1–8	2:23–28	6:1–5
13. Controversy over Sabbath healing	12:9–14	3:1–6	6:6–11
14. Healing by the sea	4:24–25 12:15–16	3:7–12	6:17–19
15. Choosing of the Twelve	10:1–4	3:13–19	6:12–16

Similarities in Parenthetical and Explanatory Material   One famous example of a shared parenthetical statement is "let the reader understand" (Matt 24:15–18; Mark 13:14–16; lacking in Luke 21:20–22). If this parenthetical statement is a note from the Gospel writer to the readers of the Gospel, the fact that both Matthew and Mark contain it would imply that one writer used the other's Gospel. But many scholars interpret the comment as Jesus' words to the readers of Daniel, in which case the statement shared by Matthew and Mark would demonstrate accuracy in reporting Jesus' words rather than literary dependence.

Those who argue that the statement is a note by the Gospel writer argue that Jesus typically referred to his audience "hearing" the OT rather than reading the OT. Since only wealthy first-century Jews had their own copies of the OT, most became familiar with the OT by hearing it read in synagogues rather than by reading it themselves (Luke 16:29,31).[20] But some scholars who affirm a literary dependence between the Gospels argue that Jesus himself uttered the words "let the reader understand" and that he addressed them to

---

[20] Ibid., 38; cf. E. Best, "The Gospel of Mark: Who Was the Reader?" *IBS* 11 (1989): 124–32.

readers of Daniel. This seems confirmed by Jesus' rather frequent references to reading the OT (Matt 12:3,5; 19:4; 21:16,42; 22:31; Mark 12:10,26; Luke 10:26).[21]

Table 3.4: Synoptic Comparison of Use of Old Testament

OT	Matt 11:10	Mark 1:2	Luke 7:27
Exod 23:20 (LXX)			
Look, I [myself] am sending my messenger before You	Look, I [myself] am sending my messenger ahead of You;	Look, I am sending My messenger ahead of You,	Look, I am sending My messenger ahead of You;
Mal 3:1 (LXX)			
And he will examine the way before Me	he will prepare Your way before You	who will prepare Your way	he will prepare Your way before You
Mal 3:1 (MT)			
and he will clear the way before Me			

Explanations of the Similarities Between the Gospels

The similarities in wording, order, editorial comments, and OT references described above have been explained in several different ways in the history of NT scholarship.

Literary Independence Some scholars argue that these similarities are products of the divine inspiration of the Synoptic Gospels rather than indicating the use of one Gospel by another. Similarly, other scholars argue that the similarities between the Gospels simply reflect history.

On one hand, if divine inspiration alone accounts for the similarities between the Synoptics, it is difficult to account for the differences between the Synoptics and especially the differences between the Synoptics and John. On the other hand, a merely historical explanation does not account for the parallels in parenthetical references and editorial comments, or the similarities in OT quotations described earlier.

Literary Interdependence A better and the most commonly accepted explanation of the similarities between the Synoptic Gospels is that the later Synoptic writers used the earlier Synoptic Gospel(s). Theories of literary dependence between the Gospels can be traced back to as early as the fifth century.[22] For example, Augustine suggested that the

---

[21] For commentators who affirm that the parenthetical statement was Jesus' call to careful interpretation of Daniel, see D. A. Carson, "Matthew," in *Matthew and Mark,* EBC 9, rev. ed. (Grand Rapids: Zondervan, 2010), 562; C. Keener, *A Commentary on the Gospel of Matthew* (Grand Rapids: Eerdmans, 1999), 576; W. D. Davies and D. Allison, *Matthew 19–28,* ICC (London: T&T Clark, 1997), 346. J. Nolland (*The Gospel of Matthew,* NICGT [Grand Rapids: Eerdmans, 2005], 972) argued that the words refer to readers of Daniel rather than the Gospels but that they were inserted by the evangelists.

[22] See the brief history of the early church discussion in D. Bock, *Studying the Historical Jesus: A Guide to Sources and Methods* (Grand Rapids: Baker, 2002), 164–67.

canonical order of the Gospels (Matthew, Mark, Luke, John) was the order in which the Gospels were written. The later writers used the material of the earlier writers: "Each of them is found not to have desired to write in ignorance of his predecessor" (*De Consensu Evangelistarum* 1.4). According to this theory Matthew, an eyewitness, wrote the first Gospel, Mark used Matthew in the compilation of his Gospel, and Luke used Matthew (and Mark) in the compilation of his Gospel.

Illustration 3.1: Augustinian View

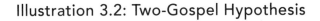

Augustine's solution to the Synoptic Problem has a few modern supporters; most scholars hold one of the following two theories.

The first is the two-gospel hypothesis proposed by J. J. Griesbach in 1783. In contrast with Augustine, Griesbach argued that Luke was the second Gospel and Mark the third. Griesbach's view regarding Luke's possible usage of Matthew is unclear. More importantly, Griesbach argued that Mark was the last of the Synoptics and that he used both Matthew and Luke in writing his Gospel.

Illustration 3.2: Two-Gospel Hypothesis

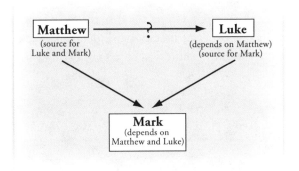

The second theory is known as ***Markan priority***. This view recognizes that Mark has a special relationship to both Matthew and Luke. Mark shares more material and verbatim agreement with Matthew and Luke than they share with each other. The special relationship of Mark to Matthew and Luke has commonly been explained in two opposite ways. Some assert that the similarity results from Mark's using both Matthew and Luke in his Gospel. The Markan priority hypothesis suggests that Mark served as a primary source for both Matthew and Luke.

Generally, differences between the Synoptics can be more reasonably explained when one assumes Markan priority. For example, Matthew and Luke place greater emphasis on high Christology than Mark does. They both apply the title "Lord" to Jesus far more frequently than Mark. It seems more likely for Matthew and Luke to adapt Mark in order to highlight Jesus' deity than for Mark to edit such material out.[23]

Finally, certain stylistic features in Mark appear in Matthew almost exclusively in the material he has in common with Mark. Mark was particularly fond of using the temporal adverb "immediately," which appears 41 times in his Gospel. The adverb appears 18 times in Matthew's Gospel. Fourteen of these occurrences appear in material that Matthew shares with Mark. R. Stein has calculated that the adverb appears once for every 778 words in material shared with Mark but only once for every 1,848 words in the material not shared by Mark. This suggests that the frequency of occurrences of the adverb "immediately" in Matthew was influenced by his dependency on Mark.[24]

Illustration 3.3: Markan Priority

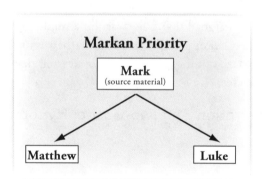

---

[23] See especially P. M. Head, *Christology and the Synoptic Problem: An Argument for Markan Priority*, SNTSMS 94 (Cambridge: University Press, 1997); cf. M. C. Williams, *Two Gospels from One: A Comprehensive Text-Critical Analysis of the Synoptic Gospels* (Grand Rapids: Kregel, 2006).

[24] R. Stein, "Synoptic Problem," in *Dictionary of Jesus and the Gospels*, 787.

STUDY QUESTIONS

1. From where is this quote taken? "Therefore, to squelch the rumor, Nero created scapegoats and subjected to the most refined tortures those whom the common people called 'Christians.'"
2. What are the most likely dates for Jesus' birth and death, and what are critical data for dating these events?
3. What are the two major possibilities regarding the relationship between the Synoptic Gospels?
4. In what order were the Gospels written according to the two-Gospel hypothesis?
5. In what order were the Gospels written according to the Markan priority view?

FOR FURTHER STUDY

Jesus

Bock, D. L. *Jesus According to Scripture: Restoring the Portrait from the Gospels.* Downers Grove: InterVarsity, 2002.

_____. *Studying the Historical Jesus: A Guide to Sources and Methods.* Grand Rapids: Baker, 2002.

Bock, D. L., and G. J. Herrick, eds. *Jesus in Context: Background Readings for Gospel Study.* Grand Rapids: Baker, 2005.

Bowman, R., J. E. Komoszewski, and R. M. Bowman Jr. *Putting Jesus in His Place: The Case for the Deity of Christ.* Grand Rapids: Kregel, 2007.

Boyd, G. A., and P. R. Eddy. *Lord or Legend? Wrestling with the Jesus Dilemma.* Grand Rapids: Baker, 2007.

Dunn, J. D. G., and S. McKnight, eds. *The Historical Jesus in Recent Research.* Sources for Biblical and Theological Study. Winona Lake: Eisenbrauns, 2005.

Eddy, P. R., and G. A. Boyd. *The Jesus Legend: A Case for the Historical Reliability of the Synoptic Tradition.* Grand Rapids: Baker, 2007.

Evans, C. A. "Jesus in Non-Christian Sources." Pages 364–68 in *Dictionary of Jesus and the Gospels.* Edited by J. B. Green, S. McKnight, and I. H. Marshall. Downers Grove: InterVarsity, 1992.

Hoehner, H. W. *Chronological Aspects of the Life of Christ.* Grand Rapids: Zondervan, 1977.

_____. "Chronology." Pages 118–22 in *Dictionary of Jesus and the Gospels.* Edited by J. B. Green, S. McKnight, and I. H. Marshall. Downers Grove: InterVarsity, 1992.

Köstenberger, M. E. *Jesus and the Feminists: Who Do They Say That He Is?* Wheaton: Crossway, 2008.

Piper, J. *What Jesus Demands from the World.* Wheaton: Crossway, 2006.

Schlatter, A. *Do We Know Jesus?* Translated by A. J. Köstenberger and R. W. Yarbrough. Grand Rapids: Kregel, 2005 [1938].

Stein, R. H. *The Method and Message of Jesus' Teachings.* Louisville: Westminster John Knox, 1978.

Van Voorst, R. E. *Jesus Outside the New Testament: An Introduction to the Ancient Evidence.* Grand Rapids: Eerdmans, 2000.

Wilkins, M. J., and J. P. Moreland, eds. *Jesus Under Fire.* Grand Rapids: Zondervan, 1995.

The Gospels

Bauckham, R. *Jesus and the Eyewitnesses: The Gospels as Eyewitness Testimony.* Grand Rapids: Eerdmans, 2006.

Bauckham, R., ed. *The Gospels for All Christians: Rethinking the Gospel Audiences.* Grand Rapids: Eerdmans, 1997.

Blomberg, C. L. *The Historical Reliability of the Gospels.* 2nd ed. Downers Grove: InterVarsity, 2007.

Burridge, R. A. *What Are the Gospels? A Comparison with Graeco-Roman Biography.* 2nd ed. Grand Rapids: Eerdmans, 2004.

France, R. T. "The Authenticity of the Sayings of Jesus." Pages 101–41 in *History, Criticism, and Faith*. Edited by Colin Brown. Downers Grove: InterVarsity, 1976.

Green, J. B. *How to Read the Gospels and Acts*. Downers Grove: InterVarsity, 1987.

Green, J. B., S. McKnight, and I. H. Marshall, eds. *Dictionary of Jesus and the Gospels*. Downers Grove: InterVarsity, 1992.

Hengel, M. *The Four Gospels and the One Gospel of Jesus Christ*. Harrisburg: Trinity Press, 2000.

McKnight, S. *Interpreting the Synoptic Gospels*. Guides to New Testament Exegesis 2. Grand Rapids: Baker, 1988.

Porter, S. E., ed. *Reading the Gospels Today*. McMaster New Testament Studies. Grand Rapids: Eerdmans, 2004.

Roberts, M. D. *Can We Trust the Gospels? Investigating the Reliability of Matthew, Mark, Luke, and John*. Wheaton: Crossway, 2007.

Stein, R. H. "Synoptic Problem." Pages 784–92 in *Dictionary of Jesus and the Gospels*. Edited by J. B. Green, S. McKnight, and I. H. Marshall. Downers Grove: InterVarsity, 1992.

_____. *The Synoptic Problem: An Introduction*. Grand Rapids: Baker, 1987.

_____. *Studying the Synoptic Gospels: Origin and Interpretation*. Grand Rapids: Baker, 2001.

Chapter 4

The Gospel According to Matthew

CORE KNOWLEDGE

Students should know the key facts of Matthew's Gospel. With regard to history, students should be able to identify the Gospel's author, date, provenance, destination, and purpose. With regard to literature, they should be able to provide a basic outline of the book and identify core elements of the book's content found in the unit-by-unit discussion. With regard to theology, students should be able to identify Matthew's major theological themes.

KEY FACTS	
Author:	Matthew
Date:	50s or 60s
Provenance:	Unknown
Destination:	Jewish audience in unknown location
Purpose:	To demonstrate that Jesus is the Messiah predicted in the OT
Theme:	Jesus is Immanuel, the Messiah, and the Savior of God's people
Key Verses:	16:13–20

CONTRIBUTION TO THE CANON

- Genealogy of Jesus Christ, the son of Abraham, the son of David (1:1–17)
- Account of the virgin birth of Christ (1:18–25)
- Fulfillment quotations showing that Jesus is the Messiah (1–4)
- Five major discourses or teaching sections of Jesus, including the Sermon on the Mount (5–7), the Commissioning of the Twelve (10), Jesus' parables of the kingdom (13; 18), and his final teachings, including the Olivet Discourse on the end time (24–25)
- The Great Commission (28:16–20)

INTRODUCTION

IT IS LITTLE wonder that Matthew's Gospel quickly became the favorite Gospel of the early church. It is one of only two Gospels written directly by one of the 12 disciples and is richly theological with a great emphasis on such truths as Jesus' identity as the virgin-born Immanuel. With its frequent citations of the OT, Matthew's Gospel emphasizes Jesus' fulfillment of God's messianic promises. Thus it provides a connecting link between the OT and the NT.

Despite differences in order from the other Gospels, Matthew finds first place in lists of Gospel books and collections of Gospel texts in the early church.[1] For this reason R. T. France wrote, "It is a fact that mainstream Christianity was, from the early second century on, to a great extent Matthean Christianity."[2] Matthew's Gospel is also a remarkable piece of literature. Matthew communicated his message not only through explicit statements but through his structure and literary devices.

Matthew's Gospel contains rich material on Jesus' infancy, the Sermon on the Mount (only partly paralleled in Luke), and a valuable collection of Jesus' parables. It demonstrates with special clarity that Jesus' death was sacrificial and that he rescued his disciples from the penalty for their sins. Thus E. Renan identified Matthew's Gospel as the most important book ever written.[3] Careful study of Matthew uncovers a message of such theological depth and literary artistry as to convince the reader that Renan's assessment was hardly an exaggeration.

HISTORY

Author

Like the other canonical Gospels, Matthew is formally anonymous, since the author of this Gospel did not explicitly identify himself in the body of the book. However, the title that ascribes the Gospel to Matthew is clearly early if not original.[4] The title would have been necessary to distinguish one Gospel from the other Gospels when the four Gospels began to circulate as a single collection. Especially if the author were aware of an earlier Gospel and used it in the composition of his own work as most scholars suspect, he may have felt that a title was necessary to distinguish his book from the earlier writing (Mark, on the assumption of Markan priority).

---

[1] R. V. G. Tasker (*The Gospel According to St. Matthew*, TNTC [London: Tyndale, 1961], 15–16) pointed out that this is probably due to more than a conviction that Matthew's Gospel was the first to be written. The priority of Matthew in the canon was inspired by the conviction that Matthew formed an appropriate bridge between the Testaments.

[2] R. T. France, *Matthew: Evangelist and Teacher* (Grand Rapids: Zondervan, 1989), 16.

[3] L. Morris, *The Gospel According to Matthew*, PNTC (Grand Rapids: Eerdmans, 1992), 1.

[4] M. Hengel argued that the Gospels have always had their headings and that "according to" implies authorship. See Hengel, *The Four Gospels and the One Gospel of Jesus Christ: An Investigation of the Collection and Origin of the Canonical Gospels*, trans. J. Bowden (Harrisburg: Trinity Press International, 2000), 48–53, 77. Compare with France, *Matthew: Evangelist and Teacher*, 50–80; and the discussion of objections to Hengel's proposal in D. A. Carson and D. J. Moo, *An Introduction to the New Testament*, 2nd ed. (Grand Rapids: Zondervan, 2005), 141–42.

The earliest external evidence—that is, evidence derived from sources outside the Gospel—for the authorship of the Gospel is from a statement of Papias, bishop of Hierapolis, in his *Expositions of the Lord's Sayings*.[5] Papias's testimony is especially significant because he claims to have received his information directly from those who personally heard Jesus' closest disciples, including Matthew.[6] Irenaeus (c. 130–c. 200) claimed that Papias was a disciple of the apostle John who had direct access to John's testimony regarding the early years of the Christian church (*Against Heresies* 5.33.4). Papias wrote: "Therefore, on the one hand Matthew arranged in order the sayings in the Hebrew dialect; on the other hand, each translated these as he was able" (Eusebius, *Eccl. Hist.* 3.39).

Clues from the Gospel itself (internal evidence) tend to confirm the early church's ascription to Matthew. Based on the internal evidence of the Gospel, most scholars recognize that the author was a Jewish Christian. Although the internal evidence is not specific enough to trace the identity of the author, it is compatible with and suggestive of Matthean authorship as affirmed by Papias. First, Matthew affirmed that the tax collector named "Levi" whom Jesus appointed to be one of the 12 apostles (see Mark 2:14; Luke 5:27) was also called "Matthew" (Matt 9:9). Matthew, a Hebrew name meaning "gift of Yahweh" or "gift of the Lord," appears to be the apostolic name that Jesus gave to the tax collector after he chose him to follow Christ much like Jesus renamed Simon "Peter" (John 1:42; reaffirmed in Matt 16:18). The use of the name here may be Matthew's personal touch.

Second, in the discussion of the payment of the imperial taxes (Matt 22:15–22), Mark and Luke both used the Greek term *denarion*, but Matthew also included the more precise term *nomisma* ("state coin"). The use of more precise terminology in referring to currency may suggest the expertise of a former tax collector.[7] Based on the impressive external and internal evidence for Matthean authorship, modern readers may confidently affirm Matthew's authorship of this Gospel and recognize it as a testimony to the life of Jesus written by both an eyewitness and an apostle.

Date

Internal Evidence   According to Matt 24:2 and parallels, Jesus predicted the fall of Jerusalem. Some scholars, however, argue that Matthew must have written this prediction after the fall (i.e., mid-to-late 80s) and deceptively presented it to his readers as prophecy. Yet, if one believes that Jesus was capable of predictive prophecy (and abundant evidence supports this conviction), a date prior to 70 is plausible.

---

[5] Papias's works have not survived but are quoted by Eusebius of Caesarea in his *Ecclesiastical History* from the early fourth century.

[6] See the discussion in R. H. Gundry, *Matthew: A Commentary on His Handbook for a Mixed Church Under Persecution*, 2nd ed. (Grand Rapids: Eerdmans, 1994), 611–17. For the argument that Papias had actually heard the teachings of two eyewitnesses to Jesus' ministry, see R. Bauckham, *Jesus and the Eyewitnesses: The Gospels as Eyewitness Testimony* (Grand Rapids: Eerdmans, 2006), 12–38.

[7] D. Guthrie, *New Testament Introduction*, rev. ed. (Downers Grove: InterVarsity, 1990), 52–53.

Other evidence in Matthew suggests that the Gospel was written before 70 when Roman armies destroyed the Jerusalem temple and devastated the Holy City. Matthew 17:24–27 contains Jesus' instruction regarding the payment of the two-drachma temple tax. Jesus taught that his disciples should pay the tax in order to avoid offending fellow Jews. However, after the destruction of the temple, the temple tax was collected by the Romans in order to support the pagan temple of Jupiter Capitolinus in Rome.[8] It is doubtful that Matthew would have included the account in his Gospel at a date at which it would have been interpreted as support for pagan idolatry (see Matt 4:10).[9]

Matthew's special references to sacrifice also make the most sense if written before the fall of Jerusalem. Matthew consistently portrayed such sacrifices as gifts that expressed gratitude to God rather than rituals that effected atonement. He further taught that Jesus was the fulfillment of Isaiah 53, the Suffering Servant whose sacrificial death accomplished atonement for sin. Matthew's carefully articulated sacrificial theology and particularly his concern for clarifying the significance of temple offerings fit best with a date of composition before 70 when the temple was destroyed and the sacrificial system ended.

External Evidence   External evidence requires a first-century date of composition. If Matthew used Mark's Gospel, Matthew may have written his Gospel anytime beginning in the mid-50s or, perhaps more likely, in the early 60s. The earliest historical evidence is consistent with this opinion since Irenaeus (c. 130–200) claimed that Matthew wrote his Gospel while Peter and Paul were preaching in Rome (early 60s).[10]

These clues and many others suggest a date for Matthew sometime prior to the destruction of Jerusalem in the year 70.[11] This pre-AD 70 date for the Gospel of Matthew thus increases the likelihood that Matthew's Gospel preserves accounts of Jesus' life and teachings that are accurate in detail.

Provenance and Destination

Scholars have proposed a variety of theories regarding possible places of origin for Matthew's Gospel. Suggestions include Jerusalem or Palestine, Caesarea Maritima, Phoenicia, Alexandria, Pella, Edessa, Syria, and Antioch. Allison correctly noted: "Given the nature of the available evidence, it is quite impossible to be fully persuaded on the issue at hand. We shall never know beyond a reasonable doubt where the autograph of Matthew was completed."[12] Yet, the theories of origin that have gained the most scholarly support view the Gospel as written in either Palestine or Syria with the majority of scholars today opting for Syria, specifically Antioch of Syria, as the place of origin.

---

[8] Josephus, *Jewish War* 7.218; Dio Cassius, 65.7.2; Suetonius, *Domitian* 12. Consequently, *m. Sheq.* 8.8 taught that the shekel laws applied only as long as the temple stood.

[9] Gundry, *Matthew*, 606.

[10] Irenaeus, *Against Heresies* 3.1.1.

[11] See the extensive and compelling defense of the early date of Matthew in Gundry (*Matthew*, 599–609), who concluded that Matthew was probably written during the 50s or early 60s.

[12] W. D. Davies and D. C. Allison, *Matthew*, 3 vols., ICC (Edinburgh: T&T Clark, 1988–1997), 1:139.

The questions of the provenance and destination of this Gospel are closely linked. Scholars who accept a Palestinian provenance generally see the church in Palestine as the intended audience. Likewise, scholars who accept a Syrian provenance generally see the church in Syria as the intended audience. Regardless of one's view of the provenance and original audience, Matthew's Gospel clearly circulated widely soon after its composition. This is demonstrated by the geographical distribution of early quotations of the book that appear in the writings of Ignatius (c. 35–110; Antioch), Polycarp (c. 69–155; Smyrna), Pseudo-Barnabas (c. 135?; possibly Alexandria), Justin Martyr (c. 100–165; Ephesus), and *2 Clement* (probably Alexandria) in the late first or early second century.

Purpose

In part because Matthew's Gospel itself does not include an explicit purpose statement, some scholars have proposed that Matthew should be read as a theological rather than a historical document.[13] However, this does not best explain the data. In particular, Matthew's insistence that certain events in Jesus' life happened in order to fulfill the OT indicates that Matthew wrote a careful record of actual events.

With this historical basis in mind, Matthew's primary focus was Jesus' identity. Matthew's Gospel stressed four aspects.[14] First, Jesus is the Messiah, the long-awaited King of God's people. Second, Jesus is the new Abraham, the founder of a new spiritual Israel consisting of all people who choose to follow him, including both Jews and Gentiles. Third, Jesus is the new Moses, the deliverer and instructor of God's people. Fourth, Jesus is the Immanuel, the virgin-born Son of God who fulfills the promises of the OT. Matthew was concerned not only to preserve Jesus' teachings, record his deeds, or commend his example, but especially to explain who Jesus was. Matthew's Gospel might best be described as a "theological biography," a historical account of Jesus' life and teachings that explains his spiritual significance.

Although Matthew's Gospel functions primarily as a theological biography, the Gospel was also written to serve as a manual for discipleship. Matthew's topical arrangement of lengthy discourses, his emphasis on the ethical demands of the kingdom of God, and especially the climactic statement regarding teaching new disciples to observe all Jesus' commands—all of these combine to offer guidance for Christian living.

LITERATURE

Literary Plan

In addition to commenting on its authorship, Papias also remarked on the literary structure of Matthew's Gospel. According to Papias, "Matthew arranged in order the sayings [of

---

[13] See especially M. D. Goulder, *Midrash and Lection in Matthew: The Speaker's Lectures in Biblical Studies* 1969–71 (London: SPCK, 1974); Gundry, *Matthew*, whose commentary was originally subtitled, "A Commentary on His Literary and Theological Art."

[14] See the similar discussion in Carson and Moo, *Introduction to the New Testament*, 158.

Jesus]" (Eusebius, *Eccl. Hist.* 3.39). Most likely, Papias meant that Matthew's Gospel had a more orderly arrangement than Mark's. Since Matthew generally shares the same order of pericopes as Mark when the two overlap, Papias probably referred to the fact that Matthew began with a genealogy and an account of Jesus' birth, gave a more thorough treatment of Jesus' post-resurrection appearances, and arranged Jesus' teaching into five major sections.

As shown below, scholars widely agree that the structure of Matthew's Gospel centers on the five major discourses that present the essence of Jesus' teachings (5–7; 10:5–42; 13:1–52; 18:1–35; and 23–25). Hence narrative portions and discourse sections alternate in the flow of Matthew's Gospel. Each of these discourses is set off from the adjacent narrative portions by concluding phrases that read roughly as follows: "When Jesus had finished saying these things" (7:28; 11:1; 13:53; 19:1; 26:1).

These five "books of Jesus" in Matthew's Gospel appear to be designed to evoke memories of the five books of Moses (Genesis to Deuteronomy). Throughout Matthew's Gospel, Jesus is presented as the new Moses, whereby the first discourse, the Sermon on the Mount in chapters 5–7, invokes the memory of Moses' receiving the law at Sinai. Beyond this, it is not necessary or advisable to press the content of Jesus' five discourses in Matthew's Gospel into direct conformity to Moses' parting instructions to Israel in Deuteronomy. Although portions of Matthew's Gospel are clearly arranged topically, the Gospel follows a general chronological order: genealogy, birth, baptism, Galilean ministry, journey to Jerusalem, trial, crucifixion, and resurrection,[15] with the five discourses linking Jesus' teaching with Jesus' life.

OUTLINE
  I. INTRODUCTION (1:1–4:11)
      A. The Ancestry, Birth, and Early Boyhood of Jesus (1–2)
      B. The Background of Jesus' Ministry (3:1–4:11)
  II. JESUS' GALILEAN MINISTRY (4:12–18:35)
      A. First Part of Galilean Ministry (4:12–25)
      Discourse 1: Sermon on the Mount (5–7)
      B. Second Part of Galilean Ministry (8–9)
      Discourse 2: Instruction to the Twelve (10)
      C. Third Part of Galilean Ministry (11–12)
      Discourse 3: Parables of the Kingdom (13:1–53)
      D. Galilean Ministry Extended to the North (13:54–17:27)
      Discourse 4: Parables of the Kingdom (18)
  III. JESUS' JUDEAN MINISTRY AND HIS PASSION (19–28)
      A. Judean Ministry (19–20)
      B. Final Ministry in Jerusalem (21–22)
      C. Jesus' Denunciation of the Pharisees (23)

---

[15] See D. A. Hagner, *Matthew 1–13*, WBC 33a (Dallas: Word, 1993), liii.

Discourse 5: Olivet Discourse, Kingdom Parables (24–25)

D. The Passion (26–27)

E. The Resurrection and the Great Commission (28)

Table 4.1: The Five Discourses in the Gospel of Matthew

Discourse	Reference	Theme
1. Sermon on the Mount	5–7	A description of the surpassing righteousness that will characterize Jesus' disciples
2. Instruction of the Twelve	10	Disciples are to spread gospel; warning of coming persecution
3. Parables of the Kingdom	13	Explains rejection of gospel by some and presence of evil; growth and ministry of the kingdom of God in the face of opposition
4. Parables of the Kingdom	18	Explains how disciples are to relate to Jesus and to each other
5. Olivet Discourse, More Kingdom Parables	24–25	Prophecy of destruction of the temple and events preceding the Second Coming

UNIT-BY-UNIT DISCUSSION

I. Introduction (1:1–4:11)

A. The Ancestry, Birth, and Early Boyhood of Jesus (1–2) Matthew begins his Gospel with a genealogy of Jesus (1:1–17). This genealogy stresses Jesus' identity as the son of Abraham, the recipient of the divine promise that through him all the nations of the earth would be blessed (Gen 12:1–3), and as the promised King from the line of David who will rule over God's people. It also underscores his supremacy over the OT patriarchs; and his redemptive mission first to Jews but also to Gentiles.

The account of Jesus' conception and birth (1:18–25) portrays these events as absolutely unique. It demonstrates that Jesus was the fulfillment of God's promises given through the OT prophets and, more importantly, emphasizes Jesus' identity as the virgin-born Immanuel, God living among human beings, and the Savior who would rescue his people from their sins. The reference to Isa 7:14 in Matt 1:22–23 is the first in a series of fulfillment quotations that document the fact that virtually every major event in Jesus' life took place in order to fulfill, and in keeping with, OT Scripture.[16]

The visit of the Magi to worship the infant Jesus (2:1–12) demonstrates that, though Jesus' mission was first directed to the Jews, its scope transcended Israel and reached to Gentiles as well. Their time-consuming and difficult journey from the east to Bethlehem,

---

[16] See the chart under Major Theological Themes below. On Jesus as "Immanuel," see D. D. Kupp, *Matthew's Emmanuel: Divine Presence and God's People in the First Gospel*, SNTSMS 90 (Cambridge: University Press, 1996).

their valuable gifts, and especially their worship of Jesus highlight his supremacy and imply his deity. The failure of the chief priests and scribes to travel to Bethlehem in search of Jesus betrays indifference toward the Messiah that later developed into animosity.

The flight from Herod and the slaughter of the innocents (2:13–18) are reminiscent of the murder of Hebrew children at the order of Pharaoh and the flight of Moses (Exodus 1–2) and is in keeping with OT prophecy (Jer 31:15 cited in Matt 2:18). The account begins a portrayal of Jesus as the new Moses, the instructor and deliverer of God's people. The temporal relationship of Jesus' birth to Herod's death is the most significant factor in establishing a chronology of Jesus' early life.[17]

The account of Jesus' infancy ends with a description of the holy family settling in Nazareth (Matt 2:19–23). Matthew saw a connection between the name of the town and the similar-sounding Hebrew word for "branch" (Hb. *netser*). The connection portrayed Jesus as the fulfillment of the "Branch prophecies" of the OT (Isa 4:2; 11:1; Jer 23:5; 33:15), emphasizing his Davidic lineage and messianic identity.

B. *The Background of Jesus' Ministry (3:1–4:11)* This section begins with a description of the ministry of John the Baptist, again in keeping with OT expectation (3:1–6). John is a "voice of one crying out in the wilderness" (Isa. 40:3), calling the Jewish people to repentance and thus preparing the way for God himself to come in the person of Jesus the Messiah. The way of the Lord is associated with the way of Jesus to highlight his divine status.

John announced the coming kingdom and called his Jewish hearers to repentance (3:7–12). In particular, he urged them to abandon the assumption that physical descent from Abraham guaranteed salvation. He called on them to express their repentance by accepting his baptism and producing the fruit of good works, and promised that another person would come after him who was more powerful and vastly superior. This messianic figure would offer sinners a choice between two baptisms: either a baptism effected by the Spirit that would transform them or a baptism of fire that would burn them like fire burned wheat chaff.

Matthew's description of Jesus' baptism (3:13–17) is packed with theological significance. When Jesus approached John requesting baptism, John identified Jesus as the one he had promised by arguing that it was more appropriate for Jesus to baptize John than for John to baptize Jesus. The descent of the Holy Spirit on Jesus like a dove may indicate that Jesus possessed the power of new creation (Gen 1:1–2; cf. Gen 8:8–12). The voice of the heavenly Father described Jesus using two OT texts that identified Jesus as the Messiah and the Suffering Servant who would provide forgiveness to sinners by becoming their sacrifice (Ps 2:7; Isa 42:1).

---

[17] See the discussion on the chronology of Jesus' life in chap. 3 above.

Jesus' 40 days of temptation (4:1–11) demonstrated that Jesus truly did come to "fulfill all righteousness" (3:15).[18] The temptation experience also demonstrated Jesus' authority over Satan and his supremacy over the angels.

II. Jesus' Galilean Ministry (4:12–18:35)

A. First Part of Galilean Ministry (4:12–25) Jesus then established his ministry headquarters in Capernaum in "Galilee of the Gentiles" (4:12–16). This location confirmed God's intention to include Gentiles in his redemptive plan, a major theme of Matthew's Gospel. Jesus began to proclaim a message identical to John's: "Repent, because the kingdom of heaven has come near" (4:17; see 3:2). After this, Jesus began to call his first disciples, two pairs of brothers who were fishermen: Peter and Andrew, and James and John (4:18–22). Their willingness to abandon their occupation and leave their families to follow Jesus demonstrates that Jesus was worthy of any sacrifice that he called his followers to make. Jesus then commenced to preach the gospel of the kingdom throughout Galilee (4:23–25). Great crowds followed him in response to his powerful preaching and amazing healing miracles.

Discourse 1: The Sermon on the Mount (5–7) The introduction to Jesus' first discourse, the Sermon on the Mount (5–7), clearly portrays him as the new Moses. Jesus' ascent of the mountain is reminiscent of Moses' ascent of Mount Sinai (Exod 19:3; 24:13,18). As in the OT (e.g., Mount Sinai; Exod 19:3), mountains in Matthew are places of divine revelation (e.g., the Mount of Transfiguration; 17:1–3, with Moses and Elijah joining Jesus).[19] Moreover, the blessings pronounced by Jesus recall Moses' blessing on the tribe of Israel (Deut 33:29). The Beatitudes (5:3–12) identify Jesus' disciples as the new true spiritual Israel on whom God's blessings rest. In this his inaugural address, Jesus describes the surpassing righteousness that will characterize his disciples who have participated in the new exodus (liberation from slavery to sin), received the benefits of the new covenant (God's Law written on the heart), and experienced the miracle of new creation.

Jesus urged his disciples to live lives that were characterized by purity to glorify God. In this way they will be "salt" and "light" in the world (5:13–16). Unless their righteousness exceeds that of the Pharisees, Jesus' followers will be unable to enter God's kingdom (5:17–20). Rightly interpreted, the OT demands that disciples control their tempers, pursue sexual purity, honor the covenant of marriage, speak with integrity, refrain from acts of vengeance, and love their enemies (5:21–48). Jesus insisted that only his disciples were capable of such righteousness since he graciously imparted this righteousness to his followers by his blessing (5:6).

---

[18] "Righteousness" is an important theme in Matthew's Gospel, especially in the early portions of Matthew: see the reference to those who "hunger and thirst for righteousness" (5:6); Jesus' requirement that his followers' "righteousness" exceed that of the Pharisees (5:20); and his injunction that his disciples seek first "the kingdom of God and His righteousness" (6:33).

[19] See T. L. Donaldson, *Jesus on the Mountain: A Study in Matthean Theology*, JSNTSup 8 (Sheffield: Almond, 1985).

Jesus also gave instructions regarding the so-called three pillars of Judaism: prayer, fasting, and almsgiving (6:1–18). He especially cautioned his disciples against performing acts of religious devotion in order to please a human audience. He stressed that true acts of devotion must be focused exclusively on pleasing God. He promised that God would reward such expressions of genuine piety. Jesus urged his disciples to value eternal and spiritual matters above temporal and material things. He commanded his disciples to be free from anxiety by trusting in God's ability to provide for their needs and by letting God's priorities define theirs (6:19–34).

Jesus prohibited hypocritical judgment of others (7:1–6). He taught that disciples may assist others in conquering sinful habits only as they gain victory over their own. Jesus promised his disciples that those who asked for good gifts would receive them. Those who sought the kingdom would find it (cf. 6:33). However, Jesus warned that the life of the true disciple would entail difficulty and persecution. Few people would be willing to suffer this hardship for the sake of receiving eternal life (7:7–14).

Jesus warned his disciples about false prophets and false disciples (7:15–23). Disciples could recognize these counterfeits by their "fruits," the actions and words that attested to their true inner character. Jesus taught that false disciples would be exposed on judgment day for what they truly were. He would personally unmask them and banish them from the kingdom of heaven. Jesus concluded the Sermon on the Mount with a parable that taught that hearing and obeying Jesus' teaching were the only effective means of preparing for eschatological judgment. Matthew noted that the people recognized the unusual authority of Jesus' teaching in comparison with their scribes and teachers of the law (7:24–29).

B. Second Part of Jesus' Galilean Ministry (8–9)   The narrative section that follows the Sermon on the Mount is saturated with accounts of Jesus' miracles. He cleansed a leper, healed the paralyzed servant of a Roman centurion, cooled the fevered brow of Simon's mother-in-law, controlled the weather by his mere command, delivered the man from Gadara from a legion of demons, raised a synagogue ruler's daughter from the dead, stopped a woman from hemorrhaging when she simply touched the hem of his garments, gave sight to the blind, and enabled a mute man to speak.

These miracles confirmed Jesus' identity as God the Savior in keeping with Isa 35:5–6; demonstrated Christ's compassion to Gentiles and clearly stated God's intention to grant them salvation (esp. Matt 8:28–34); showed that Jesus was the Servant of the Lord who would offer his life as a sacrifice to atone for the sins of God's people (Matt 8:17 quoting Isa 53:4); clearly expressed Jesus' authority to forgive sins (Matt 9:1–8); and, finally, displayed his compassion toward people regarded as unclean, treated as untouchable and rejected by the religious community. Jesus' grace and mercy extended even to the most despised and unworthy people.

Table 4.2: Jesus' Twelve Disciples

Name	Key Scriptures	Description
Simon Peter	Matt 4:18; 16:13–17,21–23; Luke 22:54–62; John 21:15–19	Fisherman before called to discipleship; one of inner circle of disciples; often brash and hotheaded
Andrew	Matt 4:18; John 1:40; 6:8; 12:22	Peter's brother; fisherman prior to following Jesus; disciple of John the Baptist before following Jesus
James	Matt 4:21; Mark 3:17; 9:2; 14:33; Acts 12:1–5	Former fisherman; John's brother; one of the two "Sons of Thunder" possibly due to temper; one of inner circle of disciples; martyred at the hand of Herod
John	Matt 4:21; Mark 3:17; 9:2; 14:33; John 1:35–39; 13:23; etc.; 21:2	Former fisherman; one of the two "Sons of Thunder" possibly due to temper, but also called "disciple whom Jesus loved"; one of inner circle of disciples
Philip	John 1:43–48; 6:5–7; 12:21–22; Acts 8:4–25,26–40	Called as disciple and brought Nathanael to Jesus; enjoyed great success preaching in Samaria, evangelized Ethiopian eunuch
Bartholomew (Nathanael)	Matt 10:3 pars.; John 1:43–49	Also known as Nathanael; seen by Jesus "under the fig tree," confessing Jesus as "Son of God" and "King of Israel"
Thomas	John 11:16; 14:5; 20:24–29	Well known as a "doubter," but later called Jesus "my Lord and my God"
Matthew (Levi)	Matt 9:9–13; 10:3; Mark 2:18; Luke 6:15	Former tax collector who left all to follow Jesus; brother of James the son of Alphaeus?
James son of Alphaeus	Matt 10:3; Mark 3:18; Luke 6:15; Acts 1:13	Brother of Matthew?
Thaddaeus (Judas son of James)	Matt 10:3; Mark 3:18; Luke 6:16; John 14:22; Acts 1:13	Also known as Judas son of James; the "other Judas" (not Iscariot; see below)
Simon the Zealot	Matt 10:4; Mark 3:18; Luke 6:15; Acts 1:13	Former zealot (Jewish freedom fighter/terrorist) who instead preached an otherworldly kingdom coming to earth
Judas Iscariot	Matt 10:4; 26:14–16; 27:3–10; John 6:70–71; 12:4–6; 13:21–30; 17:12; Acts 1:16–20	The traitor; keeper of the disciples' moneybag who eventually betrayed Jesus for 30 pieces of silver and subsequently hanged himself

This section concludes with Jesus' observation that the crowds were like sheep without a shepherd (9:35–38; see Num 27:17 with reference to the leadership transition from Moses to Joshua), an indictment against the Jewish leaders (see Ezek 34:5).

Discourse 2: Instruction of the Twelve (10)   Jesus followed his indictment of the Jewish leaders with the appointment of the Twelve to serve as shepherds of the lost sheep of the house of Israel. These 12 disciples would serve as the nucleus of a newly reconstituted spiritual Israel. Jesus commanded the disciples to proclaim the message of the coming kingdom, to perform miracles similar to his to demonstrate that the messianic age had dawned, and to live in dependence on God's gracious provisions, and warned them about persecutions they would have to endure because of their association with him. Yet these persecutions would give them opportunity for witness empowered by the Holy Spirit.

C. Third Part of Jesus' Galilean Ministry (11–12)   This section describes the wide variety of responses to Jesus' ministry ranging from the doubt of figures such as John the Baptist to his hearers' refusal to repent. Jesus alleviated John's doubts by pointing to his miraculous works that fulfilled OT prophecy and confirmed his messianic identity (11:1–19). Jesus identified John as the Messiah's forerunner, thereby implicitly identifying himself as the Messiah.

Jesus warned unrepentant cities of the terrifying judgment that awaited them if they did not repent of their rejection of Jesus (11:20–24). He explained that no one knows God the Father except Jesus his Son and "anyone to whom the Son desires to reveal him" (11:25–30). The following pericopes display the intensifying rejection of Jesus by the Jewish leaders. The Pharisees first challenged Jesus' disciples for breaking one of their Sabbath laws. Jesus replied by identifying himself as the Lord of the Sabbath, a title the Pharisees would have recognized as belonging to Yahweh alone. When Jesus later healed a paralyzed man on the Sabbath, the Pharisees began to plot to take Jesus' life (12:1–14).

Jesus is again identified as the Servant of Yahweh (see 8:17), here fulfilling OT messianic promises in the meek and humble manner of his ministry (12:15–21). Yet, the Pharisees' rejection of Jesus climaxed when they claimed the ruler of the demons was the source of Jesus' ability to cast out demons (12:22–37). Jesus warned them that ascribing the activities of the Spirit through his ministry to Satan constituted the sin of blasphemy against the Spirit, a sin for which no forgiveness was offered. He further warned that the words of the Pharisees would result in their condemnation on judgment day.

The Pharisees asked Jesus to perform a sign for them to confirm his claims (12:38–45). Jesus replied that the only sign that they would be given was his own resurrection (the "sign of Jonah"; this is the only "sign" of Jesus in the Synoptics, while John features a series of signs to show that Jesus is the promised Messiah). However, Jesus warned that the Pharisees and many others of that generation would reject that sign and that their spiritual condition would only grow worse, like a man liberated from one demon only to be inhabited by numerous more evil spirits. Finally, Jesus taught another lesson on faith and discipleship by identifying all those who performed his Father's will as his spiritual brothers and sisters (12:46–50).

Discourse 3: Parables of the Kingdom (13) In his third major discourse, Jesus told a number of parables related to the kingdom of God.[20] The parable of the sower (13:1–23) explained the reasons for which many rejected Jesus' message. Jesus' parable of the weeds (13:24–30,36–43) demonstrated that Jesus was not the source of evil in the world (compare 13:27–28 with 13:36–39), that the entire world belongs to the Son of Man, that the devil had no right to bring evil into the world, and that the Son of Man would assert his kingship over the world by punishing the wicked and blessing the righteous at the appropriate time.

The parables of the mustard seed and the leaven (13:31–35) portray the remarkable growth of the kingdom and its extensive influence on the world. The parables of the hidden treasure and the valuable pearl (13:44–46) show that the kingdom of God is worthy of any sacrifice Jesus' disciples may be called upon to make.

The parable of the dragnet (13:47–51) portrayed the separation of Jesus' righteous disciples from the wicked people of the world in final judgment and the punishment that the wicked will face. The parable of the scribe (13:52) depicted Jesus' disciples as better qualified than the scribes and Pharisees to serve as teachers of the law. In their storeroom of instruction, they had both old (the OT) and new treasures (the teachings of Jesus).

D. Galilean Ministry Extended to the North (13–17) This section of the Gospel begins with another reference to the rejection of Jesus by his own people, this time the people of Nazareth, his own hometown (13:53–58). The beginning of the close of the Galilean ministry is further signaled by the execution of John the Baptist by Herod the Tetrarch (14:1–12). In God's plan John's mission as a voice preparing the way for the Lord in the wilderness has been fulfilled, and he passes from the scene, with Jesus actively engaged in fulfilling his mission.

Jesus sought to retreat to a place of solitude after John's death, but the crowds followed him wherever he went. He provided for the crowds through the miracle of the loaves and the fish (14:13–21). He also amazed his disciples by the miracle of walking on the water (14:22–36). The two miracles were reminiscent of the provision of the manna in the wilderness and the crossing of the Red Sea and thus contribute to Matthew's emphasis on Jesus' identity as the new Moses.

Jesus' popularity among commoners due to such miracles stirred the resentment of the Pharisees and scribes (15:1–20). Jesus denounced the scribes and Pharisees as hypocrites who elevated their own traditions above the commandments of God, and thus cared more about Jewish rituals than the condition of their hearts. In contrast, the story of the Canaanite woman (15:21–28), and Jesus' words "Your faith is great" imply that Jesus

---

[20] Note that Matthew's preferred term is "kingdom of heaven" (used 32 times, though "kingdom of God" does occur five times; Mark, Luke, and John do not use the term "kingdom of heaven"). "Heaven" is most likely used to avoid overt reference to God, in typical Jewish fashion, though both expressions appear to be used synonymously. See C. C. Caragounis, "Kingdom of God/Heaven," in *Dictionary of Jesus and the Gospels*, ed. J. B. Green, S. McKnight, and I. H. Marshall (Downers Grove: InterVarsity, 1992), 417–30, esp. 435–29.

would call disciples from among the Gentiles as well as from among the Jews. Still, Jesus affirms the salvation-historical privilege of the Jews and indicates that they are the primary focus of his earthly mission (15:24,26; see 10:5–6).

Table 4.3: Parables of Jesus in the Synoptics

Parable	Mark	Matthew	Luke
Guests of the Bridegroom	2:19–20	9:15	5:33–39
Unshrunk Cloth	2:21	9:16	5:36
New Wine in Old Wineskins	2:22	9:17	5:37–39
Strong Man	3:22–27	12:29–30	11:21–23
The Sower	4:1–9,13–20	13:1–9,18–23	8:4–8,11–15
A Lamp Under a Bowl	4:21–25	5:14–15	8:16–18
Secretly Growing Seed	4:26–29		
Mustard Seed	4:30–32	13:31–32	13:18–19
Wicked Tenants	12:1–12	21:33–46	20:9–19
Budding Fig Tree	13:28–32	24:32–36	21:29–33
Watchful Servants	13:34–37		12:35–38
Father and Son		7:9–11	11:11–13
Two Gates		7:13–14	13:23–27
Good and Bad Trees		7:16–20	
Wise and Foolish Builders		7:24–27	6:47–49
Weeds Among Wheat		13:24–30,36–43	
Yeast		13:33	13:20–21
Hidden Treasure		13:44	
Pearls		13:45–46	
The Net		13:47–50	
Owner of a House		13:52	
The Lost Sheep		18:12–14	15:1–7
Unmerciful Servant		18:23–35	
Workers in the Vineyard		20:1–16	
Two Sons		21:28–32	
Wedding Feast		22:1–14	14:15–24

Parable	Mark	Matthew	Luke
Thief in the Night		24:42–44	12:39–40
Faithful and Wise Servant		24:45–51	12:42–46
Wise and Foolish Maidens		25:1–13	
The Talents		25:14–30	19:11–27
Sheep and Goats		25:31–46	
Two Debtors			7:41–50
The Good Samaritan			10:25–37
The Persistent Friend			11:5–8
Rich Fool			12:13–21
Unfruitful Fig Tree			13:6–9
Lowest Seat			14:7–14
Great Banquet			14:16–24
Tower Builder			14:28–30
Warring King			14:31–33
Lost Sheep			15:1–7
Lost Coin			15:8–10
Lost Son			15:11–32
Shrewd Manager			16:1–8
Rich Man and Lazarus			16:19–31
Humble Servant			17:7–10
Persistent Widow			18:1–8
Pharisee and Tax Collector			18:9–14

Jesus continued his miraculous ministry by ascending a mountain and healing people who suffered from various conditions, and performed another miraculous feeding reminiscent of Moses' ministry in the wilderness (15:29–39). Despite these frequent, public miracles, the Pharisees and Sadducees approached Jesus and requested another miraculous sign (16:1–12). Jesus insisted again that they would receive only one sign, the sign of Jonah mentioned earlier, Jesus' resurrection.

Contrary to the Pharisees and Sadducees, Jesus' disciples, particularly Peter (16:13–20), recognized Jesus' identity as God's Son. According to Jesus, Peter's confession at Caesarea Philippi was the result of divine revelation, and he would build his messianic community[21] on Peter because of his confession. However, when Jesus began to predict his suffering, death, and resurrection, Peter protested. Thus, despite his confession of Jesus as the Messiah, Peter still did not understand that the Messiah must suffer. Jesus explained further that all his disciples had to be prepared to bear their own cross just as Jesus was prepared to bear his.

The promised dawn of the kingdom to his disciples arrived six days later during the transfiguration of Jesus (17:1–13). Several features of the event are paralleled in Exod 34:29–35. Moreover, the description of Jesus echoes descriptions of God in the OT and strongly implies Jesus' deity. Jesus proceeded to cast out a demon which his disciples were unable to expel because, according to Jesus, they lacked faith the size of a mustard seed.

The section concludes with the account of Jesus' paying the temple tax (17:24–27). Jesus described himself as the Son of the heavenly king and thus under no obligation to pay the tax. But he performed a miracle that displayed his authority over the animal kingdom so that he and Peter could pay the tax and avoid unnecessarily offending the Jews.

Discourse 4: Parables of the Kingdom (18)   Jesus began the fourth major discourse in Matthew by describing the childlike humility of his disciples, which enabled them to submit to Jesus' authority like a child submitted to his parents' authority (18:1–9). He also warned that those who attempted to bring about the downfall of his disciples would be severely punished because of his disciples' importance to God. Even though they may wander from him, his true disciples will not be permanently lost (18:10–14). Jesus therefore outlined a disciplinary process that would encourage true disciples to repent and isolate false disciples from the Christian fellowship (18:15–20), and promised his presence with them when they made decisions about proper behavior for his disciples.

Finally, Jesus used a powerful parable to urge his disciples to offer gracious forgiveness to others (18:21–35). True disciples will forgive others. Those who refuse to forgive others who repent demonstrate by their refusal that they are not true disciples. They will suffer God's wrath for their hypocrisy.

III. Jesus' Judean Ministry and His Passion (19–28)

A. Judean Ministry (19–20)   Jesus ended his ministry in Galilee and crossed the Jordan River to enter Judea and begin his journey to Jerusalem. The Pharisees sought to trap Jesus with a question regarding divorce (19:1–12) but Jesus affirmed the sanctity and permanence of marriage. He taught that divorce had been permitted in OT law because of the hardheartedness of God's people. Yet, since Jesus' disciples were characterized by pure hearts (see 5:8), they were capable of marital love that fulfilled God's original ideal.

After blessing the children that were brought to him (19:13–15), Jesus explained to a questioner the requirements for inheriting eternal life (19:16–30). Jesus urged him to keep

---

[21] Note that this is one of only two instances of *ekklēsia* in the Gospels (the other reference is in Matt 18:17). For this reason a nontechnical translation such as "messianic community" seems preferable to the standard rendering "church" in Matt 16:18 and 18:17.

the commandments and named all of the commandments from the second table except for the tenth, which was related to possessions. Jesus' command, "[S]ell your belongings. . . . Then come, follow Me," was designed to show the young man that he defied the spirit of the Tenth Commandment by his covetousness and the commandment to love his neighbor by his neglect of the poor. Kingdom entrance, however, required giving up this self-dependence and humbly relying on the gracious forgiveness of God.

Jesus also taught that the sacrifices his disciples made to follow him would be rewarded. The disciples would reign over the 12 tribes of Israel and receive back 100 times more than what they had sacrificed for him as pictured in the parable of a rich landowner (20:1–16). Jesus then gathered his disciples privately and foretold explicitly his betrayal, trial, mockery, scourging, crucifixion, and resurrection (20:17–19). After the mother of James and John asked Jesus that her sons be granted special positions in the kingdom (20:20–28), Jesus urged his disciples to offer humble service to others rather than seek to dominate others, for he would die as a ransom for many. As Jesus passed through Jericho, he healed two blind men by touching their eyes (20:29–34).

B. Final Ministry (21–22)   As Jesus and his disciples approached Jerusalem, Jesus fulfilled OT prophecy by riding a donkey into the city in triumphal procession (21:1–11; see Zech 9:9). The crowds in Jerusalem praised Jesus both as a prophet and as the Son of David, the long-awaited Messiah. Jesus entered the temple and threw out those who sold currency that was acceptable for temple offerings and animals acceptable for temple sacrifice (21:12–17), and he quoted Isa 56:7 as justification for his actions. He also healed the blind and the lame in the temple. Jesus' display of miraculous power and the praises of the children who proclaimed him as the Son of David incited the anger of the Jewish leaders. Their anger was epitomized by the many traps they laid for Jesus, which were met by Jesus' superior understanding and interpretation of the OT.

On his way from Jerusalem back to Bethany, Jesus cursed a fig tree whose green leaves gave it the appearance of life but which produced no figs (21:18–22), and the tree immediately withered. The cursing of the fig tree foreshadowed the destruction of Jerusalem, which had failed to produce the fruits of righteousness that God expected of it. Evading an initial trap (21:23–27), Jesus then contrasted the Jewish leaders with his own disciples by telling a parable about two sons (21:28–32). Jesus compared the first son to sinners who repented in response to John's preaching, and the second son to the Jewish leaders who refused to believe and obey John's message.

Jesus then told the parable of the wicked tenants, which describes the Jewish leaders' abuse of the OT prophets and their murder of God's Son (21:33–46). Jesus warned that God would punish the Jewish leaders by stripping his kingdom from their hands and entrusting it to Jesus' disciples, who would produce the righteousness that God expected. The parable enraged the Jewish leaders, and they resolved again to kill Jesus. The parable of the wedding feast reiterated Jesus' warning by portraying the Jewish leaders as those who insulted the heavenly King by refusing an invitation to honor his Son and by mistreating and killing his servants, the OT prophets (22:1–14). The King destroyed both them and their city, thus foreshadowing the impending destruction of the city of Jerusalem. The King then invited other guests, who represent Jesus' disciples, to participate in the great messianic feast.

Another trap was laid when the Pharisees asked Jesus whether they should pay taxes to the Roman emperor (22:15–22). If so, he would have acknowledged the Romans' right to tax God's people. If not, they would have had grounds to accuse Jesus of political subversion against Rome. Jesus cleverly, and memorably, responded that people must give to Caesar what is Caesar's and to God what is God's. Jesus' reply evaded the trap and taught the important principle that since human beings were created in the image and likeness of God, all they have and are belong to God.[22] The Sadducees also attempted to trap Jesus by offering what they thought was irrefutable evidence against the doctrine of the resurrection, but Jesus demonstrated from the law of Moses that individuals continued to exist even after death (22:23–33).

The Pharisees attempted to trap Jesus again with a question regarding the most important commandment (22:34–40). He replied that the most important commandments required wholehearted devotion to God and love for others and that all other aspects of the law were related to and dependent on these two central commands. Finally, Jesus questioned the Pharisees about the lineage of the Messiah, which they could not answer. He demonstrated that the Messiah was superior to David and was recognized by David himself as Lord (22:41–45). Jesus' response so thwarted the Jewish leaders' ploys that no one dared to challenge Jesus' teaching in a public forum again (22:46).

C. Jesus' Denunciation of the Pharisees (23)   In a series of blistering woes, Jesus warned the crowds that although the teaching of the scribes and Pharisees was generally reliable, their example should not be followed since their lives were not consistent with their teaching (23:1–39). He challenged the egotistical way in which these religious leaders sought honor from other people and thus urged his followers to be characterized by humility. Jesus pronounced judgment on the scribes and Pharisees for the way they prevented others from entering the kingdom, sentenced those who embraced their teaching to destruction, used legal loopholes to evade the clear demands of the commandments, and focused on the minutiae of the law to the neglect of the more important matters such as justice, mercy, and faith. He rebuked them for focusing on matters related to external purity and for giving no attention to their inner corruption. Although the Jewish leaders piously claimed to be morally superior to their ancestors, Jesus insisted that their abuse of his disciples would make them accountable for the blood of all righteous martyrs that had been shed in human history. Jesus concluded his cry against the Jewish leaders with a warning that God would abandon the temple and that Jesus would not return to Jerusalem until his Second Coming.

---

[22] It also taught that we should pay our taxes.

Discourse 5: The Olivet Discourse, Kingdom Parables (24–25) Jesus' final discourse in Matthew commences with a section on the impending destruction of the Jerusalem temple, which would occur within one generation, and the Second Coming, which would occur in the distant future. He prophesied that the temple would be destroyed, and then he outlined the events that would precede this destruction. He explained the horrible suffering that his people would endure during that period of tribulation and assured them that he would shorten the period of suffering for their sakes. He also assured his chosen ones that they would not be deceived by the false messiahs and false prophets who would appear. Jesus' own coming would be unmistakable and easily distinguished from the appearance of the false messiahs. Thus, Jesus taught his disciples to be constantly prepared (24:42–50).

The parable of the 10 virgins (25:1–13) warned the disciples to prepare immediately for the Second Coming but to anticipate a lengthy delay. The parable of the talents (25:14–30) emphasized the importance of living faithfully and responsibly during the lengthy delay before the Lord's return. The parable of the sheep and goats (25:31–46) demonstrated that one of the most important steps in preparing for Jesus' return was treating Jesus' followers kindly and compassionately.

D. The Passion (26–27) After the conclusion of Jesus' final discourse, several Matthean features indicate that Jesus' death is drawing close. Jesus offered another prediction of his crucifixion (26:1–2). The Jewish leaders met to conspire to kill him (26:3–5). A woman anointed Jesus with myrrh in preparation for his burial (26:6–16). One of Jesus' own disciples approached the Jewish leaders offering to betray Jesus for a price (26:17–25). While Jesus shared the Passover meal with his disciples, he announced that one of them would betray him (26:26–30) and specifically identified Judas as the betrayer. Jesus then instituted the Lord's Supper by using the bread and cup from the Passover to portray his body and blood that would be sacrificed to seal the new covenant and to provide forgiveness of sins.

After this, Jesus quoted an OT prophecy to demonstrate that his disciples would abandon him after his arrest (26:31–35). Peter and the other disciples strongly denied that this was possible, yet Jesus predicted that Peter would deny him three times before the rooster crowed at sunrise. At this Jesus led his disciples into the garden of Gethsemane (26:36–46), gathering his inner circle (Peter, James, and John) to join him in prayer. Jesus asked that the Father might allow him to escape the cross, but he submitted himself to the Father's will whatever it might be. Then Jesus approached the disciples, and when he found them sleeping, he urged them to be alert and to pray.

This scene was repeated three times until Judas entered Gethsemane accompanied by an armed mob that had been dispatched by the Jewish officials (26:47–56). Judas identified Jesus by greeting him with the kiss of friendship, and Jesus was seized by the mob. One of the disciples intervened, drew his sword, and struck off the ear of a servant of the high priest. Jesus rebuked the disciple and reminded him that his Father was more than capable of rescuing him if he chose to do so but that his arrest and death were necessary to fulfill the promises of the Scripture.

After this Jesus was led to Caiaphas, the high priest, and an assembly of the scribes and elders (26:57–68). Peter followed closely but discretely and waited in the courtyard to hear the outcome of the proceedings. The Jewish leaders sought false witnesses whose testimony might justify executing Jesus. Two witnesses appeared who charged that Jesus had claimed that he was able to destroy the temple and rebuild it in three days. Jesus remained silent in the face of the charges until the high priest placed him under oath and demanded to know if he were the Messiah, the Son of God. Jesus replied by quoting Ps 110:1 and Dan 7:13. The high priest accused Jesus of blasphemy. Then the assembly sentenced Jesus to death. Members of the assembly began to abuse Jesus by spitting in his face, punching him with their fists, and slapping him.

In the meantime others present in the courtyard recognized Peter as a disciple of Jesus (26:69–75). He denied knowing Jesus three different times. Each denial was more adamant and angrier than the previous denial. Immediately after the third denial, the rooster crowed, signaling the fulfillment of Jesus' prophecy and sending Peter out to weep.

While Jesus was led away to Pilate, Judas regretted his decision to betray Jesus (27:1–10). He returned the betrayal price to the Jewish leaders, proclaimed Jesus' innocence, and then hanged himself. The Jewish leaders used the money to purchase a plot of land for the burial of foreigners who visited Jerusalem.

When Jesus was questioned by Pilate and accused by the Jewish leaders, he remained silent (27:11–26). Although Pilate attempted to release Jesus, the people, prompted by their leaders, pled for Pilate to release Barabbas instead and to crucify Jesus. Pilate washed his hands in a symbolic attempt to alleviate his guilt in Jesus' execution while the Jews accepted full responsibility for Jesus' death, then he had Jesus scourged, and handed him over to be crucified.

Soldiers from the Roman cohort responsible for Jesus' execution stripped him and ridiculed his messianic claims by adorning him with a mock robe, crown, and scepter, and bowing before him in fake homage (27:27–50). They then spit on Jesus and brutally beat him. Since Jesus was weak from his severe scourging and unable to carry his cross to the place of execution, the soldiers forced Simon of Cyrene to carry the cross for him. Jesus was offered a mixture that could have diminished his sufferings, but he refused to drink it. While he was suffering, onlookers mocked Jesus, particularly the chief priests, scribes, and elders, as well as those crucified along with him.

Several remarkable signs accompanied Jesus' sufferings and death (27:51–56). While he hung on the cross, the sky was black although it was midday. When Jesus died, the heavy curtain that separated the holy of holies from the rest of the temple complex was torn from the top to the bottom while an earthquake split the rocks and opened the tombs of the city. The Roman centurion and his soldiers who supervised the crucifixion were terrified by these supernatural events and confessed that Jesus truly was the Son of God.

Joseph of Arimathea buried Jesus in his own new tomb and sealed it with a stone (27:57–66). Mary Magdalene and Mary, mother of two of Jesus' disciples, observed the burial and thus were aware of the location of the tomb. This familiarity with its location ensured that the tomb that they later found empty was, in fact, the tomb where Jesus had been buried. At the request of the Pharisees, Pilate secured and sealed Jesus' tomb and ordered a Roman *custodia* to guard it in order to prevent Jesus' disciples from stealing the body and staging a resurrection.

E. The Resurrection and the Great Commission (28) At dawn on Sunday morning, the two women who observed Jesus' burial returned to the tomb (28:1–10). An earthquake occurred as an angel appeared and rolled back the stone that sealed Jesus' tomb. The Roman guard was immobilized with terror. The angel announced that Jesus had risen from the dead and commanded the women to report this to the disciples and to urge them to travel to Galilee where Jesus would meet them. As they raced to the disciples, Jesus himself intercepted them. The women fell to the ground, threw their arms around Jesus' feet, and worshipped him.

Meanwhile, some of the soldiers from the Roman *custodia* reported to the chief priests what had happened (28:11–15). The Sanhedrin gathered and decided to bribe the soldiers to give the false report that the disciples had stolen Jesus' body while they were asleep. Later, Jesus appeared to his disciples in Galilee and commanded them to acknowledge his authority over both heaven and earth by making disciples of people from all ethnic groups (28:16–20). These new disciples should be baptized and taught to obey all of Jesus' commands. Jesus promised his presence would empower his disciples to fulfill this commission.

THEOLOGY

Theological Themes

Jesus as the Fulfillment of Old Testament Messianic Predictions One of the most significant theological themes in Matthew's Gospel is that Jesus is the Messiah predicted in the Hebrew Scriptures. This fulfillment is highlighted especially in Matthew 1–4 in the form of several fulfillment quotations. Yet, according to Matthew, virtually every significant event in Jesus' life is shown to fulfill Scripture:

At the beginning Matthew presented Jesus as *the son of David and the son of Abraham* (1:1–18). Jesus is also *the new Moses*, who in his "inaugural address" in the Gospel, the Sermon on the Mount, ascends a mountain and instructs his followers in his new law (chaps. 5–7).

Also related to Jesus' fulfillment of the OT is the *kingdom of God*. While the exact phrase "kingdom of God" is not found in the OT, the concept is. At the height of Israel's history, the nation was ruled by King David and King Solomon. Ultimately, God himself was the King and Ruler of his people.

Table 4.4: Jesus' Fulfillment of OT Prophecy in Matthew's Gospel

Event in Jesus' Life	Matthew	OT Passage
The virgin birth and name of Jesus	1:22–23	Isa 7:14; 8:8,10
Jesus' birthplace, Bethlehem	2:5–6	Mic 5:2
The flight to Egypt	2:15	Hos 11:1
The slaying of infants by Herod	2:18	Jer 31:15
Jesus called a Nazarene ("branch")	2:23	Isa 11:1; 53:2
John the Baptist's ministry	3:3; 11:10	Isa 40:3; Mal 3:1
The temptation of Jesus	4:1–11	Deut 6:13,16; 8:3
The beginning of Jesus' ministry	4:15–16	Isa 9:1–2
Jesus' healing ministry	8:17; 11:5; 12:17–21	Isa 53:4; 35:5–6; 42:18; 61:1
Division brought by Jesus	10:35–36	Mic 7:6
Jesus' gentle style of ministry	12:17–21	Isa 42:1–4
Jesus' death, burial, resurrection	12:40	Jonah 1:17
Hardened response to Jesus	13:14–15; 15:7–9; 21:33,42	Isa 5:1–2; 6:9–10; 29:13; Ps 118:22–23
Jesus' teaching in parables	13:35	Ps 78:2
Jesus' triumphal entry	21:5,9	Isa 62:11; Ps 118:26
Jesus' cleansing of the temple	21:13	Isa 56:7; Jer 7:11
Jesus as Son and Lord of David	1:1; 22:44	Ps 110:1
Lament over Jerusalem	23:38–39	Jer 12:7; 22:5; Ps 118:26
Judas's betrayal of Jesus	26:15	Zech 11:12
Peter's denial	26:31	Zech 13:7
Jesus' arrest	26:54,56	The Scriptures, the Prophets
Judas's death	27:9–10	Zech 11:12–13; Jer 32:6–9
Jesus the righteous sufferer	27:34–35,39,43,46,48	Pss 22:1,7–8,18; 69:21

The Great Commission and the Inclusion of the Gentiles While Matthew originally wrote his Gospel for a predominantly Jewish Christian audience, one of his purposes was to demonstrate that Israel's Messiah did not come for the benefit of Israel alone. Rather, Jesus came to offer salvation to all the peoples of the earth.[23] Throughout Jesus' ministry, Gentiles are drawn to him, especially when he ministered in Gentile territory (e.g., Matt 4:24–25;

---

[23] See A. J. Köstenberger and P. T. O'Brien, *Salvation to the Ends of the Earth: A Biblical Theology of Mission*, NSBT 11 (Downers Grove: InterVarsity, 2001), 87–109 (with further bibliographical references).

15:21–31). Matthew 12:15–21 identifies Jesus as the fulfillment of Isa 42:1–4, a prophecy that climaxes with the promise "the nations will put their hope in His name."

The theme of God's inclusion of the Gentiles climaxed at Jesus' crucifixion with the confession of the Roman centurion and his guards who exclaimed, "This man really was God's Son" (27:54). Their bold confession is in stark contrast with the refusal of the Jewish leaders to believe even after the soldiers reported Jesus' resurrection. Finally, the theme was clearly stated in the Great Commission in which Jesus urged his followers to make disciples of "all nations" (28:19–20).

POINTS OF APPLICATION

- Believe in Jesus the Messiah (16:16)
- Imitate the character of God (5:48)
- Follow Jesus' call of discipleship to pick up your cross and follow him (16:24)
- Thank Jesus for paying the penalty for your sins (26:26–29)
- Obey the Great Commission (28:18–20)

STUDY QUESTIONS

1. When did Matthew most likely write his Gospel? Why is an early date significant?
2. What are the primary and secondary purposes of Matthew's Gospel?
3. What are the chapters in Matthew that correspond to the Sermon on the Mount and the final eschatological discourse?
4. Which literary and theological feature is particularly prominent in Matthew 1–4?
5. What are some texts that demonstrate Matthew's concern for the "Great Commission"?

FOR FURTHER STUDY

Allison, D. C., Jr. *The New Moses: A Matthean Typology*. Minneapolis: Fortress, 1993.

Blomberg, C. L. *Matthew*. New American Commentary 22. Nashville: Broadman, 1992.

Carson, D. A. "Matthew." Pages 3–602 in *Matthew, Mark, Luke*. Vol. 8 of *The Expositor's Bible Commentary*. Grand Rapids: Zondervan, 1984.

France, R. T. *Matthew*. Tyndale New Testament Commentary. Grand Rapids: Eerdmans, 1985.

Hagner, D. A. *Matthew*. 2 vols. Word Biblical Commentary 33. Dallas: Word, 1993.

Keener, C. S. *A Commentary on the Gospel of Matthew*. Grand Rapids: Eerdmans, 1999.

Morris, L. *The Gospel According to Matthew*. Pillar New Testament Commentary. Grand Rapids: Eerdmans, 1992.

Nolland, J. *The Gospel of Matthew*. New International Greek Testament Commentary. Grand Rapids: Eerdmans, 2005.

Turner, D. L. *Matthew*. Baker Exegetical Commentary on the New Testament. Grand Rapids: Baker, 2008.

Wilkins, M. J. *Matthew*. NIV Application Commentary. Grand Rapids: Zondervan, 2004.

Chapter 5

The Gospel According to Mark

CORE KNOWLEDGE

Basic Knowledge: Students should know the key facts of Mark's Gospel. With regard to history, students should be able to identify the Gospel's author, date, provenance, destination, and purpose. With regard to literature, they should be able to provide a basic outline of the book and identify core elements of the book's content found in the unit-by-unit discussion. With regard to theology, students should be able to identify Mark's major theological themes.

KEY FACTS	
Author:	John Mark, "interpreter" of Peter
Date:	Mid- to late 50s
Provenance:	Rome
Destination:	Gentiles in Rome
Purpose:	Apology for the cross, discipleship
Theme:	Jesus is the authoritative, miracle-working Son of God
Key Verses:	10:45; 15:39

CONTRIBUTION TO THE CANON

- Presentation of a Gospel of Jesus narrating his ministry from Galilee to Jerusalem
- Jesus as the miracle-working Son of God (1:1,11; 5:7; 9:7; 15:39)
- Jesus' displaying his power over nature, demons, sickness, and death (4:35–5:43)
- Discipleship failure (4:40; 6:51–52; 8:16–21,33; 9:18–19; 14:66–72; 16:8)
- Jesus' sacrificial, vicarious death as a ransom for many (10:45)

INTRODUCTION

THE GOSPEL OF Mark is the shortest of the four Gospels and has the least unique material. While it does not use the word "gospel" (*euangelion*) as a title, it is the only Gospel to refer to its message about Jesus as the "gospel" (1:1).[1] It is regarded by many as foundational to the other two Synoptic Gospels, Matthew and Luke. About 92 percent of it is paralleled in Matthew, about 48 percent in Luke, and about 95 percent in Matthew and Luke combined.

The Gospel of Mark is a fast-paced portrayal of the life of Jesus Christ, most likely patterned after the blueprint of Peter's preaching. Peter's sermon in Acts 10:34–43 provides us with a brief summary of the basic structure of the four canonical Gospels.[2] It tells us a story, the "Gospel," about Jesus (1:1). Mark emphasizes Jesus' identity as the Son of God by focusing on his miraculous feats rather than on the parables. At the same time, Mark notes the lack of understanding of Jesus' true identity by his first followers.

HISTORY

Author

Like the other Gospels, Mark is formally anonymous, since the author of this Gospel did not explicitly identify himself. But, as is the case of Matthew and the other Gospels, the title that ascribes the Gospel to Mark is clearly very early if not original. If Mark was the first to write his Gospel (a theory commonly called "Markan priority"; see chap. 3) and affixed the title to the Gospel himself, the other evangelists would have likely followed suit. In any case, the titles would have become necessary as soon as the Gospels were gathered and began to circulate in a single collection.

Mark's Gospel claims to be based on the witness of the apostle Peter (see the references to Peter in 1:16 and 16:7), which is also supported by evidence from the early church fathers.[3] Another feature, the "plural-to-singular device," which singles out one individual from a group in order to tell an account from that individual's perspective, makes Peter's the dominant perspective in the narrative, reproducing his eyewitness recollection in first-person terms.[4]

External Evidence Ancient tradition has consistently attributed this Gospel to Mark, who was believed to have been closely associated with the apostle Peter. The earliest and most important witness is that of Papias, bishop of Hierapolis in Phrygia in Asia Minor (c. 60–130), whose five-volume work *Expositions of the Lord's Sayings* was cited by Eusebius

---

[1] While it is possible that this phrase serves as the title for the Gospel as a whole, it most likely refers, as in Paul, to the saving message about Jesus and the salvation he provides.

[2] R. A. Guelich, "Mark, Gospel of," in *Dictionary of Jesus and the Gospels*, ed. J. B. Green, S. McKnight, and I. H. Marshall (Downers Grove: InterVarsity, 1992), 513.

[3] R. Bauckham, *Jesus and the Eyewitnesses: The Gospels as Eyewitness Testimony* (Grand Rapids: Eerdmans, 2006), chaps. 6–7, calls this the "inclusio of eyewitness testimony": the practice of naming the major eyewitness underlying an account first and last in the document.

[4] Ibid., 156–64.

in the early fourth century (*Eccl. Hist.* 3.39). Papias claimed to have learned of Mark's authorship from an individual he referred to as "the Elder" or "the Presbyter," thus preserving a tradition that dates at least as far back as the early second century.[5]

Later testimony from the middle and late second century appears to rely on this tradition. Clement of Alexandria (c. 150–215; cited by Eusebius, *Eccl. Hist.* 6.14), Tertullian (c. 160–225), and Origen (c. 185–254) all believed that Mark wrote this Gospel and that Peter was his source.[6] Tradition may vary with respect to certain details, such as Peter's exact role in connection with the composition of the Gospel and the date of authorship, but all agree that Mark wrote this Gospel and that Peter's preaching in Rome played a central role.[7]

Portrait of Mark   Who was Mark? While the name was common in Roman circles (Marcus), the association of Mark with Peter by both Papias and church tradition suggests that this Mark is most likely the John Mark mentioned by Luke (Acts 12:12,25; 13:13; 15:37–39), Peter (1 Pet 5:13), and Paul (Col 4:10; Phlm 24; 2 Tim 4:11).[8] Mark's mother was a prominent member of the early Jerusalem church (Acts 12:12). It was this same Mark who accompanied his uncle Barnabas and Paul on the first missionary journey (Acts 12:25). The book of Acts records that his failure to complete this journey resulted in a breach between Barnabas and Paul over Mark, which was later mended (Acts 13:13; 15:37–40; see Phlm 24; Col 4:10). In 2 Tim 4:11, Paul wrote of his desire to have Mark join him in Rome, showing that God can restore those who have previously failed to effective Christian ministry.

Date

A date in the 50s and no later than 60 is most likely on the basis of Peter's presence in Rome in the 50s. If, as tradition suggests, Peter had significant input in Mark's Gospel, then a very early date is unlikely because Peter probably did not arrive in Rome much before 62.

If Mark was the first to write his Gospel and if Luke used Mark in writing his Gospel, and since the book of Acts was likely written in the early 60s and Luke before that, then all these factors would place the most probable date for the writing of Mark's Gospel in the second half of the 50s.

Provenance

It is difficult to determine where Mark was when he wrote his Gospel. For the most part, tradition associates Mark's Gospel with Peter and consequently with Rome. Although internal evidence is scanty, what little there is points to an origin in Rome. Mark used a

---

[5] W. L. Lane, *The Gospel According to Mark* (Grand Rapids: Eerdmans, 1974), 8.

[6] J. A. Brooks, *Mark*, NAC 23 (Nashville: Broadman, 1991), 18.

[7] W. Hendriksen, *Exposition of the Gospel According to Mark*, New Testament Commentary (Grand Rapids: Baker, 1975), 12–13.

[8] Guelich, "Mark, Gospel of," 514.

considerable number of Latinisms. For instance, the two copper coins (*lepta*) that the poor widow cast into the offering box are explained as amounting to one Roman *quadrans* (also called "penny," *padram*; 12:42), and the palace (*aulē*) into which the soldiers led Jesus is called the *praetorium* (the governor's official residence; 15:16).[9]

Another possible piece of evidence pointing to a Roman provenance is the reference to Rufus in 15:21. As Hendriksen said, "Mark is also the only Gospel that informs us (15:21) that Simon of Cyrene was 'the father of Alexander and Rufus,' who were evidently well-known in Rome (see Rom 16:13)."[10] Mark also reckoned time in accordance with the Roman method, referring to the four watches of the night rather than the traditional three in Jewish reckoning (6:48; 13:35).[11] For these and other reasons an origin in Rome is most likely.

Destination

The universal character of this Gospel makes it difficult to pinpoint a specific audience for Mark's Gospel. A non-Jewish destination is supported by the fact that several Aramaic terms and expressions are translated into Greek: *boanerges* ("sons of thunder"; 3:17), *talitha cumi* ("Little girl, I say to you, get up!"; 5:41), *Corban* ("a gift committed to the temple"; 7:11), *Ephphatha* ("Be opened!"; 7:34), *Bartimaios* ("son of Timaeus"; 10:46), *Abba* ("Father"; 14:36), *Golgotha* ("Skull Place"; 15:22), and *Elōi, Elōi, lemá sabachtháni?* ("My God, My God, why have You forsaken me?"; 15:34).

In addition, Jewish laws and customs are often explained, such as the washing of hands (7:3–5), the custom to sacrifice the Passover lamb on the first day of the Feast of Unleavened Bread (14:12), and the "day of preparation" being the day before the Sabbath (15:42).[12] Moreover, Mark displayed an interest in the cessation of ritual elements in the Mosaic law, especially food laws (see 7:19).[13] Finally, the Gospel reaches its climax in the confession of Jesus' deity by a *Roman centurion* (15:39).

The frequent Latinisms, the reference to Rufus, and the use of the Roman method of reckoning time all point not only to the Gospel's origin in Rome but to a Roman destination as well. It follows that Mark's first readers were most likely Greek-speaking individuals who did not know Aramaic or Hebrew and were for the most part unfamiliar with certain Jewish customs. At the same time, they seem to have possessed at least a basic knowledge of the OT and a familiarity with early Christian traditions about Jesus. Mark's intended audience was most likely comprised of Gentile Christians situated in Rome. Beyond this, the Gospel is addressed to "all Christians" who care to read it.[14]

---

[9] Hendriksen, *Mark*, 13.

[10] Ibid.

[11] Lane, *Gospel of Mark*, 24.

[12] Hendriksen, *Mark*, 13.

[13] D. A. Carson and D. J. Moo, *An Introduction to the New Testament*, 2nd ed. (Grand Rapids: Zondervan, 2005), 183.

[14] R. Bauckham, ed., *The Gospels for All Christians: Rethinking the Gospel Audiences* (Grand Rapids: Eerdmans, 1997).

Purpose

As with the other Gospel writers, the primary problem confronting Mark is to account for Jesus' crucifixion. Why should anyone believe in a miracle-working messianic pretender who ended up being crucified as a common criminal? In response to this objection, Mark wrote "an apology [or apologetic] for the cross,"[15] contending that it is precisely as the Crucified that Jesus proved himself to be the messianic King and the Son of God. Not only was the Messiah's death predicted in OT Scripture, it was also repeatedly predicted by Jesus himself (8:31; 9:31; 10:33–34), and it was required as "a ransom for many" (10:45), that is, as a substitutionary, atoning sacrifice for sin.

An indication into Mark's likely purpose is the opening statement of his Gospel, which indicates that Mark's narrative primarily aims to demonstrate that Jesus is the Son of God (1:1).[16] In the Gospel, God (who refers to Jesus as his "beloved Son" at Jesus' baptism and the transfiguration; 1:11; 9:7); demons (1:25; 3:11–12; 5:7); Jesus himself (12:6; 14:61); and a Roman centurion (15:39) all agree that Jesus is the Son of God.[17] In support of this claim, Mark's Roman audience was treated to a dazzling display of Jesus' miracle-working power that shows his authority over the realms of nature, sickness, and death, and even the supernatural (4:35–5:43).[18]

Overall, then, we can note four interrelated purposes in Mark's Gospel, all of which revolve around Jesus' identity as Son of God: (1) a *pastoral* purpose: to teach Christians about the nature of discipleship; (2) a *missionary-training* purpose: to explain how Jesus prepared his followers to take on his mission and to show others how to do so as well; (3) an *apologetic* purpose: to demonstrate to non-Christians that Jesus is the Son of God because of his great power and in spite of his crucifixion; and (4) an *anti-imperial* purpose: to show that Jesus, not Caesar, is the true Son of God, Savior, and Lord.

LITERATURE

Literary Plan

Mark is an action-rich Gospel whose style is compact, concrete, vivid, and orderly. Mark's frequent use of the word "immediately," particularly in the first half of the Gospel, advances the narrative at a fast pace, while his more detailed descriptions add color (see shorter parallel accounts in 2:1–12; 5:1–20). Mark also has the least polished Greek of the four Gospels, and his sentences are often simple and straightforward. Rather than take this as an example of unrefined style, we can take this as a fine accommodation of Jesus'

---

[15] This is the subtitle of R. Gundry's commentary on Mark's Gospel: *Mark: A Commentary on His Apology for the Cross* (Grand Rapids: Eerdmans, 1993).

[16] Guelich, "Mark, Gospel of," 513. See Peter's sermon in Acts 10:34–43.

[17] A. J. Köstenberger and P. T. O'Brien, *Salvation to the Ends of the Earth: A Biblical Theology of Mission*, NSBT 11 (Downers Grove: InterVarsity, 2001), 74. See "Jesus as the Son of God" and Table 5.1 below.

[18] See Gundry, *Mark*, 237; R. A. Guelich, *Mark 1–8:26*, WBC 34A (Dallas: Word, 1989), 261–63.

life and ministry in the vernacular of the day.[19] Throughout his Gospel, Mark sought to demonstrate by way of both direct quotations and allusions from the OT that the coming of Jesus constituted the fulfillment of OT prophecy and that his powerful acts proved that he was the Son of God.

Mark's Gospel consists of two main sections that portray Jesus as the powerful Messiah (1:1–8:26) and the Suffering Servant (8:27–16:8). The plot is centered on the "Gospel of Jesus Christ, the Son of God" (1:1). The development of this plot involves conflict over the question of Jesus' identity complicated by Jesus' own injunctions to have his identity kept secret (the "messianic secret") and the failure of the disciples to comprehend who Jesus really was (the "discipleship failure" and "misunderstanding" motifs). However, as Rhoads and Michie explained, "Although Jesus is the immediate cause of the conflicts, the story shows that God is the ultimate origin of many of the actions and events of the story."[20]

Mark's emphasis on Jesus as the Son of God, beginning with the opening sentence in 1:1 and peaking with the centurion's confession at 15:39, represents the key thread running through his Gospel (see 1:11; 3:11; 5:7; 9:7; 12:6; 13:32; 14:61). The main story is set between Jesus' baptism and his death, within shifting geographical locales in Galilee and the surrounding regions. Events come to a dramatic close in Jerusalem. The first section is action packed and centers on Jesus' miracles and stories that focus on healings, controversies, and parables. The major turning point is Peter's confession of Jesus on the road to Caesarea Philippi (8:27–30). In the second half of his narrative, Mark focused on Jesus' teaching concerning his impending suffering and death, culminating in the account of Jesus' crucifixion.

Outline

The structure of Mark's Gospel presents itself as follows.[21]

I. JESUS THE SON OF GOD AS THE POWERFUL MESSIAH (1:1–8:26)
    A. Preparation for Jesus' Ministry in the Wilderness (1:1–13)
    B. Jesus' Initial Ministry in Galilee (1:14–3:35)
    C. Jesus' Ministry on and around the Sea of Galilee (4:1–8:26)
II. JESUS THE SON OF GOD AS THE SUFFERING SERVANT (8:27–16:8)
    A. Jesus' Ministry on the Way to Jerusalem (8:27–10:52)
    B. Jesus' Ministry at the Temple (11:1–13:37)
    C. Jesus' Death on the Cross and Resurrection (14:1–16:8)

---

[19] See Lane, *Gospel of Mark*, 26.

[20] D. M. Rhoads and D. M. Michie, *Mark as Story: An Introduction to the Narrative of a Gospel* (Philadelphia: Fortress, 1982), 74. See their entire discussion on pp. 73–100.

[21] The broad contours of the outline below are adapted from J. F. Williams, "Does Mark's Gospel Have an Outline?" *JETS* 49 (2006): 505–25.

UNIT-BY-UNIT DISCUSSION

I. Jesus as the Powerful Messiah (1:1–8:26)

A. Preparation for Jesus' Ministry in the Wilderness (1:1–13) The first words of Mark's Gospel immediately inform the reader that the evangelist is about to narrate a story that focuses on "Jesus Christ, the Son of God" (1:1). He began with the OT, in the words of Isaiah the prophet (actually a combination of Mal 3:1 and Isa 40:3), effectively announcing that "John's ministry fulfills divine prophecy and then identifies Jesus as the beloved Son and the conveyer of the Spirit."[22] John the Baptist performed his God-ordained role as he baptized in the desert, a significant locale due to its symbolism as a place of new beginnings and renewal.[23] His baptism was the means of preparation for God's coming Messiah and kingdom. Thus, before Jesus began his work, he was baptized by John, at which point God himself declared Jesus' sonship as the Holy Spirit descended on Jesus (Mark 1:11). He was then driven into the desert by the Holy Spirit to undergo a period of temptation by Satan. His victory over Satan sets the pattern for the narrative that continues to unfold.

B. Jesus' Ministry in Galilee (1:14–3:35) In Mark's account of Jesus' activities in Galilee, Jesus' preaching and healing ministry is held up as the pattern for his disciples to emulate (see 1:14–15,21–28,34; and 6:12–13).[24] As the narrative progresses, Jesus drew his followers more fully into his own messianic mission: he called them away from their natural vocation to follow him (1:16–20; 2:13–17); he chose the Twelve "to be with him" (3:13–19); and at the climax of the first section he sent them on a mission (6:6b–13). Early in his ministry, Jesus dissociated himself from blood ties and affirmed new forms of kinship. He redefined who his true mother and brothers are (3:31–35) and was rejected in his hometown of Nazareth (see 6:1–6a). This important principle of access on the basis of spiritual rather than ethnic identity paves the way for the future extension of the gospel to non-Jews.[25] It also demonstrates the nature of true discipleship: following Jesus involves conflict, rejection by one's own, even the bearing of one's cross.

C. Jesus' Ministry on and around the Sea of Galilee (4:1–8:26) Already in 3:6, the reader is told of the Pharisees' plot with the Herodians to kill Jesus (cf. 8:15; 12:13). While this rejection of Jesus by the official representatives of Judaism did not cause him to forsake his mission to the Jews, it did give him increased exposure to Gentiles.[26] This includes Jesus' healing of the Gerasene demoniac in 5:1–20; his encounter with the Syrophoenician woman in 7:24–30; and his feeding of the multitude in 8:1–10, which is reminiscent of Elisha's miraculous feeding of Gentiles in 2 Kgs 4:42–44. Nevertheless, when Jesus, for

---

[22] D. E. Garland, *Mark*, NIVAC (Grand Rapids: Zondervan, 1996), 207.

[23] See Exod 2:15; 1 Sam 23:14; 1 Kgs 19:3–4.

[24] Note the *inclusio* of 1:14 and 6:29, which records John's imprisonment and death at Herod's hands.

[25] D. Senior and C. Stuhlmueller, *Biblical Foundations for Mission* (Maryknoll: Orbis, 1983), 222.

[26] W. Telford, "Introduction: The Gospel of Mark," in *The Interpretation of Mark*, IRT 7, ed. W. Telford (Philadelphia: Fortress, 1985), 23; F. Hahn, *Mission in the New Testament*, SBT 47 (London: SCM, 1965), 113.

instance, restored the Gerasene demoniac to sanity, he did not invite the healed Gentile to join his messianic mission but sent him home to tell his own people what had happened to him.

In his account of the sending of the Twelve, Mark, unlike Matthew (Matt 10:5–6), did not explicitly limit their mission to Israel (6:6b–13). Nevertheless, Jesus' ministry in the first part of the Gospel is primarily devoted to the Jews (see esp. 7:26a). After Herod's mistaken identification of Jesus as the resurrected John the Baptist (6:14–29), Jesus' feeding of the five thousand, and his walking on the water (6:30–52), mounting opposition to Jesus caused him to withdraw from Galilee. He first moved to the region of Tyre and Sidon north of Galilee (7:24–30), then to the Decapolis east of Galilee (7:31–8:12), and finally to the far north in Caesarea Philippi (8:27–9:32). Throughout his narrative Mark not only emphasized the disciples' misunderstanding and hardness of heart, but he also portrayed their increased involvement in Jesus' mission (see 6:41).

II. Jesus as the Suffering Son of God (8:27–16:8)

A. Jesus' Ministry on the Way to Jerusalem (8:27–10:52)   Subsequent to Peter's confession of Jesus as the Christ (8:29–30)—which occasions a thrice-repeated pattern of passion prediction, discipleship failure, and instruction regarding true discipleship (8:27–9:1; 9:30–41; 10:32–45)—the "messianic secret" is gradually lifted, at least for the disciples (1:34,44–45; 3:12; 5:43; 7:36–37; 8:26,29–30; 9:9). Nevertheless, as long as the disciples fail to understand the inner dynamics of the cross, they do not yet recognize their mission, since this mission is contingent upon the disciples' following Jesus in the way of the cross (see 8:34).[27]

Up to 8:26 Jesus ministered in Galilee and did not leave it permanently until 10:1. The entire section of 8:27–10:52 is cast as a journey from Caesarea Philippi to Jerusalem (see 9:30,33; 10:1,17,32,46,52).[28] Intriguingly, Mark limited instances of gospel proclamation entirely to Galilee (see 1:14,38–39,45; 3:14; 5:20; 6:12; 7:36). The only two references to preaching the gospel in the Jerusalem section of Mark refer to the *future* proclamation of the good news to the Gentiles. Moreover, a future meeting between Jesus and the disciples is intimated in 14:28 and 16:7, which further directs the reader's attention to Galilee.

B. Jesus' Ministry at the Temple (11:1–13:37)   Following Jesus' entry into Jerusalem (11:1–11), Mark used scenes surrounding the Jewish temple to draw attention to the marked shift that would ensue as a result of Jesus' ministry and his rejection by the Jews.[29] Thus Mark referred to the temple as a house of prayer *for all the nations* (see the quotation of Isa 56:7 in 11:17), indicating that the temple would soon be replaced by an

---

[27] Senior and Stuhlmueller, *Biblical Foundations for Mission*, 226.

[28] See W. Kelber, *The Kingdom in Mark* (Philadelphia: Fortress, 1974), 67–85, for the "way" or "journey" motif in Mark.

[29] J. R. Donahue, *Are You the Christ?* SBLDS 10 (Missoula: SBL, 1973), 137; D. Juel, *Messiah and Temple*, SBLDS 31 (Missoula: SBL, 1977), 212.

eschatological "house of prayer."[30] The cursing of the fig tree (11:12–14,20–26; 13:28–31) likewise draws attention to the rejection of the Jews as a result of their rejection of Jesus as Messiah.

The climax is reached in the parable of the tenants of the vineyard (12:1–2), where Jesus declared that God's vineyard would be taken away from the Jews and given *to others* (see 12:9). These "others" come into view particularly during Jesus' eschatological discourse in chap. 13, which is once again occasioned by a scene at the temple. Jesus, after predicting the destruction of the temple, informed his disciples that the glorious coming of the Son of Man would be preceded by the preaching of the gospel to *all the nations.*

C. Jesus' Death on the Cross and Resurrection (14:1–16:8)   The last major section of Mark's Gospel begins with Jesus' anointing and the institution of the Lord's Supper. This intimate scene is contrasted with the harsh reality of Jesus' trial before the Sanhedrin (14:53–65). At the high point of the Jewish trial, Jesus responded to the high priest's question of whether he is the Messiah (v. 61), the Son of the Blessed One (see John 20:30–31), in the affirmative. In contrast, Jesus refrained from answering Pilate's question of whether he is the king of the Jews, presumably due to the term's political overtones (15:2). Thus the reader is led to understand that Jesus is the Messiah in terms of Jewish OT expectations but not a king in Roman political terms (see John 18:36).

Finally, at the climax of Mark's Gospel, the Roman centurion exclaimed at the foot of the cross, "This man was really God's Son" (15:39), indicating that now the messianic secret has been lifted even for the (Roman) Gentiles, so that the missionary power of Jesus' suffering and death has been extended also to non-Jews. If there is a genuinely Markan equivalent to the Matthean "Great Commission," the centurion's confession would certainly qualify. At the same time, it is certainly no coincidence that a Christological confession by a Gentile (see Peter's "Jewish" confession in 8:29) is not issued until *after* Jesus' death. If 16:8 is indeed the original ending of Mark's Gospel, the account concludes on a note of fearfulness on the part of Jesus' followers, a state of affairs that may resemble the state of Christianity in Rome at the time of writing. The abrupt ending leaves open for the reader how Jesus' announcement that he would meet the disciples in Galilee would be fulfilled (see 14:28; 16:7).

THEOLOGY

Theological Themes

Jesus as the Son of God   The preeminent theological theme in Mark's Gospel is that Jesus is the miracle-working, authoritative Son of God. The following chart displays the references in Mark's Gospel to Jesus as the Son of God and also includes the respective person or persons who uttered the statement.

---

[30] See Telford, *Mark*, 224–25; Donahue, *Are You the Christ?* 114; Senior and Stuhlmueller, *Biblical Foundations for Mission*, 223.

Table 5.1: Jesus as the Son of God in Mark's Gospel

Introduction		Galilean Ministry		Way to the Cross		Trial and Crucifixion	
1:1	1:11	3:11	5:7	9:7	13:32	14:61	15:39
Mark	God	Demons	Demons	God	Jesus	Caiaphas	Roman Centurion

The chart indicates that this theme forms the all-inclusive bookends of the Markan narrative, from the opening verse to the Roman centurion's climactic confession in 15:39. This is no coincidence since Mark's audience was the church in Rome, and it is only appropriate that the final reference to Jesus as Son of God in the Gospel should be uttered by a Roman. In a context where Roman emperors frequently ascribed deity to themselves, Mark's presentation of Jesus as the Son of God is profoundly countercultural.

The Nature of Discipleship and Discipleship Failure Progressively throughout his narrative, Mark revealed the nature of true discipleship: following Jesus involves conflict, rejection by one's own, even the bearing of one's cross. By distancing himself from his own family, and through the cross, Jesus modeled in his own life a stance toward kingdom membership that the disciples are to emulate in their relationships with one another and in their mission. As J. Williams wrote, "Following a Messiah who came to die on a cross involves sacrifice, suffering and service."[31]

The initial picture of the disciples is soon overshadowed by Mark's portrayal of their frequent failures and misunderstandings (4:11–13,33–34, 40; 6:51–52; 8:4,14–21; 9:14–21; 8:22–26; 10:46–52). Peter, too, is cast in a negative light after his confession for failing to leave room in it for a suffering Messiah (8:33). Other instances of discipleship failure are Peter's denial, Judas's betrayal, and Jesus' desertion by the rest of the disciples (chaps. 14–15).

The disciples' failure to grasp Jesus' true identity prior to the crucifixion not merely clouded their understanding as to who Jesus was and what he would do for them on the cross. As long as the disciples failed to understand the true identity of Jesus, the nature of his mission, and the meaning of the cross, they also would be unable to grasp the essence of their own mission which required following Jesus in the way of the cross (8:34).[32]

POINTS OF APPLICATION

- Believe that Jesus is the Son of God, not just a mere human (1:1)
- Believe that Jesus has power over nature, demons, sickness, and death (4:35–5:43)
- Identify with Jesus and be prepared to suffer with him if necessary (8:34–38)

---

[31] See J. F. Williams, "Mission in Mark," In *Mission in the New Testament: An Evangelical Approach*, ed. W. J. Larkin Jr. and J. F. Williams (Maryknoll: Orbis, 1998), 146.

[32] Senior and Stuhlmueller, *Biblical Foundations for Mission*, 226.

- Believe that Jesus died as a ransom for your sins (10:45)
- Know that Jesus is willing and able to restore you when you fail (14:66–72; 16:8)

STUDY QUESTIONS

1. Who does ancient tradition suggest wrote Mark's Gospel? Who was believed to be his close associate?
2. What is the major Christological title in Mark?
3. According to this chapter, what are four interrelated purposes of Mark's Gospel?
4. Why is Mark's Gospel called "action rich"?
5. How many major parts are there in the structure of Mark's Gospel, and which verse is the turning point?
6. To what does the "messianic secret" refer?

FOR FURTHER STUDY

Brooks, J. A. *Mark*. The New American Commentary 23. Nashville: Broadman, 1991.

Evans, C. A. *Mark 8:27–16:20*. Word Biblical Commentary. Nashville: Thomas Nelson, 2001.

France, R. T. *The Gospel of Mark: A Commentary on the Greek Text*. New International Greek Testament Commentary. Grand Rapids: Eerdmans, 2002.

Garland, D. E. "Mark." In *Zondervan Illustrated Bible Backgrounds Commentary*. Vol. 1. Edited by C. E. Arnold. Grand Rapids: Zondervan, 2002.

_____. *Mark*. NIV Application Commentary. Grand Rapids: Zondervan, 1996.

Guelich, R. A. *Mark 1–8:26*. Word Biblical Commentary. Volume 34A. Dallas: Word, 1989.

_____. "Mark, Gospel of." Pages 511–25 in *Dictionary of Jesus and the Gospels*. Edited by J. B. Green, S. McKnight, and I. H. Marshall. Downers Grove: InterVarsity, 1992.

Gundry, R. H. *Mark: A Commentary on His Apology for the Cross*. Grand Rapids: Eerdmans, 1993.

Köstenberger, A. J., and P. T. O'Brien, *Salvation to the Ends of the Earth: A Biblical Theology of Mission*, NSBT 11. Downers Grove: InterVarsity, 2001.

Lane, W. L. *The Gospel According to Mark: The English Text with Introduction, Exposition, and Notes*. Grand Rapids: Eerdmans, 1974.

Martin, R. *Mark: Evangelist and Theologian*. Grand Rapids: Zondervan, 1972.

Rhoads, D. M., and D. M. Michie. *Mark as Story: An Introduction to the Narrative of a Gospel*. Philadelphia: Fortress, 1982.

Stein, R. H. *Mark*. Baker Exegetical Commentary on the New Testament. Grand Rapids: Baker, 2008.

Chapter 6

The Gospel According to Luke

CORE KNOWLEDGE

Students should know the key facts of Luke's Gospel. With regard to history, students should be able to identify the Gospel's author, date, provenance, destination, and purpose. With regard to literature, they should be able to provide a basic outline of the book and identify core elements of the book's content found in the unit-by-unit discussion. With regard to theology, students should be able to identify Luke's major theological themes.

KEY FACTS	
Author:	Luke, the beloved physician
Date:	c. 58–60
Provenance:	Rome, perhaps Achaia
Destination:	Theophilus
Purpose:	A defense of the Christian faith, useful for both evangelism and discipleship
Theme:	Jesus brings universal salvation in fulfillment of OT promises to Israel
Key Verse:	19:10

CONTRIBUTION TO THE CANON

- Jesus as the son of Adam, the son of God (3:37)
- Jesus as the Spirit-anointed suffering Servant (4:18–19)
- Jesus as the compassionate healer and physician (5:31–32)

- Jesus as the Messiah sent to the poor, Gentiles, women, children, sick, and others of low status in society
- Jesus as the "friend of tax collectors and sinners" (7:34) and seeker of the lost (19:10)

INTRODUCTION

THE GOSPEL OF Luke is the longest book in the NT. It comprises a little over 14 percent of the NT and is almost 10 percent longer than the second longest NT book, the book of Acts. By contributing these two volumes, Luke composed 27 percent of the NT. Luke wrote in an elegant Greek, mastered the vocabulary and prose of an educated man, and was able to employ a variety of genres and styles. It is no wonder E. Renan called the Gospel of Luke "the most beautiful book" ever written.[1]

Luke contributed to the Gospel portrait of Jesus an emphasis on his concern for the poor, women, children, the sick, and others of low status in society. Jesus is the "friend of . . . sinners" who came "to seek and to save the lost" (19:10), the physician who came to heal not the healthy but the sick and to provide righteousness to those who knew themselves to be poor spiritually while resisting the spiritually proud and self-sufficient.

While Luke was not an eyewitness of Jesus' ministry, he carefully investigated these matters from those who were (1:1–4), especially Peter (5:3) and the women who followed Jesus from Galilee (8:2–3).[2] He was careful to relate major events in the Christian story to world history, such as Jesus' birth in relation to Caesar Augustus and the governor Quirinius (2:1), and the beginning of John the Baptist's and Jesus' ministries to Tiberius Caesar, the governor Pontius Pilate, Herod Antipas, and others (3:1). Thus, as will be seen below, Luke is both a historian *and* a theologian.

HISTORY

Author

The traditional view is that Luke, Paul's beloved physician, wrote both this Gospel and the book of Acts. If so, Paul referred to this Luke three times in the NT (Col 4:14; 2 Tim 4:11; Phlm 24), and Luke indirectly referred to himself repeatedly in the book of Acts in the "we passages." Although the author remains unnamed in both the Gospel and Acts, this does not necessarily mean that these writings were originally anonymous[3] since

---

[1] E. Renan, *Les Évangiles et la seconde génération chrétienne* (Paris: Calmann Lévy, 1877), 283 (English translation *The Gospels* [London: Mathieson, n.d.]).

[2] See Richard Bauckham, *Jesus and the Eyewitnesses: The Gospels as Eyewitness Testimony* (Grand Rapids: Eerdmans, 2006), 114–24, 129–32.

[3] See D. A. Carson and D. J. Moo, *An Introduction to the New Testament*, rev. ed. (Grand Rapids: Zondervan, 2005), 205–6 (citing M. Dibelius, *Studies in the Acts of the Apostles* [London: SCM, 1956], 89 and 148), who noted "that it is unlikely that the books ever circulated without a name attached to them in some way."

one can assume that Theophilus, to whom the book was dedicated, and its first readers knew who the writer was.

Whoever this Luke was, the stylistic Greek of the preface points to an author who was well educated.[4] Furthermore the author was male,[5] had access to a variety of sources about the life of Jesus, was not an eyewitness of Jesus' ministry, and had the opportunity to investigate the story about Jesus fully (v. 3). There is internal and the external evidence that argues for the common authorship of Luke and Acts by Luke, the physician.

Internal Evidence The common authorship of Luke and Acts is commonly defended by scholars for the following reasons.[6] First, the preface to the book of Acts appears to introduce a sequel (Acts 1:1 refers to "the first narrative"). Second, both books are dedicated to Theophilus (Luke 1:3; Acts 1:1). Third, Acts readily follows the story of Jesus presented in Luke (see the reference to "all that Jesus *began* to do and teach" in Acts 1:1). Fourth, Luke ends and Acts begins with Jesus' ascension. Hence, both books display similar styles and interests.[7]

The strongest evidence for Lukan authorship is the "we passages" in Acts (16:10–17; 20:5–15; 21:1–18; 27:1–28:16). Taken plainly, these references suggest that the author was a traveling companion of Paul, a view attested as early as Irenaeus (c. 130–200; see *Against Heresies* 3.1.2).[8] By comparing certain texts (see Acts 16:19; 20:4), we know that neither Paul nor others mentioned by name in Acts wrote it. We also know that Paul mentioned several coworkers who were with him during his first Roman imprisonment (see Col 4:10–17). It is possible one of these wrote Acts, and of these only Luke fits the bill. Thus, by process of elimination this leaves Luke as the best viable candidate.

External Evidence The early church clearly understood the author of Luke-Acts to be Paul's "beloved physician." This is attested in the title "according to Luke" at the end of the earliest manuscripts (e.g., 𝔓[75]); in the stated opinion of the early church fathers such as Irenaeus (c. 130–200), Theophilus of Antioch (later second century), and Justin Martyr (c. 100–165); the naming of Luke as author by Polycarp (c. 69–155) and Papias (c. 60–130; cited in Eusebius, *Eccl. Hist.* 3.24.5–13); and in early canonical lists, especially the Muratorian Canon (later second century). One of the earliest extrabiblical indications of authorship comes from Justin Martyr (c. 100–165), who mentioned a quote from Luke as from one who followed the apostles (*Dial.* 103).

---

[4] See Luke 1:1–4.

[5] The Greek participle *parēkolouthēkoti* ("having carefully investigated") in 1:3 is masculine.

[6] E.g., J. Verheyden, "The Unity of Luke-Acts: What Are We Up To?" in *The Unity of Luke-Acts*, ed. J. Verheyden (Leuven: Univ. Press, 1999), 3.

[7] L. Morris, *The Gospel According to St. Luke: An Introduction and Commentary*, TNTC 3 (Grand Rapids: Eerdmans, 1974), 14.

[8] E.g., Carson and Moo, *Introduction to the New Testament*, 204; F. F. Bruce, *The Acts of the Apostles* (Grand Rapids: Eerdmans, 1951), 2–3.

Notably, no candidate other than Luke has ever been set forth in the history of the church as the author of this book. Cumulatively, these data provide strong evidence for Luke as the author of the Gospel and the book of Acts, especially since it seems highly unlikely that the early church would have attributed these weighty books to an otherwise unheralded fellow worker of Paul unless he were the real author. The fact that he was not an eyewitness but depended upon eyewitnesses (Luke 1:1–4) argues for, not against, Lukan authorship. Luke is by far the best candidate for author of Luke and Acts.

Date

Since Luke and Acts are related volumes, it is necessary to discuss both in order to assess accurately the date of Luke. While some have argued that Acts precedes Luke, this is highly unlikely.[9] The "first narrative" mentioned in Acts 1:1 doubtless refers to the Gospel of Luke. Thus, Luke's Gospel predates the book of Acts, and hence the date of writing for Acts is to some extent predicated upon the date of composition for Luke.

The historical evidence in Luke's Gospel and especially in the book of Acts provides an independent point of reference for the dating of these two books.[10] Dates proposed for the book of Acts fall into three broad eras: (1) prior to 70; (2) around 80; and (3) near the end of the first century or in the early second century.[11] But the evidence for an early date for Luke-Acts (prior to 70) is compelling for the following six reasons.

First, Luke does not mention any significant event subsequent to the early 60s in the book of Acts,[12] such as the persecution of the church by Nero, the destruction of Jerusalem, and the deaths of Peter, Paul, and James the Just. Second, the stance toward the Roman Empire in the book of Acts is decidedly neutral if not friendly, favoring a time prior to Nero's persecution of Christians (64–66).

Third, the lack of reference to Jerusalem's destruction in Luke's Gospel also favors a pre-70 date. Since Luke consistently noted the fulfillment of prophecy, both written and oral,[13] why would he not mention that Jesus' prediction of the destruction of the Jerusalem temple had been fulfilled? Moreover, the temple plays a prominent role in both Luke and Acts; in fact, Luke's Gospel begins and ends in the temple (1:9; 24:53).

Fourth, Paul's letters are not mentioned in Acts. As L. T. Johnson stated, "It is far more likely for Paul's letters to be ignored before the time of their collection and canonization than after."[14] The fifth reason is the conclusion to the two volumes (Acts 28:30–31). Paul finally reaches Rome under the protection of the emperor, preaching the gospel without hindrance, but the reader is left without knowing the outcome of the trial, leading us to

---

[9] J. A. Fitzmyer, *The Gospel According to Luke I–IX* (Garden City: Doubleday, 1981), 53.

[10] See Carson and Moo, *Introduction to the New Testament*, 180.

[11] Hemer, *Book of Acts in the Setting of Hellenistic History*, 365.

[12] Morris, *Gospel According to St. Luke*, 22.

[13] E.g., Luke 7:20 see Isa 28:18; 35:5; 61:1; Luke 7:27 see Mal 3:1; Luke 24:6 see Luke 9:21–44; 18:31–33; Acts 11:28; and Acts 21:10–14.

[14] L. T. Johnson, "Book of Luke-Acts," *ABD* 4:404.

conclude that when Luke finished Acts, Paul was still under house arrest in Rome and awaiting trial before the Emperor Nero.

Sixth, in Acts 20:25 Paul told the Ephesian elders that he would never see them again. However, the Pastoral Epistles suggest that Paul continued to sustain close ties with the Ephesian church after his release from the first Roman imprisonment (1 Tim 1:3). The inclusion of this statement in Acts 20 is difficult to explain if it was written after the Pastorals. Therefore, the most likely date for Luke is sometime before the composition of the book of Acts, which was probably written in the early 60s.

If Luke conceived of Luke-Acts as a two-volume work (see Acts 1:1–3), it would seem reasonable to conclude that Luke wrote his Gospel and the book of Acts within a few years of each other. If Luke used Mark, as well as other written and oral sources, in writing his Gospel (see Luke 1:1–4), and Mark is dated in the mid-50s, this would narrow the most likely window for the composition of Luke's Gospel to the mid-to-late 50s.[15]

Provenance

Internally, the Gospel gives no indication of its place of origin. Externally, early church sources[16] claim that the Gospel was written from Achaia (Greece). Yet, Fitzmyer was on target when he stated that the provenance of Luke's Gospel is "anyone's guess."[17] If it is correct that Luke compiled his sources while Paul was in prison in Caesarea and was with Paul during the first Roman imprisonment (as is indicated by Col 4:14), the Gospel of Luke could have been written anywhere between Caesarea and Rome.

Destination

The recipient of Luke's Gospel is clearly Theophilus (Luke 1:3). Luke's preface tells us at least three things about Theophilus. First, he was a man of high rank, for Luke addressed him as "most honorable" (*kratistos*; Luke 1:3), a term that is used elsewhere in the NT only by the same author in Acts with reference to the Roman government officials Felix and Festus (see Acts 23:26; 24:3; 26:25). Second, Theophilus had received previous instruction regarding the Christian faith ("you have been instructed"; Luke 1:4). Third, Luke offered his Gospel to give Theophilus further assurance regarding this instruction ("so that you may know the certainty"; Luke 1:4).

Most likely, then, Theophilus was Luke's literary patron who supported the production of the books and made them available for viewing and copying.[18] The stated purpose (Luke 1:4) implies that Theophilus was more than merely interested but had received some

---

[15] See the discussions in Bock, *Luke*, 16–18; Carson and Moo, *Introduction to the New Testament*, 208; I. H. Marshall, *The Gospel of Luke: A Commentary on the Greek Text*, NIGTC (Grand Rapids: Eerdmans, 1978), 33–35; and Morris, *Luke*, 22–26.

[16] The Anti-Marcionite Prologue to Luke (allegedly written against Marcion; c. 160–180) and the Monarchian Prologue (short introductions prefixed in many Latin manuscripts to the four Gospels, probably written in the fourth or fifth century).

[17] Fitzmyer, *Luke*, 57.

[18] It was customary in ancient historiography for the patron's name to appear in the preface of a work. See Josephus's reference in two subsequent books to a "most excellent" and "most esteemed" Epaphroditus (*Against Apion 1.1; 2.1*).

previous Christian instruction, although it is impossible to determine his precise spiritual status. While Luke specifically addressed his Gospel to Theophilus and it has a Gentile flavor, it is unlikely that he limited his audience to just one person. Luke most likely wrote his Gospel for all, Gentiles and Jews, who would read it.[19]

Purpose

It seems most natural to allow Luke's stated purpose in his preface in correlation with the Gospel's structure to dictate the book's purpose. Indeed, Luke's Gospel does contain a purpose clause. In his preface Luke stated that he wrote his treatise to Theophilus "so that you may know the certainty of the things about which you have been instructed" (Luke 1:4). The word "instructed" indicates that Theophilus, and perhaps Luke's target audience, had been instructed but not necessarily converted. The word *asphaleia* ("certainty") indicates absolute certainty but also carries the nuance of stability. Thus Luke wanted Theophilus to know that the message about Jesus was reliable. This would imply that both Theophilus and Luke's larger audience were about to read a treatise defending the truthfulness of Christianity, evidenced by the appeal to eyewitnesses (Luke 1:2) and Jesus' statement to the witnesses of his resurrection (Luke 24:48). Luke's thorough investigation of Jesus' life and teachings (Luke 1:3; cf. Acts 1:1) indicates that Luke intended primarily to write a historically accurate and theologically significant Gospel to instruct Gentile Christians.

LITERATURE

Literary Plan

Overall, Luke followed a geographical pattern in his presentation of Jesus' ministry similar to that of Mark. Luke began his Gospel with a birth narrative and provided a genealogy of Jesus. Unlike Matthew, however, Luke's Gospel reflects Mary's and Elizabeth's perspectives on Jesus' birth rather than Joseph's, and Luke placed Jesus' genealogy not at the beginning of his Gospel but just prior to the beginning of Jesus' ministry (3:23–38). Tracing Jesus' genealogy back to Adam, the first human being, stresses the universal impact of this Jesus.[20]

Luke, like Matthew, provided an account of Jesus' temptation by the devil, though he presents a different order than Matthew (Luke 4:1–13). Jesus' inaugural sermon at his hometown synagogue of Nazareth (Luke 4:16–27) is Luke's functional substitute for Matthew's Sermon on the Mount (Matt 5–7). Luke presented Jesus as Isaiah's Servant of the Lord who was endowed with the Spirit and anointed to preach good news to the poor (Luke 4:18–19, citing Isa 61:1–2). Jesus' coming to the poor, along with other lowly and outcast figures in society, becomes a major theme in Luke.

---

[19] See Blomberg, *Jesus and the Gospels*, 152.

[20] For a thorough comparison between Matthew's and Luke's genealogies, see D. S. Huffman, "Genealogy," in *Dictionary of Jesus and the Gospels*, 253–59.

Luke then traced the stages of Jesus' initial ministry in Galilee, including major teachings and healings, similar to the pattern seen in Mark's Gospel. Some of these healings, such as that of a widow's son in the town of Nain (7:11–17), are unique to Luke. Luke also documented Jesus' calling of his disciples and his support by a number of devoted women (8:1–3) who followed Jesus all the way to the cross (23:49). As in Matthew and Mark, Peter's confession of Jesus as the Messiah is a watershed moment (9:18–20) and is followed by predictions of Jesus' passion with important implications for discipleship (9:21–27).

Luke's lengthy "Travel Narrative" (9:51–19:27), however, is where he truly broke new ground in his presentation of Jesus. This section is introduced by a curious reference to Jesus' ascension well before his actual ascension (9:51) and records in considerable detail Jesus' approach to Jerusalem. Luke also featured a large amount of unique teaching material, including parables such as the Good Samaritan (10:25–37) and the Prodigal Son (15:11–32), in this narrative. Zacchaeus is another unique, beloved character in Luke's Gospel. His interaction with Jesus prompted Jesus' programmatic declaration that "the Son of Man has come to seek and to save the lost" (19:10).

Luke's passion narrative also follows the familiar format of Mark and Matthew. Yet, Luke's inclusion of Jesus' appearance to two disciples on the road to Emmaus (one of whose names was Cleopas, the possible source of this narrative, 24:13–35) is a resurrection account unique to Luke. Luke's Gospel, similar to Matthew's, ends with a conclusion containing a commissioning narrative (24:46–49). References to the giving of the Spirit and the disciples' witness to all the nations, beginning in Jerusalem, and to Jesus' ascension prepare the reader for Luke's second volume, the book of Acts.

OUTLINE
Preface: Luke's Purpose (1:1–4)
  I. INTRODUCTION TO JESUS AND HIS MISSION (1:5–4:13)
    A. John the Baptist and Jesus (1:5–2:52)
    B. Preliminaries to Jesus' Ministry (3:1–4:13)
 II. JESUS' GALILEAN MINISTRY (4:14–9:50)
    A. First Part of Galilean Ministry (4:14–7:50)
    B. Second Part of Galilean Ministry (8:1–39)
    C. Third Part of Galilean Ministry and Withdrawal (8:40–9:50)
III. JESUS' JOURNEY TO JERUSALEM AND HIS PASSION (9:51–24:53)
    A. The Journey to Jerusalem (9:51–19:27)
    B. Final Ministry in Jerusalem (19:28–22:38)
    C. Jesus' Crucifixion, Resurrection, and Ascension (22:39–24:51)
Epilogue: The Disciples Return to Jerusalem (24:52–53)

UNIT-BY-UNIT DISCUSSION

Preface: Luke's Purpose (1:1–4)

In his elegantly worded preface, Luke set the ministry of Jesus in the scope of God's plan of salvation and stated his reason and purpose for taking up his narrative. He announced the continuity of what happened in and through Jesus with God's past dealings with his people, the thoroughness of his research, and his plan to write an orderly account in order to give assurance to Theophilus regarding the truthfulness of Christianity.

I. INTRODUCTION TO JESUS AND HIS MISSION (1:5–4:13)

A. John the Baptist and Jesus (1:5–2:52)

This portion of the Gospel provides the foundation for Jesus and his messianic mission. Luke described Jesus' supernatural birth via the pronouncements of several messengers. The angel Gabriel told Zechariah that his son John would come in the power of Elijah and that "he will turn many of the sons of Israel to the Lord their God" (1:16). Gabriel also announced to Mary that her virgin-born child is the Son of the Most High God (1:32). Zechariah prophesied that the Lord would bring salvation to his people and that John would proclaim the forgiveness of sins (1:77).

Jesus' birth is identified as that of the Savior born in Bethlehem by the angelic hosts (2:11) and the Messiah of Jews and Gentiles by Simeon (2:30–32). Anna the prophetess then declared the redemption of Israel (2:36–38). Finally, Jesus at age 12 was already fully aware of his true identity and calling: he had to be in his Father's house, the temple, and be about his Father's business (2:49).

B. Preliminaries to Jesus' Ministry (3:1–4:13)

The first steps of the narrative—the baptism, the genealogy, and the temptation account—identify Jesus as the Coming One who would save his people from their sins. Luke began this new section by fast-forwarding from Jesus at age 12 to the presentation of John in the wilderness. Although Luke included information on John's teaching, his primary emphasis is on John's declaration about Jesus. After this transition in the Gospel, Luke's emphasis shifted from John to Jesus. Hence Luke chose to place Jesus' genealogy (3:23–38) at the onset of Jesus' ministry rather than at the beginning of his book as Matthew did (see Matt 1:1–17).

The final preliminary to Jesus' ministry is his temptation by the devil (4:1–13), which follows a different sequence for the three temptations than Matthew (4:1–11): (1) turning stones into bread; (2) worshipping Satan in exchange for all the world's kingdoms; and (3) jumping off the pinnacle of the temple to be protected by angels. Most assume that Matthew followed the chronological order[21] and that Luke inverted the last two temptations.[22]

II. JESUS' GALILEAN MINISTRY (4:14–9:50)

A. First Part of Galilean Ministry (4:14–7:50)

Jesus' Galilean ministry began with his inaugural sermon in the synagogue at Nazareth (4:14–30) where Jesus presented himself as Isaiah's Servant of the Lord (see Isa 61:1–2) and publicly announced the onset of his mission to a hostile and unbelieving congregation in his hometown. Then Jesus cast out demons and healed Peter's mother-in-law and many others (4:31–41). After this Luke provided a summary of the results of Jesus' preaching and a statement of his purpose (4:43), echoing the Isaiah quote in 4:18.

In this first stage of the Galilean ministry Jesus also calls his first disciples: Simon Peter and his partners, the sons of Zebedee (5:1–11), and Levi, the tax collector (5:27–32). Following a controversy over Jesus' healing of an invalid on the Sabbath (6:1–11), the selection of Jesus' 12 apostles (6:12–16) ensues. Luke also documented a series of instructions that Jesus gave his disciples that culminates in the Sermon on the Plain (6:17–49; cf. Matt 5–7), in which Jesus advocated a rejection of worldly pleasures and goods, a love for others, and radically following him.

Another set of major healings follows: the centurion's servant is restored to health (7:1–10) and a widow's son is raised from the dead (7:11–17). At this John the Baptist expressed doubts, so Jesus pointed to the fulfillment of OT messianic prophecy in his ministry to reassure the Baptist (7:18–35), who apparently was unsettled by the popular understanding of Jesus as a mere prophet. The unit concludes with Jesus' anointing by a sinful woman in the house of Simon the Pharisee (7:36–50).

B. Second Part of Galilean Ministry (8:1–39)

The second part of Jesus' Galilean ministry begins with a reference to a group of faithful women who sacrificed to minister to Jesus out of their own means (8:1–3).[23] This is followed by the parable of the soils, which highlights the proper reception of Jesus by those who, "having heard the word with an honest and good heart, hold on to it" (8:15). After the brief parable on "the light on a lampstand" (8:16–18), the theme of proper response to Jesus continues as he identifies "those who hear and do the word of God" as his true family (8:21).

After this Luke shows Jesus journeying across Galilee (8:22–39), highlighting his authority. At the "Stilling of the Storm," Jesus calmed a strong wind on the Lake of Tiberias

---

[21] Matthew employed several chronological markers in his version of the temptation narrative: "then" in vv. 5, 10 and "again" in v. 8.

[22] The temptations seem to parallel Gen 3:6: (1) stone to bread/"good for food"; (2) kingdoms of the world/"delightful to look at"; (3) pinnacle of the temple/"desirable for obtaining wisdom."

[23] So Bock, *Luke*, 629.

(8:22–25). His authority is implicitly pronounced, "Who can this be? He commands even the winds and the waves, and they obey Him!" (8:25), and this sets the course for the narrative that follows. Jesus' encounter with the infested Gadarene demoniac makes clear he also had authority over demons (8:26–39).

C. Third Part of Galilean Ministry and Withdrawal (8:40–9:50)

Luke's account of the third part of Jesus' Galilean ministry further emphasizes Jesus' authority over disease and death. The pericope of the woman with the issue of blood (8:43–48) interrupts the raising of the daughter of Jairus where Jesus showed his authority over death (8:40–42,49–56). Jesus granted authority over demons and disease (but not nature or death) to the Twelve (9:1–6), and their mission is so successful it even perturbed Herod Antipas (9:7–9).

Jesus then withdrew with his disciples (9:10) before the feeding of the 5,000 (9:10–17), which is followed by several narrative units dealing with the nature of discipleship. Peter's confession of Jesus as the Messiah (9:18–27) marks a significant transition in Jesus' preaching and ministry. Until this point Jesus had sought to reveal himself to his disciples, but here he turned his attention to preparing his disciples for his impending death in Jerusalem.

In the wake of Peter's confession, Jesus explained to his disciples that they must deny themselves and "take up [their] cross daily" as they followed Jesus. In fact, some would see the kingdom of God. This likely anticipated the transfiguration of Jesus (9:28–36) when Moses and Elijah appeared and spoke with Jesus about his upcoming "departure" (9:31 NIV; Gk. *exodos*). Jesus' death would therefore provide deliverance for God's people as the exodus for Israel.

As Jesus went down the Mount of Transfiguration, he exorcised a demon from a boy whom his disciples could not help. Jesus castigated them for being part of an "unbelieving and rebellious generation" (9:41). Jesus also confronted a spirit of self-aggrandizement in the disciples as they argued about who was the greatest (9:46–48). Jesus rebuked them for their ungodly attitude and told them not to prevent others from casting out demons in his name (9:49–50). These accounts show Jesus' response to inadequate discipleship.

III. Jesus' Journey to Jerusalem and His Passion (9:51–24:51)

A. The Journey to Jerusalem (9:51–19:27)

The first portion of the Lukan travel narrative discusses the nature of discipleship. The key thematic thread running through 10:42 is that following Jesus often requires a separation from the familiar and comfortable and a commitment to proclaim the kingdom of God. The journey began when Jesus and his disciples went through a Samaritan village that did not receive Jesus. Jesus rebuked his followers who wanted him to destroy the village supernaturally (9:52–56).

Following Jesus requires would-be disciples to be willing to leave behind their familiar surroundings, occupation, and loved ones (9:57–62). After this comes the mission of the 70 whom Jesus sent out after giving them specific instructions (10:1–20). Jesus' private instruction to his disciples is followed by a question from a scribe, which Jesus answered in the parable of the Good Samaritan (10:25–37). Subsequently Jesus visited Mary and Martha and commended Mary for making the right choice by sitting at his feet (10:38–42).

Jesus then taught in Judea while still on his journey to Jerusalem (11:1–13:21). The unit begins with the Lukan version of the Model Prayer (11:1–4) and continues with an encouragement to be faithful in prayer (11:5–13). The distinctive thread from 11:14 through 11:54 is the call for a proper response to Jesus, given in the context of several controversies. For instance, he answered the question regarding the source of his power in the Beelzebul controversy: it is from God (11:14–26).

After commending those who "hear the word of God and keep it" (11:27–28), Jesus berated his generation for seeking signs, pointing them to "the sign of Jonah" (11:29–36). Rather than demanding additional signs, people should recognize that with the Son of Man, "something greater than Jonah is here" (11:32). Jesus also pronounced woes against the Pharisees and experts in the law (11:37–54), castigating the Jewish leaders for rank hypocrisy and for leading people to destruction. The result was that the Pharisees started seeking to trap Jesus in his own words (11:54).

The events Luke selected in the next portion of the journey highlight the necessity of responding to Jesus in faith. In particular, Jesus identified three obstacles to the reception of his message: hypocrisy, greed, and sluggishness. First, he warned against the "leaven" of the Pharisees, that is, hypocrisy (12:1–12). Second, he took the opportunity provided by a request from the crowd to settle a family dispute to speak out against greed (12:13–34), urging his followers to be about the business of the kingdom: "For where your treasure is, there your heart will be also" (12:34). Finally, he enjoined watchfulness because he will return at an unexpected time (12:49–59). This is particularly relevant because he will come to "bring fire on the earth"—judgment is coming (12:49). Consequently, 13:1–9 focuses on the urgent necessity of repentance in light of God's patience.

The next phase of the journey sustains a long thread of teaching concerning the question of who is allowed to enter God's kingdom. Another Sabbath controversy ensued in a stern warning against the hypocrisy of the religious leaders (13:10–17). The section focuses on the marked reversal of expectations brought by Jesus' ministry. Contrary to popular expectations, only a few will be saved. What is more, the few who are saved are not the religious leaders but those who "enter through the narrow door" (13:24–30). Ironically, Jerusalem herself is the owner of a desolate house (13:35).

While attending a banquet, Jesus shared his wisdom with the guests. The Pharisees are a foil for Jesus' teaching on the proper attitude of those who inherit the kingdom. He began by noting the pride of jockeying for exalted positions at the banquet and counseled that "everyone who exalts himself will be humbled, and the one who humbles himself will be exalted" (14:11). He proceeded to instruct his listeners to invite those who cannot repay so that their reward will come at the resurrection.

Jesus' teaching regarding ministering to the outcast resulted in controversy: "This man welcomes sinners and eats with them!" (15:2). The answer is given by way of the famous trio of parables on "lost things"—a sheep, a coin, and a son—highlighting people's joy over finding that which was lost. This series of parables constitutes a defense of Jesus' practices of fraternizing with "sinners" and a response to the sustained criticism of the Pharisees embodied in the older son in the final parable.

Chapter 16 returns to the matter of wealth (the subject of the second warning at 12:13–34). The surprising hero of Jesus' parable is the shrewd manager who conveys the lesson that one's wealth should be used in ways that count for eternity (16:9). The Pharisees are again the foil as they scoff at Jesus because they were "lovers of money" (16:14). The parable of Lazarus and the Rich Man points to the folly and idolatry of serving money.

The disciples were then warned not to cause others to sin or to harbor an attitude of bitterness or self-aggrandizement (17:1–10). The final portion of the journey to Jerusalem focused on several aspects of the kingdom. At 17:11–19, 10 lepers are healed, but only one Samaritan among them is grateful. When the Pharisees asked Jesus about the coming of God's kingdom, he declared that the kingdom is both a present and a future reality to which many are oblivious, just as were the contemporaries of Noah and Lot.

Next, Jesus enjoined his hearers to faithful prayer through the parable of the unjust judge and the persistent widow (18:1–8). The parable is still related to the coming of the Son of Man, for Jesus asked, "When the Son of Man comes, will He find that faith on earth?" (18:8). The parable of the Pharisee and the tax collector (18:9–14) prohibits self-righteous prayer, "because everyone who exalts himself will be humbled, but the one who humbles himself will be exalted" (18:14). Little children are the preeminent example of those who come to the kingdom (18:15–17).

Luke proceeded to cite the negative example of the rich young ruler, who turned away sad because he could not part with his wealth (18:18–23). Jesus then made the point that there is "no one who has left a house, wife or brothers, parents or children because of the kingdom of God, who will not receive many times more at this time, and eternal life in the age to come" (18:29–30).

The concluding portion of the journey shows Jesus bringing salvation to Jerusalem. Luke 18:31–34 contains yet another announcement of why Jesus was going to Jerusalem: to be beaten, killed, and raised the third day, in fulfillment of the message of the prophets and thus in keeping with the plan of God. This announcement set the stage for the final segment of the journey. Jesus first healed a blind beggar (18:35–34, Mark's Bartimaeus) as the first aspect of salvation emphasized by Luke, a humble cry for mercy.

The second aspect is highlighted by Zacchaeus (19:1–10): repentance evidenced by works, in his case restoration of defrauded gain and giving the rest to the poor. The parable of the pounds addressed the expectation by some that the kingdom would come immediately (19:11–27). The parable demonstrates not only that there will be a delay but also stresses the need for faithfulness in the interim.

B. Final Ministry in Jerusalem (19:28–22:38)

The triumphal entry (19:28–44) marks the end of the journey section and the beginning of the end for Jesus in accomplishing salvation. Jesus first mounted a donkey and rode into Jerusalem in fulfillment of prophecy (Zech 9:9), entering the city not to assume kingship but to announce it (19:38, citing Ps 118:26). The Pharisees objected to this display of royalty, and Jesus promptly rebuked them (19:39–40). Finally, Jesus lamented the impending fate of Jerusalem (19:41–48). Fully cognizant of what would soon happen to him, Jesus grieved over the great devastation to come upon Jerusalem because of its part in the crucifixion and rejection of Jesus.

The following sections show the opposition of the Jewish leadership and the ultimate consequences of the nation's rejection of the Messiah (19:45–48; chap. 20). When Jesus arrived in Jerusalem, he cleared the temple and made it the center of his teaching. His enemies could not take him into custody because the crowd was "captivated by what they heard" (19:48). This set the stage for the temple controversy (20:1–8), where Jesus reminded the Jewish leaders that John had witnessed to them about him.

This controversy, in turn, led to the parable of the Wicked Tenants (20:9–19). In this parable the tenants of a vineyard mistreat the farmer's servants and kill his heir, which rightly makes them the object of the farmer's wrath. The leaders immediately recognized that the parable was addressed to them. Jesus then appealed to Ps 118:22–23, "The stone that the builders rejected has become the cornerstone," and ominously noted that this stone will crush those who oppose it. The following section chronicles several attempts to trap Jesus, all in vain (20:20–40). The unit ends with another denunciation of the pride and hypocrisy of the scribes (20:41–47).

With his demise imminent, Jesus delivered the Olivet Discourse in which he outlined the scenario for the end time (21:1–36). First, he announced the impending destruction of the temple. The disciples asked a twofold question: When will these things be, and what are the warning signs? Jesus' answers pertained to the temple's destruction and his return. There will be false messiahs, wars, and natural disasters, but first the disciples will be persecuted. Jesus encouraged them to endure (21:19).

When Jerusalem is surrounded by armies, the end will be near. Jerusalem will be trampled until the time of the Gentiles is completed—a reference to the intervening time between the destruction of Jerusalem and Jesus' return (21:20–24). Jesus' return will be preceded by terrifying supernatural environmental disasters that make the world faint from fear, and then the Son of Man will appear with power and great glory. Jesus' concluding call for watchfulness (21:34–36) is prefaced by the parable of the Fig Tree (21:29–33).

In chapter 22, Luke began to relate the events leading up to the crucifixion. His narration essentially has three parts: preparation, confrontation, and crucifixion. First is the preparation for the event. This includes both the betrayal and the last Passover. Satan entered Judas to betray Jesus (22:1–6). Jesus also prepared the disciples for his crucifixion and subsequent absence by transforming the Passover meal (22:7–38). He announced Judas's betrayal and squelched a debate about who would be the greatest. He also told the disciples to be prepared for his departure, referring to the ensuing persecution and Peter's denial.

C. Jesus' Crucifixion, Resurrection, and Ascension (22:39–24:51)

The arrest and trials of Jesus mark the beginning of Jesus' demise. Jesus endured the agony at Gethsemane (22:39–46), and then he was betrayed and arrested. He did not allow his disciples to resist the arrest, and he considered it appropriate that the chief priests would seize him in the dark because darkness is their domain (22:53). Peter's denials are recorded as the trial phase begins (22:55–62).

The trial emphasized Jesus' innocence and the guilt of those who condemned him. At the trial before the Sanhedrin (22:63–71), the charge against Jesus was blasphemy for claiming to be the Son of God. Yet since the Sanhedrin lacked the power of capital punishment, they sent him to Pilate (23:1–7). Pilate found no guilt in Jesus, declaring him to be innocent three times. Neither did Herod (23:15), but Pilate succumbed to the demands of the bloodthirsty mob. Hence a triangle of enemies—Pilate, Herod, and the Jewish leaders—have come together to execute this plot.

Table 6.1: Phases of Jesus' Trial

Trial	Scripture	Description
Trial Before Annas	John 18:19–23	Annas questions Jesus about his teaching; Jesus is struck in face and challenges his accusers for striking him illegally; no witnesses produced
Trial Before Caiaphas	Matt 26:57–68; Mark 14:53–65; John 18:24–28	When asked if he is the Messiah, Jesus claims to be the divine Son of Man; convicted of blasphemy and sent to Pilate
Trial Before Pilate	Luke 23:1–6	Jesus falsely accused; affirms his messianic status; sent to Herod
Trial Before Herod	Luke 23:7–11	False charges against Jesus; Herod finds no guilt; Jesus sent to Pilate
Trial Before Pilate (continued)	Matt 27:1–25; Mark 15:1–15; Luke 23:12–25; John 18:29–19:6	No formal charges brought against Jesus; no witnesses produced; Jesus sentenced to crucifixion without conviction from Pilate (Pilate states three times that he finds no fault in Jesus)

The rest of chapter 23 records the events surrounding the crucifixion. Jesus was crucified and mocked repeatedly (23:24–33). He was mocked by the soldiers who crucified him, the thieves on either side of him, and the scribes and Pharisees. But it is apparent that something more than a criminal execution was taking place as the sun darkened and the veil of the temple was torn (23:44–46). Thus the mood changed: a soldier declared Jesus' righteousness, and the crowds left beating their breasts (23:47–48).

The resurrection appearances serve to reinforce and explain the meaning of the cross. An angel confronted the women at the (startlingly) empty tomb and reminded them of Jesus' claim that he would rise again (24:1–8). The apostles' response to the report is not laudatory, but Peter did examine the empty tomb. The most prominent event is Jesus' appearance to two disciples on the road to Emmaus (24:13–33). The fact that this was God's plan is pointedly reinforced (esp. at 24:26). Jesus then appeared to the Eleven in Jerusalem and established that he was really resurrected and not a ghost (24:34–49). For the second time Jesus interpreted the Scriptures to his disciples. Finally, the fulfillment of 9:51 occurs at 24:50–51: Jesus ascended into heaven from Bethany near Jerusalem.

Epilogue: The Disciples Return to Jerusalem (24:52–53) The final two verses form an epilogue to the book. The disciples returned to Jerusalem rejoicing. When they arrived, they went to the temple, continually blessing God. This ending prepares the reader for the second treatise, the book of Acts, which continues the Gospel's emphasis on God's plan of salvation in history and its fulfillment in Jesus.

THEOLOGY

Theological Themes

Salvation and Salvation History Many of the major themes in Luke are related to the fulfillment of God's purposes in Jesus as the culmination of salvation history. God is the architect of all human history, which is driven by his purposes and will. Luke's conception of salvation history may be described along the lines of "promise and fulfillment," with John the Baptist marking the end of the period of promise (16:16) and the following stages denoting the fulfillment of that promise (Jesus and the church).[24] The beginning of the Gospel implies that, through Jesus, God was fulfilling his previously planned purpose of salvation (see 1:1). It is not long until the reader is told that what God has fulfilled by sending Jesus is the provision of a Savior (1:31–33; see 1:68–71).

Indeed, salvation is one of the most prominent themes in this Gospel. The word "salvation" is used four times in Luke; it is not used in Matthew or Mark and only once in John. The first three of these references occur in Zechariah's song, where the ministry of the coming Messiah is described (1:69,71,77; the fourth reference is 19:9). Both God and Jesus are called "Savior" (1:47; 2:11; again, the word is not used in Matthew and Mark and only once in John). The verb "to save" is often used as a synonym for conversion (see 7:50; 8:12; 13:23; also frequent in Matthew and Mark). In 19:10, Jesus defined his mission as follows:

---

[24] F. Thielman, *Theology of the New Testament: A Canonical and Synthetic Approach* (Grand Rapids: Zondervan, 2005), 117.

"For the Son of Man has come to seek and to save the lost." As shown below, the salvation provided by Jesus encompasses all people, and in particular those of low status in society.

Table 6.2: Jesus' Resurrection Appearances

Recipients/ Location	Date/ Time	Matt	Mark	Luke	John	Acts	1 Cor
Number of appearances		2	0	4	4	2	4 [5]
First Sunday							
1. The women/ Tomb	Early morning	28:8–10					
2. Mary Magdalene/Tomb	Early morning				20:11–18		
3. Peter/Jerusalem	Late morning?			24:34			15:5
4. Two Disciples/ Emmaus Road	Midday/ Afternoon			24:13–32			
5. Ten Disciples/ Upper Room	Evening			24:36–43	20:19–25		
Second Sunday (One Week Later)							
6. Eleven/Upper Room	Evening				20:26–29		15:5
Subsequently							
7. Seven Disciples/Sea of Galilee	Daybreak				21:1–23		
8. Eleven/Mountain in Galilee	Sometime later	28:16–20					
9. More than 500	Sometime later						15:6
10. James	Sometime later						15:7
11. Disciples/ Mount of Olives	40 days later			24:44–49		1:3–8	
12. Paul/Road to Damascus	Sometime later					9:3–6	[15:8]

Jesus' Concern for the Lowly   Among the evangelists, it is especially Luke who emphasized Jesus' concern for those of lowly status in society—Gentiles, the poor, tax collectors and "sinners," the sick and disabled, women and children. This is part of Luke's understanding of the salvation brought by Jesus, a salvation that is inclusive of all people, whether Jew or Gentile (2:32; 4:25–27; 7:9; 10:30–37; 17:16; cf. Gal 3:28).

Luke's emphasis on the universality of salvation brought by Jesus extends most notably to *the poor*.[25] Luke witnesses to a "great reversal" brought about by Jesus' ministry: the humble would be exalted and the lofty would be humbled (1:48–49; cf. 18:14). Jesus stated in his first sermon that he was sent to "preach good news to the poor," in fulfillment of Isaiah's prophecy about the Servant of the Lord (4:18; see 7:22).

Thus, Luke consistently emphasized that Jesus strongly opposed the notion that wealth and position were indicative of a person's status before God. Instead, Jesus accepted anyone who repented and turned to him. In fact, one's possessions, status, and power constitute major obstacles to the reception of Jesus' message (12:13–21; 16:19–31).

Throughout his Gospel, Luke also emphasized Jesus' teaching among the outcasts in society: the hated *tax collectors* who were despised as traitors due to their service to the Roman authorities, and *"sinners"* (e.g., 5:30,32). Among the people Jesus was known as "the friend of . . . sinners" (7:34; see 7:36–50). Jesus was such a friend of sinners because he came "to seek and to save the lost" (19:7).

Yet another part of this "great reversal" brought about by Jesus' coming involves *women*. Luke's Gospel mentions 13 women not featured in the other Gospels.[26] Many of these women are characterized by unusual devotion to Jesus (7:36–50; 8:2–3; 10:38–42; 23:55–24:10). The considerable number of women among Jesus' followers stood in contrast with the male-oriented ministry of other Jewish rabbis in Jesus' day.

Table 6.2: Jesus and the Lowly in Luke's Gospel

Group of People	Passages in Luke's Gospel
Gentiles	2:10,32; 4:25–27; 7:9; 10:30–37; 14:23; 17:16
The poor	1:46–55; 4:18; 6:20–23; 7:22; 14:13,21–24; 16:19–31; 21:1–4
Tax collectors and "sinners"	5:27–32; 7:28,30,34,36–50; 15:1–2; 19:7
The sick and disabled	4:31–41; 5:12–26; 6:6–11,17–19; 7:1–17; 8:26–9:2; 9:37–43; 17:11–19; 18:35–43
Women	7:36–50; 8:1–3,48; 10:38–42; 13:10–17; 24:1–12
Children	2:17,27,40; 9:46–48; 17:2; 18:15–17

POINTS OF APPLICATION

- Like Luke, defend the faith, knowing that it is borne out by the facts (1:1–4)
- Put your faith in Christ, the Prince of Peace, not politics (2:1,13–14)

---

[25] See especially C. L. Blomberg, *Neither Poverty nor Riches: A Biblical Theology of Material Possessions*, NSBT (Grand Rapids: Eerdmans, 1999), 111–46, 160–74.

[26] M. Strauss, *Four Portraits, One Jesus: An Introduction to Jesus and the Gospels* (Grand Rapids: Zondervan, 2006), 339.

- Help the poor and tell them the good news about Jesus (4:18; 6:20; 7:22)
- Befriend unbelievers and social outcasts like Jesus did (5:27–32)
- Do not discriminate, mindful that Jesus came to save all kinds of people (19:7)

STUDY QUESTIONS

1. What internal evidence supports Lukan authorship?
2. To whom is Luke-Acts dedicated? What is the recipient's likely identity and on what basis?
3. What is the most natural way, according to the authors, to understand Luke's purpose in writing?
4. What is Luke's "Travel Narrative," and why do the authors suggest that it "breaks new ground"?
5. What are the phases of Jesus' trial?

FOR FURTHER STUDY

Bartholomew, C. G., J. B. Green, and A. C. Thiselton, eds. *Reading Luke: Interpretation, Reflection, Formation.* Scripture and Hermeneutics 6. Grand Rapids: Zondervan, 2005.
Bock, D. L. *Luke.* 2 vols. Baker Exegetical Commentary on the New Testament. Grand Rapids: Baker, 1994.
_____. "Luke, Gospel of." Pages 495–510 in *Dictionary of Jesus and the Gospels.* Edited by J. B. Green, S. McKnight, and I. H. Marshall. Downers Grove: InterVarsity, 1992.
Green, J. B. *The Gospel of Luke.* New International Commentary on the New Testament. Rev. ed. Grand Rapids: Eerdmans, 1997.
Liefeld, W. L., and D. W. Pao. "Luke." In *The Expositor's Bible Commentary.* Rev. ed. Vol. 10. Grand Rapids: Zondervan, 2007.
Marshall, I. H. *Commentary on Luke.* New International Greek Testament Commentary. Grand Rapids: Eerdmans, 1978.
_____. *Luke: Historian and Theologian.* 2nd ed. Grand Rapids: Zondervan, 1988.
Morris, L. *The Gospel According to St. Luke: An Introduction and Commentary.* Tyndale New Testament Commentary. 2nd ed. Grand Rapids: Eerdmans, 1988.
Nolland, J. *Luke.* Word Biblical Commentary. 3 vols. Dallas: Word, 1990–93.
Strauss, M. *Four Portraits, One Jesus: An Introduction to Jesus and the Gospels.* Grand Rapids: Zondervan, 2006.

Chapter 7

The Gospel According to John

CORE KNOWLEDGE

Students should know the key facts of John's Gospel. With regard to history, students should be able to identify the Gospel's author, date, provenance, destination, and purpose. With regard to literature, they should be able to provide a basic outline of the book and identify core elements of the book's content found in the unit-by-unit discussion. With regard to theology, students should be able to identify John's major theological themes.

KEY FACTS	
Author:	John
Date:	Mid- or late 80s or early 90s
Provenance:	Ephesus
Destination:	Ephesus; ultimately, universal audience
Purpose:	To demonstrate that Jesus is the Messiah so that people would believe in him and have eternal life (20:30–31)
Theme:	Selected signs show that Jesus is the Messiah
Key Verse:	3:16

CONTRIBUTION TO THE CANON

- Jesus as the preexistent Word made flesh (1:1,14)
- Jesus as the One and Only Son of the Father (1:14,18; 3:16,18)
- Jesus as the Lamb of God who took away the sins of the world (1:29,36)
- Jesus as the glorified, exalted Lord who directs the mission of his followers through the "Other Counselor," the Holy Spirit (14:12–18)
- Jesus as the Messiah who performed a series of startling signs (20:30–31)

INTRODUCTION

JOHN'S GOSPEL AND the book of Romans may well be considered the two high-est peaks in the landscape of NT theology. John soars like an eagle over more pedes-trian depictions of the life of Christ.[1] It likely was written by John the apostle at the culmination of his long life and ministry. John's Gospel penetrates more deeply into the mystery of God's revelation in his Son than the other canonical Gospels and perhaps more deeply than any other biblical book. From the majestic prologue to the probing epilogue, the evangelist's words are as carefully chosen as they must be thoughtfully pondered by every reader of his magnificent work.

Over the course of history, John's Gospel has exercised a remarkable influence com-mensurate with the profundity of its message. John's Christology, particularly affirmations of Jesus' deity and of his human and divine natures, has decisively shaped the formula-tions adopted by the early church councils and creeds.[2] Many of the great minds of the Christian church, from the early church fathers to modern times, have written commen-taries or monographs on John's Gospel. John's Gospel stands as a masterful, reliable witness to the life, words, and deeds of our Lord Jesus Christ.

HISTORY

Author

John's Gospel, like the Synoptics, is formally anonymous. But the author left tantaliz-ing clues in his Gospel, which, when examined in conjunction with the testimony of the early church fathers, points convincingly to authorship by John, the son of Zebedee and apostle of Jesus Christ.

Internal Evidence The author identified himself as "the disciple Jesus loved" (21:20,24; frequently referred to as "the disciple whom Jesus loved"), a prominent figure in the Johannine narrative (13:23; 19:26; 20:2; 21:7,20). Although this disciple's identity is elusive, he left sufficient clues in the narrative to ascertain it beyond reasonable doubt. In 1:14, the author used the first person, "we have observed His glory," revealing that he was an eyewitness to the accounts contained in his Gospel. The "we" of 1:14 refers to the same people as does 2:11, Jesus' disciples.[3] Thus, the writer was an apostle, an eyewitness, and a disciple of Jesus.

---

[1] A. J. Köstenberger, "John," in *New Dictionary of Biblical Theology*, ed. T. D. Alexander and B. S. Rosner (Downers Grove: InterVarsity, 2000), 280–85. Taking their point of reference from the four beasts in Ezek 1:10 and Rev 4:6–15, the Fathers described John as an eagle.

[2] See J. N. Sanders, *The Fourth Gospel in the Early Church* (Cambridge: University Press, 1943); T. E. Pollard, *Johannine Christology and the Early Church*, SNTSMS 13 (Cambridge: University Press, 1970).

[3] The connection between "we" and "his disciples" is clear because of the parallel between the related references to "his [Jesus'] glory" in 1:14 and 2:11. For a discussion on John's use of "we" (21:24) and "I" (21:25), see G. L. Borchert, *John 1–11*, NAC 25A (Nashville: B&H, 1996), 89–90.

An examination of the phrase "the disciple Jesus loved" later on in the Gospel offers further clues to his identity.[4] The expression first appears in 13:23 at the Last Supper where only the Twelve were gathered (Matt 26:20; Mark 14:17; Luke 22:14), indicating "the disciple Jesus loved" must have been one of the Twelve. Since the author never referred to himself by name, he cannot be any of the named disciples at the Last Supper: Judas Iscariot (13:2, 26–27), Peter (13:6–9), Thomas (14:5), Philip (14:8–9), or Judas the son of James (14:22).[5]

The writer offered more clues to his identity in the final chapter of the Gospel, where he mentioned "the disciple, the one Jesus loved" as one of seven other apostles: "Simon Peter, Thomas (called 'Twin'), Nathanael from Cana of Galilee, Zebedee's sons, and two others of His disciples" (21:2; see 21:7). In addition to Peter and Thomas who have already been eliminated (see above), Nathanael is also eliminated as a possible author since, as previously noted, the author remains unnamed in John's Gospel.

Thus the author must be either one of "Zebedee's [two] sons" or one of the "two other of [Jesus'] disciples." Of the two sons of Zebedee, James and John, James can safely be ruled out since he was martyred in the year 42 (see Acts 12:2). The remaining three possibilities are John the son of Zebedee and the "two other disciples." These latter two could be Matthew (Levi), Simon the Zealot, James the son of Alphaeus, Bartholomew, or Thaddaeus.[6] Matthew is an unlikely candidate since a Gospel is already attributed to him. Simon the Zealot, James the son of Alphaeus, Bartholomew, and Thaddaeus are unlikely candidates due to their historical obscurity and lack of historical support (see "External Evidence" below). This leaves John the son of Zebedee as the most likely option.

External Evidence   During the second half of the second century, Irenaeus (c. 130–200) attributed John's Gospel to John the apostle: "John the disciple of the Lord, who leaned back on his breast, published the Gospel while he was a resident at Ephesus in Asia" (*Against Heresies* 3.1.2). Clement of Alexandria (c. 150–215) followed suit: "John, last of all . . . composed a spiritual Gospel" (quoted by Eusebius, *Eccl. Hist.* 6.14.7). From this point forward, the church unanimously attributed authorship to the apostle John for almost 18 centuries with virtually no dissent.

The Synoptic Gospels and Paul's letters also provide corroborating data for John's authorship. The author of John's Gospel consistently shows "the disciple Jesus loved" to be a close companion of Peter (13:23–24; 18:15–16; 20:2–9; 21:7,20–23), while other NT writers also note the close companionship of the apostles John and Peter (Luke 22:8; Acts 1:13; 3:1–4:23; 8:14–25; Gal 2:9). Taken by itself, this connection may be inconclusive. In conjunction with the internal and external evidence adduced above, however, it further

---

[4] The epithet "the disciple Jesus loved" is plausibly understood as an instance of authorial modesty.

[5] A. J. Köstenberger, *Encountering the Gospel of John: The Gospel in Historical, Literary, and Theological Perspective* (Grand Rapids: Baker, 1999), 22.

[6] For a list of all the named apostles in the Gospels and Acts, see R. Bauckham, *Jesus and the Eyewitnesses: The Gospels as Eyewitness Testimony* (Grand Rapids: Eerdmans, 2006), 113.

confirms the likelihood of John's authorship, since, as the "disciple Jesus loved," John was the most likely close companion of Peter and thus the author of the Fourth Gospel.

Therefore, a close examination of all the available internal and external evidence provides plausible grounds for the following three conclusions about the authorship of John's Gospel: [7] (1) the author is an apostle and eyewitness (1:14; see 2:11; 19:35); (2) he is one of the Twelve (13:23; see Mark 14:17; Luke 22:14); (3) he is John, the son of Zebedee.

Date

The date for John's Gospel depends on a complex matrix of questions regarding the author, his original audience, his purpose, his occasion for writing, and other factors. In the quest for the most likely date of composition, 65 and 135 serve, respectively, as the earliest and the latest plausible dates. The first of these dates is established by John's reference to Peter's martyrdom (21:19), which occurred in 65 or 66, and by John's depiction of Jesus as the replacement for the temple, whose destruction took place in the year 70. The second date is determined by the twentieth-century discovery of the earliest NT manuscript to date ($\mathfrak{P}^{52}$, c. 135), containing John 18:31–32,37–38.

Within this time frame John most likely wrote his Gospel in the mid-80s or early 90s based on the following evidence.[8] First, John's language seems closer to reflecting that sufficient time had elapsed after Jesus' resurrection in order for John to articulate his theology in terms of Jesus' divinity. Second, if the reconstruction of John's occasion for writing—the destruction of the temple—below is correct, the Gospel was most likely written 10 to 20 years after the year 70, since a certain amount of time had to pass between the temple destruction and its composition.[9] Third, John's Gospel lacks reference to the Sadducees.[10] Since they play such an important role in the Synoptics (written prior to John) and since they were less influential after the destruction of the temple, their omission in John makes sense if he wrote subsequent to the temple's demise.

Fourth, John's use of the designation "Sea of Tiberias" in clarifying the "Sea of Galilee" (6:1; 21:1) suggests a mid-80s/early 90s date of composition. On a popular level the shift from "Sea of Tiberias" to "Sea of Galilee" probably took place in the 80s or 90s.[11] Fifth, if Thomas's confession of Jesus as "my Lord and my God" is intended to evoke associations of emperor worship under Domitian (81–96), this would seem to require a date subsequent to 81.[12] Thus a date of composition in the mid-80s or early 90s best fits all the evidence.

---

[7] Köstenberger, "John," 280.

[8] See D. A. Croteau, "An Analysis of the Arguments for the Dating of the Fourth Gospel," *Faith and Mission* 20/3 (2003): 47–80.

[9] See D. A. Carson, *Gospel According to John*, PNTC (Grand Rapids: Eerdmans, 1991), 85.

[10] Adolf Schlatter, *Evangelist Johannes*, 2nd ed. (Stuttgart: Calwer, 1948), 44, but note Carson's caution (*Gospel According to John*, 84).

[11] See Köstenberger, *John*, 199.

[12] Ibid., 8.

Provenance

Early patristic testimony lends support to the notion that John wrote his Gospel in Ephesus. Eusebius stated that after the Jewish War (66–73) dispersed the early apostles, John went to serve in Asia (*Eccl. Hist.* 3.1.1), which placed him in or near Ephesus during the 80s and 90s. Irenaeus wrote that "John, the disciple of the Lord . . . published the gospel while living in Ephesus in Asia" (*Against Heresies* 3.1.2 [c. 130–200]). Overall, Eusebius and Irenaeus provided the most reliable, albeit less than conclusive, data available. John most likely wrote in Ephesus in the province of Asia Minor.

Destination

If Irenaeus and others are correct that John was the author of the Gospel and that he wrote in Ephesus (see above), it is reasonable to assume that people living in and around Ephesus, primarily Diaspora Jews and Gentiles, were at least part of his intended readership.[13] Beyond this, John's Gospel was likely written for "all Christians" rather than for readers in only one geographical location[14] because in the end, "John's Gospel is a *Gospel*, heralding the universal good news of salvation in Christ."[15]

Occasion

The destruction of the Jerusalem temple in AD 70 was a traumatic event that created a national and religious void in Judaism and caused Jews to look for ways to continue their ritual and worship.[16] The destruction of the temple threw late first-century Jews into turmoil, just as the Babylonian exile (586 BC) had, since their faith was inextricably connected with the temple through the sacrificial system and the priesthood; a major reorientation of Jewish ritual was required. This likely served as one of the major catalysts for John to write his Gospel. John likely saw a window of opportunity for Jewish evangelism, seeking to encourage fellow believers to reach out to their Jewish and Gentile neighbors in the Diaspora.[17] He did so by arguing that the crucified and risen Messiah providentially replaced the temple (2:18–22; see 1:14; 4:21–24) and fulfilled the symbolism inherent in Jewish festivals (esp. 5–12).

In addition to the temple's destruction, the early Christian Gentile mission (Acts 9:16; Rom 1:13) and the emergence of early gnostic thought likely served as part of the matrix that occasioned the writing of John's Gospel. Since John wrote 50 years after the formation of the church when the Gentile mission was well underway, it stands to reason that this mission directly affected John's writing. Gnosticism, which did not come to full fruition until the second century, provided part of the backdrop as well. Though John did not

---

[13] See Carson, *Gospel According to John*, 91.

[14] Richard Bauckham, *The Gospels for All Christians: Rethinking Gospel Audiences* (Grand Rapids: Eerdmans, 1998), 9–48.

[15] Köstenberger, *Encountering the Gospel of John*, 26.

[16] See A. J. Köstenberger, "The Destruction of the Second Temple and the Composition of the Fourth Gospel," *TrinJ* 26 NS (2005): 205–42; slightly revised in *Challenging Perspectives on the Gospel of John*, ed. J. Lierman, WUNT 2/219 (Tübingen: Mohr Siebeck, 2006), 69–108.

[17] See Bauckham, *Gospels for All Christians*.

embrace or promote gnostic teachings, he used the conceptual categories of his audience, as a good missionary does, to contextualize his message (see John 1:1,14). These three important factors—the temple's destruction, the Gentile mission, and gnostic thought—combined as possible occasions for John's Gospel.

Purpose

Toward the end of his Gospel, John stated his purpose as follows: "But these [signs] are written so that you may believe Jesus is the Messiah, the Son of God, and by believing you may have life in his name" (20:31). Initially, "so that you may believe" suggests an evangelistic purpose; that is, John wanted to bring his readers to initial faith in Jesus as Messiah. At the same time, John's Gospel seems to presuppose an audience that is already familiar with Scripture since it contains detailed instructions for believers, especially in the second half of the Gospel. Moreover, there are few examples of directly evangelistic first-century documents. Thus it seems that John's purpose encompassed both evangelism of unbelievers and edification of believers.[18] According to 20:31, John's purpose was to set forth the evidence that Jesus is the Messiah, the Son of God, so that people might believe in him and as a result have life in his name (cf. 1:1–3,14,29,34,41). This purpose, then, can have the effect of calling unbelievers to faith in the name of Jesus, the Messiah.

LITERATURE

Literary Plan

John's Gospel breaks down into an introduction (1:1–18), a first major unit frequently called "The Book of Signs" (1:19–12:50; focusing on Jesus' messianic "signs" for the Jews), a second major unit best termed "The Book of Exaltation" (13:1–20:31; anticipating Jesus' exaltation with the Father subsequent to his crucifixion, burial, and resurrection), and an epilogue (chap. 21). Chapters 11–12 most likely represent a transition from "The Book of Signs" to "The Book of Exaltation," featuring Jesus' climactic "sign," the raising of Lazarus, which, in turn, foreshadows Jesus' own resurrection.[19] John thus achieved his purpose of demonstrating that Jesus is the Messiah, the Son of God (20:30–31; see "Purpose" above) by weaving together several narrative sections that function within an overall structure. The introduction to John's Gospel places the entire narrative in the framework of the eternal, preexistent Word made flesh in Jesus (1:1–18).

"The Book of Signs," by way of literary *inclusios*, consists of two major cycles narrating Jesus' ministry, a "Cana cycle" (2:1–4:54; see 2:11; 4:54) and a "festival cycle" (5:1–10:42; see 1:19–34; 10:40–41).[20] In addition, the watershed defection of many of Jesus' followers at the end of chap. 6 may constitute a division between chaps. 5–6 and

---

[18] See Bauckham, *Gospels for All Christians*, 10.

[19] Carson, *Gospel According to John*, 106–7; Ridderbos (*Gospel of John*, viii) called John 11–12 "Prelude to the Passion Narrative"; as did Keener (*Gospel of John*, xvii), who labeled the unit "Introducing the Passion."

[20] F. J. Moloney, *Gospel of John* (Sacra Pagina; Collegeville: Liturgical Press, 1998), v–vi.

chaps. 7–10. "The Book of Signs" in full sets forth evidence for Jesus' messiahship in the form of seven selected signs (1:19–12:50; see esp. 12:37–40; cf. 20:30–31).[21] John also includes Jesus' seven "I am" sayings (see chart below) and calls numerous (seven?) witnesses in support of Jesus' claims, including Moses and the Scriptures, John the Baptist, the Father, Jesus and his works, the Spirit, the disciples, and the evangelist himself. Certain questions concerning Jesus' messiahship lead the Gospel's readers to the author's intended conclusion, namely that Jesus is the Messiah (e.g., 1:41; 4:25; 7:27,31,52; 10:24; 11:27; 12:34).

Table 7.1: The "I Am" Sayings of Jesus in John's Gospel

Statement	Reference in John's Gospel
"I am the bread of life."	6:35,48,51
"I am the light of the world."	8:12; 9:5
"I am the door."	10:7,9
"I am the good shepherd."	10:11,14
"I am the resurrection and the life."	11:25
"I am the way, the truth, and the life."	14:6
"I am the true vine."	15:1

"The Book of Exaltation" comprises the Farewell Discourse (13–17), which can be subdivided into a preamble (13:1–30), the Farewell Discourse proper (13:31–16:33), and Jesus' final prayer (17), and the Passion Narrative (18–20), culminating in a declaration of John's purpose (20:30–31). The Farewell Discourse (13–17) shows how Jesus ensured the continuation of his mission by preparing his new messianic community for its mission as they are cleansed, prepared, and prayed for. The cleansing is effected by the footwashing and Judas' departure (chap. 13); the disciples' preparation involves instructions regarding the coming of the Holy Spirit (chaps. 14–16); and Jesus' followers are prayed for in his final prayer (chap. 17).

John's Passion Narrative (18–19) presents Jesus' death both as an atonement for sin (see 1:29,36; 6:48–58; 10:15,17–18), though largely without the Synoptic emphasis on shame and humiliation, and as a preface to Jesus' return to the Father (see 13:1; 16:28). The resurrection appearances and the disciples' commissioning constitute the focal point of John's penultimate chapter (chap. 20), where Jesus is cast as the paradigmatic "Sent One" (see 9:7), who now sends the representatives of his new messianic community (20:21–23).

---

[21] A. J. Köstenberger, "The Seventh Johannine Sign: A Study in John's Christology," *BBR* 5 (1995): 87–103.

The purpose statement of 20:30–31 then reiterates the major motifs of the Gospel: signs, believing, (eternal) life, and the identity of Jesus as Messiah and Son of God.

The Epilogue portrays the relationship between Peter and "the disciple whom Jesus loved" in terms of differing yet equally legitimate roles of service within the believing community. This brings closure to the joint characterization of Peter and the "disciple Jesus loved" especially in the second half of John's Gospel, compares and contrasts their respective callings in ministry, and offers a further glimpse into the identity of the Gospel's author. Thus, John's Gospel reveals a deliberate literary plan that reflects the evangelist's theological message.

OUTLINE
   I. INTRODUCTION: THE WORD MADE FLESH (1:1–18)
   II. THE BOOK OF SIGNS: THE SIGNS OF THE MESSIAH (1:19–12:50)
    A. The Forerunner and the Coming of the Messiah (1:19–51)
    B. The Cana Cycle: Jesus' Inaugural Signs and Representative Conversations (2:1–4:54)
    C. The Festival Cycle: Additional Signs amid Mounting Unbelief (5–10)
    D. Final Passover: Climactic Sign, the Raising of Lazarus, and Other Events (11–12)
   III. THE BOOK OF EXALTATION: PREPARING THE NEW MESSIANIC COMMUNITY AND THE PASSION OF JESUS (13–20)
    A. The Cleansing and Instruction of the New Covenant Community, including Jesus' Final Prayer (13–17)
    B. The Passion Narrative (18–19)
    C. Jesus' Resurrection and Appearances, Commissioning of Disciples (20:1–29)
    D. Concluding Purpose Statement (20:30–31)
   IV. EPILOGUE: THE COMPLEMENTARY ROLES OF PETER AND THE BELOVED DISCIPLE (21)

UNIT-BY-UNIT DISCUSSION

I. Introduction: The Word Made Flesh (1:1–18)

John's striking prologue sets the course for his entire Gospel by drawing a road map for the reader that projects in eloquent language the path on which the Gospel will travel. From 1:1 onward, John makes a startling assertion: Jesus is God. This God "became flesh" and "took up residence" (literally, "pitched his tent") among God's people (1:14) as the "One and Only Son from the Father" (1:14,18). Going beyond Matthew and Luke, who linked Jesus with Abraham and/or Adam, John traced Jesus' origins back to creation (see Gen 1:1), anchoring him not only in historical events but in eternity past.

John anticipates the later unbelief and rejection of Jesus as Messiah by both the Jews and the world (chaps. 5–10, 18–19). Thus, he distinguished between those who recognize the incarnate Word (1:12–13; believers) and those who do not (1:10–11; unbelievers). All must respond to Jesus based on John the Baptist's testimony (1:6–9,15) and the Fourth Evangelist's presentation of Jesus (see 20:30–31).

II. The Book of Signs: The Signs of the Messiah (1:19–12:50)

After introducing Jesus as the Word made flesh in the introduction, John started "The Book of Signs" (1:19–12:50), the first of his two "books." This first book establishes by way of seven selected signs that Jesus is the Messiah sent from God (2:1–11,13–22; 4:46–54; 5:1–15; 6:1–15; 9:1–41; 11:1–44).

A. The Forerunner and the Coming of the Messiah (1:19–51) John began the narrative proper by expounding upon the testimony of John the Baptist (1:19–36; see 1:6–8,15). To a delegation from Jerusalem, the Baptist gave witness regarding his own identity (1:19–28): he was not the Messiah but the "voice of one crying out in the wilderness" envisioned by the OT prophet Isaiah (1:23; see Isa 40:3; cf. Matt 3:3; Mark 1:3; Luke 3:4). He also directed his followers to Jesus, "the Lamb of God, who takes away the sin of the world" (1:29; see 1:36) and made clear that the purpose of his ministry of baptism was so that Christ "might be revealed to Israel" (1:31). The remainder of the chapter shows Jesus calling his first disciples and identifying himself to them as the new Bethel, the place where God revealed himself to Jacob who was later renamed "Israel" (1:50–51; cf. Gen 28:12).[22]

B. The Cana Cycle: Jesus' Inaugural Signs and Representative Conversations (2–4) After these introductory matters, Jesus' ministry begins in earnest. Jesus' signs and conversations with individuals intermingle in this section. Jesus' first sign in Cana—turning water into wine—"displayed his glory," so that his disciples "believed in him" (2:11). Another possible sign, the clearing of the temple (2:13–22), anticipated Jesus' resurrection (2:19) and signaled the temple's replacement with Jesus (2:20). After conversations with Nicodemus, the Jewish rabbi (3:1–21), and a Samaritan woman (4:1–42), Jesus performed another sign at Cana, healing an official's son (4:43–54), which closes the Cana cycle.

C. The Festival Cycle: Additional Signs amid Mounting Unbelief (5–10) In this cycle, Jesus' public ministry continues amid escalating controversy due to unbelief foreshadowed in 1:10–11 and 2:24–25 and further exposed by Jesus' additional messianic signs. His fourth sign, the healing of a lame man (5:1–15), took place at an unnamed feast (possibly Tabernacles) and was performed on the Sabbath, resulting in the Jews' persecution of Jesus (5:16). In the ensuing controversy, Jesus defended himself against the charge of blasphemy, calling upon God the Father, his own works, John the Baptist, Moses, and others as his witnesses (5:17–47).

---

[22] See the discussion in Köstenberger, *John*, 84–87.

Table 7.2: Jesus' Fulfillment of Old Testament Festivals

Festival	Scripture	Description/Fulfillment
Feast of Passover	Exod 12:1–4; Lev 23:4–5; John 1:29–36; 2:13; 6:4; 11:55; 12:1	Also known as *Pesach*; a lamb was killed in commemoration of God's deliverance of Israel from Egypt. **Fulfillment:** Jesus is the lamb of God whose death causes God to pass over judging those covered by the blood of Jesus.
Feast of Unleavened Bread	Exod 12:15–20; Lev 23:6–8	Also known as *Hag Hamatzot*; Israel must eat unleavened bread for 7 days; leaven often represents sin in Scripture. **Fulfillment:** Jesus is the bread of life who is free from sin (leaven).
Feast of Firstfruits	Lev 23:9–14	Also known as *Yom HaBikkurim*; Israel offered first ripe sheaf of barley to the Lord; the sheaf was set aside on Passover and offered on the third day of the Passover feast. **Fulfillment:** Jesus rose on the third day of the Passover feast as the "firstfruits of those who have fallen asleep" (1 Cor 15:20).
Feast of Pentecost	Lev 23:15–22; Acts 2:1–40	Also known as "Feast of Weeks" or *Shavnot*; occurs 50 days after Sabbath of Unleavened Bread; Israel offered new grain of summer harvest. **Fulfillment:** Holy Spirit poured out on disciples 49 days after Jesus' resurrection (50 days after the Sabbath preceding it).
Feast of Trumpets	Lev 23:23–35; Num 29:1–11; Matt 24:31; 1 Cor 15:51–52; 1 Thess 4:16–17	Also called *Rosh HaShana*; trumpet blown to call people into a time of introspection and repentance. **Fulfillment:** Traditionally associated with judgment and the Book of Life, represents the second coming of Jesus as judge; Jesus' coming will be announced by a trumpet blast.
Day of Atonement	Lev 23:26–32, 44–46; Rom 3:21–25; Heb 9:11–28	Also called *Yom Kippur*; high priest makes atonement for sin in the holy of holies where the ark of the covenant rested; final day of 10 days of repentance of Feast of Trumpets; two goats (atonement sacrifice and scapegoat) represented atonement of Israel's sin for another year. **Fulfillment:** Jesus as High Priest entered heaven (the holy of holies) and made eternal atonement for sin with his blood.
Festival of Tabernacles	Lev 23:34–43; John 1:14; 7:38–39; 8:12; 9:5	Also called *Sukkot*; the Jews dwelled in tents for one week; reminder of God's protection during Israel's wilderness wanderings; priest would pour out water to symbolize the world knowing God at coming of Messiah. **Fulfillment:** Jesus made his dwelling among us; Jesus as source of living water that will flow from believers (Jesus' address at Festival of Tabernacles).

D. Final Passover: Climactic Sign, the Raising of Lazarus, and Other Events (11–12) In this bridge section the evangelist narrates Jesus' climactic sign, the raising of Lazarus (11:1–44), as well as mounting opposition to Jesus by the Jewish authorities (11:45–57). The startling demonstration of Jesus' messiahship at the raising of Lazarus adds the final exclamation point to Jesus' claim of being the messianic Son of God (see 12:36–41; 20:30–31). In light of the mounting pressure following Jesus' final sign in this Gospel, Jesus decided to avoid the open public and withdrew with his disciples (11:54).

With the seven signs behind Jesus and with the plot against him escalating, John narrated Mary's anointing of Jesus at Bethany (12:1–8), which anticipated his death and burial; Jesus' triumphal entry into Jerusalem, which underscored his messianic identity (12:12–19); and the coming of some Greeks, which signified the dawning age of the Gentiles (12:20–36). These three public events preceded the final indictment of Jewish rejection (12:37–50). This transitions the reader from the "Book of Signs" (1:19–12:50) to the "Book of Exaltation" (chaps. 13–20), and with this Jesus shifted his focus from his revelation to Israel to the preparation of his new messianic community.

Table 7.3: Jesus' Signs in John's Gospel

Sign	Reference
1. Changing water to wine	2:1–11
2. Clearing of the temple	2:13–22
3. Healing of official's son	4:46–54
4. Healing of lame man	5:1–15
5. Feeding of multitude	6:1–15
6. Healing of blind man	9:1–41
7. Raising of Lazarus	11:1–44

III. The Book of Exaltation: Preparing the New Messianic Community and Jesus' Passion (13–20)

Following the "Book of Signs," then, John anticipated Jesus' resurrection and ascension in "The Book of Exaltation" (chaps. 13–20). The focus is squarely on Jesus' preparation of the new messianic community, which is followed by an account of Jesus' passion, including his arrest, crucifixion, and burial, and the first two of his resurrection appearances. A purpose statement concludes the narrative proper (20:30–31).

A. The Cleansing and Instruction of the New Community (13–17)   With the line of demarcation between believers and unbelievers now clearly drawn, Jesus turned his attention to the Twelve (or Eleven) in order to prepare them for the time after his departure. Commonly called the "Upper Room Discourse" or "Farewell Discourse" (chaps. 13–17), this section describes Jesus' preparation in three stages: (1) Jesus cleansed the community (13:1–30); (2) Jesus offered an encouraging and challenging farewell (13:31–16:33); and (3) Jesus uttered a parting prayer (chap. 17).

First, the new messianic community was cleansed, both literally through his washing the disciples feet (13:1–17) and spiritually through the removal of Judas the traitor from the disciples' midst (13:18–30). With the community cleansed and Jesus' departure imminent, he instructed the Eleven in order to prepare them for the time when he would no longer be physically present (13:31–16:33). In this John presented Jesus' parting instructions to his followers against the backdrop of Moses' farewell in Deuteronomy.[23]

After this announcement, Jesus comforted his disciples by telling them that he was going to prepare a place for them in his "Father's house" (14:2). In order to follow him there, they must remember that Jesus is the only way to the Father (14:6). Jesus further comforted his followers by promising to send "another Counselor" (14:16), "the Spirit of truth" (14:17). Once Jesus was exalted, the disciples must remain connected to the "true vine" (15:1), for apart from him they could do nothing (15:5). They must witness to a world that will hate and persecute them (15:18–16:33), knowing that Jesus' victory had already been secured (16:33).

While the community's cleansing served as a preamble to Jesus' Farewell Discourse, his parting prayer (17:1–26) provided a postlude. Jesus first prayed for himself (17:1–5); then for his disciples (17:6–19); and finally for all those who were going to believe on account of his disciples' proclamation (17:20–26). This provided a fitting conclusion to the Farewell Discourse and a suitable introduction to the events of the Passion Narrative that ensued in rapid order.

B. The Passion Narrative (18–19)   After praying, Jesus, knowing what was about to happen to him (18:4), was arrested under the cover of night by a group of soldiers aided by Judas the betrayer. Johannine irony thickens as the passion events unfold. From the world's perspective, the high priest's questioning of Jesus (18:19–24), Peter's denials (18:15–18,25–27), and Pilate's sentencing (18:28–19:16) revealed the misfortunes of a Jewish pretender who sought to mislead his followers by claiming to be the long-awaited Messiah. From John's perspective, however, Jesus was the otherworldly king who had come to this world as a witness to the truth; he was the one who would one day serve as its Judge but who now was to give his life for the sins of the world; and he was the crucified, buried,

---

[23] See 6:14–15; and Jesus' "signs." Possible precursors of Jesus' Farewell Discourse in John's Gospel include Moses' farewell discourse (Deuteronomy 31–33), other similar OT and Second Temple farewells (see *Jub.* 22:1–30; 1 Macc 2:49–70), and the patriarchal deathbed blessings and final words. See Köstenberger, *John*, 396–97.

and risen Messiah, whose resurrection constituted the final act of the "elusive Christ" who had continued to evade the world's grasp.[24]

As the Fourth Evangelist made clear, all of these final events in Jesus' earthly ministry unfold according to the predetermined, sovereign plan of God (12:37–41; 13:1–3; 18:4). This is particularly evident throughout the Passion Narrative.[25] At the trial and crucifixion, the Jews join the world in its unbelief and rejection of the Messiah. The carefully planned structure of an oscillating pattern of outdoor/indoor scenes of Jesus' trial (18:28–19:16a)[26] is intended "to exhibit the paradoxical outcome of the whole process—how they [Pilate and the Jewish leaders] found each other in a single unprincipled alliance against Jesus,"[27] which led to Jesus' crucifixion (19:16b–42).

C. Jesus' Resurrection and Appearances, and His Commissioning the Disciples (20) Jesus' resurrection and resurrection appearances conclude the Passion Narrative prior to the Gospel's conclusion. The empty tomb offered the first hopeful glimmer of the return that Jesus promised in the Farewell Discourse (20:1–10). This glimmer of hope reached its initial fruition in Jesus' encounter with Mary Magdalene (20:11–18). Jesus then appeared to the disciples without (20:19–23) and then with (20:24–29) Thomas.

Climaxing the "sending" motif in this Gospel, Jesus commissioned his disciples (20:21), breathing on them and, in a symbolic gesture, conferring on them the Holy Spirit (20:22) and a message of forgiveness (20:23).[28] Jesus' appearance to Thomas concluded with the latter's climactic confession, "My Lord and my God!" (20:28), which recalled the opening identification of Jesus as God in the prologue (1:1,18).

D. Concluding Purpose Statement (20:30–31) The concluding purpose statement in 20:30–31 features virtually every major theme from the preceding narrative: (1) certain selected signs; (2) the necessity of believing that Jesus is the Messiah and the Son of God; and (3) the promise of life, both present and eternal.[29]

IV. Epilogue: The Complementary Roles of Peter and the Beloved Disciple (21)

At a first glance it seems that John's Gospel concludes with the purpose statement in 20:30–31 and that the epilogue was most likely added by a later writer. However, most likely the epilogue serves as the closing bookend that corresponds to the opening bookend of the prologue. The epilogue resolves the relationship between Peter and the "disciple

---

[24] M. W. G. Stibbe, *John as Storyteller: Narrative Criticism and the Fourth Gospel*, SNTSMS 73 (Cambridge: University Press, 1992), 111–12.

[25] See especially the fulfillment of OT texts in 19:24,28,36–37; Köstenberger, "John," in *Commentary on the New Testament Use of the Old Testament*, 500–6.

[26] Outside (18:29–32); inside (18:33–38a); outside (18:38b-40); inside (19:1–3); outside (19:4–7); inside (19:8–11); and outside (19:12–15).

[27] Ridderbos, *Gospel According to John*, 587.

[28] For a book-length study, see A. J. Köstenberger, *The Missions of Jesus and the Disciples According to the Fourth Gospel* (Grand Rapids: Eerdmans, 1998).

[29] See Köstenberger, *John*, 581–82.

Jesus loved" in terms of noncompetition and clarifies the identity of Johannine authorship. Thus the epilogue most likely came from John's hand: its language and style are similar to chaps. 1–20; no textual evidence exists that John's Gospel ever circulated without it. Therefore, John's epilogue appears to be part of John's overall literary plan.[30]

Table 7.4: The Seven Words of Jesus at the Cross

Sayings of Jesus	NT Reference
"Father, forgive them, because they do not know what they are doing."	Luke 23:34
"I assure you: Today you will be with Me in paradise."	Luke 23:43
"Woman, here is your son. . . . Here is your mother."	John 19:26–27
"*Eloi, Eloi, lemá sabachtháni?*" ("My God, My God, why have You forsaken Me?")	Matt 27:46// Mark 15:34
"I'm thirsty!"	John 19:28
"It is finished!"	John 19:30
"Father, into Your hands I entrust My spirit."	Luke 23:46

A. Jesus' Third Appearance (21:1–14)   After appearing to the disciples, Jesus showed himself to them a third time, further validating his resurrection.[31] The disciples returned to the Sea of Tiberias (the Sea of Galilee; see 6:1,23) to fish.[32] When Jesus called to them from the shore, they did not recognize him (21:4). Yet after he instructed them on where to cast their net, the "disciple Jesus loved" did recognize the "Lord," prompting Peter to plunge into the water to swim ashore.

B. Jesus and Peter (21:15–19)   Earlier, Peter had openly denied knowing Jesus three times (18:15–18,25–27). Now, Jesus openly affirmed and commissioned Peter before his fellow disciples. Despite his failure, Peter would become the leader of the church (see Matt 16:16–19; Acts 1–12) and glorify God by dying a death similar to that of his Lord (21:18–19).

C. Jesus and the Disciple Jesus Loved (21:20–25)   The Fourth Evangelist concluded his Gospel with an interchange between Jesus, Peter, and the "disciple Jesus loved." The rumor was dispelled that this disciple would not die prior to Jesus' return (21:23), and the "disciple Jesus loved" was identified as the author of the Gospel (21:24; see 21:20; 13:23; cf. "Author" above). This brings proper closure to Peter's relationship with the disciple

---

[30] See ibid., 583–86.

[31] See 21:14: "This was now the third time Jesus appeared to the disciples after he was raised from the dead" (cf. 20:19–23,24–29). Note that this numbering does not include Jesus' appearance to Mary Magdalene (20:11–18), indicating that the Fourth Evangelist did not include her among Jesus' disciples known as the Twelve (or Eleven).

[32] As this was Peter's former profession (see Matt 4:18), the disciples' return to fishing may indicate unbelief. This is also suggested by the fact that they catch no fish. See the discussion in Köstenberger, *John*, 588–89.

"whom Jesus loved" and the author of the Gospel. John's concluding statement that the whole world could not contain the books that would need to be written if everything Jesus had done and said were recorded (21:25) provides a fitting conclusion to his Gospel and to all four Gospels.

THEOLOGY

Theological Themes[33]

Jesus as the Word, the Lamb of God, and the Messianic Son of God John's Gospel makes an indispensable contribution to the NT canon, for it portrays Jesus as the Word who was in the beginning with God and who was God (1:1) who became flesh (1:14), "the lamb of God" to take away the sins of the world (1:29, 36). John thus presented Jesus as both divine (1:1; 8:58; 12:41; 17:5; 20:28) and human (4:6–7; 11:33,35; 19:28).[34]

At the outset, John's account is based on the "Old Testament understanding that God sends his Word (see 1:1: *logos*) to accomplish his purposes (see Isa 55:10–11)."[35] Jesus is presented as the Word sent from heaven to accomplish a mission and, once the mission had been accomplished, to return to the place from which he came (1:1,14; 13:1–3; 16:28; see Isa 55:11). Throughout his Gospel, therefore, John furnishes proof that Jesus is the messianic Son of God (20:30–31) sent by the Father.

Jesus is also the "Lamb of God" (1:29,36) who takes away the sin of the world. John here echoed OT theology: just as the Passover lamb provided the remedy for people's sin, so does Jesus (see 8:24,34). The sacrificial and substitutionary nature of Jesus' death is also highlighted in references to Jesus as "the bread of life" given for the life of the world (6:31–59) and as the "good shepherd" who gives his life for his sheep (10:11–17). A vital part of Jesus' mission, therefore, is the sacrificial removal of sin.

The Signs The significance of the signs in John's Gospel can hardly be overstated. Jesus' performance of selected messianic signs dominates the first half of John's Gospel (chaps. 1–12) as it builds inexorably to its first climax, the Jewish rejection of Jesus as Messiah (12:36b–41). Jesus' messianic signs culminate in the raising of Lazarus, anticipating his own resurrection. Overall it appears that John's selection of particular acts of Jesus as signs proceeded on the criterion of particularly startling or stunning displays of Jesus' messianic power. In each case this is made clear by specific references provided by the evangelist, often involving (large) numbers (2:6,19–20; 4:52–53; 5:38; 6:13; 9:1; 11:39).

All of these features underscore the amazing nature of Jesus' displays of his messianic identity, which rendered Jewish unbelief all the more inexcusable. The significance of the signs in John's Gospel is further highlighted by the strategic references to Jesus' signs at the

---

[33] For a monograph-length treatment of Johannine theology see A. J. Köstenberger, *A Theology of John's Gospel and Letters: The Word, the Christ, the Son of God*, BTNT (Grand Rapids: Zondervan, 2009).

[34] See A. J. Köstenberger and S. R. Swain, *Father, Son and Spirit: The Trinity and John's Gospel*, NSBT (Leicester, UK: InterVarsity, 2008), who argued that John's Christology neither minimizes nor sacrifices his Jewish monotheistic views.

[35] Köstenberger, *John*, 39.

end of the first half of John's Gospel (12:36–40) and in the purpose statement (20:30–31). This shows that, for John, the signs were both a key Christological motif and a structural component of his Gospel. In John, his signs serve as evidence for his identity and as an aid to lead unbelievers to faith because the desired outcome of Jesus' mission is that people would believe in him as the Messiah.

POINTS OF APPLICATION

- Believe that Jesus is the eternal Word through whom God created all things (1:1)
- Realize that eternal, abundant life starts already in the here and now (10:10)
- Be confident in your faith; Jesus proved himself by many signs (12:37; 20:30–31)
- Be obedient and faithful; Jesus sent you as the Father sent him (20:21–22)
- To believe or not to believe, that's the question (20:30–31)

STUDY QUESTIONS

1. Who is "the disciple Jesus loved"?
2. What are the two major divisions that comprise the structure of John's Gospel?
3. How does John 1:1–18 serve as a road map for the entire Gospel?
4. What is the major purpose of the signs included in the first half of John's Gospel?
5. What is the major purpose of the "I am" statements?
6. What are the implications of Jesus' being the sent Son of God?

FOR FURTHER STUDY

Barrett, C. K. *The Gospel According to St. John*. 2nd ed. Philadelphia: Westminster, 1978.
Beasley-Murray, G. R. *John*. Word Biblical Commentary 36. 2nd ed. Waco: Word, 1998 [1987].
Blomberg, C. L. *The Historical Reliability of John's Gospel*. Downers Grove: InterVarsity, 2002.
Carson, D. A. *The Gospel According to John*. Pillar New Testament Commentary. Grand Rapids: Eerdmans, 1991.
Keener, C. S. *The Gospel of John: A Commentary*. 2 vols. Peabody: Hendrickson, 2003.
Köstenberger, A. J. *Encountering John: The Gospel in Its Historical, Literary, and Theological Perspective*. Encountering Biblical Studies. Grand Rapids: Baker, 1999.
_____. *John*. Baker Exegetical Commentary on the New Testament. Grand Rapids: Baker, 2004.
_____. "John." Pages 1–216 in *Zondervan Illustrated Bible Backgrounds Commentary*, vol. 2. Edited by C. E. Arnold. Grand Rapids: Zondervan, 2001.
_____. *A Theology of John's Gospel and Letters: The Word, the Christ, the Son of God*. Biblical Theology of the New Testament. Grand Rapids: Zondervan, 2009.
Köstenberger, A. J., and S. R. Swain. *Father, Son and Spirit: The Trinity and John's Gospel*. New Studies in Biblical Theology 24. Downers Grove: InterVarsity, 2008.
Lincoln, A. T. *Truth on Trial: The Lawsuit Motif in the Fourth Gospel*. Peabody: Hendrickson, 2000.
Morris, L. *The Gospel According to John*. New International Commentary on the New Testament. Rev. ed. Grand Rapids: Eerdmans, 1995.
_____. *Jesus Is the Christ*. Grand Rapids: Eerdmans, 1989.
Pryor, J. W. *John: Evangelist of the Covenant People: The Narrative and Themes of the Fourth Gospel*. Downers Grove: InterVarsity, 1992.
Ridderbos, H. N. *The Gospel of John: A Theological Commentary*. Grand Rapids: Eerdmans, 1997.

Part Three

THE EARLY CHURCH AND PAUL

IN THIS PORTION of this work, the book of Acts (chap. 8) forms the basic framework for the discussion of Paul's life and ministry (chap. 9) and subsequent chapters treating Paul's letters in chronological sequence in their presumed order of writing (chaps. 10–15): Galatians; 1 & 2 Thessalonians; 1 & 2 Corinthians; Romans; the Prison Epistles (Philippians, Ephesians, Colossians, and Philemon); and the Pastoral Epistles (1 & 2 Timothy; Titus).

Organizing the material in this way enables us to get a sense of the development of the early church and first-century Christianity throughout Paul's missionary career. Since Paul wrote 13 of the 27 books of the NT, and since his letters probe the major implications of Jesus' mission and saving cross-work for NT believers, part 3 forms the heart of this introduction to the NT. It is complemented and completed by the discussion of the General Epistles and the book of Revelation in part 4 (chaps. 16–20).

Chapter 8

The Book of Acts

CORE KNOWLEDGE

Students should know the key facts about the book of Acts. With regard to history, students should be able to identify the book's author, date, provenance, destination, and purpose. With regard to literature, they should be able to provide a basic outline of the book and identify core elements of the book's content found in the unit-by-unit discussion. With regard to theology, students should be able to identify the major theological themes in the book of Acts.

KEY FACTS	
Author:	Luke
Date:	Early 60s
Provenance:	Rome
Destination:	Theophilus
Purpose:	A defense of the Christian faith showing the expansion of the early church from a Jewish sect to a worldwide movement
Theme:	Salvation history: the birth and mission of the early church
Key Verse:	1:8

CONTRIBUTION TO THE CANON

- Volume 2 of Luke-Acts: what Jesus continued to do through the Holy Spirit (1:1)
- Account of the spread of Christianity from Jerusalem to Rome (1:8) and of the life and practices of the early church (see 2:42)
- Giving of the Spirit at Pentecost and birth of the NT church (chap. 2)
- Ministry of Peter, John, James (Jesus' half brother), and others (chaps. 1–12)

- Inclusion of the Gentiles by decree of the Jerusalem Council (chap. 15)
- Ministry of Paul "to the Jew first and also to the Gentiles" in locations to which Paul addressed letters included in the canon (chaps. 13–28; see especially 28:23–28)

INTRODUCTION

WHEN OSCAR WILDE was studying the classics at Oxford, he had to take an oral exam to test his knowledge of Greek. The examiners looked at him, sensed that he was "an effete and 'difficult' young man," and assigned him the most difficult text to translate in the Greek NT: the account of Paul's shipwreck in Acts 27 with its extensive use of nautical language. "That will be all, Mr. Wilde," the examiners said, when Oscar, a brilliant Greek student, provided an effortless translation. "Oh, please," exclaimed Wilde, "do let me go on—I am longing to know how the story finishes."[1]

This anecdote illustrates two facets of the book of Acts. To begin with, it is the account of a grand adventure, taking us from Palestine to the center of the Gentile world: Rome. Along the way, it includes the exciting story of encounters with hostile people and governments, sailing adventures and shipwrecks, and even courtroom dramas. No doubt about it, the book of Acts is an exciting adventure. But the anecdote not only underlines the exciting tale that is the book of Acts, it also leaves us (like Wilde) longing to know how the story finished after the end of the book since Paul remained under arrest in Rome awaiting trial.

HISTORY

Author

In a previous chapter, we identified Luke the beloved physician as the author of both the Gospel and the book of Acts. To recapitulate, Luke was a well-educated man, steeped in the OT (especially the LXX). He knew the geography of Palestine and the Mediterranean world. He was not an original disciple (see Luke 1:2) but a traveling companion of Paul (thus the use of the first-person plural pronoun in the "we" passages starting at Acts 16:8–17; see Table 8.1 below) and revealed great respect for Paul in his writings. Thus while Luke was not an eyewitness of the events recorded in his Gospel, he witnessed a significant portion of events narrated in the second half of the book of Acts. Luke's close association with the apostle Paul ensured that the canonical criterion of apostolicity was met.

---

[1] A. N. Wilson, *Paul: The Mind of the Apostle* (New York: W. W. Norton, 1997), 21–22. Ironically, of course, Wilde would *not* have found out how the story finishes even *if* he had read through the end of the book of Acts, since the story is open-ended.

Table 8.1: The "We" Passages in Acts

Passages in Acts	Journeys and Locations	Event
16:8–17	Troas to Philippi	Ministry in Philippi
20:5–15	Philippi to Troas to Miletus	On way to Jerusalem
21:1–18	Miletus to Jerusalem via Caesarea	On way to Jerusalem
27:1–28:16	Caesarea to Rome	All the way to Rome

Date

Like its authorship, the date of the book of Acts was established in the chapter on the Gospel of Luke. An early date remains the best option for the book of Acts. The abrupt ending; the neutral, if not friendly, presentation of the Roman Empire; the lack of mention of the Pauline Letters; and the lack of mention of the Jewish war and its events all point to an early date for Acts.[2] The ending of Acts is best explained as Luke having recorded everything that has happened up to this point in Paul's mission. Although not universally accepted, an early date is the most plausible in light of the available evidence.

If Paul (1) was released from his first Roman imprisonment in which he found himself at the end of the book of Acts; (2) engaged in several years of further missionary travels and ministry as the Pastorals suggest; (3) his martyrdom was preceded by a second, significantly harsher, Roman imprisonment as 2 Timothy seems to indicate; and (4) as tradition indicates, was martyred in c. 65/66 during the persecution under Nero (54–68) subsequent to the great fire in Rome (64), 60 is the most reasonable date for the conclusion of the book of Acts and a date of composition shortly thereafter.

Provenance

Given a date of 60, the only option for the provenance of the book is the city of Rome. If Luke had caught up in time with Paul so that the apostle was awaiting trial in Rome at the time of writing and if the "we sections" are an indication of personal involvement, then Luke was with Paul when he wrote the book. This was the view of Irenaeus (c. 130–200), Eusebius (c. 260–340), and Jerome (c. 345–420).[3] Like Irenaeus, Jerome, and Eusebius, one may deduce from the ending that Luke was with Paul in Rome at the time of writing without staking any undue weight on this deduction. (Also, at a later point, Luke is said to be the only one left with Paul in Rome; see 2 Tim 4:11.)

---

[2] For a slightly different track to reach the same conclusion, see A. J. Matill Jr., "The Date and Purpose of Luke-Acts: Rackham Reconsidered," *CBQ* 40 (1978): 335–50.

[3] Irenaeus, *Against Heresies* 3.1.1; 3.14.1; Eusebius, *Eccl. Hist.* 2.22.6; and Jerome, *De Viris Illustribus* 7.

Destination

Theophilus, like Josephus's Epaphroditus, goes unnamed in the rest of the narrative. As discussed in chap. 6 on Luke's Gospel, little is known about him other than that he may have been a Roman official (see "most excellent" in Luke 1:3; cf. Acts 23:26; 24:3; 26:25 with reference to Felix and Festus) and that he had received previous information regarding the Christian faith (Luke 1:4). Most likely, he was Luke's literary patron.

Luke also likely had a target audience beyond Theophilus. To discern this audience, it is instructive to look at the kind of information that Luke expected or did not expect his audience to know. On the one hand, he did not expect his readers to know the basic details of Judean topography (see Acts 1:12), or the local language, Aramaic (see 1:12,19; 4:36; 9:36; 13:8). At the same time, he did not explain Jewish institutions such as Pentecost (2:1; 20:16), "a Sabbath day's journey" (1:12), uncleanness (10:14), and "Passover" (12:4), which suggests that Luke expected his audience to be familiar with this kind of information.[4] Acts is a book that would resonate well with non-Aramaic speakers familiar with the Greek OT (LXX). This would have included Gentile Christians, and it would not have ruled out Diaspora Jews or Jewish Christians living outside Palestine. Beyond this, anyone interested in the nature and phenomenal rise of Christianity in the first few decades of the church would have found the book of Acts valuable and informative.

Purpose

In considering the purpose of Acts, it must be remembered that the work is a sequel to Luke's Gospel. This does not necessarily mean that the purpose of Acts is identical to the purpose of Luke's Gospel; it means that the former should be related appropriately to the latter (see esp. Acts 1:1). If the preface to Luke applies to Acts as well—and given the brevity of Acts' preface, this is most likely the case—then Luke set out to write an orderly account and to provide assurance and an apology or defense of the Christian faith. But what kind of defense did Luke provide?

The first and best indication is the literary structure of Acts, which revolves around showing the early expansion of the church from a local sect to a worldwide movement as empowered by God. Each expansion is brought about by the leading of the Holy Spirit rather than by the disciples' own initiative. In this theological emphasis, the book manifests the same focus on God's plan (including promise and fulfillment) that is prominent in Luke's Gospel. This also answers the question of why a sequel to Luke's Gospel was needed in the first place. The Gospel is "about all that Jesus began to do and teach" (Acts 1:1), and Acts narrates the continuation of that which was begun in the Gospel. The story of Jesus is not complete until the gospel has moved from the Jewish capital to "the ends of the earth"—all the way to Rome (Acts 1:8).

The book of Acts thus *spirals* out from Jerusalem and Palestine. In the second half of the book, Paul continually returns to Jerusalem, only to set out deeper and deeper into the

---

[4] Hemer, *Book of Acts in the Setting of Hellenistic History*, 107.

Gentile world. A pattern of Jewish rejection of the Messiah followed by Gentile inclusion develops: the apologetic for Gentile inclusion in the first part of the book, which culminated in the Jerusalem Council (Acts 15:1–29), Paul's consistent pattern of preaching in the local synagogue in each city before moving on to the Gentiles, and Paul's repeated returns to Jerusalem. In Acts 28:25–27, Paul spoke to Jewish leaders and some believed in the Messiah. However, for those who did not, Paul cited Isa 6:9–10:

> The Holy Spirit correctly spoke through the prophet Isaiah to your forefathers when He said, "Go to this people and say: 'You will listen and listen, yet never understand; and you will look and look, yet never perceive. For this people's heart has grown callous, their ears are hard of hearing, and they have shut their eyes; otherwise they might see with their eyes and hear with their ears, understand with their heart, and be converted—and I would heal them.'"

Having thus explained the rejection of the gospel by the Jews, Paul drew the following implication: "Therefore, let it be known to you that this saving work of God has been sent to the Gentiles; they will listen!" (28:28). With this, the book of Acts closes. By this structure, Luke's purpose was to write an accurate historical narrative designed to edify his Christian readers and to help them evangelize unbelievers, including Diaspora Jews and non-Aramaic speakers familiar with the OT.

LITERATURE

Genre

The question regarding the genre of Acts is more than merely a matter of curiosity. The answer to this question helps one to identify the expectations one should have when approaching the book. Certain genres of literature have no or little expectation of trustworthiness or historical veracity (e.g., a fairy tale or a novel). It matters, therefore, whether the book of Acts was written as a collection of legends or as a serious historical narrative. Thus, identifying the genre of Acts is a significant aid in understanding Luke's purpose.

Similar to the Gospels, the literary genre of Acts is difficult to determine with certainty. The Gospels have been identified by some as a specialized form of biography, with the words and deeds of Jesus at the center. If so, at first sight, Luke's second volume does not seem to fit this description, as it features the deeds of more than one person: Peter, Stephen, Philip, Paul, and focus shifts from person to person. Stephen is only important in Acts 6 and 7, Philip in Acts 8. After Acts 15, Peter drops off the scene altogether; and then the main character is Paul, as the gospel moves through the known world. It seems that the personalities involved serve a purpose other than chronicling their lives. As such, there is one, and only one, major divine agent underlying the entire plot of the book of Acts: the Holy Spirit. For this reason, rather than identifying the book as presenting the "Acts of the Apostles," it may be more accurate to say that at its heart are the "Acts of the Holy Spirit."

In fact, this unity of what Jesus began to do during his earthly ministry and what he began to do in the power of the Holy Spirit following his ascension seems to be precisely what Luke implies in the opening verse of Acts: "I wrote the first narrative, Theophilus, about all that Jesus began to do and teach until the day He was taken up, after He had given orders through the Holy Spirit to the apostles whom He had chosen" (Acts 1:1–2). This may constitute the common ground between Luke's Gospel and Acts and mark both books as a literary unity.

The genre of Acts is also similar to OT historiography, wherein history is ancient historiography with a theological focus. Blomberg called it a "theological history,"[5] which seems to be a satisfying way of capturing the nature of the book. If so, the reader should expect the book to set forth a historical narrative that strives not only for accuracy in its portrayal of events but also to be God-centered in its approach to history. In Acts, God is engendering salvation history.

Literary Plan

The basic blueprint of Acts is given at Acts 1:8: "But you will receive power when the Holy Spirit has come upon you, and you will be my witnesses in Jerusalem, in all Judea and Samaria, and to the ends of the earth." The rest of the book shows the fulfillment of Jesus' command and the unfolding of God's plan from the church in Jerusalem and Judea (1:1–6:7) to Samaria (6:8–9:31) and to the ends of the earth (9:32–28:31).[6] Luke took pains to show that the expansion of Christianity was at God's direction, including the Gentiles, while at the same time continuing salvation "to the Jews first."

At the heart of the book is the Jerusalem Council (chap. 15) where the church regulated the inclusion of the Gentiles in the rapidly growing Christian movement. Paul's ministry is presented through three missionary journeys (one before and two after the Jerusalem Council). Similar to Luke's Gospel, where the extended "Lukan Travel Narrative" shows Jesus on his way to Jerusalem, the action slows down during the last quarter of the book of Acts as Paul made his way to trial in Rome. Unlike Luke's Gospel—where Jesus is arrested, tried, and crucified, and on the third day rises from the dead—Acts ends on an inconclusive note, with Paul still awaiting trial in Rome.[7]

OUTLINE

I. FOUNDATIONS FOR THE CHURCH AND ITS MISSION (1:1–2:47)
    A. Preface (1:1–5)
    B. Jerusalem: Waiting for the Spirit (1:6–26)

---

[5] C. L. Blomberg, *From Pentecost to Patmos: An Introduction to Acts Through Revelation* (Nashville: B&H, 2006), 17.

[6] Commentators outline the book in slightly different ways. See, e.g., F. F. Bruce, *The Book of Acts*, NICNT, rev. ed. (Grand Rapids: Eerdmans, 1988), vii–xiv; and D. L. Bock, *Acts*, BECNT (Grand Rapids: Baker, 2007), vii–viii. For other outlines see I. H. Marshall, *The Acts of the Apostles*, TNTC (Grand Rapids: Eerdmans, 1980), 51–54; J. R. W. Stott, *The Spirit, the Church, and the World: The Message of Acts* (Downers Grove: InterVarsity, 1990), 3–4; and W. J. Larkin Jr., *Acts*, IVPNTC (Downers Grove: InterVarsity, 1995), 34–36.

[7] A few of the headings in the outline below are borrowed from the useful book by H. A. Kent Jr., *Jerusalem to Rome: Studies in Acts* (Grand Rapids: Baker, 1972), 7.

C. Pentecost: The Church Is Born (2:1–47)

II. THE CHURCH IN JERUSALEM (3:1–6:7)
A. A Miracle and Its Aftermath (3:1–4:31)
B. Trouble Within and Without (4:32–6:7)

III. WIDER HORIZONS FOR THE CHURCH: STEPHEN, SAMARIA, AND SAUL (6:8–9:31)
A. Suffering: One of the Servants Arrested and Martyred (6:8–7:60)
B. Palestine and Syria: Philip, Saul, and Peter (8:1–9:30)
C. Summary: Judea, Galilee, and Samaria (9:31)

IV. PETER AND THE FIRST GENTILE CONVERT (9:32–12:24)
A. The Proof of Gentile Conversion (9:32–11:18)
B. Gentile Conversion in Antioch and the Return of Paul (11:19–26)
C. Events in Jerusalem (11:27–12:24)

V. PAUL TURNS TO THE GENTILES (12:25–16:5)
A. First Missionary Journey (12:25–14:28)
B. Jerusalem Council (15:1–35)
C. Second Missionary Journey Begins (15:36–16:5)

VI. FURTHER PENETRATION INTO THE GENTILE WORLD (16:6–19:20)
A. Second Missionary Journey (16:6–18:22)
B. Third Missionary Journey (18:23–19:20)

VII. ON TO ROME (19:21–28:31)
A. From Ephesus to Jerusalem (19:21–21:16)
B. Paul's Final Visit to Jerusalem and His Removal to Caesarea (21:17–23:35)
C. Paul's Defenses Before Felix, Festus, and Agrippa (24:1–26:32)
D. Paul's Trip to Rome (27:1–28:31)

UNIT-BY-UNIT DISCUSSION

I. Foundations for the Church and Its Mission (1:1–2:41)

A. Preface (1:1–5)   The book of Acts opens by referring to the "first narrative," Luke's Gospel, which narrated that which Jesus began to do and teach. By implication, Acts, the sequel, sets forth the continuation of God's plan by recording what Jesus *continued* to do and teach through the Holy Spirit and the apostolic church. The resurrected Jesus reminded the disciples of the promised Holy Spirit and commanded them to wait for his imminent coming in Jerusalem.

B. Jerusalem: Waiting for the Spirit (1:6–26)   The disciples asked when Jesus would establish his kingdom, but Jesus just told them that they would be his Spirit-empowered witnesses. A period of waiting and praying followed as the early believers prepared for the coming of the Spirit (1:6–14). Acts 1:15–26 shows the replacement of Judas by the Eleven. After setting the ground rules, Matthias was selected by lot.

C. Pentecost: The Church Is Born (2:1–47)   When the day of Pentecost arrived, the gathered disciples experienced the coming of the Holy Spirit (2:1–13), which took place in fulfillment of Jesus' promise (see 1:8). Because devout Jews from every nation were present, all Israel was represented. These worshippers heard the word of God in their own languages and witnessed the power of the Spirit, a sign of the end time. In this way the coming of the Spirit at Pentecost highlights the worldwide implications of the gospel, reversing the confusion of languages that ensued at the tower of Babel incident (Gen 11:1–9).

Peter explained the significance of the events that had transpired (2:14–40). In essence, the logic of Peter's address is as follows: (1) the Spirit had now been poured out; (2) Jesus predicted that this would occur once he had been exalted with God subsequent to his ascension (Luke 24:49; see Acts 1:8–9); (3) hence the coming of the Spirit proved that Jesus had now been exalted: "Therefore, since He has been exalted to the right hand of God and has received from the Father the promised Holy Spirit, he has poured out what you both see and hear" (2:33).

Peter quoted the prophecy of Joel 2:28–32 to explain that this was the promised coming of the Holy Spirit (2:14–21). The last line of Joel's prophecy, "Then whoever calls on the name of the Lord will be saved," transitions into Peter's evangelistic appeal (2:22–36). He concluded with a call to repentance (2:37–40), with the result that 3,000 were converted. The citation of Joel 2:28–32 can be compared to the citation of Isa 61:1–2 in Luke 4:18–19 in that it sets the stage for the rest of the book by narrating the coming of the Spirit to all those who called on the name of the Lord.

Luke concluded his account of these preliminary events with the first of several summaries that mark the transitions (2:41–47). The church devoted itself to the apostles' teaching (the standard of doctrinal orthodoxy prior to the formation of the NT), to fellowship, to the breaking of bread (i.e., celebrating the Lord's Supper), and to prayers (note the plural in the original Greek, which may suggest set prayers). Many miraculous signs and wonders were performed by the apostles. The believers shared everything in common, worshipped God in gladness, and continually grew in numbers.

II. The Church in Jerusalem (3:1–6:7)

A. A Miracle and Its Aftermath (3:1–4:31)   God performed a remarkable miracle through Peter who, together with John, was on his way to the hour of prayer in the temple (3:1–10). When approached for money by a man born lame, Peter healed the man, whose great rejoicing drew a large crowd. Peter's ensuing speech at the temple (3:13–26) charged the people with putting Jesus to death but acknowledged that they had done so out of ignorance. Peter told the crowd that they would experience "times of refreshing" if they repented and followed Jesus.

At this, Peter and John were seized by the Jewish leaders (4:1–4). This gave Peter the opportunity to extend a similar message to the Sanhedrin, albeit without an appeal to repent. Subsequently, Peter and John were released with orders to stop talking about Jesus

(4:5–22). Upon their return to the community of believers, the place was shaken, and the believers were all filled with the Holy Spirit to "speak God's message with boldness" (4:31).

B. Trouble Within and Without (4:32–6:7) This section of Acts shows the nature of the new community and the lengths to which God was prepared to go to protect her purity. Barnabas, first mentioned here, sold a piece of property and donated the proceeds to the church (4:32–37). This spurred a couple in the church, Ananias and Sapphira, to do the same but to keep back a portion for themselves. By itself, this was unobjectionable, but lying about it in order to increase one's stature was an affront to God. The couple was severely judged: first Ananias and then his wife were struck dead on the spot (5:1–11). As a result, great fear came upon the church.

Undaunted, the apostles preached continually in the temple, boldly healing in Jesus' name (5:12–16). Once more the apostles were arrested but freed by an angel who told them to go on so they could "tell the people all about this life" (5:20). When arrested again and forbidden to preach about Jesus, the apostles retorted, "We must obey God rather than men" (5:29). Gamaliel's advice to his fellow Sanhedrin members was to wait and see. If this movement was not from God, it would fail, as other movements had done in the past. After receiving a flogging, the apostles returned joyfully to preaching the word, in direct disobedience to the Sanhedrin (5:40) but in obedience to God.

The section concludes with a return to the community life of the young church. A potential crisis was averted by the church's selection of seven qualified, Spirit-filled men to meet the needs of a group of Hellenistic widows (6:1–7). Stephen, the main character of chap. 7, is introduced as a man full of faith and the Holy Spirit. Luke summarized the state of the church by highlighting the effective witness borne in Jerusalem. In particular, Luke noted that even a large number of priests came to the faith (6:7).

III. Wider Horizons for the Church: Stephen, Samaria, and Saul (6:8–9:31)

A. Suffering: One of the Servants Arrested and Martyred (Acts 6:8–7:60) Stephen, introduced in the previous section, was falsely accused of speaking against "Moses and God" before the Sanhedrin by those of "the Freedmen's Synagogue" (6:8–15). Stephen's defense (chap. 7) shows how throughout Israel's history, the nation opposed God's plan and persecuted its own. In a sense, this unit serves as the completion of the last section in its emphasis on Jewish responsibility. Stephen's martyrdom and vision led to the events that are narrated in the following chapters.

B. Palestine and Syria: Philip, Saul, and Peter (8:1–9:31) Stephen's death sparked a period of great persecution for the church. Saul, who had played a major role in Stephen's stoning, was ravaging the church (8:1–3). The believers, except for the apostles, were scattered throughout the surrounding regions, which resulted in the extension of the gospel beyond Judea to Samaria, in fulfillment of Jesus' mandate (see 1:8).

Philip, one of the seven (6:5), performed signs in Samaria and preached Christ to the Samaritans (8:4–8). However, the Samaritans did not receive the Spirit upon salvation until Peter and John, representing the apostles, came and laid hands on the Samaritan believers. This served to authenticate God's work among them. In the process, Simon the sorcerer, who sought to purchase the power of the Holy Spirit from Peter for money, was rebuked (8:9–25).

Subsequently, Philip, again at the direction of the Holy Spirit, encountered a court official for Candace, the queen of Ethiopia, and led him to Christ (8:26–38). Although Gentile by birth, he was probably a proselyte (God-fearer?). The Holy Spirit miraculously transported Philip to Azotus, where he evangelized the coastal regions all the way to Caesarea (8:39–40). The gospel then moved throughout the regions of Judea and Samaria.

The final chapter in this section records the conversion of Saul in preparation for the Gentile mission (9:1–31). While on the road to Damascus to persecute Christians, Saul encountered the risen Christ and was converted. This marks a momentous occasion in the mission of the early church. The major opponent of Christianity became the greatest protagonist of the church's mission, and he would take the gospel to the "ends of the earth."

To Ananias, a disciple charged with ministering to Saul, Jesus described Saul as his "chosen instrument to carry My name before Gentiles, kings, and the sons of Israel" (9:15). Although first met with skepticism, Saul preached the gospel powerfully in Damascus. Later, the Jerusalem church received him at the intercession of Barnabas. Saul preached boldly in the name of Jesus until an assassination attempt forced the brothers to take him to Tarsus via Caesarea.

Luke concluded this section with a summary that includes a reference to the church enjoying a period of peace and increase in numbers. Thus, Luke chronicled the plan of God as expressed in 1:8, taking the gospel through Jerusalem and Judea and Samaria. His next step was to provide a clear demonstration that Gentiles can be saved without converting to Judaism first, and this is the subject of the next two major sections.

IV. Peter and the First Gentile Convert (9:32–12:24)

A. The Proof of Gentile Conversion (9:32–11:18) Peter apparently had an itinerant ministry in Palestine. The healing of Aeneas the paralytic in Lydda led to raising Dorcas in Joppa (9:32–43). It also set up the account of the encounter with the Roman centurion Cornelius (chap. 10). While in Joppa, Peter received a vision which impressed on him that he should not consider anyone "unclean" (10:9–29). Meanwhile, Cornelius received a vision to call for Peter in Joppa. When Cornelius believed, Peter was convinced that God had accepted a Gentile into the church (10:24–48). Peter, in turn, convinced skeptics among the Jewish Christians that Cornelius's conversion was genuine (11:1–18).

B. Gentile Conversion in Antioch and the Return of Paul (11:19–26) Those scattered because of the persecution of Stephen reached Syrian Antioch, preaching only to Jews. But men from Cyprus and Cyrene preached to the Gentiles (the term "Hellenists" means "speakers of Greek," which refers to Gentiles). The Lord was with them, and a large number were converted. Barnabas was sent to investigate, observed the genuineness of the conversion, and sought out Saul in Tarsus, teaching daily for the period of a year. Also, believers were first called "Christians" in Antioch.

C. Events in Jerusalem (11:27–12:24)   The events in Jerusalem are sandwiched between references to Saul and Barnabas's relief mission in response to a famine (11:27–30; 12:25), indicating not only the solidarity the new Gentile believers had with the Jerusalem church but also that God was still moving among the Jews.

Peter's miraculous release apparently so infuriated Herod Agrippa I that when he could not find Peter, he executed the guards and left town. Having given an oration and received the adoration of men as a god, Herod was "infected with worms and died" (12:1–23).

Another Lukan summary statement concludes the section, noting that the word of God continued to spread. Barnabas and Saul returned to Antioch from their mission to Jerusalem, accompanied by John Mark, who would later go with them on the first part of their first missionary journey and, later still, write the Second Gospel.

V. Paul Turns to the Gentiles (13:1–16:5)

A. First Missionary Journey (13:1–14:28)   The gospel's penetration into the Gentile world began with a specific call by the Holy Spirit through the prophets at Antioch to set aside Barnabas and Saul for the missionary enterprise. Ironically, what Saul, prior to his conversion, sought to prevent by persecuting Christians in Damascus (also in Syria), he now actively brought about: the spread of the gospel to Syria and beyond. Once commissioned, they began their journey at Barnabas's home on the island of Cyprus (13:4; see 4:26). Paul blinded Elymas the sorcerer because he "opposed them and tried to turn the proconsul away from the faith" (13:8). But the proconsul Sergius Paulus was converted.

Paul and Barnabas then traveled through Pisidian Antioch, and 13:16–41 details Paul's sermon in the local synagogue. The Jews and proselytes begged Paul to preach again the next Sabbath, and the ensuing crowds sparked jealousy and derision from the members of the synagogue. Paul then turned to the Gentiles, and the gospel spread throughout the area. But the Jews instigated a persecution against Paul and Barnabas, expelling them from the region. This, then, forms the pattern throughout the first journey: synagogue, reception, rejection, persecution.

The results in Iconium were similar to Pisidian Antioch (14:1–7). Paul preached in the synagogue and then suffered persecution. At Lystra, Barnabas and Paul were met with a warm reception that almost turned to idolatry after the healing of a man who had been lame from birth. But the Jews from Iconium and Antioch swayed the crowds to stone Paul, and they left him for dead. Paul then evangelized Derbe (14:8–20) and made a return trip through Derbe, Iconium, and Lystra, establishing elders in every church, on his way to Antioch in Syria (14:21–28).

B. Jerusalem Council (15:1–35)   The Jerusalem Council is a pivotal event for the Gentile mission. The question of Gentile converts is settled by this special meeting of the apostles and elders in Jerusalem. The issue was whether Gentiles had to become Jewish proselytes before they could become Christians (see 15:1,5). The issue was settled by the testimonies of Peter, Paul, and Barnabas, and ultimately James adjudicated the matter by citing Amos 9:11. At the conclusion of the meeting, a letter was sent (see 15:23–29) that encouraged the Gentiles to abstain from things particularly repulsive to Jews (15:20,29).

C. Second Missionary Journey Begins (15:36–16:5)   Traditionally, 15:36 has been seen as marking the beginning of Paul's second missionary journey. This journey is presented in terms of encouraging the church in Syrian Antioch and the young churches planted during the first journey. The letter mentioned in the previous section was taken to the churches of South Galatia. Silas replaced Barnabas after Barnabas and Paul disagreed on whether to take John Mark with them. Paul said no because of Mark's desertion early in the first missionary journey. But Barnabas wanted to give his nephew another chance, so they parted company. While in Lystra, Timothy was highly recommended by the churches and joined Paul and Silas. The section concludes with a summary that notes the growth and encouragement of the churches.

VI. Further Penetration into the Gentile World (16:6–19:20)

A. Second Missionary Journey (16:6–18:22)   Like every genuine new movement of the gospel into new lands or people groups, God is the one who instigated the irresistible spread of the gospel in the mission of the early church. Paul's plan was to continue through Asia Minor, but the Spirit prevented him from doing so. When he had a dream about a Macedonian calling him for help, he proceeded to go there, "concluding that God had called us to evangelize them" (16:10).

Paul's first stop after crossing the Hellespont was Philippi, where the first "we section" occurs (starting in 16:10). Paul's pattern, consistent with God's salvation-historical plan, was to begin with the Jewish residents of a given city or region and then turn to the Gentiles. The first convert to the Christian gospel in Europe was Lydia, a merchant selling an expensive purple cloth.

The confrontation with a demon-possessed young woman led to a painful but fruitful encounter with the magistrates of the city. Paul and his companions were jailed but found this incident to be a platform for the gospel. The jailer was converted, and the magistrates offered to release Paul. But Paul, appealing to his Roman citizenship, would not let the magistrates beat him and his associates in public and then release them secretly. Paul demanded, and received, a public apology, but he and his coworkers were urged to leave town.

In Thessalonica, Paul stayed consistent in following the pattern "to the Jew first, and also to the Gentile" (see 17:2: "as usual"). Preaching in the synagogue for at least three Sabbaths, Paul showed people from the Scriptures "that the Messiah had to suffer and rise from the dead" and that the Messiah was Jesus (17:3). When Gentiles came to Christ in large numbers, the Jews became jealous and hired scoundrels to persecute the believers. When this was brought to the attention of the magistrates, they fined Paul's host while Paul and the missionary team departed for Berea. After early success, the Jews from Thessalonica followed them to Berea and stirred up more violence until Paul was forced to go to Athens.

Athens, a major intellectual center, provided Paul with a great challenge in his missionary preaching. He found the city full of idols and reasoned with Epicurean and Stoic philosophers, who considered the apostle a "pseudo-intellectual" (literally, a "seed picker," that is, one who picks up scraps; 17:18). Some thought Paul spoke of "foreign deities" because he proclaimed Jesus and the resurrection (17:18). Paul began his address by referring to an altar he had observed that bore the inscription "To an unknown God" (17:23). From this Paul declared the good news of Jesus and his resurrection from the dead. Some ridiculed Paul, but a few believed, among them Dionysius the Areopagite and a woman named Damaris (17:34). On the whole, Paul met with less positive response than on other occasions in his missionary preaching.

The next stop was Corinth, where Paul met with Aquila and Priscilla, Jewish Christians recently expelled from Rome. Again Paul reasoned in the synagogues. When the people there steadfastly resisted, Paul turned to the Gentiles. Crispus, the leader of the synagogue, was converted along with many Corinthians. Paul stayed in Corinth for 18 months. Ultimately, the conflict with the Jews ended up with Paul standing before the Roman proconsul Gallio, who decided he had no jurisdiction in Jewish religious matters. Paul then left for Syria via Ephesus.

B. Third Missionary Journey (18:23–19:20)   Although from here on Paul traveled to Jerusalem and on to Antioch, the focus is on Ephesus. When Paul left Corinth, he briefly went to Ephesus. After preaching in the synagogue, Paul was asked to stay longer but declined, saying, "I'll come back to you again, if God wills" (18:21). His return occurred two verses later. In the meantime, he traveled to Caesarea, Jerusalem, Antioch, and back, visiting some of the churches of the first journey, and then arrived back in Ephesus. There Paul encountered a residual John the Baptist movement (18:24–19:7), engaged in some initial missionary work (19:8–10), and performed extraordinary acts of ministry (19:11–20).

VII. On to Rome (19:21–28:31)

A. From Ephesus to Jerusalem (19:21–21:16)   Paul planned to go to Rome after visiting Macedonia, Achaia, and Jerusalem, and this itinerary dominates the concluding section of the book. Paul's later vision (see 23:11) reinforces this plan, and Rome is the target on the horizon throughout this last section of the book. Before Paul departed from Ephesus, however, there was a strong pagan uprising. Once again, the Christians brought before the crowd were shown to be innocent of the charges brought against them. Paul traveled through Macedonia and Greece and set sail for Miletus. There he met with the Ephesian elders and gave them farewell instructions. The final unit of this section (21:1–16) marks the beginning of Paul's last journey before his arrest, and at every stop he was warned about difficulties awaiting him in Jerusalem.

B. Arrival, Unrest, and Arrest in Jerusalem (21:17–23:35) Upon arriving in Jerusalem, Paul was invited to pay for a Jewish vow to alleviate suspicion among the Jewish believers. But a charge from Jews of Asia Minor that Paul brought a Gentile into the temple created a riot. Paul was seized by the Roman soldiers garrisoned at the fortress of Antonia. (Ironically, the false charge that Paul brought a Gentile into the temple caused Gentiles to enter the temple to rescue Paul.)

C. Paul's Defenses Before Felix, Festus, and Agrippa (24:1–26:32) After being allowed to give his defense before the crowd, Paul, over a period of at least two years, was brought before Felix (24:1–27), Porcius Festus (25:1–12), and Agrippa (25:13–27). Paul's appeal to Caesar necessitated the trip to Rome even though Paul was declared innocent of the charges at each interrogation (26:1–32).

D. Paul's Trip to Rome (27:1–28:31) The actual seafaring journey comprises almost two-thirds of the final two chapters of the book. Just as God had been the major impetus behind the church's missionary expansion, he was also the driving force on the journey to Rome. While Paul was not in control of his movements, neither were the Romans. God's providence is clearly accentuated through this final section of the book. It ultimately brought Paul to Rome and proved God powerful throughout the journey.

When Paul arrived in Rome, he followed the pattern set throughout his ministry and met with the Jews first, with moderate success. Regarding those who rejected the message, Paul cited Isa 6:9–10 in order to show that the rejection of the Jews was not unexpected. After this, the Gentiles were invited to trust in Christ. Thus Luke concluded the book with Paul under house arrest in Rome yet preaching unhindered to all who would hear, Jews and Gentiles alike.

THEOLOGY

Theological Themes

The Holy Spirit Acts emphasizes that just as God is sovereign in moving the gospel forward the Holy Spirit is the agent of the church's life and growth. Luke described his Gospel as recording "all that Jesus began to do and teach" (Acts 1:1), implying that the book of Acts is about the continuing activity of Christ. This activity was accomplished through the Holy Spirit.[8] Hence, the disciples were commanded to wait for the promise of the Spirit (1:4,8). His coming at Pentecost signaled the beginning of the church's advance (2:1–4,33), and his reception is proof of salvation (2:4; 8:16; 10:46; cf. 19:6).

---

[8] A few times in Acts the Lord Jesus himself appears and communicates (1:4–8; 7:56; 9:1–18; and 23:11), although these occasions can hardly be separated from the ministry of the Holy Spirit.

The Holy Spirit was the one who sovereignly directed and empowered the Christian mission. Jesus gave orders through the Holy Spirit (1:2). Peter's citation of Joel 2:28 (2:16–21) connects Pentecost to the fulfillment of Scripture and is programmatic for the entire book. Philip was ordered by the Holy Spirit (8:29,39) just as Peter was instructed to receive Gentiles (10:19–20). Barnabas and Saul were set apart and directed by the Holy Spirit (13:2,4), who later initiated Paul's departure to the Greek peninsula (16:6–10; cf. 20:22–23,28; 21:4). Indeed, it is hard to overstate the Spirit's post-Easter role in salvation history.[9]

The Resurrection and Ascension of Jesus   The key juncture in salvation history is the death, resurrection, and exaltation of Jesus. In the proclamation of the gospel, this cluster of significant events is the pivot point of history and the culmination of God's plan from long ago. This plan was commanded by God (4:23), predicted by the prophets (26:22), accomplished in Christ (13:28–39), and proclaimed by faithful witnesses (4:33). The resurrection of Jesus is the proof of Jesus' claims (see 3:15; 5:20; 25:19). It is also the guarantee of a personal resurrection for chosen humanity (see 24:15; 26:23).

Luke's teaching on the resurrection of Christ entails not merely a restoration from the dead but an unprecedented exaltation, for Jesus was elevated to the right hand of God. Strategic references to the ascension in Luke–Acts at the end of the Gospel and at the beginning of Acts demonstrate its importance in Luke's theology (see also 13:33–34). Jesus reigns as God's Messiah from the heavenly throne. For this reason, Jesus' resurrection is also the starting point for the restoration of Israel—it is the "hope of Israel" (28:20), a restoration that begins with faith in the Messiah and reconstitutes God's people by bringing together into one body both believing Jews and Gentiles (4:10–12).[10]

POINTS OF APPLICATION

- Follow the leading of the Holy Spirit (1:5; chap. 2; 13:3–4)
- Be part of the movement spreading the gospel to the ends of the earth (1:8)
- Realize that the church's mission is fueled by the power of Christ's resurrection (2:32)
- Do not erect any unnecessary barriers for people to come to faith (chaps. 10 and 15)
- When reading and interpreting Acts, realize that it is historical narrative and not everything written in the book is necessarily normative for the church today

---

[9] Although Luke understood that the Spirit was involved in the writing of the OT (e.g., some OT passages are identified as having come through the Holy Spirit: 1:16; 4:25–26; 28:25), the reception of the Spirit is clearly an end-time event.

[10] See the fine treatment in F. Thielman, *Theology of the New Testament: A Canonical and Synthetic Approach* (Grand Rapids: Zondervan, 2005), 123–24.

STUDY QUESTIONS

1. Who wrote Acts? Was the author an apostle? What ensures that the criterion of apostolicity was met?
2. Who was Theophilus, how do we know who he was, and what was his likely role with regard to Luke/Acts?
3. Why is the question regarding genre important for studying Acts?
4. What is the basic "blueprint" for Acts, and why?
5. What was the major issue discussed at the Jerusalem Council?
6. What role does the Holy Spirit play in Acts?

FOR FURTHER STUDY

Barnett, P. *The Birth of Christianity: The First Twenty Years*. Vol. 1: *After Jesus*. Grand Rapids: Eerdmans, 2005.

Bauckham, R., ed. *The Book of Acts in Its First Century Setting*. Vol. 4: *Palestinian Setting*. Grand Rapids: Eerdmans, 1995.

Blomberg, C. L. *From Pentecost to Patmos: An Introduction to Acts through Revelation*. Nashville: B&H, 2006.

Bock, D. L. *Acts*. Baker Exegetical Commentary on the New Testament. Grand Rapids: Baker, 2007.

Bruce, F. F. *The Book of Acts*. Rev. ed. New International Commentary on the New Testament. Grand Rapids: Eerdmans, 1988.

Gill, D. W. J., and C. Gempf, eds. *The Book of Acts in Its First Century Setting*. Vol. 2: *Greco-Roman Setting*. Grand Rapids: Eerdmans, 1994.

Köstenberger, A. J., and P. T. O'Brien. *Salvation to the Ends of the Earth*. New Studies in Biblical Theology 11. Downers Grove: InterVarsity, 2001.

Larkin, W. J. *Acts*. IVP New Testament Commentary. Downers Grove: InterVarsity, 1995.

Levinskaya, I. *The Book of Acts in Its First Century Setting*. Vol. 5: *Diaspora Setting*. Grand Rapids: Eerdmans, 1996.

Longenecker, R. N. "Acts." In *The Expositor's Bible Commentary*. Rev. ed. Vol. 10. Grand Rapids: Zondervan, 2007.

Marshall, I. H. *The Acts of the Apostles*. Tyndale New Testament Commentary. Grand Rapids: Eerdmans, 1980.

Marshall, I. H., and D. Peterson, eds. *Witness to the Gospel: The Theology of Acts*. Grand Rapids: Eerdmans, 1998.

Polhill, J. *Acts*. New American Commentary 26. Nashville: B&H, 1992.

Rapske, B. *The Book of Acts in Its First Century Setting*. Vol. 3: *The Book of Acts and Paul in Roman Custody*. Grand Rapids: Eerdmans, 2004.

Schlatter, A. *The Theology of the Apostles: The Development of New Testament Theology*. Translated by A. J. Köstenberger. Grand Rapids: Baker, 1999.

Schnabel, E. J. *Early Christian Mission*. 2 vols. Downers Grove: InterVarsity, 2004.

Stott, J. R. W. *The Spirit, the Church, and the World: The Message of Acts*. Downers Grove: InterVarsity, 1990.

Chapter 9

Introduction to Paul and His Letters

CORE KNOWLEDGE

Students should be able to list several of Paul's quotations of and allusions to Jesus' teachings. They should be prepared to describe Paul's conversion and his gospel. They should know the major dates associated with Paul's life, including his conversion, missionary journeys, imprisonments, and death.

INTRODUCTION

ONE CANNOT MASTER the content of the NT and ignore the apostle Paul. After encountering the risen Jesus on the road to Damascus, Saul of Tarsus became the outstanding missionary, theologian, and writer of the early church.[1] He was a central figure both in the NT and in the history of Christianity. He wrote 13 letters that comprise almost one-fourth of the NT. Approximately 16 chapters of the book of Acts (13–28) focus on his missionary labors, describing him as the most effective missionary in all of history. Consequently, Paul was the author or subject of nearly one-third of the NT and the most influential interpreter of the teachings of Christ and of the significance of his life, death, and resurrection. This chapter introduces this important man and his message.

PAUL'S RELATIONSHIP TO JESUS

Introduction

Most readers of the NT automatically assume that Jesus was the founder of Christianity and that Paul was a faithful follower of Jesus who propagated Jesus' teachings throughout

---

[1] See esp. Eckhard J. Schnabel, *Paul the Missionary: Realities, Strategies, and Methods* (Downers Grove: InterVarsity, 2008).

the world. Although some have questioned this view,[2] by asserting that Paul, not Jesus, was the founder of Christianity,[3] the traditional view remains the best reading of the evidence. Indeed, there is significant evidence for Paul's dependence on the teachings of Jesus.

Allusions to Jesus' teachings in Paul's letters are a primary piece of this evidence, and, as such, far more extensive and frequent than many scholars have recognized. Allusions are likely when (1) Paul used an explicit tradition indicator such as "the Lord commanded" or "word from the Lord"; (2) the suspected allusion contains linguistic or thematic echoes from the Gospels; or (3) a series of several possible allusions appears in a particular context.

An investigation by D. Wenham concluded that "there is massive evidence of Pauline knowledge of Jesus-traditions."[4] Wenham categorized allusions in Paul to the sayings of Jesus as highly probable, probable, or plausible. The chart below summarizes some of the most important of Wenham's findings.

Table 9.1: Highly Probable Allusions to Jesus in Paul's Letters

Sayings and Acts of Jesus	Allusions by Paul
Last Supper (Matt 26:26–30; Mark 14:22–26; esp. Luke 22:14–23)	1 Cor 11:23–26
Resurrection narratives (Luke 24:36–49; John 20:19–29; 21:1–14)	1 Cor 15:3–5,35–57; Phil 3:21
Divorce (Mark 10:1–12; Matt 19:1–12)	1 Cor 7:10–11
Support of preachers (Matt 10:10; Luke 10:7)	1 Cor 9:14; 1 Tim 5:18
Eschatological teaching (Matthew 24; Mark 13; esp. Luke 21)	2 Thess 2:1–12
Eschatological parables: Thief in the night (Matt 24:43–44) Watchman (Luke 12:36–38) Stewards (Matt 24:45–51; Luke 12:42–48) Wise and foolish virgins (Matt 25:1–13)	1 Thess 4:1–5:11
Mountain-moving faith (Matt 17:20)	1 Cor 13:2
Nonretaliation (Matt 5:38–42; Luke 6:29–30)	Rom 12:14
Love and the law (Matt 22:37–40)	Rom 13:8–10; Gal 5:14
Nothing unclean (Matt 15:10–20; Mark 7:17–23)	Rom 14:14
Abba (Mark 14:36)	Rom 8:15; Gal 4:6

---

[2] Beginning in 1845 (original German edition) with F. C. Baur, *Paul, the Apostle of Jesus Christ*, trans. A. Menzies, 2 vols. (London: Williams & Norgate, 1875), and continued by W. Wrede's *Paul* (London: Green, 1907) and R. Bultmann, "Jesus and Paul," in *Existence and Faith* (London: Hodder & Stoughton, 1936).

[3] This organically develops from the quest for the historical Jesus (see chap. 3 above). If there is a discontinuity between the "Jesus of history" and the "Christ of faith," the question naturally arises, "From where did Paul get his religion?"

[4] David Wenham, *Paul: Follower of Jesus or Founder of Christianity?* (Grand Rapids: Eerdmans, 1995), 381.

Continuity and Development

Although Paul stands in continuity with Jesus' teachings, several important factors in the mission of Paul required him both to develop and to modify the message of Jesus. (1) Jesus' passion, resurrection, and glorification demanded an emphasis on the exalted Christ. (2) The death and exaltation of the Messiah and the outpouring of the Spirit introduced a new eschatological era and enacted a new covenant between God and his people. (3) The differences between Jesus' Jewish audience and Paul's Gentile audience required Paul to use different idioms and thought forms in order to relate to his own cultural context.[5] Nevertheless, J. M. G. Barclay concluded that "there is sufficient evidence to show that, whether consciously or otherwise, Paul did develop the central insights of the teaching of Jesus and the central meaning of his life and death in a way that truly represented their dynamic and fullest significance."[6]

Although Paul's contributions to the Christian faith should not be underestimated, Paul should be recognized as a faithful follower of Jesus Christ rather than as the founder of a form of Christianity that deviated drastically from the teachings of Jesus. Paul's teachings originated from his reflection on the life and teachings of Jesus, his study of the OT, and his contemplation on the significance of his Damascus road experience.[7] Although the major motifs of his theology are rooted in the message of Jesus himself, Paul was necessarily an innovator who pored over the Hebrew Scriptures as he addressed the unique challenges raised by the churches that he influenced.

The fact that Paul's mission primarily addressed Gentile congregations whereas Jesus' ministry was primarily focused on Palestinian Jews meant that Paul often had to look beyond Jesus back to the OT to present the implications of Jesus' death, burial, and resurrection for his audience. However, the differences between Jesus' teaching and Paul's letters are like the difference between the seed and the mature plant, the foundation and the superstructure built upon it. In Paul's letters to the churches, one hears not only the voice of the Spirit that inspired the OT Scriptures but also the voice of Jesus, Paul's Savior and Lord.

THE LIFE OF PAUL

Introduction

Saul of Tarsus became the apostle Paul, the outstanding missionary, theologian, and writer of the early church.[8] He was the author or subject of nearly one-third of the NT and

---

[5] See J. M. G. Barclay, "Jesus and Paul," in *Dictionary of Paul and His Letters*, ed. G. F. Hawthorne, R. P. Martin, and D. G. Reid (Downers Grove: InterVarsity, 1993), 502; A. J. Köstenberger, "Review of David Wenham, *Paul: Follower of Jesus or Founder of Christianity?*" *TrinJ* NS 16 (1995): 259–62.

[6] Barclay, "Jesus and Paul," 502.

[7] For the significance of the Damascus road experience for Paul's theology, see S. Kim, *The Origin of Paul's Gospel* (Grand Rapids: Eerdmans: 1982). For the significance of the OT for Paul and his methods of OT exegesis, see E. E. Ellis, *Paul's Use of the Old Testament* (Grand Rapids: Baker, 1981).

[8] On Paul as a missionary, see especially A. J. Köstenberger and P. T. O'Brien, *Salvation to the Ends of the Earth: A Biblical Theology of Mission*, NSBT 11 (Downers Grove: InterVarsity, 2001), chap. 7. Cf. E. J. Schnabel, *Early Christian*

the most important interpreter of the teachings of Christ and of the significance of his life, death, and resurrection. This section provides a brief biography of Paul and describes the gospel he proclaimed. His proclamation of the gospel demonstrated his continuity with and obedience to Jesus Christ.

Early Life and Training (1–33)

Birth and Family Background Paul was born in a Jewish family in Tarsus of Cilicia (Acts 22:3), probably early in the first decade of the first century. According to a tradition recorded by Jerome (c. 345–420), Paul's family had moved to Tarsus from Gischala in Galilee.[9] Paul's family was of the tribe of Benjamin (Phil 3:5). His parents named him Saul in honor of the most prominent member of the tribe in Jewish history—King Saul. Paul came from a family of tent makers or leatherworkers and, according to Jewish custom, was taught this trade by his father.[10] Apparently, the business thrived, and Paul's family became moderately wealthy. Paul was a citizen of the city of Tarsus, "an important city" (Acts 21:39). According to one ancient writer, the monetary requirement for Tarsian citizenship was 500 drachmae, a year and a half's wages (Dio Chrysostom, *Orations* 34.1–23).

Roman Citizenship More importantly, Paul was born a Roman citizen. Many interpreters speculate that Paul's father or grandfather was honored with citizenship because of some special service rendered to a military proconsul.[11] However, early Christian tradition (preserved by Jerome; see also Photius, ninth century) states that Paul's parents had been carried as prisoners of war from Gischala to Tarsus, enslaved to a Roman citizen, and then freed and granted citizenship.[12] Regardless of how Paul's parents received their citizenship, Acts states three times that Paul possessed Roman citizenship, and this privilege was accompanied by important rights that would benefit him in his missionary labors. The Roman citizen had the right of appeal after a trial, exemption from imperial service, right to choose between a local or Roman trial, and protection from degrading forms of punishment such as scourging and crucifixion. Paul might have carried a wax tablet that functioned as a birth certificate or certificate of citizenship in order to prove his Roman citizenship. However, most people who claimed citizenship were trusted since the penalty for impersonating a Roman citizen was death.

Paul's Name Ancient Romans were formally designated by a *praenomen* (first name), *nomen* (family name), father's *praenomen*, Roman tribe, and *cognomen* (extra name like the modern middle name) in official documents. Roman citizens had to register with

---

Mission, vol. 2: *Paul and the Early Church* (Downers Grove: InterVarsity, 2004), 923–1485; and R. L. Plummer, *Paul's Understanding of the Church's Mission*, Paternoster Biblical Monographs (Milton Keynes, UK: Paternoster, 2006).

[9] Jerome, *Commentary on the Epistle to the Philippians*, on v. 23; *De Viris Illustribus* 5.

[10] See Acts 18:3. Although Paul's letters make many references to his working at a trade in order to support himself (1 Cor 4:12; 9:1–18; 2 Cor 6:5; 11:23,27; 1 Thess 2:9; 2 Thess 3:8), only Acts mentions the specific trade. Paul probably made tents from leather. He was probably skilled in making and repairing a wide range of leather and woven goods. See R. F. Hock, *The Social Context of Paul's Mission* (Philadelphia: Fortress, 1980), 20–21.

[11] E.g., F. F. Bruce, *Paul: Apostle of the Heart Set Free* (Grand Rapids: Eerdmans, 1977), 37.

[12] Jerome, *Commentary on the Epistle to the Philippians*, on v. 23; *De viris illustribus* 5; Photius, *Quaest. Amphil,* 116.

the government using the *trianomina* consisting of the *praenomen, nomen gentile,* and *cognomen.* The NT refers to the apostle only informally as "Paul" or "Saul." Paul was the apostle's cognomen; Saul was his Hebrew name. The name "Paul" was common in the Roman world (Acts 13:7) and meant "small" in Latin. Later traditions probably inferred that Paul was short from the meaning of his Latin name, but one cannot determine Paul's stature from the name since the name was given to him at his birth.[13]

Rabbinic Training   Acts 22:3 shows that Paul was "brought up" in Jerusalem "at the feet of Gamaliel," the member of the Sanhedrin mentioned in Acts 5:33–39 and, according to the earliest traditions, the founder of his own rabbinic school. Although the verb "brought up" (*anatrephō*) may refer to being raised from the time of infancy (Acts 7:21), in this context it probably means nothing more than that Paul received his rabbinic training under Gamaliel after moving to Jerusalem, probably some time in his teenage years.[14] Paul used this fact to prove that he was not one of the Diaspora Jews, those who were more influenced by Gentile culture than Jewish ways. In Jerusalem, Paul was educated in the Jewish religion according to the traditions of his ancestors (Acts 22:3). A century and a half after Paul, Rabbi Judah ben Tema taught, "At five years old [one is fit] for the Scripture, at ten years for the Mishnah, at thirteen [for the fulfilling of] the commandments, at fifteen for the Talmud, at eighteen for the bride-chamber, at twenty for pursuing a calling, at thirty for authority" (*m. Avot* 5:21). Judah's words are probably an accurate description of the regimen of training that Paul experienced. This regimen led Paul to become an even more radical interpreter of the law than Gamaliel (see Gal 5:3; Acts 5:34–39). As is often the case, students become more radical than their teachers.

Paul thus quickly excelled as a Jewish rabbinical student. Paul said, "I advanced in Judaism beyond many contemporaries among my people, because I was extremely zealous for the traditions of my ancestors" (Gal 1:14). Paul described himself as "circumcised the eighth day; of the nation of Israel, of the tribe of Benjamin, a Hebrew born of Hebrews; as to the law, a Pharisee; as to zeal, persecuting the church; as to the righteousness that is in the law, blameless" (Phil 3:5–6). He also identified himself with the sect of the Pharisees, which he described as the "strictest party of our religion" (Acts 26:5). Paul's father had also been a Pharisee (Acts 23:6).

Persecution of Christians   As an ideal Pharisee, Paul may have been active as a Jewish missionary, winning Gentiles as proselytes to the Jewish faith. He may have been like the Pharisees Jesus described who "travel over land and sea to make one proselyte" (Matt 23:15). Paul's words, "If I still preach circumcision," may allude to his past as a Jewish missionary (Gal 5:11). Paul, more than his mentor Gamaliel (Acts 5:34–39), recognized the serious threat Christianity posed to the Jewish religion. Paul was probably in his thirties when he, with authorization from the chief priest, began to imprison Christians first in the synagogues of Jerusalem and then later in more remote areas like Damascus.

---

[13] For a detailed discussion of Paul's name, see C. Hemer, "The Name of Paul," *TynB* 36 (1985): 179–83.

[14] See J. McRay, *Paul: His Life and Teaching* (Grand Rapids: Baker, 2003), 44.

One cannot underestimate Paul's aggression and viciousness in persecuting the church that was inspired by his misguided zeal. When Paul described his efforts to persecute the church, he used the language of warfare and made clear that his intention was to obliterate the church (Gal 1:13). Luke described Paul's destruction of the church using the Greek verb *lumainomai*, a verb used in the Septuagint (Greek OT) to speak of a wild animal such as a lion, bear, or leopard tearing at raw flesh.[15] Paul's zeal in persecuting the church was like the savage rage of a hungry predator frenzied by the taste of blood.

Perhaps Paul's clearest description of his activities as a persecutor is found in Acts 26:9–11: "In fact, I myself supposed it was necessary to do many things in opposition to the name of Jesus the Nazarene. This I actually did in Jerusalem, and I locked up many of the saints in prison, since I had received authority for that from the chief priests. When they were put to death, I cast my vote against them. In all the synagogues I often tried to make them blaspheme by punishing them. Being greatly enraged at them, I even pursued them to foreign cities." The statement, "casting a vote," is probably a metaphor implying that Paul consented to the execution of Christians, or it suggests that he was a member of a committee appointed by the Sanhedrin and vested with this authority.[16]

Paul's initial and adamant rejection of Jesus Christ as the Messiah may largely have been motivated by Christ's ignoble death. Paul knew that death by crucifixion was indicative of a divine curse (Deut 21:23). It was inconceivable to him that the Messiah could die under the curse of God. But when Paul wrote his first letter, he had come to recognize this death curse as the grounds for substitutionary atonement (Gal 3:10–14). Jesus had suffered the curse that sinners deserved in their place. In 1 Corinthians, Paul explained that the idea of a crucified Messiah was a stumbling block to the Jews (see 1:23). Paul was likely speaking from his own past experience.

Paul's Conversion (34)

While Saul was on his way to Damascus to arrest and imprison Christians, the resurrected and glorified Christ appeared to him with blinding radiance. Christ's words, "It is hard for you to kick against the goads" (Acts 26:14), indicate that God had already begun to prompt Saul to follow Jesus as Messiah. Like an ox kicking against a sharpened prod in the hand of the ox driver, Paul had been resisting divine guidance resulting in his own harm and pain. At the appearance of Christ, Saul immediately surrendered to his authority and went into the city to await further orders from his Master. There his blindness was healed, he received the Holy Spirit, and he accepted believer's baptism. No doubt Ananias shared with Saul the message that the Lord had given him in a vision, "This man is My chosen instrument to carry My name before Gentiles, kings, and the sons of Israel. I will certainly show him how much he must suffer for My name" (Acts 9:15). After this Saul spent a few days with the disciples in Damascus.

---

[15] See Isa 65:25; Sir 28:23; and Theodotion's rendering of Dan 6:23.

[16] J. B. Polhill, *Acts*, NAC 26 (Nashville: B&H, 1992), 501.

Paul's Missionary Travels (34–58)

Early Travels (34–47) Soon after his conversion, Paul traveled to Arabia where he began evangelization of the Nabatean Arabs (Gal 1:17; 2 Cor 11:32–33) and probably experienced his first opposition to the gospel from political authorities. He then returned to Damascus where he began to go into the synagogues to preach the message that had been revealed to him on the Damascus road: Jesus is the Son of God and the promised Messiah. The governor in Damascus had the city gates guarded in order to arrest Paul, and he had to escape through a window in the wall by being lowered in a basket.

Paul then traveled to Jerusalem where he spent 15 days visiting with Peter and James, the Lord's brother, and doubtless heard them describe Jesus' life and teachings, though Paul's gospel was already clearly defined even before this visit. Church leaders were initially suspicious of Paul, but Barnabas intervened on his behalf (Acts 9:26–30; Gal 1:18). After 15 days in Jerusalem, Paul returned to Tarsus, evangelizing Syria and Cilicia for several years. While in Syria, Barnabas contacted Paul and invited him to become involved in the outreach of the Antioch church where large numbers of Gentiles were responding to the gospel. The church at Antioch collected money to carry to the Christians who suffered in Judea during a period of famine. Barnabas and Paul were chosen by the church to carry the gift to Jerusalem (Acts 11:27–30). This probably was the occasion of the conference described by Paul in Gal 2:1–10. Some equate this with the Jerusalem Council, but this is unlikely. If Galatians were written after an official ruling at the Jerusalem Council, Paul could have just displayed the letter from the apostles to discredit the Judaizers. Moreover, the encounter described in Gal 2:1–10 appears to have been a private meeting rather than a public affair. The pillars of the Jerusalem church, Peter, John, and James the brother of Jesus, approved the no-law gospel preached by Paul and his focus on Gentile evangelism.

First Missionary Journey (47–48) Paul and Barnabas soon began their first missionary journey, traveling through Cyprus and Anatolia probably during the years 47–48. The missionary team carried the gospel to the cities of Pisidian Antioch, Iconium, Lystra, and Derbe. These cities were located in the Roman province of Galatia, and the letter to the Galatians is probably addressed to these churches in South Galatia. *Galatians* was most likely written from Antioch shortly after this journey.

Jerusalem Council (49) When Paul returned to Antioch from the first missionary journey, he immediately found himself embroiled in controversy over requirements for Gentile salvation. Peter and even Barnabas were vacillating on the issue of Jew-Gentile relationships. Even worse, some false teachers from the Jerusalem church had infiltrated congregations in Antioch and were teaching, "Unless you are circumcised according to the custom prescribed by Moses, you cannot be saved" (Acts 15:1). The church appointed Paul and Barnabas to go to Jerusalem and settle the matter. A council was convened in the year 49 that included the missionary team, those who insisted upon circumcision as a requirement for salvation, and the apostles. The apostle Peter and James the brother of Jesus spoke in defense of Paul's law-free gospel, and a letter was sent to the Gentile churches confirming the official Christian view. Paul returned to Antioch.

Second Missionary Journey (49–51) The second missionary journey carried Paul through Anatolia, Macedonia, and Achaia in 49–51. Paul and Barnabas parted company at this point in a disagreement about the role of Barnabas's nephew John Mark in the second missionary journey. Mark had abandoned the team on the first journey (Acts 15:38). Paul took Silas on this journey and established churches in Philippi, Thessalonica, and Berea. Paul also spent 18 months in Corinth strengthening a fledgling church there. Four of Paul's letters are addressed to churches known from this second journey. Most scholars believe that *1 and 2 Thessalonians* were written during this journey.

Third Missionary Journey (51–54) Paul's third missionary journey focused on the city of Ephesus where Paul spent the better part of three years (51–54). Toward the end of this journey Paul worked hard to collect another relief offering for the Jerusalem Christians. Paul wrote *1 and 2 Corinthians* and *Romans* during this journey.

Final Years (55–65/66) Paul carried the relief offering to Jerusalem. While in the temple performing a ritual to demonstrate his Jewish identity to some of the Jerusalem Christians, Jewish opponents incited a riot, and Paul was arrested (55). Paul was sent to Caesarea to stand trial before the procurator Felix. After two years of procrastination on the part of his detainers, Paul finally appealed to the Roman emperor for trial. After arriving in Rome, Paul spent two years under house arrest awaiting his trial. Paul wrote *Ephesians, Philippians, Colossians,* and *Philemon* during this first Roman imprisonment (c. 58–60).[17]

The record of Acts ends at this point, so information as to the outcome of the trial is sketchy. Early church tradition suggests that Paul was acquitted (c. 60) or exiled and may possibly have fulfilled the dream expressed in Rom 15:23–29 of carrying the gospel to Spain (60–66).[18] Paul wrote *1 Timothy* and *Titus* during the period between his acquittal and a second Roman imprisonment, and he wrote *2 Timothy* during the second Roman imprisonment. According to church tradition, Paul was arrested again and subjected to a harsher imprisonment. He was condemned by the Emperor Nero and beheaded with the sword at the third milestone on the Ostian Way at a place called Aquae Salviae and lies buried on the site covered by the Basilica of St. Paul Outside the Walls. His execution probably occurred in 66 or 67.

Paul's Appearance

No biblical record of the appearance of Paul or his physical condition exists. He must have been a hearty individual to endure the abuses and trials that he suffered as an apostle (2 Cor 11:23–29). He was evidently the victim of some serious eye disease (Gal 4:12–16). This may account for his characteristically large signature that he appended to letters that

---

[17] The precise order in which these four epistles were written is unknown.

[18] For a thorough discussion of Paul's possible missionary work in Spain, see Schnabel, *Early Christian Mission*, 1271–83.

were likely penned by a secretary (Gal 6:11). The earliest description of Paul's appearance appears in a book from the NT Apocrypha, which says that Paul was "a man small of stature, with a bald head and crooked legs, in a good state of body, with eyebrows meeting and nose somewhat hooked, full of friendliness; for now he appeared like a man, and now he had the face of an angel."[19] The writer attributes the description of Paul to Titus, and it may have some historical basis. Although it sounds unflattering to moderns, several of the physical features mentioned were considered to be traits of the ideal Roman.

Table 9.2: A Chronology of Paul's Life and Letters

Event	Approximate Date	Scripture Reference
Paul's Birth	c. AD 1	
Jesus' Crucifixion, Resurrection, Ascension, and Pentecost	Spring 33	Acts 1–2
Paul's Conversion	34	Acts 9:1–19
First Missionary Journey	47–48	Acts 13–14
Authorship of Galatians	48	
Jerusalem Council	49	Acts 15
Second Missionary Journey Antioch to Corinth Thessalonian Letters from Corinth Appearance Before Gallio	49–51	Acts 16–18 Acts 18:11 Acts 18:12
Third Missionary Journey Stay in Ephesus Corinthians A 1 Corinthians Corinthians C 2 Corinthians Stay in Corinth Romans	51–54	Acts 19–21 Acts 20:31 1 Cor 5:9,11 Acts 19:10 2 Cor 2:4; 7:8 Acts 20:1–2 2 Cor 13:1–2 Rom 16:1–2,23
Jerusalem Arrest	55	Acts 21–23 Acts 21:27–40
Imprisonment in Caesarea	55–57	Acts 24–27
Journey to Rome Voyage and Shipwreck Winter in Malta	57–58	Acts 27 Acts 27:27–40

---

[19] *Acts of Paul* 3:3 in E. Hennecke and W. Schneemelcher, *Writings Relating to the Apostles, Apocalypses and Related Subjects*, vol. 2 of *New Testament Apocrypha*, trans. and ed. R. M. Wilson (Philadelphia: Westminster, 1964), 354.

Event	Approximate Date	Scripture Reference
First Roman Imprisonment Prison Epistles: Ephesians, Philippians, Colossians, Philemon	58–60	Acts 28
Paul's Release	60	
Fourth Missionary Journey Titus 1 Timothy	60–66	
Great Fire in Rome	64	
Paul's Arrest and Second Roman Imprisonment 2 Timothy	66	
Paul's Death	66 or 67	

Paul's Gospel

Paul's gospel indicted all humanity for the crime of rejecting God and his rightful authority.[20] Suffering the consequences of Adam's sin, mankind plunged into the depths of depravity so that they were utterly unable to fulfill the righteous demands of God (Rom 1:18–32; 3:9–20; 9:12–19) and deserved only the wrath of God (Rom 1:18; 2:5–16). The sinner was alienated from God and at enmity with him (Rom 5:10; Col 1:21). Consequently, the sinner's only hope was the gospel that embodied God's power to save those who had faith in Christ (Rom 1:16).

The focus of Paul's gospel was Jesus Christ (Rom 1:3–4). Paul affirmed Jesus' humanity and his deity. Christ was a physical descendent from the line of David (Rom 1:3), came in the likeness of sinful man (Rom 8:3), assuming the form of a humble, obedient servant (Phil 2:7–8). Yet he was the visible form of the invisible God (Col 1:15), all the fullness of deity living in him in bodily form (Col 2:9). Jesus was in very nature God (Phil 2:6) and possessed the title "Lord" (Greek title for the God of the OT), the name above all names (Phil 2:9–11). Paul believed that by virtue of his sinlessness, Jesus was qualified to be the sacrifice that made sinners right with God (2 Cor 5:21). In his death on the cross, Jesus had become the curse for sin (Gal 3:10–14), and the righteous had died for the unrighteous (Rom 5:6–8).

Salvation is a free gift granted to believers and grounded solely in God's grace. Salvation is not dependent on human merit, activity, or effort but only on God's undeserved love (Rom 6:23; Eph 2:8–10). Those who trust Jesus for their salvation, confess him as Lord,

---

[20] See the discussion of "The Gospel Paul Preached" in Köstenberger and O'Brien, *Salvation to the Ends of the Earth*, 173–84.

and believe that God raised him from the dead (Rom 10:9) will be saved from God's wrath, become righteous in God's sight (Rom 5:9), are adopted as God's children (Rom 8:15–17; Eph 1:5), and are transformed by the Spirit's power (Gal 5:22–24). At the coming of Christ believers will be resurrected (1 Cor 15:12–57), partake fully of the Son's righteous character (Phil 3:20–21), and live forever with their Lord (1 Thess 4:17).

By their union with Christ through faith, believers participate spiritually in Christ's death, resurrection, and ascension (Rom 6:1–7:6; Eph 2:4–5; Col 3:1–4). Consequently, the believer has been liberated from the power of sin, death, and the law. He is a new, though imperfect, creation that is continually being made more like Christ (2 Cor 5:17; Col 3:9–10). Although the believer is no longer under the authority of the written law, the Holy Spirit functions as a new internal law leading him naturally and spontaneously to fulfill the law's righteous demands (Rom 8:1–4). As a result, the law-free gospel does not encourage unrighteous behavior in believers. Such behavior is contrary to their new identity in Christ.

The union of believers with Christ brings them into union with other believers in the body of Christ, the church. Believers exercise their spiritual gifts in order to help each other mature, to serve Christ and glorify him, the church's highest purpose (Eph 3:21; 4:11–13). Christ now rules over the church as its Head, its highest authority (Eph 1:22). When Christ comes again, his reign over the world will be consummated, and all that exists will be placed under his absolute authority (Eph 1:10; Phil 4:20). He will raise the dead, unbelievers for judgment and punishment, believers for glorification and reward (2 Thess 1:5–10).

STUDY QUESTIONS

1. How many letters of Paul are included in the NT?
2. What kind of evidence did Wenham advance to support his claim that Paul was a follower of Jesus?
3. Which legal status enabled Paul to appeal to the Roman emperor?
4. Where was Paul from?
5. Who was Paul's teacher?
6. What does the name *Paul* mean?
7. When Paul was converted, what was the central tenet in his belief system that had to change?
8. What was the focus of Paul's gospel?

FOR FURTHER STUDY

Barnett, P. *Paul: Missionary of Jesus.* After Jesus, vol. 2. Grand Rapids: Eerdmans, 2008.

Barrett, C. K. *Paul: An Introduction to His Thought.* Louisville: Westminster John Knox, 1994.

Bruce, F. F. *Paul: Apostle of the Heart Set Free.* Grand Rapids: Eerdmans, 1977.

Hawthorne, G. F., R. P. Martin, and D. G. Reid, eds. *Dictionary of Paul and His Letters.* Downers Grove: InterVarsity, 1993.

Kim, S. Y. *The Origin of Paul's Gospel.* Grand Rapids: Eerdmans, 1982.

Köstenberger, A. J., and P. T. O'Brien. *Salvation to the Ends of the Earth: A Biblical Theology of Mission*. NSBT 11. Downers Grove: InterVarsity, 2001.

Longenecker, R. N. *The Ministry and Message of Paul*. Grand Rapids: Zondervan, 1971.

Polhill, J. B. *Paul and His Letters*. Nashville: B&H, 1999.

Ridderbos, H. *Paul: An Outline of His Theology*. Translated by J. R. De Witt. Grand Rapids: Eerdmans, 1975.

Riesner, R. *Paul's Early Period: Chronology, Mission Strategy, Theology*. Grand Rapids: Eerdmans, 1998.

Schnabel, E. *Early Christian Mission*. 2 vols. Downers Grove: InterVarsity, 2004.

_____. *Paul the Missionary: Realities, Strategies, and Methods*. Downers Grove: InterVarsity, 2008.

Schreiner, T. R. *Paul: Apostle of God's Glory in Christ: A Pauline Theology*. Downers Grove: InterVarsity, 2001.

Thielman, F. *Paul and the Law: A Contextual Approach*. Downers Grove: InterVarsity, 1994.

Wenham, D. *Paul: Follower of Jesus or Founder of Christianity?* Grand Rapids: Eerdmans, 1995.

Chapter 10

Paul's Letter to the Galatians

CORE KNOWLEDGE

Students should know the key facts of Galatians. With regard to history, students should be able to identify the letter's author, date, provenance, destination, and purpose. With regard to literature, they should be able to provide a basic outline of the book and identify core elements of the book's content found in the unit-by-unit discussion. With regard to theology, students should be able to identify the major theological themes in Galatians.

KEY FACTS	
Author:	Paul
Date:	48 or 49
Provenance:	Possibly Antioch, Jerusalem, or the route between the two cities
Destination:	Churches of South Galatia visited by Paul during first missionary journey
Occasion:	False teaching (Judaizing heresy)
Purpose:	To defend the one true gospel
Theme:	Both Jews and Gentiles are saved through faith in Jesus Christ, not by works of the law
Key Verses:	3:10–14

CONTRIBUTION TO THE CANON

- Gentiles included in the church on equal terms with the Jews (3:28); circumcision not required, contrary to the "false gospel" of the Judaizers (1:6–9; 6:15)
- Paul's confrontation of Peter regarding the inclusion of the Gentiles, most likely prior to the Jerusalem Council (2:11–14; see Acts 15)

- Justification by faith apart from works of the law (see 2:16; 3:24); demonstration from Scripture that Abraham was also justified by faith apart from works (3:1–4:7, esp. 3:6 citing Gen 15:6)
- Defense of Christian freedom from the demands of the law (5:1–15)
- Teaching on life in the Spirit and the fruit of the Spirit (5:16–26)

INTRODUCTION

THE LETTER TO the Galatians is in all likelihood the first letter Paul wrote that is included in the NT, and since this Introduction follows a chronological approach with regard to Paul's letters, Galatians is the place to start. Although the letter is relatively short, it has exerted enormous influence on Christianity. The early church fathers wrote more commentaries on Galatians than on any other NT book.[1] The letter was a favorite of the Protestant Reformer Martin Luther, who described it as dear to him as his own precious wife and called it "my own epistle, to which I have plighted my troth [i.e., pledged my truthfulness]; my Katie von Bora."[2] G. Duncan described the letter as the "magna carta of Evangelical Christianity."[3]

Indeed, Galatians makes numerous and significant contributions to NT theology and ethics. The most important contribution of the letter is its exposition of the doctrine of justification. This short letter attacks all notions, both ancient and modern, that one's eternal destiny is dependent on one's personal actions, participation in rituals, or conformity to group norms. Instead, the letter liberates the believer from slavery to the law and expounds a higher righteousness that is prompted and empowered by the indwelling Spirit.[4] The letter also addresses the Spirit's transforming work in the believer and the nature of Christ's substitutionary atonement, and it also expresses an early but high Christology.

HISTORY

Author

The letter to the Galatians is regarded as an authentic letter of the apostle Paul by all but the most radical critics. Acceptance of Paul's authorship is so widespread that extended discussion of the issue is unnecessary. The early church unanimously accepted Paul's authorship of the letter. Allusions to Galatians appear in the works of Clement of Rome (c. 96), Ignatius (c. 35–110), Polycarp (c. 69–155), and Justin Martyr (c. 100–165). Galatians was included in the ancient canonical lists and in the ancient versions. It was quoted directly and was explicitly ascribed to Paul by Irenaeus (c. 130–200), Clement of

---

[1] C. B. Cousar, *Galatians*, Interpretation (Atlanta: John Knox, 1982), 1.

[2] G. W. Hansen, "Galatians, Letter to the," in *Dictionary of Paul and His Letters*, ed. G. F. Hawthorne, R. P. Martin, and D. G. Reid (Downers Grove: InterVarsity, 1993), 323.

[3] G. Duncan, *The Epistle of Paul to the Galatians* (London: Hodder & Stoughton, 1934), xvii.

[4] L. Morris's description of Galatians is apt when he called the letter "Paul's charter of Christian freedom" (the subtitle of *Galatians: Paul's Charter of Christian Freedom* [Downers Grove: InterVarsity, 1996]).

Alexandria (c. 150–215), Origen (c. 185–254), and Tertullian (c. 160–225).[5] The author identified himself as Paul in Gal 1:1 and appealed to his personal signature in Gal 6:11 as confirmation of the authenticity of the letter. Paul's authorship of the epistle may be accepted with great confidence. As R. Longenecker noted, "If Galatians is not by Paul, no NT letter is by him, for none has any better claim."[6]

Provenance

The provenance of Galatians is inextricably related to the identity of the addressees and the date of authorship. Most NT introductions and commentaries do not even venture a guess as to the place of authorship. However, if one affirms the South Galatian theory (see below) and accepts a date of authorship between the first missionary journey and the Jerusalem Conference, Paul probably wrote the letter either from Antioch, Jerusalem, or some location en route between these two cities.[7]

Destination

While Paul's authorship of Galatians is widely accepted, scholars differ in their opinions regarding those to whom the letter was addressed. It is clear that the letter was addressed to the Galatians (1:2; 3:1), but precise identification of the Galatians is difficult. The term *Galatia* could be used in the first century in either an ethnic sense or a provincial sense. The issue is complicated but the study is worthwhile. Pinpointing the precise location of the Galatian churches addressed in the letter is crucial for determining its date.

In the ethnic sense, the term *Galatia* could be used to describe the area inhabited by the Gauls or Celts who invaded north central Asia Minor from Central Europe in 278 BC and were of the same ethnic origin as the Celts of France and Britain. If Paul intended this sense in his address, he was writing to churches in northern Galatia, possibly in such cities as Ancyra, Pessinus, and Tavium. The theory that Paul addressed his letter to churches in these northern cities is called the North Galatian theory.

The North Galatian theory was the view of the early church fathers, medieval commentators, and the Protestant reformers. While the evidence from the early church fathers is impressive, they may have imposed their own contemporary geography on Paul's address. In the year 74, Vespasian detached most of Pisidia from the Galatian province. In the year 137, the Lyconian portion of the province was transferred to Cilicia, and in c. 297, the remaining southern portions were transferred to a new province of Pisidia. When the early church fathers read the word *Galatia*, geographical boundaries had changed, and the prominent Galatian cities that Paul visited during his first missionary journey were no longer considered Galatia.[8] Reading the geography of their day back into the NT would have

---

[5] J. B. Lightfoot, *St. Paul's Epistle to the Galatians*, 10th ed. (London: Macmillan, 1921), 57–62. Cf. E. De Witt Burton, *A Critical and Exegetical Commentary on the Epistle to the Galatians*, ICC (Edinburgh: T&T Clark, 1921), lxviii-lxix.

[6] R. N. Longenecker, *Galatians*, WBC 41 (Dallas: Word, 1990), lviii.

[7] A. Cole, *The Epistle of St. Paul to the Galatians* (Grand Rapids: Eerdmans, 1965), 23.

[8] Hansen, "Galatians," 323.

been an easy mistake. This would be much like interpreting Louisiana in the Louisiana Purchase to refer only to the small area contained in the present state rather than the vast lands of Louisiana in 1803.

If, however, Paul's address refers to the Roman province of Galatia, he could be writing to churches in southern Galatia. In 64 BC, Pompey rewarded the Galatians for their support in his battle against Mithradates V by making them a client kingdom. Over the next several decades, the kingdom was enlarged toward the south and the east. In 25 BC, Augustus reorganized the area into a Roman province. During Paul's time, the province extended from Pontus on the Black Sea to Pamphylia on the Mediterranean. The Roman province included cities such as Antioch of Pisidia, Iconium, Lystra and Derbe. Paul visited these cities during his first missionary journey. The theory that Paul addressed the letter to the churches in these cities is called the South Galatian theory.

Scholars adduce the following evidence to support this view. First, Paul obviously knew the Galatian readers personally (Gal 1:8; 4:11–15,19). Acts contains large amounts of information about Paul's work among the churches of South Galatia, and yet no information exists (unless Acts 16:6 and 18:23 are exceptions) about his work in North Galatia. The silence of Acts regarding a Pauline ministry in North Galatia does seem significant. Second, the route described in Acts 16:6 and 18:23 seems to be a South Galatian route. Third, "Galatia" was the only word that would have encompassed Antioch, Lystra, Iconium, and Derbe. Antioch was in the region of Pisidia; Lystra and Iconium were in Lycaonia. Moreover, Paul normally used Roman imperial names for provinces.[9]

Fourth, in 1 Cor 16:1 Paul referred to the Galatian churches as among the contributors to the collection for Jerusalem. Acts 20:4 mentions a Berean, two Thessalonians, two south Galatians, and two Asians who appear to represent the churches presenting the gift. This suggests that the Galatian churches Paul mentioned in 1 Corinthians were South Galatian churches. If Paul used the term *Galatia* consistently, then the letter to the Galatians was addressed to South Galatians.

Fifth, Barnabas is mentioned three times in Galatians (2:1,9,13). Barnabas accompanied Paul only on the first missionary journey through cities in South Galatia. He did not accompany Paul on the second or third journeys, so very likely he did not visit Northern Galatia, although this is not conclusive.

To conclude, both theories have their strengths and weaknesses. Neither can be proven or disproven conclusively. The balance of the evidence weighs in favor of the South Galatian theory. Perhaps most importantly, there is no biblical evidence that Paul ever visited the North Galatian cities, while Acts records Paul planting churches in South Galatia. Also, as discussed, the reference to the Galatian churches in 1 Cor 16:1 and the repeated mention of Barnabas in Galatians (2:1,9,13) seem to favor a South Galatian destination.

---

[9] F. F. Bruce, *The Epistle to the Galatians*, NIGTC (Grand Rapids: Eerdmans, 1982), 15.

Date

The date for Galatians depends largely on three factors: (1) the question of destination; (2) the relationship of Paul's two visits to Jerusalem mentioned in Galatians (1:18; 2:1–10) with the four visits to Jerusalem mentioned in Acts (Acts 9:26–30; 11:30; 15:1–30; 21:15–17); and (3) the number of visits to the Galatian churches made before the letter was written as implied in Gal 4:13. The determination of destination makes the greatest difference in date. Those who espouse the South Galatian theory normally affirm a relatively early date for the letter: either shortly after Paul's first missionary journey or just before or shortly after the Jerusalem Council. Those who accept the North Galatian theory typically affirm a later date, usually during Paul's third missionary journey.

Though the debate is lively, the evidence favors the equation of the famine relief visit in Acts 11:30, not the Jerusalem Council of Acts 15, with the visit recounted in Gal 2:1–10. Although superficial similarities between Acts 15:1–20 and Gal 2:1–10 exist, close examination of the data suggests that the Gal 2:1–10 visit holds more in common with the famine relief visit of Acts 11:30. Hence, Galatians was most likely written in approximately 48 or 49.

Table 10.1: Events Surrounding the Writing of Galatians

Event	Likely Date	NT Passage
1. Famine relief visit to Jerusalem	47	Acts 11:30 = Gal 2:1–10
2. First missionary journey	47–48	Acts 13:4–14:28
3. Paul wrote Galatians	48/49	Galatians
4. Jerusalem Council	49	Acts 15:1–20

Occasion and Purpose

Assuming the South Galatian theory, Acts 13–14 combined with scattered references in Galatians charts Paul's church-starting work in the churches of South Galatia. Paul's initial evangelistic work among the Galatians was complicated by an illness that harmed his vision (Gal 4:13–16). Yet the Galatians gave Paul a warm reception, recognized that his message was of divine origin, and welcomed Paul as if he were an angel or even Christ himself. Many believed Paul's gospel, thereby demonstrating their divine appointment for eternal life (Acts 13:48; 14:4,21). The Galatians' love for Paul was so great that they would have sacrificed their eyes to restore Paul's vision if that had been possible.

Paul clearly proclaimed the gospel of grace from the very beginning of his Galatian ministry. According to Acts 13:38–39, Paul offered the Jews and the Gentiles who worshipped God in the synagogue of Pisidian Antioch forgiveness of sins through Jesus: "Everyone who believes in Him is justified from everything, which you could not be justified from through the law of Moses." Paul's work met with heavy opposition from the Jews of the area. Their opposition was initially motivated by jealousy over Paul's success and popularity with the people (Acts 13:45). But personal rivalry was quickly overwhelmed by religious disputes. The statement in Acts 14:3 that the Lord "testified to the message of His grace" through miraculous signs and wonders implies that the Jewish opposition had focused their campaign against Paul's teaching about grace. Thus, the issue of salvation by grace versus the law of Moses permeated Paul's Galatian ministry and was the crux that divided Christian disciples from Galatian Jews.

Soon after Paul left the area, false teachers infiltrated the church preaching a different gospel—a gospel that insisted that keeping the law of Moses, in particular receiving circumcision, rather than faith in the gospel of grace alone was essential to salvation. The false teachers were probably Jews who considered themselves Christians, but Paul was emphatic that imposition of the law as a requirement for salvation was inconsistent with genuine Christianity (Gal 1:6–9). Scholars typically label these false teachers as "Judaizers" since they sought to impose Judaism on new Christian converts. The Judaizers proclaimed a message akin to the one expressed in Acts 15:1, "Unless you are circumcised according to the custom prescribed by Moses, you cannot be saved." The Judaizers may not have insisted that the Galatians keep the entire law. Circumcision was their main focus. But Paul warned that requiring circumcision for salvation ultimately made the entire OT law obligatory (Gal 5:3). Thus Paul often defended the gospel against the necessity of observing the law generally (Gal 1:16,21; 2:2,5,10; etc.).

Paul's proclamation of the gospel of grace had been so clear that insistence on circumcision and the observance of the law could not be made without rejection of Paul's apostleship. This led to the Judaizers' charge that Paul's apostleship was somehow inferior to the other apostles. These opponents twisted Scripture and claimed that their doctrines were imbued with true authority—the authority of the original apostles in the Jerusalem church. The members of the Galatian church defected from the true gospel and began to resent Paul and his teaching and to reject the apostle's authority.

Paul, then, wrote Galatians to defend the gospel of justification by faith alone against the false gospel of the Judaizers. In the process, he had to defend his apostolic authority against the Judaizers' attack. Finally, since some readers might interpret Paul's defense of the gospel of grace as justification for immoral or unethical behavior, Paul wrote to defend the consistency of the Spirit-led life with the law's righteous demands.

LITERATURE

Literary Plan

Although some scholars have suggested that Galatians is an impassioned letter composed in the heat of controversy and thus lacking a clear and planned structure, recent research suggests that the letter was much more carefully composed.[10] Like most letters

---

[10] H. D. Betz, *Galatians*, Hermeneia (Philadelphia: Fortress, 1979), 312, pointed out that Paul's use of a personal secretary or professional letter writer implies a careful process of composition: "It is apparent that the very employment of an

from the period, Galatians has an obvious introduction (1:1–9), body (1:10–6:10), and conclusion (6:11–18). Older commentators generally see the body of the letter as breaking down into three major parts: a historical section (1:10–2:21), a theological section (3:1–5:1), and an ethical section (5:2–6:10).[11] The historical section validates the divine origin of Paul's gospel—his encounter with the risen Christ on the road to Damascus. The theological section defends the gospel of justification by faith apart from the works of the law. The ethical section describes the lifestyle prompted by the Spirit in those justified by faith. The outline below represents an adaptation of R. Longenecker's proposed structure of Galatians, which describes Galatians as a letter of rebuke and request akin to other such letters found in the first century.[12]

OUTLINE
  I. OPENING (1:1–5)
  II. REBUKE: PAUL'S GOSPEL AND THE "OTHER GOSPEL" (1:6–4:11)
    A.Historical Section (1:6–2:21)
    B.Theological Section (3:1–4:11)
  III. APPEAL: CHOOSE THE LIBERTY OF LIFE IN THE SPIRIT (4:12–6:10)
    A.Children of the Free Woman (4:12–31)
    B.Living a Life of Liberty (5:1–6:10)
  IV. CONCLUSION (6:11–18)

UNIT-BY-UNIT DISCUSSION

I. Opening (1:1–5)
The need of the Galatian churches was so urgent that Paul did not wait until the body of his letter to begin to address their confusion. Even as he identified the sender and addressees of the letter and greeted his readers, he touched on the key issues that he would address more fully later. First, Paul defended his genuine apostleship. An "apostle" is one who is commissioned for a task by another and entrusted with authority to carry out that task. Paul stressed that his commissioning for service did not come from a body of people, nor was his commissioning communicated through a human who acted on God's behalf. Paul was commissioned for ministry by Jesus Christ and the Father.

By contrasting Jesus with human beings and by placing Jesus Christ beside the Father as the two sources of his commission, Paul implied the deity of Christ as well as affirming his own divine commission. Paul's mention of the resurrection should have led readers to recall that Paul's commissioning came from the glorified and resurrected Jesus so that

---

amanuensis [secretary] rules out a haphazard writing of the letter and suggests the existence of Paul's draft and the copy by an amanuensis, or a sequence of draft, composition, and copy."

[11] E.g., Lightfoot, *Galatians*, 5–6; Cole, *Galatians*, 27.

[12] Longenecker, *Galatians*, c-cix. Demetrius's handbook *On Style* describes 21 different kinds of letters written in the first century.

his own apostleship was in no way inferior to that of the Twelve. Paul also referred to his co-laborers who accompanied him on his travels to demonstrate that his gospel was not an idiosyncrasy affirmed only by him but that it was also embraced by other devout men.

Paul identified Jesus Christ from whom grace and peace come by appealing to his sacrificial death. Christ gave himself for our sins, bearing the curse that our sins deserved in our place so that we might escape that curse (see 3:13). Paul's opponents might have argued that the view that forgiveness is based on Christ's substitutionary atonement alone fosters reckless and immoral behavior. Paul anticipated the objection even before it was raised and insisted that Jesus' sacrificial death was intended not only to grant the believer forgiveness but also to rescue him from the corrupting influences of a depraved age.

This and nothing less fulfilled God's will for the believer. The believer is rescued from the present evil age when he recognizes that he belongs to the coming age and begins to live in light of this awareness. The coming age is the resurrection age in which the believer will be fully delivered from his corruption and is the age in which Christ will bring all things into subjection. Paul's brief summary of the gospel prompted him to burst into doxology, and rightly so. The gospel with its message about forgiveness and transformation displays God's eternal glory and urges his creatures to praise him as nothing else does.

II. Rebuke: Paul's Gospel and the "Other Gospel" (1:6–4:11)

Paul rebuked the Galatians for abandoning the one true gospel by accepting the Judaizers' claim that circumcision is necessary for salvation.

A. Historical Section (1:6–2:21) Because the Judaizers dismissed the gospel that Paul preached, Paul demonstrated that his gospel was of divine, not human, origin. Jesus Christ had himself revealed this gospel to Paul. Paul's gospel clearly was not derived from his Jewish background. His loyalty to Jewish tradition only prompted him to seek to destroy the church and the faith. Likewise, Paul's gospel was not derived from the other apostles or the leaders of the Jerusalem church (1:11–12). In fact, he did not consult with these prominent Christian believers until years after his conversion.

When he did finally consult with the apostles and the leaders of the Jerusalem church, they heartily approved Paul's gospel and encouraged his continued ministry to the Gentiles. Moreover, Paul discovered that some of these prominent church leaders did not behave in a manner that was consistent with the gospel that they all proclaimed. Paul had been forced to challenge the church leaders for this hypocrisy (2:11–14). Paul's challenge demonstrated that his apostolic authority was in no way inferior to theirs.

Paul reminded these Christian Jews that even they were saved by faith in Jesus Christ and not by obedience to the law. If even Jews were not saved by the law, surely the law was not the means of Gentile salvation. By their union with Christ, believers have participated in Jesus' death. They have died to the law and the law no longer exercises authority over them. But Christ indwells believers, which enables them to live righteously. The believer's gratitude for Christ's great love and enormous sacrifice motivates the believer's righteous living.

B. *Theological Section (3:1–4:11)*   Paul continued his assault on the false gospel of the Judaizers with a series of theological arguments. First, the Galatians' own religious experience confirmed the centrality of faith rather than the law (3:1–5). The Holy Spirit was conferred on the believers when they believed the gospel. His presence in them was proven by the occurrence of miracles. This implied that faith, not the law, was the real basis for salvation. Second, the law's description of Abraham demonstrated that faith was the means by which a person was declared righteous by God (3:6–9). Although Abraham was known as the father of the Jews, the OT foretold that people of all nations would share the blessing of justification by faith.

Third, salvation by the works of the law requires complete and absolute obedience. A person who does not keep all of the law all of the time is actually cursed by the law. In his substitutionary death, Jesus bore this curse for sinners in order to free them from the law's curse. Fourth, God's covenant with Abraham, which was based on faith, preceded the giving of the law by 430 years (3:15–16). The covenant based on faith still takes precedence.

Fifth, the law was not given in the first place to provide salvation but to lead sinners to Christ (3:19–26). The law brought about knowledge of sin and condemned all humanity for that sin; thus the law was intended to drive sinners to look to Christ for salvation. Sixth, Gentile believers are not second-class citizens of God's family (3:27–4:7). Christ has abolished spiritual distinctions among believers. God has adopted believers, both Jews and Gentiles, as his children, and they have equal status with God. Seventh, observing the Jewish ritual calendar as a means of salvation was nothing more than a lapse back into the paganism from which the Galatians had been delivered (4:8–11).

III. Appeal: Choose the Liberty of Life in the Spirit (4:12–6:10)

After explaining the faults of the Judaizing heresy, Paul appealed to the Galatians to return to the true gospel (4:12–20). He began his appeal by reminding the Galatians of the intimate relationship that he had shared with them, warning them that the Judaizers did not care for them the way Paul did. In fact, the Judaizers' ministry to the Galatians had selfish ulterior motives.

The apostle used an allegory about Sarah and Hagar to teach that the true children of Abraham were free, not enslaved to the law, and that they had always been persecuted by the false children of Abraham who lived in slavery (4:21–31). He urged the Galatians to expel the Judaizers from their congregations, warning that circumcision could not be separated from the other demands of the law. If circumcision were required for salvation, the entire law became obligatory.

The apostle thwarted suspicions that faith without law led to immoral living by appealing to three sources of righteousness for the believer: the Spirit, faith, and the influence of the church (5:15–26). The righteousness that the law demanded was produced by the

Spirit through faith. Faith working through love is what pleases God and fulfills the law. The life that the Spirit produces is characterized by love, joy, peace, patience, kindness, goodness, faith, gentleness, and self-control. This lifestyle was fully consistent with the law's moral demands. Moreover, if a believer lived sinfully, fellow believers in the church had the responsibility to restore the believer to righteous living.

IV. Conclusion (6:11–18)

Paul concluded the letter with his characteristic signature. His concluding remarks reminded the Galatians again of the selfish motives of the Judaizers, humanity's inability to keep the law, and the necessity of experiencing the new creation (transformation through the Spirit's activity) in order to belong to the true Israel. Finally, Paul pointed to the scars that he had received in his ministry for Christ as marks proving his identity as a true servant of Christ.

THEOLOGY

Theological Themes

Justification by Faith and the Substitutionary Atonement   Paul stressed that a person is justified by faith apart from the works of the law. Since the Protestant Reformation, texts such as Gal 2:15–16 and 3:6–14 have been interpreted as teaching that, because of Jesus' sacrificial death, sinners are declared righteous by the heavenly judge through faith in Christ rather than by personal acts of obedience. Galatians teaches that believers are declared righteous by God, both now and in eschatological judgment, based on Christ's sacrifice and in response to their faith in Jesus and not through obedience to the OT law.

Galatians 3:10–14 is one of the clearest statements in the NT on the substitutionary nature of Jesus' death. Those who rely on the works of the law for salvation are under a divine curse. In order to be deemed righteous through one's fidelity to the law, a person has to fulfill all of the law all of the time. Interpreted in light of Deut 27:26, the fact that Jesus died by crucifixion demonstrates that he bore the curse of believing sinners in their place. Thus, Jesus granted forgiveness to sinners by suffering the penalty for their sins so that they might escape God's wrath.

The Transformation of the Believer   Paul's Jewish opponents in Galatia likely argued that the law was necessary to restrain the sinful conduct of believers. They contended that since believers are saved through faith alone, their personal lifestyles do not matter to God. Paul countered both errors in Galatians by stressing the dramatic change that takes place in the life of the believer. Paul reminded the believers that God had granted his Spirit to them when they placed their faith in Christ (3:2). The Spirit had manifested his presence among them through amazing miracles (3:5). The indwelling Spirit was the source of the personal righteousness for which true believers aspire (5:5).

The Spirit leads the believer to live a life characterized by spiritual fruit, which satisfies and even exceeds the law's moral demands (5:22). The fact that love is the primary expression of the Spirit is significant because love is the essence of the law (5:13–15; see Lev 19:18). This transformation produced by the Spirit is so dramatic and radical that Paul described it as "a new creation" (6:15), echoing the new covenant promises of Ezek 11:19–20; 36:26–27. The new creation effected by the Spirit in the believer serves as the standard, the rule, according to which the believer lives (Gal 6:16).[13] Consequently, the gospel that Paul preached was not a license for sinful behavior but the impetus for righteous living.

POINTS OF APPLICATION

- Let no one deter you from the gospel of God's grace in Jesus Christ (1:6–9)
- Beware of slipping into legalism in your Christian faith (3:2)
- Remember that just like salvation is by grace through faith, so is growth in Christ (3:3)
- Know that the gospel has deep OT roots; people were always saved by grace through faith (3:6)
- Thank God for the amazing privilege of being his child through faith in Christ (3:26)

STUDY QUESTIONS

1. What are some indications that Galatians has exerted enormous influence on Christianity?
2. What are the two possible destinations for Galatians?
3. Was Galatians written most likely before or after the Jerusalem Council?
4. What was Paul's primary purpose in writing Galatians?
5. Who were the Judaizers and what was their message?
6. Why did Paul rebuke the Galatians?
7. What did Paul teach in Galatians concerning justification by faith?

FOR FURTHER STUDY

Bruce, F. F. *The Epistle to the Galatians*. New International Greek Testament Commentary. Grand Rapids: Eerdmans, 1982.

Dunn, J. D. G. *The Epistle to the Galatians*. Black's New Testament Commentary. Peabody: Hendrickson, 1993.

Fung, R. Y. K. *The Epistle to the Galatians*. New International Commentary on the New Testament. Grand Rapids: Eerdmans, 1988.

George, T. *Galatians*. New American Commentary. Nashville: B&H, 1994.

Hansen, G. W. "Galatians, Letter to the." Pages 323–34 in *Dictionary of Paul and His Letters*. Edited by G. F. Hawthorne, R. P. Martin, and D. G. Reid. Downers Grove: InterVarsity, 1993.

---

[13] Martyn, *Galatians*, 567. See also A. J. Köstenberger, "The Identity of the Israel of God in Galatians 6:16," *Faith and Mission* 19/1 (2001): 3–24.

Longenecker, B. W. *The Triumph of Abraham's God: The Transformation of Identity in Galatians.* Edinburgh: T&T Clark, 1998.

Longenecker, R. N. *Galatians.* Word Biblical Commentary 41. Dallas: Word, 1990.

Morris, L. *Galatians: Paul's Charter of Christian Freedom.* Downers Grove: InterVarsity, 1996.

Silva, M. *Interpreting Galatians: Explorations in Exegetical Method.* 2nd ed. Grand Rapids: Baker, 2001.

Thielman, F. *From Plight to Solution: A Jewish Framework for Understanding Paul's View of the Law in Galatians and Romans.* Novum Testamentum Supplement 61. Leiden: Brill, 1989.

Witherington, B., III. *Grace in Galatia: A Commentary on Paul's Letter to the Galatians.* Grand Rapids: Eerdmans, 1998.

Chapter 11

Paul's Thessalonian Correspondence: 1–2 Thessalonians

CORE KNOWLEDGE

Students should know the key facts of 1 and 2 Thessalonians. With regard to history, students should be able to identify each book's author, date, provenance, destination, and purpose. With regard to literature, they should be able to provide a basic outline of each book and identify core elements of each book's content found in the unit-by-unit discussion. With regard to theology, students should be able to identify the major theological themes in 1 and 2 Thessalonians.

KEY FACTS	
Author:	Paul
Date:	50
Provenance:	Corinth
Destination:	Church at Thessalonica in Macedonia
Occasion:	Persecution of the Thessalonians and confusion regarding the end time
Purpose:	To encourage persecuted believers, defend Paul's integrity, and clarify Paul's eschatological teaching
Theme:	Persecuted believers should be encouraged by the anticipation of Jesus' return
Key Verses:	1 Thess 4:13–18

CONTRIBUTION TO THE CANON

- Teaching regarding the events immediately preceding the second coming of Christ, including the rapture (1 Thess 4:13–18)
- Teaching on the "man of lawlessness," the Antichrist (2 Thess 2:3–4), and "the one now restraining," whose identity is disputed (2 Thess 2:7)
- Believers' election and calling by God (1 Thess 1:4; 2 Thess 2:13–15)
- The importance of a Christian work ethic (1 Thess 5:12–14; 2 Thess 3:6–13)
- Teaching on how to live expectantly in the light of Christ's return (e.g., 1 Thess 5:1–22)

INTRODUCTION

THE THESSALONIAN LETTERS are probably among the more neglected of Paul's letters. This is partly due to the modest amount of discussion in the letters regarding salvation compared with works like Romans and Galatians. It is also partly due to their brevity and to questions about the authorship of 2 Thessalonians. But these letters are significant for providing insight into the missionary methods and message of the great apostle. They are invaluable for the insights that they offer regarding the return of Jesus Christ, the resurrection of believers, the eternal punishment of the wicked, and the events immediately preceding Jesus' return. They also offer helpful instructions regarding sanctification, election, and the Christian work ethic.

Paul's letters to the Thessalonians are also among the earliest letters written by Paul. Those who affirm the North Galatian theory of provenance for Galatians typically view the Thessalonian correspondence as the earliest samples of Pauline literature. Most of those who hold to the South Galatian theory place 1 and 2 Thessalonians after Galatians. Since Paul's letters are treated here in likely chronological order, and since the South Galatian theory has been established as more plausible than the North Galatian one, Paul's Thessalonian correspondence is discussed subsequent to Galatians. In any event, the letters offer important information about the foundational truths of the apostle's theology.

HISTORY

Author

Modern NT scholars generally recognize 1 Thessalonians as an authentic letter of Paul. The Pauline authorship of the letters attributed to him in the NT is of considerable importance since these letters tie the Thessalonian correspondence to Paul, the one who was called and commissioned by the risen Christ himself. At least from the time of Irenaeus (c. 130–200), the early church unanimously accepted the letter as both Pauline and canonical. Irenaeus quoted 1 Thess 5:23 and identified that quotation as the words of the "apostle" in "his first epistle to the Thessalonians" (*Against Heresies* 6.5.1). Clement of

Alexandria (c. 150–215; *Paedagogus* 5) and Tertullian (c. 160–225; *Against Marcion* 5.15) also acknowledged that the letter was Paul's own composition.[1]

Unlike the first letter, the majority of modern scholars doubt, if not wholly reject, Pauline authorship of 2 Thessalonians.[2] However, the letter claims to have been written by Paul (2 Thess 1:1), describes letters falsely ascribed to the apostle as deception (2 Thess 2:2–3), and confirms Paul's own authorship with a distinctive autograph (2 Thess 3:17). The letter cannot be accepted as written by a person of integrity who writes in the name of Paul to express what he believed to be Pauline doctrine as some scholars have claimed. Either the letter is a genuine document written by the apostle Paul, or it is a forgery written by someone who intentionally deceived his readers. As R. Jewett noted, "The improbability of a forgery is extremely high."[3] Both the external and internal evidence affirm Paul's authorship of the letter. Those who study the letter in greatest detail typically affirm the authenticity of the letter.[4] Modern readers may be confident that the early church was correct in ascribing this letter to Paul.

Date

First Thessalonians was written by Paul during his second missionary journey soon after he fled Thessalonica in the face of severe persecution (Acts 17:5–10). If Paul wrote the letter from Corinth, he probably did so in the year 50. Paul's 18 months in Corinth can be dated in light of the Gallio Inscription that indicates Gallio served as proconsul from July 1, AD 51, to July 1, AD 52. Paul probably appeared before Gallio shortly after he assumed power, because Paul's opponents most likely would have brought their charges to a new and untested proconsul in hopes that he might be influenced to rule in their favor. Thus Paul's appearance before Gallio probably occurred in the late summer or early fall of the year 51 toward the end of Paul's 18 months in Corinth.[5]

Timothy remained in Berea while Paul was escorted to Athens (Acts 17:13–14). Paul apparently used these escorts, who returned to Berea as Paul was entering Athens, to deliver his instructions for Timothy to return to Thessalonica. The journey from Athens back to Berea probably took the couriers several weeks. One must then allow several weeks for Timothy's journey from Berea to Thessalonica and his stay in Thessalonica. His travel from Thessalonica back to Paul in Corinth probably took approximately one month. A period of two and a half to three months likely transpired between the time of Paul's entrance into Athens and Timothy's return to Paul.

---

[1] See D. Guthrie, *New Testament Introduction*, 2nd ed. (Downers Grove: InterVarsity, 1990), 589.

[2] Modern doubt of the Pauline authorship of 2 Thessalonians began with J. E. C. Schmidt in 1801; see G. Milligan, *St. Paul's Epistles to the Thessalonians* (London: Macmillan, 1908), lxxviii.

[3] R. Jewett, *The Thessalonian Correspondence: Pauline Rhetoric and Millenarian Piety* (Philadelphia: Fortress, 1986), 18.

[4] E. Best, *A Commentary on the First and Second Epistles to the Thessalonians* (London: A. and C. Black, 1977), 52.

[5] Both assumptions are supported by C. J. Hemer, *The Book of Acts in the Setting of Hellenistic History* (Tübingen: Mohr Siebeck, 1989), 119.

Paul probably wrote 1 Thessalonians soon after Timothy's arrival in Corinth. This suggests that Paul wrote 1 Thessalonians several months after personally arriving in Corinth. Thus, he could have composed the letter anytime between midspring and midsummer 50. If Paul appeared before Gallio later in his proconsulate, a date of composition up to one year later is possible. A date within this range or a few months later is also compatible with the theory, held by a few scholars, that Paul wrote 2 Thessalonians before 1 Thessalonians.

Second Thessalonians was probably written several months after the earlier letter, perhaps in the winter of 50. Interpreters who accept the priority of 2 Thessalonians generally suggest that Timothy served as the courier for the letter and that it accompanied him on his trip from Athens to Thessalonica, in which case the letter was composed while Paul was in Athens early in the spring of 50.

Provenance

The internal evidence of the letter and the account of Paul's second missionary journey in Acts suggest that Corinth is the likely location of writing. First Thessalonians 3:1–10 explains that Paul decided to remain in Athens alone and to send Timothy to Thessalonica to encourage the church and to find out how the church was faring in Paul's absence. A comparison of 1 Thessalonians 3 and Acts 17 suggests that although Paul was in Athens, he sent instructions through his escorts to Timothy in Berea. Timothy was to travel to Thessalonica and then reconnect with Paul in Athens. But by the time Timothy returned from Thessalonica, Paul had already moved on to Corinth (Acts 17:14–16; 18:5) where Timothy eventually rejoined Paul with his report of the situation in Thessalonica that prompted Paul to write 1 Thessalonians. Since 1 Thessalonians names Timothy as a coauthor of the letter, the letter was likely from Corinth.

The large majority of contemporary scholars who affirm Paul's authorship of the letter argue that 2 Thessalonians was written from Corinth several months after the first letter. Second Thessalonians 1:1 identifies Paul, Timothy, and Silas as coauthors. According to the testimony of Acts, these three men traveled together only during the second missionary journey. Second Corinthians 1:9 confirms that Paul and Timothy resided together in Corinth, and Silas is probably also among the "brothers from Macedonia" mentioned in 2 Cor 11:7–11. Paul was probably not in Athens long enough to have written 1 Thessalonians there. It is even less likely that he composed his second letter in Athens. So 2 Thessalonians was probably written within a few months of the first letter, and Paul's 18 months in Corinth afford more than enough time for the letter to have been written there.

Destination

Both 1 and 2 Thessalonians were addressed to believers in the recently planted church in Thessalonica. Thessalonica, modern Thessaloniki or Salonica, was strategically located. It was situated at the head of the Gulf of Therme on the finest natural harbor on the Aegean Sea and became the chief port city for Macedonia. It also lay on the Via Egnatia, the main Roman road between Asia Minor and Dyrrachium, a port on the coast of the Adriatic Sea from which one could sail across the Adriatic to the port at Brundisium and then follow the Via Appia directly to Rome. Thessalonica was thus the largest and most important city in Macedonia during the time of the apostle Paul.[6]

Thessalonica was a cosmopolitan city inhabited by both Greeks and Romans, and a significant Jewish population lived there (Acts 17). Most of Paul's readers had been pagan idolaters before their conversion to Christianity (1 Thess 1:9). They may have worshipped a number of the various gods of Thessalonica including Dionysius, Sarapis, Kabiros, and Caesar.[7] The congregation in Thessalonica was a mixed one that included new believers from both Jewish and pagan backgrounds.

Occasion

Acts 17:1–10 records Paul's founding of the church at Thessalonica. After Paul was expelled from Philippi, he continued westward on the Via Egnatia to Thessalonica. There, for three consecutive Sabbaths, he spoke in the Jewish synagogue and sought to convince the Jews that Jesus is the Messiah and that he "had to suffer and rise from the dead" (Acts 17:3). Some of the hearers embraced the gospel not because of the persuasiveness of Paul's arguments but because of God's own mysterious activity among the Thessalonians. Paul had no doubt that God had chosen them because his gospel "did not come to you in word only, but also in power, in the Holy Spirit, and with much assurance" (1 Thess 1:5).

Although Paul's ministry in the synagogue only lasted a few weeks, evidence from the Thessalonian letters suggests that he may have continued his ministry in his workshop (1 Thess 2:9). Paul mentioned receiving financial support from the Philippians at least twice during his stay in Thessalonica (Phil 4:16), thus implying a longer stay in the city than a superficial reading of Acts 17 might suggest. While Paul was in Thessalonica, persecution against the missionary team and the new believers erupted. Acts 17:5 suggests that Jews incited the persecution but that the entire city was quickly caught up with anti-Christian sentiments. The Jews stirred the anger of "scoundrels from the marketplace" who formed a mob and "set the city in an uproar." Their complaints against the Christians were brought to the city magistrates and invoked Caesar's decrees. The magistrates viewed the matter as serious enough to require them to take a security bond from some of the new believers.

Recognizing that Paul's presence would only continue to inflame the animosity against Christians in the city, the Thessalonians urged Paul and Silas to depart for Berea. Paul later departed for Athens where he preached his famous sermon before the Areopagus. While Paul was in Athens, he sent Timothy back to Thessalonica to inspect the state of the church there. Timothy met up with Paul again in Corinth. He gave Paul a report concerning the

---

[6] C. Wanamaker, *Commentary on 1 and 2 Thessalonians*, NIGTC (Grand Rapids: Eerdmans, 1990), 3.

[7] See especially C. Edson, "Cults of Thessalonica," *HTR* 41 (1948): 153–204; and K. P. Donfried, "The Cults of Thessalonica and the Thessalonian Correspondence," *NTS* 31 (1985): 336–56.

church and may have even delivered a letter from the Thessalonians to Paul. The phrase "now concerning" (*peri de*) may imply that Paul was answering questions raised by the Thessalonians in their correspondence to him.[8]

Paul wrote his first letter to the Thessalonians in response to Timothy's report and, possibly, correspondence from the Thessalonians that Timothy delivered. This led Paul to address the issues we discuss in the "Purpose" below. Second Thessalonians deals with some of the same problems, though he expands his treatment of the end time and further addresses the problem of the "idle" in the church.

Purpose

Both 1 and 2 Thessalonians are pastoral letters written to address the specific needs of the church of Thessalonica. First Thessalonians was written to (1) encourage the church during a time of persecution; (2) defend the purity of Paul's motives behind his mission to the Thessalonians; (3) urge the church to live holy lives characterized by sexual purity; (4) define a Christian work ethic; (5) correct confusion about the return of Christ; and (6) prompt the church to respect its leaders.

Second Thessalonians was written to address issues in the church about which Paul appears to have learned through an oral report (2 Thess 3:11). He wrote the letter to (1) encourage a persecuted church with the promise of final vindication; (2) correct confused views about the end time caused by misrepresentations of Paul's teaching; and (3) give the church more extensive directions for dealing with the "idle."

LITERATURE

Literary Plan

Modern-day letter writers use certain literary conventions like the greeting "Dear" or the closing "Sincerely." The format of a modern letter is dependent to some degree upon its purpose. A personal letter typically assumes one format and a business letter another. Similarly, ancient speeches and letters used particular conventions and formats: Aristotle described three major genres of rhetoric. Grasping these can help the interpreter better understand ancient communication and so the function of these letters.[9]

First Thessalonians is best classified as epideictic (praise or blame) rhetoric, a genre in which an author reinforces and celebrates values or ideas shared with his audience. Such rhetoric could be either positive or negative. On the one hand, it might use praise to persuade the audience to continue present behavior. On the other hand, it might use blame to dissuade the audience from continuing present behavior. Most scholars classify

---

[8] Compare 1 Thess 4:9; 5:1 with 1 Cor 7:1,25; 8:1.

[9] For a good introduction to the basic format of Paul's letters, see P. T. O'Brien, "Letters, Letter Forms," in *Dictionary of Paul and His Letters*, 550–53.

1 Thessalonians as epideictic because Paul's praise and thanksgiving for the Thessalonians are so dominant throughout the letter.[10]

Second Thessalonians is best described as deliberative rhetoric. This genre sought to persuade people to follow a particular course of action in the future, so 2 Thessalonians is classified as deliberative because Paul sought to persuade the Thessalonians to adopt a different understanding of the Day of the Lord and to abandon their idleness.[11]

OUTLINES

1 Thessalonians
I.   INTRODUCTION (1:1)
II. EXPRESSIONS OF THANKS AND LOVE FOR THE THESSALONIANS (1:2–3:13)
    A.   First Prayer of Thanksgiving for the Thessalonians (1:2–10)
    B.   Paul's Relationship with the Thessalonians During His Visit Demonstrating the Purity of His Motives for the Thessalonian Ministry (2:1–12)
    C.   Second Prayer of Thanksgiving for the Thessalonians (2:13–16)
    D.   Paul's Relationship with the Thessalonians After His Departure (2:17–3:10)
    E.   Third Prayer of Thanksgiving Introducing the Three Major Topics of the Next Section: Personal Holiness, Christian Love, and the Second Coming (3:11–13)
III. EXHORTATIONS AND INSTRUCTIONS (4:1–5:22)
    A.   Introduction to Exhortations (4:1–2)
    B.   Exhortation to Personal Holiness and Sexual Purity (4:3–8)
    C.   Exhortation to Christian Love and Responsible Living (4:9–12)
    D.   Instructions about the Second Coming (4:13–18)
    E.   Exhortations Related to the Second Coming (5:1–11)
    F.   General Exhortations (5:12–22)
IV. CONCLUSION (5:23–28)

2 Thessalonians
I.   INTRODUCTION (1:1–12)
II. THESIS STATEMENT: THE DAY OF THE LORD HAS NOT OCCURRED AND TRUE BELIEVERS NEED NOT FEAR IT (2:1–2)
III. PROOFS SUPPORTING PAUL'S THESIS (2:3–17)
    A.   First Proof: Day of the Lord Has Not Occurred (2:3–12)
    B.   Second Proof: Christians Can Have Hope and Confidence as They Anticipate the End Time (2:13–17)
IV. EXHORTATIONS (3:1–15)
    A.   Exhortation to Pray (3:1–5)

---

[10] Jewett, *Thessalonian Correspondence*, 71–72; G. Lyons, *Pauline Autobiography: Toward a New Understanding*, SBLDS 73 (Atlanta: Scholars Press, 1985), 219–21; Wanamaker, *Thessalonians*, 47.

[11] F. W. Hughes, *Early Christian Rhetoric and 2 Thessalonians*, JSNTSup 30 (Sheffield: JSOT, 1989), 55; Jewett, *Thessalonian Correspondence*, 82; G. A. Kennedy, *New Testament Interpretation Through Rhetorical Criticism* (Chapel Hill: University of North Carolina, 1984), 144; Wanamaker, *Thessalonians*, 48.

B.　Exhortations Related to the Idle (3:6–15)
V.　CONCLUSION (3:16–18)

UNIT-BY-UNIT DISCUSSIONS

1 THESSALONIANS

I. Introduction (1:1)

II. Expressions of Thanks and Love for the Thessalonians (1:2–3:13)

In his first major section, Paul assured the Thessalonians of his love for them and the purity of his motives for his mission in Thessalonica. He apparently did so in response to claims by his opponents that his mission was driven by selfish motives and that he had abandoned the church when it needed him most. The criticism was, of course, untrue. Luke clearly indicated that Paul fled Thessalonica at the church's request (Acts 17:10). The new church evidently thought that Paul's departure would defuse the growing anti-Christian sentiments in the city. But now that Paul was gone, his opponents probably argued that Paul had incited the wrath of the city and then conveniently disappeared at the first sign of trouble.

A. First Prayer of Thanksgiving for the Thessalonians (1:2–10)　　Paul's first letter to the Thessalonians is peppered with prayers of thanksgiving that demonstrate Paul's love for the congregation. In this first prayer, Paul thanked God for the evidences of his gracious election of the believers (1:2–4). Their election and authentic conversion were evidenced by the miracles that accompanied Paul's message and had confirmed the truthfulness of his gospel and the Holy Spirit's activity in persuading them to embrace the truth (1:5–7). The Thessalonians had abandoned their idols to serve God and were an example to other believers in their Christian service, evangelistic zeal, and faithfulness in the face of persecution (1:8–10). The prayer introduces the major themes of the letter by reminding the Thessalonians of (1) the effects of Paul's ministry that confirmed God's approval of Paul; (2) the Thessalonians' perseverance in the face of persecution; and (3) the believers' eager anticipation of Christ's return.

B. Paul's Relationship with the Thessalonians during His Visit (2:1–12)　　Paul responded to his opponents' attack against his motives by reminding the Thessalonians of the characteristics of his ministry (2:1–4). Paul had preached at great risk with integrity and sincerity and without receiving any financial support from the new believers (2:5–9). Paul appealed to both the Thessalonians and to God as witnesses who testified to his devotion and blamelessness (2:10–12).

C. Second Prayer of Thanksgiving for the Thessalonians (2:13–16)　　Paul's second prayer of thanksgiving confirmed the divine origin of Paul's gospel. It reminded the Thessalonians that they were not alone in their sufferings for Christ. It encouraged the Thessalonians to persevere with the assurance that God would judge their persecutors.

D. Paul's Relationship with the Thessalonians After His Departure (2:17–3:10)   Paul's love for the Thessalonian church had been displayed by his efforts to return to Thessalonica (2:17–20) and by sending Timothy to strengthen and encourage the church while he remained in Athens (3:1–5; cf. Acts 17). Paul expresses gratitude for Timothy's positive report about the Thessalonians' faith and love and assures them of his earnest and constant prayers for them (3:6–10).

E. Third Prayer of Thanksgiving (3:11–13)   Paul's third prayer of thanksgiving and petition for the church introduced the three main topics of the next main section. The prayer "may the Lord cause you to increase and overflow with love for one another and for everyone" (v. 12) anticipates the discussion of brotherly love in 4:9–12. The petition "May he make your hearts blameless in holiness before our God and Father" (v. 13) anticipates the discussion of personal holiness in 4:1–8. The reference to the "coming of our Lord Jesus with all His saints" (v. 13) introduces the eschatological discussion in 4:13–5:11 and hints that deceased believers will accompany Christ at the time of his return.

III. Exhortations and Instructions (4:1–5:22)

This major section is permeated by numerous commands to the church along with supporting arguments.

A. Introduction to Exhortations (4:1–2)   Paul urged the church to pursue a moral and ethical lifestyle that was pleasing to God. He reminded the Thessalonians that the commands that he gave ultimately came from Christ himself.

B. Exhortation to Personal Holiness and Sexual Purity (4:3–8)   Paul urged the church to abstain from sexual immorality (4:3). He went so far as to define sexual purity as the essence of God's will for the believer and a goal of the process of sanctification. Sexual immorality was pagan behavior and inappropriate for followers of Jesus. After insisting earlier that his moral teaching came from Christ (4:2), Paul now insisted that it came from God through the Holy Spirit (4:8). Consequently, a lifestyle of immorality defied the commands of the triune God and invited his holy vengeance.

C. Exhortation to Christian Love and Responsible Living (4:9–12)   The Thessalonians naturally and spontaneously expressed love to each other as a by-product of the Spirit's transforming work in them (4:9). Paul urged them to do so even more (4:10). Love for others demanded that one live responsibly and work for a living rather than depending on the generosity of other believers (4:11). This insistence was aimed at the idle who were mentioned again in 5:14 and would be addressed in greater detail in Paul's second letter. Paul warned that failure to live compassionately and responsibly would thwart the church's witness to outsiders (4:12).

D. Instructions About the Second Coming (4:13–18)   Paul prepared his audience for exhortations related to the Second Coming by first clearing up some confusion about events accompanying Christ's return. The church was apparently concerned about the fate of believers who died before the Second Coming and feared that the dead believers might not be able to enjoy the dramatic and exciting events related to Jesus' return (4:13). Paul encouraged the church by assuring them that believers who had died would be raised as Jesus descended to consummate his reign over the earth (4:14–16). Those who were alive at Christ's return would be "caught up" together with them in the clouds to meet the Lord in the air (the "rapture") and so forever be with the Lord (4:17).

E. Exhortations Related to the Second Coming (5:1–11)   Paul urged the Thessalonians to be alert and vigilant because Jesus' return would be sudden (5:1–8). He comforted the church with the assurance that God's people would escape God's wrath because of Jesus' sacrificial death. Thus they could anticipate Jesus' return with joy rather than dread (5:9–11).

F. General Exhortations (5:12–22)   Paul urged the church to support and respect spiritual leaders, show love and forgiveness to others, and be faithful in prayer (5:12–18). He also commanded the church to value the gift of prophecy by which God revealed his truth through gifted individuals in the church but to test prophetic pronouncements and to accept only those that were good, that is, that were consistent with the truth Christ revealed through Paul (5:19–22).

IV. Conclusion (5:23–28)

Paul's final prayer encapsulates the two greatest concerns of the letter by focusing on the purity of God's people in anticipation of the Second Coming. The letter ends on the confident note that the congregation would be found blameless at the time of Jesus' return because of God's faithfulness to those whom he called. God called his people to sanctification (see 4:7), and he would accomplish it (5:24).

2 THESSALONIANS

I. Introduction (1:1–12)

Following his customary greeting (1:1–2), Paul sought to encourage the Thessalonians to remain faithful as they endured persecution (1:3–4). In divine retribution, God would torment those who tormented his people and give rest to those who were suffering (1:5–7a). This judgment would occur in conjunction with the Second Coming when sinners would confront the same glorious divine presence that would slay the antichrist (1:7b–10; cf. 2:8). As Paul anticipated that great event, he prayed that the believers would be characterized by goodness and thus bring glory to Christ (1:11–12).

II. Thesis Statement: The Day of the Lord Has Not Occurred and True Believers Need Not Fear It (2:1–2)

Paul announced two topics that dominate the second chapter of his letter: Christ's return and the gathering of believers. Somehow, whether by a spirit or a spoken word or a letter seeming to be from Paul and his associates, the Thessalonians had begun to suspect that the Day of the Lord had already occurred or that it was already occurring.

III. Proofs Supporting Paul's Thesis (2:3–17)

Paul wrote to insist that the Day of the Lord had not yet taken place and to describe events that must transpire prior to Christ's return.

A. First Proof: The Day of the Lord Has Not Occurred (2:3–12) The Day of the Lord, which encompasses such important eschatological events as the Second Coming, the resurrection of the dead, and the final judgment, would be preceded by widespread apostasy inspired by the "man of lawlessness" (i.e., the antichrist; 2:3). This figure would enthrone himself in the place of God in the Jerusalem temple and would deceive unbelievers with amazing counterfeit miracles (2:4,9–12). Ultimately, the man of lawlessness would be destroyed by Christ at his return. Some unnamed person and power were restraining lawlessness, and the man of lawlessness would not appear until the restrainer was removed (2:5–8).

B. Second Proof: Christians Can Have Hope and Confidence as They Anticipate the End Time (2:13–17) Paul recognized that his warning about the great delusion that would accompany the coming of the man of lawlessness might have frightened his readers. Paul encouraged the believers to stand firm by reminding them that God had chosen them for salvation and that he had called them for final glorification (2:13–15). This gracious election and powerful call assured them that God would strengthen and protect them until his plan for them was fulfilled (2:16–17). Paul repeated this assurance in 3:3–5.

IV. Exhortations (3:1–15)

Paul concluded his letter by tackling some of the practical problems in the church at Thessalonica.

A. Exhortation to Pray (3:1–5) First, Paul exhorted the church to pray for the spread and positive reception of the gospel. Paul was convinced that the effectiveness of his ministry was dependent on the exercise of God's gracious power and not his own skills or abilities. Paul also asked the church to pray for the protection of the missionary team.

B. Exhortations Related to the Idle (3:6–15) Second, Paul instructed the church on how to handle the idle. These individuals were living irresponsibly by refusing to work and depending on the generosity of other members of the church for their survival (3:6). This lifestyle might somehow be linked to the confused eschatology of the church or represent a separate issue. Paul appealed to both Christian tradition and his own example to argue that believers must work for a living (3:7–13). Church members should disassociate themselves from the idle and no longer support them financially in hopes that they would repent and begin to live responsibly (3:14–15).

V. Conclusion (3:16–18) Paul prayed that the church would experience both the peace and grace of the Lord Jesus. He also explained how he authenticated his letters so that the church could now distinguish letters actually authored by the apostle from those fraudulently ascribed to him.

THEOLOGY

Theological Themes

The Second Coming   Both letters to the Thessalonians were written to address questions or false assumptions about the end time and thus provide Paul's most explicit teaching about the Second Coming. Paul's teaching in 1 Thess 4:13–18 was derived from "a revelation from the Lord," whether Jesus' eschatological teachings during his earthly ministry (see Matthew 24–25; Mark 13) or revelation from Christian prophets in the early church.[12]

At the Second Coming, the Lord Jesus will descend from heaven. The accompanying shout of the Messiah (John 5:25) will raise the dead. The voice of the archangel and the blast of a trumpet (Matt 24:29–31; 1 Cor 15:52) serve as signals to the angels to gather God's people both dead and living for final transformation. The newly resurrected believers and the believers who had not experienced death will be caught up together in the clouds to meet the Lord in the air.

The word "meet" (*apantesis*) was often used to speak of a group who went out to meet an approaching dignitary and then turned around and escorted him or her into their city or home (Matt 25:6; Acts 28:15). The approach of the dignitary was sometimes called the *parousia*, the word used here to describe the coming of Christ.[13] The close connection of the passage to Jesus' descriptions of the Second Coming (see esp. Matt 24:30–31) and the likely sense of the words *apantesis* and *parousia* in 1 Thess 4:13–18 favor a posttribulational rapture.

First Thessalonians 5:1–11 describes the Second Coming as belonging to the Day of the Lord predicted by the OT prophets (e.g., Amos 5:18–20; Obadiah 15; Zeph 1:2–18). Paul insisted that the Day of the Lord would come suddenly, taking unbelievers, though not God's people, by surprise. Second Thessalonians 1:3–12 stresses the horrors experienced by unbelievers when Jesus returns. Believers will escape this frightening outpouring of divine wrath but ought to prepare for Jesus' return by cultivating Christian character.

A Christian Work Ethic   Because of the unique challenge posed by the presence of the "lazy" (1 Thess 5:14) who lived "irresponsibly" (2 Thess 3:6–15), Paul emphasized the importance of a Christian work ethic in these letters. The "lazy" were apparently refusing to work and were taking advantage of the generosity of other members of the church, all because of their confused eschatology. Perhaps, like some end-time enthusiasts today, they quit their jobs and climbed on their rooftops to sit and wait for Christ's return. Whatever the motivations for their behavior, Paul insisted that such behavior was contrary to Christian teaching and to the apostle's own example (see 1 Thess 1:9–12).

---

[12] E.g., G. K. Beale, *1–2 Thessalonians* (Downers Grove: InterVarsity, 2003), 136–38; Wanamaker, *Thessalonians*, 170–71; and I. H. Marshall, *1 and 2 Thessalonians*, NCBC (London: Marshall, Morgan, and Scott, 1983), 125–27.

[13] Several commentators argue that the interplay of the noun "coming" that could speak of the approach of the king and the noun "meet" imply that believers meet Christ in the heavens and then escort him back to earth in royal procession. E.g., F. F. Bruce, *1 and 2 Thessalonians*, WBC 45 (Waco: Word, 1982), 102–3.

Paul listed several damaging consequences of the behavior of the idle: They used their free time to interfere with the work of others (2 Thess 3:11); they placed an undue financial burden on generous brothers and sisters; and, their behavior earned the disrespect of unbelievers or "outsiders" (1 Thess 4:10–12). Thus, Paul insisted that the church must not support the idle and even urged the church to initiate a process of compassionate church discipline in order to encourage the idle to change their behavior. Shaped by a right understanding of the Day of the Lord, Paul's teaching demonstrates the importance of believers working hard to provide for themselves and their families and become a positive testimony to unbelievers.

POINTS OF APPLICATION

- Work hard rather than being a burden to others (1 Thess 4:11–12; 2 Thess 3:10)
- Don't be uninformed regarding end-time events such as the rapture or the coming of the antichrist and get ready for Christ's return (1 Thess 4:13–16; 2 Thess 2:3–12)
- Pray constantly (1 Thess 5:17)
- Give thanks in everything (1 Thess 5:18)
- Don't stifle the Spirit (1 Thess 5:19)

STUDY QUESTIONS

1. Why are the Thessalonian letters often neglected? Why are they significant?
2. When was 1 Thessalonians likely written? How long was 2 Thessalonians written after 1 Thessalonians?
3. What are some of the primary reasons Paul wrote the Thessalonian letters?
4. What was the cause of the Thessalonians' deficient work ethic?
5. Which position regarding the rapture finds most support in 1 Thessalonians and why?
6. What is the most significant contribution of the Thessalonian letters to the NT canon?

FOR FURTHER STUDY

Beale, G. K. *1–2 Thessalonians*. IVP New Testament Commentary. Downers Grove: InterVarsity, 2003.

Bruce, F. F. *1 and 2 Thessalonians*. Word Biblical Commentary 45. Waco: Word, 1982.

Green, G. *The Letters to the Thessalonians*. Pillar New Testament Commentary. Grand Rapids: Eerdmans, 2002.

Holmes, M. W. *1 and 2 Thessalonians*. NIV Application Commentary. Grand Rapids: Zondervan, 1998.

Jewett, R. *The Thessalonian Correspondence: Pauline Rhetoric and Millenarian Piety*. Foundations and Facets: New Testament. Philadelphia: Fortress, 1986.

Marshall, I. H. *I and II Thessalonians*. New Century Bible. Grand Rapids: Eerdmans, 1983.

Martin, D. M. *1, 2 Thessalonians*. New American Commentary 33. Nashville: B&H, 1995.

Morris, L. *The First and Second Epistles to the Thessalonians*. Rev. ed. New International Commentary on the New Testament. Grand Rapids: Eerdmans, 1991.

Wanamaker, C. A. *Commentary on 1 and 2 Thessalonians*. New International Greek Testament Commentary. Grand Rapids: Eerdmans, 1990.

Weima, J. A. D., and S. E. Porter. *An Annotated Bibliography of 1 and 2 Thessalonians*. Leiden: Brill, 1998.

Chapter 12

Paul's Corinthian Correspondence: 1–2 Corinthians

CORE KNOWLEDGE

Students should know the key facts of 1 and 2 Corinthians. With regard to history, students should be able to identify the author, date, provenance, destination, and purpose for each book. With regard to literature, they should be able to provide a basic outline of each book and identify core elements of the book's content found in the unit-by-unit discussion. With regard to theology, students should be able to identify the major theological themes in 1 and 2 Corinthians.

KEY FACTS	
1 Corinthians	
Author:	Paul
Date:	53 or 54
Provenance:	Ephesus
Destination:	The church at Corinth
Occasion:	Oral reports and a letter from the Corinthians
Purpose:	To address practical issues such as schisms in the church, lawsuits in local courts, the exercise of church discipline, questions related to idolatry, Christian marriage, the ordinances, spiritual gifts, and theological issues such as the nature of salvation and the doctrine of resurrection
Key Verses:	13:1–3

Key Facts	
2 Corinthians	
Author:	Paul
Date:	54 or 55
Provenance:	Macedonia, perhaps Philippi
Destination:	Churches in Corinth and throughout the province of Achaia
Occasion:	Titus's report on the condition of the church followed by additional information regarding the intrusion of false apostles
Purpose:	To defend Paul's apostolic authority, explain the nature of the new covenant, encourage sacrificial giving to the relief offering, and challenge the claims of false apostles
Key Verses:	5:16–21

CONTRIBUTION TO THE CANON

- Dealing with division and spiritual immaturity in the church (1 Corinthians 1–4)
- Church discipline (1 Corinthians 5; 2 Cor 2:5–11)
- The respective advantages of singleness and marriage (1 Corinthians 7)
- Principles for NT giving (1 Corinthians 9; 16:1–4; 2 Corinthians 9)
- Spiritual gifts and the supremacy of love (1 Corinthians 12–14)
- The resurrection of Christ and believers and the nature of the resurrection body (1 Corinthians 15)
- The redemptive grace of suffering and the revelation of God's power in human weakness (2 Cor 1:3–11; 4:7–18; 12:1–10)
- Paul's defense of his apostolic ministry (2 Corinthians, esp. chaps. 10–13)

INTRODUCTION

PAUL'S LETTERS TO the church at Corinth are among the most theologically rich and most practically helpful books in the NT. They are most likely next in chronological sequence after Galatians and the Thessalonian letters. In his Corinthian correspondence Paul addressed numerous problems in a church plagued by many troubles. Paul's response to these problems applies his thoughtful theology to very practical issues and demonstrates that theology for Paul was not static. It was dynamic and made a practical difference in daily living. The Corinthian letters show Paul's remarkable integration of faith and practice.

First Corinthians contains Paul's most extensive discussion of topics such as Christian unity, Christian morality, the ordinances of the church, spiritual gifts, and the resurrection of believers. It challenges the development of personality cliques in the church, guides church leaders in the exercise of church discipline, and explains ways to conduct worship decently and in order. It also addresses issues of importance in contemporary society such as the abiding distinction between the genders and the limits of personal freedom.

The contribution of 2 Corinthians to the NT is considerable as well. The letter is invaluable in guiding interpreters to understand Paul's theology of the new covenant. The letter also aids students of the Bible in constructing a theology of suffering like no other NT book. Just as importantly, the Corinthian letters, especially 2 Corinthians, aid in developing a theology of ministry that emphasizes compassion, sacrifice, humility, and dependence on God. In an era in which spiritual leaders are being turned into celebrities and humility is viewed as an undesirable trait, 2 Corinthians may be more important than ever.[1]

HISTORY

Author

1 Corinthians   Paul's authorship of 1 Corinthians is so widely accepted that some prominent commentaries on the letter do not even treat the issue of authorship.[2] The ancient external evidence for the authenticity of the letter is also compelling. Clement of Rome quoted from 1 Corinthians and ascribed the quote to "the epistle of the blessed apostle Paul" around the year 96. He did so, remarkably, in a letter also addressed to the church at Corinth.[3] There are also frequent echoes of 1 Corinthians in the letters of Ignatius that were composed prior to 110.[4]

2 Corinthians   Paul's authorship of 2 Corinthians has not been seriously contested. The external attestation of 2 Corinthians is not as strong as that for 1 Corinthians. Echoes of 2 Corinthians may appear in the letters of Ignatius (prior to 110) and the *Epistle of Barnabas* (c. 135).[5] But the possible parallels are not close enough to demonstrate dependence on 2 Corinthians.[6] Polycarp's letter to the Philippians almost certainly contains a loose paraphrase of 2 Cor 5:10, and other statements in the letter imply Polycarp's familiarity with 2 Corinthians.[7] Polycarp wrote this letter some time near the death of Ignatius,

---

[1] R. V. G. Tasker, *The Second Epistle to the Corinthians: Introduction and Commentary*, TNTC (Grand Rapids: Eerdmans, 1958), 12–13.

[2] E.g., G. D. Fee, *The First Epistle to the Corinthians*, NICNT (Grand Rapids: Eerdmans, 1987); D. E. Garland, *1 Corinthians*, BECNT (Grand Rapids: Baker, 2003); and C. K. Barrett, *The First Epistle to the Corinthians*, HNTC (Peabody: Hendrickson, 1968), 11.

[3] *1 Clement* 47:1–3 alludes to the discussion of factions in 1 Cor 1:10–17 and in chap. 3; *1 Clement* 49 contains a hymn about love based on 1 Corinthians 13.

[4] *To the Ephesians* 16:1; 18:1; *To the Romans* 4:3; 5:1; 9:2; and *To the Philadelphians* 3:3.

[5] See Ignatius, *To the Ephesians* 15:3 (2 Cor 6:16); *To the Trallians* 9:2 (2 Cor 4:14); *To the Philadelphians* 6:3 (2 Cor 1:12; 2:5; 11:9–10; 12:16); *To Barnabas* 4:11–13 (2 Cor 5:10); 6:11–12 (2 Cor 5:17).

[6] V. P. Furnish, *II Corinthians*, AB (Garden City: Doubleday, 1984), 29–30.

[7] Polycarp (*Phil.* 4:1) may have quoted 2 Cor 6:7 ("weapons of righteousness") and Phil 2:2, and he probably alluded to 2 Cor 4:14. M. J. Harris (*Second Epistle to the Corinthians*, NIGTC [Grand Rapids: Eerdmans, 2005], 3) sees "three or four clearer allusions" to 2 Corinthians in Polycarp's letter.

which is typically dated during the reign of Trajan (98–117).[8] Thus Polycarp showed an awareness of the existence and authority of 2 Corinthians in the early second century. According to Tertullian (c. 160–225; *Against Marcion* 5.11–12), Marcion also included 2 Corinthians in his canon in the same general time period. By the late second century, 2 Corinthians was listed in the Muratorian Canon (c. later second century) and widely quoted and ascribed to Paul. The weaker external attestation for 2 Corinthians is not sufficient to raise suspicions regarding its authenticity. The letter is so thoroughly Pauline in form, style, and content that Paul's authorship of 2 Corinthians is practically indisputable.

In 1 Cor 1:1 Paul listed Sosthenes as a cosender. Some have inferred from the use of the first person plural pronoun "we" in the letter that Sosthenes had a greater role in composing the letter than was normally the case for Paul. Sosthenes is not mentioned elsewhere in Paul's letters. But it is possible that the Sosthenes of 1 Corinthians is the same Sosthenes mentioned in Acts 18:17, the ruler of the synagogue who was beaten by bystanders after the Jews accused Paul before Gallio in Corinth. If so, Sosthenes was a follower of Christ at the time of the writing of 1 Corinthians and supported and encouraged the ministry of the apostle he once persecuted.

In 2 Cor 1:1 Paul listed Timothy as a cosender. In contrast with Sosthenes, much is known about Timothy and his relationship to Paul. Paul met Timothy on his second missionary journey (Acts 16:1), and the two became life-long friends. Two of Paul's letters, 1 and 2 Timothy, are personally addressed to him. Moreover, Timothy was named as cosender of more of Paul's letters than any other individual. In addition to 2 Corinthians, he was Paul's cosender of five other letters: Philippians, Colossians, 1 and 2 Thessalonians, and Philemon.

Date and Provenance

Paul's history with the Corinthians is complex, but it is possible to reconstruct the course of the apostle's dealings with this difficult congregation from the available evidence in Acts and 1 and 2 Corinthians with a high degree of plausibility. As the following list shows, Paul made at least three visits to Corinth and wrote at least four letters, only two of which have been preserved in the Christian canon. The sequence of these visits and letters presents itself as follows.

1 Corinthians   According to 1 Cor 16:8, Paul wrote 1 Corinthians during his third missionary journey when he was well into his two-and-a-half-year stay in Ephesus. Based on the Delphi Inscription, Paul's appearance before Gallio in Corinth on the second missionary journey can be dated to late 51. Paul then returned to Antioch and later traveled through Galatia and Achaia to Ephesus where he remained for two and a half to three years. Paul probably wrote 1 Corinthians shortly before Pentecost either in late 53 or early 54.[9]

---

[8] See the discussion in M. W. Holmes, *The Apostolic Fathers: Greek Texts and English Translations*, 3rd ed. (Grand Rapids: Baker, 2007), 170, 276.

[9] For similar views on the dating of 1 Corinthians, see Barrett, *First Epistle to the Corinthians*, 5; Fee, *First Epistle to the Corinthians*, 4–5; and B. Witherington, *Conflict and Community in Corinth: A Socio-Rhetorical Commentary on 1 and*

Table 12.1: Paul's Visits and Letters to the Church at Corinth

1.	First visit: Paul planted the church in Corinth in 50–52 (Acts 18)
2.	Paul wrote the "previous letter" (1 Cor 5:9,11; "Corinthians A")
3.	Paul wrote 1 Corinthians from Ephesus in 53/54 (1 Cor 16:8; "Corinthians B")
4.	Paul wrote the "severe letter" (2 Cor 2:4; 7:8; "Corinthians C")
5.	Second visit: the "painful visit" (2 Cor 2:1; see 12:14; 13:1–2)
6.	Paul wrote 2 Corinthians from Macedonia in 54/55 (2 Cor 7:5; 8:1; 9:2; "Corinthians D")
7.	Third visit (Acts 20:2)

2 Corinthians Paul wrote 2 Corinthians from Macedonia (2 Cor 7:5; 8:1; 9:2). The subscription in several ancient manuscripts of the letter states more specifically that Paul wrote the letter from Philippi. This is a plausible provenance but remains uncertain unless more evidence becomes available. Second Corinthians 9:2 implies that the Corinthians had been preparing for the Jerusalem relief offering "since last year." This seems to require a date of composition in late 54 or perhaps early 55. The letter was delivered to Corinth by Titus and two other church representatives who later accompanied Paul to Jerusalem with the relief offering.[10]

Destination

Paul addressed the Corinthian letters to "God's church at Corinth, to those who are sanctified in Christ Jesus and called as saints" (1 Cor 1:2) and to "God's church at Corinth" (2 Cor 1:1). Although the church at Corinth was the primary intended recipient of the letters, Paul wanted the letters to be read by many congregations, particularly those in Achaia. First Corinthians was coaddressed to "all those in every place who call on the name of Jesus Christ our Lord—theirs and ours" (1:2). Similarly, 2 Corinthians was co-addressed to "all the saints who are throughout Achaia" (1:1).

Paul planted the churches in the province of Achaia in cities such as Athens and Corinth during his second missionary journey (Acts 17:16–18:17). He revisited the area during his third missionary journey (Acts 20:1–6). He returned again after his release from his first Roman imprisonment (2 Tim 4:20).

In Paul's day, the population was probably about 200,000, although some scholars and ancient writers suggest that it was much larger.[11] Since even conservative estimates make Corinth eight times larger than Athens, the enormous population of Corinth probably explains why Paul left Athens for Corinth after only a brief ministry there during the second missionary journey. It may also explain why Paul felt compelled to serve in Corinth

---

2 Corinthians (Grand Rapids: Eerdmans, 1995), 73.

[10] Many commentators date 2 Corinthians one year later, in the year 56; see the discussion in Harris, *Second Epistle to the Corinthians*, 67. Those accepting this later date typically assume a later date for 1 Corinthians than we think possible. This later date for 2 Corinthians also conflicts with the numismatic evidence that Felix succeeded Festus in the year 56.

[11] W. J. Larkin Jr., *Acts*, IVPNTC 5 (Downers Grove: InterVarsity, 1995), 262. Some scholars estimate the population to have been significantly higher. See W. McRae, *Archaeology and the New Testament* (Grand Rapids: Baker, 1991), 312.

for an entire 18 months. Corinth's political importance also exceeded that of other cities in the region. Since 27 BC, Corinth had been the administrative center for the province of Achaia.[12]

Corinth's prosperity was due in part to its strategic location. The city was located on the isthmus that connected the Peloponnesus, the southern peninsula of Greece, to mainland Greece. This isthmus was also the location of ancient Isthmia, the site of the famous Isthmian games. These games were held every two years, the years both before and after the Olympics, and attracted athletes from all over the ancient world to compete in contests. Several ancient writers note that the games were an important boost to Corinth's economy and enabled the city to prosper when other Greek cities like Athens were languishing.[13] First Corinthians is rich with athletic imagery (see esp. 1 Cor 9:24–27), and Paul may have used this imagery in part because of the prominence of the Isthmian games in Corinth's history.

Corinth was infamous for its immorality. Because of the numerous vices that characterized the city, an ancient Greek proverb said, "Not for every man is the voyage to Corinth!" (Strabo, *Geography* 8.6.2). Aristophanes (450–385 BC) demonstrated the immorality of ancient Corinth when he coined the term "Corinthianize" to describe the act of fornication. Plato used the term "Corinthian girl" as a euphemism for a prostitute.[14] Strabo, who wrote only a few decades before Paul's visit, claimed that one thousand prostitutes served as slaves for the temple of Aphrodite in Corinth (Strabo, *Geography* 8.6.20). The Corinthians and the numerous visitors to the city worshipped the goddess of love by engaging in immoral acts with the prostitutes.

Corinth was known for other vices too. A common figure in ancient Greek plays was a drunk who typically wore a Corinthian hat.[15] This implies that the Corinthians were notorious for their tendency to drink too much wine. Thus, it is not surprising that Paul had to combat heinous immorality including incest, prostitution, and drunkenness among the Corinthians in his letters.

Although not as religious as Athens, Corinth's landscape was also dotted with temples and shrines. Looming over the city on the Acrocorinth was the temple of Aphrodite, the goddess of love, lust, and beauty. Near the Forum in Corinth was a temple of Apollo or Athena, one of the oldest temples in Greece. Just inside the northern city wall stood a sanctuary of Asclepius, the god of healing. A huge structure at the western end of the forum is believed to have been a temple dedicated to the worship of the emperor.[16] These and other centers of pagan religion also figure prominently in the Corinthian letters, such as in Paul's discussion of whether the Corinthian believers should continue to participate

---

[12] D. Bock, *Acts*, BECNT (Grand Rapids: Baker, 2007), 577.

[13] Strabo, *Geography* 8.4; Plutarch, *Quaestiones conviviales* 5.3.1–3; 8.4.1; Pausanias, *Description of Greece* 2.2.

[14] J. Murphy-O'Connor, *St Paul's Corinth: Texts and Archaeology* (Wilmington, DE: Glazier, 1983), 56.

[15] C. E. Fant and M. G. Reddish, *A Guide to Biblical Sites in Greece and Turkey* (Oxford: University Press, 2003), 54.

[16] McRae, *Archaeology and the New Testament*, 322–24.

in pagan feasts in the temples of the city (1 Cor 8:1–13; 10:1–22; 2 Cor 6:14–7:1) and whether they should eat the meat left over from the feasts that was sold in Corinth's markets (1 Cor 10:25–11:1).

Although Gentile believers composed the large majority of the membership, the church at Corinth was a mixed congregation with both Jewish and Gentile believers. The city of Corinth had at least one synagogue, and the Jews who gathered there were the focus of Paul's initial ministry in the city (Acts 18:4). Although Paul abandoned his synagogue ministry due to opposition from the Jews, Paul's outreach to the Jews and God--fearers in the synagogue was effective. Even Crispus, the leader of the synagogue, embraced the gospel and was baptized together with his entire family (Acts 18:8). After his conversion, he was replaced by Sosthenes as leader of the synagogue (Acts 18:17). Sosthenes may have eventually followed Crispus in his new faith, since this Sosthenes may be the "brother" of the same name whom Paul identified as the cosender of 1 Corinthians (1:1).

The church also had members from very different social and economic strata. Some were slaves (1 Cor 7:21–23), while many others were very prosperous (1 Cor 4:6–8). Paul's discussion of the collection for the saints implies that the church in Corinth had few economic worries compared with the financial struggles of the believers in Macedonia (2 Cor 8:1–7,13–15). Erastus, one of the members of the church at Corinth, was the treasurer for the city (Rom 16:23). This appears to be the city official who was honored in an inscription in front of the ancient Corinthian theater for paving one of the streets of the city at his own expense.[17] Erastus was probably only one of several high-ranking, wealthy, and influential members of the church. The material prosperity of the church would eventually create problems for Paul. Some members of the church questioned Paul's spirituality because of his poverty (1 Cor 4:10–13).[18]

The rampant immorality, the prominence of pagan religion, the economic, social, and racial diversity of the city of Corinth help explain many of the unique challenges that Paul faced in Corinth. These factors provide helpful insights that guide the interpretation of the Corinthian letters.

Occasion

Paul had a long and somewhat complicated relationship with the church at Corinth. He established the church at Corinth during his second missionary journey. After traveling from Athens to Corinth, Paul met Aquila and Priscilla and worked as their partner in his tent-making trade. He preached each Sabbath in the synagogue until some of the Jews blasphemed Jesus. Paul then continued his missionary work next door to the synagogue in the home of Titus Justus, a Gentile who frequented the synagogue and embraced

---

[17] Ibid., 331–33.

[18] For an excellent summary of the history of Corinth and its religious and cultural background, see Garland, *1 Corinthians*, 1–14. For an almost exhaustive treatment of Corinth, see Murphy-O'Connor, *St Paul's Corinth: Texts and Archaeology*.

Paul's gospel. Crispus, the leader of the synagogue, together with his entire family, and many other Corinthians believed the message that Paul preached and received Christian baptism. Some of Paul's Jewish opponents accused Paul before Gallio, the proconsul of Achaia. He dismissed Paul's case as irrelevant to Roman law and drove the accusers away. After spending a total of 18 months in Corinth, Paul sailed to Syria. After a very brief stay in Ephesus, he journeyed to Antioch by way of Caesarea and Jerusalem to report to the church there (see Acts 18:1–22).

Paul then traveled through Galatia and Phrygia until he finally arrived at Ephesus, where he remained for approximately two and a half years (see Acts 18:23–20:1). Perhaps some time early in Paul's stay at Ephesus, he received news of trouble in the church at Corinth. Evidently the church was facing problems with sexual immorality within the fellowship. In response, Paul wrote a letter urging the Corinthians to avoid associating with sexually immoral people who claimed to be Christians. This letter, which is mentioned in 1 Cor 5:9, is generally referred to by scholars as "Corinthians A" since it has not been preserved either in our NT or in any presently known manuscript. According to 1 Cor 5:10–13, some of the church members misunderstood the letter and assumed that Paul was demanding that believers retreat from pagan society and isolate themselves from all interaction with immoral people.

Meanwhile, Apollos, a disciple of Aquila and Priscilla, was preaching in Corinth with great effect, and some of the Christians at Corinth began rallying around him. Soon church members began to compare Apollos with Paul. Some felt Apollos was superior to Paul, and others felt he was inferior to the apostle. Soon the church had divided into four major factions: a Paul group, an Apollos group, a Cephas (Peter) group, and a Christ group. Other problems arose. A church member began to live in an incestuous relationship with his stepmother. Some members of the church developed confused ideas about marriage, sexual relationships, and gender roles. They were also practicing a form of the Lord's Supper that was more akin to celebrations in pagan temples than to the ordinance commanded by Christ. Church members were taking other church members to court to settle disputes. The church became obsessed with the more spectacular spiritual gifts and neglected Christian compassion. Moreover, the church had begun to doubt the doctrine of bodily resurrection. On top of all this, some members of the church had challenged Paul's apostolic authority.

Paul received information about the church's condition from at least two sources. First, a group of people identified as "members of Chloe's household" (1 Cor 1:11; lit. "those of Chloe") reported to Paul about the personality cults in the church that were ripping it apart. Second, Stephanus, Fortunatus, and Achaicus (1 Cor 16:15–18), three official delegates from the church, delivered a letter from the church to Paul that raised a number of doctrinal and practical questions. No doubt the three delegates supplemented the letter with their own verbal reports on the condition of the church so that Paul had a very clear understanding of the church's situation. Paul wrote a second letter to the church that answered the questions raised in the Corinthian correspondence and responded to other issues Paul knew about through the verbal reports. This letter is now known as 1 Corinthians and is identified by scholars as "Corinthians B."[19]

According to 1 Cor 16:5–11, when Paul wrote Corinthians B, he intended to remain in Ephesus until Pentecost and then travel through Macedonia to Corinth where he might spend the entire winter. Paul would then send church representatives chosen by the Corinthians to Jerusalem with the relief offering. In the meantime, Paul sent Timothy to the Corinthians (1 Cor 16:10–11). When Timothy arrived in Corinth, he was unsettled by the severity of their crises. He somehow informed Paul of the situation, and Paul determined to visit the Corinthians as soon as possible. Corinthians B contained a warning that if their problems were not soon corrected, Paul might be forced to "come to you with a rod [of discipline]" (1 Cor 4:21).

When Paul learned of the church's reaction to Corinthians B, he determined that the time for such disciplinary action had clearly arrived. Paul later characterized this personal confrontation with the church as his "painful visit" (2 Cor 2:1). The visit was painful not only for the Corinthians but also for Paul. He returned to Ephesus doubting that his visit had provided any real remedy to their crises and with "an extremely troubled and anguished heart" (2 Cor 2:2–4).

Paul's abandonment of his earlier plan to spend the winter in Corinth prompted some of his opponents in the church to charge him with vacillation. Paul defended his change of plans and explained his reasons for the change in 2 Cor 1:15–24. Paul felt that he could handle the situation better by letter than by another face-to-face confrontation with his opponents in the church. His tear-stained letter (2 Cor 2:4) is now lost. It is generally identified by scholars as "Corinthians C." In the absence of the letter, scholars can reconstruct its contents only by a few obscure references to the letter in 2 Corinthians. At the very least, the letter called for the church to prove its obedient character by disciplining one of the opponents who had personally maligned Paul (2 Cor 2:3–9; 7:8–12). Titus delivered the letter and worked to encourage the church's contribution to the relief offering that the Gentile churches were collecting for the church in Jerusalem.

In the meantime the "wide door for effective ministry" in Ephesus (1 Cor 16:9) began to close for Paul. Paul began to suffer such great affliction that he was "completely overwhelmed" and "even despaired of life." The great affliction could refer to the Demetrius riot (Acts 19:23–20:1) or could indicate that the town clerk's dismissal of the mob in the

---

[19] D. A. Carson and D. J. Moo, *An Introduction to the New Testament*, 2nd ed. (Grand Rapids: Zondervan, 2005), 420–25. Some use a different scheme borrowed from Paul's own descriptions. Letter 1 is the "previous letter"; Letter 2 is 1 Corinthians; Letter 3 is the "sorrowful letter"; and Letter 4 is 2 Corinthians. See D. Guthrie, *New Testament Introduction*, rev. ed. (Downers Grove: InterVarsity, 1990), 437.

Ephesian theater did not end the anti-Christian persecution in Ephesus but was only the prelude to even more intense persecution. Owing to this great affliction, Paul was forced to flee from Ephesus. He traveled to Troas, where he hoped to preach the gospel and to be reunited with Titus who would report on the situation at Corinth. Paul's ministry in Troas enjoyed encouraging results (2 Cor 2:12). However, Titus was nowhere to be found (2 Cor 2:13). Paul decided to leave Troas and travel throughout Macedonia. As he passed through the cities of Macedonia, he proclaimed the gospel, encouraged new believers, and organized the collection of the relief offering for the believers in Jerusalem (2 Cor 8:1–4; 9:2). These churches were suffering intense persecution, which Paul described as "a severe testing by affliction" (2 Cor 8:2). This severe persecution had an economic impact on the believers and left many of them in "deep poverty." But the Macedonian believers gave eagerly, generously, even "beyond their ability," to aid the believers in Jerusalem.

Paul was disturbed that Titus had still not appeared. When Titus finally met up with Paul in Macedonia, he delivered such an encouraging report about the Corinthians' response to Corinthians C that Paul was ecstatic. Paul had feared that his letter might have been too harsh and might have ended all hopes of restoring his relationship with the Corinthians. In the end it had the desired effect: to produce a godly sorrow in the Corinthians that moved them to repentance (2 Cor 7:10). Paul hurried to write a final letter to the Corinthians that expressed his joy at their change of heart. This letter has been traditionally identified as 2 Corinthians, and scholars refer to it as "Corinthians D."

Unfortunately, during a pause in his dictation of Corinthians D, Paul somehow received disturbing new information about the situation in Corinth. When he dictated the final three chapters of Corinthians D (or possibly took up the pen himself), his writing exhibits a noticeable shift in tone that suggests that Paul's fears for the Corinthians had returned. Paul's concerns related primarily to the influence that a group of false apostles bore over the congregation. These "superapostles" (2 Cor 12:11) boasted that their apostolic credentials exceeded Paul's and that he was unworthy to exercise leadership over the congregation. They apparently preached "another Jesus" and "a different gospel" than that proclaimed by Paul (2 Cor 11:1–4).

The letters of Paul and the history in Acts do not indicate whether the Corinthians responded to Paul's correction with repentance. *First Clement*, written by Clement of Rome to the Corinthians (c. 96), implies that the letter was effective and that the church of Corinth became a model congregation for nearly half a century. Interestingly, when problems erupted in the church again at the end of the first century, the issues that threatened the church were very similar to those that Paul had addressed: rejecting legitimate spiritual authority in order to be manipulated by a few headstrong and arrogant leaders and lacking the unity that should characterize the body of Christ.[20]

Purpose

1 Corinthians   Paul wrote 1 Corinthians to respond to oral reports he had received from those associated with Chloe (1 Cor 1:11) and elsewhere and to answer questions raised by the Corinthians in a letter that they wrote to him (1 Cor 7:1). The oral report focused primarily on the disunity of the Corinthian church. The church had divided into several factions, each of which celebrated a particular Christian leader. Paul wrote 1 Corinthians to urge the church to seek unity and to follow Christ rather than idolizing a human leader such as Paul, Apollos, or Cephas (1 Cor 1:12; see 1:10–4:21). Paul recognized that the glorification of human leaders indicated that the Corinthians did not understand the nature of divine grace and that they had a flawed view of the nature of human leadership. God's grace uses unlikely people for great purposes to display his power and wisdom. This promotes God's glory and diminishes human pride.

Paul had also heard from several different sources that a member of the church of Corinth was living in an incestuous relationship with his stepmother. Paul urged the church to repent of its casual acceptance of such immorality. He commanded the church to exercise discipline in hopes of encouraging the immoral church member to repent and of preventing the spread of immorality throughout the congregation (1 Cor 5:1–13). Paul also wrote to clarify the doctrine of Christian liberty and to demonstrate that freedom in Christ was not a license for immoral behavior (1 Cor 6:12–20).

Paul also knew that believers were taking fellow believers to court to settle disputes. Paul recognized that this was a poor witness to unbelievers in the local court systems and that justice was more likely to be found in decisions made by believers than by unbelievers. Paul thus urged the Corinthians to settle their disputes through arbitrators who were fellow believers.

Several issues were raised by the Corinthians' letter to Paul, and his reply to these concerns begins in chap. 7 and extends at least through chap. 14 and possibly through chap. 15. These concerns include questions about Christian marital relationships (chap. 7), participation in pagan feasts in various temples in Corinth and eating food formerly sacrificed to idols (chaps. 8–10), proper dress and decorum during worship and the Lord's Supper (chap. 11), and the exercise of spiritual gifts (chaps. 12–14).

Some of the Corinthians had rejected the doctrine of the bodily resurrection of believers. This rejection had a significant impact on their moral as well as their theological views. Paul wrote to defend the doctrine of the resurrection and to show the crucial nature of this doctrine to the Christian gospel (chap. 15).

---

[20] See *1 Clement*, otherwise known as the "Letter of the Romans to the Corinthians." The Greek text with an updated English translation and a helpful introduction is available in Holmes, *Apostolic Fathers*, 44–131.

Finally, Paul gave the church practical instructions for the collection of the relief offering for believers in Jerusalem and informed the Corinthians of his tentative travel plans (chap. 16).

2 Corinthians Although 2 Corinthians constitutes a single letter rather than a composite of several different Pauline letters, a letter of this length was likely composed over a period of several days or weeks. The needs of the churches to which Paul traveled, the demands of his occupation as a tentmaker, and the limited availability of secretaries with the skills needed to produce such a letter probably required Paul to dictate various portions of the letter at different times and possibly different places. This chapter has suggested that when Paul dictated chaps. 1–9 he was greatly encouraged by the positive report about the Corinthians that he received from Titus. But, after dictating the first nine chapters, he may have received more news from Corinth that alarmed him again and prompted him to write the final chapters of the letter with a different tone.[21] Some suggest that a secretary was not available for the last three chapters and that Paul actually penned chaps. 10–13 with his own hand.[22]

Paul wrote chaps. 1–9 for four major purposes. First, Paul's change in travel plans had made him vulnerable to his opponents' charge that he was inconsistent and unworthy of the Corinthians' trust. Paul wrote to defend his reliability and to explain the reasons for his change in plans. Second, Paul wrote to encourage the Corinthians to restore a church member who had been disciplined by the congregation for vicious attacks on the apostle. Third, Paul wrote to clarify the nature of his apostolic ministry and his qualifications for that ministry. Under the influence of new leaders who boasted that their apostolic qualifications were superior to Paul's, his credentials had been scrutinized and rejected by a growing number of Corinthian believers. Paul attempted to demonstrate that his qualifications for spiritual leadership exceeded those of his opponents in every way. This defense of Paul's apostleship is the primary motivation for the earlier section of the letter, and Paul seems confident that the Corinthians would be convinced by his defense. Fourth, Paul wrote to encourage the Corinthians to fulfill their pledge to contribute generously to the relief offering for the Jerusalem believers.

In chaps. 10–13, Paul's defense of his apostolic authority becomes much more intense. Paul was no longer confident that the Corinthians would recognize the false apostles for what they were or that they would reaffirm his own apostolic authority. Paul wrote these chapters to urge the Corinthians to reject the false apostles and their message and to

---

[21] See D. A. Carson, D. J. Moo, and L. Morris, *An Introduction to the New Testament* (Grand Rapids: Zondervan, 1992), 271–72; T. D. Lea, *The New Testament: Its Background and Message* (Nashville: B&H, 1996), 426–27; Guthrie, *New Testament Introduction*, 456–57 (influenced by W. Ramsey); and Harris, *Second Epistle to the Corinthians*, 50–51. F. F. Bruce (*1 and 2 Corinthians* [London: Oliphants, 1971], 170) even suggested that chaps. 10–13 were a separate letter that was dispatched slightly later than chaps. 1–9. Alternatively, R. Gundry, *A Survey of the New Testament*, 3rd ed. (Grand Rapids: Zondervan, 1994), 371, proposed that chaps. 1–9 are addressed to the repentant majority and chaps. 10–13 to a reactionary minority, but few have adopted his view.

[22] L. L. Belleville, *2 Corinthians* (Downers Grove: InterVarsity, 1996), 33.

embrace again the gospel that Paul had preached. Paul also wrote to announce his plans to make a third visit to Corinth. Finally, he wrote to urge the Corinthians to examine their faith to determine whether it was authentic.

LITERATURE

Literary Plan

The literary plan of 1 Corinthians is in some ways much simpler than that of other Pauline letters. After his introduction and customary prayer of thanksgiving, Paul systematically addressed issues of concern from oral reports relayed to Paul by those of Chloe and representatives of the Corinthian church. Paul then addressed questions posed to him in a letter from the Corinthians. The responses to questions from the letter begin in 1 Cor 7:1 as indicated by the introduction "About the things you wrote." New topics culled from the Corinthians' letter are introduced using the construction "now concerning," which appears in 1 Cor 7:1,25,37; 8:1; 12:1; and 16:1,12. Paul concluded his letter with his customary greeting and blessing.

Efforts to understand the literary plan of 2 Corinthians are complicated by the many theories of interpolation that regard 2 Corinthians as a composite of several different letters rather than a single literary document. Several scholars have attempted rhetorical classifications of 2 Corinthians and have sought to understand the structure of the letter based on rhetorical analyses. Other scholars have attempted to analyze the chiastic structure of the letter. No single analysis has won the favor of a large number of scholars. The majority of commentators prefer to analyze the structure of the letter based on content alone. Such a procedure divides the letter into three major sections consisting of chaps. 1–7, 8–9, and 10–13.

OUTLINES

1 CORINTHIANS

I. INTRODUCTION (1:1–9)
   A. Salutation (1:1–3)
   B. Prayer of Thanksgiving (1:4–9)
II. RESPONSE TO ORAL REPORTS (1:10–6:20)
   A. A Proper Perspective on Christian Ministers and Ministry (1:10–4:20)
   B. Immorality in the Church (5:1–13)
   C. Disputes Between Believers (6:1–11)
   D. Limitations on Freedom in Christ (6:12–20)
III. RESPONSES TO A LETTER FROM THE CORINTHIANS (7:1–16:4)
   A. Matters Related to Sex and Marriage (7:1–40)
   B. Matters Related to Idol Feasts (8:1–11:1)
   C. Matters Related to Christian Worship (11:2–34)

    D. Matters Related to Spiritual Gifts (12:1–14:40)
    E. Matters Related to the Resurrection (15:1–58)
    F. Matters Related to the Relief Offering (16:1–4)
IV. CONCLUSION (16:5–24)
    A. Paul's Travel Plans (16:5–12)
    B. Final Exhortations (16:13–18)
    C. Closing (16:19–24)

2 CORINTHIANS

  I. INTRODUCTION (1:1–11)
    A. Salutation (1:1–2)
    B. Prayer of Thanksgiving (1:3–7)
    C. Explanation of Paul's Thanksgiving (1:8–11)
 II. PAUL'S RELATIONSHIP WITH THE CORINTHIANS (1:12–2:11)
    A. Paul's Pure Conduct (1:12–14)
    B. Paul's Change in Plans (1:15–22)
    C. The Reason for the Change in Plans (1:23–2:4)
    D. Forgiveness to the Repentant Sinner (2:5–11)
III. PAUL'S DEFENSE OF HIS MINISTRY (2:12–7:16)
    A. Paul's Ministry in Troas and Macedonia (2:12–17)
    B. Paul's Letters of Commendation (3:1–3)
    C. Paul's Competence (3:4–6)
    D. Ministry of the New Covenant (3:7–18)
    E. The Unveiled Truth (4:1–6)
    F. Treasure in Clay Jars (4:7–18)
    G. The Coming Resurrection (5:1–10)
    H. The Ministry of Reconciliation (5:11–6:2)
    I. Catalog of Paul's Sufferings (6:3–13)
    J. Call to Separate from Paul's Opponents (6:14–7:1)
    K. Paul's Final Defense (7:2–16)
IV. THE COLLECTION FOR THE BELIEVERS IN JERUSALEM (8:1–9:15)
    A. Example of the Churches in Macedonia (8:1–7)
    B. Examples of Christ's Sacrifice and the Old Testament (8:8–15)
    C. Administration of the Offering (8:16–24)
    D. Importance of Having the Offering Ready (9:1–5)
    E. Principles Motivating Generous Giving (9:6–15)
  V. PAUL'S RENEWED DEFENSE OF HIS APOSTLESHIP (10:1–13:4)
    A. The Tone of Paul's Appeal (10:1–11)
    B. Divine Commendation of Paul's Ministry (10:12–18)
    C. Danger of the False Apostles (11:1–15)
    D. Paul's Sufferings (11:16–33)
    E. Paul's Visions and Revelations (12:1–10)

F.   Paul's Miracles (12:11–13)
    G.   Paul's Final Defense (12:14–13:4)
VI. FINAL EXHORTATIONS (13:5–12)
VII. CLOSING (13:13)

UNIT-BY-UNIT DISCUSSIONS

1 CORINTHIANS

I. Introduction (1:1–9)

A. Salutation (1:1–3)   Paul opened his letter, as was the custom, by identifying the author and intended recipients. His self-description, "called as an apostle of Christ Jesus by God's will," confirmed Paul's apostleship to a church that was apparently beginning to question Paul's apostolic authority and would ultimately deny his apostolic authority. The address emphasizes the importance of Jesus Christ to the church. Jesus Christ is both the agent of the church's sanctification and the object of her confession.

B. Prayer of Thanksgiving (1:4–9)   Paul's prayer offers thanks to God for the numerous spiritual gifts enjoyed by the Corinthian church. The prayer thus encouraged a significant change in the Corinthians' outlook on these gifts. Rather than being an object of personal pride and an incentive for boasting, the gifts were to be recognized as graciously imparted to the believers by God and thus incentives for thanksgiving and praise to him alone.

Paul's "grace and peace" is his typical greeting.[23] However, it may take on a slightly different significance in this church that had depreciated divine grace through its boasting in human accomplishments and had traded peace for heated conflict.

Paul also expressed his confidence that the gracious God who called the Corinthians to fellowship with his Son would ensure that they passed the scrutiny of final judgment. His reference to the "day of our Lord Jesus Christ" borrows the familiar phrase "day of the Lord/Yahweh" from the OT and applies it to Jesus' second coming. The application of this phrase that describes the coming of Yahweh in judgment to Jesus' return strongly implies the deity of Jesus and confirms that the title "Lord" used of Jesus frequently in 1 Corinthians (six times in the introduction alone: see 1:2,3,7,8,9,10) functions as a title of deity rather than mere authority.

II. Response to Oral Reports (1:10–4:20)

A. A Proper Perspective on Christian Ministers and Ministry (1:10–4:20)   Paul indicated that he had received word from people associated with Chloe that the church had divided into four major factions (1:10–17). Three of these factions wrongly idolized individuals and gave them a standing dangerously close to that of Jesus himself. This was terribly wrong since Jesus' role in the church was unique. Only he had suffered crucifixion

---

[23] See Rom 1:5; 2 Cor 1:2; Gal 1:3; Eph 1:2; Phil 1:2; Col 1:2; 1 Thess 1:1; 2 Thess 1:2; Titus 1:4; Phlm 3.

for their sake, and only he was the Messiah in whose name believers were baptized. Moreover, the Corinthians' celebration of human skills and abilities emptied the cross of its effect in ways that Paul soon described.

By turning Christian servants into celebrities based on their speaking and intellectual abilities, the Corinthians had shown a complete lack of understanding of the economy of God (1:18–25). God uses weak, foolish, and ignoble people and an apparently foolish and scandalous message to save sinners. This displays the supremacy of God's power and wisdom and reduces human wisdom and power to mere foolishness and weakness. The makeup of the Corinthian church confirmed Paul's description of the divine economy. An understanding of God's ways eliminated human boasting and drove sinners to praise God alone (1:26–31).

Paul's ministry to the Corinthians illustrated the principles that Paul had just explained (2:1–5). Paul did not seek to impress people with rhetorical abilities or his persona. Instead, a weak man who trembled before God preached a simple message about God's provision of forgiveness through Jesus' sacrificial death. The Corinthians had embraced this message not because Paul's wisdom was on display but because God's power was at work.

The worldly wisdom that the Corinthians prized was no true wisdom at all (2:6–16). Those responsible for Jesus' crucifixion touted themselves as wise men, but they did not even recognize who Jesus was. True wisdom was granted only through the revealing work of God's Spirit. Paul's ministry was an expression of this revelatory work. However, only those who were indwelled and influenced by God's Spirit could understand spiritual matters.

Paul had been forced to explain only the most elementary truths of the Christian faith to the Corinthians because they lacked the spiritual maturity to understand more difficult truths (3:1–9). Their disunity confirmed their immaturity. If they had been mature, they would have understood that the Christian servants they celebrated were only instruments in the hands of God and that God alone was to be glorified for the harvest produced through their ministries.

God gave Paul the resources needed to lay the foundation for the Corinthian church, and another person was building on that foundation (3:10–17). Those who were involved in the ministries of the church needed to make sure that Jesus Christ remained the focal point of those ministries. Those who served needed to be mindful that their service would be evaluated by God and unworthy contributions to the ministry would be destroyed. The church is God's holy temple, and God will justly punish those who desecrate that temple.

True wisdom came only through embracing the message that the world viewed as foolishness (3:18–23). But God viewed the world's wisdom as foolishness. God's evaluation of the worldly wisdom that prompted boasting and stirred dissension should silence all human boasting at last.

Paul's own ministry exemplified the principles that he had just explained (4:1–20). He desired others to view him as a servant and a manager, not as a celebrity. His only aim was to be faithful to the Master he served. It mattered little to him whether he passed the judgment of others, but it was of supreme importance that he pleased God. Consequently, no room remained for personal pride and arrogance based on one's giftedness or the results of his ministry. With biting sarcasm, Paul contrasted the experience of the apostles with the Corinthians' own arrogant self-appraisal. He presented the humility, self-sacrifice, and self-obeisance of the apostles as a model fit for all believers to follow.

Paul's earlier sarcasm was not intended to shame the Corinthians. He loved them like a father loves his children. Indeed, they were his spiritual children since he had first preached the gospel to them. Now they should seek to imitate him like a little boy imitates his father. Timothy, who would soon visit the Corinthians, was also Paul's spiritual son who exemplified the love and faithfulness to the Lord that was appropriate for one of Paul's children. He would remind the Corinthians of Paul's example. Paul would eventually come to Corinth and was prepared to use the rod of discipline on the arrogant and divisive members of the family as a father must sometimes do.

B. Immorality in the Church (5:1–13)   Paul had heard reports that a member of the church in Corinth was committing incest with his stepmother. This sin was so deplorable that not even pagans tolerated it. Yet the church celebrated this sin in a confused attempt to flaunt its freedom in Christ. Paul called the church to repent and to expel this person from the church. This expulsion had two major purposes. First, it would hopefully lead to the sinner's repentance and restoration. Second, it would protect the church from an immoral influence that might corrupt the entire congregation.

Although it was both impractical and unnecessary for believers to attempt to dissociate themselves from unbelievers who lived sinfully, believers should break fellowship with so-called believers who live immorally. As OT Israel expelled certain individuals from the congregation for particularly heinous sins (5:13 quotes Deut 17:7), so the Christian church must expel those who are characterized by wickedness.

C. Disputes Between Believers (6:1–11)   Paul scolded believers in Corinth for attempting to settle disputes between one another in the civil courts. Fellow believers were far better qualified to make just and righteous decisions in such disputes than unbelievers were. Moreover, taking Christian disputes to the civil courts flaunted Christian disunity before unbelievers in a way that damaged Christian witness. In such cases everyone lost. Believers should prefer being wronged or defrauded to triumphing over fellow believers in court. But Paul warned those who wronged and defrauded their brothers and sisters that such actions were completely inconsistent with genuine Christianity. Those who practiced particularly heinous sins would not inherit the kingdom of God. Though the Corinthians had once practiced such sins, they had been dramatically transformed by Christ and rescued from these wicked lifestyles.

D. Limitations on Freedom in Christ (6:12–20)   The Corinthians' toleration of incest and fraud among members of the church indicated that they had a perverted view of Christian liberty. Paul insisted that freedom in Christ was not absolute. Christians should not engage in any behavior that was not beneficial for others or that had the potential of dominating their lives. They should recognize that their bodies were created to glorify God. God's intention to resurrect their bodies demonstrated that the body, and what one does with it, is important to him. Believers should also recognize that their connection with Christ necessarily involved him in all of their activities. The body of the believer was now God's temple and should be regarded as holy. Finally, all notions of Christian freedom should be tempered by the consideration that believers are slaves of the Lord Jesus who have been bought with the redemptive price of his blood.

III. Responses to a Letter from the Corinthians (7:1–16:4)

A. Matters Related to Sex and Marriage (7:1–40) Perhaps because of a confused view of the end times, some Corinthian believers were seeking to practice abstinence within marriage (7:1–7). Paul critiqued this practice on both theological and practical grounds. First, a married person's body belongs to his or her spouse. Withholding the body defrauds the spouse of what rightfully belongs to him or her. Second, such abstinence is risky business because it makes the spouse more vulnerable to sexual temptation.

Believers who had no sexual compulsion for marriage should remain single (7:8). Believers should not divorce unbelieving spouses on religious grounds as if a believer were corrupted by the relationship (7:10–16). If the unbeliever decided to leave the believer, the believer should permit him or her to do so. But a believer married to an unbeliever should seek to preserve the marriage in the hope of having a positive spiritual influence on the unbelieving spouse.

Paul's general advice was for believers to remain in the situation in which they lived at the time of their conversion, particularly with regard to slavery and circumcision (7:17–24). Because of the nearness of Jesus' return and the distress believers would experience as that time approached, unmarried believers should remain unmarried. This would enable believers to focus their concerns on the things of the Lord and prevent them from being distracted from their devotion to him. However, when two unmarried believers felt passionately for each other and struggled to control themselves, marriage was the best option.

Marriage is a lifelong covenant, which means that widows are no longer bound to their deceased spouses. Widows may be happier if they remain single, but they are free to marry another believer if they so desire (7:25–40).

B. Matters Related to Idol Feasts (8:1–11:1) Many of the Corinthian believers had formerly worshipped in idol temples. Some of these believers had now sworn off any association with pagan idolatry. They refused to participate in the idol feasts or even to eat meat formally sacrificed to idols that was later sold in Corinthian markets. Others avoided the idol feasts but felt free to purchase and enjoy the food that had been devoted to the idol. Still others felt free to participate even in the feasts based on their conviction that the idol gods did not exist anyway.

Paul confirmed the theological premise of those who felt free to attend the idol feasts but challenged the conclusion that they drew from that premise. Paul agreed that there is only one true God, quoting the Shema of Deut 6:4, "The LORD our God, the LORD is One." Strikingly, he interpreted this confession as an expression of a high Christology in which the Father is the one true God and Jesus is the one true Lord who created all that exists. This Christological interpretation of the Shema is one of the clearest and most stunning affirmations of the deity of Jesus in Paul's letters.

However, Christian rejection of polytheism and the existence of idol gods did not necessarily lead to unqualified approval of eating food formerly sacrificed to idols. Believers needed to be aware that others might follow their example of eating food sacrificed to idols only to suffer a tormented conscience. They ought to be sensitive to how other believers perceived their actions and the potential impact of others following their example (8:1–13).

Although some believers might resent this limitation on their Christian liberty, Paul himself willingly sacrificed some of his liberties as an apostle as well. He relinquished his right to financial support from the churches that he served even though secular examples, OT law, and the teaching of Jesus confirmed his right to that support. Paul also sacrificed other freedoms in order to relate better to the people whom he was attempting to reach. Paul was concerned that some Corinthians viewed Christian liberty as a throwing off of all restraints on their behavior. He used several athletic examples that were familiar to them from the nearby Isthmian Games to remind them that self-control and personal restraint are practical necessities in all areas of life (9:1–27).

Paul suspected that the Corinthian view of Christian liberty was related to their sacramental theology. The Corinthians apparently believed that reception of baptism and participation in the Lord's Supper guaranteed salvation. Those who received those ordinances were free to live in any way they wanted without fear of divine judgment. Paul attacked this sacramental theology by arguing that the Israelites had participated in events analogous to baptism and a spiritual meal. However, all but two of the Israelites died in the wilderness wanderings as a result of divine judgment. Moreover, they fell under divine judgment because they had committed the very same sins in which the Corinthians were now engaged: idolatry, sexual immorality, and rejection of the authority of divinely appointed leaders. The example of the Israelites functioned as a warning to the Corinthians. They must not presume that the ordinances guaranteed salvation, and they must beware of falling into temptation (10:1–13).

Although the idol gods did not actually exist, those who participated in the idol feasts thus became partners with demons (10:14–22). This was inconsistent with the Corinthians' Christian commitment and could only provoke the Lord's jealousy as the Second Commandment warned (Exod 20:4). Because believers should only do what is helpful, edifying, and beneficial for other believers, they ought to limit their freedom to eat idol meat for the sake of those with weaker consciences. In the privacy of their own homes, they were free to eat the meat. However, in public settings where people were present who might be disturbed by the consumption of idol meat, believers should refrain from eating it. The believer's primary concern is to glorify God rather than exercise his own freedom. Thus he should avoid giving unnecessary offense to others by his actions. This was in keeping with the examples of both Paul and Christ who lived for the benefit of others rather than their own pleasure (10:23–11:1).

C. Matters Related to Christian Worship (11:2–34) The first relevant issue was gender distractions in worship (11:2–16). Some believers in the church at Corinth were apparently practicing gender role reversal. This practice probably resulted from their confused eschatology, the influence of their pagan backgrounds, and misunderstandings of Paul's own teaching. Women in the church began to dress in a masculine fashion, and some men possibly dressed in a feminine manner. In response, Paul argued that the distinction between men and women had been ordained by God. These distinctions should be reflected in the dress and hairstyles of believers, with women being in proper subjection to men.

The second issue was behavior during the Lord's Supper (11:17–34). Paul also expressed concern about abuses of the sacred ordinance of the Lord's Supper (11:17–22). During the Supper, the church was divided into personality cliques. Some members overindulged in both food and wine, while others, particularly the poorer members of the congregation, remained hungry and thirsty. In doing so, they desecrated the Supper that should have been a celebration of the new covenant, a remembrance of Jesus' sacrifice, and an anticipation of his return. Paul urged the Corinthians to examine themselves to ensure that they partook of the Supper in a worthy manner (11:27–34). They should gratefully reflect on the body and blood of the Lord that had been sacrificed for them in their observance of the Supper. Paul warned that sickness or even death might result (and in fact already had resulted) from the sacrilege of the Corinthians with regard to the Lord's Supper.

D. Matters Related to Spiritual Gifts (12:1–14:40) The Corinthians evidently had very confused notions about the nature, importance, and proper exercise of spiritual gifts. Apparently, some in the congregation who thought that they were exercising the gift of prophecy had actually cursed Jesus in corporate worship (12:1–3). Paul saw the need to correct the Corinthians' confused views. He explained that the same Spirit had bestowed different gifts to different people for the benefit of the church (12:4–11). The fact that the different gifts all came from the same source implied that the gifts were all equally "spiritual" and no gift was unimportant. Paul confirmed this by comparing the different gifts to the various abilities of different members of the human body (12:12–31). All gifts, like all physical abilities, were necessary and important. No individual would have all the gifts. However, he should exercise whatever gift God granted him without comparing his gift to someone else's.

Paul urged the Corinthians to cultivate the attribute of love, which is more important than the exercise of any spiritual gift (13:1–13). Love is more important than the gifts of human or heavenly speech, miracle-working faith, liberal generosity, or even the faithfulness that motivated a person to embrace martyrdom. Paul's prose soared into poetry as he beautifully described this patient, kind, humble, forgiving, and virtuous love. This kind of love exceeded all spiritual gifts, even the gifts of tongues, prophecy, and faith, because only the gift of love would endure after Jesus' return and would continue to be exercised throughout eternity.

Paul encouraged the Corinthians to aspire to the gift of prophecy and demonstrated that prophecy was superior to the gift of languages in many ways (14:1–6). Evidence suggests that the Corinthians had confused the true gift of languages given at Pentecost with ecstatic utterances common in the pagan religions of Corinth (14:6–12). The gift of languages described here seems different from the gift exhibited in Acts 2 since the spoken languages were not intelligible to others or apparently even to the speaker himself without an added gift of interpretation. Because the utterances communicated no message to the hearer, they were like shrills from a flute that lacked a clear melody or blasts from a bugle that communicated no meaningful message to the troops (14:8–10). Whereas the Acts 2 display of languages transformed foreigners who could not communicate with one another into friends and brothers who spoke the same language, this gift of languages turned friends and brothers who spoke the same language into foreigners who could not communicate.

Paul also expressed concern that the Corinthian view of the gift of languages involved utterances that were unintelligible to the speaker himself (14:13–19). He urged the Corinthians to exercise the gift only when the utterance was intelligible to the speaker and when someone could interpret the message in an intelligible manner to the others who were present. Paul preferred five intelligible words understood by the speaker that instructed others to 10,000 words that no one understood. Paul quoted Isa 28:11–12 to argue that unintelligible utterances were actually a sign of divine judgment on unbelievers (14:21). Moreover, the Corinthian practice of languages might give visitors to the church the impression that believers had lost their minds. However, prophecy revealed the secret sins of the unbeliever, drove him to his knees in repentance, and displayed to him the presence of God (14:20–25).

Finally, Paul offered instructions about maintaining order in corporate worship (14:26–33a). Worship services should be organized. Those who prophesied should maintain their composure and self-control rather than attempting to work themselves into a frenzy like pagan prophets in the idol temples. The congregation should evaluate the prophets and silence those who departed from the truth.

Paul also silenced women in the church whose speech in the setting of corporate worship somehow undermined the authority of their husbands and publicly embarrassed them (14:33b-36). Possibly, some wives were questioning or challenging the legitimacy of the prophecies of their husbands or other leaders of the church, thereby seizing a role that Paul recognized as inconsistent with the wife's role of submission. Paul's general guideline for the conduct of public worship was that all things should be done "decently and in order" (14:37–40).

   E. Matters Related to the Resurrection (15:1–58)   Under the influence of the dualism that pervaded much of the ancient pagan world, some Corinthians denied the doctrine of bodily resurrection of individuals (15:1–2,9–11). This denial was probably accompanied by an eschatological view that said believers experienced a spiritual resurrection at the moment they believed or were baptized. But in the Corinthians' view, believers were to expect no future bodily resurrection.

   In response to doubts about the possibility of the bodily resurrection, Paul affirmed that the gospel he received testified to Christ's death, burial, and resurrection "according to the Scriptures," that is, in fulfillment of OT prophecy (15:3–4). He also cited numerous appearances of the resurrected Jesus to various audiences (including "over 500 brothers at one time," v. 6), including many who were still living at the time of writing (15:5–8), and last but not least to Paul himself on the road to Damascus.[24]

   Paul wrote at length to defend the doctrine of bodily resurrection. He demonstrated that Jesus' bodily resurrection was intrinsic to the gospel (15:12–19). Denial of bodily resurrection required denial of Jesus' resurrection, and without a resurrected Jesus the entire Christian faith collapsed. Moreover, Jesus' resurrection was the prelude to the resurrection of believers, which would occur at the Second Coming when Jesus would conquer death once and for all (15:20–28). Paul's willingness to risk his own life on an hourly basis to proclaim the gospel demonstrates the depth of his own belief in a coming bodily resurrection.

   Paul clarified that the body Jesus raised from the dead would be dramatically transformed and significantly different from the believer's present body (15:35–49). The resurrection body would be incorruptible, glorious, powerful, and perfectly adapted for a life controlled by the Spirit in which the old battle between flesh and Spirit ceased at last. Through the dramatic transformation that Christ brought about through the resurrection, believers would have complete and final victory over both sin and death (15:50–58). The doctrine of resurrection serves as a reminder to believers that their work for the Lord is not in vain but will be rewarded in eternity.

   F. Matters Related to the Relief Offering (16:1–4)   Paul gave the Corinthians practical instructions about the collection of the relief offering for believers in Jerusalem. These instructions ensured that the Corinthian offering would be ready when Paul arrived and that it would be handled with integrity.

IV. Conclusion (16:5–24)

   A. Paul's Travel Plans (16:5–12)   Paul announced his intentions to remain in Ephesus until Pentecost and then travel to Corinth by way of Macedonia. He also urged

---

[24] For a defense of the historicity of this passage, see K. R. MacGregor, "1 Corinthians 15:3b–6a,7 and the Bodily Resurrection of Jesus," *JETS* 49 (2006): 225–34.

the Corinthians to treat Timothy respectfully since he would arrive in Corinth ahead of Paul.

B. Final Exhortations (16:13–18)   Paul concluded the letter by urging the Corinthians to stand firm in their faith and to do all things with the love he described in chap. 13. He urged the Corinthians to acknowledge the authority of their spiritual leaders.

C. Closing (16:19–24)   Paul sent greetings from those with him and pronounced a blessing on the church.

2 CORINTHIANS

I. Introduction (1:1–11)

A. Salutation (1:1–2)   In addition to features that are typical of Paul's greetings, Paul identified Timothy as cosender of this letter. He also addressed the letter not only to believers in Corinth but to those scattered throughout the entire province of Achaia.

B. Prayer of Thanksgiving (1:3–7)   Paul's opponents in Corinth probably argued that the great difficulties that Paul experienced in his ministry proved that he did not enjoy God's blessing on his ministry. But Paul viewed his sufferings as essential to his ministry and as an authentication of his divine call. Paul thanked God for comforting him in his afflictions so that he could use his experiences of suffering to bring comfort to others. Paul viewed his suffering as a continuation of the suffering endured by Christ. Paul also antici-pated sharing in Christ's comfort through resurrection.

C. Explanation of Paul's Thanksgiving (1:8–11)   Paul recounted the suffering and brush with death he had experienced in Asia, which strengthened his trust in the com-ing resurrection. Paul knew that the God who had delivered him from death by sparing his life in Asia would ultimately deliver him from death by raising him. Paul urged the Corinthians to thank God for sparing his life.

II. Paul's Relationship with the Corinthians (1:12–2:11)

A. Paul's Pure Conduct (1:12–14)   Despite attacks on Paul's ministry by his oppo-nents, Paul's conscience was clear. He had conducted himself with sincerity and purity that came from God in his ministry toward the Corinthians. He wrote clearly and plainly to the Corinthians because he had nothing to hide from them. He also had nothing to hide from God. Thus he looked confidently to the day that Christ would evaluate his ministry to the Corinthians.

B. Paul's Change in Plans (1:15–22)   Paul's opponents in Corinth evidently argued that Paul could not be trusted since he had not followed through with the travel plans he had announced earlier. Paul argued that the Corinthians must distinguish the gospel that he preached from his travel plans. His travel plans were subject to change, but his gospel was consistent and unchanging. Paul had not vacillated in the least with regard to his message.

C. The Reason for the Change in Plans (1:23–2:4)   Paul had not changed his travel plans on a mere whim. He had refrained from visiting the Corinthians to avoid hurting them and being hurt by them. He had decided that he could best address the problems in Corinth by a letter rather than by another personal visit.

D. Forgiveness to the Repentant Sinner (2:5–11)   Paul demonstrated that his change in plans had produced the desired result. In response to his tearful letter, the Corinthians had disciplined the church member who led the congregation to reject Paul's apostolic authority. That church member had now repented, and Paul urged the church to forgive and restore him in a display of Christian love.

III. Paul's Defense of His Ministry (2:12–7:16)

A. Paul's Ministry in Troas and Macedonia (2:12–17)   God's guidance in changing his travel plans was further confirmed by the fruits of his ministry in Troas where God opened a door for effective ministry. But Paul's concern to find Titus and to hear his report about the situation at Corinth quickly prompted him to travel to Macedonia.

Paul used the analogy of the Roman triumph in which a victorious general marched his conquered enemy through the streets of the capital and ultimately to his death to describe God's work in his own life. God had conquered his enemy, Saul of Tarsus, on the road to Damascus. Paul was now God's prisoner in chains, driven wherever God willed. Just as the defeat of the conquered enemy brought the victorious general great glory, Paul's defeat and subjection glorified God.

Paul's ministry was like the OT incense offering (see Exod 29:18). Whether Paul's ministry was an attractive scent or repulsive odor to others, it was a pleasing fragrance to God. Paul's ministry was pleasing to God because it was prompted by sincere motives, empowered by God, and performed in anticipation of divine judgment. Through Paul's ministry, the world had the opportunity to know God.

B. Paul's Letters of Commendation (3:1–3)   Paul's opponents evidently appealed to letters of commendation from impressive church leaders, perhaps leaders of the church in Jerusalem, for their authority. They criticized Paul's lack of such letters. Paul countered that the Corinthian believers themselves functioned as his letters of recommendation that confirmed the legitimacy of his apostleship. Paul's contrast between letters written with ink on tablets of stone (see Exod 24:12; 31:18; 32:15; 34:1; Deut 9:10) and those written by the Spirit on the tablets of the human heart (see Ezek 11:19; 36:26–27) recalls OT descriptions of the old covenant and new covenant respectively and paves the way for Paul's description of his role as a minister of the new covenant.

C. Paul's Competence (3:4–6)   God made Paul competent to serve as a minister of the new covenant. Although the old covenant, the law, could only produce death because it demanded a righteousness from sinners that they could not achieve, the new covenant grants the Holy Spirit to believers, and this Spirit imparts life to them.

D. Ministry of the New Covenant (3:7–18)   Although the old covenant was glorious, the glory of the new covenant greatly surpasses that of the old. The old covenant only produced condemnation of sinners since it was incapable of making them righteous. But the new covenant actually makes sinners righteous. Moreover, the old covenant was only temporary; the new covenant is eternal.

After Moses received the old covenant, he veiled his face to prevent the Israelites from gazing on the reflection of God's glory that frightened them. That demonstrated that the old covenant only condemned sinners and sentenced them to death. Moses also veiled his face because he did not want the Israelites to see the final glimmers of glory ebb from his face when the glory faded. The fading glory displayed the temporary nature of the old covenant.

Although the sons of Israel had a veil over their hearts that prevented them from understanding the writings of Moses, the veil was removed for those who turned to the Lord. Those who turned to the Lord and received the promises of the new covenant would be transformed by the Spirit so that the image of God is restored in them with an ever-increasing glory.

E. The Unveiled Truth (4:1–6)   Because of the glorious ministry entrusted to Paul, he had no reason to adopt the underhanded techniques of his opponents. His legitimate apostleship was confirmed by his "open display of the truth." If his gospel appeared to be veiled, it was only because Satan had blinded the minds of unbelievers. The glory of God shone from the face of Jesus in the hearts of those who believe.

F. Treasure in Clay Jars (4:7–18)   The great treasure of the message about Jesus Christ was housed in a suffering apostle, a vessel made of clay—weak, fragile, and vulnerable. By using so weak a vessel as Paul to bear the glorious good news, God put his great power on display. Although the gospel ministry constantly exposed the apostle to the threat of death, he pressed on, assured that God would resurrect his body and that his sufferings were only the prelude to an "absolutely incomparable eternal weight of glory."

G. The Coming Resurrection (5:1–10)   Paul knew that when his body was destroyed, he would be given a new resurrection body. The indwelling Spirit was a down payment that guaranteed that final transformation and glorification. Paul's aim was to please God in all things because he knew that the deeds of all people will one day be judged by God.

H. The Ministry of Reconciliation (5:11–6:2)   Driven by anticipation of this judgment and by Christian love, Paul sought to persuade others that Jesus died for them and that they died together with him so that they were liberated from their old selfish way of life to live for the crucified and resurrected Jesus.

Paul had abandoned his pre-Christian view of Jesus, which saw him as a mere human sufferer and nothing more. He now saw Christ as the one who initiated the new creation. Christ both radically transformed believers and was the one through whom God reconciled to himself those alienated from him by sin.[25]

---

[25] Translations such as the NIV render 2 Cor 5:20 as follows: "We implore *you* on Christ's behalf: Be reconciled to God." But there is no equivalent for the word rendered "you" in the Greek original. Nor would it make sense for Paul to implore

Jesus took the guilt of believers' sins upon himself and endured the penalty for those sins so that believers might be counted righteous by God. Paul pled with sinners on Christ's behalf to be reconciled to God and insisted that the day of salvation had come at last.

I. Catalog of Paul's Sufferings (6:3–13)   Although Paul's opponents probably argued that a true apostle would be divinely protected from suffering, Paul argued that his sufferings actually confirmed the legitimacy of his apostleship. He listed the sufferings and sacrifices he had endured in the fulfillment of his divine call.

J. Call to Separate from Paul's Opponents (6:14–7:1)   Paul addressed the relationship of believers to unbelievers. The unbelievers in this context are Paul's opponents who have rejected his apostleship and his gospel. Paul urged the Corinthians to separate themselves from these lawless, evil, and impure persons so that they might cleanse themselves of every impurity in both flesh and spirit and be the pure sanctuary of the living God.

K. Paul's Final Defense (7:2–16)   Paul affirmed again his innocence in the face of the ludicrous charges against him by his opponents. He urged the Corinthians to embrace him with their very hearts. Paul expressed his joy at the report from Titus concerning the repentance of the Corinthians and the renewal of their affection for Paul. Paul joyfully exclaimed that his complete confidence in the Corinthians had been restored.

IV. The Collection for the Believers in Jerusalem (8:1–9:15)

A. Example of the Churches in Macedonia (8:1–7)   Paul turned his attention from his opponents in the church at Corinth to the collection of a relief offering for believers in Palestine, a topic that he addressed briefly in 1 Corinthians 16. Paul appealed to the example of giving by the impoverished churches in Macedonia to motivate the Corinthians to give more sacrificially.

B. Examples of Christ's Sacrifice and the Old Testament (8:8–15)   Gratitude for Jesus' sacrifice should motivate the Corinthians to give sacrificially and joyfully. Paul did not want the Corinthians to relieve the believers in Jerusalem by imposing hardship on themselves. But he did believe that there should be a general equality among believers as illustrated by the gathering of the manna in the OT.

C. Administration of the Offering (8:16–24)   Some of Paul's opponents apparently argued that Paul intended to misuse the relief offering that the Corinthians were collecting. Paul assured the Corinthians that the funds would be used for their designated purpose. Both Titus and a representative appointed by the churches would oversee the collection and distribution of the gift "so that no one can find fault with us."

---

the Corinthians to be reconciled to God since, for all their failings, Paul addressed the Corinthians generally as believers (see 2 Cor 1:1). For this reason it is preferable to understand 2 Cor 5:20 as a description of Paul's message of reconciliation in his evangelistic preaching in general: "Therefore, we are ambassadors for Christ; certain that God is appealing through us, we plead on Christ's behalf, 'Be reconciled to God'" (HCSB). See A. J. Köstenberger, "'We Plead on Christ's Behalf: "Be Reconciled to God"': Correcting the Common Mistranslation of 2 Corinthians 5:20," *BT* 48 (1997): 328–31, followed by J. Piper, *The Future of Justification: A Critique of N. T. Wright* (Wheaton: Crossway, 2007), 178n32.

D. Importance of Having the Offering Ready (9:1–5)   Paul had already informed the Macedonians that the Corinthians had begun their collection of the offering. This made it especially important to have the offering ready when the church representatives arrived so that the Corinthians would not appear reluctant to give.

E. Principles Motivating Generous Giving (9:6–15)   The Corinthians should give generously because God would reward them in proportion to their generosity. They should give cheerfully because God loves a cheerful giver. God would provide for their needs so they could give liberally. Their generosity would not only express their gratitude to God but would also prompt the Jerusalem Christians to glorify God and pray more fervently for Gentile believers.

V. Paul's Renewed Defense of His Apostleship (10:1–13:4)

A. The Tone of Paul's Appeal (10:1–11)   Paul concluded his earlier defense of his apostleship by expressing complete confidence that the Corinthians would separate from his opponents and affirm his authority and his gospel. But as Paul wrapped up chap. 9, he evidently received fresh news of problems in Corinth that prompted him to readdress the issue of his apostleship with a much sterner tone.

Paul's opponents argued that he was weak because he was willing to speak sternly only through his letters written from a distance. They evidently used this inconsistency to argue that Paul walked "in a fleshly way." Paul countered that he sought to relate to the Corinthians with the gentleness and graciousness of Christ, but he warned that he could adopt a much sterner posture if necessary.

B. Divine Commendation of Paul's Ministry (10:12–18)   Unlike his opponents who sought to commend themselves with competitive comparisons, Paul appealed only to divine commendation of his ministry. God had assigned to Paul a ministry that extended to Corinth and would ultimately extend far beyond it. Paul's appeal to the effectiveness of his ministry to confirm his apostolic authority did not constitute self-commendation. Paul sought only to glorify God and to be commended by him.

C. Danger of the False Apostles (11:1–15)   Paul was concerned that the false apostles were wooing the Corinthians from their devotion to Christ like an immoral man might seek to allure a bride from the one to whom she was promised. Like Satan had deceived Eve, the false apostles deceived the Corinthians by preaching another Jesus, a different spirit, and a different gospel.

The false apostles claimed to be "superapostles" who exceeded Paul in speaking ability, knowledge, and status. Their superiority was demonstrated in that they felt worthy to demand financial support of the Corinthians while Paul did not. Paul argued that he had forfeited his right to financial support to avoid being a burden to the Corinthians and in a display of his love for them. Paul warned the Corinthians that the false apostles were servants of Satan disguised as servants of righteousness.

D. Paul's Sufferings (11:16–33)   Paul's opponents argued that they had a more impressive religious background than Paul did. Paul's opponents argued that their own protection from suffering demonstrated that God's blessing was upon them and, conversely, that the suffering Paul endured showed that he did not enjoy divine favor. Paul countered that his religious background was actually more impressive than that of his opponents. Moreover, his suffering for Christ and for the church authenticated rather than diminished his apostolic ministry.

E. Paul's Visions and Revelations (12:1–10)   Paul's opponents also contended that they had spiritual gifts that Paul lacked. In particular, they had experienced visions and revelations that Paul had not. Paul countered that he had spiritual experiences that he did not typically publicize. On one occasion he had been caught up to paradise and heard a revelation that he dared not even repeat. However, God humbled Paul by giving him a thorn in the flesh that prevented him from exalting himself. This "thorn" (whose identity is debated) left Paul weak and forced him to live in dependence on God's great power.

F. Paul's Miracles (12:11–13)   Paul also reminded the Corinthians that they had personally witnessed his signs, wonders, and miracles during his stay in Corinth. These were "the signs of an apostle" that confirmed the legitimacy of Paul's apostleship.

G. Paul's Final Defense (12:14–13:4)   Paul insisted that neither he nor those associated with him had taken advantage of the Corinthians in any way. Although he appeared to be defending himself, his real concern was to build up the church. This required him to confront sin and the false teaching that sought to justify it. Paul warned the Corinthians that his third visit to them might serve as a third witness against them. He alerted the Corinthians that he would sternly confront their sin without leniency in display of the power of Christ.

VI. Final Exhortations (13:5–12)

Paul urged the Corinthians to examine themselves to determine whether they truly possessed authentic Christian faith. Paul prayed that the Corinthians would grow toward spiritual maturity and commanded them to pursue Christian unity.

VII. Closing (13:13)

Paul's final words in his canonical correspondence with the Corinthians are a concluding blessing, commending these believers to the grace of Christ, the love of God, and the fellowship of the Holy Spirit (a trinitarian formula). This expresses the apostle's hope and confidence that only the triune God was able to do a spiritual work in this congregation.

THEOLOGY

Theological Themes

The Nature of the Resurrection Body   The most detailed discussion of the resurrection in Paul's letters and in the entire NT is found in 1 Corinthians 15. Paul most likely wrote this chapter to combat wrong ideas about the Christian teaching concerning the resurrection that were influenced by Greek philosophy. Apparently, some in Corinth denied the bodily resurrection and taught instead that believers' experience of spiritual resurrection at conversion was the only resurrection they would ever experience (cf. 2 Tim 2:16–19).

Some apparently believed that this spiritual resurrection made them like the angels. Thus they attempted to live a sexless existence (1 Cor 7:1–5), endeavored to abolish distinctions between genders (1 Cor 11:2–6), and ventured to speak in angelic languages (1 Cor 13:1). Paul realized that much of the confused theology and many of the unbiblical practices of the Corinthians were related to their denial of bodily resurrection. Paul's argument ran as follows.

First, Paul argued that the resurrection of Jesus had been prophesied in the OT and proclaimed by eyewitnesses of Jesus' ministry. Denying the possibility of bodily resurrection entailed denial of the resurrection of Jesus and a dismissal of the reliability of OT prophecy and apostolic testimony. Such a denial reduced both the apostles and the Scripture to the status of false witnesses.

Second, Paul argued that the Christian faith was worthless without the resurrection of Jesus. Participation in Jesus' resurrection effectively ends the sinner's old life and begins a new and different life. Consequently, without the resurrection of Jesus, believers are "still in [their] sins."

Third, Paul argued that Jesus' resurrection was the prelude (the firstfruits) of the resurrection of all believers. The resurrection of the people of Christ was to occur "afterward, at His coming" (1 Cor 15:23). He also contended that Corinthian practices such as proxy baptism for the dead (however misguided) and his own willingness to risk martyrdom implied the veracity of the doctrine of bodily resurrection.

After defending the doctrine of bodily resurrection, Paul devoted the second half of his discussion to a treatment of the nature of the resurrection body. His primary point was that the resurrection body will have continuity with the body that is buried in some ways but will also be dramatically different in other ways. He illustrated this by pointing to a seed, which is both continuous with and yet radically dissimilar from a living plant.

Confusion about the doctrine of the resurrection impacted the Corinthians' ethics as much as their views on the end times. They apparently argued that since God was going to destroy the body in the end, it did not matter what or how much they ate or in which kinds of sexual activities believers engaged and with whom. As Paul maintained, however, the resurrection made clear that the body has enduring significance to God. Thus it matters what believers do with their bodies.[26]

The New versus the Old Covenant   Second Corinthians 3 contains the most explicit discussion of the new covenant in Paul's letters. The new covenant was promised by God

---

[26] For an incisive treatment of this passage against the backdrop of pagan views of sexuality, see P. Jones, "Paul Confronts Paganism in the Church: A Case Study of First Corinthians 15:45," *JETS* 49 (2006): 713–37.

through the prophets in such passages as Jer 31:31–34 and Ezek 36:24–30. Echoes of these OT texts in 2 Corinthians show that these OT promises were foundational to Paul's theology in these letters.

Paul contrasted the old and new covenants to highlight the supremacy of the new covenant. The old covenant resulted in death and condemnation because sinners were incapable of fulfilling its demands and were thus destined to be declared guilty by God and punished; the new covenant resulted in life and righteousness. Finally, while the old covenant was temporary, the new covenant was eternal. Thus the glory of the new covenant completely eclipsed that of the old.

Paul illustrated the fact that the old covenant resulted in death and condemnation by reminding his readers that after Moses received the old covenant, he had to veil his face to prevent the Israelites from being destroyed by the mere reflection of the divine glory (Exod 34:29–35), even though that glory, like the covenant it represented, was already in the process of being abolished.[27]

The veil that hid the abolishment of the old covenant was still over the eyes of many of Paul's contemporary Jews when they read the books of Moses. But Christ removed the veil. When a sinner turned to the Lord and came under the power of the new covenant, the veil masking the demise of the old covenant was destroyed. Then the believer was privileged to look on and reflect the glory of the Lord.

POINTS OF APPLICATION

- Work for unity in the church and confront divisiveness (1 Corinthians 1–4)
- Identify and exercise your spiritual gifts for the benefit of others (1 Corinthians 12, 14)
- Be a man or woman of love, recognizing that love is the supreme Christian virtue (1 Corinthians 13)
- Make sure you understand the biblical teaching on believers' bodily resurrection (1 Corinthians 15)
- Don't discredit the God-given authority of church leaders (2 Corinthians 10–13)

STUDY QUESTIONS

1. Why are the Corinthian letters especially practical for the modern church?
2. How many letters did Paul write to the Corinthian church? How are they designated in this chapter? How do the letters coincide with Paul's visits? List the letters and the visits together in chronological order.

---

[27] This interpretation conflicts with the one suggested by many English translations. For an extensive defense of the interpretation, see S. J. Hafemann, *2 Corinthians*, NAC (Nashville: B&H, 1999), 147–49; P. Hughes, *The Second Epistle to the Corinthians*, NICNT (Grand Rapids: Eerdmans, 1962), 108. For the interpretation suggested by the translations, see Belleville, *2 Corinthians*, 99.

3. From where did Paul receive information about the church's condition?
4. What is the dual purpose of 1 Corinthians, and what is the main purpose of 2 Corinthians?
5. What is the basic literary plan of 1 Corinthians?
6. What will be the nature of the believers' resurrection body?
7. What is the relationship between the new and old covenants in 2 Corinthians?

FOR FURTHER STUDY

1 Corinthians

Barrett, C. K. *A Commentary on the First Epistle to the Corinthians.* Harper New Testament Commentary. New York: Harper, 1968.

Blomberg, C. *1 Corinthians.* NIV Application Commentary. Grand Rapids: Zondervan, 1994.

Fee, G. D. *The First Epistle to the Corinthians.* New International Commentary on the New Testament. Grand Rapids: Eerdmans, 1987.

Garland, D. E. *1 Corinthians.* Baker Exegetical Commentary on the New Testament. Grand Rapids: Baker, 2003.

Morris, L. *The First Epistle of Paul to the Corinthians: An Introduction and Commentary.* 2nd ed. Tyndale New Testament Commentary. Grand Rapids: Eerdmans, 1985.

Thiselton, A. C. *The First Epistle to the Corinthians: A Commentary on the Greek Text.* New International Greek Testament Commentary. Grand Rapids: Eerdmans, 2000.

2 Corinthians

Barnett, P. *The Second Epistle to the Corinthians.* New International Commentary on the New Testament. Grand Rapids: Eerdmans, 1997.

Garland, D. E. *2 Corinthians.* New American Commentary. Nashville: B&H, 1999.

Hafemann, S. J. *2 Corinthians.* NIV Application Commentary. Grand Rapids: Zondervan, 2000.

Harris, M. J. "2 Cointhians." Pages 415–545 in *The Expositor's Bible Commentary.* Rev. ed. Vol. 11: *Romans-Galatians.* Grand Rapids: Zondervan, 2008.

_____. *The Second Epistle to the Corinthians.* New International Greek Testament Commentary. Grand Rapids: Eerdmans, 2005.

Kruse, C. *2 Corinthians.* Tyndale New Testament Commentary. Grand Rapids: Eerdmans, 1987.

Chapter 13

Paul's Letter to the Romans

CORE KNOWLEDGE

Students should know the key facts of Paul's letter to the Romans. With regard to history, students should be able to identify the book's author, date, provenance, destination, and purpose. With regard to literature, they should be able to provide a basic outline of the book and identify core elements of the book's content found in the unit-by-unit discussion. With regard to theology, students should be able to identify the major theological themes in the book of Romans.

KEY FACTS	
Author:	Paul
Date:	Mid- to late 50s
Provenance:	Greece, probably Corinth
Destination:	Several congregations in Rome
Occasion:	Preparation for Paul's journey through Rome to Spain
Purpose:	To promote Jewish-Gentile unity in the church by setting forth Paul's gospel
Theme:	The gospel proclaims that God acquits both Jews and Gentiles who believe in Jesus on the basis of Jesus' sacrificial death
Key Verses:	1:16–17; 3:21–26

CONTRIBUTION TO THE CANON

- The gospel—promised through the prophets and preached by Paul (1:1–4,16–17; see Hab 2:4)

- Justification by faith apart from works of the law (1:17; 3:21–5:2; see esp. 4:3,9,22–23, citing Gen 15:6)
- Promotion of Jew-Gentile unity on the basis of the universality of sin (1:18–3:20; 3:23); the free gift of salvation through Jesus Christ (6:23); and God's all-encompassing plan of salvation (chaps. 9–11)
- The impossibility of keeping the law, and new life in the Spirit (chaps. 6–8)
- God's salvation-historical plan for Jews and Gentiles past, present, and future (chaps. 9–11)

INTRODUCTION

PAUL WROTE THE letter to the Romans after his letters to the Galatians, Thessalonians, and Corinthians. Romans is the product of Paul's mature theological thought and a thorough presentation of his gospel. In fact, the book of Romans may be the most important letter ever penned in human history. Countless multitudes in modern times have confessed faith in Jesus as the risen Savior after being led through a series of texts known as the "Roman Road" taken from this letter (3:23; 5:8; 6:23; 10:9). Although some of the truths of this letter still baffle learned scholars, its basic assertions are clear enough to guide children as well as adults to faith in Christ. Thus it is no surprise that this letter is a favorite NT book for many.

Some of the most influential theologians and Christian leaders in church history were converted to Christianity while studying this book. In the summer of 386, Aurelius Augustinus, professor of rhetoric at Milan, was weeping in the garden of his friend Alypius as he struggled with the choice over whether to embrace the Christian faith. He heard a child in a nearby house singing *"Tolle, lege! Tolle, lege!"* ("Take up and read! Take up and read!"). He rushed to a bench where there lay a scroll of the letter to the Romans, picked it up, began to read the powerful words of Rom 13:13–14, and immediately resolved to follow Christ.

Also while reading Romans, Martin Luther, an Augustinian monk and professor of biblical theology at the University of Wittenberg, discovered that the "righteousness of God" was not God's justice that motivated him to punish the wicked but "that by which the just lives by a gift of God, namely by faith." At this, Luther "felt that I was altogether born again and had entered paradise itself through open gates. There a totally other face of all Scripture showed itself to me."[1] Luther's dramatic discovery would forever change the course of history by sparking the Protestant Reformation. The book warrants detailed study by both believers and unbelievers. All who study the book should be prepared to be changed by it.

---

[1] M. Luther, *Luther's Works*, ed. J. Pelikan and H. Lehman (Philadelphia: Fortress, 1958–86), 34:336–37.

HISTORY

Author

The letter to the Romans claims to have been written by Paul. Historically, NT scholarship has been so certain of Paul's authorship of the book that it has served as an important standard for evaluating the claim of Paul's authorship in other letters. Charles Hodge, a commentator in the mid-nineteenth century, surveyed the strong internal and external evidence for Paul's authorship and concluded: "There is . . . no book in the Bible, and there is no ancient book in the world, of which the authenticity is more certain than that of this epistle."[2]

In the late nineteenth century, Paul's authorship of Romans was disputed by some, but their arguments were deemed unconvincing by the large majority of scholars. Half a century ago, C. H. Dodd confidently stated: "The authenticity of the Epistle to the Romans is a closed question."[3] The question of authorship was closed because the internal evidence for Paul's authorship, particularly the language, style, and theology of the book, was so compelling. Moreover, all ancient sources who mention the author of Romans identify him as the apostle Paul. These include Marcion's *Apostolicon* as quoted by Tertullian (c. 160–225), the Muratorian Canon (later second century), the canons of the Council of Laodicea (363–364), as well as the writings of Athanasius (c. 296–373) and Amphilochus (c. 340–395).[4] Although the question of Paul's authorship has been settled, one related issue is worthy of discussion.

Some scholars have suggested that Paul's role as author needs to be redefined. Romans 16:22 demonstrates that Paul used Tertius as an amanuensis or personal secretary to pen the letter to the Romans. O. Roller showed that an author who used an amanuensis could approach his task in a number of different ways. Sometimes authors dictated their work to the amanuensis who penned the material *verbatim* either in longhand or in shorthand in preparation for a final longhand edition. At other times, an author summarized his ideas to the amanuensis, and the latter took responsibility for the wording and form in which the ideas were expressed in writing. Paul may have used Tertius's services in the latter manner.

Several lines of evidence strongly suggest that Paul dictated the letter to Tertius. The language and style of Romans is very similar to Paul's other letters. If Tertius were responsible for the wording of Romans, one could only account for the high degree of similarity between Paul's letters by claiming that Tertius was responsible for the wording of Paul's other letters as well. But no evidence exists that Tertius served as Paul's amanuensis for letters other than Romans. The degree of similarity between Romans and Paul's other letters is best explained by assuming that Paul dictated Romans.

---

[2] C. Hodge, *Commentary on the Epistle to the Romans* (Grand Rapids: Eerdmans, 1976), 9.

[3] C. H. Dodd, *The Epistle of Paul to the Romans* (London: Fontana Books, 1959; repr. of 1932 edition), 9.

[4] J. Fitzmyer, *Romans*, AB (Garden City: Doubleday, 1993), 40.

Date

Romans 15 contains important details about Paul's travel plans that are helpful in dating the composition of the letter. Romans 15:25 indicates that Paul was about to begin or had just begun his journey to Jerusalem to deliver the relief offering to the impoverished believers there. Romans 15:19,23 show that Paul viewed his work in the regions between Jerusalem and Illyricum as complete. Paul had determined to carry the gospel to Spain (Rom 15:24,28) and would pass through Rome on his trip from Jerusalem to Western Europe. Paul had already completed the collection of the relief offering in Macedonia and Achaia (Rom 15:26).

These details readily coalesce with details in Acts 20. Acts 19:21 records that Paul resolved to pass through Macedonia and Achaia on his way to Jerusalem from Ephesus. Paul traveled through Macedonia to Greece where he stayed for three months (Acts 20:1–3). He likely stayed in Corinth during most of this period in which he wrote the letter to the Romans. While in Corinth, Paul discovered a plot that had been devised by his Jewish opponents that led to a change in his travel plans. Rather than sailing from the port in Cenchrea near Corinth to Syria as he originally planned, he reversed course and traveled back through Macedonia, sailed to Troas, Miletus, Cos, Patara, and then to Tyre, Ptolemais, and Caesarea to travel overland to Jerusalem.

Paul's third missionary journey probably extended from around 51 to the winter of 54–55. The key factors for dating this journey are the dates of Paul's stay in Corinth during the second missionary journey that are established by the Delphi Inscription, and the probable date of Paul's arrest in Jerusalem that can be calculated based on the Roman tribune's statement in Acts 21:38 and the ascension of Festus. Paul probably wrote the letter to the Romans in the winter of 54–55.[5]

One factor may complicate this date. At the time Paul wrote this letter, Aquila and Priscilla had taken up residence in Rome again, and a church was meeting in their home. They had likely been in Rome long enough to become familiar with the situation of the churches there and to correspond with Paul about that situation. If Jews were not allowed to return to Rome until after the death of Claudius in the year 54, this date for the composition of Romans is probably too early to allow time for the couple to become aware of Claudius's death, move to Rome, become informed about the churches' situations, and correspond with Paul. But it is likely that the ban of Jews in Rome began to be relaxed toward the end of Claudius's reign. If so, these factors do not necessarily preclude this early date.[6] After all things are considered, it is wisest to content oneself with a general estimate that Romans was written in the mid- to late 50s.

---

[5] This date is supported by J. Finegan, *Handbook of Biblical Chronology: Principles of Time-Reckoning in the Ancient World and Problems of Chronology in the Bible*, rev. ed. (Peabody: Hendrickson, 1998), 396–97, §687; L. Morris, *The Epistle to the Romans* (Grand Rapids: Eerdmans, 1988), 6–7; and C. K. Barrett, *A Commentary on the Epistle to the Romans*, Harper's NT Commentaries (New York: Harper & Row, 1957), 5. Most recent discussions date the letter a year or two after the date proposed here.

[6] S. Mason suggested that the expulsion of the Jews from Rome was not comprehensive in the first place. See Mason, "'For I am not ashamed of the Gospel' (Rom 1:16): The Gospel and the First Readers of Romans," in *The Gospel in Paul*, ed. L. A. Jarvis and P. Richardson (Sheffield: Sheffield Academic Press, 1994), 254–87.

Provenance

Scholars have suggested a variety of cities as the probable location in which the letter to the Romans was written. Suggestions include Corinth, Athens, Ephesus, Philippi, Thessalonica, or the province of Macedonia.[7] Two views of the provenance of the letter were affirmed in the early church. Some versions of the Marcionite Prologue preserved in a few manuscripts of the Vulgate assign the letter to Athens. But two early subscriptions to the letter in ancient Greek manuscripts stated that Paul wrote Romans from Corinth. An early scribe who corrected Codex Vaticanus added a subscription that reads, "It was written to the Romans from Corinth." Another scribe who corrected Codex Claromontanus added an identical subscription to that manuscript. Several later manuscripts mention a Corinthian provenance as well.

The same clues that suggest Paul wrote Romans at the end of his third missionary journey while en route to Jerusalem also point to Greece as the place that the letter was composed. Paul's three months in Greece (Acts 20:3), during which he stayed in the home of Gaius (Rom 16:23), probably afforded rare opportunities for the careful and prolonged reflection necessary for such an extensive project as well as daily access to an amanuensis to assist in writing the work. Although Acts does not specifically mention where Paul primarily stayed during the three months in Greece, several considerations point to Corinth as the most likely place of composition for Romans.

First, the NT mentions four men by the name of Gaius: (1) one from Derbe (Acts 20:4); (2) one from Macedonia who was with Paul in Ephesus (Acts 19:29); (3) one from Corinth who was one of the few persons Paul baptized there (1 Cor 1:14); and (4) the recipient of 3 John who is not known to be associated with Paul (3 John 1). The Gaius of Romans 16 is likely Gaius of Corinth.

Second, Paul sent greetings from Erastus, the city treasurer or manager, who is probably the person by the same name mentioned in Acts 19:22 and 2 Tim 4:20. Paul probably mentioned Erastus here because he was a prominent member of the church of Corinth largely due to his authority in the local government. A Latin inscription that dates to the mid-first century AD and that remains in its original location in the paved square near the Corinthian theater refers to an Erastus who paved the square: "Erastus, in return for his aedileship, laid the pavement at his own expense." This Erastus who served as *aedilis coloniae* ("city treasurer") of Corinth is generally recognized to be the same person mentioned in Rom 16:23.[8]

Third, Rom 16:1–2 serves as a letter of recommendation for Phoebe to the church of Rome. According to subscriptions to Romans in some Greek manuscripts, Phoebe also served as the courier for the letter. Paul mentioned that Phoebe was "a servant [*diakonos*]

---

[7] Fitzmyer, *Romans*, 85.

[8] J. Murphy-O'Connor, *Saint Paul's Corinth* (Collegeville: Liturgical Press, 2002), 37; J. H. Kent, *Ancient Corinth: A Guide to the Excavations* (Athens: American School of Classical Studies at Athens, 1954), 74; V. P. Furnish, "Corinth in Paul's Time: What Can Archaeology Tell Us?" *BAR* 14/3 (1988): 14–27.

of the church in Cenchreae." Cenchreae was a port city that was located only a few miles from ancient Corinth.

The question of the provenance of the letter is closely connected with the question of the integrity of the letter. If chap. 16 was not a part of the original form of the letter as composed by Paul, insufficient evidence exists to determine the provenance. But strong evidence supports the integrity of the letter. Thus most scholars today affirm the legitimacy of using clues from chap. 16 to pinpoint the city from which Romans was written. Phoebe, Erastus, and Gaius were with Paul when he wrote this letter. They are associated with Corinth or a city close by. Thus Corinth is the most likely provenance of the letter. This evidence is sufficient to allow J. D. G. Dunn to make the confident assertion that there is "scarcely any dispute" today over the Corinthian provenance.[9]

Destination

As the present title of the letter indicates, this letter was addressed to Christians who lived in Rome, the capital of the Roman Empire. The address of the letter in Rom 1:7, "To all who are in Rome, loved by God, called as saints," and in Rom 1:15, "who are in Rome," clearly identifies the addressees as believers in Rome. Rome was the capital of the great Roman Empire. It rivaled Alexandria in Egypt, Corinth in Greece, and Antioch in Syria as the most important city of the Mediterranean world during the lifetime of Paul. In the first century, the city of Rome had a population of approximately one million people from every corner of the empire and the strange lands beyond its borders.[10] The population included 40,000 to 50,000 Jews.

The mixture of cultures in the city ensured that the city would be home to a great variety of religions. Worship of the traditional Roman pantheon and the imperial cult thrived in the city. But many Romans gave foreign religions like Mithraism, Judaism, and Christianity a warm reception as well. When Christianity first reached Rome, the worship of Jupiter, Juno, and Minerva in the large temple on the Capitolium dominated the city.[11]

Like Corinth and other large population centers of the Mediterranean world, Rome was known for its decadence and immorality. Tacitus described Rome during the reign of Nero as "the City, where all degraded and shameful practices collect from all over and become the vogue" (*Annals* 15.44). When Paul wrote Romans, the Emperor Nero had not yet begun his war of terror against the Christians of the city. Even early in his reign, however, the emperor was known to "practice every kind of obscenity." Suetonius (*Nero* 28–29) described in vivid detail Nero's sins with mistresses and prostitutes and his unthinkable

---

[9] Commentators who affirm a Corinthian provenance include T. R. Schreiner, *Romans*, BECNT (Grand Rapids: Baker, 1998), 4; D. J. Moo, *The Epistle to the Romans*, NICNT (Grand Rapids: Eerdmans, 1996), 2–3; J. D. G. Dunn, *Romans*, WBC 38A-B, 2 vols. (Dallas: Word, 1988), 1:xliv; Fitzmyer, *Romans*, 85–87.

[10] M. Reasoner, "Rome and Roman Christianity," in *Dictionary of Paul and His Letters*, ed. G. F. Hawthorne, R. P. Martin, and D. G. Reid (Downers Grove: InterVarsity, 1993), 850–55, esp. 851.

[11] Ibid., 851.

perversions. This was Rome's noble leader, and his conduct was undoubtedly a reflection, though perhaps an exaggerated one, of the immoral culture in which he lived.

Amazingly, Christianity began to thrive in Rome very early. The origins of the church in Rome are unknown. It is clear that Paul did not found the church. Perhaps the church began when Jewish pilgrims from Rome traveled to Jerusalem for one of the major feasts and heard the gospel from Jesus' disciples (possibly as early as Pentecost; Acts 2:10). Perhaps the church began when Christians from other cities migrated to Rome. Christians were clearly present in Rome by the late 40s. Suetonius claimed that Claudius expelled the Jews from Rome in the year 49 because of disturbances that arose in the instigation of "Chrestus." Apparently, Jews and Jewish Christians were debating whether Jesus was the Christ and these debates led to serious conflict that upset the capital (see Acts 18:1–2).

Unlike Paul's Thessalonian and Corinthian correspondence, Romans is addressed generally to all believers throughout the city of Rome rather than to a single congregation. Paul was aware that multiple Christian congregations existed in the city. He later mentioned a church that met in the home of Aquila and Priscilla (Rom 16:5), a group of Christians associated with Asyncritus, Phlegon, Hermes, Patrobas, and Hermas (Rom 16:14), and another group of Christians associated with Philologus, Julia, Nereus, and his sister (Rom 16:15). The Christians in the households of Aristobulus and Narcissus may also have met together as a group for worship in these homes. If so, Paul mentioned five congregations of believers in Rome. Other congregations unknown to Paul likely existed in Rome as well.[12]

Scholars debate whether the churches in Rome were predominantly Jewish or Gentile. In favor of a Gentile composition is Paul's discussion of his witness among Gentiles in Rom 1:5–6, and 1:15 clearly includes the addressees in that group. Paul directly addressed Gentiles using the second person in Rom 11:13,31 in a rebuke of Gentile pride over their election by God. Paul's discussion of the strong and the weak in Rom 14:1–15:13 is primarily addressed to the strong, almost certainly Gentile believers who had a stronger sense of liberty in Christ than some of their brothers from a Jewish background.

On the other hand, Paul addressed many issues in the letter that would have been of concern primarily to Jewish Christians, such as the role of the law in salvation and the place of Israel in God's redemptive plan. Moreover, Paul's rebuke of Jewish pride and hypocritical self-righteousness in Romans 2 frequently uses the second person and implies that Paul was directly addressing people of Jewish origin. Paul closely associated his readers with the Mosaic law in texts such as Rom 6:14; 7:1,4. He also referred to Abraham as "our forefather according to the flesh" (Rom 4:1) in a manner that implies that his original readers included physical descendants of Abraham. These features demonstrate that Christianity in Rome was of mixed composition with believers from both Jewish and Gentile backgrounds.

---

[12] See especially Dunn, *Romans*, 1:lii.

The discussion of the occasion of the letter to the Romans in the next section suggests that the Roman churches were dominated by Gentiles during the five years or so preceding the letter. However, a sudden influx of Jewish believers into the Christian community caused conflict to erupt that threatened the unity of God's people in Rome. The historical circumstances suggest that the church was of mixed composition, predominantly Gentile but with a growing number of Jewish believers.[13]

Occasion

Paul wrote Romans shortly before his final recorded journey to Jerusalem (Rom 15:25–29). He wanted to travel to Jerusalem in order to present the money that had been collected by the Gentile churches in Macedonia and Achaia to help meet the needs of poor Christians in Jerusalem (15:26). The relief offering was partially motivated by a desire to promote good relations between Jewish Christian and Gentile Christian churches. This concern is related to some of the topics that Paul addressed in Romans 9–11 and 14–15.

Paul planned to travel from Jerusalem through Rome to Spain due to his longing to "preach the gospel where Christ was not known" (Rom 15:20 NIV). This information fits very well with Luke's description of Paul's travels at the close of the third missionary journey (Acts 19:21; 20:16). Acts 20:3 shows that Paul spent three months in Greece during his trip from Macedonia and Achaia to Jerusalem. Paul wrote Romans at this time, and it served as a formal introduction of Paul and his gospel to the church in Rome in preparation for his eventual visit to the church.

Additional clues regarding the occasion of the letter can be gleaned from extrabiblical sources. Several sources document Claudius's expulsion of the Jews from Rome around 49. After Jewish Christians evacuated Rome, the leadership of the Roman churches fell entirely to Gentile believers. Some Jews likely began to return to Rome during the final years of Claudius's reign. They returned to find that the very churches they formerly dominated were now controlled and led by Gentile Christians. They likely felt that Gentile Christian leaders were not appropriately appreciative of and sensitive to their own rich Jewish heritage. Gentile Christians resented pressure from their Jewish brothers and sisters to adopt Jewish ways and restrict their freedom in Christ. These factors in the historical setting help explain why much of the letter to the Romans addresses issues of importance to the relationship between Jewish and Gentile Christians.[14]

Purpose

Some interpreters have felt that Romans is a theological treatise or a compendium of Christian doctrine. The earliest comment on the purpose of Romans appears in the Muratorian Canon, which probably dates to the later second century: "then to the Romans he [Paul] wrote at length, explaining the order (or, plan) of the Scriptures, and also that

---

[13] This is the view of most modern commentators (e.g., Moo, *Romans*, 12–13).

[14] So also Schreiner, *Romans*, 13–14; Moo, *Romans*, 4–5; Dunn, *Romans*, 1:liii–liv.

Christ is their principle (or, main theme)."[15] Although the author of the fragment viewed 1 Corinthians and Galatians as occasional documents that addressed specific problems in a particular congregation (heretical schisms and circumcision, respectively), he viewed Romans as a summary of Christocentric biblical doctrine. The view of Romans as a compendium of Christian doctrine was later advanced by Philip Melanchthon in his *Loci Communes* (1521) and his commentary on Romans (1532). Romans has generally been viewed as a summary of Christian theology ever since.

Although Romans is an intensely theological letter, most scholars today view it not as a general treatise but as an occasional document, that is, a letter written to address the particular needs of a specific group of churches. They point out that the letter does not expound some important aspects of Paul's theology such as his doctrine of the Lord's Supper (1 Cor 11:17–24), the Second Coming (1 Thess 4:13–5:11), or the doctrine of the church that is explicated in far greater detail in Ephesians and 1 Corinthians. This silence is indeed hard to explain if the letter were written to be a general theological treatise.

Moreover, Paul also gave a lot of attention in this letter to matters such as the wrath of God (Rom 1:18–32) and the Jews' rejection of Jesus (Romans 9–11), which he did not discuss extensively in his other letters. Several aspects of the letter, such as the discussion about the way in which believers should relate to the government (Rom 13:1–7) and the discussion of the weak and the strong (Rom 14:1–15:6), seem to reflect the specific struggles faced by this particular congregation. Thus Romans should not be viewed as a textbook of systematic theology written to total strangers.

An examination of the entirety of the letter demonstrates that Paul had several reasons for writing this book. First, Paul wanted to remind the Roman believers of some of the fundamental truths of the gospel in fulfillment of his priestly duty of proclaiming the gospel to the Gentiles (Rom 15:14–16). Paul was well aware of the many ways in which his message might be misunderstood or misapplied. He wrote to clarify important aspects of his message to those who had heard about him and his gospel only indirectly. Moreover, Rom 16:17–20 shows that Paul was concerned about false teachers infiltrating the Roman church. In the face of this danger, a careful articulation of the essentials of Paul's gospel was needed.

Second, Paul wanted to address several of the problems faced by the Roman church. In particular, he wanted to call the churches to unity. He was aware that some of the differences in outlook between the Jewish and Gentile Christians had produced disunity in the congregations at Rome. These differences emerged in arguments about obligations to OT dietary laws and the observance of Jewish holy days. Perhaps at the heart of the debate was the larger question: Did the inclusion of the Gentiles among the people of God mean that God had abandoned his promises to Israel (see esp. Romans 9–11)? In dealing with this question, Paul's letter stressed the equality between Jewish and Gentile believers. He insisted that Jews and Gentiles alike were condemned as sinners (Rom 2:9; 3:9,23) and

---

[15] This translation is from B. Metzger, *The Canon of the New Testament* (Oxford: Clarendon, 1987), 305–7.

that both Jews and Gentiles were saved by grace through faith apart from the works of the law (Rom 3:22,28–30).[16] He explained the different roles for Jews and Gentiles during different phases of God's redemptive plan (Romans 9–11). He also directly addressed issues such as diet and calendar observances that were apparently the immediate sources of tension between Jewish and Gentile believers (Rom 14:1–15:13).

Third, Paul wanted formally to introduce himself to the Roman churches and solicit their support for his Spanish mission. Paul had fully proclaimed the gospel through the eastern half of the Roman Empire, "from Jerusalem all the way around to Illyricum" (Rom 15:19). Now he was planning to introduce the gospel in Spain in the far west of the empire. After Paul left Jerusalem, he would travel to Spain by way of Rome. Paul hoped to receive a material gift from the Roman church to assist him in his missionary endeavors in Spain (Rom 15:24).

Most scholars affirm these three purposes for the letter. The multiple purposes of the book are clearly interrelated. To affirm one and neglect another leads to an impoverished view of the letter. Paul's intention to introduce his gospel to churches about which he knew fairly little resulted in a letter that was more general and directly applicable to the Christian church at large and throughout all time. The general character of the message of Romans makes it directly applicable and particularly helpful to modern believers.

LITERATURE

Literary Plan

Recent scholars have made numerous attempts to classify the genre of Romans. Several objective features of the letter aid interpreters in understanding its intended structure, and most scholars agree on its major divisions. The letter opens with an epistolary prescript (1:1–7), which summarizes Paul's gospel, followed by an expression of thanksgiving (1:8–9). Next is the proem containing preliminary comments (1:10–15) followed by the programmatic statement that summarizes the message of the letter (1:16–17). This programmatic statement begins the doctrinal section of the letter (1:16–11:36), which is followed by a hortatory or ethical section (12:1–15:13). Paul included a summary of his travel plans and some requests for prayer (15:14–33), followed by a letter of recommendation for Phoebe and greetings to various groups and individuals in Rome (16:1–23). The letter concludes with a doxology (16:25–27).

The major debate regarding the structure of Romans concerns the divisions of the doctrinal section. Scholars generally agree that the major divisions are chapters 1–8 and 9–16. They further agree that 1:16–4:25 and 6:1–8:39 constitute major units in the first division, but there is considerable disagreement on the placement of chap. 5. The evidence for 5:1–8:39 as a major section of the letter is based on both the topic of the chapters

---

[16] Schreiner (*Romans*, 19) stated: "The majority position is now that Paul wrote to resolve the disunity between Jews and Gentiles," citing numerous scholars as representatives of this view.

and important structural markers. After an introductory paragraph (5:1–11), the section addresses three important freedoms for believers: freedom from sin and death (5:12–21), freedom from sin and self (chap. 6), and freedom from the law (chap. 7). The discussion of these areas of freedom naturally flows into a discussion of life in the Spirit. Moreover, the section divisions in chaps. 5–8 are marked by a concluding formula that appears at the end of chaps. 5, 6, 7, and 8 with only slight variation: "through Jesus Christ our Lord" (5:21; 7:23) and "in Christ Jesus our Lord" (6:23; 8:39).[17]

OUTLINE

I. INTRODUCTION (1:1–15)
    A. Jesus Christ Is the Focus of the Gospel, and Paul Is Qualified to Proclaim It (1:1–7)
    B. Paul Thanks God for the Roman Christians and Expresses His Love for Them (1:8–15)
II. THEME: THE GOSPEL REVEALS GOD'S POWER FOR SALVATION AND HIS RIGHTEOUSNESS (1:16–17)
III. THE RIGHTEOUSNESS OF MAN: UNIVERSAL SINFULNESS AND JUSTIFICATION BY FAITH IN CHRIST (1:18–4:25)
    A. Man's Need for Justification (1:18–3:20)
    B. God's Gift of Justification (3:21–4:25)
IV. THE BENEFITS CONFERRED BY THE GOSPEL (5:1–8:39)
    A. The Believer Has Peace, Righteousness, and Joy (5:1–11)
    B. The Believer Escapes the Consequences of Adam's Transgression, the Reign of Sin in Death (5:12–21)
    C. The Believer Is Liberated from Slavery to Sin (6:1–23)
    D. The Believer Is Liberated from Bondage to the Law (7:1–25)
    E. The Believer Lives a Righteous Life Through the Power of the Spirit (8:1–17)
    F. The Believer Will Ultimately Enjoy Complete Victory over Corruption (8:18–39)
V. THE RIGHTEOUSNESS OF GOD AND ISRAEL'S REJECTION OF THE GOSPEL (9:1–11:36)
    A. Israel Has Rejected Christ (9:1–5)
    B. Israel's Temporary Rejection of Christ Is Consistent with God's Eternal Plan (9:6–29)
    C. Israel's Temporary Rejection of Christ Is Due to Her Own Stubborn Pursuit of Self-Righteousness (9:30–10:21)
    D. God Has Chosen a Present Remnant of the Jews for Salvation While Hardening the Rest (11:1–10)
    E. God Will Ultimately Save the Nation of Israel (11:11–32)
    F. God's Plan Is Mysterious and Wise (11:33–36)
VI. THE PRACTICAL IMPLICATIONS OF THE GOSPEL (12:1–15:13)
    A. Christians Should Respond to God's Mercy by Living Transformed Lives (12:1–2)
    B. Transformed Living Will Impact Relationships in the Church (12:3–21)

---

[17] See the more thorough treatment of the structure in Fitzmyer, *Romans*, 96–98; C. E. B. Cranfield, *A Critical and Exegetical Commentary on the Epistle to the Romans*, ICC, 2 vols. (Edinburgh: T&T Clark, 1975–79), 1:252–54.

C. Transformed Living Will Affect Relationships with Political Authorities (13:1–7)

D. Transformed Living Is Urgent Because of the Nearness of Christ's Return (13:8–14)

E. Transformed Living Will Lead to Mutual Acceptance of Stronger and Weaker Christians (14:1–15:13)

VII. CONCLUSION (15:14–16:27)

A. Paul's Travel Plans: Visiting Rome on the Way to Spain (15:14–33)

B. Commendation of Phoebe and Greetings to Roman Christians (16:1–16)

C. Final Warning (16:17–18)

D. Final Commendation and Greetings (16:19–24)

E. Concluding Benediction (16:25–27)

UNIT-BY-UNIT DISCUSSION

I. Introduction (1:1–15)

A. Jesus Christ Is the Focus of the Gospel, and Paul Is Qualified to Proclaim It (1:1–7) The introduction of the letter includes a brief summary of the gospel that highlights its foundation in the OT and its focus on Christ. Paul maintained at the very outset that the gospel he preached was not his message but God's ("God's good news," 1:1) and that God had promised this gospel "long ago through His prophets in the Holy Scriptures" (1:2). The specific prophetic passage Paul cited at the end of the preface to Romans was Hab 2:4, which affirmed that "the righteous will live by faith" (1:17).

In essence, Paul devoted a significant portion of his letter to an exposition of this crucial passage, showing later that the same teaching was not even original with OT prophets such as Habakkuk but found already in the law—specifically in Gen 15:6, which stated that Abraham was righteous on the basis of his faith in God. Hence what is at stake is nothing other than the consistency of God's way of saving people and the truthfulness of his promises. Rightly understood, there was only one way of salvation—faith in God apart from works—and this saving plan had now come to its climactic fulfillment in Jesus' death on the cross as the culminating expression of God's covenant-keeping faithfulness.

As Paul noted at the outset, Christ's Davidic lineage confirmed his right to rule as Messiah-King. By virtue of his resurrection, Jesus was also "the powerful Son of God" (1:4). Since the next occurrence of "power" in Romans refers to God's saving power (1:16), the title signified that Jesus possessed the power to save because of his resurrection (see 4:25; 1 Cor 15:14,17,20). Finally, Jesus was called "our Lord," a title that clearly denoted deity (see 10:9,13; Joel 2:32). Thus the introduction to the gospel focused on Jesus' identity, power, and authority as Messiah-King, Savior, and Lord-God. In addition, Paul briefly alluded to his Damascus road experience and apostolic call. He explained that Christ appointed him as an apostle in order to produce obedience among the Gentiles to the gospel command to believe the good news. This ministry was motivated by zeal for Jesus' name, a desire to see Christ glorified among all the peoples of the earth.

**B. Paul Thanks God for the Roman Christians and Expresses His Love for Them
(1:8–15)**   Paul explained that his failure to visit the churches of Rome did not imply his lack of concern for them. He prayed for them incessantly and thanked God for their faith that was acclaimed throughout the entire Christian world (1:8–10). He longed to preach the gospel in Rome due to a deep sense of obligation to proclaim Christ to all kinds of people.

II. Theme: The Gospel Reveals God's Power for Salvation and His Righteousness (1:16–17)

Romans 1:16–17 expresses the theme of the letter. Paul was not ashamed to proclaim the gospel because the gospel is God's saving power that accomplishes salvation for all who believe, whether they are Jews or Gentiles. The gospel reveals God's righteousness in declaring sinners to be righteous despite their misdeeds based on Jesus' sacrificial death— a truth more fully developed in 3:21–26 (see below). Paul reminded his readers that salvation by faith was not a new message but in fact constituted the central message of the OT prophets (1:17, citing Hab 2:4, which is also cited at Gal 3:11; cf. Rom 1:1–2). For both OT and NT believers, the righteousness that resulted in life had always been imputed on the basis of an individual's faith.

III. The Righteousness of Man: Universal Sinfulness and Justification by Faith in Christ (1:18–4:25)

A. Man's Need for Justification (1:18–3:20)   Beginning in 1:18, Paul explained that all individuals need justification since all are sinners who are justly condemned by God. Paul first addressed the sinfulness of Gentiles, then that of Jews, and then all humankind generally. Especially if Jewish-Gentile conflict is one of the major pastoral concerns that prompted Paul to take up his pen, this emphasis on humanity's universal sinfulness was designed to level the playing field at the beginning of Paul's letter. Jews and Gentiles alike must recognize themselves first and foremost as sinners saved by grace. Neither ethnic privilege nor numeric majority is a proper basis for arrogance. Hence Jews and Gentiles are to find their unity in their common justification by faith on the basis of Jesus' substitutionary death on the cross, which is an expression of God's covenant-keeping love and faithfulness.

According to Paul, Gentiles deserved God's wrath because their sins were not committed in ignorance but involved suppression of the truths about God that were apparent to all (1:18). Man's chief sin is failure to give God the glory that he deserves. God expresses his wrath by releasing humanity to the corrupting power of sin so that man's sinful behavior becomes progressively more heinous and repulsive. Gentiles experience a spiritual and moral devolution that leads them to idolatry, sexual perversion, and complete moral decadence (1:26–27). They choose to live in rebellion against God despite their clear understanding that sin results in death.

Although the Jews may have felt that their moral superiority to Gentiles would benefit them in judgment, Paul warned that condemning others did not prevent God from noticing one's own guilt (2:1). God's kindness to Israel did not imply that the Jews were righteous in and of themselves so that they had no need to repent. On the contrary, God's kindness to Israel was a summons to repentance (2:4). God would judge each person fairly and give him either the punishment or reward that his deeds deserve. He would judge Jews and Gentiles equally, fairly, and justly because God's judgment was not based on favoritism. Ignorance of the written law did not exempt a person from judgment since God inscribed the requirements of the law on the heart of every person.

Hence Jews as well as Gentiles deserve God's wrath (2:5). Though the Jews preach and teach the law, they fail to obey the law and thereby dishonor God and blaspheme his name. Circumcision, likewise, grants no protection against divine judgment and was rendered meaningless by the transgression of the law (2:25). Conversely, an uncircumcised Gentile who keeps the law of God should be viewed as a circumcised Jew and a member of the covenant people (2:27). The true Jew whom God will praise in judgment is one who has been internally transformed (2:28–29).

Jews do possess certain advantages over Gentiles. God chose to grant them the OT Scriptures, and he has remained faithful to his promises to Israel (3:1–4). Still, God's justice is not compromised by his punishment of the sins of Jews, but it would be diminished if he failed to punish their sins. Although the sinfulness of humanity accentuates the glorious righteousness, faithfulness, and truthfulness of God, it does not excuse sin, nor does it encourage it (3:7–8).

In fact, the descriptions of the Jews in the OT itself demonstrate their intense sinfulness and show that Jews are no better than Gentiles (3:9). The law that Israel possesses is not a means of salvation. Rather, it demonstrates man's sinfulness so that he despairs of saving himself by his own righteousness. All people, both Jews and Gentiles, are justly condemned as sinners by God (3:19–20). Grace can come only when people see their desperate need for it; those who are spiritually poor will inherit the kingdom of heaven (Matt 5:3).

B. God's Gift of Justification (3:21–4:25)   Having established the universal sinfulness of Jews and Gentiles alike—the "plight" of humanity—Paul proceeded to state the solution: justification by faith in Jesus Christ. The present section elaborates more fully on Paul's comments in the introduction. Both the Law (esp. Gen 15:6; see below) and the Prophets (esp. Hab 2:4; see above) testify that God declares sinners righteous in his sight if they believe in Jesus Christ (1:1–2,16–17), and he did this for those who failed to keep the law. In a startling pronouncement, Paul declared, "But now, apart from the law, God's righteousness has been revealed—attested by the Law and the Prophets—that is, God's righteousness through faith in Jesus Christ, to all who believe, since there is no distinction. For all have sinned and fall short of the glory of God" (3:21–23).

The phrase "apart from the law" introduces a stunning disjunction between the previous point of reference of God's people—the law—and his new gracious act of saving people on the basis of the atoning sacrifice of Jesus Christ. God's declaration of righteousness precludes any human pride and places Jews and Gentiles on an equal footing (3:22). Jesus' sacrificial death displayed the justice of God in declaring sinners to be righteous on the basis of faith alone (3:25). If God were simply to overlook the sins of his creatures, he would not be righteous. However, in Jesus' death for sinners, God's righteousness was beautifully expressed because sin was punished (see 2 Cor 5:21) *and* God was able to forgive and justify sinners without compromising his own holiness.

At the same time, the gospel proclamation that righteousness comes through faith in Christ rather than by keeping the law does not dispense with the law altogether—though it did put its role into proper perspective (see esp. 10:4 below). On the contrary, it affirmed what the law had said about salvation all along (3:31). The law states plainly that Abraham, the father of the Jews, was declared righteous in God's sight through faith (Rom 4:3, citing Gen 15:6; cf. Gal 3:6). This righteousness was not a standing that Abraham achieved through his good works but a gift he received. Psalm 32:1–2 also describes this imputed righteousness. Hence the OT Scriptures upheld the gospel preached by Paul.

This righteousness was imputed to Abraham before he was circumcised (4:10). Thus God credited this righteousness to a person based on faith alone, apart from circumcision. This righteousness was also credited to Abraham before the Mosaic law was given, further demonstrating that God granted this righteousness on the basis of faith and not observance of the law (4:13–15). The promises to Abraham's offspring (which included receiving a righteous standing and life in the world to come) were granted to believers, both Jews and Gentiles, in fulfillment of the promise that Abraham would be the father of many nations (4:18).

Abraham's faith paralleled Christian faith. Abraham believed that God could bring "life out of death," a promised son out of aged people who were as good as dead (4:19; see Heb 11:12). Christians likewise believe that God raised Jesus from the dead, thereby exhibiting Abraham's faith and receiving the promise of imputed righteousness. Moreover, as Hebrews points out, Abraham also exercised faith in the God who raises the dead when he was willing to offer up Isaac, the promised son, on the altar rather than holding him back because "he considered God to be able even to raise someone from the dead" (Heb 11:19).

IV. The Benefits Conferred by the Gospel (5:1–8:39)

A. The Believer Has Peace, Righteousness, and Joy (5:1–11) In Rom 5:1 Paul began to describe the benefits conferred on the believer through the gospel. This description of benefits occupied his attention for four entire chapters. To begin with, because of justification, believers are at peace with God and joyfully anticipate their full and final transformation (5:1–5). While sinners were in a wretched spiritual condition—weak, unable to save themselves, ungodly, and sinful—Christ died for them (5:6). Through Jesus' sacrificial and substitutionary death, believers who were formerly God's enemies have been reconciled to God. Those doomed to suffer his eternal wrath have been rescued from condemnation, and those who were judged to be sinners have been declared righteous (5:9–11).

B. The Believer Escapes the Consequences of Adam's Transgression, the Reign of Sin in Death (5:12–21) The impact of Adam's disobedience on the human race offers a negative parallel to the impact of Christ's obedience on believers (5:12). Due to Adam's sin, all people die. Even those who lived before the giving of the law and who had no explicit commandment to defy died (5:13). Clearly, a single act by one person can have a universal and eternal impact. However, the obedience of Jesus Christ had the power to cancel the consequences of Adam's disobedience. If the disobedience of one man could cause the death of many others, Christ's obedience could likewise grant righteousness and life to many (5:15). Just as the effects of Adam's disobedience were universal, the effects of Christ's obedience were also universal in that Christ granted righteousness and life to those who believe, whether Jews or Gentiles. The law did not introduce death into the world. It offered Adam's descendants explicit commandments to defy just as Adam had done (5:20). This made sin more rampant and more heinous. This pervasive and intense sinfulness magnifies the abundance and greatness of God's grace (5:21).

C. The Believer Is Liberated from Slavery to Sin (6:1–23) One should not conclude from this, as some of Paul's opponents charged him as teaching, that sin served a positive purpose and should be continued (6:1–2). The believer's union with Christ in his death, burial, and resurrection is inconsistent with a sinful lifestyle. The person the believer had been has died with Christ (6:3). Now the believer has been liberated from sin's mastery. Eventually, the believer's union with Christ will result in his resurrection and complete liberation from sin. In the present, believers should live in light of the fact that sin's mastery has been broken. They should offer themselves to God as instruments for righteousness (6:11–14). Salvation by grace does not grant license for sinful behavior. The believer has a new spiritual master—righteousness, so he should live as a slave to righteousness (6:18). Slavery to sin grants no benefits to the sinner; it condemns him to die. Slavery to righteousness produces holiness and results in eternal life.

D. The Believer Is Liberated from Bondage to the Law (7:1–25) The believer has been liberated from the law. Death nullifies a marriage covenant so that it is no longer legally binding (7:1). After a spouse has died, the surviving spouse is liberated from the law of marriage and free to marry someone else. In a similar way, death nullified the power of the law (7:4). By his union with Christ in his death, the believer was liberated from the law and freed to devote himself to God. Liberation from the law, union with God in Christ, and empowerment by the Spirit enabled the believer to live a righteous life, something that the law could not accomplish.

The law actually aggravated and aroused sin in unbelievers, but this did not mean that the law was bad (7:7). The law was holy, righteous, and good, but the sinful nature used the law as a weapon to destroy the sinner. Paul illustrated this truth by presenting the example of a person striving to obey the law perfectly. He showed that the law still served a positive function by demonstrating the person's utter corruption and slavery to sin. At the same time, the law was powerless to save the person from his slavery to sin (7:13). Anyone who tries to fulfill the law's demands apart from the enabling of the Holy Spirit was engaged in a frustrating exercise of futility. Such a person is caught in a constant tug-of-war between that part of him that delights in God's law and that part of him that is dominated by sin (7:14–25). Only crucifixion with Christ and resurrection with him can resolve this desperate struggle.

E. The Believer Lives a Righteous Life Through the Power of the Spirit (8:1–17)   Yet the believer enjoys present victory over sin. The Spirit accomplishes for the believer that which the law cannot do. The Spirit, who enables this new life in Christ, thus replaces the old law as a reference point in the life of the believer (8:2; see 10:4). The Spirit liberates the believer from his slavery to sin and moves him to fulfill naturally and spontaneously the law's righteous demands (8:9). The Spirit exercises the same power that he used to raise Jesus from the dead in order to produce new life in the believer. Those who live by God's Spirit are God's children and thus heirs who will share in God's glory (8:17).

F. The Believer Will Ultimately Enjoy Complete Victory over Corruption (8:18–39)   The whole creation eagerly awaits the glorification of God's people (8:18). Believers long for the completion of their adoption through the redemption of the body when their transformation will be complete and their struggle with sin comes to an end. In the present, God works through every circumstance to accomplish the spiritual good of believers (8:28). God's eternal purpose will not be thwarted, and he will unfailingly make those whom he loved from eternity past to become like his Son (8:29–30). The completion of the believer's salvation through his justification at the final judgment and at his glorification are absolutely certain because God will make sure all these things occur for the people he loves.

V. The Righteousness of God and Israel's Rejection of the Gospel (9:1–11:36)

A. Israel Has Rejected Christ (9:1–5)   While Romans 1–8 is primarily concerned with the justification of man—accomplished through faith in Christ on the basis of his atoning death—chaps. 9–11 move on to a more important topic still (anticipated in chaps. 1–8)—the justification of God. By this is meant what scholars call "theodicy," the demonstration that, contrary to what some might allege, God was just and righteous in all he did. In the present case, the alleged congruity in God's purposes was the fact that the majority of Jews had not believed in Jesus as Messiah. Hence, many Jews charged, God had reneged on his covenant promises.

Not so, Paul countered. Despite what could appear to be a change in God's mode of operation, God's promises to Israel continue unabated. At the same time, God now includes the Gentiles in the Abrahamic promise that in him "all the peoples on earth will be blessed" (Gen 12:3). Hence "it is not as though the word of God has failed" (9:6). In this regard, Paul himself, who was known as the apostle to the Gentiles, was deeply torn within, for he still dearly loved his fellow Israelites. In fact, he says that he could wish that he himself "were cursed and cut off from the Messiah" for the benefit of his fellow Jews (9:3).

B. Israel's Temporary Rejection of Christ Is Consistent with God's Eternal Plan (9:6–29)   Although Israel's rejection of Christ might seem to contradict the infallibility of God's promises and shake the believer's hopes, God's promises to Israel have not failed (9:6). The remainder of chaps. 9–11 is devoted to demonstrating the truthfulness of Paul's assertion. To begin with, not all physical descendants of Abraham are true Israelites. God's promises apply only to those whom he has chosen. His choice, in turn, is based, not on human character or behavior but on God's mysterious purpose (9:14–18).

For this reason one must not charge God with injustice (9:19–21). This would be to reverse improperly the roles of creature and Creator (see the book of Job). God is free to show his mercy to whomever he wills because in his utter sovereignty the Creator has complete authority over his creatures. Nor is it proper to challenge God's character if he glorified himself by expressing his wrath against some people while lavishing his mercy on others. God would have been just if he had saved no one. He is certainly just if by sheer grace he chose to save many without saving all.

C. Israel's Temporary Rejection of Christ Is Due to Her Own Stubborn Pursuit of Self-Righteousness (9:30–10:21)   Still, Israel was fully responsible for its spiritual condition. Gentiles obtained true righteousness by faith while Israel sought righteousness but did not attain it because she attempted to establish her own righteousness through obedience to the law rather than through faith in Christ (9:30–32). Hence, despite all her efforts, Israel did not find true righteousness because the law was fulfilled only through faith in Christ. As the OT demonstrates, salvation comes only through confession of faith in Jesus Christ (9:33, citing Isa 8:14; 28:16).

In truth, Israel did not fail to confess faith in Christ because she was uninformed about Christ (10:1–4). All Israel heard the message about Christ, but most rejected the message in stubborn disobedience. Yet Christ is "the end of the law." In context, this means that Christ ends for the believer the attempt to achieve righteousness through keeping the law. Unlike Israel, the believer ceases from seeking to establish his own righteousness (8:3). The believer gives up the vain hope of receiving life by doing the things written in the law (8:5). As "the end of the law," Christ is the ultimate goal to which the OT prophetically pointed in its entirety. He is also literally the end of the law in that he, in his own person, fulfilled the law. As a result, the law is embodied in Christ, and believers can look to the one who has fulfilled the law as they live their Christian lives through the enablement of the Spirit.

Paul proceeded to cite additional OT texts in order to demonstrate that the salvation of both Jews and Gentiles clearly followed from the OT message. This salvation, in turn, was predicated upon confession that "Jesus is Lord" and upon faith that God raised him from the dead (10:9). This was the essence of faith and fulfilled the premise that "everyone who calls on the name of the Lord will be saved" (10:13, citing Joel 2:32)—Jew as well as Gentile. Moreover, if faith in Christ is required for salvation, then there must be messengers telling people the good news of salvation in Christ (10:14–21; see Isa 52:7; 53:1).

D. God Has Chosen a Present Remnant of the Jews for Salvation While Hardening the Rest (11:1–10) Thus far Paul's "justification of God" has been largely devoted to the demonstration that God was right to condemn Jews for seeking to establish a righteousness of their own rather than submitting to the way of salvation God has established (10:3). This opened the door for the salvation of a large number of Gentiles who had no such ambition and who had previously been far off (10:20, citing Isa 65:1), perhaps provoking Israel to jealousy (10:19, citing Deut 32:21). Yet, as Paul proceeded to show in chap. 11, God has not rejected Israel entirely. God has chosen a portion of Israel by his grace for salvation. This remnant will obtain the righteousness Israel had sought.

E. God Will Ultimately Save the Nation of Israel (11:11–32) Thus God used Israel's rejection of the gospel for his gracious purposes to bring salvation to the Gentiles (11:11–12). Now God uses the Gentiles' reception of the gospel to make the Jews envious and move some of them to faith in Christ. At the same time, Gentiles should not be arrogant toward Jews (11:17–21). Their salvation rests on God's promises to Israel and is predicated on faith. God is ready to accept the rest of Israel when they repent of their unbelief.

Gentiles, Paul warned, should not assume that they have favored status with God. At the appointed time, God would shift his focus to national Israel again. Great masses of Jews will be saved. This was necessary because God's gifts and call are irrevocable. Hence Paul's argument has come full circle, and he has established that God's word is true (9:6). God's righteous salvation-historical purposes for both Jews and Gentiles proved to be coherent and consistent, though ultimately beyond complete human comprehension.

F. God's Plan Is Mysterious and Wise (11:33–36) Appropriately, therefore, Paul concluded his demonstration of the righteousness of God in chaps. 9–11 with a doxology, affirming the mystery and wisdom of God's ways. As the apostle explained, God wondrously displayed his mysterious wisdom by using Gentiles and Jews to prompt one another to believe in Christ. This realization should drive all believers to praise the depth of God's wisdom and acknowledge that God is glorious in all he does, whether or not they now fully understand all of his purposes.

VI. The Practical Implications of the Gospel (12:1–15:13)

A. Christians Should Respond to God's Mercy by Living Transformed Lives (12:1–2) On the basis of Paul's foregoing arguments ("Therefore," 12:1), he called on believers to respond to God's mercy by devoting their lives completely to him and by having renewed minds that know God's will. They are to do so, not by bringing a variety of sacrifices as people did in OT times but by presenting themselves—their very own bodies in their entirety—as a "living sacrifice, holy and pleasing to God." This will be their "spiritual worship," and this is how they will be able to discern "the good, pleasing, and perfect will of God" (12:2).

B. Transformed Living Will Impact Relationships in the Church (12:3–21)   The renewed mind is characterized by humility. It recognizes the interdependency of the different members of the church and does not establish a church hierarchy based on spiritual gifts (12:3–8). The renewed mind is also characterized by love. This love expresses itself through forgiveness, sympathy, harmony, humility, and kindness (12:9–21).

C. Transformed Living Will Affect Relationships with Political Authorities (13:1–7)   Another important implication of the gospel Paul preached is that all believers should submit themselves to governing authorities. Governmental authority has been appointed by God, preserves order, and thwarts lawlessness. For this reason, believers should conscientiously pay their taxes and show respect for political leaders. These words take on special significance in light of the fact that they were written during the tenure of Emperor Nero (54–68), whose ignominious reign would be responsible for the martyrdom of numerous Christians, including Paul himself.

D. Transformed Living Is Urgent Because of the Nearness of Christ's Return (13:8–14)   Believers should fulfill the law by expressing love for others. Expressing love for others and living righteously are especially important since Christ's return is fast approaching.

E. Transformed Living Will Lead to Mutual Acceptance of Stronger and Weaker Christians (14:1–15:13)   Believers should accept one another in love even when they disagree over issues of conscience such as diet and the observance of holy days (14:1–8). They should follow their own consciences in this regard while taking care not to allow their behavior to disturb other believers who hold different convictions. What is more, they should make sure not to encourage other believers to do something that they do not believe is right. It is wrong to eat, drink, or do anything that disturbs another's conscience.

Jewish and Gentile Christians, the weak and the strong, should live in unity and try to build up one another (14:19). They should learn to glorify God with one heart and one voice. Jesus himself came into the world as a servant to the Jews, fulfilling the promises to the Jews and yet including Gentiles in God's plan, so that they might glorify God as was foretold in the OT Scriptures.

VII. Conclusion (15:14–16:27)

The conclusion of Paul's letter to the Romans is longer than those in his other letters, yet it is appropriate in light of the length of the entire letter and in view of the fact that Paul had neither planted the church in Rome nor yet paid a visit to it. Especially noteworthy is the large number of individuals greeted by Paul in 16:1–16.

A. Paul's Travel Plans: Visiting Rome on the Way to Spain (15:14–33)   At long last, Paul elaborated on one of the major purposes for writing the letter: his plan to visit Rome on his way to Spain (15:24). Rather than making Rome the final destination of his impending visit, Paul intended for Rome to be merely a stop on his way to the far western frontiers of his European mission. In this Paul serves as a model of a frontier missionary, his aim being "to evangelize where Christ has not been named, in order that I will not be building on someone else's foundation" (15:20). Paul also asked for prayer that he would be rescued from unbelievers in Judea and for a successful delivery of the Gentile offering for the Jerusalem church (15:30–32). But as the book of Acts makes clear, Paul was arrested in Jerusalem and eventually arrived in Rome, though not the way he had originally envisioned (Acts 21–28).

B. Commendation of Phoebe and Greetings to Roman Christians (16:1–16)   At the end of the letter, Paul first commended the likely carrier of the letter, Phoebe, a servant or deaconess (*diakonos*) of the church in Cenchrea and a benefactress or patroness for many, including Paul (16:1–2).[18] Paul also greeted his trusted coworkers, Priscilla and Aquila (who had apparently returned to Rome), including the church that met in their house (16:3–5; see Acts 18:2). This is followed by a long list of greetings to various individuals and house churches, including a surprisingly large number of women.[19]

C. Final Warning (16:17–18)   A final warning is issued against those who cause divisions. Believers are implored to avoid these individuals and not to be deceived by their smooth talk or flattering words.

D. Final Commendation and Greetings (16:19–24)   The believers in Rome are commended for their obedience and urged to be wise about what is good and innocent about what is evil. God will soon crush Satan under his feet. Timothy and others sent greetings, as did Tertius (Paul's amanuensis), Gaius (Paul's host), and Erastus (the city-treasurer), among others.

E. Concluding Benediction (16:25–27)   A glorious benediction concludes the letter. It includes Paul's final reference to his gospel and to God's revelation of the "sacred secret" that was anticipated in the prophetic Scriptures, according to which "the obedience of faith among all nations" was now advancing through Paul and his associates to the glory of God in Christ.

THEOLOGY

Theological Themes

The Gospel   Paul's letter to the Romans makes an enormous contribution to the NT canon. This letter contains the most extensive presentation of Paul's gospel. Romans 1:18–3:20 is Paul's most thorough and sustained treatment of the universal sinfulness of

---

[18] See the discussion of Phoebe in A. J. Köstenberger, "Women in the Pauline Mission," in *The Gospel to the Nations: Perspectives on Paul's Mission*, ed. P. Bolt and M. Thompson (Downers Grove: InterVarsity, 2000), 228–29. Cf. Moo, *Romans*, 912–16; and Schreiner, *Romans*, 786–88, both of whom, while also complementarian in their view of gender roles, leaned toward identifying Phoebe as a deacon. Among translations, the HCSB has "servant" in the text, with a footnote saying, "Others interpret this term in a technical sense: *deacon, or deaconess, or minister.*" Similarly, both the NASB and the NIV have "servant" in the text and a footnote: "Or *deaconess*"; the situation is reversed in the NIV2010 which identifies Phoebe as a "deacon" (footnote: "Or *servant*").

[19] See Köstenberger, "Women in the Pauline Mission," 221–47.

humanity. Paul's portrait of the sinner is a graphic depiction of the creature's rebellion against the Creator, a depiction that unmasks his deep depravity. Rarely does one see the horrific ugliness of his soul with such shocking clarity as in these riveting verses.

Further, Rom 3:21–4:20 contains Paul's most developed exposition of his doctrine of justification. Paul discussed this doctrine extensively in Galatians. Romans adds specific details to the discussion of justification that the earlier treatment in Galatians did not include, such as the point that Abraham was justified before he was circumcised; that Abraham's faith closely parallels Christian faith in the God who resurrected Jesus and who justifies sinners; and that all three major sections of the OT affirm justification by faith.

Also, Rom 5:1–8:39 contains Paul's most developed discussion of the believer's new spiritual state, particularly his liberation from death, sin, the law, and corruption. Then in 12:1–15:13, Paul described in vivid detail the practical implications of this new spiritual state. Although Romans is frequently associated with the doctrine of justification by faith alone, it must not be overlooked that Paul sees justification as leading inevitably to sanctification in which the Spirit prompts and empowers the believer to fulfill God's righteous demands in fulfillment of the new covenant promises (8:1–4).

Finally, Romans contains what is by far Paul's most complete treatment of God's relationship to national Israel. Romans 9–11 discusses in great detail Israel's gracious election, God's faithfulness to his covenant, Israel's rejection of God's grace, the positive purpose of this rejection in redemptive history, and the future salvation of Israel. These chapters express the love of the "apostle of the Gentiles" for the people of Israel more powerfully and passionately than any other text that he penned.

The "Righteousness of God"   One of the major themes of Romans is the insistence that individuals are viewed by God as righteous only on the basis of faith rather than by the works of the law. This theme is so prominent that many interpreters since the Protestant Reformation have viewed justification by faith as the primary focus of the letter. Although many now insist that justification cannot be singled out as the central theme of the entire book, most still acknowledge that it is at least the focus of 1:1–4:25 where Paul explained that believers are declared righteous on the basis of Jesus' sacrificial death and that this is the only means of salvation since all have failed to live up to the standard of the law.

Paul was emphatic that the doctrine of justification by faith was not a novelty of his own invention. God's gracious justification of believers had been clearly attested in the OT. "The Law and the Prophets" witnessed to "God's righteousness through faith in Jesus Christ" (3:21–22). This theme is also prominent in the programmatic statement of the letter. Romans 1:17 confirms the claim that God's justifying righteousness was revealed "from faith to faith" by citing Hab 2:4 and introducing the quotation with the words "just as it is written."

In chap. 4 Paul added to this citation from the Prophets a confirmation from the Pentateuch (4:3) to which he referred no less than three times in this single chapter and a citation from the Writings (Ps 32:1–2). Paul appears to have been using a rabbinic method of proving an argument by demonstrating that all three major portions of the OT—the Law, the Prophets, and the Writings—affirm a particular truth (see also 1:2).[20]

At the conclusion of his discussion of justification, Paul described Jesus as the one who "was delivered up for our trespasses" (Rom 4:25), a description that echoes Isa 53:12 (LXX). The idea is that Jesus was handed over to the judge in order to suffer the penalty for the believer's trespasses. It is on these grounds that the judge may pronounce the verdict that the sinner is "not guilty." Divine justice has been fully satisfied through the substitutionary suffering of God's Son.

The faith required for justification in Romans is a faith in which sinners believe in Jesus' identity as the Messiah, the Savior whose sacrificial death secures the believer's acquittal, and the eternal and almighty God. Such faith acknowledges both that Jesus died a sacrificial death and that he rose from the dead. Only this Christ-centered faith is sufficient for the gracious acquittal of the sinner.

POINTS OF APPLICATION

- Admit that you are a sinner in the eyes of a holy God (3:23)
- Believe that God saved you in Christ apart from anything you did (5:8)
- Confess that Jesus is Lord and believe in him in your heart (10:9–10)
- Deliver the good news to others who haven't yet heard (10:14–17)
- Exercise your spiritual gifts (12:3–8)

STUDY QUESTIONS

1. Why is Paul's authorship of Romans so certain among scholars?
2. Why are Paul's travel plans so important in dating the book of Romans?
3. Why did Paul write Romans?
4. On what major divisions of Romans do most scholars agree?
5. When Paul says in Romans 3:23 that "all have sinned and fall short of the glory of God," whom does he have in mind when referring to "all"?
6. How are individuals viewed as righteous by God in Romans?

FOR FURTHER STUDY

Bruce, F. F. *The Letter of Paul to the Romans: An Introduction and Commentary*. Tyndale New Testament Commentaries. Rev. ed. Grand Rapids: Eerdmans, 1985.

Harrison, E. F., and D. A. Hagner. "Romans." Pages 19–237 in *The Expositor's Bible Commentary*. Rev. ed. Vol. 11: *Romans—Galatians*. Grand Rapids: Zondervan, 2008.

Moo, D. J. *Encountering the Book of Romans: A Theological Survey*. Encountering Biblical Studies. Grand Rapids: Baker, 2002.

_____. *The Epistle to the Romans*. The New International Commentary on the New Testament. Grand Rapids: Eerdmans, 1996.

---

[20] E. E. Ellis, *Paul's Use of the Old Testament* (Grand Rapids: Baker, 1981), 46.

Morris, L. *The Epistle to the Romans*. Grand Rapids: Eerdmans, 1988.
Schlatter, A. *Romans: The Righteousness of God*. Translated by S. Schatzmann. Peabody: Hendrickson, 1995.
Schreiner, T. R. *Romans*. Baker Exegetical Commentary on the New Testament. Grand Rapids: Baker, 1998.
Wright, N. T. "The Letter to the Romans." Pages 393–770 in *The New Interpreter's Bible*. Vol. 10. Nashville: Abingdon, 2002.

Chapter 14

The Prison Epistles: Philippians, Ephesians, Colossians, and Philemon

CORE KNOWLEDGE

Students should know the key facts of Philippians, Ephesians, Colossians, and Philemon. With regard to history, students should be able to identify each book's author, date, provenance, destination, and purpose. With regard to literature, they should be able to provide a basic outline of each book and identify core elements of each book's content found in the unit-by-unit discussion. With regard to theology, students should be able to identify the major theological themes in Philippians, Ephesians, Colossians, and Philemon.

INTRODUCTION

AS THE BOOK of Acts makes clear, Paul established several local congregations in major urban centers on at least three missionary journeys. Toward the end of his distinguished apostolic ministry, and after writing Galatians, 1 and 2 Thessalonians, 1 and 2 Corinthians, and Romans, Paul engaged in additional correspondence with several churches and individuals during his first Roman imprisonment (58–60). Paul's letters to the Philippians, Ephesians, Colossians, and Philemon (commonly called the Prison Epistles) date to this period.

Most likely Philippians was written prior to the other letters. In Phlm 22, Paul expected to be released from prison soon, while in Phil 1:21–25 he inferred what the future held based on spiritual principles, but he had no idea as to the timing of his release.

Ephesians, Colossians, and Philemon were all related to the return of Onesimus and were most likely written roughly at the same time and under similar circumstances. But the precise sequence in which these letters were penned is unknown. Because Ephesians and

231

Colossians are connected via Tychicus (Eph 6:21; Col 4:7), and Colossians and Philemon via Onesimus (Col 4:9; Phlm 10) and Epaphras (Col 1:7; 4:12; Phlm 23), and because Ephesians, Colossians, Philemon is the order in which the letters are included in the NT canon, we will discuss these three letters in that same order.

CONTRIBUTION TO THE CANON[1]

- The centrality of the gospel of Christ and partnership in the gospel (Phil 1:5; 4:15)
- Christ's self-humiliation *(kenōsis)* and subsequent exaltation (Phil 2:5–12)
- The supremacy of Christ, the cosmic reconciling work of Christ, and spiritual warfare (Eph 1:10,20–23; 6:10–18; Col 1:15–20)
- The subjection of all things to Christ's lordship and the present implications of Christ's victory for believers (Eph 1:10; 4:1–6:9; Col 3:1–4:1)
- The unity of the church as the body of Christ consisting of Jews and Gentiles (Eph 2:11–22; 3:1–13; 4:1–6; Col 1:24–2:3; 3:12–17)
- Christian joy and thanksgiving (Phil 1:12–20; 4:4; Col 1:9–12; 2:6–7; 3:17; 4:2)
- The Christian transformation of socioeconomic structures such as slavery (Philemon)
- Social relationships (Eph 5:22–6:9; Col 3:18–4:1)

PHILIPPIANS

KEY FACTS	
Author:	Paul
Date:	Around 59 (most likely prior to Ephesians, Colossians, and Philemon)
Provenance:	Roman imprisonment
Destination:	The church at Philippi
Occasion:	Thanksgiving for the Philippians' partnership in the gospel and warnings against disunity and false teaching as hindrances to the spread of the gospel
Purpose:	To promote gospel-centered unity for the sake of advancing the gospel
Theme:	Partnership in the gospel and walking worthy of the gospel
Key Verses:	1:27–30

---

[1] The Contribution to the Canon, Study Questions, and For Further Study sections cover all four Prison Epistles.

INTRODUCTION

PHILIPPIANS STANDS AS a favorite among Paul's letters for many because of its inspiring message of joy in the midst of trying circumstances (e.g., imprisonment). Some students may know Philippians in piecemeal fashion because of the numerous memorable phrases or expressions found in the letter. Familiar phrases include: "For me, living is Christ and dying is gain" (1:21); "so that at the name of Jesus every knee should bow . . . and every tongue confess that Jesus Christ is Lord" (2:10–11); "I am able to do all things through Him who strengthens me" (4:13); and "rejoice in the Lord always. I will say it again: Rejoice!" (4:4). However, this "bits and pieces" approach to Philippians does justice neither to the depth of the letter nor to Paul's overall purpose for writing. One must see how the pieces fit together into a coherent whole in order to appreciate truly the profound message of the letter.

HISTORY

Author

Most scholars regard Philippians as an authentic letter written by Paul. Scholarly acceptance of Paul's authorship is so widespread that an extended discussion is unnecessary. The reasons for accepting authenticity are as follows: (1) the letter opens by identifying the author as Paul; (2) the early church accepted Paul as the author without dissent; and (3) the letter is intensely personal, suggesting that the author was well known to the church of Philippi. The early church fathers Polycarp (c. 69–155), Irenaeus (c. 130–200), Clement of Alexandria (c. 150–215), and Tertullian (c. 160–225) unanimously accepted Pauline authorship.

Date

The date for Philippians depends on the place of writing. Dates as early as 50 or as late as 63 are possible. If Paul wrote the letter during his first Roman imprisonment, he probably wrote in the late 50s (early 60s in the conventional reckoning). If he wrote the letter during his Caesarean imprisonment, the letter should be dated 55–57 (58–60 in the conventional reckoning). If he wrote from Ephesus, Paul wrote between the years 51 and 54 (54 and 57 in the conventional reckoning). Although the issues are complex, the evidence for a Roman provenance is most persuasive. Philippians appears to have been written somewhat earlier than the other Prison Epistles. Paul appears to have written Colossians, Philemon, and Ephesians at about the same time. Philemon implies that Paul's release from prison was imminent (Phlm 21). However, when Paul wrote Philippians, he seemed less certain about the outcome of his trial and was contemplating the possibility that he would be martyred (Phil 1:21–26). On the other hand, Paul's extensive outreach (Phil 1:12–14) and the widespread knowledge of Paul's circumstances suggest that he had been imprisoned in Rome for at least several months at the time that he wrote Philippians.

These factors suggest that the composition of Philippians should be dated to around the midpoint of the Roman imprisonment in or around the year 59.

Provenance

The question of provenance is one of the most contested issues in Philippians. Paul clearly identified himself as a prisoner (1:7,13,17), but he did not explicitly state the location of this imprisonment. Presumably, the Philippians knew where Paul was imprisoned and thus did not need to be told. Three different answers commend themselves as worthy of consideration: (1) Rome;[2] (2) Caesarea; and (3) Ephesus.[3]

The traditional view places Paul's imprisonment in Rome. A Roman imprisonment hypothesis would account for (1) the mention of the Praetorium (1:13) and Caesar's household (4:22); (2) the loose restrictions implied by his activity during his imprisonment (see Acts 28:16,30–31); (3) references to a seemingly well-established church (1:14); (4) external evidence such as the subscription added by the first corrector of Codex Vaticanus and the comments in the Marcionite Prologue;[4] and (5) the "life or death" nature of the imprisonment (Paul could have appealed to Caesar while under any other imprisonment).

Until recently the Roman hypothesis held almost universal sway. But scholars began to note two primary weaknesses in the traditional hypothesis related to geography and Paul's travel plans. First, the distance between Philippi and Rome (about 1,200 miles) renders the number of journeys implied in Philippians (perhaps as many as seven) problematic.[5] Second, the letter to the Romans mentions Paul's intention to travel to Spain (Rom 15:24,28), while Philippians states that Paul planned to visit Philippi after his release (Phil 2:24).

Despite these weaknesses, however, the hypothesis of the Roman provenance of the Prison Epistles is persuasive because it depends on a known imprisonment, enjoys more abundant external evidence than alternative locations such as Ephesus or Caesarea, and has a long-standing tradition.[6] In fact, the hypothesis of a Roman provenance for Philippians

---

[2] M. Bockmuehl, *The Epistle to the Philippians*, BNTC 11 (Peabody: Hendrickson, 1998), 25–32; G. D. Fee, *Paul's Letter to the Philippians*, NICNT (Grand Rapids: Eerdmans, 1995), 34–37; M. Silva, *Philippians*, 2nd ed., BECNT (Grand Rapids: Baker, 2005), 5–7; P. T. O'Brien, *Philippians*, NIGTC (Grand Rapids: Eerdmans, 1991), 19–26.

[3] F. Thielman, "Ephesus and the Literary Setting of Philippians," in *New Testament Greek and Exegesis, Essays in Honor of Gerald F. Hawthorne*, ed. A. M. Donaldson and T. B. Sailors (Grand Rapids: Eerdmans, 2003), 205–23; id., *Theology of the New Testament* (Grand Rapids: Zondervan, 2005), 307. D. A. Carson and D. J. Moo (*An Introduction to the New Testament*, 2nd ed. [Grand Rapids: Zondervan, 2005], 506) cautiously said that "there is a little more to be said for Ephesus than for Rome, but we can say no more than this (and many would hold that we are not entitled to say even this)."

[4] "The Philippians are Macedonians. These, having received the word of truth, remained steadfast in the faith. The apostle commends them, writing to them from prison in Rome."

[5] O'Brien (*Philippians*, 25) correctly calculated that as few as three journeys between Rome and Philippi are possible before Paul penned the letter depending on where Epaphroditus was when he became ill. If Paul wrote Philippians toward the end of his two-year imprisonment in Rome, there is more than adequate time for the required trips. The three one-way trips to Philippi by Epaphroditus, Timothy, and Paul, respectively, do not pose a real problem for a Roman provenance. Concern should focus on the number of trips between the beginning of Paul's incarceration and the penning of the letter.

[6] F. F. Bruce, *Philippians*, NIBC (Peabody: Hendrickson, 1989), 11–16.

is stronger than that for the other Prison Epistles due to the references to the Praetorium (Phil 1:13) and Caesar's household (Phil 4:22). Fortunately, questions of provenance do not drastically alter one's interpretation of the message of the letter.

Destination

Philippians 1:1 indicates that Paul addressed the letter to the believers in Christ Jesus "who are in Philippi." The straightforward nature of this declaration has created a consensus among NT scholars that Philippi is the destination of the letter. The Acts narrative reveals that Philippi represents the first church Paul planted in Europe (Acts 16:6–40) on his second missionary journey in c. 49–51.[7]

The city of Philippi was best known in the ancient world as the site of the battle in which Antony and Octavian emerged victorious over Brutus and Cassius (who helped assassinate Julius Caesar) in 42 BC. Octavian later defeated Antony (31 BC) and rebuilt Philippi and gave it the *ius italicum* ("law of Italy"), which was the highest privilege a colony could obtain. The city was a site of historical interest long before these events.[8] It was founded by Philip II of Macedon, who named it after himself. It was situated in a very fertile region eight miles from the Macedonian Sea and enjoyed an abundance of springs and gold (Strabo, *Geography* 7.331). Philippi became part of the Roman Empire in 168 BC and prospered due to its strategic location along the Via Egnatia, the main land route between Rome and the East.

Occasion

The text of Philippians suggests several possible reasons for writing. It is important to note that Paul addressed both pastoral problems and personal concerns. Two major pastoral problems surface in Philippians. First, Paul had apparently heard a report of disunity among the Philippians, which included a specific conflict between two women in the church, Euodia and Syntyche. Paul urged them to be united to live in harmony together in the Lord (4:2). Second, Paul sounded a serious warning against false teachers and their teachings.[9]

Paul also included numerous personal concerns. To begin with, the apostle sought to provide the Philippians with an update regarding his own circumstances and the advancement of the gospel since he regarded them as partners in the gospel (1:5) who labored in prayer for him (1:19). In addition, the evidence suggests three other personal concerns:

---

[7] Acts 16:14 records that Lydia was the first convert. She and her family responded to the gospel and were baptized (Acts 16:15). Her house also functioned as the meeting place for the church. The Acts account also mentions the conversion of the Philippian jailer and his family (16:30–33). G. F. Hawthorne (*Philippians*, WBC 43 [Waco: Word, 1983], xxxv) noted that the names in Philippians (Epaphroditus, Euodia, Syntyche, and Clement) reveal that the church was made up largely of Gentiles.

[8] L. M. McDonald, "Philippi," in *Dictionary of New Testament Background*, ed. C. A. Evans and S. E. Porter (Downers Grove: InterVarsity, 2000), 787–89.

[9] There is a debate over whether the false teachers were present in Philippi or Paul was warning the church about a potential threat.

(1) a commendation of Timothy in order that the Philippians would welcome him upon his arrival (2:19–23); (2) an announcement of Paul's desire to visit the church in the future (2:24); and (3) a report on Epaphroditus and his illness (2:25–30).

Purpose

Paul's main purpose in Philippians is connected to the main theme of the letter: partnership in the gospel and walking worthy of the gospel. "Partnership" or "fellowship" is the customary rendering here for the Greek word *koinōnia*. The Philippians' partnership in the gospel should be understood in an active, not passive, sense.[10] D. A. Carson captured the sense well when he wrote, "Christian fellowship, then, is self-sacrificing conformity to the gospel. There may be overtones of warmth and intimacy, but the heart of the matter is this shared vision of what is of transcendent importance, a vision that calls forth our commitment."[11] This partnership involved, but was not limited to, the Philippians' financial support for Paul's missionary work (4:15–16).

"Living one's life in a manner worthy of the gospel" (1:27) is shorthand for living in a manner that befits the greatness of the gospel. This "worthy walk" involves both Christian unity and a willingness to suffer for the advancement of the gospel. This necessary unity was not "peace at any cost" but was instead a unity that was inspired by a shared faith in the gospel message. Paul called believers to stand together as one in a battle for faith in the gospel. This stand involved resisting false teachings that compromised the message of the gospel, courageous suffering of persecution for the sake of the gospel, and being undaunted in the proclamation of the gospel.

LITERATURE

Literary Plan

Some scholars have identified Philippians as a "letter of friendship."[12] Others have compared the book to the genre of "family letters."[13] Many, most notably J. T. Reed, have analyzed Philippians at the discourse level and concluded that the letter is a unified and coherent composition from start to finish.[14] The unity and internal coherence of Paul's

---

[10] See especially the excellent discussion in O'Brien (*Philippians*, 61–63), who highlighted the "many-sided activity" of the Philippians in their partnership in the gospel. He said it probably included (1) proclamation of the gospel to outsiders (1:27–28); (2) suffering for the gospel with Paul (1:30; 4:14–15); (3) intercessory prayer (1:19); and (4) their cooperation with Paul in the gospel (1:5) demonstrated by their financial assistance in the past (4:15–16) and the present (4:10).

[11] D. A. Carson, *Basics for Believers: An Exposition of Philippians* (Grand Rapids: Baker, 1996), 16.

[12] See Fee, *Philippians*, 2–7; B. Witherington III, *Friendship and Finances in Philippi* (Valley Forge: Trinity Press International, 1994); S. K. Stowers, "Friends and Enemies in the Politics of Heaven: Reading Theology in Philippians," in *Pauline Theology: Thessalonians, Philippians, Galatians, Philemon*, vol. 1, ed. J. M. Bassler (Minneapolis: Fortress, 1991), 105–21, esp. 107–14.

[13] L. Alexander, "Hellenistic Letter-Forms and the Structure of Philippians," *JSNT* 37 (1989): 87–101.

[14] J. T. Reed, A *Discourse Analysis of Philippians: Method and Rhetoric in the Debate over Literary Integrity*, JSNTSup 136 (Sheffield: Sheffield Academic Press, 1997).

letter to the Philippians are further demonstrated in the outline and unit-by-unit discussion below.

OUTLINE
I. INTRODUCTION: GREETINGS TO THE PHILIPPIANS (1:1–2)
II. BODY: THE PHILIPPIANS' PARTNERSHIP WITH PAUL IN THE GOSPEL (1:3–4:20)
    A. Opening: Thanksgiving and Prayer for the Philippians (1:3–11)
    B. Body Proper: Exhortation to Unity for the Sake of the Gospel (1:12–4:9)
    C. Closing: Thanksgiving for the Philippians' Present and Previous Gifts (4:10–20)
III. CONCLUSION: FINAL GREETINGS (4:21–23)

UNIT-BY-UNIT DISCUSSION

I. Introduction: Greetings to the Philippians (1:1–2)
Following standard epistolary conventions, Paul identified himself as the sender and Timothy as a cosender of the letter.[15] He referred to the recipients of the letter in Philippi and specifically mentioned the elders and deacons of the church at Philippi (1:1). In the salutation, Paul, as customary, changed the standard greeting (*chairein*) to the theologically pregnant grace-wish (*charis*, 1:2).

II. Body: The Philippians' Partnership with Paul in the Gospel (1:3–4:20)
The body of the letter centers on the theme of gospel partnership. Paul stressed the urgent need for unity in the cause of the gospel. This unity not only arises as a natural outgrowth of the gospel; it also remains necessary for continued growth of the gospel. Paul urged the Philippians to unite against those things that threatened the progress of the gospel.

A. Opening: Thanksgiving and Prayer for the Philippians (1:3–11) Paul's thanksgiving centers on the Philippians' participation and partnership in the gospel. The apostle rejoiced that this partnership which extended from the past into the present (1:5) would continue to the end because the one who began the work could be trusted to complete it (1:6). He commented on how fitting these feelings were in light of his firm conviction that the Philippians were fellow recipients of divine grace together with Paul in his work of defending and confirming the gospel (1:7). Paul also called God as witness to the sincerity of these affections for the Philippians (1:8). He concluded this section with a prayer for the continued growth of the Philippians in the gospel (1:9–11).

---

[15] Some scholars minimize the importance of Paul's mention of Timothy. Acts portrays Timothy in a significant ministry role throughout Macedonia. Silva (*Philippians*, 39) is probably correct in stating that good reasons exist to believe that "the Philippians had a strong attachment to Timothy." Carson and Moo (*Introduction to the New Testament*, 507) took a very different tack in saying that Paul's later commendation of Timothy (2:19–24) implies that "the Philippians did not know him well."

B. Body Proper: Exhortation to Unity for the Sake of the Gospel (1:12–4:9)   Paul provided the Philippians with four biographical vignettes in 1:12–2:30. The lives of Paul (1:12–26), Jesus (2:5–11), Timothy (2:19–24), and Epaphroditus (2:25–30) serve as examples to the Philippians because they demonstrated humility by putting the needs of others first, even in the face of potential (1:20–24; 2:27,30) or actual death (2:8). The testimony of these lives provided models for the Philippians to emulate as they sought the greater progress of the gospel amid their own hardships. They served to strengthen the Philippians so that they too could endure the suffering (1:29) they faced at the hands of their opponents (1:28). Paul even referred to this hardship as a gracious gift from God (1:29).

The call to emulation continues in 3:17 and 4:9, but in 3:1–4:9 this call differs in that it focuses on two grave threats against the gospel: (1) false teachers, and (2) disunity among the Philippians. Paul's note of urgency throughout this section reads like a call to mobilize in the fight for the gospel.

The threat from the false teachers was much more serious than the threat posed by the evangelists mentioned earlier by Paul (1:15–17). The evangelists preached the right message with the wrong motives. They preached because they envied Paul and wished to increase his suffering. If they had doctrinal differences with Paul, those were relatively minor so that Paul could still rejoice that they proclaimed the gospel. The present unit makes clear that these false teachers got their message very wrong. It contained disturbing departures from the true gospel that Paul had to confront.[16]

Paul rebuked their zeal for a false gospel that apparently viewed circumcision and OT dietary laws as necessary for salvation. In a biting irony, Paul turned the tables on the false teachers and demonstrated that their indictment of Gentile believers was in fact a self-indictment. Jews would call non-Jews "unclean," partly because they ate a forbidden diet, much like dogs who fed on carrion and garbage. Paul called the false teachers "dogs" in order to show that they did not belong to the true people of God.

In a play on words, Paul described the false teachers' circumcision as mutilation, which referred to the pagan cuttings of the body like the self-inflicted wounds of the prophets of Baal (1 Kgs 18:28) that were forbidden in OT law (Lev 19:28; 21:5; Deut 14:1; Isa 15:2; Hos 7:14). Paul's point was that the false teachers' dependence on circumcision for salvation demonstrated that they did not understand God's grace and were in fact pagans rather than the chosen people of God. Christians are the true circumcision who worship God in the Spirit and forsake confidence in the flesh (3:1–3). In fact, Paul reminded the Philippians that if anyone had reason to put stock in the flesh, it was he (3:4–6).

Yet after his conversion to Christ, he came to relegate those former things (3:7), and indeed all things (3:8), to the loss side of the ledger in comparison with the surpassing value of gaining and knowing Christ (3:8) and being found righteous in him by faith

---

[16] See Silva, *Philippians*, 64–65; Fee, *Philippians*, 122–23; and Bockmuehl, *Philippians*, 77–78.

(3:9). Paul's passion was now knowing Christ in the power of his resurrection and the fellowship of his sufferings (3:10), so that Paul might eventually follow Christ in experiencing resurrection (3:11).

Paul reminded the Philippians that he had not attained the goal of the resurrection or become perfect (3:12). He intentionally forgot about the qualifications that he once depended on for salvation and now pressed on in pursuit of the heavenly prize (3:12–14). This perspective represented the mark of mature thinking for Christians (3:15), which God would reveal even to those who disagreed (3:16). The apostle presented himself and those who took the same perspective as examples to emulate in contrast with the behavior of the opponents who were enemies of the cross (3:17–19). The apostle drew a stark contrast between their focus on "earthly things" (3:19) and believers' "citizenship in heaven" (3:20). Paul showed that these contrasting focal points would lead to contrasting outcomes: destruction for the opponents (3:19) and glorified bodies for believers (3:20–21). Believers "eagerly wait" for Jesus the Savior (3:20) who will transform them by his almighty power (3:21).

The second threat to the gospel is disunity. Philippians 4 begins with a charge to stand firm in the Lord (4:1). Paul continued his charge by urging two prominent women in the church to "agree in the Lord" (4:2). Disunity obviously threatened "partnership" in the gospel, so Paul asked the Philippians to help these women who contended for the gospel at Paul's side like Clement and the rest of Paul's coworkers (4:3). Rejoicing in the Lord (4:4), prayer (4:6), and the heart-guarding power of the peace of God (4:7) represent the cure for disunity. Paul concluded by urging the Philippians to concentrate on excellent things (4:8) and to emulate Paul's teaching and lifestyle (4:9).

C. Closing: Thanksgiving for the Philippians' Partnership in the Gospel (4:10–20)   Paul rejoiced with thanksgiving for the Philippians' present (4:10,14,18) and past (4:15–16) financial gifts. He did not rejoice in the gift itself so much as in what the gift represented: the Philippians' partnership with Paul in the gospel. The apostle testified that Christ's strength enabled him (4:13) to be content in every circumstance (4:11), whether poverty or abundance (4:12). He reminded the Philippians that their gifts to Paul were in reality sacrifices of praise to God (4:18), who would supply all their needs according to his riches in glory in Christ Jesus (4:19). Therefore, Paul closed with a fitting doxology in which he gave God all the glory (4:20).

III. Conclusion: Final Greetings (4:21–23)

Paul urged the Philippians to greet all the believers in Christ Jesus. He also reminded them that all the believers sent their greetings, including the brothers who were with Paul. Among those in the category of "all believers," Paul especially highlighted "Caesar's household" (4:22). Paul followed these greetings with the grace benediction: "the grace of our Lord Jesus Christ be with your spirit" (4:23).

THEOLOGY

Theological Themes

Christian Unity   Paul repeatedly stressed the special relationship he had with the Philippian church (1:5–6; 4:15). Yet not all was well in the Philippian church. Not only were there external threats in the form of false teachers (3:2), there was also internal disunity that threatened to divide the church. This problem was epitomized by Euodia and Syntyche (4:2), who had been coworkers of Paul but who now were in need of a mediator to work out their differences (4:3; cf. 1:27).

Earlier in the letter, Paul exhorted the Philippians to "[d]o nothing out of rivalry or conceit, but in humility consider others as more important than yourselves. Everyone should look out not only for his own interests, but also for the interests of others" (2:3–4). This is followed by a moving and poetic description of Jesus Christ, who renounced all his privileges in order to meet humanity's desperate need for salvation, as the supreme example of such humility (2:5–11).

Consequently, believers are exhorted to work out their salvation with fear and trembling, for it is God who is at work in them (2:12–13). Paul's concern was for the unity of believers so that the gospel proclamation would not be hindered. Internal disunity continues to be a major tool of Satan hindering effective Christian ministry. The gospel will go forth, and God will be glorified, if only people in the church will lay aside their differences and "agree in the Lord" (4:2).

Joy in Christ in the Context of Christian Suffering   Paul used the "joy" word family 16 times in this short letter. Thus Philippians testifies to the deep-rooted reality of joy in the life of a follower of Christ. One should not regard delight in Christ as an "icing on the cake" version of Christianity but as an essential outgrowth of union with Christ in the gospel. Joy is an inevitable overflow of progressively perceiving the "surpassing value" of knowing Christ Jesus as Lord through faith in the gospel of Christ.[17]

This joy often finds expression in the midst of suffering (see Acts 16:16–25).[18] Paul's trying circumstances had served to advance the gospel (1:12–13), and both Paul and Epaphroditus faced the prospect of death in their ministry (1:20–21; 2:27). In the Philippians' fight for the faith, they would meet suffering as well (1:27–28). Christ suffered on the cross (2:8), and Paul regarded his own suffering as a fellowship in Christ's sufferings (3:11). Paul could endure suffering, such as hunger and poverty, through the strength that Christ provided (4:12–13).

---

[17] F. Thielman, *Theology of the New Testament: A Canonical and Synthetic Approach* (Grand Rapids: Zondervan, 2005), 321.

[18] P. Oakes, *Philippians: From People to Letter*, SNTSMS 110 (Cambridge: University Press, 2001), 59–96. Oakes said that the Philippians suffered economically and physically for their refusal to join in pagan religious rituals.

EPHESIANS

KEY FACTS	
Author:	Paul
Date:	Around 60
Provenance:	Roman imprisonment
Destination:	Circular letter or Ephesus
Occasion:	Not clearly identifiable
Purpose:	To declare and promote cosmic reconciliation and unity in Christ
Theme:	The summing up of all things in Christ
Key Verses:	1:3–14, especially 1:9–10

INTRODUCTION

EPHESIANS IS A magisterial summary of Paul's teaching and was Calvin's favorite letter of Paul.[19] R. Brown claimed that only Romans has exercised more influence on Christian thought throughout church history.[20] The letter continues to encourage Christians today with the cosmic scale of Christ's reconciling work and to challenge believers to maintain the unity of the church that Christ purchased and that the Spirit produced.

Ephesians makes numerous and significant contributions to the canon. First, Paul presented the theme of subjecting all things to Christ's lordship most clearly and articulately in Ephesians. Paul developed this cosmic realignment of proper submission to God's authority along the lines of the reconciling work of Christ in two spheres: the heavens and the earth.

Second, perhaps only Colossians can compare with Ephesians' emphasis on the staggering aspects of Christ's victory that believers already enjoy in Christ. Christ is exalted above all other powers to the point that they will all serve as the footstool for his feet. A unified church consisting of Jews and Gentiles shares that victory as the church sits and reigns with Christ.

Third, Ephesians contains perhaps the most developed discussion of and vision for the church. This same church that already shares in Christ's victory serves as a herald or foreshadowing of God's great plan to "bring all things back together under one head," the Lord Jesus Christ (1:10, author's translation). Therefore, the unified church testifies to the unified universe in God's new creation when he will place all hostile forces under the feet of his Son.

---

[19] For an excellent survey of accolades ascribed to Ephesians (including the Calvin reference), see H. W. Hoehner, *Ephesians: An Exegetical Commentary* (Grand Rapids: Baker, 2003), 1–2.

[20] R. E. Brown, *An Introduction to the New Testament* (New York: Doubleday, 1997), 620. For an extensive look at the influence exercised by Ephesians, see R. Schnackenburg, *Ephesians: A Commentary* (Edinburgh: T&T Clark, 1996), 311–42.

Fourth, Ephesians also contains the most developed discussion of spiritual warfare in the NT (6:10–18; see 2 Cor 10:3–6). The church plays a crucial role in these times as all things are being subjected to the authority of Christ. The two realms clash in warfare as the hostile heavenly powers wage war against the redeemed forces of humanity upon the earth. Believers advance by standing united in God's armor.

HISTORY

Author

It has become fashionable to speak of three tiers within the "Pauline" corpus: (1) undisputed letters (Romans, 1 and 2 Corinthians, Galatians, Philippians, 1 Thessalonians, Philemon); (2) Deutero-Pauline letters (Ephesians, Colossians, 2 Thessalonians); and (3) pseudonymous letters (1 and 2 Timothy, Titus). Many modern scholars reject the traditional view that Ephesians is an authentic Pauline letter, citing concerns with the letter's theology, vocabulary, literary style, relationship to Colossians, and impersonal nature.

However, when all arguments are weighed, the Pauline authorship of Ephesians rests upon a firm foundation. Paul's authorship of Ephesians rests most securely upon two early and influential claims for authenticity: (1) the claim of the letter, and (2) the testimony of the early church.[21] The case against authenticity is further plagued by questions surrounding the practice and validity of pseudonymity.[22] The overall weight of the evidence decisively favors Pauline authorship.

Date

The date for Ephesians depends on complex questions concerning authorship and provenance. If the letter was written during Paul's Roman imprisonment, then it dates to 58–60 (60–62 in the conventional reckoning).[23] Since Ephesians, Colossians, and Philemon appear to have been written at approximately the same time and since Philemon belongs to the final phase of Paul's imprisonment, a date around the year 60 is reasonable. If one places Ephesians earlier in Paul's ministry, then it dates to the early or mid-50s. Most who see the letter as non-Pauline or post-Pauline date the letter somewhere between 70 and 90.[24]

---

[21] C. L. Mitton (*Ephesians*, NCB [London: Oliphants, 1976], 15–16) wrote, "The external evidence is wholly on the side of those who maintain Pauline authorship. Among all the early writers of the Christian Church there is never the slightest hint that questions it." Clement of Rome (c. 95) appears to be the first church father to allude to Ephesians (*1 Clem.* 46:6). It appears that Ignatius (died c. 110), Irenaeus (c. 180), Polycarp (c. 155), Clement of Alexandria (c. 200), and Tertullian (d. 225) knew Ephesians and confirmed its authenticity. Ephesians can also be found in Marcion's canon and the Muratorian canon. See Hoehner's excellent survey of Ephesians in the early church (*Ephesians*, 2–6).

[22] See the excellent discussion on pseudonymity and pseudepigraphy in Carson and Moo, *Introduction to the New Testament*, 337–53.

[23] P. T. O'Brien (*The Epistle to the Ephesians*, PNTC [Grand Rapids: Eerdmans, 1999], 57) opted for 61–62.

[24] Carson and Moo (*Introduction to the New Testament*, 487) noted that the latest possible date appears to be approximately 90 because it appears that Clement of Rome referred to Ephesians in his letter, which is usually dated to the year 96.

Provenance

The provenance of Ephesians is inextricably related to issues such as authorship, the identity of the addressees, and the date. Many hold that Ephesians was written from the same place as Colossians and Philemon, and possibly Philippians.

Destination

The fact that some important manuscripts do not include "at Ephesus" (1:1) poses problems for identifying a destination.[25] Prominent textual critics such as B. Metzger doubt the integrity of the phrase "at Ephesus."[26] Therefore, some scholars have theorized that Ephesians was a circular letter.[27] This assumption coheres with some of the internal evidence of the letter. The impersonal tone throughout Ephesians is surprising in light of the considerable amount of time that Paul spent in Ephesus (Acts 19:8,10; 20:31). Moreover, some texts seem to imply that the author did not even know the readers (Eph 3:2; 4:21).

However, one should also note that the circular letter hypothesis is not without problems in that even the manuscripts that do not contain the phrase "at Ephesus" have "Ephesus" in the title.[28] What is more, even those who adhere to the circular letter hypothesis admit that the omission of "at Ephesus" creates an awkward grammatical construction: "to the saints and believers in Christ Jesus." This debate seems somewhat inconsequential because some scholars who think that "at Ephesus" is part of the original text still believe that the letter circulated to the churches in Asia Minor as well.[29]

Occasion

Paul's letters are not expressions of theoretical theology. They are pastoral letters that address specific congregational circumstances. But Ephesians appears to break this mold, and thus it is difficult to detect a clear occasion for the letter.[30] Most agree that Gentile readers are the primary audience, but the consensus quickly begins to crumble after that observation. In contrast with the tone and content of Colossians, Ephesians does not read like a response to false teaching. Some have questioned the search for an occasion to the extent that they doubt whether Ephesians is a letter at all. These scholars prefer to describe it as a homily or a speech.[31]

---

[25] "At Ephesus" is omitted by key early texts and church fathers. Other text traditions support the inclusion of "at Ephesus."

[26] B. M. Metzger, *A Textual Commentary on the Greek New Testament*, 2nd ed. (Stuttgart: United Bible Societies, 1994), 532.

[27] Ibid.; F. F. Bruce, *The Epistle to the Colossians, to Philemon, and to the Ephesians*, NICNT (Grand Rapids: Eerdmans, 1984), 250; O'Brien, *Ephesians*, 5, 86–87.

[28] Hoehner, *Ephesians*, 147.

[29] Ibid., 79.

[30] So also Carson and Moo, *Introduction to the New Testament*, 490.

[31] E. Best, *A Critical and Exegetical Commentary on Ephesians*, ICC (Edinburgh: T&T Clark, 1998), 61–63.

If one assumes the circular nature of the letter, Ephesians represents a careful summary and exposition of Paul's thought. If the letter was addressed to the Ephesians, then questions concerning the occasion of the letter largely become educated guesses culled from the content of Ephesians. Among those who argue for Pauline authenticity, most stress that there is no specific crisis in view. Paul had time to write a positive exposition of his theology while under house arrest in Rome.[32] Others identify specific needs that Christians in Asia Minor would have had.

F. Thielman argued that Christians possibly facing suffering in Asia Minor would have needed an encouraging reminder of all that God had done for them in Christ and a challenge to live in a manner consistent with God's purposes for the church in summing up all things in Christ.[33] C. E. Arnold stated that Christians in Asia Minor would have required positive grounding in Paul's gospel because they were converts from a pagan past saturated with magic, astrology, and mystery religions. Their pagan past also necessitated moral guidance for living a life consistent with the lordship of Christ.[34]

Purpose

Despite the variegated proposals for the life setting of the letter, most scholars agree on the main themes in Ephesians. They see Ephesians emphasizing cosmic reconciliation in Christ and stressing the need for (1) unity in the church, (2) a distinctive Christian ethic, and (3) vigilance in spiritual warfare.[35] As noted above, various exegetes take these emphases and then attempt to develop points of contact with possible concrete needs.

The attempt to ascertain a specific purpose may engender a variety of proposals, but most would acknowledge, as Carson and Moo pointed out, that Ephesians is "an important statement of the gospel that may have been greatly needed in more than one first-century situation."[36] The general nature of Ephesians renders it particularly suitable for application by present-day believers.

LITERATURE

Literary Plan

Recent works have set forth a variety of proposals regarding the literary plan of Ephesians. Though a number of these studies are insightful and thought provoking, many rightly remain unpersuaded by these analyses because of the ever-present danger of pressing Paul's letters into preconceived models.

---

[32] J. A. Robinson, *St. Paul's Epistle to the Ephesians*, 2nd ed. (London: Macmillan, 1907), 10–11.

[33] Thielman, *Theology of the New Testament*, 394.

[34] C. E. Arnold, "Ephesians, Letter to the," in *Dictionary of Paul and His Letters*, ed. G. F. Hawthorne, R. P. Martin, and D. G. Reid (Downers Grove: InterVarsity, 1993), 246.

[35] O'Brien, *Ephesians*, 58–65.

[36] Carson and Moo, *Introduction to the New Testament*, 491.

OUTLINE

  I. OPENING (1:1–2)
 II. BODY: SEATED WITH CHRIST, WALKING WITH CHRIST, STANDING FOR
      CHRIST (1:3–6:20)
      A. Shared Spiritual Blessings in Union with Christ and Unity in Christ (1:3–3:21)
      B. Walk with Christ and Stand for Christ (4:1–6:20)
III. CLOSING (6:21–24)

UNIT-BY-UNIT DISCUSSION

I. Opening (1:1–2)

Ephesians begins with the three customary elements that introduce an epistle:
(1) author, (2) recipient, and (3) greeting.

II. Body: Seated with Christ, Walking with Christ, Standing for Christ (1:3–6:20)

The body of the letter naturally subdivides into an indicative section conveying general
theological truths regarding the recipients of the letter (1:15–3:21) and an imperative section (4:1–6:20) issuing a series of commands and exhortations on the basis of these realities. The key terms appear to be "sit," "walk," and "stand." The first half of the letter lays
the proper foundation by defining believers' identity in Christ. On the basis of their spiritual status, they are in the second half exhorted to attain to the unity and maturity in the
Spirit that are already theirs in Christ. In this way, as the key verse of the entire letter states
(1:10), Christ, the centerpiece of God's salvation-historical purposes, will be restored to his
rightful place of supremacy and preeminence in all things in the church and the cosmos.

*A. Shared Spiritual Blessings in Union with Christ and Unity in Christ (1:3–
3:21)*   In this section Paul (1) unpacked the spiritual blessings that believers have because
they are seated with Christ in the heavenly realms (1:3–14); (2) prayed for his readers
(1:15–23); (3) described conversion as a change from spiritual death to spiritual life (2:1–
10); (4) portrayed the gospel-centered unity of the church (2:11–22); (5) highlighted his
own role in this unity as the minister to the Gentiles entrusted with the mystery of the
gospel (3:1–13); and (6) ended with a concluding prayer and doxology (3:14–21).

The letter's lengthy eulogy (1:3–14) is one sentence in the Greek text, and in it Paul
explained the spiritual blessings believers possess in Christ (1:3). These blessings center
upon the work of the Trinity in the salvation of believers and elicit the praise of God's
glory. God the Father plans salvation (1:4–5) for his glory (1:6). God the Son procures
salvation (1:7–12) for the praise of God's glory (1:12). God the Spirit seals salvation (1:13)
and serves as the down payment of the believer's inheritance for the praise of God's glory
(1:14).

Paul followed the eulogy with an opening prayer for his readers (1:15–23) and concluded the section with a closing prayer (3:14–21). The opening prayer pleads that God

would give believers a spirit of wisdom and revelation and that he would open the eyes of their hearts so that they would be enabled fully to grasp their hope in the glorious riches of his inheritance and his immeasurably great power at work in believers. Paul compared this power to the power that raised Christ from the dead and seated him at God's right hand above all rule and authority (1:20–23).

The next three sections portray the unity that God has created through the gospel from three different angles: (1) the heavenly angle where God gives life to the spiritually dead and raises them up so they are spiritually seated together with Christ in the heavenly realms (2:1–10); (2) the cross-centered angle that depicts the cross of Christ demolishing old barriers in order to create the church as the one new man and the one new building (2:11–22); and (3) Paul's apostolic ministry angle that highlights the role of Paul in bringing to light the mystery of the spiritual equality of Gentiles with Jews in the body of Christ (3:1–13). Paul's closing prayer and doxology again stress unity as he prayed for believers to be able to grasp the love of Christ "with all the saints" (3:18) and as he exulted in the God who is glorified "in the church" (3:21).

Ephesians 2:1–10 and 2:11–22 both use the "once-now" schema, which rehearses the readers' condition before and after their conversion to Christ. Ephesians 2:1–10 speaks of the spiritual separation between God and men in soteriological terms, while 2:11–22 portrays this separation in the context of salvation history.

Ephesians 2:1–10 moves from the sphere of spiritual death and the status of unbelievers as "children of wrath" to the realm of spiritual life and the state of salvation. This ultimate "rags to riches" experience rests on God's amazing grace apart from any human works (2:4–5). Paul linked his earlier description of the experience of Christ (1:20–23) with the experience of the believer in Christ (2:6). The believers' union with Christ means that just as he was raised up and seated at God's right hand (1:20), so believers are made alive with Christ, raised up with him, and seated with him in the heavenly places (2:6). The joy of this present experience can only be exceeded by the experience in the ages to come when God will "show the surpassing riches of His grace in kindness" to believers in Christ (2:7 NASB). Paul also stressed the unmerited nature of salvation as a gift of God's grace, which is received by faith (2:8). This salvation precludes human boasting because it is based on the work of God and not the works of man (2:8–9). Though salvation does not result from good works, good works flow from salvation (2:10).

In 2:11–12 Paul described the plight of his readers' past. Paul called them to remember their former condition as Gentiles. Specifically, Paul stated that they were formerly separated from (1) Christ, (2) citizenship in Israel, (3) covenants of promise, (4) hope, and (5) God. But Christ has established peace and unity between Jews and Gentiles by abolishing the dividing wall through the cross (2:14–15) and by creating in himself one new man, the church (2:15), which is a united building or sanctuary for God's dwelling place in the Spirit (2:21–22).

Paul highlighted his apostolic ministry to the Gentiles as the "mystery" of the gospel (3:1–13). God's "mystery," formerly hidden and now revealed to the apostles and prophets, is the spiritual equality of Gentiles with Jews in the body of Christ through the gospel (3:5–6). God empowered Paul to bring his plan to pass (3:8–9), so that through the church God's wisdom will be revealed "to the rulers and authorities in the heavens" (3:10; see 1:21).

Paul's closing prayer (3:14–21) petitions God to empower believers so they will be able "to comprehend with all the saints what is the breadth and width, height and depth, and to know the Messiah's love that surpasses knowledge, so you may be filled with all the fullness of God" (3:18–19). Paul closed with a doxology to God as the one who works with power beyond all we could ask or imagine (3:20–21).

B. Walk with Christ and Stand for Christ (4:1–6:20)   The indicative section (chaps. 1–3) provides the basis ("therefore"; 4:1) for the imperative section. The two key words in this section appear to be "walk" (4:1,17 [twice]; 5:2,8,15) and "stand" (6:11,13,14). Hoehner's proposed structure of the "walk" section is pedagogically helpful. Paul called the church to walk in (1) unity (4:1–16), (2) holiness (4:17–32), (3) love (5:1–6), (4) light (5:7–14), and (5) wisdom (5:15–6:9).[37] Ephesians 6:10–20 constitutes a call for believers to stand in spiritual warfare against the dark forces of wickedness by accessing God's power in God's armor (6:10–17) and in prayer (6:18–20).

Ephesians 4:1–16 highlights diversity in unity (4:1–13) in the church for the maturity (4:13), stability (4:14), and growth (4:15–16) of the body of Christ. Ephesians 4:1–6 specifically outlines *what* Christians are called to do (walk worthy of their calling as Christians); *how* they are to do it (with humility, gentleness, patience, loving forbearance, maintaining the unity of the Spirit); and *why* (because of the sevenfold "oneness" of the faith). Ephesians 4:7–13 adds the observation that "oneness" does not imply "sameness." Believers are not called to be "cookie-cutter" Christians, because Christ graciously gives a variety of gifts as the booty of his victory (4:7–10) for the sake of the church (4:11–12), so that the body will be built up and attain unity, maturity, and fullness in the faith (4:12–13).[38]

This unity and maturity will guard the body not only from false teaching (4:14) but also from false living (4:17–19). Christians must not walk in darkness like the Gentiles (4:17–19; 5:6–7), but must "walk as children of light" (5:8–10) and remain separate from dark deeds and expose them by bringing them into the light (5:11–14). They walk in light (5:6–14) and in wisdom (5:15–17).

---

[37] See the outline in Hoehner, *Ephesians*, 66–68.

[38] Scholars have wrestled with the apparent verb change ("he received gifts") in Ps 68:8 (LXX 67:19; MT 68:19) to "he gave gifts" in Eph 4:8. For an extensive survey of approaches to this text, see W. Hall Harris III, *The Descent of Christ: Ephesians 4:7–11 and Traditional Hebrew Imagery*, AGJU 32 (Leiden: Brill, 1996), 64–122.

Paul commanded Christians to be continually filled by the Spirit,[39] which is contrasted with drunkenness (5:18). A series of dependent participles[40] follows the command to be filled by the Spirit in order that the reader will see that "being filled" by the Spirit has effects such as wholehearted praise (v. 19), thanksgiving (v. 20), and submission (v. 21). Paul developed the specifics of this submission in the form of a domestic code, which delineates the various roles and responsibilities of the members of the household (5:22–6:9).[41]

As a result of "being filled by the Spirit," wives are enjoined to submit to their husbands (5:22), children to obey their parents (6:1), and slaves to obey their masters (6:5). Paul also stressed what Spirit-filled behavior entails for those in positions of authority: husbands are called to love their wives as Christ loves his bride, the church (5:28); fathers ought not provoke their children to anger but bring them up in the training and instruction of the Lord (6:4); and masters should treat those under their authority fairly and not threaten them (6:9).

The last clarion call is for believers to stand firm for Christ (6:10–20). The text consists of three parts: (1) verses 10–13 provide an introductory admonition for believers to be strong in the Lord and to put on the full armor of God in light of the hostile forces arrayed against them; (2) verses 14–17 build upon ("therefore") and reinforce the introductory admonition and further specify the pieces that constitute the "full armor"; and (3) verses 18–20 call on believers to access God's power in prayer for all believers (6:18), including Paul (6:19–20). The word for "stand" occurs three times (6:11,13,14) as a call to stand strong in God's power (i.e., the full armor of God) against the devil and the spiritual powers of wickedness.

Ephesians 6:10–20 serves as a climax for the letter. Therefore, the reader finds many earlier themes repeated and made more emphatic. The list of armor pieces that believers use in spiritual warfare (6:14–17) was already prominent in Ephesians: truth (1:13; 4:15,21,24–25; 5:9); righteousness (4:24; 5:9); peace (1:2; 2:14–18; 4:3); the gospel (1:13; 3:6); the word of God (1:13; 5:26); salvation (1:13; 2:5,8; 5:23); and faith (1:1,13,15,19; 2:8; 3:12,17; 4:5,13). The lexical and conceptual links between 1:3–14 and 6:10–20 are also pronounced, especially the cluster of key theological terms between 1:13 and 6:14–17. Importantly, as in the case of the command to be "filled with the Spirit" (5:18), the Ephesian "spiritual warfare" passage has important corporate as well as

---

[39] Paul wanted to see the distinctively Christian solution of "being filled *by* the Spirit." See especially D. B. Wallace, *Greek Grammar Beyond the Basics* (Grand Rapids: Zondervan, 1996), 375; O'Brien, *Ephesians*, 391–92; and Hoehner, *Ephesians*, 702–4. For a survey of various proposals, see A. J. Köstenberger, "What Does It Mean to Be Filled with the Spirit? A Biblical Investigation," *JETS* 40 (1997): 231–35.

[40] The five participles convey result. So also A. T. Lincoln, *Ephesians*, WBC 42 (Dallas: Word, 1990), 345; Wallace, *Greek Grammar Beyond the Basics*, 639. Paul's grammar highlights the cause-and-effect relationship between "being filled by the Spirit" (5:18) and the godly characteristics that follow (5:19–21). These are not independent realities believers are called to create by their own willpower; instead, they are dependent on the Spirit's work (cf. the fruit of the Spirit in Gal 5:22–23).

[41] See T. G. Gombis, "A Radically New Humanity: The Function of the *Haustafel* in Ephesians," *JETS* 48 (2005): 317–30.

individual dimensions. Both individual believers and the church *as a whole* must be spiritually equipped to engage in spiritual warfare.[42]

III. Closing (6:21–24)

Paul concluded the letter with some brief references regarding his travel plans and a standard closing formula. He stated that he was sending Tychicus to inform the readers regarding Paul's personal affairs (6:21–22) and to encourage them (6:22). Paul closed the letter with a wish for peace and love from God the Father and the Lord Jesus Christ (6:23) and with the grace benediction (6:24).

THEOLOGY

Theological Themes

The Lordship of Christ   The "[bringing back of] all things . . . together again under one head" (*anakephalaioō*, 1:10 NIV), the Lord Jesus Christ, is the central theme of the whole letter. God progressively brings about this realignment of proper authority and submission in two spheres: the heavens (1:3,10,20; 2:6; 3:10; 6:12) and the earth (1:10; 3:15; 4:9; 6:3).[43] Each realm has its own representative: the powers in the heavens and the church upon the earth.[44] Therefore, God's subjection of all things to Christ becomes a progressive reality through Christ's supremacy over and defeat of the evil powers (1:19–22) and his gathering together of both Jews and Gentiles into one body (2:11–22).

Though the theme is the subjection of all things to the lordship of *Christ*, Paul stressed the unified work of all three members of the Trinity in bringing this goal to its fulfillment. This thematic theological center is expressed through four theological themes: soteriology, ecclesiology, ethics, and spiritual warfare. References to the united work of the Trinity emerge in eight passages: 1:4–14; 1:17; 2:18; 2:22; 3:4–5; 3:14–17; 4:4–6; 5:18–20.[45] The first two passages (1:4–14,17) are related to soteriology; the next five passages (2:18,22; 3:4–5,14–17; 4:4–6) to ecclesiology; and the last (5:18–20) to ethics.

The Church   Ephesians places a marked emphasis on the nature of the church. Discussions of ecclesiology must follow after soteriology because the trinitarian work of salvation has massive implications for the church. This dynamic comes across succinctly in 2:18: "*through Him* [Christ] we both have access *by one Spirit to the Father*" (see also 2:22; 3:4–5,14–19). Christ has broken down the dividing wall through the cross and created the church as one new man (2:13–22).

This redeeming work of Christ reconciles God's people to the Father (2:16). Believers are "fellow citizens with the saints, and members of God's household" (2:19). Paul also

---

[42] See D. R. Reinhard, "Ephesians 6:10–18: A Call to Personal Piety or Another Way of Describing Union with Christ?" *JETS* 48 (2005): 521–32.

[43] See O'Brien, *Ephesians*, 58; Thielman, *Theology of the New Testament*, 394.

[44] See the excellent treatment by C. C. Caragounis, *The Ephesian Mysterion: Meaning and Content* (Lund: Gleerup, 1977), 144–46.

[45] Hoehner (*Ephesians*, 106–7) said that "Ephesians is known as the Trinitarian letter."

called believers to maintain—not create—unity because the Spirit has produced unity (4:3). Oneness in the church is a top priority because of the oneness of the Trinity and other dimensions of oneness (4:4–6). If the unity of the body is based on the unity of the Godhead, then dividing the church is as unthinkable and heinous as dividing the Trinity.

Paul's teaching on spiritual gifts also addresses the theme of ecclesiology (cf. 1 Corinthians 12–14; Rom 12:4–8). Paul stressed that spiritual gifts are connected to the work of Christ as the booty of his victory. Christ bestowed these gifts on individual believers for the sake of the growth of the corporate body, not just the individual. The building up of the body of Christ is essential for attaining unity in the faith (4:13).

COLOSSIANS

KEY FACTS	
Author:	Paul
Date:	Around 60
Provenance:	Imprisonment in Rome
Destination:	Colossae
Occasion:	False teaching
Purpose:	Combat false teaching with the supremacy and sufficiency of Christ
Theme:	Christ is complete in every way and thus believers are complete in Christ
Key Verses:	2:6–10

INTRODUCTION

PAUL'S LETTER TO the Colossians is perhaps the most Christ-centered letter in the NT. Colossians offers a strong corrective to the false teachings in the Lycus Valley that minimized the importance of the person and work of Christ. Paul firmly placed the emphasis back on the centrality of Christ in all things. The letter clearly and passionately argues for the supremacy of Christ, the sufficiency of his work for the believer, and the application of Christ's lordship to every aspect of the Christian life. Colossians thus serves as a stringent reminder of the serious problems that arise when one's focus is taken off Christ and he is displaced from the center of the Christian life.

The letter also demonstrates that gratitude to Christ for the great salvation he provided serves as a principal motivation for the Christian life. Although Colossian legalists may have pursued righteousness out of a sense of obligation and fear, Paul stressed that the believer lives his life in a manner worthy of his calling motivated by joyful thanksgiving to the Father who adopted him, rescued him from Satan's dominion, delivered him from punishment, and forgave his sins.[46] Perhaps more than any other Pauline letter, Colossians presents the Christian life as an unrestrainable outburst of joy, praise, and thanksgiving, in which all that the believer says and does is an expression of grateful worship of an all-supreme Lord who has provided an all-sufficient salvation.

HISTORY

Author

The following discussion bears many striking similarities to the debate over the authorship of Ephesians, so it is not necessary to tread all of the same terrain again. The letter opens with a claim that Paul was the author (1:1) and contains two further expressions of personal identification in 1:23 ("I, Paul") and 4:18 ("I, Paul, write this greeting in my own hand," NIV). The letter also refers to Timothy, Epaphras, John Mark, and Barnabas, who were companions of Paul as documented in the book of Acts. The closing of the letter makes many personal references that would not be expected in a pseudepigraphal writing. Paul's authorship was also affirmed by the unbroken testimony of the early church.

Once again, however, despite strong evidence for authenticity, the authorship of the letter is heavily debated. Such challenges notwithstanding, Paul's authorship primarily rests on the strength of four pillars: (1) the letter's own claim to authenticity; (2) the unbroken tradition throughout church history; (3) the close connections between Colossians and Philemon, a letter which almost all accept as authentic;[47] and (4) the questions surrounding the practice and acceptance of pseudonymity.

Date

The date for Colossians is difficult to determine with precision, especially because it depends on the letter's authorship and provenance. If written by Paul from Caesarea or Ephesus, then the letter has a date sometime in the 50s. If written by Paul from Rome, then one must place the composition of the letter at around 58–60 according to the chronology of Paul suggested in this text.[48] If one rejects the authenticity of Colossians, then the book should be dated about 70–100. However, this late date is problematic because of the earthquake that presumably destroyed Colossae in 60–61.

Provenance

Many difficulties surround the provenance of the letter as well. Debate about the provenance of the letter clearly began in ancient times. Although subscriptions in many

---

[46] Every chapter of Colossians mentions thanksgiving: thanksgiving is the motivation for the life that pleases God (1:9–12); the programmatic statement of the letter stresses that walking in Christ Jesus is prompted by overflowing thanksgiving (2:6–7); Christian thanksgiving motivates all that the believer says and does (3:17); Paul urged the Colossians to make sure that their prayers, like his (1:3–8), were permeated with a spirit of thanksgiving (4:2).

[47] J. D. G. Dunn (*The Epistles to the Colossians and to Philemon*, NIGTC [Grand Rapids: Eerdmans, 1996], 37–38) listed some of the similarities between Colossians and Philemon.

[48] Many scholars date the first Roman imprisonment in the early 60s.

manuscripts, including Alexandrinus (fifth century) and the first corrector of Vaticanus, assign the letter to Rome, and no subscriptions suggest any other provenance, the Marcionite Prologue (c. 160–180) stated that the letter was written from Ephesus.

The presence of Luke, Aristarchus, Timothy, and other coworkers with Paul at the time of writing are important clues for the provenance of Colossians.[49] The presence of Luke appears to support a Roman hypothesis because Acts places Luke with Paul in Rome, while Paul's Ephesian ministry is not one of the "we" passages in Acts. Acts 27:2 also indicates that Aristarchus accompanied Paul to Italy and most likely all the way to Rome. Although Acts does not mention the presence of Timothy in Rome, the Acts narrative closes without identifying by name any persons who visited Paul in Rome during his house arrest. In light of the close relationship shared by Paul and Timothy, one would expect Timothy to visit Paul sometime during the two-year Roman imprisonment. Although good arguments can be made for Ephesus, the balance of the evidence favors a Roman provenance.

Destination

The destination is not in question. J. D. G. Dunn could say that there is "no dispute regarding where and to whom the letter was addressed: 'to the saints in Colossae.'" [50] J. B. Lightfoot provided a wealth of information about Colossae.[51] The city was a mixed population of Phrygians, Romans involved in political affairs, and Jews of the Diaspora. Though no one knows when the city was established, Herodotus called Colossae a "great city of Phrygia" as early as 480 BC. The greatness of the city was due to its location in the Lycus valley (modern-day Turkey) on the main east-west road from Ephesus to the east.[52] The lush Lycus valley provided plenty of food for grazing sheep, and the wool from the sheep supported a large clothing industry.

Two neighboring towns, Laodicea and Hierapolis, eclipsed Colossae in importance by the time of Paul. The Romans made Laodicea the *conventus* (capital in a district of 25 towns) and changed the road system so that Laodicea was located on the junction between four other roads and the east-west highway. While Laodicea prospered as a commercial center, Hierapolis increased as a place of luxury and pleasure because of its mineral baths. Strabo, writing about 20 years before Paul, testified to the diminished importance of Colossae when he described it as a "small town." As mentioned above, the demise of all three cities came in the form of a mighty earthquake in 60–61 (though Laodicea was rebuilt; see Rev 3:14–22).

---

[49] Dunn (*Epistles to the Colossians and Philemon*, 41) and P. T. O'Brien (*Colossians, Philemon*, WBC 44 [Dallas: Word, 1982], xlix-liv) favored the Roman hypothesis for Colossians.

[50] Dunn, *Epistles to the Colossians and Philemon*, 20.

[51] J. B. Lightfoot, *St. Paul's Epistle to the Colossians and to Philemon*, 9th ed. (London: Macmillan, 1890), 1–72; cf. L. M. McDonald, "Colossae," in *Dictionary of New Testament Background*, 225–26.

[52] Travelers would journey on the main route from Antioch to Tarsus, through the Cilician Gates to Derbe, Lystra, Iconium, and then to Colossae and its neighboring towns, Laodicea and Hierapolis. One would then journey about 100 miles to Ephesus and between 1,000 and 1,200 land miles to Rome.

Occasion

The occasion of the letter is the most complex introductory issue. Paul addressed a false teaching some have called the "Colossian heresy." The identity of the teachers and their teachings is debated. Scholars have noted some of the distinguishing marks of the teaching through a "mirror reading" of Colossians. At the formal level, it is identified as a "philosophy" that has a long-standing pedigree of support in "human tradition" (2:8). It is more difficult to detect certain catchwords of this philosophy in Colossians, but a few phrases stand out: "the entire fullness" (2:9); "insisting on ascetic practices and the worship of angels" (2:18); "claiming access to a visionary realm" (2:18); "don't handle, don't taste, don't touch" (2:21); and "ascetic practices, humility, and severe treatment of the body" (2:23). There also seems to be an emphasis on circumcision, food laws, Sabbaths, and purity regulations (2:11,13,16,20–21).

Scholars have studied these strands and attempted to locate a group or movement in the first century that matches all the criteria. However, Paul's opponents were notoriously difficult to identify with precision. In the most up-to-date work on the subject, I. K. Smith surveyed four main proposals: (1) Essene Judaism and Gnosticism, (2) Hellenism, (3) paganism, and (4) Judaism.[53] Smith's own proposal locates the philosophy firmly within the stream of apocalyptic Judaism. Perhaps all one can conclude at this point is that Paul faced some form of Jewish legalism and mysticism.

Purpose

While, as mentioned, the precise identity of those perpetrating the Colossian heresy is hard to pinpoint, one can easily see that Colossians serves as a Christ-centered correction to the Colossian errorists, whatever the exact nature of their teaching. Most would acknowledge that Paul made at least three main points in Colossians: (1) all the fullness dwells in the preeminent Christ (1:15–20); (2) believers are complete in Christ (2:10); and thus (3) they should seek to know more of Christ in his fullness by seeking the things above where he dwells, not the things on the earth (3:1–2). Background questions may help clarify Paul's rebuke. For example, if Paul was responding to mystical ascents in Colossians, the irony is that "their desire to witness the worship rendered by angels is not a heavenly pursuit, but worldly, as it focuses on regulations that are destined to perish."[54] It is also fleshly in that these ascents and the visions associated with them do not offer help in overcoming the flesh, because they lead to spiritual elitism and divisions.

---

[53] I. K. Smith, *Heavenly Perspective: A Study of Paul's Response to a Jewish Mystical Movement at Colossae*, LSNTS 326 (Edinburgh: T&T Clark, 2007), 19.

[54] Ibid., 207.

LITERATURE

Literary Plan

Colossians is best classified as a letter written for the purpose of exhortation and encouragement. As far as the overall literary structure is concerned, it seems best to divide the text along epistolary lines that conform to the common Pauline tendency to begin with a doctrinal section and end with a paraenetic (hortatory) section.

OUTLINE

I. INTRODUCTION (1:1–8)
   A. Opening (1:1–2)
   B. Thanksgiving (1:3–8)
II. BODY: THE SUPREMACY AND ALL-SUFFICIENCY OF CHRIST (1:9–4:6)
   A. The Centrality of Christ and the Colossian Heresy (1:9–2:23)
   B. Believers' New Life in Christ (3:1–4:6)
III. CLOSING (4:7–18)
   A. Commendation of Tychicus and Onesimus (4:7–9)
   B. Greetings from Paul's Coworkers (4:10–14)
   C. Final Instructions (4:15–17)
   D. Final Greetings and Benediction (4:18)

UNIT-BY-UNIT DISCUSSION

I. Introduction (1:1–8)

The introduction to Paul's letter to the Colossians consists of an opening statement (1:1–2) and a thanksgiving section (1:3–8).

A. Opening (1:1–2)   Paul opened the letter with the customary identification of the author, recipients, and the grace salutation.

B. Thanksgiving (1:3–8)   Paul offered thanks to God for the Colossians' faith, love, and hope (1:4–5), which he had heard from Epaphras, who had apparently founded the Colossian church (1:7). Paul also rejoiced in the spread of the gospel among the Colossians (1:5–6) and beyond them to the entire world (1:6).

II. Body: The Supremacy and All-Sufficiency of Christ (1:9–4:6)

A. The Centrality of Christ and the Colossian Heresy (1:9–2:23)   Paul began the letter body with a prayer that God would fill the Colossians with the knowledge of God's will (1:9) and that the overflow of this knowledge would result in a worthy way of life, that is, a moral and ethical lifestyle that was pleasing to the Lord. Such a lifestyle is characterized by bearing the fruit of good works, continuing to grow in the knowledge of God, being strengthened by his power for perseverance, and joyfully giving thanks to the Father (1:10–12). God is worthy of thanksgiving because he qualified Christians to share in the heavenly inheritance, rescued them from the dominion of darkness, and transferred them into the kingdom of his dearly loved Son (1:12–13), in whom they have the forgiveness of sins (1:14).

Paul highlighted the supremacy of Christ in 1:15–20. The structure of the passage is debated, but most scholars recognize two central structural points: (1) Christ as head over creation (1:15–17) and (2) Christ as head over the church (1:18–20). This staggering supremacy of Jesus is seen not only in his lordship over creation and the church but also in his equality with God: he is the image of the invisible God (1:15), and all the fullness of deity dwells in him (1:19; 2:9). Because Jesus is over everything, he has first place in everything (1:18), and thus God effects the cosmic reconciliation of all things to himself through Christ (1:20).

Paul moved from the sweeping reconciliation of all things in Christ to the specific reconciliation of believers to God through Christ (1:21–23). Paul's readers were formerly alienated from and hostile to God, yet now God had reconciled them through his body of flesh through death in order that believers might stand holy and blameless before God (1:21–22). This glorious work of salvation is a reality only in those who persevere until the end in the faith and the hope of the gospel that they heard and that Paul proclaimed as a minister (1:23).

Paul expanded on his own unique contribution as a minister of the mystery of reconciliation (1:24–2:5). He emphasized his unique role as a sufferer for (1:24) and steward of (1:25) the formerly hidden but now manifest mystery (1:26) of God's good news to the Gentiles: "Christ in you, the hope of glory" (1:27). Paul proclaimed Christ to everyone, so that everyone might be presented complete in Christ (1:28), a task that God empowered Paul to perform (1:29).

The apostle also informed his readers of his struggle on their behalf so that they and others (2:1) would have full assurance in the knowledge of God's mystery, namely Christ (2:2), in whom were all the treasures of wisdom and knowledge (2:3). This reminder served as a safeguard against the deluding force of false teaching (2:4), and Paul rejoiced to see their stability in the faith (2:5).

Colossians 2:6–23 builds on this teaching by laying out its implications for the readers. Verses 6–7 show that they must walk in the Christ they have received and in whom they have become rooted and established. Verse 8 directly warns against captivity to the errorists' philosophy and empty deception. Paul's response was first to repeat his earlier argument: all the fullness of deity dwells bodily in Christ (2:9; see 1:19). Paul applied this point to the believer in 2:10: therefore those who are in Christ "have been made complete" (NASB). In other words, if *all* the fullness dwells in Christ, and the believer is in Christ, then the believer is complete in Christ and does not need any supplements. Just as in the mathematical realm one cannot add anything to infinity, so in the spiritual realm nothing can be added to Christ who is infinite.

Paul focused on the great spiritual change that Christ's cross had effected for believers in their union with him in his crucifixion, burial, and resurrection (2:11–12). God granted them new life even when they were dead in transgressions (2:13), which he forgave and canceled by nailing the sinner's IOU to the cross (2:14). Christ's cross also thoroughly and publicly spelled the defeat of the evil forces aligned against believers (2:15). The supremacy of Christ's person and work severely undercut the false teachers and their message. Therefore, they did not need to worry about supplementing their Christian faith with the ceremonial law (2:16–17), self-abasement, angelic worship, boasting in visions (2:18–19), or man-made decrees (2:20–23).

   B. Believers' New Life in Christ (3:1–4:6)   Paul built upon the foundational indicative concerning the person and work of Christ by adding the imperative call for bringing every area of life under that lordship. The cosmic scope of Christ's lordship must now be applied to the individual believer by pursuing the things above (3:1–4), and putting earthly things to death (3:5–8). Believers should put to death their old deeds because they have put off the old self and put on the new self (3:9–11). What is more, because they have experienced the forgiving grace of Christ, they can now express this same grace to others (3:12–17). Paul also exhorted his readers to bring the Christian household under the realm of Christ's lordship (3:18–4:1). He concluded the imperative section by focusing on prayer (4:2–4) and interaction with outsiders (4:5–6).

III. Closing (4:7–18)

   Paul concluded the letter in four ways.

   A. Commendation of Tychicus and Onesimus (4:7–9)   First, Paul informed the Colossians that Tychicus and Onesimus (the converted runaway slave featured in Philemon), who were charged with carrying the letter back to the church at Colossae, would fill them in on his current situation.

   B. Personal Greetings from Paul's Coworkers (4:10–14)   Second, Paul passed along some personal greetings from his coworkers, including Aristarchus, Mark, Jesus Justus, Epaphras, Luke, and Demas. Notably, two of the four evangelists are with Paul at this point in his ministry, visiting him in prison.

   C. Final Instructions (4:15–17)   Third, Paul issued final instructions regarding the church at Laodicea, a church meeting at the house of a woman named Nympha, and a certain Archippus (see Phlm 2).

   D. Final Greeting and Benediction (4:18)   Fourth, Paul greeted the Colossians, signing the letter with his own hand and offering a concluding grace benediction.

THEOLOGY

Theological Themes

   The Supremacy of Christ   The overriding theological premise undergirding Paul's letter to the Colossians is the supremacy of Christ. Christ's preeminence comes to the forefront especially in 1:15–20, which contains one of the most exalted depictions of Christ in the entire NT.

Paul first described Jesus as the "image of the invisible God" (1:15), that is, as a visible manifestation or tangible expression of God's attributes (cf. 2 Cor 4:4). Paul also called Jesus the "firstborn over all creation" (1:15) and later asserted that "He is before [in time] all things" (1:17). Since Jesus existed prior to creation, he has authority over all things.[55]

Paul also explained why Christ is supreme over all creation. First and foremost, Jesus is the agent of creation. He is the one through whom the Father made all that exists. He not only created the material universe, the visible world, he also created the spiritual world, including angelic beings of all kinds, four of which are thrones, dominions, rulers, and authorities (1:16).

Paul added that Jesus is the purpose of creation: "All things were created for him" (1:16). Every created thing exists for the pleasure of Christ and for his glory. Not only is Jesus the purpose of creation, he is also the sustainer of the entire universe: "by him all things hold together" (1:17).

Christ's preeminence in all things further extends to his lordship over God's new creation. Jesus is the head of the church by virtue of his resurrection from the dead (1:18). Jesus' qualification as the "firstborn from the dead" serves to identify him as the beginning of the church, the founder of a new humanity. Jesus' resurrection is the key to the transformation of rebellious sinners into the holy people of God and the promise of final redemption.

Proper Christian Conduct The indicative explanations in Colossians 1–2 of who Christ is and what he has done leads to the imperative proclamation in chaps. 3–4 of who believers are and what they are to do.[56] Paul established the cosmic scope of Christ's lordship and the complete scope of the believer's salvation in him (chaps. 1–2); he applied these two points in three broad ways (chaps. 3–4).

First, the complete scope of Christ's sufficient work and believers' spiritual union with him means that they can keep pursuing the things above where Christ dwells (3:1–2). Though believers are complete in Christ, the Christian life is not static. Believers should have a passion to pursue Christ, and that pursuit necessitates looking away from earthly things and putting to death earthly passions and deeds that belong to the old way of life (3:5).

Second, union with Christ means that the believer is a new creature and acts accordingly. The believer has "put off the old man with his practices" (3:9) and has "put on the new man" (3:10). Paul stated earlier that Christ is the image of God (1:15) and the Creator (1:16), and now in union with Christ the believer is made anew according to the image of the Creator (3:10). Thus the believer is being transformed so that he becomes more and more like Christ.

---

[55] Elsewhere Paul used the argument from priority in time to demonstrate man's authority over the woman (see 1 Cor 11:8–9).

[56] E. Lohse, *Colossians and Philemon*, Hermeneia, ed. W. R. Poehlmann and R. J. Karris (Philadelphia: Fortress, 1971), 178.

Third, the cosmic scope of Christ's lordship has staggering implications for his lordship over every aspect of the believer's life, which is especially emphasized in the household code in 3:18–4:1.[57] Christ's lordship extends to one's personal holiness, family life, work life, and everything in between ("whatever you do, in word or in deed," 3:17).

PHILEMON

KEY FACTS	
Author:	Paul
Date:	Around 60
Provenance:	Roman imprisonment
Destination:	Philemon
Occasion:	Philemon's slave escapes, meets Paul, becomes a believer, and is sent back to his owner
Purpose:	To encourage Philemon to accept Onesimus as a brother and to send him back to Paul and possibly grant him his freedom
Theme:	Love and reconciliation in the body of Christ
Key Verses:	17–20

INTRODUCTION

EVEN THOUGH PHILEMON is separated in the NT canon from the book of Colossians, it shares with Colossians its likely destination and its presumed date of writing during Paul's first Roman imprisonment with Philippians, Ephesians, and Colossians. For this reason it is appropriate to group Philemon with the other Prison Epistles (Philippians, Ephesians, and Colossians) and to discuss the letter under the present rubric.

Philemon bears the distinction of being the shortest Pauline letter with its 335 words in the Greek text.[58] Carson and Moo also characterized Philemon as the "most personal" letter of Paul.[59] The issue of slavery is probably the first thought that comes to mind when the average Christian thinks about Philemon, but Paul's letter is not a position paper on slavery. Rather, it makes a much more multifaceted contribution to the canon than a superficial reading of the letter might suggest.

While Philemon may be the shortest Pauline letter, it still makes a significant contribution to NT theology. It effectively takes Colossians' concept of cosmic reconciliation

---

[57] See the analysis of A. R. Bevere (*Sharing in the Inheritance: Identity and the Moral Life in Colossians*, JSNTSup 226 [London: Sheffield Academic Press, 2003], 225–54, esp. 240), who argued that the household code is an integral piece of the entire letter in light of the lordship of Christ.

[58] A. G. Patzia, "Philemon, Letter to," in *Dictionary of Paul and His Letters*, 703.

[59] Carson and Moo, *Introduction to the New Testament*, 589.

through the cross of Christ and translates it into a specific setting of reconciliation between two individuals. The gospel message does not stand alone; it has an important message on how to deal with real-life issues. In a very real sense, relationships in the body of Christ are gospel relationships, and social issues such as slavery are gospel issues.

HISTORY

Author

Philemon is almost universally recognized as an authentic letter of the apostle Paul. The only sustained case against Pauline authorship was made by the Tübingen School in the nineteenth century. As mentioned previously, F. C. Baur affirmed the authenticity of only four letters ascribed to Paul—Romans, 1–2 Corinthians, and Galatians—which he categorically called the *Hauptbriefe* (German for "major epistles").[60] His arguments against authenticity are now dismissed by virtually all Pauline scholars.[61]

Date

The date for Philemon depends largely on the date assigned to Colossians. The evidence for the close relationship between the two letters is as follows: (1) Colossians refers to Onesimus (Col 4:9); (2) both letters have Timothy as the cosender (Phlm 1; Col 1:1); (3) both letters refer to Epaphras (Phlm 23; Col 1:7) and Archippus (Phlm 2; Col 4:17); and (4) both letters include Mark, Aristarchus, Demas, and Luke among Paul's companions (Phlm 24; Col 4:10,14). Assuming the Roman provenance of Colossians, the letter should be dated to around the year 60.

Destination

Paul addressed the letter to Philemon, whom Paul called his "dear friend and co-worker" (v. 1). Virtually everyone accepts this destination. John Knox suggested that Philemon was the initial recipient of the letter, while Archippus was the ultimate recipient, but his view has generated little acceptance.[62]

Philemon was the master of a slave named Onesimus. The letter provides a number of possible biographical details concerning Philemon. First, Paul presented Philemon in glowing terms as a cherished coworker (v. 1) and a model of love and faith toward Jesus (v. 5). Philemon's love and faith had also overflowed to all the believers (v. 5), whom he had often refreshed (v. 7). Second, the apostle Paul probably played a significant role in Philemon's conversion (v. 19) because Paul parenthetically commented that Philemon owed his "own self" to the apostle.[63] Third, Philemon was probably wealthy since he

---

[60] F. C. Baur, *Paul: His Life and Works* (London: Williams and Norgate, 1875), 1:246.

[61] E.g., O'Brien, *Colossians, Philemon*, xli-liv.

[62] J. Knox, *Philemon Among the Letters of Paul*, 2nd ed. (New York: Abingdon, 1959).

[63] From early times (e.g., Theodoret), it has been conjectured that Apphia was Philemon's wife since her name appears beside his own (v. 2). See O'Brien, *Colossians, Philemon*, 273 ("probably correctly"). Some theorized further that Archippus was Philemon's and Apphia's son, though this is impossible to verify (ibid.: "possibly").

hosted the church (v. 2) in Colossae (see Col 4:9) and was able to provide a guest room for Paul (v. 22).[64]

Provenance

Questions concerning the provenance of Philemon are dependent on the provenance of Colossians. Paul was in prison when he wrote both letters. In addition to the other similarities sketched above, Colossians indicates that Onesimus was a resident of Colossae (Col 4:9). Thus one may safely infer that Philemon resided in the same place as his slave. Many scholars conclude that these similarities between the two letters suggest that they were written at the same time and place and were sent together to Colossae. The time and place, however, continue to be vigorously contested.

The three major proposals regarding the provenance of Philemon are Rome, Ephesus, and Caesarea, with Rome and Ephesus being the most seriously debated. In favor of Rome, external evidence dating to the fourth and fifth centuries "uniformly attributes" the provenance of Philemon to Rome.[65] Other scholars believe that two factors in Philemon favor an Ephesian imprisonment: (1) it is more likely that Onesimus would flee to Ephesus as the nearest metropolis, not the distant city of Rome; and (2) Paul's request to Philemon for a room in the near future (Phlm 22) fits more readily with the shorter distance between Ephesus and Colossae.[66]

Those who hold to a Roman imprisonment make two points in response. First, the proximity of Ephesus to Colossae cuts both ways. It may be that Onesimus would seek the anonymity found within the capital of the Roman Empire because a place like Ephesus was too close for comfort. Second, Paul's request for lodging does not preclude a Roman imprisonment because he could still make the trip in about five weeks. Carson and Moo argued that the reference to an imminent arrival could have been a way to put further pressure on Philemon and to obtain a favorable decision from him.[67]

Occasion

The traditional hypothesis regarding the letter's occasion can be sketched as follows. Philemon had a runaway slave named Onesimus, who may have added to his crime of desertion by stealing from his master (v. 18). Subsequent to his escape, Onesimus encountered Paul in prison (or house arrest). The apostle befriended Onesimus and eventually led him to Christ. Though Paul desired to keep Onesimus with him, he knew that he must send the slave back to Philemon. But he did so with the expressed expectation that Philemon would return Onesimus to Paul in order to provide him with further assistance,

---

[64] Dunn, *Colossians and Philemon*, 300–1.

[65] Ibid., 308; cf. Metzger, *Textual Commentary*, 589–90.

[66] D. A. DeSilva, *An Introduction to the New Testament: Contexts, Methods & Ministry Formation* (Downers Grove: InterVarsity, 2004), 668.

[67] Carson and Moo, *Introduction to the New Testament*, 592. Dunn (*Colossians and Philemon*, 308) also claimed that one should observe the note of uncertainty in v. 22 and contended that Paul may simply have said, "Keep a room ready for me; you never know when I might turn up."

perhaps with the additional hope that Philemon would grant freedom to his slave, who was now a fellow slave of Christ with Philemon and thus a brother in Christ.[68]

This portrayal has come under fire recently because of the improbability that Onesimus just happened to stumble on Philemon's close friend, Paul. Carson and Moo capture this attitude well in saying that "[s]uch a coincidence seems more in keeping with a Dickens novel than with sober history."[69] Yet, as Carson and Moo rightly noted, the traditional view allows for other possibilities. Perhaps, for example, Onesimus fled to Rome and then subsequently had second thoughts about his escape, so he sought out Paul for refuge or mediation.[70] In any case, questions such as these do not materially affect the understanding and appreciation of the overall message of the book.

LITERATURE

Literary Plan

Recent research on Philemon focuses on a study of the letter as a rhetorical device aimed "to demonstrate love or friendship and to induce sympathy or goodwill, in order to dispose the hearer favorably to the merits of one's case."[71] Others have argued along epistolary lines that Philemon is a letter of mediation or intercession.[72]

The hardest decision for the outline of the letter is where the body ends and the closing begins. Many think the body extends from verses 8 to 22 and the final greetings begin in verse 23.[73] Though certainty is nearly impossible, it may be preferable to read verse 20 as the end of the letter body, with verses 21–25 forming the closing.

OUTLINE

I. OPENING (1–7)
   A. Salutation (1–3)
   B. Thanksgiving and Prayer (4–7)
II. BODY: THREE APPEALS FOR ONESIMUS (8–20)
   A. Initial Appeal: He is Useful for Both You and Me (8–11)
   B. Second Appeal: Accept Him as a Brother in Christ (12–16)
   C. Third Appeal: Refresh My Heart by Sending Onesimus Back (17–20)
III. CLOSING (21–25)

---

[68] J. G. Nordling, "Onesimus Fugitivus: A Defense of the Runaway Slave Hypothesis in Philemon," *JSNT* 41 (1999): 97–119.

[69] Carson and Moo, *Introduction to the New Testament*, 590.

[70] Ibid., 592.

[71] F. F. Church, "Rhetorical Structure and Design in Paul's Letter to Philemon," *HTR* 71 (1978): 19–20.

[72] S. K. Stowers, *Letter Writing in Greco-Roman Antiquity* (Philadelphia: Westminster, 1986), 153–65.

[73] Patzia, "Philemon," 703.

UNIT-BY-UNIT DISCUSSION

I. Opening (1–7)

A. Salutation (1–3)   The letter opens with the customary identification of the senders (Paul and Timothy; v. 1) and the recipients (Philemon, Apphia, Archippus, and the house church; v. 2) as well as the grace salutation (v. 3).

B. Thanksgiving and Prayer (4–7)   Paul offered thanks to God (v. 4) for the report of Philemon's love and faith (v. 5). He also prayed that Philemon's participation in the faith would be effective through knowledge (v. 6). Philemon's act of refreshing the hearts of the believers brought joy and encouragement to Paul (v. 7).

II. Body: Three Appeals for Onesimus (8–20)

A. First Appeal: He Is Useful for Both You and Me (8–11)   Paul lovingly issued a series of fatherly pleas to Philemon on behalf of Onesimus as Paul's son (v. 10). Paul appealed to Philemon as an aged and imprisoned man, not as an authoritarian apostle (vv. 8–9). The first appeal focused on the current usefulness of Onesimus to both Philemon and Paul, which is contrasted with the former uselessness of Onesimus to Philemon (v. 11). The expression involves a pun involving Onesimus's name, which means "profitable" or "useful." Previously, he had been "useless" (*achrēston*), but now he had become "useful" (*euchrēston*) to Philemon as well as Paul.[74]

B. Second Appeal: Accept Him as a Brother in Christ (12–16)   The second appeal (vv. 12–16) petitioned Philemon to accept Onesimus back as a beloved brother, not a slave (vv. 15–16). Paul sent Onesimus back for this purpose, though Paul would have preferred to keep Onesimus, who could take Philemon's place in ministering to Paul in prison (v. 13). Paul did not act according to this desire because he wanted Philemon's free and heartfelt consent to this good deed (v. 14).

C. Third Appeal: Refresh My Heart by Sending Onesimus Back (17–20)   The third appeal (vv. 17–20) again asked for the acceptance of Onesimus (v. 17) in light of the partnership between Paul and Philemon. The apostle assumed a fatherly role in that anything that Onesimus owed to Philemon could be charged to Paul, even though Philemon was already a debtor who owed Paul everything (vv. 18–19). Paul expressed confidence that Philemon would refresh his heart (v. 20), just as Philemon had previously refreshed the hearts of the believers (v. 7).

III. Closing (21–25)

Paul concluded the letter with the confident expectation that Philemon would exceed his expectant appeals (v. 21), which many take as veiled reference to granting Onesimus his freedom. He also urged Philemon to prepare a place for him in light of his hope that Philemon's

---

[74] See O'Brien (*Colossians, Philemon*, 291–92), who noted that there are many extrabiblical instances of the play on words involving "useless" and "useful."

own prayers for Paul's release would be answered (v. 22). Paul also extended greetings to Philemon from others (vv. 23–24), followed by the familiar grace benediction (v. 25).

THEOLOGY

Theological Themes

Mutual Love and Brotherhood in the Body of Christ   Paul not only asked for Philemon's brotherly acceptance of Onesimus in the gospel; he also modeled brotherly love in the act of asking for it. The aged apostle could command Philemon and easily attain forced or feigned obedience, but Paul opted for a fatherly approach in the form of a series of tender appeals. Paul also highlighted the mutuality of Christian relationships. Philemon had refreshed the believers in the past (v. 7), and now he had a chance to refresh the heart of another fellow believer (Paul) by accepting Onesimus as a fellow Christian (v. 20). Paul willingly assumed all of Onesimus's possible debts to Philemon (v. 18), but he also asked Philemon to remember his own indebtedness to Paul (v. 19). The family ethos of the letter stems from the fact that the author saw Onesimus not only as his child (v. 10) but also as a part of himself—"his very heart" (v. 12 NASB).

A Christian Approach to Slavery and Other Social Issues   Though Paul did not *directly* tackle social issues such as slavery in Philemon, he did suggest that the gospel had important implications for issues such as slavery. Paul asked Philemon to accept Onesimus as a brother in Christ. Equality before God through the gospel challenges the very heart and soul of slavery as the ownership of one human by another.[75]

This approach closely coheres with Paul's teaching in Colossians. Colossians 4:1 urges Christian masters to pay their slaves that which was right and fair and to treat their slaves as they wished to be treated by their master, Jesus Christ. If masters heeded Paul's words, the institution of slavery within the church would have been transformed from a master-slave relationship to an employer-employee relationship or, even better, to a brother-brother relationship.

Relationships at the social level (masters and slaves) look much different in the redefining light of relationships enjoyed at the spiritual level (fellow brothers and slaves of Christ). The social convention of slavery can only wilt and die when the gospel uproots the concept that grounds it and establishes its growth. Carson and Moo said it well: "That it took so long for this to happen is a sad chapter in Christian blindness to the implications of the gospel."[76]

---

[75] For excellent treatments of slavery in the ancient Near East, the OT, and the Greco-Roman world, see the entries by M. A. Dandamayev and S. S. Bartchy in *ABD* 6:56–73.

[76] Carson and Moo, *Introduction to the New Testament*, 594.

POINTS OF APPLICATION

- Diligently keep the unity of the Spirit in the bond of peace (Eph 4:3)
- Husbands, love your wives; wives, submit to your husbands; children, obey your parents (Eph 5:21–6:4)
- Put on the full armor of God and stand firm in your faith (Eph 6:10–18)
- Be humble and consider not only your own interests but also those of others (Phil 2:3–4)
- Rejoice in the Lord always (Phil 4:4)
- Don't be anxious but commit everything to the Lord in prayer (Phil 4:6–7)
- Learn the secret of being content in all circumstances (Phil 4:11–12)
- Realize that Christ is all you need and give him first place in everything (Col 1:18; 2:9)
- Be filled with the Spirit—at church, at home, and at work (Eph 5:18–6:9)
- Embrace the gospel truth that faith transcends all social or economic barriers (Philemon)

STUDY QUESTIONS

1. What are the probable date, provenance, destination, occasion, and purpose of each of the four Prison Epistles?
2. What is the central theological theme in Ephesians?
3. What is the occasion and purpose of Ephesians?
4. What is the "Colossian heresy" and how does it relate to the occasion of Colossians?
5. What are the three main points that Paul made in Colossians?
6. Why is Philemon included with the discussions of Ephesians, Philippians, and Colossians when it is canonically separated from them?

FOR FURTHER STUDY

Arnold, C. E. "Ephesians, Letter to the." Pages 238–49 in *Dictionary of Paul and His Letters*. Edited by G. F. Hawthorne, R. P. Martin, and D. G. Reid. Downers Grove: InterVarsity, 1993.

Bockmuehl, M. *The Epistle to the Philippians*. Black's New Testament Commentaries 11. Peabody: Hendrickson, 1998. Paperback ed. New York: Continuum, 2006.

Bruce, F. F. *The Epistles to the Colossians, to Philemon, and to the Ephesians*. New International Commentary on the New Testament. Grand Rapids: Eerdmans, 1984.

_____. *Philippians*. New International Bible Commentary. Peabody: Hendrickson, 1989.

Carson, D. A. *Basics for Believers: An Exposition of Philippians*. Grand Rapids: Baker, 1996.

Fee, G. D. *Paul's Letter to the Philippians*. New International Commentary on the New Testament. Grand Rapids: Eerdmans, 1995.

Garland, D. E. *Colossians and Philemon*. NIV Application Commentary. Grand Rapids: Zondervan, 1998.

Klein, W. W. "Ephesians." Pages 19–173 in *The Expositor's Bible Commentary*. Rev. ed. Vol. 12: *Ephesians-Philemon*. Grand Rapids: Zondervan, 2005.

Melick, R. R. *Philippians, Colossians, Philemon*. New American Commentary. Nashville: Broadman, 1991.

Moo, D. J. *The Letters to the Colossians and to Philemon.* Pillar New Testament Commentary. Grand Rapids: Eerdmans, 2008.

O'Brien, P. T. *Colossians, Philemon.* Word Biblical Commentary 44. Dallas: Word, 1982.

_____. *The Epistle to the Ephesians.* The Pillar New Testament Commentary. Grand Rapids: Eerdmans, 1999.

_____. *Philippians.* New International Greek Testament Commentary. Grand Rapids: Eerdmans, 1991.

Silva, M. *Philippians.* 2nd ed. Baker Exegetical Commentary on the New Testament. Grand Rapids: Baker, 2005.

Thielman, F. S. *Philippians.* NIV Application Commentary. Grand Rapids: Zondervan, 1995.

_____. *Ephesians.* Baker Exegetical Commentary on the New Testament. Grand Rapids: Baker, 2010.

Wright, N. T. *The Epistles of Paul to the Colossians and to Philemon.* Tyndale New Testament Commentary. Grand Rapids: Eerdmans, 1986.

Chapter 15

The Pastoral Epistles: 1–2 Timothy, Titus

CORE KNOWLEDGE

Students should know the key facts of 1 and 2 Timothy and Titus. With regard to history, students should be able to identify each book's author, date, provenance, destination, and purpose. With regard to literature, they should be able to provide a basic outline of each book and identify core elements of each book's content found in the unit-by-unit Discussion. With regard to theology, students should be able to identify the major theological themes found in the Pastoral Epistles.

KEY FACTS	
Author:	Paul
Date:	Early to mid-60s
Provenance:	Macedonia (1 Timothy); Rome (2 Timothy); unknown (Titus)
Destination:	Ephesus (1 Timothy; 2 Timothy); Crete (Titus)
Occasion:	Instructions for apostolic delegates on how to deal with various issues in the church
Purpose:	To instruct and equip Timothy and Titus in their role as apostolic delegates
Theme:	Establishing the church for the postapostolic period
Key Verses:	2 Tim 4:1–2

CONTRIBUTION TO THE CANON

- God our Savior and salvation in Christ (1 Tim 2:3–4; 4:10; 2 Tim 1:10; Titus 1:3–4)
- Qualifications for church leaders (1 Tim 3:1–12; Titus 1:6–9) and the role of women in the church (1 Tim 2:9–15)
- Preservation of sound doctrine and refutation of false teachers (1 Tim 4:16)
- The importance of pursuing godliness, self-control, and Christian virtues (1 Tim 4:11–16; 6:6; 2 Tim 2:22)
- Trustworthy sayings (see Table 15.1 later in the chapter)

INTRODUCTION

THE PASTORAL EPISTLES, 1 and 2 Timothy and Titus, make a unique and indispensable contribution to the writings of the NT.[1] Supplementing Acts, they provide vital instructions regarding qualifications for church leaders and other important matters for governing and administering the church. Most likely, they were the last letters Paul wrote during his long missionary career toward the end of his apostolic ministry. As early as in the Muratorian Canon (later second century), the special character of the Pastorals was acknowledged, and they were designated as having to do with "the regulation of ecclesiastical discipline."[2] The designation "Pastoral Epistles" apparently dates back to D. N. Berdot, who called Titus a "Pastoral Epistle" in 1703, and P. Anton of Halle, who in 1726 delivered a series of lectures on 1 and 2 Timothy and Titus titled "The Pastoral Epistles."[3]

Timothy and Titus are often viewed as paradigmatic (senior) pastors of local congregations. It should be noted, however, that, technically, Timothy's and Titus's role was not actually that of a permanent, resident pastor of a church. Rather, the men were Paul's apostolic delegates who were temporarily assigned to their locations in order to deal with particular problems that had arisen and needed special attention.[4] For this reason the Pastorals are not merely letters giving advice to younger ministers or manuals of church order. They are Paul's instructions to his special delegates, set toward the closing of the apostolic era at a time when the aging apostle would have felt a keen responsibility to ensure the orderly transition from the apostolic to the postapostolic period. As such, they contain relevant and authoritative apostolic instruction for the governance of the church at any time and place.

---

[1] Parts of this chapter draw on A. J. Köstenberger, "1–2 Timothy, Titus," in *Expositor's Bible Commentary*, vol. 12: *Ephesians—Philemon*, rev. ed. (Grand Rapids: Zondervan, 2005), 487–625.

[2] L. T. Johnson, *Letters to Paul's Delegates: 1 Timothy, 2 Timothy, Titus*, The New Testament in Context (Valley Forge: Trinity Press International, 1996), 3; G. W. Knight, *Commentary on the Pastoral Epistles*, NIGTC (Grand Rapids: Eerdmans, 1992), 3.

[3] D. Guthrie, *The Pastoral Epistles*, TNTC, 2nd ed. (Grand Rapids: Eerdmans, 1990), 11.

[4] See G. D. Fee, *1 and 2 Timothy, Titus*, NIBCNT 13 (Peabody: Hendrickson, 1988), 21.

As discussed below, it appears that 1 Timothy and Titus were written subsequent to Paul's release from his first Roman imprisonment (see chap. 14 on the Prison Epistles above) but prior to a second, considerably more severe, Roman imprisonment, during which Paul composed 2 Timothy and which turned out to be his final letter included in the canon. It is not known whether 1 Timothy or Titus was written first.[5] In the canon, the order is "1 Timothy-2 Timothy-Titus," even though the actual chronological order of writing was almost certainly "1 Timothy-Titus-2 Timothy" or "Titus-1 Timothy-2 Timothy."[6] For our present purposes, we follow the canonical order, treating 2 Timothy prior to Titus and in conjunction with 1 Timothy, since 1 and 2 Timothy are addressed to the same individual and the same church, and thus both letters entail a similar set of introductory issues that are best discussed jointly.[7]

HISTORY

Author

External Evidence The authenticity of Paul's correspondence with Timothy and Titus went unchallenged until the nineteenth century.[8] In all probability Paul's letters to Timothy were known to Polycarp (c. 117), who may have cited 1 Tim 6:7,10 (*Philippians* 4.1).[9] The first unmistakable attestations are found in Athenagoras (*Supplication* 37.1; c. 180) and Theophilus (*To Autolycus* 3.14; later second century), both of whom cite 1 Tim 2:1–2 and allude to other passages in the Pastoral Epistles. Irenaeus (c. 130–200), in several passages in his work *Against Heresies* (see 1.pref.; 1.23.4; 2.14.7; 3.1.1), cited each of the letters and identified their author as the apostle Paul. Clement of Alexandria (c. 150–215; *Stromateis* 2.11) noted that some Gnostics who perceived themselves to be the targets of the denunciation of 1 Tim 6:20–21 rejected Paul's letters to Timothy. The Muratorian Canon (later second century?) included all three letters in the Pauline corpus.

---

[5] See W. D. Mounce, *The Pastoral Epistles*, WBC 46 (Waco: Word, 2000), lxi. He added, "It is not possible to determine whether Paul wrote 1 Timothy or Titus first. All that I am comfortable saying is that the similarity of language between 1 Timothy and Titus may suggest that they were written at approximately the same time" (p. lxii).

[6] Mounce (*Pastoral Epistles*, lxii) noted that the Muratorian Canon (later second century) has the order Titus, 1 Timothy, 2 Timothy, presumably in order to place 2 Timothy last as Paul's final letter. He also pointed out that J. D. Quinn (*The Letter to Titus*, AB 35 [Garden City: Doubleday, 1990]) sought to make a case for the priority of Titus, referring also to W. G. Doty ("The Classification of Epistolary Literature," *CBQ* 31 [1969]: 192–98). Against I. H. Marshall (*Pastoral Epistles*, ICC [Edinburgh: T&T Clark, 1999], 92), who hypothesized that 2 Timothy was written first, and 1 Timothy and Titus were written by someone other than Paul after his death. Similarly, Johnson (*Letters to Paul's Delegates*) dealt first with 2 Timothy and then 1 Timothy and Titus.

[7] The sections on Authorship, Date and Provenance, and Occasion integrate a discussion of all three Pastoral Epistles under a single heading due to the interrelated nature of the questions addressed by these particular introductory issues.

[8] For brief surveys, see R. F. Collins, *Letters That Paul Did Not Write* (Wilmington: Michael Glazier, 1988), 89–90. Collins named as the earliest challengers of the Pastorals' authenticity Schmidt (1804), Schleiermacher (1807), Eichhorn (1912), Baur (1835), and Holtzmann (1885); cf. E. E. Ellis, "Pastoral Letters," in *Dictionary of Paul and His Letters*, ed. G. F. Hawthorne, R. P. Martin, and D. G. Reid (Downers Grove: InterVarsity, 1993), 659.

[9] See the discussion in Marshall, *Pastoral Epistles*, 3–8 (including the tables on pp. 4–5).

Marshall's overall assessment of the patristic evidence regarding the Pastorals is noteworthy especially since he did not hold to Paul's authorship: "It can be concluded that the PE [Pastoral Epistles] were known to Christian writers from early in the second century and that there is no evidence of rejection of them by any writers except for Marcion."[10] Consequently, the Pastorals became part of the established NT canon of the church, and Paul's authorship of the Pastorals was not seriously questioned for a millennium and a half.

Pseudonymity and Internal Evidence It was only in the nineteenth century that an increasing number of commentators began to allege that the Pastoral Epistles constituted an instance of pseudonymous writing in which a later follower attributed his own work to his revered teacher in order to perpetuate that person's teaching and influence.[11] At first, this view may seem surprising since all three Pastoral Epistles open with the unequivocal attribution, "Paul, an apostle of Christ Jesus," or a similar phrase (1 Tim 1:1; 2 Tim 1:1; Titus 1:1). It seems hard to fathom how someone other than the apostle Paul could have written those letters that he falsely attributed to the apostle, with these letters being accepted into the NT canon as Pauline. And all of this supposedly took place without any intent to deceive or any error on the church's part.

Indeed, as will be seen, Paul's authorship of the Pastoral Epistles is by far the best conclusion based on all the available evidence and on several major problems attached to any pseudonymity or allonymity position.[12] The question is primarily a historical one. Is pseudonymous letter-writing attested in the first century? If so, was such a practice as ethically unobjectionable and devoid of deceptive intent as is often alleged?[13] Could pseudonymous letters have been acceptable to the early church? If so, is pseudonymity more plausible than authenticity in the case of the Pastorals?[14]

Attention has frequently been drawn to the differences in style and vocabulary between the Pastorals and the other Pauline letters.[15] The Pastorals feature words not used elsewhere in Paul, such as "godliness" (*eusebeia*), "self-controlled" (*sōphrōn*), or *epiphaneia* rather

---

[10] Ibid., 8. Cf. G. W. Knight III, *Commentary on the Pastoral Epistles*, NIGTC (Grand Rapids: Eerdmans, 1992), 14. He noted that from the end of the second century, the Pastorals were regarded without question as Pauline and were attested as strongly as most of the other Pauline letters.

[11] See the thorough survey and adjudication in T. L. Wilder, "Pseudonymity and the New Testament," in *Interpreting the New Testament: Essays on Methods and Issues*, ed. D. A. Black and D. S. Dockery (Nashville: B&H, 2001), 296–335; id., *Pseudonymity, the New Testament, and Deception: An Inquiry into Intention and Reception* (Lanham: University Press of America, 2004). Cf. D. A. Carson, "Pseudonymity and Pseudepigraphy," in *Dictionary of New Testament Background*, ed. C. A. Evans and S. E. Porter (Downers Grove: InterVarsity, 2000), 856–64.

[12] The label "allonymity" or "allepigraphy" (the view that the Pastorals were written "under another name" without intent to deceive) was introduced by Marshall, *Pastoral Epistles*, 83–84.

[13] For a forceful argument against this contention, see E. E. Ellis, "Pseudonymity and Canonicity of New Testament Documents," in *Worship, Theology and Ministry in the Early Church*, ed. M. J. Wilkins and T. Page, JSNTSup 87 (Sheffield: JSOT, 1992), 212–24; cf. Wilder, *Pseudonymity*.

[14] For a thorough discussion of these issues, see especially D. Guthrie, *New Testament Introduction*, 2nd ed. (Downers Grove: InterVarsity, 1990), 607–49, 1011–28.

[15] See Mounce, *Pastoral Epistles*, xcix–cxviii; and Marshall, *Pastoral Epistles*, 60–61. Other common objections to Paul's authorship of the Pastorals are the difficulty in harmonizing Paul's movements mentioned in the Pastorals with those recorded in Acts and the alleged late church structures reflected in the Pastorals (see discussion below).

than *parousia* to refer to Christ's return (but see 2 Thess 2:8), while characteristic Pauline terminology is omitted: "freedom" (*eleutheria*), "flesh" (*sarx*, especially used versus Spirit), "cross" (*stauros*), "righteousness of God" (*dikaiosynē theou*).[16] However, conclusions regarding authorship based on stylistic differences are highly precarious because the sample size is too small for definitive conclusions on the basis of word statistics alone.[17] Moreover, there is the difference between public letters sent to congregations (the 10 Pauline letters) and personal correspondence such as the Pastorals.[18] Also, Paul felt that he was nearing the end of his life and that there was an urgent need to ensure the preservation of sound doctrine for the postapostolic period, which accounts for the Pastoral Epistles' emphasis on qualifications for leadership, church organization, and the faithful passing on of apostolic tradition.

What is more, while pseudonymity was not uncommon for apocalyptic writings, gospels, or even acts, pseudonymous *letters* are exceedingly rare.[19] Of the two extant Jewish sources, the *Epistle of Jeremy* and the *Letter of Aristeas* are really misnomers, for neither can properly be classified as a letter.[20] In the apostolic era, far from an acceptance of pseudonymous letters, there was actually considerable concern that letters might be forged (2 Thess 2:2: "a letter seeming to be from us," author's translation). Thus Paul referred to the distinguishing mark in all his letters (1 Cor 16:21; Gal 6:11; Col 4:18; 2 Thess 3:17; Phlm 19). In the second century, Tertullian (c. 160–225) reported that an Asian presbyter was removed from office for forging a letter in Paul's name (*On Baptism* 17). Both *3 Corinthians* and the *Epistle to the Laodiceans* are transparent attempts to fill in a perceived gap in canonical revelation (see 1 Cor 5:9; 2 Cor 2:4; 7:8; Col 4:16).[21] Toward the end of the second century, Serapion, the bishop of Antioch (died 211), sharply distinguished between apostolic writings and those that "falsely bear their names" (*pseudepigrapha*; cited in Eusebius, *Eccl. Hist.* 6.12.3). On the basis of this evidence it seems doubtful that the early church would have been prepared to accept pseudonymous letters into the Christian canon.[22]

---

[16] Cf. the list in Marshall, *Pastoral Epistles*, 104–6; and the discussion in Mounce, *Pastoral Epistles*, lxxxviii-xcvii (including the chart on p. xc).

[17] For an incisive treatment, see B. M. Metzger, "A Reconsideration of Certain Arguments Against the Pauline Authorship of the Pastoral Epistles," *ExpTim* 70 (1958): 91–94 (see esp. the four questions listed on p. 93).

[18] See esp. M. Prior, *Paul the Letter-Writer and the Second Letter to Timothy*, JSNTSup 23 (Sheffield: JSOT, 1989), and P. H. Towner, *1–2 Timothy and Titus*, IVPNTC (Downers Grove: InterVarsity, 1994), 34–35.

[19] R. Bauckham ("Pseudo-Apostolic Letters," *JBL* 107 [1988]: 487) observed the rarity of apocryphal or pseudepigraphical apostolic letters in relation to other genres and conjectured that the reason for this "may well have been the sheer difficulty of using a pseudepigraphical letter to perform the same functions as an authentic letter." He concluded that "among the letters surveyed there is no really good example of a pseudepigraphical letter that achieves didactic relevance by the generality of its contents."

[20] Bauckham (ibid., 478) considered it "misclassified" and a "dedicated treatise." He also discussed several didactic letters (*1 Enoch* 92–105; *Epistle of Jeremiah*; *Baruch*; *2 Baruch* 78–87).

[21] Bauckham (ibid., 485) called *Laodiceans* "a remarkably incompetent attempt to fill the gap. . . . nothing but a patchwork of Pauline sentences and phrases from other letters, mainly Philippians." *Third Corinthians* is part of the late second-century *Acts of Paul*.

[22] See especially J. Duff, "A Reconsideration of Pseudepigraphy in Early Christianity" (Ph.D. thesis, Oxford University, 1998), who concluded that the value of a text was closely linked to its true authorship, that pseudonymity was generally

Another important issue is the significant number of historical particularities featured in the Pastorals. While it is possible that a later imitator of Paul fabricated these pieces of information to lend greater verisimilitude to his letter, it seems much more credible to see these references as authentic instances in Paul's life and ministry. For this reason Carson and Moo are surely right that "[t]he Pastorals are much more akin to the accepted letters of Paul than they are to the known pseudonymous documents that circulated in the early church."[23] This, of course, in no way obviates the possibility that Paul may have employed an amanuensis, as he frequently did in other instances.[24]

Destination

1–2 Timothy   Paul wrote in 1 Tim 1:3, "As I urged you when I went into Macedonia, remain in Ephesus." This indicates that Timothy had been put in charge of the church in this important city. Ephesus was situated on the west coast of Asia Minor (modern Turkey).[25] Josephus calls Ephesus "the chief city of Asia" (*Ant.* 14.224). Similar to Corinth, the city's location along a major trade route made it a primary prospect for planting a church that could serve as a beachhead for other congregations over the Roman Empire. The city was famous for its cult and temple dedicated to the Greek goddess Artemis (see Acts 19:28–41). As a center of pagan worship, Ephesus presented a considerable challenge for the Christian mission. The Ephesian church was started during Paul's three years in the city (Acts 19:8; see 20:31) and probably consisted of several house churches (see 1 Cor 16:19). Ephesus also boasted a considerable Jewish population. There is no indication in 2 Timothy of any difference of location with regard to Timothy's ministry, and there is every reason to assume that Timothy and the church in Ephesus are also the destination of Paul's second letter to Timothy.

Timothy occupied a special place in Paul's heart and mission (1 Cor 4:17; Phil 2:20,22; 1 Tim 1:2; 2 Tim 1:2). Paul first met him in Lystra, which at that time was part of the Roman province of Galatia (modern Turkey). It is possible, but not certain, that their paths crossed during Paul's previous visit to Lystra (Acts 14:8–20; see 2 Tim 3:10–11). Timothy was the product of a mixed marriage of a Gentile father and a Jewish mother. He was a "believer" (Acts 16:1–2), having been taught the Scriptures from his youth (2 Tim 1:5; 3:15). Recommended by his local church, Timothy joined Paul on his second missionary journey and shared in the evangelization of Macedonia and Achaia (Acts 16:2; 17:14–15; 18:5). He was associated with Paul during much of his extended ministry in Ephesus (Acts 19:22), traveled with him from Ephesus to Macedonia, to Corinth, back to

---

viewed as a deceitful practice, and that texts thought to be pseudonymous were marginalized.

[23] D. A. Carson and D. J. Moo, *An Introduction to the New Testament*, 2nd ed. (Grand Rapids: Zondervan, 2005), 563. Similarly, D. Guthrie, "The Development of the Idea of Canonical Pseudepigrapha in New Testament Criticism," *Vox Evangelica* 1 (1962): 43–59.

[24] See R. N. Longenecker, "Ancient Amanuenses and the Pauline Epistles," in *New Dimensions in New Testament Study*, ed. R. N. Longenecker and M. C. Tenney (Grand Rapids: Zondervan, 1974), 281–97; E. R. Richards, *The Secretary in the Letters of Paul*, WUNT 2/42 (Tübingen: Mohr-Siebeck, 1991); and Ellis, "Pastoral Letters," 663–64.

[25] See C. E. Arnold, "Ephesus," in *Dictionary of Paul and His Letters*, 249–53.

Macedonia, and to Asia Minor (Acts 20:1–6), and was with Paul during his first Roman imprisonment (Phil 1:1; Col 1:1; Phlm 1).

Timothy also served as Paul's emissary on at least three occasions prior to his current assignment in Ephesus: to Thessalonica (c. 50), Corinth (c. 53–54), and Philippi (c. 60–62). Paul frequently called him "co-worker" (Rom 16:21; 1 Cor 16:10; Phil 2:22; 1 Thess 3:2) and referred to him as coauthor of six of his apostolic letters (2 Corinthians, Philippians, Colossians, 1 and 2 Thessalonians, Philemon; see esp. Phil 2:19–22; cf. 1 Cor 16:10). The author of Hebrews mentioned Timothy's release from an otherwise unknown imprisonment (Heb 13:23). Due to his mixed Jewish-Gentile heritage (Acts 16:1), Timothy was an ideal choice for ministering in a Hellenistic-Jewish environment and for dealing with a Jewish proto-gnostic heresy. Even at the time 1 Timothy was written, Timothy was still fairly young (1 Tim 4:12), though he had met Paul more than 10 years earlier (Acts 16:1; c. AD 49), if not earlier. Timothy was therefore probably in his late thirties when he received 1 and 2 Timothy.

Titus As Paul's letter to Titus indicates, Titus had been left in Crete, a Mediterranean island Paul had previously passed on his sea voyage to Rome (Titus 1:5; see Acts 27:7–13). Paul indicated that the inhabitants of Crete were proverbial in that day for their dishonesty, immorality, and laziness (Titus 1:12). Paul's statement that he left Titus in Crete seems to imply that Paul had been there with him, presumably subsequent to the events in Acts. Titus had been directed by Paul to straighten out unfinished business and to appoint elders in every town (Paul's pattern—see Acts 14:21–23). Compared with Timothy's task, Titus's may have been a bit easier since Crete was no Ephesus—though it had been known for its many cities ever since Homer (*Iliad* 2.649). And, since Timothy found himself in a situation where there were already elders (some of whom at least seem to have been in need of rebuke, 1 Tim 5:19–20), Titus was charged with the fresh appointment of elders in every town. Thus it is possible that Paul and Titus planted these churches subsequent to Paul's first Roman imprisonment, with no time left to establish leadership before Paul decided to leave. Nevertheless Titus, like Timothy, faced the challenge of false teachers, "especially those from Judaism" (Titus 1:10).

While Titus was not as close to Paul as Timothy was, Titus was a trusted associate. When Paul went to discuss his gospel with the leaders of the Jerusalem church, he took Titus with him (Gal 2:1–3). Titus, a Gentile, was not compelled to be circumcised upon his conversion to Christianity, which served to illustrate the nature of Paul's gospel (Gal 2:3–5). While not mentioned in Acts, Titus surfaces repeatedly in Paul's letters as a member of the Pauline circle.[26] His commission by Paul found him on the island of Crete, where he was to take care of "what was left undone" (Titus 1:5). Cretan culture was known for its moral decay; hence Titus's task was not an easy one. Similar to 1 Timothy, Paul's letter to Titus is to encourage his delegate to complete the assignment given to him

---

[26] 2 Cor 2:12–13; 7:5–6,13–14; 8:6,16,23; 12:18; Gal 2:1–5; 2 Tim. 4:10; Titus 1:4.

in Crete by his apostolic mentor. Later, Titus was to meet Paul in Nicopolis (Titus 3:12), and after being with Paul for what was likely the last time, Titus departed for Dalmatia (2 Tim 4:10).

Date and Provenance

It may be assumed that Paul was released from his first Roman imprisonment (Acts 28) and that he engaged in a subsequent second Aegean ministry that provides the proper framework for 1 and 2 Timothy and Titus.[27] If so, Paul probably wrote his first letter to Timothy some time after the year 60 (the most likely date of Paul's release from his first Roman imprisonment), but before 66, the likely date for Paul's second Roman imprisonment that was followed by his martyrdom under Nero, who died in AD 68. The most natural reading of 1 Tim 1:3 is that Paul wrote from Macedonia. Timothy, who was at that time stationed in Ephesus, needed counsel on how to deal with the false teachers in the Ephesian church. To this end Paul interwove personal instructions with those on community life, so that Timothy received public apostolic support while it was acknowledged that he also had certain standards to meet.[28] Paul probably wrote 2 Timothy from Rome in the year 66. Titus was likely written in the interim between 1 and 2 Timothy (or possibly prior to 1 Timothy) from an unknown location.

It is often alleged that the church structure in the Pastoral Epistles reflects the church in the early second century instead of the first. This pattern can most clearly be seen in Ignatius of Antioch (c. 35–110), who advocated a monarchical episcopate and a three-tiered ecclesiastical hierarchy (see *Eph.* 2.2; *Magn.* 3.1; *Trall.* 2.2; 3.1).[29] But this is markedly different from the Pastoral Epistles, where the terms "overseer" (*episkopos*) and "elder" (*presbyteros*) refer to one and the same office (Titus 1:5,7; see Acts 20:17,28).[30] Paul and Barnabas appointed elders in the churches they had established already prior to the year 50 (Acts 14:23; see 11:30; 15:2; 20:28–31; 21:18; cf. Phil 1:1), so there is nothing novel in Paul's instruction to Titus to "appoint elders in every town" (Titus 1:5). In fact, the emphasis on qualifications for overseers and deacons in the Pastorals supports a first-century date because a second-century writer would have expected his readers already to be familiar with this kind of information.[31]

---

[27] For a tentative reconstruction of the chronology of Paul's ministry, see Ellis, "Pastoral Letters," 661–62; cf. Köstenberger, "1–2 Timothy, Titus," 596–98.

[28] So Johnson (*Letters to Paul's Delegates*, 106–7, 168), who called this the *mandata principis* ("commandments of the ruler") letter and cited several ancient parallels.

[29] See Mounce (*Pastoral Epistles*, lxxxvi–lxxxviii, 186–92), who cited Polycarp, Clement, Clement of Alexandria, and Irenaeus as referring to a two-tiered structure, using *episkopos* and *presbuteros* interchangeably.

[30] F. M. Young ("On *Episkopos* and *Presbyteros*," *JTS* 45 [1994]: 142–48) ventured the "admittedly tentative" hypothesis that the origins of the *episkopos* and the *presbuteros* are distinct. But Young's interpretation of the Pastorals in light of Ignatius (died c. 110) rather than vice versa seems precarious if not methodologically fallacious.

[31] See A. J. Köstenberger, "Church Government," in *Encyclopedia of Christian Civilization*, ed. G. T. Kurian (Oxford: Blackwell, 2011), 543–51.

Occasion

Paul's primary concern was not to describe the respective heresy in question but to refute it.[32] The nature of the false teachings combated in the Pastoral Epistles must therefore be deduced from the apostle's response. Moreover, while there are doubtless similarities between the heresies confronted in the Pastorals, one must not assume that the opponents are precisely the same in each case.[33] The teaching seems to have arisen from within the churches rather than having invaded from the outside (1 Tim 1:3; 6:2; 2 Tim 2:14; 4:2; Titus 1:13; 3:10; cf. 1 Tim 1:20; 2 Tim 2:17–18), which was in keeping with Paul's prediction (Acts 20:28–31). Some even suggest that the heretics were elders in the church, but this is uncertain.[34] There may be a connection with problems in Corinth (see 1 Cor 15:12,34) and especially in the Lycus Valley (compare 1 Tim 4:3 with Col 2:8,16–23).

Materially, the heresy involves an interest in myths and genealogies (1 Tim 1:4; 4:7; 2 Tim 4:4; Titus 1:14; 3:9) and a concern with the law (1 Tim 1:7; Titus 1:10,14; 3:9; see Col 2:16–17), which suggests that the false teachers were (Hellenistic) Jews.[35] In Ephesus at least, one finds ascetic elements such as the prohibition of marriage or the eating of certain foods (1 Tim 4:1–5; see Titus 1:15; Col 2:18–23) and the teaching that the resurrection had already taken place (2 Tim 2:17–18; see 1 Tim 1:19–20; 1 Cor 15:12),[36] which may point to a Greek-style dualism that prized spirituality over the natural order. As is the case with many forms of false teaching, the heretics displayed a tendency toward acrimony and speculation (1 Tim 1:4,6; 6:4,20; 2 Tim 2:14,16,23; Titus 1:10; 3:9), deceptiveness (1 Tim 4:1–3; 2 Tim 3:6–9,13; Titus 1:10–13; see Col 2:8), immorality (1 Tim 1:19–20; 2 Tim 2:22; 3:3–4; Titus 1:15), and greed (1 Tim 6:5; 2 Tim 3:2,4; Titus 1:11; contrast 1 Tim 3:3).

The practice of forbidding marriage was evident both in Judaism (especially among the Essenes; see Philo, *Apology* 380) and later Gnosticism (Irenaeus, *Against Heresies* 1.24.2). Even Paul himself at times extolled the advantages of celibacy (1 Cor 7:1–7).[37] Whatever the exact nature of the false teaching, what Paul apparently opposed here was an appeal to the Mosaic law in support of ascetic practices that at the root were motivated by gnostic thinking.[38] Paul denounced the various permutations of heresy in strong language as

---

[32] Two important articles on the subject are O. Skarsaune, "Heresy and the Pastoral Epistles," *Them* 20/1 (1994): 9–14; and R. J. Karris, "The Background and Significance of the Polemic of the Pastoral Epistles," *JBL* 92 (1973): 549–64.

[33] Towner, *1–2 Timothy and Titus*, 22; Mounce, *Pastoral Epistles*, lxi.

[34] Fee, *1 and 2 Timothy, Titus*, 7–9.

[35] Ignatius (died c. 110), in his epistle to the Magnesians, likewise warned his readers not to be "led astray by strange doctrines or by old fables which are profitless" (see *To Polycarp* 3.1; *To the Smyrnaeans* 6.2), linking these teachings with Judaism (*To the Magnesians* 8.1; see 9.1; 10.3; *To the Philadelphians* 6.1) involving the proper interpretation of the OT Scriptures (*To the Philadelphians* 8.2). See S. Westerholm, "The Law and the 'Just Man' (1 Tim 1,3–11)," *ST* 36 (1982): 82.

[36] See P. H. Towner, "Gnosis and Realized Eschatology in Ephesus (of the Pastoral Epistles) and the Corinthian Enthusiasm," *JSNT* 31 (1987): 95–124.

[37] Towner, *1–2 Timothy and Titus*, 25.

[38] So Westerholm, "The Law and the 'Just Man,'" 82.

"fruitless discussion" (1 Tim 1:6), "godless myths and old wives' tales" (1 Tim 4:7 NIV), "irreverent, empty speech" (1 Tim 6:20), "foolish and stupid arguments" (2 Tim 2:23 NIV), and "foolish debates" (Titus 3:9). This would have created a stereotype in believers' minds cautioning them against associating with these false teachers.[39] To some extent, Paul may have viewed the heresy as more irrelevant than false ("myths," "quarrels about words"), indicating that the "main stock-in-trade of these teachers was empty platitudes which Paul did not even consider it worthwhile to refute."[40]

Purpose

1 Timothy   Paul stated the occasion for 1 Timothy as follows: "As I urged you when I went to Macedonia, remain in Ephesus so that you may command certain people not to teach other doctrine" (1 Tim 1:3–4; see vv. 18–20). The question is whether this occasion constituted the purpose for 1 Timothy in its entirety or whether Paul had other purposes besides instructing Timothy on how to deal with these false teachers. Contrary to those who emphasize the *ad hoc* (Lat. "to this," i.e., addressed to a given circumstance only) nature of the Pastorals, it is likely that Paul's purpose was broader than merely dealing with false teachers.[41]

Specifically, 1 Timothy 1; 4–6 are concerned primarily with the challenge of the false teachers, while chaps. 2–3 focus more constructively on general organizational matters. This is suggested, first, by the phrase "First of all, then" (1 Tim 2:1) that introduces 2:1–3:16, which suggests the beginning of a new section;[42] and, second, the closing words of the same section in 3:15: "But if I should be delayed, *I have written so that you will know how people ought to act in God's household, which is the church of the living God, the pillar and foundation of the truth*" (emphasis added). This solemn affirmation and the following hymn in 1 Tim 3:16 indicate that Paul conceived of 1 Timothy not merely as occasional (i.e., as limited to this specific occasion) but as applicable to the church more broadly.

Third, in keeping with the genre of "Pastoral Epistle," Paul's office of the apostle (1 Tim 1:1; 2 Tim 1:1; Titus 1:1) would mean that his letters transcend the scope of any one local congregation. As Paul wrote elsewhere, the church is "God's household, built on the foundation of the apostles and prophets, with Christ Jesus Himself as the cornerstone" (Eph 2:19–20). Hence the Pastoral Epistles are foundational documents for the church,

---

[39] On the polemic employed by Paul, see esp. Karris, "Polemic of the Pastoral Epistles," 548–64.

[40] T. D. Lea and H. P. Griffin, Jr., *1, 2 Timothy, Titus*, NAC 34 (Nashville: B&H, 1992), 28–29, quoting Guthrie.

[41] See Fee, "Reflections on Church Order," 141–51; id., *1 and 2 Timothy, Titus*, 5–14 and throughout. Fee ("Reflections," 142–43) claimed that "the whole of 1 Timothy . . . is dominated by this singular concern" of refuting the false teachers and that "the whole of chs. 2–3 is best understood as instruction vis-à-vis the behavior and attitudes of the FT [false teachers]." But see the critique of Fee in Köstenberger ("1–2 Timothy, Titus," 514), who noted that Fee unduly diminished the structural markers in 2:1 and 3:15–16 that set off chaps. 2 and 3 from chaps. 1 and 4–6, respectively. Cf. the further interaction under the heading "Reflections" (ibid., 520).

[42] See Köstenberger ("1–2 Timothy, Titus," 510), who noted that the verb *parakaleō* ("I urge"), which is found in 1 Tim 2:1, is used regularly by Paul in transitioning to the "business portion" of a letter (1 Cor 1:19; 2 Cor 2:8; 6:1; Eph 4:1; 1 Thess 4:1; Phlm 10).

not just *ad hoc* instructions dealing with merely local circumstances that had no lasting implications for the church overall.

In 1 Tim 4:1, Paul returned to the matter of false teachers. What is more, even if the apostle addressed local circumstances requiring resolution, such as principles for the care of needy widows (1 Tim 5:3–16) or sinning elders (1 Tim 5:17–25), the truths and principles Paul enunciated as an apostle are true and therefore binding—not merely for Timothy and the church of Ephesus at the time of writing, but also for every church, "the church of the living God, the pillar and foundation of the truth" (1 Tim 3:15).[43] Hence Paul's purpose for writing 1 Timothy was both to instruct Timothy on how to deal with false teachers and to provide guidelines on a variety of matters of perennial significance for the church.[44]

2 Timothy   The most personal of Paul's letters is clearly 2 Timothy. With Paul in prison again (2 Tim 1:8) and nearing the end of his life (2 Tim 4:6–8), this book contains his final charge to Timothy to "proclaim the message" of the Christian gospel (2 Tim 4:1–2) as he passed on his mantle to his foremost disciple. In terms of salvation history, this book marks the transition from the apostolic to the subapostolic period, during which believers were charged to build on the foundation of the apostles and to guard the "good deposit" made by them (2 Tim 1:12,14 NIV). But the apostle touched on many topics of perennial significance in this letter that are not limited to the original circumstance to which they were addressed.[45]

Titus   Paul's letter to Titus was most likely written around the same time as 1 Timothy and for similar reasons. In Titus's case, the occasion is stated in Titus 1:5 as follows: "The reason I left you in Crete was to set right what was left undone and, as I directed you, to appoint elders in every town." This is followed by a set of qualifications for elders in Titus 1:6–9. While initially given to provide guidance for Titus, this passage is hardly limited to the original occasion but continues to have relevance for the church today as it ensures that its leaders meet biblical requirements. Beyond this immediate purpose, Paul provided a variety of other instructions for Titus in overseeing the life of the church. He articulated a series of important and abiding Christian doctrinal truths, such as salvation not by works, the regeneration of believers by the Holy Spirit, justification by grace, and so on (see Titus 3:4–7).

---

[43] See A. J. Köstenberger, "Women in the Church: A Response to Kevin Giles," *EvQ* 73 (2001): 205–24.

[44] This raises the issue of hermeneutical consistency. If an interpreter were to relativize Paul's instructions regarding women in church leadership in 1 Tim 2:11–15, he or she, to be consistent, would need to view Paul's instructions on qualifications for church leaders in 1 Tim 3:1–12 as relative and nonbinding for the church as well. See Mounce, *Pastoral Epistles*, 185.

[45] E.g., the affirmation in 2 Tim 1:9–10; the "trustworthy saying" in 2:11–13; and the "inscription" in 2 Tim 2:19. On the "trustworthy sayings" in the Pastorals, see the discussion under Theological Themes below.

LITERATURE

Genre

The Pastoral Epistles conform to the standard format of the ancient letter, including an opening salutation, a body with features such as thanksgiving and the main content, and a closing greeting. Beyond this, the Pastorals are often identified as exemplars of the paraenetic (hortatory) letter, which contained a series of exhortations to its recipients. Since 2 Timothy was Paul's last recorded letter—written from a second and much more severe Roman imprisonment with Paul's martyrdom apparently imminent—it thus takes on the character of a last testament (similar to 2 Peter).[46]

Yet the Pastorals are much more than a mere letter written by one individual to another for the purpose of conveying exhortation and information. As T. D. Gordon observed, "The Pastoral Epistles are the only New Testament writings that are expressly written with the purpose of providing instructions for ordering churches at the close of the apostolic era."[47] He continued:

> The very apostle who had established churches and provided for their continued oversight, doctrinal purity, and worship, now gives instructions to his coworkers regarding the organization of churches in subsequent generations. The norms and principles he himself had observed in the ordering of his churches, Paul makes explicit to his colleagues so that they, too, might order their churches correctly.[48]

Hence the genre of the Pastorals is inextricably bound to the historical life-setting of Paul's ministry as set forth in Acts and Paul's letters.

Hermeneutically, the important implication from this understanding of the genre of the Pastoral Epistles is that "[t]hese letters contain norms that are especially germane to the issues of life in the church, the 'household of God'" (see 1 Tim 3:14–15).[49] As Gordon noted, "The instructions in these letters, far from being primarily of local significance, are significant wherever there is concern for the proper ordering of God's house. Indeed, as instructions given to postapostolic ministers, the instructions contained in the Pastoral Epistles are particularly germane to other postapostolic churches."[50]

Literary Plan

1 Timothy Paul's first letter to Timothy immediately turns to the subject at hand: the need for Timothy to "command certain people not to teach other doctrine" in the church

---

[46] See the discussion in Marshall, *Pastoral Epistles*, 12–13.

[47] T. D. Gordon, "A Certain Kind of Letter: The Genre of 1 Timothy," in *Women in the Church: A Fresh Analysis of 1 Timothy 2:9–15*, ed. A. J. Köstenberger, T. R. Schreiner, and H. S. Baldwin (Grand Rapids: Baker, 1995), 59.

[48] Ibid. Gordon provided a specific list of such instructions on pp. 59–60.

[49] Ibid., 60.

[50] Ibid.

at Ephesus (1:3–4). Paul's customary thanksgiving follows his initial comments regarding these false teachers, which is in fact a thanksgiving to God for Paul's own conversion since he himself at one point persecuted the church of God (1:12–17). At the end of the first chapter, Paul mentioned two of these false teachers by name: Hymenaeus and Alexander (1:20).

After this, Paul transitioned ("First of all, then," 2:1) to a section where he set forth instructions for the church, in keeping with his purpose: "I write these things to you, hoping to come to you soon. But if I should be delayed, I have written so that you will know how people ought to act in God's household, which is the church of the living God, the pillar and foundation of the truth" (3:14–15). This makes clear that 2:1–3:16 constitutes a section apart from chap. 1 on the one hand and chaps. 4–6 on the other, both of which are dominated by Paul's concern with the false teachers. While not absent from chaps. 2–3, these chapters are taken up with Paul's more positive instructions to Timothy on how to govern the church. This includes instructions on prayer (2:1–8), women's roles in the congregation (2:9–15), and qualifications for church leadership, both overseers (3:1–7) and deacons (3:8–13). The section concludes with a presentation of the "mystery of godliness," possibly drawing on a piece of liturgy (3:16).

Chapter 4 opens with the dramatic phrase, "Now the Spirit explicitly says" (4:1), setting the work of the false teachers squarely in the context of the end time, during which things would go from bad to worse. In this context, Timothy was to set himself apart by giving close attention both to his personal life and to his doctrine, thus preserving both himself and his hearers (4:11–16). Additional instructions are given regarding the care of widows (5:3–16); dealing with elders, including those who had sinned (5:17–25); the proper conduct of Christian slaves (6:1–2); and the rich (6:3–10,17–19). Timothy, on the other hand, is to guard what has been entrusted to him, as Paul's final charge makes clear (6:11–16,20–21).

2 Timothy   Paul's second letter to Timothy opens with the customary greeting and thanksgiving (1:1–7), followed by an exhortation for Timothy not to be ashamed of Paul who is now in prison (1:8–12). After contrasting various coworkers, Paul instructed Timothy on the nature of Christian ministry by way of three metaphors: the soldier, the athlete, and the farmer. Each one has important lessons to teach regarding the proper disposition of the Lord's servant (2:1–7). Paul used three additional metaphors for Christian ministry: the workman, various instruments, and the servant (2:14–26). Further charges, recent news, and a concluding greeting round out the letter (chaps. 3–4).

Titus   Similar to 1 Timothy, Paul went straight to the point by reminding Titus why Paul left him in Crete: "to set right what was left undone and . . . to appoint elders in every town" (1:5). Also similar to 1 Timothy, Titus received various instructions on how to correct the enemies of the gospel while himself staying above the fray. Christians are to "adorn the teaching of God our Savior in everything" (2:10) and to devote themselves to "every good work" (3:1). In keeping with the personal nature of the letter, Paul concluded with some final instructions and a closing greeting (3:12–15).

OUTLINE

1 Timothy
I. OPENING (1:1–2)
II. PERSONAL CHARGE (1:3–20)
III. CONGREGATIONAL MATTERS (2:1–3:16)
IV. FURTHER CHARGES (4:1–6:2A)
V. EXTENDED FINAL EXHORTATION AND CLOSING (6:2B–21)

2 Timothy
I. OPENING (1:1–2)
II. THANKSGIVING AND PERSONAL EXHORTATION (1:3–18)
III. MINISTRY METAPHORS, PAUL'S GOSPEL, AND A TRUSTWORTHY SAYING (2:1–26)
IV. FURTHER CHARGES (3:1–4:8)
V. RECENT NEWS (4:9–18)
VI. CLOSING GREETINGS (4:19–22)

UNIT-BY-UNIT DISCUSSIONS

1 TIMOTHY

I. Opening (1:1–2)
The standard epistolary opening names Paul as the author and Timothy, his "true child in the faith," as the recipient. "Mercy" is added to the traditional greeting of "grace and peace."

II. Personal Charge (1:3–20)
At the very outset, Paul stated the occasion for writing, the challenge of the false teachers (1:3–11). Paul's testimony shows that God's grace alone separated Paul from the false teachers (1:12–17). The opening section concludes with an exhortation to Timothy and an identification by name of two false teachers, Hymenaeus and Alexander (1:18–20).

III. Congregational Matters (2:1–3:16)
With the transition, "First of all, then, I urge," Paul turned to some of the major business at hand. He addresses various issues related to congregational prayer (2:1–8) before turning to issues related to leadership in the church. Women are to dress modestly and must not teach or exercise authority over men (2:8–15). Male candidates for overseer must

meet certain qualifications (3:1–7), as do candidates for deacon, male or female (3:8–13). The section ends with a statement of the purpose of Paul's letter and a concluding confession (3:14–16).

IV. Further Charges (4:1–6:2a)

Returning to the challenge of the false teachers, Paul set this phenomenon in the larger context of latter-day apostasy (4:1–5). He instructed Timothy on being a good servant of Jesus Christ (4:6–16) and addressed several additional congregational matters, such as relating to older and younger men as well as older and younger women (5:1–2); ministering to widows who are truly in need (5:3–16); appointing or disciplining elders (5:17–25); and providing instructions for slaves (6:1–2a).

V. Extended Final Exhortation and Closing (6:2b–21)

The first part of Paul's final exhortation is taken up with a closing indictment of the false teachers (6:2b-10). This is followed by a final charge for Timothy in the sight of God to discharge his ministry in keeping with his "good confession" made in the presence of many witnesses (his ordination service?) and in light of the hope of Christ's return. A doxology (6:15–16) is followed by an exhortation to the rich (6:17–19) and one last exhortation for Timothy to oppose what is falsely called "knowledge" (perhaps incipient Gnosticism; 6:20–21).

2 TIMOTHY

I. Opening (1:1–2)

The opening of 2 Timothy closely resembles that of 1 Timothy. Again, Paul identified himself as the writer, called Timothy his "dearly loved child," and greeted Timothy with "Grace, mercy, and peace."

II. Thanksgiving and Personal Exhortation (1:3–18)

An opening thanksgiving (1:3–7) and a general call to suffering and faithfulness (1:8–14) replace the more urgent appeal found at the beginning of Paul's first letter to Timothy. Paul closed the introduction with a contrast between faithless and faithful coworkers (1:15–18).

III. Ministry Metaphors, Paul's Gospel, and a Trustworthy Saying (2:1–26)

In his exhortation of Timothy his "child," Paul drew on three metaphors illustrating the nature of Christian ministry: soldier, athlete, and farmer (2:1–7). Each of these conveys a key characteristic Paul wanted Timothy to cultivate. At the heart of this section is a carefully arranged mini-doxology (one of the several "trustworthy sayings" featured in the Pastoral Epistles), which focuses on Christ's work of salvation and its implications for

God's workers (2:8–13). The section closes with three additional ministry roles: workman, instrument, and servant (2:14–26).

IV. Further Charges (3:1–4:8)

As in 1 Timothy, about halfway through the letter Paul referred to the latter-day apostasy at work in the false teachers (3:1–9). He encouraged Timothy to stay the course (3:10–17) and to preach the Word (4:1–8). The charge to preach the Word marks the solemn, climactic concluding exhortation of Paul's two letters to Timothy, in that it is given "before God and Christ Jesus, who is going to judge the living and the dead, and by His appearing and His kingdom."

V. Recent News (4:9–18)

The letter concludes with some recent news from the apostle's busy life, even while in prison as he coordinated the mission of the early church (4:9–18), and with final greetings (4:19–22). Paul urged Timothy to come to him quickly, and if possible before winter. Only Luke was with Paul, and the apostle wanted Timothy to bring Mark with him as well, once he was relieved by Tychicus, who would stay in Ephesus and take Timothy's place after delivering the present letter to him.

VI. Closing Greetings (4:19–22)

Closing greetings are sent to Priscilla and Aquila and to the household of Onesiphorus.

OUTLINE

Titus

   I. OPENING (1:1–4)
  II. OCCASION FOR WRITING (1:5–16)
 III. INSTRUCTIONS ON TEACHING DIFFERENT GROUPS (2:1–15)
  IV. CLOSING GENERAL INSTRUCTIONS ON DOING WHAT IS GOOD (3:1–11)
   V. CLOSING COMMENTS (3:12–15)

UNIT-BY-UNIT DISCUSSION

Titus

I. Opening (1:1–4)

Paul's greeting to Titus, the third-longest opening greeting of any of his letters, bears considerable resemblance to the greeting in 1 Timothy. In addition, Paul provided an extended statement on the purpose of his apostleship.

II. Occasion for Writing (1:5–16)

The occasion is described in terms of the need to appoint qualified elders (1:5–9), which is set in the context of Titus's Cretan opposition (1:10–16). The list of qualifications for church leaders in Titus 1:6–9 is roughly equivalent to the one in 1 Tim 3:1–7, though there is no equivalent list of qualification for deacons (1 Tim 3:8–12).

III. Instructions on Teaching Different Groups (2:1–15)

Similar to his instructions to Timothy (1 Tim 5:1–2), Paul summarized how Titus should treat older men (2:1–2), older and younger women (2:3–5), and younger men (2:6–8); and he provided instructions for slaves in the church (2:9–10). Paul proceeded to identify two major incentives as Titus discharged his ministry: the grace of God and the return of Christ, "the glorious appearing of our great God and Savior, Jesus Christ," which Paul calls "the blessed hope" (2:11–14). The section concludes with an affirmation of Titus's authority (2:15).

IV. Closing General Instructions on Doing What Is Good (3:1–11)

The closing general instructions focus on being "ready for every good work." This involves comments on keeping the peace (3:1–2) and remarks on salvation in Christ and on the renewal by the Spirit, plus a final warning (3:3–11). At the outset Paul described the state of non-Christians by way of seven characteristics, making clear that it is only by God's grace that he, Titus, and other believers are any different.

V. Closing Comments (3:12–15)

The customary closing comments conclude the letter (3:12–15).

THEOLOGY

Theological Themes

Qualifications of Church Leaders   A considerable portion of the Pastoral Epistles is given to instructions on qualifications for church leaders.[51] The threat of the false teachers provided the backdrop for Paul's stipulations in this area. Since church leaders are charged with doctrinal oversight of local congregations, it is absolutely essential that they are chosen carefully in conformity to clearly articulated standards of character and integrity.

These leaders, variously called "overseers" or "elders," are to meet the following qualifications (1 Tim 3:1–7).[52] They are to be above reproach, faithful husbands,[53] self-controlled, sensible, respectable, hospitable, able to teach, not addicted to wine, not violent but gentle,

---

[51] For helpful materials on the subject, see especially P. A. Newton, *Elders in Congregational Life: Rediscovering the Biblical Model for Church Leadership* (Grand Rapids: Kregel, 2005); B. L. Merkle, *The Elder and Overseer: One Office in the Early Church*, Studies in Biblical Literature 57 (New York: Peter Lang, 2003); id., *40 Questions About Elders and Deacons* (Grand Rapids: Kregel, 2008); Köstenberger, "Church Government"; id., "1 Timothy," 521–30. For a presentation of different views, see S. B. Cowan, gen. ed., *Who Runs the Church? 4 Views on Church Government* (Grand Rapids: Zondervan, 2004); and C. O. Brand and R. S. Norman, eds., *Perspectives on Church Government: Five Views of Church Polity* (Nashville: B&H, 2004).

[52] See the comparative chart in Köstenberger, "1–2 Timothy, Titus," 523–24.

[53] See A. J. Köstenberger (with D. W. Jones), *God, Marriage and Family: Rebuilding the Biblical Foundation*, 2nd ed. (Wheaton: Crossway, 2010), 239–44 (see esp. the chart listing the different views on p. 243).

not quarrelsome, not greedy, manage their own households well, with their children in submission, not new converts, and have a good reputation with those outside the church (cf. Titus 1:6–9).[54]

The second office regulated in the Pastoral Epistles is that of deacon. Qualifications for deacons include: worthy of respect, not hypocritical, not drinking a lot of wine, not greedy for money, holding the mystery of the faith with a clear conscience, husbands of one wife, managing their children and their own households competently (1 Tim 3:8–10,12).[55] Deacons should first be tested (v. 10), and serving well brings a good standing and great eternal rewards (v. 13).

In addition to providing qualifications for church leaders, 1 Timothy and the other Pastorals provide insight into many areas of congregational life, such as the role of women (1 Tim 2:9–15),[56] caring for widows (1 Tim 5:1–16), dealing with sinning elders (1 Tim 5:17–25), or exhorting wealthy church members (1 Tim 6:2–10,17–19). All in all, the Pastorals are a treasure trove for the training of church leaders for the ministry.

The Preservation of Believers   The Pastorals exhibit a consistent concern for believers' preservation from Satan or demonic forces.[57] In 1 Tim 1:20, Paul said that he has delivered two false teachers over to Satan in order for them not to blaspheme. He mentioned that Eve was deceived at the fall, and he provided instructions for women on how to escape a similar fate (1 Tim 2:14–15; cf. 5:14–15). He warned against appointing new converts to positions of church leadership, lest they become conceited and fall into the condemnation incurred by the devil (1 Tim 3:6). This also requires that candidates for ecclesiastical office be above reproach and enjoy a good reputation with those outside the church (1 Tim 3:7).

Paul also denounced those who taught others to refrain from marriage or to abstain from certain foods because of a false dichotomy between material and spiritual things described as "teachings of demons" (1 Tim 4:1–3). Another area from which believers need to be preserved spiritually is the desire to get rich (1 Tim 6:9–10; see 2 Tim 2:26). Paul warned Timothy to guard himself against "contradictions from the 'knowledge' that falsely bears that name" (1 Tim 6:20). This apparently relates to an early form of Gnosticism, which taught a dualism between matter and spirit, disparaging all things created (see 1 Tim 2:14–15; 4:1–3).

---

[54] A separate list of qualifications is provided for deacons and women (whether women deacons or deacons' wives; 1 Tim 3:8–13; see Acts 6:1–6; Rom 16:1–2). For a discussion of these qualifications, see Köstenberger, "1–2 Timothy, Titus," 522–30, 606–8.

[55] The reference to women in 1 Tim 3:11 may denote women deacons or deacons' wives. See the discussion and literature cited in Köstenberger, "1–2 Timothy, Titus," 529–30. Among translations, the HCSB has "wives"; the NASB "women" (footnote "i.e. either deacons' wives or deaconesses"); the NIV "their wives" (footnote: "Or deaconesses"); and the NIV2010: "the women" (footnote: "Probably deacons' wives or women who are deacons").

[56] See A. J. Köstenberger and T. R. Schreiner, eds., *Women in the Church: An Analysis and Application of 1 Timothy 2:9–15*, 2nd ed. (Grand Rapids: Baker, 2005).

[57] See A. J. Köstenberger, "Ascertaining Women's God-Ordained Roles: An Interpretation of 1 Timothy 2:15," *BBR* 7 (1997): 107–44, especially 130–33.

Paul explained that the false teachers have been ensnared by the devil and held captive to do his will (2 Tim 2:26). In contrast with these heretics, Timothy was repeatedly exhorted to guard what had been entrusted to him (1 Tim 6:12; 2 Tim 1:12,14; 4:7,15,18) so that he may escape the grasp of the errorists and pursue Christian virtue (1 Tim 6:11; 2 Tim 2:22). As Paul's apostolic delegate, he is to be conscientious about himself and his teaching and to persevere in these things, for by doing so he would "preserve" (NASB) both himself and his hearers (1 Tim 4:16). By contrast, the false teachers have wandered away from the faith (1 Tim 1:6,19; 5:13,15; 6:9,10,21).

Table 15.1: The "Trustworthy Sayings" in the Pastorals

Trustworthy Saying	
1 Tim 1:15	This saying is trustworthy and deserving of full acceptance: "Christ Jesus came into the world to save sinners."
1 Tim 3:1	This saying is trustworthy: "If anyone aspires to be an overseer, he desires a noble work."
1 Tim 4:8–9	"The training of the body has a limited benefit, but godliness is beneficial in every way, since it holds promise for the present life and also for the life to come." This saying is trustworthy.
2 Tim 2:11–13	This saying is trustworthy: "For if we have died with Him, we will also live with Him; if we endure, we will also reign with Him; if we deny Him, He will also deny us; if we are faithless, He remains faithful, for He cannot deny himself."
Titus 3:4–8	"But when the goodness and love for man appeared from God our Savior, He saved us—not by works of righteousness that we had done, but according to His mercy, through the washing of regeneration and renewal by the Holy Spirit. This Spirit He poured out on us abundantly through Jesus Christ our Savior, so that having been justified by His grace, we may become heirs with the hope of eternal life." This saying is trustworthy.

POINTS OF APPLICATION

- Let mature believers mentor those who are younger in the faith (1 Tim 2:2; Titus 2:1–8)
- Embrace God's design for men's and women's roles in the church (1 Tim 2:8–3:13)
- Make sure that all church leaders are biblically qualified (1 Tim 3:1–12; Titus 1:6–9)
- Cultivate godliness (1 Tim 4:7; Titus 1:1; 2:3)
- Preach the Word, whether or not it is popular to do so (2 Tim 4:1)

STUDY QUESTIONS

1. Is it proper to call 1 and 2 Timothy and Titus "Pastoral Epistles"?

2. Which Pastoral Epistle was written from prison?

3. What is the genre of the Pastoral Epistles, and what implications does this have?

4. How many church offices are prescribed in the Pastoral Epistles?

5. What is the best description of Timothy's and Titus's ministry assignments?

6. What are the qualifications of church leaders (1 Tim 3:1–7; Titus 1:6–9)?

FOR FURTHER STUDY

Baugh, S. M. "1, 2 Timothy, Titus." Pages 444–511 in vol. 3 of *Zondervan Illustrated Bible Background Commentary*. Edited by C. E. Arnold. Grand Rapids: Zondervan, 2001.

Carson, D. A. "Pseudonymity and Pseudepigraphy." Pages 856–64 in *Dictionary of New Testament Background*. Edited by C. A. Evans and S. E. Porter. Downers Grove: InterVarsity, 2000.

Ellis, E. E. "Pastoral Letters." Pages 658–66 in *Dictionary of Paul and His Letters*. Edited by G. F. Hawthorne and R. P. Martin. Downers Grove: InterVarsity, 1993.

Gorday, J. *The Pastoral Epistles*. Ancient Christian Commentary on Scripture. Downers Grove: InterVarsity, 2000.

Guthrie, D. *The Pastoral Epistles*. Tyndale New Testament Commentaries. 2nd ed. Grand Rapids: Eerdmans, 1990.

Hughes, R. K., and B. Chapell. *1 and 2 Timothy and Titus*. Wheaton: Crossway, 2000.

Johnson, L. T. *The First and Second Letters to Timothy: A New Translation with Introduction and Commentary*. Anchor Bible 35A. New York: Doubleday, 2001.

_____. *Letters to Paul's Delegates: 1 Timothy, 2 Timothy, Titus*. Valley Forge: Trinity International, 1996.

Kelly, J. N. D. *A Commentary on the Pastoral Epistles*. Black's New Testament Commentaries. London: A&C Black, 1963.

Knight, G. W. *The Pastoral Epistles*. New International Greek Testament Commentary. Grand Rapids: Eerdmans, 1992.

Köstenberger, A. J. "1–2 Timothy, Titus." Pages 487–625 in *Expositor's Bible Commentary*. Rev. ed. Vol. 12: *Ephesians-Philemon*. Grand Rapids: Zondervan, 2005.

Köstenberger, A. J., and T. R. Schreiner, eds. *Women in the Church: An Analysis and Application of 1 Timothy 2:9–15*. 2nd ed. Grand Rapids: Baker, 2005.

Köstenberger, A. J., and T. L. Wilder, eds. *Entrusted with the Gospel: Paul's Theology in the Pastoral Epistles*. Nashville: B & H Academic, 2010.

Laniak, Timothy S. *Shepherds After My Own Heart: Pastoral Traditions and Leadership in the Bible*. New Studies in Biblical Theology 20. Downers Grove: InterVarsity, 2006.

Lea, T. D., and H. P. Griffin, Jr. *1, 2 Timothy, Titus*. New American Commentary 34. Nashville: B&H, 1992.

Merkle, B. L. *40 Questions About Elders and Deacons*. Grand Rapids: Kregel, 2008.

Mounce, W. D. *The Pastoral Epistles*. Word Biblical Commentary 46. Waco: Word, 2000.

Newton, P. A. *Elders in Congregational Life: Rediscovering the Biblical Model for Church Leadership*. Grand Rapids: Kregel, 2005.

Quinn, J. D. *The Letter to Titus*. Anchor Bible 35. Garden City: Doubleday, 1990.

Quinn, J. D., and W. C. Wacker. *The First and Second Letters to Timothy*. Eerdmans Critical Commentary. Grand Rapids/Cambridge: Eerdmans, 2000.

Towner, P. H. *1–2 Timothy and Titus*. IVP New Testament Commentary. Downers Grove: InterVarsity, 1994.

_____. *The Letters to Timothy and Titus*. New International Commentary on the New Testament. Grand Rapids: Eerdmans, 2006.

Wilder, T. L. "Pseudonymity and the New Testament." Pages 296–335 in *Interpreting the New Testament: Essays on Methods and Issues*. Edited by D. A. Black and D. S. Dockery. Nashville: B&H, 2001.

Part Four

THE GENERAL EPISTLES AND REVELATION

THIS INTRODUCTION TO the NT has provided treatments of the four Gospels, the book of Acts, and the 13 letters of Paul. Nine additional books remain to be discussed: eight letters conventionally grouped together under the rubric General Epistles and then the book of Revelation. While often not considered to be as central to the canon of the NT as the Pauline correspondence, these letters make an indispensable contribution to the biblical canon, and their study should in no way be neglected. With one minor change, the treatment of these books follows the canonical order. Chapter 16 considers the book of Hebrews; chapter 17, the book of James; chapter 18, 1 and 2 Peter and Jude; chapter 19, 1, 2, and 3 John; and chapter 20, the book of Revelation.

Each of these documents raises a unique set of questions that are discussed as appropriate. In the case of Hebrews, a difficulty pertains to the unknown identity of the author. James is a unique writing representing early Jewish Christianity in the NT. The relationship between 2 Peter and Jude and the authorship of 2 Peter also raise interesting questions that are considered. Both James and 1 John are notoriously difficult to outline, so this problem also receives attention. The relationship between the Johannine Letters and John's Gospel and Revelation is treated as well. A discussion of the historical, literary, and theological issues raised by the book of Revelation concludes the volume.

Chapter 16

The Letter to the Hebrews

CORE KNOWLEDGE

Students should know the key facts of the book of Hebrews. With regard to history, students should be able to identify the book's author, date, provenance, destination, and purpose. With regard to literature, they should be able to provide a basic outline of the book and identify core elements of the book's content found in the unit-by-unit discussion. With regard to theology, students should be able to identify the major theological themes in the book of Hebrews

KEY FACTS	
Author:	Unknown
Date:	c. 65
Provenance:	Unknown
Destination:	Jewish-Christian congregation(s) in Rome
Occasion:	Persecution of Christians causing some to revert to Judaism
Purpose:	To warn people in these Jewish-Christian congregations against reverting to Judaism in order to avoid being persecuted as Christians
Theme:	The supremacy of Christ over OT antecedent figures and other intermediaries
Key Verses:	12:1–2

CONTRIBUTION TO THE CANON
- The definitive revelation and redemption brought by Christ (1:1–4; 7:27; 8:26)
- Christian perseverance and the warning passages (e.g., 2:1–4)

- The eternal high priesthood of Christ (4:14–5:10; 7:1–28)
- The superiority of the new covenant over the old (8:1–9:25)
- The example of faith by OT believers (chap. 11)

INTRODUCTION

HEBREWS IS A book of profound contrasts and irony. Written in the most classical style of Greek in the NT, it reflects distinctly Jewish hermeneutics. The book has traditionally been known as "the letter of Paul to the Hebrews," but, as will be seen, scholars dispute almost every word of this description. The author calls the document a brief "word of exhortation" (13:22), but it is in fact one of the longest letters in the NT. While Hebrews has been acknowledged as one of the greatest works of theology in the NT, it struggled for full canonical acceptance longer than any other NT book.

Indeed, the student of Hebrews encounters a rather daunting series of unknowns, which have consistently defied resolution over the centuries.[1] What is more, studying Hebrews is taxing because understanding it requires considerable familiarity with OT teaching.[2] Yet anyone who immerses himself in the book and its message will be richly rewarded. With its emphasis on the unmatched, eternal high priesthood of Jesus Christ and the once-for-all character of his substitutionary sacrifice, Hebrews makes a vital and indispensable contribution to the Christian canon.[3]

HISTORY

Author

It has been suggested that the author of Hebrews is "one of the three great theologians of the New Testament."[4] Unfortunately, the authorship of the letter is the first in the list of unknowns regarding this book. The debate most familiar to evangelical Christians is whether Paul was its author, but it is unlikely that he was (see below). Few scholars today believe Paul wrote Hebrews.[5] Two major factors, in particular, support the near unanimous consensus in this regard. First, the language of the book is different from

---

[1] L. D. Hurst (*The Epistle to the Hebrews: Its Background of Thought*, SNTSMS 65 [New York: Cambridge Univ. Press, 1990], 1) even described the book as "something of a joke—a joke played upon a church obsessed with finding complete certainty about its origins." D. A. Black ("The Problem of the Literary Structure of Hebrews," *Grace Theological Journal* 7 [1986]: 164) noted that the book today frequently has become a collection of prooftexts and memory verses.

[2] Preparation for reading Hebrews involves, among other things, reading about the wilderness wanderings of the Israelites (esp. Numbers 13–14) and the OT sacrificial system and accessories (e.g., Exodus 25–30, 35–40). L. T. Johnson, *Hebrews: A Commentary*, NTL (Louisville: Westminster John Knox, 2006), 1.

[3] The book of Hebrews has major soteriological and missiological implications in a pluralistic world that seeks to be inclusive while Scripture teaches that salvation is found only in Jesus and his once-for-all sacrifice. See C. W. Morgan and R. A. Peterson, ed., *Faith Comes by Hearing: A Response to Inclusivism* (Downers Grove: InterVarsity, 2008).

[4] B. Lindars, *The Theology of the Letter to the Hebrews*, New Testament Theology (Cambridge: University Press, 1991), 25. Lindars did not specify the other two theologians; one surmises that one of them is Paul.

[5] But see D. A. Black, "Who Wrote Hebrews? The Internal and External Evidence Re-examined," *Faith and Mission* 18 (Spring 2002): 57–69.

Paul's in his letters. These differences extend beyond its vocabulary and style also to the book's imagery and theological motifs, such as the high priesthood of Christ. Second, and perhaps most damaging, is that the writer says that he heard the gospel from those who received it from Christ (see 2:3)—something Paul vehemently denied about himself elsewhere (Gal 1:11–16; see 1 Cor 15:8).

In lieu of Pauline authorship, a long parade of candidates has been proposed as the possible writer of Hebrews. These include Clement of Rome, Barnabas, Apollos, Luke, Silas, Priscilla, Philip, and even Mary the mother of Jesus.[6] Each of these, excluding Luke, has the same problem: we have no known documents by these authors to compare with Hebrews. Given the circumstances, therefore, it is best to admit that the authorship of Hebrews is unknown.[7]

The good news is that not one point of exegesis is dependent on knowing the identity of the person responsible for the letter. The document itself is formally anonymous, that is, the author does not name himself. At the same time it is apparent that the book was likely never intended to be an anonymous letter to its first readers. The author fully expected the recipients of his letter to know who he was, given the nature of the personal references to his readers (see 13:19–23). He may have been part of their congregation at some point in the past, and he expected to see them again in the future.

The difficulty is not just that the book is anonymous but that the early church struggled with identifying the author when they had no such struggle with other formally anonymous works in the NT (e.g., the Gospels and Acts).[8] The book first appears in the canon among the handwritten manuscripts in Paul's letters, usually between 2 Thessalonians and 1 Timothy.[9] This phenomenon is best accounted for by the tradition that Paul was the

---

[6] Clement (as Paul's amanuensis) is supported by Eusebius, *Eccl. Hist.* 3.38; Barnabas by the church father Tertullian and more recently E. Riggenbach, *Der Brief an die Hebräer: Kommentar zum Neuen Testament*, ed. T. Zahn (Wuppertal: R. Brockhaus, 1987 [1922]). Apollos was proposed by M. Luther, first in his Commentary on Genesis in 1545 (Luther's Works 8:178); as early as 1522, Luther qualified this opinion with "some say." Luke is favored by D. L. Allen, *Lukan Authorship of Hebrews*, NAC Studies in Bible & Theology (Nashville: B&H Academic, 2010). Silas was suggested by T. Hewitt, *The Epistle to the Hebrews* (Grand Rapids: Eerdmans, 1960), 26–32. Priscilla is the choice of A. von Harnack, "Probabilia über die Addresse und den Verfasser des Hebräerbriefes," *ZNW* 1 (1900): 16–41; and R. Hoppins, "The Epistle to the Hebrews Is Priscilla's Letter," in *A Feminist Companion to the Catholic Epistles and Hebrews*, ed. A.-J. Levine with M. M. Robbins, Feminist Companion to the New Testament and Early Christian Writings 8 (London: T&T Clark, 2004), 147–70. The suggestion of Philip is noted by J. Moffatt, *The Epistle to the Hebrews*, ICC (Edinburgh: T&T Clark, 1924), xx; cf. W. Ramsay, *Luke the Physician and Other Studies in the History of Religion* (New York: Hodder & Stoughton, 1908), 301–8. D. A. Hagner (*Encountering the Book of Hebrews: An Exposition*, EBS [Grand Rapids: Baker, 2002], 22) mentioned the suggestion of both Philip and Mary the mother of Jesus.

[7] This was the judgment of Origen: "But who wrote the epistle, in truth God knows" (cited in Eusebius, *Eccl. Hist.* 6.25.14).

[8] The Eastern part of the church (represented by Alexandria) affirmed the Pauline authorship of Hebrews, while recognizing the difficulty of this position. The best example is Athanasius's festal letter (367) that refers to 14 letters of Paul (including Hebrews). The Western part of the church rejected Pauline authorship. This is represented by such luminaries as Irenaeus and Hippolytus (according to Photius), who are said to have rejected it, as well as its absence in the Muratorian Canon that is careful to mention 13 letters of Paul.

[9] The oldest extant collection of Paul's letters ($\mathfrak{P}^{46}$; c. 200) has Hebrews immediately after Romans.

source of the letter. If so, it is possible that Paul was not the author of the document but that he included it in a collection of his letters on the basis that it was penned by one of his close associates, though this must of necessity remain in the realm of conjecture.

If the book is put in the Pauline corpus without Paul being the author, what is its connection to the apostle? The mention of Timothy in 13:23 recalls a prominent member of the Pauline circle, though the imprisonment mentioned there is not attested elsewhere in the NT. Also, the thematic connections are vast.[10] L. D. Hurst sketched the possible points of contact between Paul and the author of Hebrews as follows.[11] (1) Hebrews does not reflect literary borrowing from Paul by one of his followers. At the same time, one detects certain thematic similarities. (2) If these ideas were originally Pauline, the author could at some point have been a disciple of Paul. (3) Personal Pauline influence other than direct literary dependence is likely. Along similar lines, the church father Origen (c. 185–254) wrote, "If I were to venture my own opinion, I would say that the thoughts are the apostle's but the style and construction reflect someone who recalled the apostle's teachings and interpreted them" (cited in Eusebius, *Eccl. Hist.* 6.25).

What is more, while the author's identity remains elusive, it is possible to infer a few pieces of information regarding the writer from the letter itself. First, the author was male. The masculine participle "telling" (*diegeomai*) at 11:32 removes Priscilla, Mary, and any other female from consideration. Second, the author was obviously a gifted and eloquent writer, displaying an impressive command of ancient rhetoric. This points to the third characteristic, which is that the author was well educated. Fourth, he is most likely Jewish, showing familial relations with his readers. While his rhetoric was Greek, his hermeneutic was consistent with early Jewish and Christian principles of interpretation. Fifth, the writer was familiar with the Greek OT (the LXX).[12] Finally, as previously mentioned, the author was a second-generation believer (see 2:3). This is all that can be confidently said about the author.

Date

The second element of uncertainty regarding Hebrews is its date. Scholars have proposed a fairly narrow range of possibilities, spanning from the mid-60s just years prior to the destruction of the Jerusalem temple in 70 to about 90.[13] The author claims that he and his readers were second-generation Christians (2:3). He also indicated that some time had

---

[10] Hurst (*Hebrews*, 108) located at least 25 strong points of theological connection.

[11] Ibid., 124.

[12] G. Guthrie (*Hebrews*, NIVAC [Grand Rapids: Zondervan, 1998], 19) noted that there are 35 direct quotes, 34 clear allusions, 19 summaries of OT materials, and 13 times the author mentioned an OT name or topic, often without reference to a specific context. For the difficulty in assessing a strict number, see W. L. Lane (*Hebrews 1–8*, WBC 47A [Dallas: Word, 1991], cxvi), who located 31 quotations and 4 implicit quotations, 37 allusions, 19 summaries, and 13 references of names or topics that are introduced without a reference. The exact form of the LXX employed by the author is also the subject of scholarly debate.

[13] L. Gaston, *No Stone on Another: Studies in the Significance of the Fall of Jerusalem in the Synoptic Gospels*, NovTSup 23 (Leiden: Brill, 1970), 467; and T. Zahn, *Introduction to the New Testament*, trans. J. M. Trout et al. (New York: Scribner's,

elapsed after his readers' conversion (5:12) and after they had been persecuted for their faith in the past (10:32; 12:4), urging them to remember their leaders and to follow their example, "considering the outcome of their conduct" (13:7).

From these observations it is safe to assume that a date prior to 45 is unlikely.[14] The latest possible date is late in the first century since Clement of Rome (c. 96) was clearly influenced by the letter (indisputably *1 Clem.* 36:1–6, esp. 2–5). If one adds to this the fact that the letter must have been written in Timothy's lifetime (13:23) and during the life of a second-generation Christian (2:3), this places the upper limit of the letter at about the time of Clement.[15] Hence the letter must have been written between the years 45 and 95.

But it is possible to narrow the range still further. The letter was in all probability written before the Jewish War, including the destruction of the Jewish temple in the year 70 since the writer speaks of the sacerdotal ministry in the present tense (9:6–10).[16] But it is more likely that the references are to the temple. If the temple had already been destroyed and sacrifices and priesthood ceased to exist, it is virtually inconceivable that the author would have made no reference to these events.[17] The present-tense references to the temple and the lack of references to its destruction point to a date prior to the destruction of Jerusalem in AD 70.

As will be seen below, Hebrews was most likely written to a group of churches in Rome. If so, the experience of believers mentioned in the book is entirely congruent with the time period subsequent to the edict of Claudius (c. 49) and the persecution of Christians under Nero (64–66). Since these believers seem to be undergoing persecution at the time of writing, a date of composition toward the end of this time period seems most likely, yet not at the very end, for the author noted that the recipients had not yet shed any blood (12:4). On balance, therefore, a date in the mid-60s seems most likely.

Provenance

The provenance of Hebrews is unknown. The only possible internal piece of evidence is 13:24, which states, "Those who are from Italy greet you." But, as is argued below, most likely this indicates a Roman *destination* while leaving the question of the letter's provenance open. If so, perhaps the only safe conclusion is that wherever the letter was written, it was not penned in Rome since this was its probable intended destination. Especially since the author's identity itself is unknown, it is even more difficult to establish where

---

1909), 315–23. Zahn based his arguments on the interpretation of Heb 3:7–4:11, "Your fathers tested me, tried me, and saw my works for 40 years," as the years 30–70.

[14] Johnson, *Hebrews*, 39.

[15] See D. A. Carson and D. J. Moo, *An Introduction to the New Testament*, 2nd ed. (Grand Rapids: Zondervan, 2005), 605.

[16] See Brown, *Introduction to the New Testament*, 696; G. A. Barton, "The Date of the Epistle to the Hebrews," *JBL* 57 (1938): 199–200.

[17] B. Lindars, "Hebrews and the Second Temple," in *Templum Amicitiae: Essays on the Second Temple Presented to Ernst Bammel*, ed. W. Horbury (Sheffield: JSOT, 1991), 416.

that unknown author was at the time he wrote Hebrews. For this reason, to reappropriate Origen, "The provenance of Hebrews, only God knows."[18]

Destination

The third unknown is the destination of the letter. The question of the letter's destination encompasses several factors. One is the ethnic makeup of the congregation(s) being addressed. Another is the geographical location of the recipients. Yet another is any other characteristics of the original recipients or their situation at the time of writing. The first question is about the recipients' ethnic makeup. At first glance, this issue seems to be settled by the designation of the letter as "To the Hebrews." Yet while this title suggests that the recipients were Jewish Christians, scholars do not all agree that the book was written to a Jewish audience. Some contend that they were Gentiles, and they view the title as vague and misleading—something added after the knowledge of the recipients was lost. Nevertheless, while some factors are congruent with a Gentile audience, none override the cumulative impression that the original readers were Hebrew Christians.

The first major argument in favor of a Jewish Christian audience of Hebrews is bound up with the title of the book. This title, which is the only title that is extant, most likely dates to the book's inclusion in the Pauline corpus. If so, it is chronologically so close to Paul's time that any appeal to the recipients being forgotten becomes untenable. Thus the title "To the Hebrews" should be taken seriously, and it unequivocally points to Jewish readers. The question of whether these Jews lived in Palestine or the Diaspora is not addressed by the title. Some have tried to identify the recipients with the Qumran covenanters[19] or Jewish priests in Jerusalem (such as those converted in Acts 6:7),[20] but these views have not generated a great following. The fact that the readers had not heard Jesus personally (2:3), the author's exclusive use of the LXX, and the presence of linguistic features characteristic of the Hellenistic synagogue all point to readers outside Palestine.

The second major argument for a Jewish Christian audience is related to the pervasive use of the OT in the book. The author presupposed that his readers were thoroughly familiar with OT teaching, including the Levitical ritual, the priesthood, and the pattern of the tabernacle. Achtemeier, Green, and Thompson correctly stated that "it is difficult not to see Hebrews as directed toward Jewish Christians, to whom the exhortations and arguments from the exposition of so many OT passages, especially those regarding the wandering Israelites looking for the Promised Land, would have a particularly strong appeal."[21]

---

[18] It is, of course, true that presumably the first recipients of Hebrews knew who the author was, but the point of Origen's remark (which still applies today) is that this knowledge of the author was soon lost in subsequent generations.

[19] See P. E. Hughes, *A Commentary on the Epistle to the Hebrews* (Grand Rapids: Eerdmans, 1977), 10–15.

[20] C. Spicq, *L'Épître aux Hébreux* (Paris: J. Gabalda, 1952), 1:226–31.

[21] P. J. Achtemeier, J. B. Green, and M. M. Thompson, *The New Testament: Its Literature and Theology* (Grand Rapids: Eerdmans, 2001), 471.

The next question regarding the letter's destination relates to the audience's geographical location. The only possible clue in this regard is found in 13:24, which states, "Those who are from Italy greet you." This passage evidently establishes a connection between the readers and Italy. But is the reference to the location of the readers or of the writer? In other words, does the reference indicate that Italian expatriates are sending greetings back home or that the writer was in Italy at the time of writing?

Guthrie advocates the former (a Roman destination) based on the following set of arguments: (1) "from Italy" is used in Acts 18:2 for Aquila and Priscilla, who were Italian expatriates; (2) the reference to pastors as "leaders" (*hegoumenoi*) in Hebrews (13:7,17,24) is paralleled outside the NT only in *1 Clement* (c. 95) and the *Shepherd of Hermas* (early second century?), both of which are of Roman origin; (3) *1 Clement* (written in Rome) made extensive use of Hebrews, so the earliest evidence of the book's existence comes from Rome.[22] On the basis of this type of evidence, a Roman destination for Hebrews is indeed plausible, if not probable.

Beyond this, there are a few other characteristics of the audience that may be inferred from the letter. In fact, the author of the letter referred to the fact that the recipients, as well as the author, are second-generation Christians (2:3); that is, the author looked back to the apostles as belonging to the preceding spiritual generation. While they had been believers for some time, they had regressed in their growth in Christ (5:11–6:3), and some had stopped attending the weekly assembly (10:25). On the whole, however, the author was confident in his readers' salvation because of their labor of love (6:10), which includes supporting fellow Christians in need (10:34). These believers were not only under doctrinal pressure, but they also seem to have been well acquainted with persecution. They had endured "a hard struggle with sufferings" at their conversion (10:32), had their property seized, and had endured this ill treatment joyfully (10:34). Moreover, they were currently under pressure (12:3–13), though they had yet to suffer to the point of martyrdom (12:4), but there was an expectation of more severe suffering in the future (13:12–14).

All this evidence fits well with the audience being Hebrew Christians in Rome in the mid-60s. If the discussion above is accurate, the most likely date would be shortly before Nero's persecution in the last half of the 60s reached its climax. The community, having existed for some time, had previously endured persecution. Their property had been confiscated, and they had endured shame from outside their group (12:4; 13:13). All of this matches the situation in Rome from the time subsequent to the edict of Claudius in the year 49—at which time the confiscation of property was experienced when the Jews were temporarily expelled from Rome[23]—to the latter half of Nero's reign (54–68). The warning passages and the repeated exhortations to endure, as well as the author's effort to

---

[22] Guthrie, *Hebrews*, 20–21.

[23] Suetonius (*Claudius*, 25.4) stated that "[Claudius] banished from Rome all the Jews, who were continually making disturbances at the instigation of one Chrestus," which suggests that a disturbance over Christ among the synagogues had spilled out into the streets of Rome.

prevent a reverting to Judaism, indicate that this was a serious temptation for his readers. Also, by the time of Nero's persecution (c. 65–68), the state recognized the distinction between Judaism, a tolerated religion (Lat. *religio licita*) with certain leniencies, and Christianity, which was forbidden. A Jewish Christian tempted to escape persecution thus may have found it appealing to retreat back under the protective umbrella of Judaism.[24]

Purpose and Occasion

The occasion and purpose of the letter are closely connected to the judgments made about the recipients. As argued, Hebrews was most likely written to a congregation of Jewish Christians who were urged to move on to maturity (see 5:11–6:8) in the face of looming persecution. Whether the letter was written to one or several Jewish Christian congregations in Rome, two things seem certain: first, the recipients were facing continued pressure, whether social or physical; and, second, a retreat back into Judaism was viewed, at least by some, as an appealing solution to relieve the pressure. This is the temptation the author addressed.

The author described his writing as a "word of exhortation" (13:22), a phrase found elsewhere in the NT only in Acts 13:15, where it refers to a synagogue homily (sermon). This makes it likely that the genre of Hebrews is that of a written series of oral messages. Lane argued that this means the author identified his work as "an earnest passionate and personal appeal."[25] As the book unfolds, this appeal turns into a series of arguments designed to encourage the readers to move on to maturity, holding on to their Christian confession (see 6:1; 10:23).

The basis of this series of appeals is the utter superiority of the Son to all previous intermediary figures who spoke for God, whether human or angelic. Moreover, the recent revelation of God's Son, the Lord Jesus Christ, ushered in the new covenant that had been announced by the OT prophets (see 8:8–13, citing Jer 31:31–34), so that now the old Mosaic covenant had become obsolete.

The essence of the appeal can be found in the three exhortations at 10:19–25 (marked in English by "let us"). The first is "let us draw near with a true heart in full assurance of faith, our hearts sprinkled clean from an evil conscience and our bodies washed in pure water" (v. 22). The author invited his readers to draw near and approach God in trust, based on the assumption that they were believers. His primary concern was the actual conversion of his hearers and their orientation toward God. The second injunction is in verse 23: "Let us hold on to the confession of our hope without wavering, for He who promised is faithful." Thus the related concern subsequent to salvation was an authentic confession of faith in Jesus Christ. The third exhortation further enjoins believers to express that faith

---

[24] The same scenario would also obtain if the author were writing to a Greek-speaking church in Palestine. These converts certainly existed in Palestine (see Acts 6–7), and a retreat to Judaism would have provided them with an escape from Jewish persecution and ridicule.

[25] W. Lane, "Hebrews," in *Dictionary of the Later New Testament and Its Developments*, ed. R. P. Martin and P. H. Davids (Downers Grove: InterVarsity, 1997), 453.

to one another: "Let us be concerned about one another in order to promote love and good works" (10:24).

This triad of concerns climaxes at 12:1–2, where believers are encouraged to "run with endurance the race that lies before us." Thus, the purpose of Hebrews is not merely to maintain believers' confession in the face of persecution but also that they would move on to full maturity in Christ by holding fast to their confession.

LITERATURE

Genre

The genre of Hebrews has been the subject of considerable debate. The letter opens and proceeds like a work of rhetoric but closes like a letter.[26] The author himself described his piece of writing as a "word of exhortation" (13:22, cf. Acts 13:15). Whether or not a specific type of sermon can be identified, the description "homily" or "sermon" certainly seems to fit the book well. First, the author referred to himself in the first person (both singular and plural, asserting authority and identifying with his hearers). Second, he cast his activity as an act of speaking, not writing. When making such a self-reference, he generally used verbs of speaking rather than words of writing.[27] He also preferred "hearing" to "reading" in reference to his audience. Thus he created a sense of personal presence with his audience.[28] Third, he alternated exposition and exhortation, which "allows an orator to drive home points immediately without losing the hearers' attention."[29] Fourth, the author introduced a theme only to explain it later in his work. Thus Jesus' priesthood is introduced at 4:14 but not developed until 7:1–9:28, and his connection with Melchizedek is mentioned in 5:10 but not taken up in detail until 7:1.

For these reasons it may be concluded that Hebrews was in all probability first delivered as a series of oral messages and subsequently compiled and edited for publication as a letter, which included attaching an epistolary ending. Also, in keeping with the ancient notion that the written form of the letter served as a substitute for the author's presence, the letter was aimed at moving the audience persuasively to adopt the author's argument that reverting back to Judaism would be a serious mistake with disastrous spiritual consequences. Most likely, the letter would have been read to the congregation aloud, and thus the writer used several devices that enhanced the material's memorability, such as alliteration, repetition, and arguments from the lesser to the greater. Indeed, the identification of

---

[26] In this regard, only 1 John is similar in its opening. James is the exact opposite, opening like a letter but ending differently.

[27] E.g., 2:5; 5:11; 6:9; 8:1; 9:5; 11:32. The only exception is 13:22, where the author used the verb translated "to write a letter" (*epesteila*), though even this is not a real exception since 13:22 is part of the epistolary framework provided for the body of the document.

[28] Lane, *Hebrews*, lxxiv.

[29] Johnson, *Hebrews*, 10.

the letter as originating in a homily or sermon calls attention to a host of rhetorical devices and matters in the book.

Literary Plan

Turning now to the second item of literary import, the book's structure, Hebrews has proven to be difficult to outline. Scholars have suggested many different divisions of the text, some based on traditional exegesis,[30] others based on the newest literary methods. In spite of the prolonged interest, no consensus is on the horizon. The intricate structure that makes it difficult to outline the book is due to a variety of factors, including the rhetorical style and hermeneutical principles employed by the writer, but most of all it is due to the fact that the author of Hebrews employed some of the smoothest transitions in the entire NT.[31]

OUTLINE

    I. JESUS THE APOSTLE OF OUR CONFESSION (1:1–4:16)
        A. Jesus as the Heir of the Universe (1:1–2:18)
        B. Enter the Remaining Sabbath Rest (3:1–4:16)
    II. JESUS OUR HIGH PRIEST (4:11–10:25)
        A. Carry on to Maturity (4:11–5:14)
        B. Maturity Enables Hope (6:1–7:3)
        C. Drawing Near to God (7:4–10:25)
    III. JESUS THE ONE WHO RAN THE RACE BEFORE US (10:19–13:16)
        A. Run the Race (10:19–11:40)
        B. The Course Set Before Us (12:1–29)
        C. Go with Jesus outside the Camp (13:1–16)
    IV. CONCLUSION (13:17–25)

UNIT-BY-UNIT DISCUSSION

I. Jesus the Apostle of Our Confession (1:1–4:16)

Hebrews begins in a rather abrupt manner. Some have identified 1:1–4 as the introduction to the book. If so, the mention of angels at both 1:4 and 5 is an example of how the author elegantly transitions from one section to another.

A. Jesus as the Heir of the Universe (1:1–2:18) Without a formal prescript, the book opens like a rhetorical presentation rather than a letter (1:1–4). Immediately, the author drew a sharp contrast between the prophets who spoke of old and the Son through whom God speaks in the present. This section smoothly transitions into the first major section of the book.

---

[30] See F. F. Bruce, *The Epistle to the Hebrews* (Grand Rapids: Eerdmans, 1984).

[31] Lane, *Hebrews*, xc.

Hebrews 1:4 introduces the idea that "Son" is a better name than the angels, and verses 5–18 adduce seven OT quotations to prove this point (1:5–14). These are organized in the form of a pair of three quotations with a concluding quote, a common rabbinical rhetorical device called "pearl stringing."[32]

The quotations are as follows. (1) In 1:5–6 the author contrasted the position of the Son and of the angels: he is the Son, and the angels worship him (citing Ps 2:7; 2 Sam 7:14; Deut 32:43, LXX). (2) In 1:7–12 the author contrasted the work of the Son and the angels: angels are his servants, but he is the sovereign ruler of the universe (citing Pss 104:4; 45:6; 102:25–27). (3) In 1:13–14 the author concluded the string of citations with a quote of Ps 110:1, reemphasizing that the Son is the ruler while the angels are "ministering spirits."

The first of several warning passages follows on the heels of the exposition (2:1–4). The argument follows a lesser to greater pattern.[33] If just punishment was meted out for violations of the OT law (mediated through angels), how much more would this be the case for those who rejected the Son, who was manifestly greater than the angels, which points back to 1:1–4. Thus the readers should pay close attention to what God says today through the Son.

The author then cited two reasons that the recipients ought to pay close attention to his message: (1) lest they "drift away" (a constant danger for believers; notice that this does not necessarily imply apostasy); and (2) lest they fall under the discipline of the Lord.

Citing Ps 8:4–6, the author continued to demonstrate his thesis that Jesus is superior to the angels (2:5–9). "The world to come" will not be under the dominion of angels but subject to one who had become human, the Lord Jesus Christ. Through the OT citation, the author recalled that God's original intent was for human beings to subdue the earth (Gen 1:28) but that this intent had not been fulfilled. Humanity had not fully subdued the earth. Yet God's purpose would be fulfilled in Jesus (the first time that the humanity of Jesus is stressed), who had been "crowned with glory and honor because of the suffering of death" (2:9).

The author noted that it was fitting for God to perfect the source or author (*archēgos*) of humanity's salvation through suffering (as a human being) because both Christ and believers are united in their relationship to the Father as sons of God (v. 11). Christ even calls believers his brothers (vv. 12–13 set the OT foundation for this identification). The ultimate intent is that since humans and Christ share "flesh and blood," in his death on the cross Christ was able to break the power of the one who held human beings in bondage through fear of death, that is, the devil (vv. 14–15). In 2:16–18 the author explained that Jesus had to be made truly human so that he could serve as an effective high priest for God's people.

---

[32] Hb. *haraz*. See Lane, *Hebrews*, cxxii.

[33] Hb. *qal wahomer.* Ibid., cxx.

B. Enter the Remaining Sabbath Rest (3:1–4:16) The argument proceeds smoothly into the next section (3:1–2; note the conjunction "therefore"), where Jesus, the superior messenger or "apostle" (Gk *apostolos*) is contrasted with Moses, who was a servant in God's house. At the end of the previous section, the author introduced the fact that Jesus became a human being to serve as an effective high priest for God's people. The entirety of the present section functions as preparation for the development of this theme later on in the letter.

The movement from angels to Moses is best understood against the common notion in ancient Judaism that Moses was considered superior to the angels (3:1–6). The author, however, pointed his readers toward Jesus so they would consider him. The basis for the author's appeal is that Jesus is worthy of greater glory than Moses (3:3–4) and that he was faithful as a Son over the household rather than having been faithful only as a servant (an allusion to Num 12:7). The essence of "considering Jesus" is fleshed out in 3:6b. The readers must hold on to their public confession of Jesus in order to retain unhindered access to him and to attain the object of their hope. This leads directly to the next section, which represents a call to endurance and challenges the readers to be faithful as Jesus was faithful.

Hebrews 3:7–19 begins with a quotation of Ps 95:7–11 that was used weekly in the synagogue. Every week the worshippers were reminded of the tragic consequences of the rebellion in Numbers 13–14. The injunction in verses 12–13 is to "watch out" and to "encourage each other daily," lest the readers are "hardened by the deceit of sin" (v. 13, author's translation). The example from Numbers refers to a group of people (the Israelites) who were about to receive God's blessings but who did not because they would not trust God. The author warned his readers to endure to the end and trust God.

The next section (4:1–13) is made up of two paragraphs. The first describes the remaining rest and encourages the recipients of the letter to enter it. The unit is followed by a second warning passage concerning the necessity of heeding the word of God. The author shifted from a discussion of those who failed to enter the rest to a discussion of the continuing validity of a rest from God. He cited Gen 2:2 as the foundation of the Sabbath rest (which would have been the second scriptural citation given in the synagogues each Sabbath) to explain that God had invited the Israelites into his rest, but they had failed through unbelief and disobedience. Since God later through David issued another offer of rest (Ps 95:7–11), surely this "rest" was not merely the rest of conquering Canaan but a real Sabbath-type rest from God that remained for the people of God (see 4:8). The encouragement, then, was to make sure the readers had entered this remaining rest, that is, a rest from their own labors, salvation by grace. The final exhortation is to "make every effort to enter that rest, so that no one will fall into the same pattern of disobedience" (4:11).

According to the common pattern, the exhortation is followed by a warning not to drift away (4:11–16). The people of God are to heed his voice as he calls out to them "today" (see Psalm 95). The author compared God's word to a double-edged sword that pierces through all human excuses, exposing the innermost portions of the heart, painting

300 Part Four: The General Epistles and Revelation

a picture of the hearer of the word being naked so that his thoughts are laid bare. People are indeed defenseless before God when they disobey his word. Hebrews 4:11–16 forms what Westfall called a "discourse peak," concluding the first section of the letter with three inseparable exhortations: "Let us make every effort" (4:11); "Let us hold fast to the confession" (4:14); and "Let us approach the throne of grace" (4:16).[34]

Typical of the author's transitions, the movement between the major sections is seamless. The warning not to drift away (4:11–16) is both the conclusion to the present section and the introduction to the next. In theatrical terms, the author preferred a fade to a hard cut.

II. Jesus Our High Priest (4:11–10:25)

Prior to 4:13 the author referred to Jesus as "high priest" (2:17; 3:1), but now a sustained defense of the meaning and implications of his priesthood is presented. Just as the previous section was an exposition of Ps 95:7–11, so this section is an exposition of Ps 110:4, which is not cited in any other NT book: "The LORD has sworn an oath and will not take it back: 'Forever, You are a priest like Melchizedek.'"

A. Carry on to Maturity (4:11–5:14) Hebrews 4:14–16 draws a conclusion based on the humanity of Christ (mentioned in chap. 2). The readers should "hold fast" to their "confession" because they have a high priest who is familiar with their sinful condition without having succumbed to it. For this reason they are able to go before God's throne to receive mercy and find grace to help.

Having declared Christ's high priesthood, the author describes the perfection of this high priest through his earthly life and sufferings (5:1–10). He begins by noting God's intent for the Levitical high priest, who was appointed to serve God by offering gifts and sacrifices for sins on behalf of his people. It was God's intent that a human being serve in this role since he would be familiar with people's weakness, and the high priest himself is included in the sin offering. Finally, he was not self-appointed but designated by God.

Similarly, Christ was appointed by God yet not in the likeness of Aaron but according to the order of Melchizedek (5:5–6). Verses 7–8 most likely refer to Jesus' prayer in Gethsemane where his ultimate request was for God's will to be done. Thus "He learned obedience through what He suffered" (5:8).[35] From 5:11 to 6:12 the author took a temporary reprieve from his explication of the high priesthood of Christ. The reason for this is that his hearers had become slow to understand. The reason they could not understand the author's teaching on Melchizedek was not that the nature of his priesthood was impossible to grasp but that they had ceased paying attention to the teaching of God's Word and needed to go back to the ABCs of the Christian faith.

---

[34] C. L. Westfall, *A Discourse Analysis of the Letter to the Hebrews: The Relationship Between Form and Meaning,* LNTS (New York: T&T Clark, 2005), 142.

[35] Learning obedience and attaining to perfection do not imply any imperfection on Jesus' part; instead, the reference implies that Jesus had completed his course to be installed as high priest. The term *teleioō* ("to perfect") was used in the LXX to describe the installation of a priest (e.g., Exod 29:9,33).

B. Maturity Enables Hope (6:1–7:3) The "elementary doctrine of Christ" (ESV) is spelled out in 6:1–2 (another transitional passage). Instead of languishing at these elementary things, the author wanted his readers to press on to maturity. The exhortation (the only one in this entire unit) is in the passive (most likely, a "divine passive" with God as the agent of the action), conveying the sense "let us be carried on [by God]" to full maturity. This was important because it was impossible to renew those to repentance who were "recrucifying the Son of God" (6:4–12).

If it is kept in mind that the author envisioned his hearers in a similar situation as Israel in the wilderness, then the description of those who fell—"once enlightened" (v. 4), "tasted the heavenly gift" (v. 4), "partakers of the Holy Spirit" (v. 4 NASB), "tasted the good word of God" (v. 5)—does not necessarily refer to believers. Just as Israel in the wilderness saw the pillar of fire, ate the manna, witnessed the manifestation of God's power in Moses' mighty miracles, and received the divine promises of deliverance from their enemies, the readers had seen manifestations of God's reality, presence, and power all around them in the congregation of which they were, at least nominally, a part (6:4–6). Yet as is still true today, external association with a given congregation does not guarantee salvation; what is required is a heart that trusts in God and the provision he made in Christ.

The author contrasted his hearers as following in the footsteps either of Joshua and Caleb or of the disobedient generation of Israelites who perished in the desert. Those who fell away repudiated Christ similar to those who rejected him in Jerusalem—thus "recrucifying" (6:6) him does not have an atoning significance but emphasizes the rejection of Christ—and openly casts aspersions on him. Thus the illustration at 6:7–8 describes believers as those producing fruit and unbelievers as producing thorns, reinforcing the previous affirmation that true believers persevere to the end (see 3:14). Nevertheless, the author had confidence in the salvation of most of his readers (6:9–10).

The believer has assurance of enduring faith because the oath made to Abraham has application also for believers today (6:13–7:3). By two immovable realities—God's oath and his word—God established the covenant with Abraham that his seed would be innumerable. This covenant implies the endurance of the believer. Believers thus have encouragement to seize this immovable hope secured for them because Jesus entered the inner sanctuary for them as an eternal high priest like Melchizedek.

Hebrews 7:1–3 establishes who Melchizedek was and how Christ resembled him in certain respects. Melchizedek was the priest of the Most High God who received tithes from Abraham. The name *Melchizedek* means "king of righteousness," and he was the "King of Salem" (i.e., king of the city of "Salem," meaning "peace"). The author also skillfully exploited the silence of the OT and noted that Melchizedek had "neither beginning of days nor end of life" because the Genesis narrative where he is introduced mentioned neither his birth nor his death.

C. Drawing Near to God (7:4–10:25) In the prominent central section of the letter, the author developed (1) the arguments for Christ's high priesthood (7:4–28); (2) the accomplishment of Jesus' priesthood (8:1–10:18); and (3) the proper response to Jesus' priesthood (10:19–25).

Hebrews 7:4–10 establishes the greatness of Melchizedek's priesthood over the sons of Aaron, for three reasons. First, the sons of Aaron collected tithes from their brothers, but Melchizedek blessed Abraham—the possessor of the promise of God—proving that he was Abraham's superior. Second, the sons of Aaron died, but there is no mention of Melchizedek's death; thus, in a sense, he still lives. Third, Levi himself, while still in Abraham's loins, paid tithes to Melchizedek prior to Levi's birth.

Having established the superiority of Melchizedek, the author moved on to the changing of the priesthood—implying that the old covenant deals with Aaron, and the new with Melchizedek—and its superiority (7:11–19). He begins by asking the question, If perfection came through the law, why was there the need for another priest not of the Aaronic order? The answer is that there must be a change of law as well. Jesus became high priest not by a command of the law and physical descent—after all, he was from Judah—but based on the power of an indestructible life (a priest forever like Melchizedek).[36]

The words "not without an oath" (v. 20 NIV) (a litotes) emphasizes two important points (7:20–25): (1) Jesus' priesthood was confirmed by the oath of God; and (2) the Aaronic priesthood possessed no such oath. Because Jesus' priesthood was sworn by God as a permanent oath, it will never be taken away. This could not be said of the old Levitical order. The emphasis on the duration of the two sets of priests continues throughout this section. The Levites were prevented from being permanent priests through their own deaths, but not Jesus. The great benefit, of course, is that because Jesus lives forever, he is able to save forever those who come to him on account of his priesthood. Jesus is qualified to be believers' high priest in every way. He is "holy, innocent, undefiled, separated from sinners, and exalted above the heavens" (7:26); he offers a better sacrifice and serves for a better, eternal term.

Hebrews 8:1–6, the main assertion of the chapter, is supported by 8:7–13. In the former unit, the author highlighted the main point: Jesus is a superior high priest, serving in a superior (i.e., heavenly) tabernacle. Levitical priests only served in a faint copy of the heavenly tabernacle. The upshot is stated in 8:6: "But Jesus has now obtained a superior ministry, and to that degree He is the mediator of a better covenant, which has been legally enacted on better promises." At 8:7–13, the author provided scriptural support for his assertion, calling attention to the promise of the new covenant in Jer 31:31–34 and noting that the fault was not with the old covenant itself but with the old covenant community, that is, the people (8:8). Because people were unable to keep the old covenant, God promised a new covenant, indicating that the old covenant was about to disappear.

Hebrews 9:1–14 further explicates the assertions made in 8:1–6. In 9:1–10, the author described two main limitations of the old covenant. First, there were serious barricades

---

[36] Melchizedek actually drops off the scene at 7:17, having served the purpose of demonstrating that the OT made allowance for a priest not after Aaron's lineage.

separating the worshipper from God under the old covenant. The purpose of the separation of the holy place and the holy of holies was to show that the way to God's presence was not yet open (see 9:8). Thus the setup of the earthly tabernacle pointed forward to a new day. The second limitation of the old covenant was that no one was perfected by the sacrifices it required. Hence the old covenant was ultimately ineffective because the worshipper was required to repeat the same sacrifices year after year.

In 9:11–14 the contrast with the inefficacy of the old covenant is completed by showing the accomplishment of Christ in cleansing the believer. He entered the holy of holies in the more perfect tabernacle once for all, not once a year; offering his own blood, not representative animals; obtaining eternal redemption, not a temporary covering. The author then summed up his argument with an appeal from the lesser to the greater (animals versus Christ) to declare the actual cleansing of the people of God.

By his perfect sacrifice Jesus became the mediator of the new covenant (9:15–28). The reason Jesus had to die was rooted in the ancient Near Eastern practice (see Gen 15:1–18; Jer 34:18–20), where in permanent covenants animals representative of the two parties making the covenant were slain and divided between the parties establishing the agreement. The blood of the new covenant—the blood from the death of Jesus as believers' representative—ensured the permanent arrangement. As in the old covenant where the instruments of the tabernacle were cleansed by blood, so Jesus' blood effected cleansing for believers as they appeared in the heavenly tabernacle. Jesus' death was so powerful that it removed sins once for all, obtaining an eternal salvation. The next action of Jesus that believers awaited was the ultimate salvation to be effected at his (second) coming.

In 10:1–4 the author summarized his previous arguments. The old sacrifices made no one perfect; the very fact of annual sacrifices was a reminder of sin; and the blood of animals did not truly remove sin. In 10:5–10 the result was stated that these symbolic and repeated sacrifices were replaced by the all-sufficient sacrifice of Christ. The next paragraph pictured the futility of the old covenant after the advent of the new covenant was announced (10:11–14). The author pictured the Levitical priests perennially performing the obsolete offerings that could never permanently remove sins. The contrast was between the standing priests of the old order and the seated priest of the new order according to Melchizedek. Jesus completed the course of Ps 110:1–4 and was seated, awaiting the subjugation of all of his enemies. As Bruce stated, "A *seated* priest is the guarantee of a finished work and an accepted sacrifice."[37]

Finally, 10:15–18 refers again to the text of the new covenant. When God said, "I will never again remember their sins and lawless acts," this implied a completed payment for sins. There was thus no other offering for sin; the temple sacrifices achieved nothing, while Jesus' sacrifice accomplished everything that was necessary for salvation.

---

[37] Bruce, *Hebrews*, 239.

The capstone of the previous teaching is found in 10:19–25.[38] Three exhortations to the readers ("let us") mark this section as a thematic peak that both concludes this section and introduces the next section through the third exhortation. There are also several links back to the previous trio of exhortations (4:14–16). Because of what Jesus accomplished, there was no longer a series of boundaries between the believer and God since the veil had indeed been torn down. The proper response of believers is to draw near to God with confidence, knowing that their sins are forgiven; to hold on to their confession without wavering because God is faithful; and to exercise genuine care for other believers, spurring them on to love, good works, and faithful fellowship.

III. Jesus the One Who Ran the Race Before Us (10:19–13:16)

The dominant thought throughout this section is that believers are pilgrims in this life, looking forward to the life to come. Lane called this the concept of "committed pilgrimage."[39] The author began by describing the life of faith as a race.

A. Run the Race (10:19–11:40)   The entire passage is so tightly knit structurally that the discussion of "divisions" is problematic. Having given the thematic commands, the author suggested a course of action: move forward rather than drawing back. The declaration that a believer, by definition, does not draw back elicits the discussion of faith in chap. 11, which in turn is predicated on the encouragement to run the race with endurance.

The last exhortation, "And let us be concerned about one another in order to promote love and good works" (10:24), introduces the final section of the letter. It is dominated by an increased ratio of second person plural verbs ("you"), as the application of the sermon is now fully in view.[40]

The unit 10:26–39 is made up of two paragraphs: the first warns (10:26–31); the second encourages (10:32–39). Perhaps drawing on Num 15:27–31, this warning is probably the most urgent. The distinction between "unintentional" and "defiant" sins does not seem to be in view here but rather the rejection of Christ (in Num 15:30, the sinner "blasphemes the Lord"). The person who rejects Christ after hearing the gospel "has trampled on the Son of God, regarded as profane the blood of the covenant by which he was sanctified, and insulted the Spirit of grace" (10:29). The point is simply that if one rejects the sacrifice of Christ, no other sacrifice remains. The terrifying prospect is that of falling into the hands of the living, almighty God without having proper covering for one's sin.

The second paragraph (10:32–39) softens the blow with an encouragement to those who have not rejected Christ. The author called them to remember the former days when they were treated harshly but responded in joy, and he encouraged them not to throw away their confidence. Instead, they had need of endurance, which the author connected to faith (see chap. 11). Hence the writer did not put the majority of his readers in the

---

[38] See Westfall, *Discourse Analysis*, 235.

[39] See W. Lane, *Hebrews: A Call to Commitment* (Peabody, MA: Hendrickson, 1998), 162.

[40] See Westfall (*Discourse Analysis*, 242), who noted 14 pronouns, 26 finite verbs, and 18 imperatives; almost twice the number of the first two sections combined (30/58).

category of those who drew back: "But we are not those who draw back and are destroyed, but those who have faith and obtain life" (10:39).

Beginning with the definition of faith (11:1), the author recounted the faithful endurance of believers in the past in five movements.[41] The chapter includes an introduction (11:1–3); preliminary examples from the patriarchs to Abraham (11:4–12); a description of their pilgrim status (11:13–16); more examples from the patriarchs from Abraham forward (11:17–31); and finally the continuation of the faithful up to the time of the writer (11:32–40). The pivot seems to be Abraham, who is the prime example of the one who overcame "by faith" (a phrase used 18 times in this chapter). By faith, Abraham looked beyond the earthly to the heavenly city; all believers, like him, do the same.

The exhortation that flows from having such a "large cloud of witnesses" (12:1) is to follow their example and to run the race with endurance, looking to Jesus who also endured great suffering. Importantly, the kind of faith required of the readers was the exact same faith exhibited by OT believers, a powerful point to make if the recipients were Jewish Christians. Thus, the author argued that having the same faith Abraham had means to believe in Jesus, who had already come to make perfect atonement for sin. Reverting back to Judaism, therefore, is not a legitimate option because this would not only mean drawing back from Christ but also falling short of the type of faith displayed by Abraham. To be a true descendant of Abraham, subsequent to God's revelation "by His Son" (1:2), means to believe in Jesus.

B. The Course Set Before Us (12:1–40)   Hebrews 12:1–2 describes running the race set before believers. The rest of this major section describes running that race. This involves enduring the discipline of God in everyday life and making every effort to hold on to his grace. The author described the Christian life as a marathon (12:1–13) where one does not compete against the other runners but encourages them to run the race as well (the idea of the competition is resumed in 12:12–13). This paragraph describes the significance of, the purpose of, and the response to divine discipline.[42] The significance of discipline is that being subjected to such discipline proves that one is the child of God (12:4–10). The purpose of discipline is that, in due course, it yields the fruit of peace and righteousness (12:11). The proper response to the discipline of the Lord is to encourage one another to persevere and endure (12:12–13).

The final section of this unit contains three paragraphs. The first is made up of three commands pertaining to the stability of the community (12:14–17). The first command is to pursue peace and holiness (12:14). The second is to encourage others (12:15), realizing that falling short of the grace of God as a believer means not using the grace given by God to believers to pursue peace and holiness. Thus the resulting bitterness causes trouble and defiles many. The third one is to remember those who did not possess true faith, such

---

[41] See Guthrie, *Hebrews*, 373.
[42] Lane, *Call to Commitment*, 163.

as Esau, who was the antithesis of those who endured, having sold his birthright for one single meal.

The second paragraph in this section (12:18–24) builds on the previous one by giving the grounds for the exhortations found there: believers have not come to the Mount of Terror (Sinai) but to the Mount of Joy (Zion) where Jesus works in believers to accomplish his will. The final illustration is that Abel's blood cried out for vengeance, while Christ's blood cries out for grace. The third paragraph in this section (12:25–29) contains the last warning passage of the book. The warning is not to reject Christ, the one who speaks. In essence, since believers have received an unshakable kingdom, they must hold on to grace.

C. Go with Jesus Outside the Camp (13:1–16)   The first paragraph of this section (13:1–4) is an exhortation to remember brotherly love. This is spelled out as (1) remembering strangers; (2) remembering prisoners; and (3) remembering spouses (marital fidelity). The second paragraph (13:5–16) revolves around commands relating to matters of doctrine. The first command (13:5–6) urges believers to forsake the love of money. The second (13:7–8) encourages them to esteem their leaders and to imitate their lives because Jesus does not change. The third injunction (13:9–15) is to hold fast to correct doctrine. Finally, the author encourages believers to continue in good works (13:16).

IV. Conclusion (13:17–25)

The conclusion of the book makes two requests. First, the readers were enjoined to obey their leaders (13:17). Second, they were to pray for "us," whoever the intended beneficiaries of these requested prayers may be (13:18–19). Finally, the author ended with concluding exhortations and pieces of information (13:20–25), asking his readers to receive his "word of exhortation" (describing the nature and purpose of the work) and giving notice that Timothy was out of prison and was on his way to them. Final greetings and benediction close out the book.

THEOLOGY

Theological Themes

The Superiority of the Person and Work of Christ and His High Priesthood   The first major theme of the letter is the supremacy of the person and work of Christ. Christ is the eternal, preexistent Son of God, who created the world and was made human to provide atonement for his people, and then sat down in order to return at the end of time for judgment and salvation. The book opens with a series of contrasts demonstrating the superiority of Christ. Jesus is not merely a servant like the prophets; he is the unique Son of God. While God spoke in the past through various prophets, in these last days he spoke by His Son. As the maker of the universe, Christ is also its heir. The angels are merely ministering servants who worship the Son. Moses was a servant in God's house; Christ was the Son over the house.

On the basis of his uniqueness as a person, Christ also rendered a unique work, described in Hebrews against the larger backdrop of the high priesthood of Christ.[43] While this emphasis is virtually unparalleled in the NT, it does not represent an innovation by the author. To the contrary, the author's use of Ps 110:4 in his argument finds support in Jesus' own application of the figure mentioned in Ps 110:1 to himself (see Matt 22:41–45 and parallels). From this it was only a small step to conclude that the oath of God to this figure also pertained to Christ. Hence, Jesus is a priest forever like Melchizedek, as the author of Hebrews argued on the basis of the two major OT passages dealing with this priest-king (Gen 14:18–20; Ps 110:4). As a high priest, Jesus sat down at the right hand of God and lives forever to make intercession for his people.

Perseverance and Christian Assurance As the author desired to encourage believers to adhere to their confession and progress to maturity, it is necessary to address the very nature of salvation. A key component of his argument is to warn his hearers of the dangers of not heeding his call. The author accomplished this in alternating blocks of exposition and exhortation.[44] Within the exhortations of Hebrews are a group of passages (the warning passages) that sternly warn the hearers about the dangers of not heeding God's word.[45] These warnings are deemed so strong that they become a common thread in the age-old debate over the preservation of believers.[46] Most likely, the writer did not warn Christians about the possibility of apostasy but rather enjoined them to examine the condition of their faith and the repercussions of not moving on to maturity. Two critical considerations point in this direction.

First, the author affirmed the teaching of Jesus that, by definition, all true believers endure to the end (Matt 10:22 and parallel). The author stated: "For we have become companions of the Messiah if we hold firmly until the end the reality that we had at the start" (3:14). Hebrews 6:9 affirms that apostasy is not connected to salvation, that is, those who possess salvation are not those who fall away. The author asserted that Christ is able to save his own eternally because of his eternal intercession (7:25) and that believers are not among those who draw back to destruction but among those who believe resulting in the salvation of their soul (10:39). Clearly, the author of Hebrews affirmed the perseverance and eternal preservation of believers.

Second, the author acknowledged that some are related to Christ only superficially. He likened these kinds of people to the wilderness generation who rebelled (Numbers 13–14), noting that they heard the word but that this hearing did not meet with faith (4:2). In fact, the author described their actions in terms of rebellion (as does Psalm 95, which he quoted), and to be like these disobedient individuals is to have "an evil, unbelieving heart

---

[43] Nowhere else in the NT is there such a clear affirmation of the high priesthood of Christ.

[44] G. H. Guthrie, The *Structure of Hebrews: A Text-Linguistic Analysis* (New York: Brill, 1994; Grand Rapids: Baker, 1998).

[45] The five "warning passages" are 2:1–4; 3:7–4:13; 5:11–6:12; 10:19–39; and 12:14–29.

[46] See H. W. Bateman IV, gen. ed., *Four Views on the Warning Passages in Hebrews* (Grand Rapids: Kregel, 2006).

that departs from the living God" (3:12). Thus the author contrasted his hearers as falling either in the category of those who perished in the wilderness or under the rubric of those who believed and were allowed to enter God's rest, namely Joshua and Caleb. The all-important contrast, then, is between those who trusted in God and his promise and those who were connected to God only nominally, those who in truth resembled a fruitless field good only for being burnt (6:8).

POINTS OF APPLICATION

- Realize that faith in Christ is necessary for salvation (2:3)
- Heed the warnings against drifting or falling away from the faith (6:1–8)
- Be inspired by the heroes of faith who have run the race before you (chap. 11)
- As you run the Christian race, lay aside all sin and keep your eyes on Jesus (12:1–2)
- Accept God's loving, fatherly discipline (12:3–13)

STUDY QUESTIONS

1. What is the evidence against the Pauline authorship of Hebrews?
2. What do we know about the author?
3. What seems to be the latest possible date for Hebrews, and why?
4. What are the likely destination and audience of Hebrews?
5. What is the purpose of Hebrews?
6. Why were the early church fathers in the West slow to receive Hebrews into the canon?

FOR FURTHER STUDY

Bateman, Herbert W., IV, gen. ed. *Four Views on the Warning Passages in Hebrews.* Grand Rapids: Kregel, 2006.

Bruce, F. F. *The Epistle to the Hebrews.* New International Commentary on the New Testament. Rev. ed. Grand Rapids: Eerdmans, 1990.

Ellingworth, P. *The Epistle to the Hebrews.* New International Greek New Testament Commentary. Grand Rapids: Eerdmans, 1993.

France, R. T. "Hebrews." Pages 17–195 in *The Expositor's Bible Commentary.* Rev. ed. Vol. 13: *Hebrews-Revelation.* Grand Rapids: Zondervan, 2005.

Guthrie, G. *Hebrews.* NIV Application Commentary. Grand Rapids: Zondervan, 1998.

Hagner, D. A. *Encountering the Book of Hebrews: An Exposition.* Encountering Biblical Studies. Grand Rapids: Baker, 2002.

_____. *Hebrews.* New International Biblical Commentary. Peabody: Hendrickson, 1990.

Hughes, P. E. *A Commentary on the Epistle to the Hebrews.* Grand Rapids: Eerdmans, 1977.

Johnson, L. T. *Hebrews: A Commentary.* New Testament Library. Louisville: Westminster John Knox, 2006.

Lane, W. *Hebrews.* Word Biblical Commentary 47A-B. 2 vols. Dallas: Word, 1991.

_____. *Hebrews: A Call to Commitment.* Peabody, MA: Hendrickson, 1998.

Lindars, B. *The Theology of the Letter to the Hebrews.* New Testament Theology. Cambridge: University Press, 1991.

Trotter, A. H., Jr. *Interpreting the Epistle to the Hebrews.* Guides to New Testament Exegesis. Grand Rapids: Baker, 1997.

Chapter 17

The Letter of James

CORE KNOWLEDGE

Students should know the key facts of the book of James. With regard to history, students should be able to identify the book's author, date, provenance, destination, and purpose. With regard to literature, they should be able to provide a basic outline of the book and identify core elements of the book's content found in the unit-by-unit discussion. With regard to theology, students should be able to identify the major theological themes in the book of James.

KEY FACTS	
Author:	James, son of Joseph, half brother of Jesus
Date:	c. 45
Provenance:	Jerusalem?
Destination:	Diaspora Jewish Christians outside Jerusalem
Occasion:	A circular letter to believers who had fled Jerusalem because of Agrippa's persecution
Purpose:	To exhort Jewish Christians to live their Christian lives in keeping with wisdom, to act on their faith, and not to show preferential treatment to the rich
Theme:	Faith that works
Key Verses:	2:21–22

CONTRIBUTION TO THE CANON

- An exemplar of early Jewish Christianity written by James, the half brother of Jesus (1:1)

309

- The relationship between faith and works (2:14–26)
- The need for wisdom in the Christian life (1:5; 3:13–18)
- Practical exhortations related to dealing with the rich (1:9–11; 2:1–13; 5:1–6), controlling one's tongue (3:1–12), humility in planning (4:13–17), and other matters
- The abiding examples of OT men of faith such as Job or Elijah (5:11,17)

INTRODUCTION

SOME SCHOLARS, SUCH as Martin Luther, have seen little value in the book of James and have sought to relegate it to the margins of Scripture. But James does make an important contribution to the NT canon. Augmenting Paul's doctrine of justification by grace alone through faith alone, James insists that faith, if genuine, inevitably results in good works or it is not true faith at all. This sounds a warning against an undue focus on right belief (orthodoxy) at the expense of right praxis (orthopraxy), which must go together. This point, it should be noted, is not original with James; rather, it originated with Jesus himself (Matt 7:21).

With its scarcity of references to Jesus and the absence of references to the Holy Spirit, James fits somewhat uneasily in the NT canon. In essence, James represents an early form of Jewish Christianity that is firmly grounded in the soil of a Jewish wisdom ethic while having embraced Jesus as Messiah. This shows that even for Christians there is considerable value in the wisdom teaching of the OT. Indeed, Christianity shares considerable ground with Judaism. While the Jewishness of James's Christianity may make some readers uncomfortable, they should be careful not to distort James's teaching by conforming him to other NT books that are addressed to a Gentile audience.

Since the late 1990s, James has become a popular figure as an object of historical research, much of which has come in response to an amateur archaeologist's claim to have found his ossuary in Jerusalem.[1] While the academy has often found James to be controversial, many regular students of Scripture have found comfort in the book. James's ethical admonitions render the letter as applicable today as it was when it was first written. In this sense, Luther's remark that the book of James is "a right strawy epistle" (i.e., a lightweight epistle, one made of straw) is a right strawy statement itself.

---

[1] E.g., P.-A. Bernheim, *James Brother of Jesus*, trans. J. Bowden (London: SCM, 1997); J. Painter, *Just James: The Brother of Jesus in History and Tradition* (Columbia: University of South Carolina Press, 1997); R. Eisenman, *James the Brother of Jesus: The Key to Unlocking the Secrets of Early Christianity and the Dead Sea Scrolls* (New York: Viking, 1997); B. Chilton and C. A. Evans, eds., *James the Just and Christian Origins* (Leiden: Brill, 1999); B. Chilton and J. Neusner, eds., *The Brother of Jesus: James the Just and His Mission* (Louisville: Westminster John Knox, 2001); and H. Shanks and B. Witherington III, *The Brother of Jesus: The Dramatic Story and Meaning of the First Archaeological Link to Jesus and His Family* (New York: HarperCollins, 2003).

HISTORY

Author

The book of James, from a modern reader's perspective, begins with a trip through language and time. It claims to be from a certain *Iakōbus*, Greek for the Hebrew *Ia'acov* (Jacob), translated into English as "James."[2] Although the name was extremely common,[3] and several figures in the NT carry the name "James," it is virtually certain that the "James" referred to at 1:1 is the half brother of the Lord.[4] The question debated by scholars is not which James is mentioned but whether the letter could actually be from James the Just, the half brother of Jesus.

The following evidence supports the view that James was the author—James the half brother of Jesus, or "James the Just," as he came to be identified by the early church. First, the reference to "James, a slave of God and of the Lord Jesus Christ" at the beginning of the letter (1:1) suggests that this James was a person with considerable name recognition and equally great authority. Otherwise, it would have been necessary for the author to provide additional information and distinguishing characteristics about himself. James the Just, as the leader of the church in Jerusalem, fits both of these descriptions unlike any other person by that name in the first century. For another James to be so important but quickly to fade into obscurity is highly unlikely.

Second, despite claims to the contrary, the writer showed some evidence of being a Palestinian Jew. He mentioned "early and late rains" (5:7), which was demonstrably a weather phenomenon in Palestine. More significantly, the author's language is immersed in the OT Scriptures.[5]

Third, there are striking verbal similarities to Acts 15. "Greetings" occurs in Jas 1:1 and Acts 15:23 (and elsewhere in Acts only in 23:16). Strikingly, Acts 15:23 is part of the Jerusalem decree, in which James had a leading role. In both Jas 2:7 and Acts 15:17, believers are called by God's name. The exhortation for the "brothers" "to hear" occurs in Jas 2:5 and Acts 15:13. Uncommon words are found in both James and Acts in conjunction with James: "to inspect" in Jas 1:27; Acts 15:14; "to turn" in Jas 5:19; Acts 15:19; and "to keep oneself" in Jas 1:27; Acts 15:29. While not constituting conclusive proof, these linguistic parallels corroborate James's authorship.

---

[2] Often the first question asked by American students is, "How do we get 'James' from *Ia'acov*?" The answer requires a long trek through both translations and geopolitical entities. Suffice it to say that the name *Ia'acov* becomes *Iacomus* in Latin, *Giacomo* in Italian, *Gemmes* or *Jaimmes* in French, and "James" in English as a result of the Norman conquest at the battle of Hastings in 1066.

[3] According to R. Bauckham (*Jesus and the Eyewitnesses: The Gospels as Eyewitness Testimony* [Grand Rapids: Eerdmans, 2006], 85) the name "Jacob" ranked as the eleventh most popular male name among Palestinian Jews from 330 BC to AD 200.

[4] L. T. Johnson, *The Letter of James*, AB 37A (New York: Doubleday, 1995), 93.

[5] Although James only quoted the OT explicitly in five verses (1:11; 2:8,11,23; 4:6), indirect allusions abound (cf., e.g., 1:10; 2:21,23,25; 3:9; 4:6; 5:2,11,17,18).

Table 17.1: The Teachings of Jesus in James

Teaching	James	Gospels
Joy in testing	1:2	Matt 5:11–12; Luke 6:23
The call to perfection/maturity	1:4	Matt 5:48
Asking and receiving	1:5,17; 4:2–3	Matt 7:7–11; Luke 11:9–13
Endurance and salvation	1:12	Matt 10:22; 24:13
Anger and righteousness	1:20	Matt 5:22 (with v. 20)
Doers of the Word	1:22–23	Matt 7:24,26
The poor inherit God's kingdom	2:5	Matt 5:3,5; Luke 6:20
Law of liberty/neighbor's love	2:10–12	Matt 22:36–40; Luke 10:25–28
Merciless are judged	2:13	Matt 7:1
Practical care of the poor	2:14–16	Matt 25:34–35
The fruit of good works	3:12	Matt 7:16–18; Luke 6:43–44
Warning of divided loyalties	4:4	Matt 6:24; 16:13
Purity of heart	4:8	Matt 5:8
Humility and exaltation	4:10	Matt 23:12; Luke 14:11; 18:14
The dangers of wealth	5:1–3	Matt 6:19–21; Luke 12:33–34
The prophet's example	5:10	Matt 5:11–12; Luke 6:23
Oaths forbidden	5:12	Matt 5:33–37
Restoring a sinner	5:19–20	Matt 18:15

Finally, the man reflected in the letter comports well with James the half brother of Jesus as he is portrayed in the rest of the NT. This James is identified as the leader of the Jerusalem church and viewed as the guarantor of a Jewish expression of Christianity (Acts 12:17; 21:18–25; Gal 1:19).

For these reasons recent years have witnessed a trend among scholars to recognize that the internal evidence from the letter is not incompatible with James's authorship. Even many scholars who are otherwise critical of traditional views now see this letter as indeed from James the Just.[6] Without compelling evidence to the contrary, the best understanding of the author is in fact that the author of the book of James is James the son of Joseph, the half brother of the Lord Jesus.

Date

Given the absence of conventional indications of time such as references to specific individuals, places, or events, the letter is rather difficult to date. J. A. T. Robinson noted a wide spectrum of suggested dates offered in the scholarly literature, anywhere from 50 to 150.[7] If the above discussion of authorship is correct, the book was written during the lifetime of James the Just, that is, sometime before c. 62 or 63 (Josephus, *Ant.* 20.200).[8] On the other end of the spectrum, the letter must have been written subsequent to James's conversion (see 1 Cor 15:7), that is, no earlier than approximately 33. This provides a range of possible dates spanning about 30 years.

To narrow the range yet further, the letter must have been written after James became the prominent leader in the Jerusalem church. This can be dated to around 41/42 (see Acts 12:17). Several factors suggest a date of composition subsequent to this time frame, such as that some economic difficulties suggested in the letter match the time of the famine in Palestine mentioned in Acts 11:28–30. Possibly, the recipients were dispersed because of the persecution of Herod Agrippa I mentioned in Acts 12:1–4 (c. 43). At the same time, the letter shows an acquaintance with the teaching of Jesus that does not seem to be a result of mere literary knowledge, which suggests that the letter was most likely written prior to the canonical Gospels (and thus prior to the mid-50s).[9] This narrows the most likely date of composition to between 42 and the mid-50s.

In addition, the letter does not seem to address any of the issues that arose subsequent to 48/49. There is no discussion or even acknowledgement of the question of Gentile inclusion in the church (e.g., Acts 11:1–18) or the controversy spawned by the Judaizers (e.g., Acts 15:5; Gal 2:11–13), much less the resolution of these issues at the Jerusalem Council in the year 49 (Acts 15:1–21). Thus it seems that the letter was most likely written prior to the Jerusalem Council and thus prior to Paul's letters and perhaps even prior

---

[6] Johnson, *James*, 108–21; R. Bauckham, *James: Wisdom of James, Disciple of Jesus the Sage*, New Testament Readings (London: Rouledge, 1999), 11–25; id., *Jude and the Relatives of Jesus* (Edinburgh: T&T Clark, 1990), 128; M. Hengel, *Paulus und Jakobus*, WUNT 141 (Tübingen: Mohr Siebeck, 2002), 511–48; P. J. Hartin, *James*, SacPag 14 (Collegeville: Liturgical Press, 2003), 24–25; and T. C. Penner, *The Epistle of James and Eschatology: Re-Reading an Ancient Christian Letter* (Sheffield: Sheffield Academic Press, 1996), 35–103.

[7] J. A. T. Robinson, *Redating the New Testament* (London: SCM, 1976), 118–19.

[8] According to Josephus (*Ant.* 20.9.1), James's death occurred after the death of the procurator Porcius Festus and before his successor Lucceius Albinus took office. The Jewish high priest Ananus took advantage of the power vacuum and assembled the Sanhedrin. There, "a man named James, the brother of Jesus who was called the Christ," and certain others were accused of having transgressed the law and were delivered up to be stoned. Apparently, this offended some of the fair-minded, law-observant Jews who petitioned Albinus on the matter when he entered the province, and King Agrippa had Ananus replaced with Jesus, the son of Damnaeus, as high priest.

[9] See D. A. DeSilva, An *Introduction to the New Testament: Context, Methods & Ministry Formation* (Downers Grove: InterVarsity, 2004), 816.

to the Gentile mission.[10] The probable range during which the letter was written therefore spans from 42 until 49.[11]

Provenance

Those proposing a different author than James the Just have offered various locations for the source of the letter, including Rome. If our views of authorship, date, destination, and occasion are correct, then Jerusalem may be a possible place of writing, in particular since it is not known if James spent significant time outside Palestine during the early years of the church. It must be conceded that the provenance is not known, but fortunately little rests on this identification.

Destination

The letter is addressed to "the 12 tribes in the Dispersion" (1:1). Most understand these recipients to be Jewish Christians. The term "12 tribes," while elsewhere used figuratively of the people of God (see 1 Pet 1:1), in the present case most likely refers to a Jewish Christian audience. Several features point to a Jewish setting: (1) the reference to meeting in a synagogue (2:2 HCSB "meeting"); (2) the reference to "Abraham our father" (2:21); (3) the use of the OT in both direct quotations and allusions; (4) the letter's resemblance to Jewish wisdom literature; and (5) the prophetic tone.

This view is also confirmed by clear indications from the letter that the readers were expected to be familiar with conditions in Palestine. Johnson noted seven factors that point to this conclusion: (1) the effect of burning wind on vegetation (1:11); (2) proximity to a dangerous sea (1:6; 4:13); (3) salt and bitter springs (3:11); (4) agriculture featuring figs, olives, and grapes (3:12); (5) a specific Palestinian weather pattern, the early and latter rains (5:7); (6) daily workers deprived of pay (5:4); and (7) the use of the term *gehenna* (hell) in 3:6, a term found elsewhere in the NT only in the Gospels.[12]

But where are these Jewish believers? The term "Dispersion" (1:1) usually refers to Jews living outside Palestine (e.g., John 7:35), describing the people of God who were scattered due to divine judgment but who carried with them the hope of restoration (see 1 Pet 1:1,17; 2:11, with reference to believers in general). The fact that this is a letter demands a congregation at some distance from the author. Hence it is possible that the recipients were Jewish Christians somewhere in the area known as the Diaspora, perhaps in Syrian Antioch, possibly dispersed because of the persecution of Herod Agrippa I (Acts 12:1–4; c. AD 43), while the author may have been in Palestine.[13]

---

[10] E.g., in the book of James, the meeting place of Christians is still called a "synagogue" (2:2), which may indicate a time of writing prior to the launch of the Gentile mission.

[11] Robinson, *Redating*, 139.

[12] Johnson, *James*, 120–21.

[13] See Provenance above. Antioch is the tentative preference of A. Chester, "The Theology of James," in A. Chester and R. P. Martin, *The Theology of the Letters to James, Peter, and Jude*, New Testament Theology (Cambridge: Cambridge University Press, 1994), 13–15.

Occasion

The letter seems to address specific individuals (the 12 tribes) but not one specific situation. It is best to see James as a general letter (warranting its inclusion among the General Epistles in the NT canon) written to give pastoral advice to the recipients, whatever their specific circumstances. There were precedents for such a letter among Jews and early Christians (see Jeremiah 29; 2 Macc 1:1–9; Acts 15:23–29).

Given the likely date of the letter, there does seem to be a specific group and occasion that would fit the letter's contents. After the stoning of Stephen, the Jerusalem believers (quite a large number by this time) were scattered outside Jerusalem.[14] The injunctions in the letter seem appropriate for both wealthy and poor, and in particular portray wealthy landowners as oppressing poor laborers. Those displaced by persecution would certainly find themselves working essentially as migrant workers (though some might flourish). The encouragement to live out their lives fully committed to Christ's lordship would certainly be appropriate for such a group.

LITERATURE

Genre

Given the epistolary opening of the work, the intent for the letter to serve as a substitute for the writer's presence, and the document's hortatory nature, it is best to consider James a letter of some kind. While most consider James to be a letter, this category does not adequately describe it in every respect. While the book opens like a letter, no occasion behind the letter is discernible, no individuals are mentioned, and there is no epistolary ending (cf. Phil 4:10–23). The book is purposefully general and intended for a wide audience (the 12 tribes in the Dispersion).[15]

Literary Plan

There is little consensus on the structure of James. Opinions today vary from the minimalist to the maximalist end of the spectrum. Minimalists see no apparent literary structure in James,[16] while maximalists identify a discernible structure. Often this structure is identified as chiasm (an ABB´A´ pattern).[17]

The most likely proposal views James in terms of a more linear structure in which chapter 1 serves as an introduction of major themes but demurs from identifying a chiasm in it. Instead, the structure is viewed as reflecting three stages. First, following the introduction

---

[14] See Acts 11:19, where the verb used is *diaspeirō*, the verbal cognate of the noun used in Jas 1:1.

[15] Deissmann classified James as a literary letter, similar to other writings included in the General Epistles. See A. Deissmann, *Light from the Ancient East*, 2nd ed., trans. L. R. M. Strachan (London: Hodder & Stoughton, 1911), 235.

[16] Among these are M. Dibelius, *James: A Commentary on the Epistle of James*, trans. M. A. Williams, Hermeneia (Philadelphia: Fortress, 1976), 1–11; and S. Stowers, *Letter Writing in Greek Antiquity*, LEC 5 (Philadelphia: Westminster, 1986), 97.

[17] F. O. Francis, "Form and Function of the Opening and Closing Paragraphs of James and 1 John," *ZNW* 61 (1970): 118.

of major themes in chap. 1, the first major unit in the body of the letter (2:1–26) describes the nature of saving faith. Second, 3:1–4:10 contains an appeal to repentance in view of God's opposition to pride. Third, 4:11–5:11 constitutes an exhortation to patience and endurance in light of God's judgment. The book concludes without a formal epistolary closing.

OUTLINE

  I. OPENING (1:1)
  II. INTRODUCTION: THE PATH TO TRUE CHRISTIAN MATURITY (1:2–27)
      A. Introduction of Major Themes: Trials and Temptations (1:2–18)
      B. Obedience to the "Law of Liberty" as the Mark of True Piety (1:19–27)
  III. BODY: THE NATURE OF TRUE FAITH AND EXHORTATIONS TO REPENTANCE AND PATIENCE (2:1–5:11)
      A. Thesis: Genuine Faith Results in Works (2:1–26)
      B. Exhortation to Repentance in View of God's Opposition to Pride (3:1–4:10)
      C. Exhortation to Patience in View of God's Judgment (4:11–5:11)
  IV. CONCLUSION (5:12–20)
      A. The Matter of Oaths (5:12)
      B. Faithful Prayer (5:13–18)
      C. Rescue the Perishing (5:19–20)

UNIT-BY-UNIT DISCUSSION

I. Opening (1:1)

The writer introduced himself as "James, a slave of God and of the Lord Jesus Christ." As mentioned, this seems to indicate that the author was a well-known figure. If the author was Jesus' half brother, identifying himself as his slave and God's is an exceedingly humble self-identification. The letter is addressed to the 12 tribes in the Dispersion, which may refer to Jewish believers who had been scattered through the persecution of Herod Agrippa I in c. 43 (Acts 12:1–4).

II. Introduction: The Path to True Christian Maturity (1:2–27)

A. Introduction of Major Themes: Trials and Temptations (1:2–18)   James 1:2–12 is best understood as based on a play on the Greek word *peirasmos*, which, depending on the context, can mean either "trial" or "temptation." James first assured those experiencing "trials" that these serve to test and refine their faith (1:2–4). Asking for wisdom refers to wisdom needed in dealing with trying situations (1:5–8). James briefly digressed to deal with the rich and the poor (1:9–11), an issue to which he returns later (5:1–6). In verse 12 the word *peirasmos* occurs again, but the context makes clear that the meaning has now changed from "trials" to "temptations." James's major burden here is to exonerate God from any connection with this kind of *peirasmos* (see 1:2–4). God is not the source of temptation; instead, he is the giver of "every perfect gift . . . from above" (1:17). As will be shown later, this also includes "the wisdom from above" (3:17). The direct address "My dearly loved brothers" (1:16) introduces the transition to the next section, taking its point of departure from the trials/temptations of the previous unit and signaling the topic of the next section, true religion, by introducing its source: the election of God (1:18).

B. Obedience to the "Law of Liberty" as the Mark of True Piety (1:19–27) The direct address "My dearly loved brothers" (1:19; see 1:16) marks the beginning of the next section and introduces one of the major themes of the letter: true piety cannot be separated from obedience. James 1:19–20 states the general principle: "Everyone must be quick to hear, slow to speak, and slow to anger, for man's anger does not accomplish God's righteousness." Thus verse 21 draws the proper inference: believers are to rid themselves of all moral filth and evil excess and to receive humbly the "implanted word," which is able to save them.[18]

The thesis statement of this unit is in verse 22: "But be doers of the word and not hearers only, deceiving yourselves." A person who is a mere hearer of the word is compared to a man who briefly looks at a mirror and then forgets what he saw; he heard the word but forgot it. The section ends with a summary of the nature of "pure and undefiled religion" (1:26–27). Such piety involves controlling one's tongue (a subject developed more fully in 3:1–12) as well as helping orphans and widows and avoiding spiritual defilement by the world (see 4:1–5, esp. v. 4).

III. Body: The Nature of True Faith and Exhortations to Repentance and Patience (2:1–5:11)

The body of the letter consists of three major units. The first (2:1–26) sets forth James's thesis concerning the nature of true saving faith: it is the kind of faith that inexorably issues in specific works that give concrete evidence of this faith. This thesis is followed by two major exhortations that echo significant components of the thesis. Of these the first (3:1–4:10) is an exhortation to repentance and humility in light of the fact that all human pride sets itself in opposition to God. What follows (4:11–5:11) is an exhortation to patience and endurance in view of God's judgment addressed to various groups of offenders.

A. Thesis: Genuine Faith Results in Works (2:1–26) The general thrust of 2:1–26 is the nature of true saving faith. In essence, the first two paragraphs insist that true faith does not distinguish between people in the church based on their socioeconomic standing (2:1–13). It does not give preferential treatment to the wealthy in the church (2:1–7), since this represents a violation of the commands of God (2:8–13) and exposes those who do so as lawbreakers. This leads to James's second major point that true faith is shown by believers' actions rather than their mere words (2:14–26).

The topic of faith is introduced in 2:1 by way of a warning against showing favoritism in the church. Those who are partial toward the wealthy have become "judges with

---

[18] "Word" is the "hook word," occurring in both 1:21 and 22, which connects 1:19–21 with 1:22–27.

evil thoughts" (2:4), and, even more disturbingly, they are acting contrary to God's own actions, who has not chosen the rich in this world but the poor (2:5). Moreover, partiality exposes people as lawbreakers because they do not love their neighbors as themselves. Thus they fail to fulfill their obligations toward others stipulated in the law (2:8–13; see Lev 19:18).

Hence James insists that faith is useless without accompanying works, just as telling a hungry and ill-clothed man to "keep warm, and eat well" is inadequate (2:15–17). Faith without works is dead, and works are a natural outflow of faith. James substantiates this dual thesis with three illustrations. The first is negative: even the demons believe in God, but they shudder (2:19). The reader is left to draw the obvious inference in this case: the "faith" of the demons is not accompanied by works, and hence their bare confession is insufficient.

The second and third illustrations are positive: Abraham was justified by his willingness to offer Isaac on the altar (2:21; see Genesis 22; cf. the citation of Gen 15:6 in v. 23), as was Rahab the prostitute (2:25; see Joshua 2; cf. the commendation of Rahab's faith in Heb 11:31). Each of these three illustrations concludes with a declaration reiterating the basic premise: faith without works is useless (v. 20); faith is the partner of works (v. 24); and faith is dead apart from works (v. 26).

B. Exhortation to Repentance in View of God's Opposition to Pride (3:1–4:10)
Although 3:1–12 may be a self-contained essay on the tongue, the connection between the teacher (3:1) and the sage (3:13) seems to provide cohesion with the surrounding contexts. By contrast, the section on the tongue ends with completely negative results (see esp. 3:8: "no man can tame the tongue"), while wisdom from above has positive results (see 3:17–18). James then affirmed the central truth that authentic faith results in good works since it flows out of God's work in the believer's life.

The warning about desiring to be a teacher is predicated on the dangers of the tongue (see 1:26). Although very small, the tongue can accomplish great things, illustrated by the bit of a horse, the rudder of a ship, and a spark that starts a forest fire (3:3–5). Regarding the latter, the human tongue "sets the course of life on fire, and is set on fire by hell" (3:6). The untamed tongue may inconsistently bless the Lord and curse a fellow human being. Just as a spring cannot produce both fresh and salt water, or a fig tree olives, or a grapevine figs, the untamed tongue cannot be expected to produce any fruit contrary to its own nature; "it is a restless evil, full of deadly poison" (3:8). Thus James, echoing the teachings of Jesus (Matt 7:16–20; 12:33–37), made clear that a person's speech exposes the contents of his heart.

In contrast to the untamed tongue, wise and understanding church members are to be marked by good conduct and the gentleness of wisdom (3:13). The worldly wise person is characterized by bitter envy and ambition that is willing to boast and lie in promoting what James called "truth" (3:14). James identified the source of such worldly "wisdom" as demonic. By contrast, "the wisdom from above is first pure, then peace-loving, gentle, submissive, full of mercy and good fruits, without favoritism and hypocrisy" (3:17).[19] James affirmed that the end result of this "wisdom from above" is peace (3:17–18).

The call to humility in 4:1–10 flows directly from the section on wisdom in 3:1–18. Thus, in 3:1–4:10 James established the need for a humble, God-centered ministry, and offered an appeal to repentance. If the "wisdom from above" produces people who are peace-loving, gentle, submissive, full of mercy and good fruits, and without partiality, one might ask, "What is the source of disputes among believers?" The answer is that dissension stems from a sinful human heart. Covetousness (4:2), selfishness (4:3), and worldliness (4:4) place us in a hostile position toward God. But the good news is that while God resists the proud, he gives grace to the humble (4:6). The final three verses of this section constitute a call to repentance, urging people to abandon pride and arrogance and to humble themselves before God.

C. Exhortation to Patience in View of God's Judgment (4:11–5:11) This final major section of James features three examples of arrogance—slanderers, arrogant merchants, and wealthy landowners exploiting the poor—and issues a stern warning to each of these groups. Like the previous section, the present unit concludes with an exhortation—in the present case, to patience and endurance in a sinful world—based on the exposure of sinful behavior (5:7–11). In essence, this constitutes a call for believers to approach the world by faith.

Taking the discussion into a new direction by the vocative "brothers," James warned against slandering one's neighbor (4:11–12). Those who act as judges and criticize the law are guilty of the ultimate arrogance. The next warning is introduced by the address "come now." Merchants presume upon the grace of God by making great plans without submitting them to the will of God. Again James rebuked these people for their arrogance and presumption (4:16–17).

Finally, James described wealthy landowners who, while amassing a large number of possessions on earth, have heaped up a storehouse of condemnation for themselves. Speaking in end-time terms, moths ate those people's expensive clothes, and their gold and silver rusted. By gaining riches in an unrighteous manner, those wealthy landowners "fattened [their] hearts in a day of slaughter" (5:5 NASB). By this sharp denunciation, James took the stance of an OT prophet, which leads naturally into his commendation of the prophets in his ensuing call to repentance.

Closely related to the previous section by the conjunction "therefore," 5:7–11 represents an exhortation for believers to display patience and endurance. The examples of both the prophets and Job are models for Christians who live in the hostile world around them. The prophets were patient, Job endured, and both received great blessings from God (5:11). Rather than seeking to beat the world at its own game or playing by its rules,

---

[19] HCSB slightly altered. The rendering "submissive" (NIV) is preferable to "compliant" (HCSB).

believers must commit themselves and all their ways to him and look to him to give them grace. If they are arrogant, they will be judged like the world.

IV. Conclusion (5:12–20)

In staccato fashion, James concluded the letter with a series of short commands. This is marked off by the very prominent vocative, "Now above all, my brothers." There is no proper epistolary ending (cf. Heb 13:20–25).

A. The Matter of Oaths (5:12)   Rather than making pledges or vows, whether by heaven or by earth, the believer's "yes" or "no" should suffice. Like other pronouncements, this statement echoes Jesus' teaching (see Matt 5:33–37).

B. Faithful Prayer (5:13–18)   Connected, perhaps, to the previous verse by addressing situations that might lead one to make an oath, 5:13–18 cites specific scenarios involving prayer. Specifically, a call to prayer is issued to the suffering, cheerful, and sick. The teachings in 5:14–16 do not have exact NT parallels, calling for the elders of the church to come and anoint a sick member of the church and enjoining believers to confess their sins and to pray for one another. This passage led to the Roman Catholic sacraments of confession and the "last unction"—a person's anointing with oil on his deathbed. By contrast, both teachings are widely ignored in evangelical churches today. In keeping with the Jewish character of the book, the biblical example cited for persistent prayer is the OT prophet Elijah. Believers today likewise are called to fervent, righteous prayer.

C. Rescue the Perishing (5:19–20)   James concluded his letter with an exhortation for believers to rescue straying sinners, resulting in salvation. The phrase "cover a multitude of sins" in verse 20 closely resembles 1 Pet 4:8, which echoes Prov 10:12. Most likely, James's point is that such a rescue operation is prompted by love. Here the letter comes to a rather abrupt halt. The customary closing features for a letter (such as greetings, benediction, etc.) are absent. It is unclear what accounts for this departure from the standard format for ancient letters.

THEOLOGY

Theological Themes

The Relationship Between Faith and Works   James 2:14–26 is often interpreted as a repudiation of Paul's doctrine of salvation through faith alone (see Rom 3:28; Gal 2:15–16; Eph 2:8–9). Three views have appeared in the scholarly literature: (1) James disagreed with Paul and was seeking to correct him (or vice versa).[20] (2) James corrected a misunderstanding of Paul.[21] (3) James and Paul addressed two related but distinct issues.

At the very outset, the caution seems appropriate not to involve James and Paul in a necessary contradiction. Whether James sought to address Paul's teaching in the present context will never be known with certainty. The doctrine of justification by faith is found

---

[20] See Hengel, *Paulus und Jakobus*, 526–29.
[21] See J. H. Ropes, *St. James*, ICC (Edinburgh: T&T Clark, 1916), 204–6.

elsewhere in the NT and is not limited to Paul (e.g., Heb 11:7; 1 Pet 1:3–7). Paul's own contention was that the Jerusalem apostles had heard his gospel and offered him the right hand of fellowship—James included (Gal 2:9).

Taken on his own merits, James contrasted the passing with the concrete. The former does not affect the world, while the latter does. Thus a needy brother who is offered only an encouraging word has encountered the ephemeral. But one who has his needs met has encountered the concrete; the former is helpful, while the latter is not. Likewise, faith apart from works is like the ephemeral word—it accomplishes nothing and fails to produce authentic salvation.

In this sense Abraham was "justified by his works."[22] In the same way, people today show their faith by their works.[23] Most likely, therefore, James and Paul do not stand in actual conflict with one another in their teaching on the relationship between faith and works.

Table 17.2: Faith and Works: Comparing James and Paul

Doctrine	James	Paul
Faith is necessary for salvation.	2:18	Eph 2:8–9
Faith without works is not saving faith.	2:17,24	1 Cor 15:2
Saving faith is accompanied by works.	2:24	Rom 3:31; Eph 2:8–10

The person James describes is all too familiar. That person claims to have faith, and to an extent he believes all the right things about God, Jesus, and salvation. But his faith is not lived out in his daily life. It is this kind of faith that James condemns; faith without works is useless. It neither sanctifies nor saves. Saving faith—or, as James put it, faith accompanied by works—is "faith that works" in that it radically affects the way a person lives.

Wisdom and Ethics Apart from his treatment of faith and works, James is perhaps best known for his strong ethical teaching in keeping with Jewish wisdom. James's entire letter is pervaded by an emphasis on the need to deal with practical aspects of the Christian life in a godly and wise manner. This includes dealing with trials and temptations (1:2–18); helping those in need, such as widows and orphans, as an expression of a practical form of Christianity that refuses to divorce faith from works (1:19–27; see 2:14–26); avoiding preferential treatment to those of a higher socioeconomic status in society (2:1–13); controlling one's speech (3:1–12); cultivating wisdom and understanding in a

---

[22] In another sense, of course, it was Abraham's faith that was credited to him as righteousness; see Gen 15:6, cited in Jas 2:23; Gal 3:6; and Rom 4:3, in likely chronological order of writing.

[23] In 2:24 James did not say that a man is justified by works and not by faith—he added by faith *alone* (i.e., without works).

variety of good works (3:13–18); adopting an attitude of humility in one's dealings with others and in the way one goes about one's business (4:1–17); and many other practical, ethical matters (chap. 5).

James's ethical teaching is firmly grounded in the teaching of Jesus, especially the Sermon on the Mount. James is also deeply embedded in the ethical teachings of the OT, especially in wisdom literature and here particularly in Proverbs (e.g., 4:4 citing Prov 3:34). This shows the significant continuity in ethical thought between the OT, Jesus, and the NT (such as the book of James). Christians are believers in Jesus, the "glorious Lord Jesus Christ" (2:1), and they do not leave behind the ethical and moral grounding of biblical revelation in the Hebrew Scriptures. Instead, they continue to engage in conduct consistent with wise living, justice, humility, love, and mercy. This is summed up memorably in the well-known words of the prophet Micah: "He has told you . . . what is good and what it is the LORD requires of you . . . to act justly, to love faithfulness, and to walk humbly with your God" (Mic 6:8).[24]

POINTS OF APPLICATION

- Consider it great joy when you face various trials, knowing that the testing of your faith produces endurance (1:2–3; I know that's possible only by the grace of God!)
- Ask God for wisdom, especially in trying situations (1:5–7)
- In the church, don't give preferential treatment to those who are well off (1:9–11; 5:1–6)
- Don't forget what you learned in your study of God's Word—do what it says (1:22–25)
- While we are saved by faith, faith must be accompanied by works (2:14–26)

STUDY QUESTIONS

1. Which James was the author of the book of James, and which other two persons named James are less likely candidates?
2. Between what two dates was James likely written, and why?
3. Where was James most likely written and to whom?
4. What is the likely occasion for James?
5. What is the genre of James?
6. In what ways do Paul and James agree on faith and works?

---

[24] For a fuller discussion of James's ethical teaching, including aspects such as speech control, the rich and the poor, testing and suffering, and love, mercy, and humility, see Chester, "Theology of James," 16–45.

FOR FURTHER STUDY

Bauckham, R. *James: Wisdom of James, Disciple of Jesus the Sage.* New Testament Readings. New York/London: Routledge, 1999.

_____. *Jude and the Relatives of Jesus in the Early Church.* Edinburgh: T&T Clark, 1990.

Chilton, B., and C. A. Evans, eds. *James the Just and Christian Origins.* Novum Testamentum Supplement 98. Leiden: Brill, 1999.

Davids, P. H. *The Epistle of James: A Commentary on the Greek Text.* New International Greek Testament Commentary. Grand Rapids: Eerdmans, 1982.

Guthrie, G. H. "James." Pages 197–273 in *The Expositor's Bible Commentary.* Rev. ed. Vol. 13: *Hebrews-Revelation.* Grand Rapids: Zondervan, 2005.

Johnson, L. T. *The Letter of James.* Anchor Bible 37A. New York: Doubleday, 1995.

Martin, R. P. *James.* Word Biblical Commentary 48. Waco: Word, 1988.

Moo, D. J. *The Letter of James.* Pillar New Testament Commentary. Grand Rapids: Eerdmans, 2000.

_____. *The Letter of James.* Tyndale New Testament Commentary. Grand Rapids: Eerdmans, 1985.

Richardson, K. *James.* New American Commentary. Nashville: B&H, 1997.

Chapter 18

The Petrine Epistles (1–2 Peter) and the Letter of Jude

CORE KNOWLEDGE

Students should know the key facts of 1 and 2 Peter and Jude. With regard to history, students should be able to identify each book's author, date, provenance, destination, and purpose. With regard to literature, they should be able to provide a basic outline of each book and identify core elements of the book's content found in the unit-by-unit discussion. With regard to theology, students should be able to identify the major theological themes in the Petrine Epistles and the book of Jude.

1–2 Peter

KEY FACTS	
Author:	Simon Peter
Date:	c. 62–63, 65
Provenance:	Rome
Destination:	Christians in Northern Asia Minor
Occasion:	Persecution of the church (1 Peter) and false teaching (2 Peter)
Purpose:	Encourage these Christians to stay the course (1 Peter) and to combat the false teaching (2 Peter)
Theme:	Christians living in a hostile world (1 Peter) and the dangers of false teachers (2 Peter)
Key Verses:	1 Pet 3:15–17; 2 Pet 3:17–18

CONTRIBUTION TO THE CANON

- Believers as "temporary residents" in this world (1 Pet 1:1,17; 2:11)
- The continuity between OT Israel and the Christian church (1 Pet 2:1–10)
- The importance of submission to authorities (1 Pet 2:13–3:7)
- The importance of Christlike suffering (1 Pet 2:21–25; 3:13–18)
- The need to cultivate godliness and Christian virtues (2 Pet 1:3–11)
- The divine inspiration of the prophetic Scriptures (2 Pet 1:21)
- The need for perseverance and watchfulness in view of Jesus' return (2 Pet 3:1–13)
- The need to contend for the faith once for all delivered to the saints (Jude 3)

INTRODUCTION

FIRST PETER HAS long been recognized as one of the high points of NT literature and theology. Martin Luther recognized 1 Peter (along with the Gospel of John and Paul's letters) as "the true kernel and marrow of all the NT Books. For in them you . . . find depicted in masterly fashion how faith in Christ overcomes sin, death, and hell, and gives life, righteousness, and salvation."[1] This view changed as commentators in the nineteenth century and twentieth century saw the author as a Paulinist. Thanks to the work of J. H. Elliott, more modern scholars are rejecting this idea, and 1 Peter has been rehabilitated in recent years as a dependable source of Christian theology.

Second Peter is not so fortunate. In modern circles, the book's theological contribution is often diminished. J. D. G. Dunn complained that 2 Peter contains "a somewhat hollow 'orthodoxy'" by a man "who has lost all hope of an immediate parousia."[2] The most extreme example may be E. Käsemann, who considered the letter to be of "a stiff and stereotyped character" and alleged that its parts had been assembled by "embarrassment rather than force," representing an early Catholicism in the second century.[3] However, much of this low esteem for 2 Peter comes from a misapprehension of the style of the letter and from the assumption of a late and pseudonymous origin, according to which the book was written by someone other than Peter and attributed to him for some reason.[4] Understood properly, however, the contents of 2 Peter indicate that the book is worthy

---

[1] M. Luther, *Prefaces to the New Testament*, 1522, cited by J. H. Elliott, "Peter, First Epistle of," *ABD* 5:270.

[2] J. D. G. Dunn, *Unity and Diversity in the New Testament: An Inquiry into the Character of Earliest Christianity*, 2nd ed. (Valley Forge: Trinity Press International, 1990), 350.

[3] E. Käsemann, "An Apologia for Primitive Christian Eschatology," in *Essays on New Testament Themes*, SBT 41 (London: SCM, 1964), 191, 194.

[4] On the phenomenon of pseudonymity see T. L. Wilder, *Pseudonymity, the New Testament, and Deception: An Inquiry into Intention and Reception* (Lanham: University Press of America, 2004); and A. J. Köstenberger, "1 Timothy," in *The Expositor's Bible Commentary*, rev. ed. (Grand Rapids: Zondervan, 2006), 492–94 and the sources cited there. See also D. A. Carson and D. J. Moo, *An Introduction to the New Testament*, 2nd ed. (Grand Rapids: Zondervan, 2005), 337–50; D. Guthrie, *New Testament Introduction*, 2nd ed. (Downers Grove: InterVarsity, 1990), 607–49; and E. E. Ellis, "Pseudonymity and Canonicity of New Testament Documents," in *Worship, Theology and Ministry in the Early Church*, ed. M. J. Wilkins and T. Paige, JSNTSup 87 (Sheffield: Sheffield Academic Press, 1992), 212–24.

of the canonical status it achieved by the force of its arguments, in spite of initial doubts regarding its authenticity.

1 PETER

HISTORY

Author

External Evidence   The early tradition of the church was thoroughly acquainted with 1 Peter and attributed authorship of the book to the apostle Peter in an impressive way. The first clear evidence for the knowledge of the letter comes from 2 Peter; the author there said that "this is now the second letter I've written you" (2 Pet 3:1). Few would claim that he is not referring to the first letter.[5] There have been attempts to show dependence on 1 Peter in other first-century documents such as *1 Clement* (c. 96) and the *Didache* (second half of first or early second century), but the evidence is inconclusive.[6] Polycarp—a resident of Asia Minor, which was the destination of 1 Peter—showed knowledge of 1 Peter in his letter to the Philippians (c. 108).[7] According to Eusebius (c. 260–340), both Papias (c. 60–130) and Clement of Alexandria (c. 150–215) affirmed that Peter wrote this book (cited in Eusebius, *Eccl. Hist.* 2.15; 3.1.2, 39).

The first extant citation naming Peter as the author comes from Irenaeus (c. 130–200). He not only named Peter as the author but also referred to 1 Peter often (Eusebius, *Eccl. Hist.* 4.9.2; 16.5; 5.7.2). Both Clement of Alexandria and Tertullian (c. 160–225) cited 1 Peter and attributed the verses to the apostle.[8] Eusebius listed 1 Peter as the only "undisputed" book of all the General Epistles.[9] The letter is not listed in the Muratorian Canon (later second century?); however, the manuscript is fragmentary and incomplete for all the General Epistles (Eusebius, *Eccl. Hist.* 3.3.25). Thus Peter's authorship of the letter is well attested in the early church tradition. Bigg stated regarding 1 Peter, "There is no book in the New Testament which has earlier, better, or stronger attestation."[10]

Internal Evidence   Internally, the portrait of the writer is quite reserved and not characteristic of a pseudepigrapher.[11] The author drew an apparent contrast with his readers, noting that they have not seen Christ, likely implying that he had seen him (1:8). He also claimed to be a "witness of the sufferings of Christ" (5:1). Again, one notes the uncharacteristic reserve with which the author staked this claim to first-hand testimony.

---

[5] J. R. Michaels, *1 Peter*, WBC 49 (Waco: Word, 1988), xxxii.

[6] T. R. Schreiner, *1, 2 Peter, Jude*, NAC 37 (Nashville: B&H, 2003), 22.

[7] E.g., *Phil.* 1:3; 2:1–2; 6:3; 7:2; 8:1–2; 10:2–3.

[8] See *Scorpiace* 12 and 14, as well as *Orat.* 20.

[9] Eusebius, *Eccl. Hist.* 3.3.25.

[10] C. Bigg, *A Critical and Exegetical Commentary on the Epistles of St. Peter and St. Jude*, ICC (Edinburgh: T&T Clark, 1901), 7.

[11] See especially T. L. Wilder, *Pseudonymity, the New Testament, and Deception*; Guthrie, "Appendix C: Epistolary Pseudepigraphy," in *New Testament Introduction*, 1011–28.

Because there is no undisputed sample of Peter's speech and writing, little linguistic evidence exists to analyze the letter(s). But there does seem to be some internal evidence that point to the apostle Peter as the author of 1 Peter. For example, R. Gundry believed there is an almost unconscious "Petrine pattern" in the letter. In 1958, Selwyn listed 30 allusions to the words of Jesus in 1 Peter, calling these the *verba Christi* ("words of Christ").[12] Many of them occur in contexts in the Gospels associated with Peter.[13] Moreover, there are clear affinities to the speeches of Peter in Acts.[14] In addition, Acts 5:29 ("Peter and the other apostles"), Acts 10:39 ("Peter"), and 1 Pet 2:24 employ the phrase "upon a tree" (*epi xylou*) to describe the cross of Christ (as Paul did obliquely in Gal 3:13, citing Deut 21:23).

The book of 1 Peter includes no references to Gnosticism (flowering only in the second century), no depreciation of the state, no glowing honors given to Peter, "and none of the developed apparatus of pseudonymity."[15] Thus, there are no substantial grounds to resort to pseudepigraphy. Conversely, what is known of Peter does fit the letter, and the confidence of the early church—which is especially noteworthy since there were hosts of pseudepigraphical writings that claimed Peter as the author—should be given full weight.[16] Thus Robinson rightly affirmed Peter's authorship of 1 Peter, noting that "whatever the intention, [pseudepigraphy] in this case [is] a particularly motiveless exercise which in fact (unlike II Peter) deceived everyone until the 19th century."[17]

Date

The date of the letter and its authorship are tightly intertwined. Scholars who reject Peter's authorship usually posit a date in the reign of Domitian (81–96).[18] As shown above, the arguments for a late date are neither necessary nor convincing. Since the letter was composed during Peter's lifetime, the question arises concerning its exact date of composition.

There are some indications of an early date regardless of authorship. Many point to a primitive theological expression that includes the Suffering Servant of Isaiah 53, the expectation of Jesus' imminent return, and undeveloped trinitarian formulation.[19] Any

---

[12] E. G. Selwyn, *The First Epistle of St. Peter* (London: Macmillan, 1955), 23–24.

[13] R. Gundry, "*Verba Christi* in 1 Peter: Their Implications Concerning the Authorship of 1 Peter and the Authenticity of the Gospel Tradition," *NTS* 13 (1966–67): 336–50; cf. id., "Further *Verba* on *Verba Christi* in First Peter," *Bib* 55 (1974): 211–32.

[14] E.g., Acts 2:23 and 1 Pet 1:2,20; 2:4,5; Acts 2:33 and 1 Pet 1:12; 3:22; 4:1; Acts 2:36 and 1 Pet 1:11; 3:14; 4:12; Acts 2:38 and 1 Pet 3:22; and Acts 10:42 and 1 Pet 4:2.

[15] I. H. Marshall, *1 Peter*, NTC (Downers Grove: InterVarsity, 1991), 24.

[16] J. A. T. Robinson, *Redating the New Testament* (Philadelphia: Westminster, 1976), 164; cf. Marshall, *1 Peter*, 21 (no foe of pseudepigraphy), who rightly stated of 1 Peter, "If ever there was a weak case for pseudonymity, surely it is in respect to this letter."

[17] Robinson, *Redating*, 164.

[18] State-sponsored persecution of Christians is only attested for the reigns of Nero, Domitian, and Trajan. Robinson (*Redating*, 155–56) noted that Domitian was chosen as a compromise for those who could tolerate neither Nero nor Trajan.

[19] See Robinson (*Redating*, 162–63), who also named J. N. D. Kelly, *A Commentary on the Epistles of Peter and of Jude*, Harper's New Testament Commentaries (New York: Harper & Row, 1969), 30; F. L. Cross, *1 Peter: A Paschal Liturgy* (London: A. R. Mowbray, 1954), 43–44; and C. F. D. Moule, "The Nature and Purpose of I Peter," *NTS* 3 (1956–57): 11.

assessment of date should also include the reference to elders at 1 Pet 5:1 as the office of oversight in the church. At the time of Ignatius (c. 35–110), a monarchial episcopate had rapidly taken hold, which also suggests an early date because there is no mention of a two-tiered pastoral office in 1 Peter as was characteristic of the second-century church.

The best indicator as to the date of the letter, given Peter's authorship, is the reference to Rome at 1 Pet 5:13. Most agree that "Babylon" refers to Rome. If so, Peter most likely was in Rome in the mid- to late 60s. The letter gives no hint that there is ongoing persecution, by the state or otherwise, in the environment of the author. This indicates a date prior to the persecution of Nero, which began in approximately 64. Most likely, 1 Peter was written slightly before then, around 62–63, when the harbingers of this persecution were already on the horizon.[20]

Provenance

First Peter specifically mentions "Babylon" in 5:13 as the place from which the letter was sent. Three options arise from this description. First, the location could be Mesopotamian Babylon. However, at this time the city was all but deserted.[21] Second, there was a Babylon in Egypt, but it was an insignificant military outpost, and there is no evidence of any Christian mission there until much later.[22] The third and best option is Rome. In this case, the term is metaphorical, designating the center of Gentile power. Even most of those who do not hold to Peter's authorship and espouse a later date still consider Rome to be the geographical source of 1 Peter.[23]

Destination

First Peter 1:1 identifies where the recipients of the letter lived, which was northern Asia Minor (modern Turkey). Peter listed a series of Roman provinces in an unusual order, "to the temporary residents of the Dispersion in the provinces of Pontus, Galatia, Cappadocia, Asia, and Bithynia" (1:1). This would include a crescent-shaped region of northern Asia Minor.[24]

The more difficult question is, "Who were the recipients of the letter?" Some interpreters claimed that the original readers were Jewish converts, primarily on the basis of Peter's opening address, "To the temporary residents of the Dispersion" (1:1).[25] More likely, however, the reference is metaphorical (see the passages describing the readers' previous lifestyle in 1:18; 4:3).

---

[20] For a more detailed discussion of persecution in 1 Peter, see Schreiner, *1, 2 Peter and Jude*, 28–31.

[21] See P. J. Achtemeier, *1 Peter*, Hermeneia (Philadelphia: Fortress, 1996), 353. Strabo (c. AD 19) noted that the city "is so deserted that one would not hesitate to say . . . 'the Great City is a great desert'" (*Geog.* 16.1.5).

[22] W. A. Grudem, *The First Epistle of Peter*, TNTC (Grand Rapids: Eerdmans, 1997), 33.

[23] See J. H. Elliott, "Peter, First Epistle of," *ABD* 5:277.

[24] R. E. Brown, *An Introduction to the New Testament*, ABRL (New York: Doubleday, 1997), 708.

[25] So Augustine, Jerome, and Calvin.

Occasion

Persecution is a common theme in 1 Peter and serves as the occasion for the writing of this letter. While Peter may have been anticipating the persecution of Nero in Rome, his readers were most likely already experiencing private persecution or some localized state persecution. They suffered from various trials (1:6); endured grief from suffering unjustly (2:19); were accused and their Christian life denounced (3:16); were slandered (4:4); suffered fiery ordeals (4:12); shared in the sufferings of the Messiah (4:13); were ridiculed for the name of Christ (4:14); and suffered according to God's will (4:19). But they were not (yet) being executed as criminals.

Purpose

Persecution was not an abstract notion for the believers in Asia Minor; they were undergoing fierce repercussions for their faith. Peter encouraged believers to endure in the face of difficult times. He did this by promoting a biblical worldview among the believers. They needed to understand who (or whose) they were and then face their situation from this vantage point. The essence of this exhortation is in 1:5–6, "[You] are being protected by God's power through faith for a salvation that is ready to be revealed in the last time. You rejoice in this, though now for a short time you have had to be distressed by various trials."

LITERATURE

Literary Plan

Remarkably, there is virtual unanimity regarding the structure of 1 Peter in the recent scholarly literature.[26] The literary plan of 1 Peter is marked by the presence of the direct address, "dear friends," in 2:11 and 4:11, which divides the letter into three parts: 1:1–2:10; 2:11–4:11; and 4:12–5:14; 1:1–2 constitutes the opening greeting and 5:12–14 the final greeting and benediction. The major topic of the first part is believers' identity as God's chosen people due to their salvation through Christ and their rebirth by the Holy Spirit. The address in 2:11 shifts the focus from believers' identity to their consequent responsibility as "aliens and strangers" in a world hostile to Christ, which involves proper submission to authorities in the spheres of government, the workplace, and the home. The address in 4:12 (following a doxology in 4:11) introduces an appeal to submission in yet another context, the church.

Peter addressed "temporary residents" in parts of the "Diaspora" (1:1–2). The letter opens with a thanksgiving to God for his spiritual blessings bestowed on the recipients (1:3–12), followed by an exhortation to holy conduct (note esp. the quote of Lev 11:44–45;

---

[26] See the virtually identical outlines in Michaels, *1 Peter*, xxxiv–xxxvii; K. H. Jobes, *1 Peter*, BECNT (Grand Rapids: Baker, 2005), vii, 56–57; P. H. Davids, The *First Epistle of Peter*, NICNT (Grand Rapids: Eerdmans, 2006), 28–29; and Schreiner, *1, 2 Peter, Jude*, 46–48. Grudem (*1 Peter*, 44–46) saw no major break in 4:12 and divided the letter into two major units, 1:1–2:10 and 2:11–5:14. Marshall (*1 Peter*, 28) has a major break at 3:13 rather than 4:12. For a discussion and critique of alternative proposals, see Schreiner, *1, 2 Peter, Jude*, 47–48.

19:2; 20:7 in 1:16). In keeping with this continuity with OT Israel, Peter elaborated on the similarity of identity between Israel and the recipients, many of whom would have been Gentile believers, in a series of OT references applied to the readers (2:4–10).

A new section begins in 2:11 with a renewed address to the readers as "aliens and temporary residents" (see 1:1,17). In the form of a modified "house table" or "household code," Peter urged his readers to engage in proper submission to those in positions of authority, whether in government (2:13–17), the workplace (2:18–25), or the home (3:1–7). The remainder of this section contains exhortations to righteous suffering in the context of persecution in light of the fact that "the end of all things is near" (4:7; see 3:8–4:11).

Another new section begins in 4:12 with a similar address as in 2:11. Peter's readers must not be surprised "when the fiery ordeal arises among you to test you." Also in this section are further instructions on proper submission to those in authority, in the present case to the elders of the church (5:1–7), and on resisting the devil. Peter included a doxology (5:8–11) and a brief conclusion (5:12–14). The latter acknowledges the help of Silvanus in writing (or delivering) the letter; refers to "Babylon" (i.e., Rome) as the provenance of the letter, and to (John) Mark who was with Peter at this time; and contains a final greeting.

OUTLINE

I. OPENING (1:1–2)

II. THE STATUS OF THE PEOPLE OF GOD (1:3–2:10)
   A. Their Precious Standing (1:3–12)
   B. The Ethics of Their New Life (1:13–25)
   C. The Growth of Their New Life (2:1–10)

III. THE RESPONSIBILITIES OF THE PEOPLE OF GOD (2:11–4:11)
   A. The Conduct of the People of God (2:11–3:12)
   B. The Promise of Vindication (3:13–4:6)
   C. The Nearness of the End (4:7–11)

IV. THE RESPONSIBILITY OF THE CHURCH AND THE ELDERS (4:12–5:11)
   A. Response to the Fiery Ordeal (4:12–19)
   B. Relationships in the Church (5:1–11)

V. CONCLUSION (5:12–14)

UNIT-BY-UNIT DISCUSSION

I. Opening (1:1–2)

Peter identified himself as "an apostle of Jesus Christ," and he addressed the recipients of the letter as "temporary residents of the Dispersion" in different provinces (1:1) and as "set apart by the Spirit for obedience and for the sprinkling with the blood of Jesus Christ" (1:2). Thus the readers' identity is clarified both with regard to the world and to God.

II. The Status of the People of God (1:3–2:10)

The first major section of the body of the letter lays the foundation for the remainder of the letter by addressing the identity of believers as the result of their salvation in Christ and their rebirth by the Holy Spirit.

A. Their Precious Standing (1:3–12)   Peter wanted believers to appreciate fully their standing before God (1:3–12). They had joy because their salvation was protected, even though they endured trials now (1:3–6). Peter noted that this was the proof of genuine faith, which was more precious even than gold (1:7–9). Peter concluded the section by explaining that this salvation put his readers in a unique position that the prophets had predicted and had searched diligently to understand (1:10–12). Peter thus underscored the continuity of these NT believers with the people of God in the OT.

B. The Ethics of Their New Life (1:13–25)   Peter highlighted the appropriate response to believers' new identity in Christ (1:13–25). First, they were to be holy because God was holy, setting their hope on Christ's return (1:13–16). Second, they were to conduct themselves in reverence to God (1:17) because they had been redeemed from their previous empty way of life at a great price (1:17–21). Finally, they were to love one another earnestly, having joined the family of God through the new birth, knowing that their human existence was transitory (1:22–25; see Isa 40:6–8).

C. The Growth of Their New Life (2:1–10)   Similar to Paul's terminology of "putting off" and "putting on" (e.g., Col 3:8), Peter enjoined believers, after putting aside all wickedness,[27] to desire eagerly the "pure milk" of the word of God that will help them grow in their new life of faith (2:1–3; see Ps 34:8). While elsewhere in the NT believers' need of "milk" is used as an illustration of their immaturity and need for growth in Christ (1 Cor 3:1–3; Heb 5:12–14), in the present passage babies' craving for milk furnishes a positive example of believers' hunger and thirst for the nourishing qualities of God's word and as a necessary precondition for "tasting" the goodness of God (see the quotation of Ps 34:8 in 1 Pet 2:3).

Peter developed this in terms of the corporate life of the church (2:4–10). In doing so, he strung together a series of OT passages about Jesus Christ that include a reference to a "stone."[28] This Christ was the stone that the builders rejected but that had now become the cornerstone in God's new "temple," the community of believers (2:6; see Isa 28:16; cf. further below). While he turned out to be a stumbling stone for many (2:7–8; see Ps 118:22;

---

[27] The phrase in 2:1 rendered as a command, "rid yourselves," actually denotes the prerequisite action to the main command found in 2:2, "desire." Specifically enumerated are those sins that would destroy fellowship with other believers—the antithesis to the previous imperative (see Jobes, *1 Peter*, 131).

[28] See D. A. Carson, "1 Peter," in *Commentary on the New Testament Use of the Old Testament*, ed. G. K. Beale and D. A. Carson (Grand Rapids: Baker, 2007), 1023–33; and N. Hillyer, "Rock-Stone Imagery in 1 Peter," *TynBul* 22 (1971): 58–81. The word "stone" occurs in 2:4,5,6,7,8. Peter here engaged in a rabbinic practice known as "pearl-stringing," connecting a series of references on a similar topic (also known as *gezerah shawah*). Characteristically, Peter first paraphrased a given reference and then quoted it.

Isa 8:14), believers were an elect, holy, and priestly nation, God's possession, called to offer spiritual sacrifices to God (2:9–10; see Exod 19:5–6; Deut 4:20; 7:6; Isa 43:21).

Moreover, one important aspect of these "stone" references is Peter's reapplication of "temple" imagery, presenting Christ as the foundation of the new spiritual temple and believers as "living stones" (1 Pet 2:5) in that temple. This is accomplished by (1) the phrase "draw near" in 2:4 (see Ps 34:5, LXX), which is used in the LXX with reference to the Israelites "drawing near" to the OT sanctuary (e.g., Exod 12:48; 16:9; Lev 9:7–8; 10:4–5); (2) the use of "house" (*oikos*) in 2:5 (e.g., 1 Kgs 5:5; Isa 56:7; see Matt 12:4; 21:13; Mark 2:26; Luke 11:51; John 2:16); and (3) the references to "priesthood" and "sacrifices" in 2:5, all of which hark back to OT terminology regarding the temple.[29]

III. The Responsibilities of the People of God (2:11–4:11)

In this section of the letter, there is an overriding concern for the witness of the people of God. First, they are to conduct their lives in a respectable and God-honoring fashion (2:11–3:12). As temporary residents (2:11–12), they must submit to the world's government (2:13–17) and submit to masters, even unreasonable ones, following Christ's example (2:18–25); wives should submit even to unbelieving husbands (3:1–7); and thus all must be willing to suffer for doing what is right (3:8–12). Second, believers are encouraged that vindication will come in due course (3:13–4:6). Peter discussed the witness of believers (3:13–17); provided a kind of excursus on the witness of Christ (3:18–22; see 2:21–25); and issued a call to Christlike suffering (4:1–6). Third, Peter impressed on the recipients the urgency of proper Christian conduct in the midst of suffering in light of the nearness of the end (4:7–11).

A. The Conduct of the People of God (2:11–3:12)   First Peter 2:11–3:12 begins the so-called "household codes" in the book. The dual general command to these "aliens and temporary residents" is found in 2:11–12: "Abstain from fleshly desires that war against you" and "Conduct yourselves honorably among the Gentiles." This is developed in the passages that follow in terms of their need to submit to "every human institution because of the Lord" (2:13). Believers are to submit to human authorities (2:13–15, reiterated in 2:16–17). After this Peter turned to specific groups of individuals, starting with household servants (2:18). These are called to follow Christ's example in suffering and look to him as the shepherd and guardian of their souls (2:18–25).

Wives, even those of unbelieving spouses, are enjoined to submit to their husbands (3:1–6). They should adorn themselves with Christ, Sarah being the prime example. Husbands must treat their wives "with understanding of their weaker nature" (v. 7) (*kata gnōsin hōs asthenesterō skeuei*; lit. "according to knowledge as to [their wives being] a weaker vessel"), avoiding harsh treatment (see Col 3:19), and as "co-heirs of the grace of life" in Christ, so that their prayers will not be hindered (3:7).[30] The command to husbands

---

[29] See the discussion in Jobes, *1 Peter*, 144–52.

[30] For helpful discussions, see Schreiner, *1, 2 Peter, Jude*, 158–61; Michaels, *1 Peter*, 167–71.

balances Peter's previous commands to wives, making clear that the call to wives to submit to their husbands is in no way a license for the latter to treat their wives in a dominating, oppressive, or abusive manner.

This section concludes with a summary injunction to be like-minded and not to return evil for evil. Instead, in keeping with Jesus' own words, believers ought to bless those who persecute them (see Matt 5:10–11) and thus inherit a blessing, for "the face of the Lord is against those who do evil" (3:10–12; see Ps 34:12–16). This summary smoothly transitions to the next topic, the Lord's vindication of those who suffer for doing what is right.

B. *The Promise of Vindication (3:13–4:6)* The next section is introduced by a rhetorical question: "And who will harm you if you are passionate for what is good?" (3:13). Peter was concerned that persecuted Christians be bold witnesses while maintaining full integrity, "so that when you are accused, those who denounce your Christian life will be put to shame" (3:16b). The example is none other than Christ himself, who suffered while being righteous and was vindicated by God in the end. After proclaiming his victory to the fallen angels (3:19–20), he was enthroned in heaven, vindicated in the life to come (3:22), as will be believers. Thus the Christian is to have the same resolve (4:1), knowing that God will call those who persecute him to account (4:5) and give life to believers in the spiritual realm (4:6).

C. *The Nearness of the End (4:7–11)* Peter desired to impress on his recipients the urgency of the call to righteous suffering in light of the nearness of the end, that is, Christ's return and God's judgment. To this end he concluded the unit with an appeal to personal holiness and sincere love for one another. Believers are to express their care for others by exercising hospitality and by using their gifts to speak or to serve in the church (4:10–11). The point is that believers ought to glorify God through Jesus Christ in all things.

IV. The Responsibility of the Church and the Elders (4:12–5:11)

Peter concluded with instructions to those in the church, including church leaders. His final instruction to the church is to trust God while living for him, especially if one is suffering "as a Christian" (4:12–19; see esp. v. 16).[31] The elders of the church should lead humbly and by example (5:1–4), while the younger men should submit to the elders (5:5). All should exercise humility toward one another and humble themselves under God's mighty hand as they await God's vindication (5:6–7), and all should resist the devil and bear up under suffering (5:8–11).

A. *Response to the Fiery Ordeal (4:12–19)* In a solemn exhortation Peter warned believers to expect increased persecution.[32] As they share in the sufferings of the Messiah,

---

[31] The term "Christian," while extremely common today, is found only two other times in the NT. In Acts 11:26 Luke stated that the disciples were first called "Christians" in Antioch (c. 43/44). In Acts 26:28 King Agrippa used the term "Christian" (c. 58/59). Other names for Christians at the time of the early church were followers of "the Way" (Acts 9:2; 24:14) or of "the name" (i.e., God/Christ; see Acts 2:21; 4:12; Rom 10:13; Phil 2:9–10; Heb 1:4; see 1 Pet 4:16).

[32] The expression "fiery ordeal" in 4:12 refers most likely to the refinement and purification that persecution brings with regard to believers' character and confession of Christ (see 1:6–7; see Ps 66:10; Mal 3:1–4). For a helpful discussion

their response should be joy, not despair, realizing that their suffering is evidence of salvation and divine blessing. At the same time, believers should be careful not to suffer because of their own stubborn sinfulness. Peter also struck the ominous note that judgment begins with the house of God, arguing from the greater to the lesser that if judgment begins with the church and it barely escapes (citing Prov 11:31), what will the fate of sinners be? For this reason believers should entrust themselves to God, their "faithful Creator" (4:19).

B. Relationships in the Church (5:1–11)   The final section breaks down into three parts: (1) instructions pertaining to elders (5:1–7); (2) a call to alertness regarding, and resistance against, the devil (5:8–9); and (3) a final benediction to encourage those who suffer for Christ's sake (5:10–11). Peter instructed his fellow elders as an eyewitness of Christ's sufferings to shepherd the flock.[33] He employed three sets of contrasts to describe pastoral ministry: (1) not out of compulsion, but freely; (2) not for the money, but eagerly; (3) not in an authoritarian manner, but as an example (5:2–3). Those who lead in such a way will receive a great reward (5:4). Peter instructed the younger men to be subject to the elders (5:5) and all to be humble toward one another (5:6–7) and to resist the devil (5:8–9). He closed in a benediction (as he began; see 1:2) that focuses on the sovereignty of God and his promise to strengthen and restore suffering believers (5:10–11).

V. Conclusion (5:12–14)

The conclusion of the letter identifies the likely letter carrier, Silvanus, and refers to the content of the letter as a brief exhortation to "take [a] stand in" the true grace of God (5:12). Peter also sent greetings from the church in Rome ("Babylon") and issued a wish for peace in the life of those who are in Christ (5:14).

THEOLOGY

Theological Themes

Christian Suffering and the End Time   One of the major emphases and theological achievements of 1 Peter is the pervasive reference to believers' suffering in the context of the end time and in particular the second coming of Christ. From the very outset, Peter noted that believers are but "temporary residents" in this world (1:1). He reminded these suffering believers of their "living hope through the resurrection of Jesus Christ from the dead" (1:3; see 1:13,20–21) and their "inheritance that is imperishable, uncorrupted, and unfading, kept in heaven" for them (1:4), noting that their full salvation "is ready to be revealed in the last time" (1:5).

---

and further bibliographic references, see Schreiner (*1, 2 Peter, Jude*, 219–20), citing D. E. Johnson, "Fire in God's House: Imagery from Malachi 3 in Peter's Theology of Suffering (1 Peter 4:12–19)," *JETS* 29 (1986): 287–89.

[33] Interestingly, in 1 Pet 5:1 Peter referred to himself as a "witness to the sufferings of the Messiah"; in 2 Pet 1:16 he called himself one of the "eyewitnesses of His [majesty]" at the transfiguration "when He received honor and glory from God the Father" (2 Pet 1:17).

These references to eternal realities serve to put believers' sufferings into their proper context. They are to rejoice in their expectation of these soon-to-be-realized expectations, "though now for a short time" they may face the distress of various trials, which then refines their faith and makes it more valuable than gold, resulting "in praise, glory, and honor at the revelation of Jesus Christ" (1:6–7). This preamble provides an eschatological framework for believers in their sufferings that, if heeded, will render their ordeal more bearable and instill in them joy that transcends their temporary afflictions and circumstances in the hostile world around them.

In all this, Christ serves as the believer's example. After enduring great hostility from sinners as the Suffering Servant referred to in Isaiah (2:21–25), Jesus now "has gone into heaven [and] is at God's right hand, with angels, authorities, and powers subjected to Him" (3:22). On the basis of Christ's example, Peter issued the following powerful exhortation to his readers: "Therefore, since Christ suffered in the flesh, arm yourselves also with the same resolve—because the one who suffered in the flesh has finished with sin—in order to live the remaining time in the flesh no longer for human desires, but for God's will" (4:1–2).

In light of the fact that "the end of all things is near" (4:7), believers are to be clear-headed and disciplined for the purpose of prayer, to love one another, to exercise hospitality, and to exercise their spiritual gifts for the glory of God in Christ (4:7–11). Peter identified himself as a fellow "participant in the glory about to be revealed" (5:1) and spoke of his expectation of the day "when the chief Shepherd appears" and he and his readers "will receive the unfading crown of glory" (5:4). The closing benediction brings the book to a fitting end: "Now the God of all grace, who called you to His eternal glory in Christ Jesus, will personally restore, establish, strengthen, and support you after you have suffered a little. To Him be the dominion forever. Amen" (5:10–11).

The Identity of Believers and Their Witness to the World The identity of believers and their witness to the world are thoroughly intertwined in Peter's presentation. His description of the status of believers is twofold: first, he described NT believers in terms reminiscent of OT Israel, stressing the continuity of the NT church with the OT people of God; second, he emphasized the fact that believers are pilgrims and temporary residents in this world. Regarding the first aspect, Peter wrote, "But you are a chosen race, a royal priesthood, a holy nation, a people for His possession, so that you may proclaim the praises of the One who called you out of darkness into His marvelous light" (2:9). All these designations have OT antecedents.

Second, Peter addressed the letter to "the temporary residents of the Dispersion" (1:1) and called on them to conduct themselves in reverence "during this time of temporary residence" (1:17), urging them "as aliens and temporary residents to abstain from fleshly desires that war against you" (2:11). Because they are the people of God who are called to be holy in serving a holy God and because their stay in this world is merely temporary, believers ought to be good citizens of this world without compromising their purity or integrity.

Believers' status as the redeemed people of God brings with it certain expectations as to what it means to be the people of God. As obedient children, they are to be holy because God is holy (1:12–13). They are to conduct themselves honorably in the world, engaging in good works, which also involves submission to every human institution. They must be good citizens (2:13–17), fulfill their roles within the family (3:1–7), humbly love one another (3:8), and be willing to suffer for righteousness's sake (4:16), casting every care upon God (5:6–7) while resisting the devil (5:9).

Table 18.1: Submission to Authorities in 1 Peter

1 Peter	Authority to Be in Submission to	Other OT and NT References
2:13	Government authorities (instituted by God)	Rom 13:1,5; Titus 3:1
2:18	Authorities in workplace (even cruel ones)	Titus 2:9; see Eph 6:5–9
3:1	Husbands (even unbelieving ones)	Eph 5:21,24; Col 3:18; Titus 2:5
3:5	Example: Sarah and holy women in OT	Gen 18:12
3:22	Spirit world subjected to Jesus Christ	1 Cor 15:27–28; Eph 1:22; Phil 3:21
5:5	Younger men [and others] subject to elders	1 Cor 16:16; see Heb 13:17

With regard to believers' witness to the world, Peter was concerned that his readers not capitulate to the pressure of society to conform to its mores and norms. At the same time he wanted believers not to antagonize civic authorities, including the emperor, unnecessarily. Instead, they were to silence those who slandered them by being good citizens. Peter explained it this way: "Honor everyone. Love the brotherhood. Fear God. Honor the Emperor" (2:17). Peter did not want his readers to withdraw from the world but to engage it in an active witness. Instead, he told Christians to "set apart the Messiah as Lord in your hearts, and always be ready to give a defense to anyone who asks you for a reason for the hope that is in you" (3:15).[34] This requires a particularly Christian understanding of God, believers' identity, the world, and the ultimate adversary, Satan.

2 PETER

HISTORY

Author

Today, 2 Peter is widely believed to be pseudonymous.[35] Even many of those who believe Peter wrote 1 Peter have difficulty with 2 Peter.[36] Unlike 1 Peter, this opinion is not

---

[34] See F. Thielman, *Theology of the New Testament: A Canonical and Synthetic Approach* (Grand Rapids: Zondervan, 2005), 571–72.

[35] Brown, *Introduction to the New Testament*, 767.

[36] E.g., Kelly, *Epistles of Peter and of Jude*, 33, 236.

entirely a recent phenomenon. While there is no record of an overt denial of the authenticity of 2 Peter in the early church, many noted the difficulties that others had with it. In modern times the letter is widely judged to be inauthentic for at least three reasons: (1) the external evidence for Petrine authorship is very slim; (2) stylistically, the letter is very different from 1 Peter; and (3) alleged historical and doctrinal problems.

External Evidence Of all the books in the NT, 2 Peter has the least external data concerning authorship. While citations *naming* Peter as the author of 2 Peter are rather late and while there were some doubts regarding its authenticity, however, there is good evidence that 2 Peter was widely considered authoritative, which in many cases may imply belief in Peter's authorship. Thus the external evidence points to an early document, widely believed to be from Peter.[37] Later on, a host of forgeries claiming to be from Peter began to circulate.[38] That 2 Peter was recognized as canonical in the end surely means that it stood out from the rest.[39] The external evidence is in no way incompatible with Peter's authorship.

Internal Evidence The stylistic differences between 1 Peter and 2 Peter constituted the major problem that caused doubt regarding Peter's authorship of 2 Peter in the early church. Moreover, 1 Peter is generally considered to reflect a more sophisticated Greek style than 2 Peter.[40] But these negative assessments do not take into account the different styles of Greek available at the time of writing.[41] What is more, in spite of these stylistic differences, there are many subtle correspondences between 1 and 2 Peter in both thought and vocabulary that are difficult to account for if a pseudepigrapher wrote the letter.[42] Since it is unlikely that these subtle coincidences in language are the result of conscious imitation, these parallels provide significant evidence to suggest the authenticity and Petrine authorship of 2 Peter.[43]

The options for Peter's authorship are that 2 Peter was produced by an unknown pseudepigrapher subsequent to Peter's lifetime (perhaps as Peter's "last testament") or that the letter was written by the apostle Peter, most likely shortly before his death. In light of the difficulties associated with the former argument; in light of the absence of compelling external or internal evidence against Peter's authorship; and in view of the above-noted

[37] See R. E. Picirilli, "Allusions to 2 Peter in the Apostolic Fathers," *JSNT* 33 (1988): 57–83. He concluded that many of the apostolic fathers knew, alluded to, and reflected upon 2 Peter. Picirilli also noted that these fathers did not typically mention Peter by name as the author but that they did identify Paul as the author of the letters commonly attributed to him.

[38] There existed a *Gospel of Peter; Preaching of Peter; Acts of Peter; Acts of Peter and the Twelve Apostles; Epistle of Peter to Philip; Coptic Apocalypse of Peter;* and an *Apocalypse of Peter.*

[39] M. J. Kruger, "The Authenticity of 2 Peter," *JETS* 42 (1999): 662.

[40] One writer went as far as to call 2 Peter "baboo Greek"; see E. A. Abbott, "On the Second Epistle of St. Peter. I. Had the Author Read Josephus? II. Had the Author Read St. Jude? III. Was the Author St. Peter?" *The Expositor* 2/3 (1882): 204–19.

[41] T. Callan, "The Style of the Second Letter of Peter," *Bib* 84 (2003): 202–24. Cf. D. F. Watson, *Invention, Arrangement, and Style: Rhetorical Criticism of Jude and 2 Peter*, SBLDS 104 (Atlanta: Scholars Press, 1988).

[42] E.g., in 2 Pet 1:1 the author referred to "Simeon Peter," a phrase that occurs elsewhere in the NT only in Acts 15:14 (there on the lips of James). For additional examples, see M. Green, *2 Peter Reconsidered* (London: Tyndale, 1960), 12–13.

[43] Kruger, "Authenticity," 661.

convincing connections between 1 and 2 Peter, the view that the apostle Peter wrote 2 Peter is preferable.[44]

Date

Few books are attributed to such diverse dates as 2 Peter. Those who find the arguments for pseudepigraphy compelling place 2 Peter as late as the mid-second century. If 2 Peter is from the apostle, then it must have been written late in his life. Since 2 Peter probably comes from the pen of the apostle, and in light of the reference to his impending death in 2 Pet 1:14–15, it should be placed near the end of the apostle's life. Church tradition holds that Peter died during the Neronian persecution (64–66; see *1 Clem.* 5.4). The best date for Peter's death is 65 or 66.[45] Thus the letter was most likely written just prior to Peter's martyrdom.

Provenance

Second Peter makes no mention of a place of origin, but if the discussions of the authorship and the likely date of composition of 2 Peter are correct, the most plausible place of writing is Rome. If 1 Peter is authentic and was written by Peter in Rome ("Babylon"; 1 Pet 5:13) in the early or mid-60s, and if 2 Peter is authentic and was written by Peter as well, it must have been penned a few years after 1 Peter and thus likely originated in the empire's capital as well. Some have tried to adjudicate the origins of the letter based on linguistic evidence, but these attempts are not convincing.[46] People can exhibit various types of linguistic traits in myriads of places, which renders determining a place of writing on the basis of linguistic use precarious.[47] Rome continues to be by far the best option for the provenance of the letter.

Destination

Unlike 1 Peter, the second letter does not mention its recipients. However, two clues help us to identify its destination. Since this was the second letter Peter had written to this audience (2 Pet 3:1), and since he showed knowledge of Paul's letters (2 Pet 3:15), it seems reasonable to infer that the destination of 2 Peter was the same as that of 1 Peter (see 1 Pet 1:1).

Moreover, the use of the Grand Asian style of the letter suggests that the author wrote to readers who would appreciate this style of writing. This would have been the case in the eastern part of the empire (but not the western), though not at the eastern end of the

---

[44] At the very least, humility would seem to require that interpreters recognize the limited evidence that is available to adjudicate the matter and that giving Petrine authorship the benefit of the doubt is the most reasonable option. See P. H. Davids, *The Letters of 2 Peter and Jude*, PNTC (Grand Rapids: Eerdmans, 2006), 129.

[45] See especially the thorough discussion in Robinson, *Redating*, 140–50.

[46] See R. Bauckham, *Jude, 2 Peter*, WBC 50 (Waco: Word, 1983) 135–38.

[47] Many who do not consider Peter to be the author of the letter still hold Rome to be the place of origin. A case in point is Bauckham (*Jude, 2 Peter*, 159), who concluded that the letter was written from Rome on the basis of close affinities to *1 and 2 Clement* and the *Shepherd of Hermas* and the association with 1 Peter.

Mediterranean.[48] On the whole, the evidence points to the same recipients as 1 Peter, Gentile Christians in Asia Minor.

Occasion and Purpose

The occasion for writing 2 Peter was most likely that the apostle was nearing his death (1:15) and needed to address a false teaching that was circulating in the churches to which he wrote (2:1–22). Thus in 3:17–18, Peter admonished his readers to "be on your guard, so that you are not led away by the error of the immoral and fall from your own stability. But grow in the grace and knowledge of our Lord and Savior Jesus Christ."

The opponents in 2 Peter apparently considered themselves Christian teachers and not necessarily prophets (2:1,13), although Peter grouped them with false prophets of old. They gathered disciples (2:2) and attempted to draw true believers into their sphere of influence. At the heart of their teaching seems to have been eschatological skepticism.[49] These false teachers apparently denied the Second Coming and sought to undermine apostolic testimony (see 1:16; 2:18–19; 3:4). Peter's denial that the apostles followed "cleverly contrived myths when we made known to you the power and coming of our Lord Jesus Christ" (1:16) seems to respond to the charge leveled by his opponents that the apostles' teaching of the resurrection was merely a matter of human fabrication (for a similar instance, see 2 Tim 2:17–18; cf. 1 Tim 1:20; 2 Tim 4:14).

On the whole, it is best to view the opponents as advocating a philosophy otherwise not attested in the NT or extrabiblical literature, similar to the "Colossian heresy," which was likewise unique in its local expression. The internal evidence suggests that the opponents' philosophy at the very outset precluded God's intervention in the world at any time (3:3–4), whether by sending a flood (thus denying the veracity of the OT Scriptures; see Genesis 6–9) or by having Jesus return at the end of time (a denial of Jesus' own words and of the apostolic and early church's witness).

LITERATURE

Literary Plan

The unity of 2 Peter is not seriously doubted.[50] Overall, 2 Peter conforms to the standard epistolary conventions of the day, featuring opening greetings (1:1–2), the body of the letter (1:3–3:13), and concluding remarks (3:14–18). There is wide consensus that 2:1–22 and 3:1–13 constitute literary units. There is less agreement with regard to the material in chap. 1. T. Schreiner divided the letter at 1:12, while D. Moo discerned a break

---

[48] See Davids, *2 Peter, Jude*, 133.

[49] Bauckham, *Jude, 2 Peter*, 154.

[50] See the refutation of the challenge to the unity of 2 Peter by M. McNamara ("The Unity of Second Peter: A Reconsideration," *Scr* 12 [1960]: 13–19) in Schreiner, *1, 2 Peter, Jude*, 281.

at 1:16.[51] Most likely, both are right as the following outline indicates: the sections are 1:3–11; 1:12–15; and 1:16–21.

Second Peter 1:3–21 sets forth Peter's challenge to his readers to pursue Christian virtues in light of God's provision of everything required for life and godliness (1:3–11), states Peter's purpose for writing the letter (1:12–15), and issues a defense and counter-charge against allegations by the false teachers regarding Peter's preaching on Jesus' return (1:12–21). As further developed in the discussion of Jude below, chap. 2 incorporates in modified form large portions of Jude, while 3:1–13 presents the specifics of the heresy at issue and calls the readers to holy conduct and godliness as they await the Lord's return. On the whole, the letter balances Peter's concern with believers' pursuit of Christian virtues with his desire to refute the false teaching that denied the reality of the Second Coming.

The important connection between Peter's focus on holiness and the false teaching he was combating ought not to be missed. Apparently, the denial of the Second Coming led directly to an anti-law sentiment and licentious behavior. This is confirmed in the references to the judgment of the angels, those in Noah's day, and Sodom and Gomorrah (2:4–9), assuring the readers that God will hold people accountable for their actions. Hence, the example of the false teachers—whose lack of doctrinal orthodoxy led to a denial of the Second Coming, resulting in an immoral lifestyle—taught the important lesson that believers who affirm the Second Coming must cultivate holiness as they await Christ's return.

OUTLINE

I. GREETINGS (1:1–2)

II. ENCOURAGEMENT TO GROWTH IN GODLINESS (1:3–21)
    A.   The Pursuit of Christian Virtues (1:3–11)
    B.   The Nature of Peter's Letter (1:12–15)
    C.   Defense of Peter's and the Prophets' Testimony (1:16–21)

III. CONDEMNATION OF THE FALSE TEACHERS (2:1–22)
    A.   The Danger and Nature of the False Teachers (2:1–3)
    B.   God's Judgment in the Past (2:4–10a)
    C.   The False Teachers' Godless Character (2:10b–16)
    D.   The False Teachers Described (2:17–22)

IV. REFUTATION AND RESPONSE TO THE FALSE TEACHERS (3:1–13)

V. CLOSING (3:14–18)

UNIT-BY-UNIT DISCUSSION

I. Greetings (1:1–2)

Second Peter opens with a standard prescript found in first-century letters, including a "well-wish" of a spiritual nature: "May grace and peace be multiplied to you through

---

[51] See Schreiner, *1, 2 Peter, Jude*, 282; and D. J. Moo, *2 Peter, Jude*, NIVAC (Grand Rapids: Zondervan, 1996), 26.

the knowledge of God and of Jesus our Lord" (1:2). The dual reference to "grace" and "knowledge" also concludes the letter, possibly forming a literary *inclusio* (3:18), a pattern also found in 1 Peter.

II. Encouragement to Growth in Godliness (1:3–21)

A. The Pursuit of Christian Virtues (1:3–11)   Peter made the previous "well-wish" because Christ has given believers everything they need for eternal life and godliness through their knowledge of him and through God's election of believers, having called them by his own glory and goodness. By virtue of this calling, the Christian participates in the divine nature and is able to escape the corruption brought on by evil desires.

The list that follows is not mere moralism, for Peter has already stressed that the foundation that allows the effort to be effectually extended has been laid in salvation, here epitomized in the word *faith*. In this faith, the believer is to supply certain things. The verb translated "supply" or "add" usually means to provide at one's own expense, but here it is a linking verb, as if someone made an effort at gaining goodness to obtain a supply of faith, and so on.[52]

Peter followed this encouragement to pursue Christian virtues with references to the negative and positive outcomes of such an effort. If a person did not engage in the pursuit of Christian virtues, that person was nearsighted to the point of blindness. If he did, he would be rewarded with a rich entrance into God's kingdom at the appearing of the Lord Jesus Christ (1:8–11).

B. The Nature of Peter's Letter (1:12–15)   In 1:12–15, Peter stated the purpose of his letter, namely to remind believers of important spiritual truths, presumably because of the threat of the false teachers, the exact nature of whose teaching is not specified until chap. 3. Peter wrote what turned out to be his final extant letter because he was convinced that his death was imminent and because he was confident that he was speaking the truth (1:14; see 1:12). Verse 15 specifies the future benefits of the letter for the readers.

C. Defense of Peter's and the Prophets' Message (1:16–21)   The reason Peter made this effort to remind his readers of their need to pursue Christian virtues was that he and his fellow apostles were eyewitnesses of Christ's majesty (1:16–18), so that the prophetic word about the coming of Christ was strongly confirmed (1:19). Peter then affirmed that both the origin of prophecy and its interpretation came from God himself (1:20–21). This represented a thinly veiled admonition to beware of those who engaged in their own "private interpretation" of Scripture, resulting in false teaching (the subject of chaps. 2–3).

III. Condemnation of the False Teachers (2:1–22)

Peter most likely incorporated nearly the whole of Jude's letter in his condemnation of the false teachers. Thus the condemnation was applicable to the present opponents but

---

[52] So Davids, *2 Peter, Jude*, 179.

beyond this to all false teachers. It would not be until chap. 3 that the precise nature of the false teaching was addressed.

A. *The Danger and Nature of the False Teachers (2:1–3)*   False teachers were as inevitable as the false prophets of old. They were clearly unregenerate and led others to destruction with them, blaspheming the truth out of greed and resulting in the inevitability of God's judgment.

B. *God's Judgment in the Past (2:4–10a)*   The reason that God's judgment was inevitable is that God has always judged false teachers and others who failed properly to submit to authority. The fallen angels were condemned to Tartarus and kept in chains (2:4); the people who lived prior to the flood and who engaged in egregious sin were destroyed; and Sodom and Gomorrah were obliterated as well (2:5–6). In the midst of this strong note of denunciation, however, Peter—in contrast with Jude, whose portrait was entirely negative (see below)—also struck an encouraging note. He pointed out that while God had destroyed the ancient world by a flood, he had rescued Noah and his family, and he also rescued Lot and his family when he destroyed Sodom and Gomorrah. Thus God could be counted on not only to judge the unrighteous but also to rescue the righteous from the polluted spiritual state of the world (2:7–10a).

C. *The False Teachers' Godless Character (2:10b-16)* In 2:10b, Peter delved further into the godless character of these false teachers. They were bold, arrogant, profane, and slanderous; they were like the beasts of the field in their blasphemies and thus fit for destruction (2:10b-12). They had secretly infiltrated the assembly and polluted the pure doctrine of the church. They were ever seeking to seduce and devour the righteous. Peter compared them to Balaam, who had been a prophet for profit (2:15–16).

D. *The False Teachers Described (2:17–22)*   Peter described these teachers as "springs without water," who seduced those who had barely escaped from those who lived in error. It is tempting to understand these as believers who have fallen from grace, for the apostle stated that it would have been better if they had never known the truth, than having turned back from the holy commandment. But verse 22 makes clear that they were never true believers, for "a dog returns to its own vomit, and, 'a sow, after washing itself, wallows in the mud'" (2 Pet 2:22, citing Prov 26:11). Thus the true nature of these false teachers becomes apparent: their unregenerate nature had only been masked externally, but in the end it will be made clear that they were never spiritually transformed in the first place.[53]

IV. Refutation and Response to the False Teachers (3:1–13)

The specific nature of the heresy, already hinted at in 1:16, is now set forth and the error of the false teachers is refuted. These scoffers denied the truthfulness of the apostolic

---

[53] See C. L. Blomberg, *From Pentecost to Patmos: An Introduction to Acts Through Revelation* (Nashville: B&H, 2006), 481. This interpretation fits well with Peter's previous statements that God knows how to preserve the righteous in the midst of a filthy world.

teaching regarding the second coming of the Lord Jesus Christ, contending that "all things continue as they have been since the beginning of creation" (3:3–4). In response, Peter firmly rejected this teaching by noting that the underlying premise was wrong. Contrary to the false teachers, the world will not always exist, for God has already judged it once in the past with a flood (3:6) and would destroy it again by fire in the future (3:7).

In fact, from the vantage point of eternity, there was little difference between a day and 1,000 years. Moreover, the Lord was not delaying his return but patiently waiting for the last of the elect to be saved; then judgment would swiftly ensue (3:8–9). Indeed, the Day of the Lord would come on the wicked without warning; the heavens would pass away, and the earth would melt and be dissolved. Thus the opponents were wrong regarding the earth's continual existence. In light of the world's final judgment, Christians ought to be a sanctified people, waiting expectantly for the promise of the new heavens and the new earth (3:11–13).

V. Closing (3:14–18)

Peter concluded his letter by affirming that believers should view the apparent delay of the Second Coming as an opportunity for salvation. For confirmation, he called on Paul's letters (though it is not clear if he had any specific passage in mind). He concluded with a warning against the false teachers and reiterated his desire that his readers "grow in the grace and knowledge of our Lord and Savior Jesus Christ," followed by a closing doxology.

THEOLOGY

Theological Themes

The Pursuit of Christian Virtues in Light of the End Time   The growth of believers in Christian virtues is a major emphasis in 2 Peter.[54] According to Peter, people may travel on one of two paths.[55] The first is that of progressing in the faith, climbing a staircase of Christian virtues, which enables believers to lead spiritually productive lives (1:3–11; see 3:11–18). The second is that of straying from the path, resulting in destruction and condemnation, as in the case of the false teachers (2:1–3:10). Hence, the letter is permeated by a pastoral concern for the well-being of the flock and its protection from the potential harm caused by those who would twist the Word of God (1:12–21).[56]

Peter's teaching on the pursuit of Christian virtue is epitomized by the word "godliness" (*eusebeia*), which occurs three times in 1:3–7 (vv. 3,6,7; see 3:11). Peter made it clear that,

---

[54] For a modern application of Peter's teaching on virtues to the life of the Christian scholar, see A. J. Köstenberger, *Excellence: The Character of God and the Pursuit of Scholarly Virtue* (Wheaton: Crossway, 2011).

[55] See Kelly, *Epistles of Peter and of Jude*, 328; Thielman, *Theology of the New Testament*, 527. Peter used the term "way" four times (2:2,15 [twice], 21) as well as the related expressions "entrance" (1:11) and "departure" (1:15).

[56] The most unusual element of Peter's instruction is found in 1:4, where believers are said to share in the divine nature. By this Peter did not mean participation in the essence of God, but enablement to progress in Christian virtues. See Thielman, *Theology of the New Testament*, 527, citing J. M. Starr, *Sharers in the Divine Nature: 2 Peter 1:4 in Its Hellenistic Context*, ConBNT 33 (Stockholm: Almqvist & Wiksell, 2000), 47–48.

through their knowledge of God in Christ, believers have been given everything they need to live a godly life (1:3). For this reason they are to pursue godliness in conjunction with faith, goodness, knowledge, self-control, endurance, brotherly affection, and love (1:5–7).

Peter's teaching on believers' need to pursue Christian virtues also has important end-time implications. The false teachers challenged the belief that Christ will return and that God will bring about a consummation to history. Yet Peter affirmed that, in spite of apparent delays, the Lord will come again at the appointed time. He will judge all people, and the elements of this world will be dissolved and melt away (3:12). Thus believers should live in light of the end and pursue the path of Christian virtue in order to reach their final glorious destination (1:11). In this way the coming Day of the Lord (3:12) provides an incentive for moral behavior (3:14).[57]

Apostolic Eyewitness Testimony versus Heresy   Another distinctive emphasis in 2 Peter is the importance of apostolic eyewitness testimony against heresy with its reliance on human reasoning and fabricated arguments. This is borne out by the presence of two particular word groups in 2 Peter. The first is represented by the noun "eyewitness" in 1:16, which occurs only here in the NT, the particular verb "to witness" occurs only in 1 Peter in the NT (1 Pet 2:12; 3:2). The second is represented by the Greek word that forms the etymological root for the English word "heresy," which can mean "sect" or "party," such as Sadducees (Acts 5:17); Pharisees (Acts 15:5; 26:5); "the Nazarenes" or "the Way," that is, Christians (Acts 24:5,14; 28:22). It can also mean "faction" or "division" (1 Cor 11:19; Gal 5:20), or "heresy" (2 Pet 2:1). Peter's letter revolves around this contrast between "eyewitness" testimony and destructive "heresies."

Against allegations from his opponents, Peter asserted that he (unlike them) did not follow "cleverly contributed myths" in his preaching of the Second Coming; instead, "we were eyewitnesses of His majesty" (1:16). He proceeded to recount his eyewitness recollection of Jesus' transfiguration, which included hearing the divine voice from heaven utter the words, "This is My beloved Son. I take delight in him!" (1:17–18; see Matt 17:5 and parallels). This meant that Peter's message was authoritative because it was based on what really happened (similarly, 1 John 1:1–4; see 1 Tim 1:4; 4:7; 2 Tim 4:4; Titus 1:14), which was contrary to the false teachers' message that they fabricated and that was not based on actual fact (2:1–3; 3:4).

The point made in 1:19–21 is, therefore, that Peter's witness of the glorified Christ formed a strong basis for his witness to the expectation of the return of Christ in his glory at the end of time. In this, the apostle was allied with the OT prophets, and in his testimony "the prophetic word [was] strongly confirmed" (1:19). The witness of the OT prophets had not been self-induced but had been God given and Spirit inspired (1:20–21). Likewise, Peter's witness was based on what God had done, and was going to do, in Christ. This underscores the crucial importance of relying on OT and NT Scripture in one's

---

[57] Thielman, *Theology of the New Testament*, 535.

expectations of the end, and in particular Christ's return. It also inspires confidence in the accuracy and trustworthiness of the apostolic witness handed down to us in Scripture. Based on this sure foundation, believers can zealously pursue Christian virtues in order to be ready for Christ when he returns.

The Letter of Jude

KEY FACTS	
Author:	Jude, brother of James
Date:	c. 55–62
Provenance:	Unknown
Destination:	Predominantly Jewish Christian congregation (Asia Minor?)
Occasion:	False teaching (antinomianism coupled with licentiousness)
Purpose:	To contend for the faith once for all entrusted to believers
Theme:	Jude urges his readers to contend for the faith and to reject the false teaching of the heretics
Key Verse:	3

INTRODUCTION

WHILE A FEW decades ago Jude could still be called "the most neglected book of the New Testament," this short letter, placed in the canon last among the General Epistles and prior to the book of Revelation, has received considerable attention in recent years.[58] In contemporary preaching, however, Jude continues to suffer neglect. Apart from the phrase "the faith that was delivered to the saints once for all" (v. 3), it is only the concluding doxology (vv. 24–25), albeit without reference to its context in Jude, that is a regular part of the church's worship.

In an age when Christian faith and moral integrity are in short supply, Jude's message is particularly appropriate. All too commonly, local churches fail to confront false teachings or are unwilling to challenge compromises in the way people live. Frequently, tolerance is the order of the day, and church discipline is at an all-time low. Into this malaise Jude issued a clarion call to defend the faith and to confront false teaching, particularly in light of the reality of a holy God who will judge sin unless it is acknowledged and confessed.

---

[58] D. J. Rowston, "The Most Neglected Book in the New Testament," *NTS* 21 (1975): 554–63; see Bauckham, *Jude, 2 Peter*, xi: "No NT books have been more neglected by scholars than Jude and 2 Peter."

HISTORY

Author

The letter begins with a reference to "Jude, a slave of Jesus Christ, and a brother of James" (1).[59] In all probability, the author of Jude is the brother of the James mentioned in Matt 13:55. The opening self-reference by Jude as "brother" rather than the customary reference to himself as "son of" his father is unusual.[60] With regard to the expression "brother of James," it is noteworthy that only James the brother of Jesus could be mentioned simply as "James" (Jas 1:1) without a need for further identification.[61]

Jude began in a way that is reminiscent of the book of James.[62] James was much better known and had no need to identify himself further, but Jude is hardly mentioned elsewhere and needed to add the epithet "brother of James."[63] What is more, Jude called himself only "brother of James"[64] and not "brother of Jesus Christ."[65] The latter designation may have seemed inappropriate in light of Jesus' divine sonship. Rather than identifying themselves in terms of their flesh-and-blood relationship with Jesus, both James and Jude called themselves "slaves of Jesus Christ" who did his will.

The view is not uncommon that Jude's letter is pseudonymous, that it was written by someone other than Jude and attributed to him for some reason. This practice was supposedly in keeping with the ancient convention of pseudonymity, according to which a literary work was attributed to a well-known personality in order to lend it credence and to enlarge its potential audience. But the obvious question is why anyone would have wanted

---

[59] See R. Bauckham, "The Letter of Jude: An Account of Research," *Aufstieg und Niedergang der Römischen Welt* 2.25.5 (Berlin: de Gruyter, 1988), 3791–3826.

[60] R. L. Webb, "Jude," in *Dictionary of the Later New Testament and Its Developments*, ed. R. P. Martin and P. H. Davids (Downers Grove: InterVarsity, 1997), 611–21.

[61] So R. Bauckham, *Jude and the Relatives of Jesus in the Early Church* (Edinburgh: T&T Clark, 1990), 172. Bauckham noted that prior to the nineteenth century (including Calvin and the Council of Trent) Jude the apostle was considered to be the author of Jude (see Luke 6:16; Acts 1:13). However, Jude the apostle was identified with the half brother of Jesus, who is mentioned in Matt 13:55 and Mark 6:3. Jessein (1821) was the first to argue against this consensus and to distinguish Jude the half brother of Jesus and author of Jude from Jude the apostle. See the list of alternative identifications of Jude in Bauckham, *Jude and the Relatives of Jesus*, 172–73.

[62] Compare Jude 1: "Jude, a slave of Jesus Christ and a brother of James" with Jas 1:1: "James, a slave of God and of the Lord Jesus Christ."

[63] According to Gal 2:9, James, together with Peter and John, was one of the "pillars" of the Jerusalem church. James had a leading role in the Jerusalem Council (Jas 15:13; see 12:17; 21:18). Paul also mentioned that the resurrected Jesus had appeared to James (1 Cor 15:7) and called James "the Lord's brother" (Gal 1:19; see Acts 1:14; 1 Cor 9:5). Remarkably, James only called himself "a slave of God and of the Lord Jesus Christ" (1:1).

[64] Kelly (*Epistles of Peter and of Jude*, 242) believed that Jude would have identified himself as "brother of the Lord" and that the designation "brother of James" points to pseudonymity. So H. Windisch, *Die katholischen Briefe*, HNT, 3rd ed., rev. H. Preisker (Tübingen: J. C. B. Mohr [Paul Siebeck], 1951 [1911]), 38; but see the decisive response by Bauckham, *Jude, 2 Peter*, 24.

[65] This is a convincing argument against the pseudonymity of Jude. As Bauckham (*Jude and the Relatives of Jesus*, 176) observed, "The lack of reference to Jude's relationship to Jesus is much more easily explicable on the assumption of authenticity than on the assumption of pseudepigraphy."

to attribute a writing to a person as little known as Jude rather than to other disciples who were known much more widely.[66]

For this reason there is no serious doubt that Jude, the brother of James and half brother of Jesus, is the author of the book of Jude.

Date

The date for Jude depends in part on its relationship with 1 and 2 Peter, particularly the latter. A comparison between Jude's letter and 2 Peter suggests that Jude's letter was written first and that Peter in his second letter adapted Jude for his own purposes and circumstances.[67] In light of the considerable number of parallels between the letters, a literary relationship between the two is more likely than the independent use of a common source by both writers.

A detailed comparison of Jude and 2 Peter will be provided further below. For the time being, the probability of Jude's having been written prior to 2 Peter can be illustrated by the way in which these writings used Jewish apocryphal literature. Jude included three such quotations or allusions: (1) to *The Assumption of Moses* in verse 9; (2) to *1 Enoch* in verses 14–15; and (3) to an otherwise unattested saying of the apostles in verse 18. All three quotations are lacking in 2 Peter. It seems more likely that Peter avoided reference to these apocryphal works rather than that Jude added these references on the assumption of Petrine priority.[68]

Estimates of the date of composition of Jude extend from the year 50 (Bauckham) to 65–80 (Guthrie) to 100 (Kümmel).[69] The critical question here is whether the letter displays the characteristics of early Catholicism.[70] Dunn cited three such characteristics: (1) a decrease in the expectation of the imminent return of Christ; (2) an emphasis on the institutional nature of the church (as in the Pastorals); and (3) the use of liturgical elements (similar to the Pastorals).[71] However, a closer look shows that none of these elements is present in Jude.

---

[66] So rightly Bauckham, *Jude and the Relatives of Jesus*, 175; cf. id., "Account of Research," 3817–18. At times it is argued that the author of Jude was not Jude himself but rather a friend, student, or relative of Jude or that he belonged to a "circle of Judas." The argument has also been advanced that the epithet "brother of James" served to lend authority to Jude's letter. Yet these theories are far less plausible than the simpler assumption that Jude, the brother of James, was himself the author of the letter.

[67] So many (if not most) contemporary commentators. Others, however, such as D. J. Moo (*2 Peter, Jude*, NIVAC [Grand Rapids: Zondervan, 1996], 18), contended that Jude used parts of 2 Peter.

[68] Perhaps in order to compensate, Peter supplemented Jude's letter with the biblical examples of Noah (2 Pet 2:5) and Lot (2 Pet 2:7–9) and provided a more thorough presentation of Balaam (2 Pet 2:15–16).

[69] See Bauckham, *Jude and the Relatives of Jesus*, 168–69n237; id., "Account of Research," 3812–15.

[70] See, e.g., K. H. Schelkle, *Die Petrusbriefe, der Judasbrief*, HTKNT 13/2 (Freiburg: Herder, 1961). But see Bauckham, *Jude and the Relatives of Jesus*, 158–60.

[71] J. D. G. Dunn, *Unity and Diversity in the New Testament*, 2nd ed. (London/Philadelphia: Trinity Press International, 1990), 341–66.

1. The expectation of the Second Coming is given clear and repeated expression in Jude 14,21,24. The entire argument in verses 5–19 assumes that the false teachers will be judged following Christ's return.[72]
2. There is no reference to holders of ecclesiastical offices anywhere in Jude, and the manner in which the heretics are called to account stands in stark contrast with the early Catholic practice of appealing to ecclesiastical office.
3. Jude does not contain any liturgical fragments (the phrase "the faith that was delivered to the saints once for all" in verse 3 constitutes a simple reference to the gospel; see Gal 1:23).

For this reason the theory that Jude is a product of early Catholicism is untenable, which suggests the possibility, even probability, of an early date, and as shown below, possibly even a very early date in relation to the other NT letters.

Another factor is the question of a possible literary dependence between Jude and 2 Peter. If 2 Peter postdates and is dependent on Jude (a view held by most, though not all, commentators today), and 2 Peter is authentic (see the introduction to 2 Peter in this volume), the fact that Peter died a martyr's death in c. 65–66 requires the early 60s as the latest possible date for the book of Jude.[73]

Since there is no good reason to question the authenticity of 2 Peter, and since it is probable that 2 Peter is dependent on Jude rather than vice versa, 55–62 as a date of composition is most likely.[74] But it must be noted that the lack of clear internal evidence regarding the date of composition renders this estimate tentative at best.

Provenance

The provenance of Jude cannot be determined with certainty. Bauckham showed conclusively that Jude is not a product of early Catholicism but an expression of apocalyptic Palestinian Christianity.[75] This is confirmed by Jude's use of the Jewish books *The Assumption of Moses* and *1 Enoch* and by the *pesher* exegesis in verses 5–19.[76] In light of these observations, Jude has a closer affinity to James than to 2 Peter. Beyond this, it is difficult to pinpoint the provenance of Jude, so that it is best to leave this question open.

---

[72] See esp. R. L. Webb, "The Eschatology of the Epistle of Jude and Its Rhetorical and Social Functions," *BBR* 6 (1996): 139–51.

[73] Robinson (*Redating*, 197) proposed that if James had already died by the time of the writing of Jude, Jude would most likely have referred to him as "the blessed," "the good," or "the righteous." Since he did not do so, James must still have been alive. James died a martyr's death in the year 62, so Robinson suggested that Jude was written before then.

[74] If Jude's letter does reveal anti-gnostic tendencies, then 1 Tim 6:21 provides further confirmation that proto-gnostic elements were already at work in Asia Minor in the early 60s (on the assumption of Paul's authorship of the Pastorals).

[75] Bauckham, *Jude and the Relatives of Jesus*, 155, 161; D. A. Hagner, "Jewish Christianity," in *Dictionary of the Later New Testament and its Developments*, 582.

[76] Bauckham, *Jude and the Relatives of Jesus*, 161.

Destination

The general reference to "those who are the called, loved by God the Father and kept by Jesus Christ" at the beginning of the letter (v. 1b) does not allow an identification of the recipients of the letter. Judging from the internal evidence, it is possible that the letter was directed to a predominantly (though not exclusively) Jewish Christian congregation, possibly in Asia Minor.[77] Itinerant false teachers had infiltrated the church, while living a life of licentiousness and practicing a form of Christian antinomianism (lawlessness).

According to these heretics, the grace of God liberated believers from all ethical norms, so that a Christian was free to choose his own conduct without any moral restraints. These heretics were not only members of the church but also teachers (vv. 11–13). They took part in the church's worship and sought to spread their prophecies and teachings at the occasion of the church's regular "love feasts," that is, communal meals including the celebration of the Lord's Supper. Jude warned his readers against the heretics and urged them to contend for their faith (v. 3).

Occasion and Purpose

The heretics mentioned in Jude cannot be identified with any of the other false teachers mentioned in the NT.[78] In identifying their exact nature, priority should therefore be given to the internal evidence provided by the book itself. According to Jude, the false teachers "have come in[to the church] by stealth" (v. 4; see Gal 2:4). Most likely, they were therefore itinerant teachers or preachers who went from church to church and depended on the hospitality of local Christians (see 1 Cor 9:5; 2 John 10; 3 John 5–10). In their unbelief, these godless individuals denied "Jesus Christ our only Sovereign and Lord" (v. 4 NIV). Their motto was "freedom," in the sense of complete ethical autonomy (vv. 4,8; see v. 7). Possibly, these false teachers held to an overrealized eschatology, focusing on their present enjoyment of the benefits of salvation while apocalyptic elements were given short shrift (see 2 Tim 2:17–18).

Jude called the false teachers "dreamers" (v. 8), mystics who boasted of privileged access to esoteric knowledge. This may indicate the charismatic character of these itinerant preachers.[79] These claims of visionary experiences appear to have resulted also in lack of respect toward angels (vv. 9–10). It is possible that people were said to have an angelic nature and thus the distinction between humans and angels was blurred. Jude accounted for this by reference to the lack of spiritual insight on the part of the heretics: "These people blaspheme anything they don't understand" (v. 10). In truth, they do not possess the Spirit (v. 19).

These teachers are "blemishes" (v. 12 NIV) at the church's "love feasts," in which they participate without the slightest qualm (v. 12; see vv. 8,23). Their status as teachers is hinted at in verse 12, where they are called shepherds "nurturing only themselves." Like Balaam or the false shepherds in Ezekiel 34, these heretics sought nothing but their own

---

[77] See Bauckham, *Jude, 2 Peter*, 26.

[78] See the survey by Bauckham, "Account of Research," 3809–12 and the thorough treatment by G. Sellin, "Die Häretiker des Judasbriefes," *ZNW* 76–77 (1985–86): 206–25.

[79] See G. Theissen, *The First Followers of Jesus* (London: SCM, 1978).

advantage (v. 11). These individuals are as unreliable as waterless clouds or fruitless autumn trees and as unstable as the restless ocean (vv. 12–13; see Isa 57:20; Eph 4:14), leading people astray similar to stars that do not keep their course (see v. 6).

The heretics were highly critical and deeply discontent with their own fate (v. 16).[80] They utter "defiant words" (v. 15) similar to the godless mentioned in the previous quotation from *1 Enoch* (see also vv. 8,10); they were "scoffers" who displayed a mocking spirit (v. 18). They caused divisions (v. 19; see 1 Cor 1:10–4:7; Jas 3:14) and were earthly minded (v. 19; the word is *psychikoi*; see 1 Cor 2:14; Jas 3:15; 4:5). Although these charismatic itinerant preachers boasted of their visionary experiences, they were devoid of the Spirit (v. 19), thus proving their unregenerate nature (see Rom 8:9). This was impressively demonstrated by their licentious lifestyle.

These were the false teachers that Jude opposed in his letter. While he had intended to write a general and encouraging letter "about our common salvation," he instead "found it necessary to write and exhort" his readers to contend for the faith once for all entrusted to believers (v. 3). This remarkable change of plans was occasioned by the covert and subversive presence of the false teachers in the congregation to which Jude addressed his letter. Rather than acquiesce to their teachings, the believers in that congregation needed to oppose these heretics, knowing that God's judgment of such individuals is sure.

Just as God severely punished people who did such things in the past—the demonstration of which is the burden underlying Jude's reference to several OT examples in verses 5–19—he will most certainly judge these false teachers. Jude's message for his recipients is given clear expression in verses 20–23, where he called on his readers to build themselves up in their most holy faith, to pray in the Holy Spirit, and to keep themselves in God's love as they await Christ's return (one of the proto-trinitarian references in the NT, vv. 20–21). They were to show mercy toward those who doubted; save others by snatching them from the fire; and conduct themselves with holy fear, knowing that even the clothing of the false teachers was "defiled by the flesh" (vv. 22–23).

It is hard to exaggerate the utmost seriousness with which the church, according to Jude, must deal with heretics while acting redemptively toward those who may still be wrenched from the demonic grasp of these wicked, self-seeking individuals.

LITERATURE

Genre

Jude is addressed to a particular group of people (vv. 1–4). It is therefore not a "Catholic" (i.e., "General") Epistle. Nevertheless, the main body of the letter and the concluding blessing read more like a sermon composed of a commentary on various texts (vv. 5–19),

---

[80] Possibly they considered themselves fatalistically as slaves of their own destiny and shifted the responsibility for their own licentious conduct to others. So R. P. Martin, *The Theology of Jude, 1 Peter, and 2 Peter*, in *The Theology of the Letters of James, Peter, and Jude* by A. Chester and R. P. Martin (Cambridge: Cambridge University Press, 1994), 71.

an exhortation (vv. 20–23), and a doxology (vv. 24–25).[81] It may be best to characterize Jude as a "sermon in form of an epistle."[82]

Literary Plan

The letter of Jude displays the following concentric chiastic structure:[83]

Section	Introductory formula
A Greeting (1–2)	Jude to those . . .
B Occasion (3–4)	Beloved
C Reminder (5–7)	I want to remind you
D The Heretics (8–13)	In the same way, these people
D′ *1 Enoch* (14–16)	Enoch prophesied about them
C′ Reminder (17–19)	But you, beloved, remember the words
B′ Exhortation (20–23)	But you, beloved
A′ Doxology (24–25)	But to him who is able to keep you . . .

This structure contains correspondence between greeting and doxology and between occasion and exhortation, two reminders, and the two units at the heart of the letter, the section on the false teachers and the quotation from *1 Enoch*. The body of the letter (vv. 5–19) contains an extended exegetical treatment of types and prophecies for the purpose of showing "that the false teachers are people whose behavior is condemned and whose judgment is prophesied in OT types and in prophecy from the time of Enoch to the time of the apostles."[84]

Despite the length of verses 5–19, the actual purpose of the letter is Jude's exhortation that his readers contend for the faith (vv. 20–23; see v. 3). Thus verses 20–23 are not merely a concluding exhortation or a postscript but the climax to which the entire letter builds. Verses 5–19 provide the necessary background and foundation for this paraenesis (exhortation). The message of the letter is therefore a call for the readers to contend for the faith against God's adversaries who are condemned already in Scripture and who will be held accountable on the last day.

On the basis of this exhortatory message, Jude's readers must cast their lot with the "faith that was delivered to the saints once for all" (v. 3) and separate from the false teachers, seeking to salvage any doubters or others under the spell of the heretics while applying all necessary caution (vv. 20–23). Otherwise, they will share in the false teachers' sins and incur the same judgment.

---

[81] See C. A. Evans, "Midrash," in *Dictionary of Jesus and the Gospels*, ed. J. B. Green, S. McKnight, and I. H. Marshall (Downers Grove: InterVarsity, 1992), 544–48.

[82] Bauckham, *Jude, 2 Peter*, 1; D. F. Watson, "Letter, Letter Form," in *Dictionary of the Later New Testament and Its Developments*, 653.

[83] A slightly different chiastic structure is proposed by Bauckham (*Jude, 2 Peter*, 5–6), followed by Webb ("Jude," 612). On the structure of Jude, see the survey in Bauckham, "Account of Research," 3800–804.

[84] Bauckham, *Jude, 2 Peter*, 4.

OUTLINE

   I. SALUTATION (1–2)

  II. OCCASION (3–4)

 III. EXPOSITION: GOD'S JUDGMENT ON SINNERS (5–19)

      A. Reminder from the Hebrew Scriptures (5–7)

      B. The False Teachers (8–13)

      C. The Quotation from Enoch (14–16)

      D. Reminder from Apostolic Prophecy (17–19)

 IV. EXHORTATION (20–23)

  V. DOXOLOGY (24–25)

UNIT-BY-UNIT DISCUSSION

I. Salutation (1–2)

The customary salutation identifies Jude, the brother of James, as the author; includes an address of the recipients as "those who are called, loved by God the Father and kept by Jesus Christ"; and a greeting of mercy, peace, and love.

II. Occasion (3–4)

In refreshing candor, Jude explained why the letter he actually wrote was different from the one he had intended to write. Rather than penning an encouraging note regarding "our common salvation," Jude wrote a scathing rebuke of the false teachers and urged believers to "contend for the faith once for all entrusted" to them.

III. Exposition: God's Judgment on Sinners (5–19)

Jude set his denunciation of the false teachers within the framework of reminders from the Hebrew Scriptures (vv. 5–7) and from apostolic prophecy (vv. 17–19). The false teachers shared several essential characteristics with those who had sinned conspicuously in OT times and subsequently were severely judged by God (vv. 8–16). While still future from Jude's perspective, the judgment of God on the false teachers in his day was nonetheless certain.

A. Reminder from the Hebrew Scriptures (5–7) Jude's denunciation of the false teachers takes on the form of a "reminder" of how God dealt with similar offenders and rebels in the past. Exhibit 1 is God's judgment of the rebellious generation in the wilderness during the exodus from Egypt. Exhibit 2 concerns God's judgment of the fallen angels who were not content with their assigned place in God's creation but rebelled against it. Exhibit 3 is Sodom and Gomorrah, who rebelled against God's creation order by engaging in perverse sexual acts (homosexuality) and consequently were destroyed as an act of divine judgment. These three scriptural examples make clear that those who rebel against God will certainly not escape divine judgment, even if, as in the case of the false teachers in the book of Jude, this judgment was yet future.

B. The False Teachers (8–13)   This section, together with verses 14–16, is at the heart of the chiasm of the letter, focusing squarely on the false teachers. Their root sin is defiance of God's authority. The archangel Michael is cited as a positive example, contrasted with three negative predecessors of the false teachers: Cain, who murdered his brother out of jealousy; Balaam, whose error was the result of greed; and Korah, who rebelled in the wilderness. The false teachers are placed in this terrible trajectory of past rebels against God's authority who were severely judged by God; as Jude makes clear, the false teachers' punishment is likewise assured.

C. The Quotation from Enoch (14–16)   As a proof text Jude cites a passage from the apocryphal book of Enoch, attesting to the certainly of divine judgment on the ungodly. The teachers are charged with discontent, sensuality, arrogance, and flattery.

D. Reminder from Apostolic Prophecy (17–19)   The reminder from apostolic prophecy corresponds in the chiastic structure to the opening reminder from the Hebrew Scriptures in verses 5–7. With this, Jude turns to his audience ("dear friends," v. 17), reminding them that the false teachers were fulfilling end-time prophecy. The heretics are divisive, merely natural, and devoid of the Spirit.

IV. Exhortation (20–23)

On the basis of Jude's exposition regarding God's impending judgment of the false teachers in verses 5–19, the purpose of the letter, stated in verse 3, is now fleshed out in the form of a full-fledged exhortation. In this climactic section, Jude, in dramatic fashion, urged his readers to keep themselves pure while attempting to "snatch" some who doubt "from the fire," that is, from eternal judgment by God.

V. Doxology (24–25)

The concluding doxology affirms God's ability to keep believers from stumbling and celebrates the glory, majesty, and power of the only God and Savior through Jesus Christ now and forever.

THEOLOGY

Theological Theme

Contending for the Faith   In his letter, Jude issues an urgent appeal for believers to contend for the Christian faith over against false teaching that accentuated believers' alleged unfettered freedom in Christ, which leads to an immoral lifestyle. In this form of antinomianism, people appealed to God's grace as setting believers free to live any way they chose and turned it into a license for immorality (v. 4).

Today, too, many a convert wrongly concludes that the gospel of God's grace renders unnecessary a lifestyle that is characterized by trust in God and obedience to biblical morality and teaching. After all, God is a God of grace, love, and forgiveness. As Jude made clear, however, the decision to trust Christ must not issue in a life of unfettered freedom and licentious immorality. To the contrary, the believer becomes "a slave of Jesus Christ" (v. 1).

The message of Jude's letter is therefore perennially relevant. Believers in any age must be reminded of the holiness and righteousness of God, which will not allow sin to go unpunished and which requires a holy lifestyle in response to God's grace in Christ. Jude also provided diagnostic tools for spotting false teachers: an immoral lifestyle, a self-serving and self-seeking disposition, and a primarily monetary motivation.

POINTS OF APPLICATION

- Recognize that you are only a temporary resident in this world (1 Pet 1:1,17; 2:11)
- Be holy in all your conduct, because God is holy (1 Pet 1:15–16)
- Like newborn babies, crave the pure spiritual "milk" of God's Word (1 Pet 2:2)
- Submit to every human authority, as a citizen, at home, and at work, even when this involves suffering for doing what is right (1 Pet 2:13–3:7)
- Make every effort to supplement your faith with Christian virtues (2 Pet 1:3–11)
- Contend for the faith that many have died to preserve and pass on to you (Jude 3)

STUDY QUESTIONS

1. According to the authors, which was written first: 1 Peter, 2 Peter, or Jude, and why?
2. What is the most likely date for 1 Peter, and why?
3. Why did Peter write 1 Peter, and what is the major example he cites in his exhortation?
4. What is the heresy addressed in 2 Peter?
5. In what ways does Peter's teaching to pursue Christian virtues have important end-time implications?
6. Who were most likely the "false teachers" in Jude?

FOR FURTHER STUDY

Bauckham, R. *Jude, 2 Peter.* Word Biblical Commentary 50. Waco: Word, 1983.

_____. *Jude and the Relatives of Jesus in the Early Church.* Edinburgh: T&T Clark, 1990.

Charles, J. D. "1, 2 Peter." Pages 275–411 in *The Expositor's Bible Commentary.* Rev. ed. Vol. 13: *Hebrews-Revelation.* Grand Rapids: Zondervan, 2005.

_____. "Jude." Pages 539–69 in *The Expositor's Bible Commentary.* Rev. ed. Vol. 13: *Hebrews-Revelation.* Grand Rapids: Zondervan, 2005.

Davids, P. H. *The First Epistle of Peter.* New International Commentary on the New Testament. Grand Rapids: Eerdmans, 1990.

_____. *The Letters of 2 Peter and Jude.* Pillar New Testament Commentary. Grand Rapids: Eerdmans, 2006.

Elliott, J. H. *1 Peter: A New Translation with Introduction and Commentary.* Anchor Bible 37B. New York: Doubleday, 2000.

Green, E. M. B. *2 Peter Reconsidered.* London: Tyndale, 1961.

Green, G. L. *Jude and 2 Peter.* Baker Exegetical Commentary on the New Testament. Grand Rapids: Baker, 2008.

Green, M. *The Second Epistle General of Peter and the General Epistle of Jude.* 2nd ed. Grand Rapids: Eerdmans, 1987.

Grudem, W. A. *The First Epistle of Peter: An Introduction and Commentary.* Tyndale New Testament Commentary. Grand Rapids, Eerdmans, 1997.

Jobes, K. H. *1 Peter.* Baker Exegetical Commentary on the New Testament. Grand Rapids: Baker, 2005.

Kelly, J. N. D. *A Commentary on the Epistles of Peter and of Jude.* Harper's New Testament Commentaries. New York: Harper & Row, 1969.

Kruger, M. J. "The Authenticity of 2 Peter." *Journal of the Evangelical Theological Society* 42 (1999): 645–71.

Marshall, I. H. *1 Peter.* New Testament Commentary. Downers Grove: InterVarsity, 1991.

Martin, R. P. "The Theology of Jude, 1 Peter, and 2 Peter." Pages 63–163 in *The Theology of the Letters of James, Peter, and Jude* by A. Chester and R. P. Martin. Cambridge: Cambridge University Press, 1994.

Michaels, J. R. *1 Peter.* Word Biblical Commentary 49. Waco: Word, 1988.

Moo, D. J. *2 Peter, Jude.* NIV Application Commentary. Grand Rapids: Zondervan, 1996.

Reese, R. A. *2 Peter and Jude.* Two Horizons New Testament Commentary. Grand Rapids: Eerdmans, 2007.

Schreiner, T. R. *1, 2 Peter, Jude.* New American Commentary 37. Nashville: B&H, 2003.

Senior, D. P. *1 Peter, Jude, and 2 Peter.* Sacra Pagina 15. Collegeville: Liturgical Press, 2003.

Chapter 19

The Johannine Epistles: 1–3 John

CORE KNOWLEDGE

Students should know the key facts of 1, 2, and 3 John. With regard to history, students should be able to identify each book's author, date, provenance, destination, and purpose. With regard to literature, they should be able to provide a basic outline of each book and identify core elements of each book's content found in the unit-by-unit discussion. With regard to theology, students should be able to identify the major theological themes in 1, 2, and 3 John.

KEY FACTS	
Author:	John the son of Zebedee
Date:	c. 90–95
Provenance:	Asia Minor
Destination:	Churches in and around Ephesus
Occasion:	The recent departure of false teachers from the Ephesian church (1 John); itinerant false teachers (2 John); an autocratic despot named Diotrephes (3 John)
Purpose:	John encourages believers to love God and one another and reassures them that they are in the Son (1 John); instructs them not to extend hospitality to false teachers (2 John); and helps Gaius deal with the autocratic Demetrius (3 John)
Theme:	Christian reassurance and continuing to walk in love and truth
Key Verses:	1 John 5:11–12; 2 John 9–11; 3 John 4

CONTRIBUTION TO THE CANON

- Jesus Christ as the propitiation for the sins of the entire world (1 John 2:2)
- God is love (e.g., 1 John 4:16)
- Christian assurance (1 John 5:11–13)
- Prohibition against extending hospitality to false teachers (2 John)
- Warning against autocratic church leadership (3 John)

INTRODUCTION

IN HIS LECTURES on 1 John, Martin Luther declared, "I have never read a book written in simpler words than this one, and yet the words are inexpressible."[1] His fellow Reformer John Calvin remarked about the author, "At one time he admonishes us in general to a godly and holy life; and at another he gives express directions about love. Yet he does none of this systematically, but varies teaching with exhortation."[2]

These two comments reveal a measure of the paradox of the Johannine Letters: simple in expression (a vocabulary of only 303 words) but complex in thought. Especially John's first letter has proved to be both the staple of beginning Greek students and the bane of experienced commentators.

In the church and throughout history, the first letter has been read, loved, and memorized by many doubting Christians, who have fled to its contents to be comforted by the assurance it provides. William Penn was so struck by the new command given in 1 John that he named the chief city of Pennsylvania "the city of brotherly love" (Philadelphia). In contrast, the second and third letters have been, and continue to be, widely neglected, to the detriment of all who do so.

HISTORY

Author

External Evidence   Early church tradition unanimously held that the author of 1 John was the apostle John, the son of Zebedee, but 2 John and 3 John were not as strongly attested. Origen (c. 185–254) noted that some did not receive these letters, though he himself did.[3] In spite of the wavering of a few, 2 and 3 John were received into the canon on the strength of the conviction that John the apostle was the author.

More recently, however, confidence in the tradition has frequently been undermined by the claim that no explicit attribution to John as the author occurs until Irenaeus

---

[1] M. Luther, *D. Martin Luthers Werke: Kritische Gesamtausgabe, Weimarer Lutherausgabe*, vol. 28 (Cologne: Böhlau, 1903), 183.

[2] J. Calvin, *The Gospel According to St. John 11–21 and the First Epistle of John*, trans. T. H. L. Parker (Grand Rapids: Eerdmans, 1959), 231.

[3] Cited in Eusebius, *Eccl. Hist.* 6.25.10.

(c. 130–200).[4] This skepticism is often used to support a theory that the orthodox were initially apprehensive of the Johannine Letters until their rehabilitation by Irenaeus.[5]

In response, it should be noted that these kinds of statements arise from the overly rigid demand that a text must be mentioned as "from John" before it can be used in support of John's authorship. But this is an illegitimate burden imposed on the source quotation. If this is kept in mind, it becomes relevant that solid evidence of the authoritative use of these letters, very likely implying the assumption and acceptance of John's authorship, exists well before Irenaeus.[6] Polycarp (c. 69–155), Ignatius (c. 35–110), Papias (c. 60–130), the *Epistula Apostolorum* (c. 140), and the Epistle to Diognetus (second or third century), among others, all show at least a great appreciation for the Johannine Letters prior to Irenaeus. Much of this evidence instills confidence that the apostle John wrote these letters.[7]

From Irenaeus's time forward, there is a steady stream of citations that continues to express the confidence evidenced in the earliest literature. A brief inventory of the more germane evidence since Irenaeus includes the following: the Muratorian Canon (later second century?) refers to the letters (in the plural) as coming from John; Tertullian (c. 160–225) cited 1 John at least 40 times as the work of John; Clement of Alexandria (c. 150–215) referred to 1 John as the "greater epistle" (*Stromateis* 2.15.66), and he also wrote a short commentary on 2 John. Third John is first mentioned in the extant patristic works by Origen (c. 185–254). Dionysius of Alexandria (Origen's successor, died 265) held to John's authorship of 1 John but knew that there was a "reputed" 2 and 3 John (Eusebius, *Eccl. Hist.* 7.25.7–8.11).

The external data point quite early to 1 and 2 John as coming from the apostle. John's authorship of 3 John, most likely due to the letter's brevity and the lack of extant patristic works, is supported less widely. But since there is evidence to assume that the letters circulated together, it is likely that 3 John was included as well. This would be consistent with what is known of published letter collections in antiquity.[8] So the letters are cited consistently as authoritative without a single source proposing a different author.

Internal Evidence   B. H. Streeter's dictum is often repeated: "The three Epistles and the Gospel of John are so closely allied in diction, style, and general outlook that the

---

[4] R. E. Brown, *The Epistles of John*, AB 30 (Garden City: Doubleday, 1982), 6; cf. J. Painter, *1, 2, and 3 John*, SacPag (Collegeville: Liturgical Press, 2002), 40.

[5] See the comments on the external evidence for authorship in the chapter on John's Gospel for a defense against the commonly held opinion that there was a "Johannophobia" among the orthodox (a.k.a. the OJP theory).

[6] Irenaeus's quote of 2 John 7–8 occurs in a context that refers to 1 John and cites 2 John as if it were in the same letter (*Against Heresies* 3.16.8). Instead of claiming that Irenaeus was mistaken, it is more commonly held that this is evidence that at least 1 and 2 John circulated together. See Brown, *Epistles*, 10.

[7] See the impressive study by C. E. Hill, *The Johannine Corpus in the Early Church* (Oxford: Oxford University Press, 2004) for a thorough catalogue of early Johannine citations.

[8] See "Appendix A: The Collection of Paul's Letters," in D. Guthrie, *New Testament Introduction*, rev. ed. (Downers Grove: InterVarsity, 1990), 986–1000; D. Trobisch, *Paul's Letter Collection: Tracing the Origins* (Minneapolis: Fortress, 2000 [1994]); and S. E. Porter, ed., *The Pauline Canon*, Pauline Studies 1 (Leiden: Brill, 2004).

burden of proof lies with the person who would deny their common authorship."[9] The similarities are so numerous and multifaceted that they dwarf any perceived differences by comparison.

What is more, especially in the references in the prologue, the writer used sensory language that is best understood as the speech of an eyewitness. He claims to have "heard," "seen," and touched with his "hands" "the Word of life" (1 John 1:1). The latter expression, using his hands to touch the Word of life, leads us to understand that "Word of life" does not refer to the *message* of life but to the Word who *is* life—Jesus Christ (see John 1:1,14). It is hard to imagine that such language would have been used by someone who was not claiming physical contact with Jesus.

The author consistently assumed an authoritative tone that is consistent with an apostle. Although he calls himself an "elder" in 2 and 3 John, this is not inconsistent with being an apostle as 1 Pet 1:1 shows (cf. 5:1). Papias similarly referred to the apostles as "elders" (cited in Eusebius, *Eccl. Hist.* 3.39.5–7). Thus there is ample reason to believe that John could simultaneously occupy the status of both an apostle and an elder—a prophet also since he wrote Revelation. Thus in his function as an apostle, he wrote a Gospel; and in his role as an elder, he wrote letters to various congregations.

There is also an indication that the author was advanced in years. If the Johannine Letters date from the end of the first century, then any eyewitness would have reached old age by that time. In keeping with this, the author referred to the congregations addressed in John's letters as "my little children," including even those he called "fathers" (1 John 2:12–14).

In the final analysis, although there are recent objections to the apostle John's authorship of the Gospel and of the letters, no external or internal evidence has surfaced that is inconsistent with identifying the author of the Gospel with that of the letters. Coupled with the conclusions concerning the authorship of John's Gospel reached above, the apostle John remains convincingly the best candidate for author of the letters.

Date

Reliable historical tradition strongly suggests that John spent his latter years in Asia Minor in and around Ephesus (see Irenaeus, *Against Heresies* 3.1.2; Eusebius, *Eccl. Hist.* 3.1.1). The apostle's move from Palestine to Asia Minor reportedly took place sometime subsequent to the Jewish rebellion in the year 66. We concluded that John's Gospel was most likely written in the early to mid-80s (see chap. 7). So the question concerning the date of John's letters is, Were they written prior or subsequent to John's Gospel?

On balance, the latter seems more likely. While it is possible that some of the connections with John's Gospel in 1 John are based on a common tradition,[10] in a few places the

---

[9] B. H. Streeter, *The Four Gospels*, rev. ed. (London: Macmillan, 1930), 460.

[10] See A. E. Brooke, *A Critical and Exegetical Commentary on the Johannine Epistles* (New York: Scribner, 1912), xix–xxii; and K. Grayston, *The Johannine Epistles*, New Century Bible Commentary (Grand Rapids: Eerdmans, 1984), 12–14.

Gospel seems to be assumed. For example, 1 John 2:7–8 refers to and explicates the meaning of the new commandment of John 13:34–35 without naming it. In 1 John 5:6, reference is made to Jesus' coming by "water and blood," most likely referring to Jesus' baptism and crucifixion, respectively (see the verbal parallel with John 19:34).

Some, such as Carson and Moo, think the Johannine letters were written to combat heretical misinterpretations of the Gospel, which would require a date for them after the Gospel.[11] This is entirely plausible. Yet even if the purpose for the letters were construed differently, the conclusion that they postdate the Gospel would still be the most probable in light of the parallels mentioned above. The best date, given the death of John at around the turn of the century[12] and the dating of the Gospel in the early to mid-80s, is somewhere in the early to mid-90s.

Provenance

As stated above, the ancient tradition is uniform that John spent his latter years in Ephesus in Asia Minor. Polycrates, in a letter to Victor of Rome, called John one of the "luminaries" buried in Ephesus (Eusebius, *Eccl. Hist.* 3.31.3; 5.24.2). Irenaeus said that John stayed in Ephesus permanently until the reign of Trajan (98–117) and included specific statements about John's ministry in Ephesus (*Against Heresies* 3.1.1). Without solid evidence to the contrary, most scholars assume the accuracy of the Ephesus tradition.

Destination

In 1 John, John addressed various groups in the congregation as "little children," "fathers," "young men," "brothers," and "beloved" (e.g., 2:12–14; 4:1,7). These ways of addressing his audience indicate a closely established relationship between John and his readers. Since 1 John does not refer to specific names and places, contains little mention of specific events, and is general in its teaching, it seems that John focused on important truths of broad relevance to address as many believers as possible. This lends credence to the view that 1 John was a circular letter sent to predominantly Gentile churches in and around Ephesus.

Both 2 John and 3 John are personal letters. The former was written to an "elect lady and her children" (v. 1), which most likely refers to several local congregations; the latter was written to an individual named Gaius (v. 1), but we know nothing about him.[13]

---

[11] D. A. Carson and D. J. Moo, *An Introduction to the New Testament*, 2nd ed. (Grand Rapids: Zondervan, 2005), 676.

[12] Irenaeus (*Against Heresies* 22.22.5; 3.3.4; quoted by Eusebius, *Eccl. Hist.* 3.23.3–4) placed John's death during the reign of Trajan (98–117); Jerome (*Vir. Ill.* 9) said that John died in the sixty-eighth year after Jesus' passion (98 or 101).

[13] Second and Third John are more readily recognizable as examples of the first-century personal letter. Both are rather short (245 and 219 words, respectively) and would easily fit on one papyrus sheet (typical of first-century letters). For a helpful treatment, see the chapter on "New Testament Letters" in Carson and Moo, *Introduction to the New Testament*, 331–53, esp. 332–33 (including further bibliographic references).

Occasion

The churches to whom 1 John was written are under doctrinal and emotional duress. There had been a recent departure of false teachers from the church (2:19) that apparently was both painful and unpleasant and that was still evident in 2 John (v. 7). This is evident especially in the repeated charge against the secessionists that they do not love other believers (e.g., 1 John 2:9–10; 3:10; 4:7). The Christians to whom John wrote in 1 John were in need of instruction, but more importantly they needed to be reassured and comforted in light of the recent upheaval ending in the departure of the false teachers (5:13; see 2:19).

While there was clearly conflict among John's readers, its precise nature is difficult to determine because of the oblique nature of the references. Throughout the letter, John presupposed that his readers knew the issues that were at stake. Irenaeus claimed that John wrote his Gospel to refute Cerinthus—an early gnostic teacher who held that the "Christ spirit" descended on Jesus at his baptism and left him at the cross—but does not make the same claim for his Letters.[14] Some, with reference to Irenaeus, claim the letters were written to combat the same opponent.[15] But it is not at all certain that Cerinthus was the catalyst of the secession that sparked 1 John. Nascent Gnosticism of his sort was certainly afoot, and some form of it may have influenced the secession. But wholesale identification of the Ephesian secessionists with Cerinthus's followers is unwarranted.[16]

The exact nature of the false teaching is impossible to pinpoint with certainty. Schnackenburg aptly observed, "The meager hints and the formulas used in the letter are all we have to go on."[17] As Griffin showed, these may be interpreted in different ways.[18] Nevertheless, there are some clues to help us understand the broad contours of the false teaching found in 1 John. The clearest indicators of the secessionists' doctrine are in 1 John 2 where repeated reference is made to their denial that Jesus is the Messiah (2:22–23; see John 20:30–31).[19]

While certainty remains elusive, it is possible to identify several characteristics of the secessionists. First, they do not know God because they do not keep his commandments. Second, they do not conduct themselves the way Jesus did, especially with regard to the commandment to love one another. In all this, their behavior is characterized by a lack of obedience. If these references were included to condemn the conduct of the secessionists,

---

[14] Irenaeus (*Against Heresies* 3.11.1) also related a confrontation between Cerinthus and John. He noted that John refused to stay in a bath house occupied by Cerinthus and advised the people to flee, "lest even the bath house fall down." Irenaeus (ibid., 3.3.4) named Polycarp as the source of this tradition.

[15] E.g., R. Gundry (*A Survey of the New Testament*, 3rd ed. [Grand Rapids: Zondervan, 1994], 448–49) proposed that Cerinthus is the culprit. But R. Schnackenburg (*The Johannine Epistles: A Commentary* [New York: Crossroad, 1992], 21–23) noted several differences between the secessionists in 1 John and both Cerinthus and Ignatius's opponents mentioned below.

[16] So Schnackenburg, *Epistles*, 21–23.

[17] Ibid., 17.

[18] T. Griffith (*Keep Yourselves from Idols: A New Look at 1 John* [London: Sheffield Academic Press, 2002]) asserted that the secessionists were reverting back to Judaism and that "in the flesh" does not refer to a docetic theology but merely represents a way of expressing the incarnation.

[19] The statement in 2:26 ("I have written these things to you about those who are trying to deceive you") goes back at least as far as 2:18. In 2:22, it is stated that the opponents denied that Jesus was the Messiah (though the exact nature of this denial is not specified). The references to denying and confessing the Son in 2:23 are also general in nature.

the series of contrasts in 1:6–10 probably alludes to them as well. If so, the secessionists were "walking in darkness" while rejecting the notion of sin. This lack of ethical orientation is borne out in chap. 3 where they are identified as "children of the devil" (3:10 KJV) upon an examination of their deeds.

The secessionists, or a group distinguished from them, denied that Jesus had come in the flesh (1 John 4:2–3; cf. 2 John 7). This may (though not necessarily) reflect a docetic Christology. In what follows, rather than reinforcing the humanity of Jesus, the author simply defined the denial as the failure to confess Jesus. The same pattern continues later in the letter (see 4:15; 5:1,5). It seems that the major emphasis lies not so much on refuting a docetic Christology but on the rejection or confession of Jesus.[20] At any rate, the underlying denial is that Jesus is the Messiah. As to the exact nature of the denial, it is hard to be certain.

Another possibility is that the secessionists subscribed to a Christology that denied the atoning merit of the cross. This is hinted at in the confession in 1 John 5:6, "He is the One who came by water and blood; not by water only, but by water and by blood." Again, John was scrupulous to deny an understanding of Christ that viewed him as having come "by water only" and not also "by blood," which seems to indicate a rejection of the sacrificial and substitutionary nature of Jesus' death for others. This flowed from a rejection of the notion of sin.

So what can be said about the secessionists' doctrine? First, it seems that they rejected the apostolic witness (1 John 1:1–5). They had a defective Christology that denied that Jesus was the Messiah, though the reason for this is unclear. Moreover, they were disobedient to the commands of God, especially the love command (see 3:10–15). This led to a doctrine that minimized the reality or at least the seriousness of sin. Thus, the false teachers showed they were not truly children of God. D. Akin described the false teaching well: they flaunted a new theology that "compromised the uniqueness of the person and work of Jesus Christ"; a new morality that "minimized the importance of sin; they claimed to have fellowship with God despite their unrighteous behavior"; and, finally, a new spirituality that "resulted in spiritual arrogance; consequently they did not show love to others."[21]

But there was more than secession prior to John's writing. The controversy continued, and 2 John 8–9 indicates the status of the controversy: "Watch yourselves so that you don't lose what we have worked for, but you may receive a full reward. Anyone who does not remain in the teaching about Christ, but goes beyond it, does not have God. The one who remains in that teaching, this one has both the Father and the Son." It seems that the itinerant teaching of the opponents was ongoing (1 John 2:26).[22] Thus the secessionists

---

[20] For this reason the reference to Jesus having "come in the flesh" in 1 John 4:2 may resemble the affirmation that God "was revealed in the flesh" in 1 Tim 3:16 (NASB).

[21] D. L. Akin, *1, 2, 3 John*, NAC 38 (Nashville: B&H, 2001), 31.

[22] The phrase "those who are trying to deceive you" in 1 John 2:26 is in the present tense, suggesting that, at the time of writing of 1 John, the false teachers were still trying to infiltrate the churches with their false doctrine.

were aggressively seeking to infiltrate the churches in and around Ephesus with their "progressive" theology, and that the aged apostle John (see "the elder" in 2 John 1; 3 John 1) took up his pen to address this situation.

Purpose

First John is similar to John's Gospel in that the purpose statement occurs near, but not at, the very end of the book (see John 20:30–31). In 1 John, the purpose statement occurs at 5:13: "I have written these things to you who believe in the name of the Son of God, so that you may know that you have eternal life." While there are two other passages that declare John's purpose for writing (2:1; 2:12–14), they do not carry the same global weight as 5:13. Thus the reassurance of all genuine Christians in the church(es) addressed is the primary purpose of the book. Nevertheless, reassurance is only part of John's purpose. The book also displays a pronounced emphasis on exhortation, which is indicated by the fact that many verbs are either formal or implied imperatives. There is therefore little doubt that exhortation is an important part of John's purpose for writing his first letter.[23]

Introductory Matters Unique to 2 John and 3 John

The prescripts of 2 John and 3 John differ from 1 John in that the recipients and sender are named, albeit imprecisely. The sender is identified in both letters simply as "the elder." The similarity in language and themes to 1 John makes it virtually certain they are from the same person. The use of the term "elder" here is similar to the prologue in 1 John 1:1–4 in that the writer is so well known that the simplest of ascriptions is sufficient to identify him to the readers.[24]

The designation of the recipients in 2 John as "the elect lady and her children" (2 John 1; cf. v. 13) is also imprecise. These recipients have been variously interpreted as an actual woman and her offspring or as a figurative reference to a (series of) local congregation(s), with the latter of these being preferable.[25] John's language is not appropriate in referring to a real person (e.g., v. 5: "So now I urge you, lady . . . that we love one another"). Also, the scenario underlying verses 7–11 was more appropriate to a local congregation than to a single home in it. The conspicuous absence of personal names in 2 John—compared with the references to Gaius, Demetrius, and Diotrephes in 3 John—suggests that the intended recipient is a local congregation rather than an individual lady and her children. It is unclear why John chose not to name the location of the church. The omission may have been motivated by John's desire to lend his letter universal application or to protect the specific identity of the church for some other reason.[26]

---

[23] See 1 John 2:4–5,12–15 and the repeated exhortations to "remain" in Christ (1 John 2:24,27–28; 3:17; 4:13; 2 John 1:9; see 1 John 3:14).

[24] Schnackenburg, *Epistles*, 270.

[25] So Carson and Moo, *Introduction to the New Testament*, 677; Brown, *Epistles*, 655; C. G. Kruse, *The Letters of John*, PNTC (Grand Rapids: Eerdmans, 2000), 38; I. H. Marshall, *The Epistles of John*, NICNT (Grand Rapids: Eerdmans, 1978), 60; Brooke, *Epistles*, 167–70.

[26] For a judicious treatment, see J. R. W. Stott, *Letters of John*, TNTC, rev. ed. (Grand Rapids: Eerdmans, 1988), 203–5.

The occasion of 2 John may have been the return of a delegation sent by the church to the apostle. In verse 4, John commended "some" as "walking in truth." If related to 1 John (see esp. 2:19), the author may have intended to warn the church against welcoming the secessionists into their homes (see 2 John 8–11). Achtemeier, Green, and Thompson explained it well: "If in 1 John we see the problem from the vantage point of the church from which the false prophets 'went out,' in 2 John we see the problem with the eyes of the church in which they may then have showed up to preach and teach."[27] If so, John wrote to encourage this local congregation to beware of these false teachers.

Third John is specifically written "to my dear friend Gaius" (v. 1), an otherwise unknown individual.[28] John did not specifically mention the secession or problems associated with it. Instead, he commended Gaius for receiving the brothers sent from the apostle (apparently itinerant preachers) and commended Demetrius as one of them (3 John 12). Diotrephes, on the other hand, opposed "the brothers" and did not support the apostolic missionaries (vv. 9–10).[29] Thus it is safe to conclude that one of the major purposes of 3 John was to provide a letter of recommendation for the elder's emissaries in general and for Demetrius in particular, as well as to put Diotrephes in his place prior to John's anticipated visit.

LITERATURE

Genre

The genre of 1 John is difficult to discern. The document contains few formal characteristics that would classify it as a letter. There is no prescript, well-wish/prayer, closing, or formulaic farewell. In fact, both the opening "[t]hat which was from the beginning" (NIV) and the closing "keep yourselves from idols" (5:21 NIV) are highly unconventional. In between the preface and the concluding statement, the elder teaches in a somewhat cyclical manner, frequently returning to a topic he has already addressed only to discuss it in somewhat similar though not identical terms. In this regard, 1 John is similar to Hebrews, which likewise opens with a kind of preface rather than an epistolary opening, and like James, which also concludes without a formal epistolary closing. By comparison, 1 John conforms even less to the standard first-century epistolary format than either Hebrews or James, for the former features at least an epistolary closing and the latter an epistolary opening, while 1 John has neither.

So what is the genre of 1 John? Despite the lack of standard formal epistolary features, it is best to understand it in broad terms as a letter since Greco-Roman letters exhibited a considerable degree of diversity. The work is from a single authoritative source (an apostle),

---

[27] P. J. Achtemeier, J. B. Green, and M. M. Thompson, *Introducing the New Testament: Its Literature and Theology* (Grand Rapids: Eerdmans, 2001), 548.

[28] As Carson and Moo (*Introduction to the New Testament*, 677) observed, this Gaius is likely neither the Gaius of Corinth (Rom 16:23; 1 Cor 1:14) nor the Gaius of Macedonia (Acts 19:29) nor the Gaius of Derbe (Acts 20:4; against the fourth-century *Apostolic Constitutions* 7.46.9).

[29] Nothing is known about Demetrius or Diotrephes apart from the references to these individuals in 2 John.

but the recipients are identified only in general (and figurative) terms as "little children." There is more specific information regarding the secessionists. It seems that the letter was designed to address a situation germane to a number of congregations in the area.

Without imposing external categories on the letter, it is probably best to understand 1 John in terms of a circular letter similar to Ephesians or James. There is abundant evidence for this type of letter in antiquity, especially among the Jews. Jeremiah 29:4–13; Acts 15:23–29; James; and Revelation 2–3 contain exemplars of this type of genre. If so, 1 John is a situational letter written to instruct and encourage the apostolic Christians in and around Ephesus regarding the nature of the gospel and their part in it.

Matters are much more straightforward with 2 and 3 John. Both are prototypical examples of the first-century letter and may be some of the most situational in the NT.[30] There is an opening prescript featuring sender and recipient (in the dative) without benefit of a verb (assuming some form of "I write"), a health wish, a body, closing greeting, and a formulaic farewell. Moreover, unlike most Christian letters, and like most Greco-Roman letters, they are quite brief.[31] Third John may even be classified further as a letter of recommendation for Demetrius. Thus there is wide consensus for identifying the genre of 2 John and 3 John as simple, straightforward *letters*.

Literary Plan

The outline of 2 John and 3 John is predictable and easily discernible. As typical first-century letters, both follow the simple pattern: "introduction—body—conclusion." But the outline of 1 John has generated much debate,[32] and to date no scholarly consensus has been reached. The options range from those who see an intricate macro-chiasm to those who reject any coherent structure.[33]

What makes the structure of 1 John so difficult to discern? In a word, the answer is *subtlety*. The topical transitions are virtually seamless, and the various subjects recur in cyclical intervals throughout the letter. Nevertheless, given the clear structure of John's Gospel and Revelation, as well as the careful nuances displayed within the various paragraphs, it seems unlikely that the author had no plan in mind when writing the letter.[34]

---

[30] J. L. White, "Ancient Greek Letters," in *Greco-Roman Literature and the New Testament*, ed. D. E. Aune, SBLSBS 21 (Atlanta: Scholars Press, 1988), 100; cf. J. A. D. Weima, "Letters, Greco-Roman," in *Dictionary of New Testament Background*, ed. C. A. Evans and S. E. Porter (Downers Grove: InterVarsity, 2000), 640–44.

[31] D. Aune, *The New Testament in Its Literary Environment* (Philadelphia: Westminster, 1987), 163–64.

[32] For a survey of recent options see B. Olsson, "First John: Discourse Analyses and Interpretations," in *Discourse Analysis and the New Testament: Approaches and Results*, ed. S. E. Porter and J. T. Reed, JSNTSup 170, Studies in New Testament Greek 4 (Sheffield: Sheffield Academic Press, 1999), 369–91.

[33] E.g., P. J. van Staden ("The Debate on the Structure of 1 John," *Hervormde Teologiese Studies* 47 [1991]: 487–502) argued for a macro-chiasm. Marshall (*Epistles*, 26) suggested that there is no coherent structure, and Kruse (*Letters of John*, 32) said his analysis of the letter does not "trace any developing argument through the letter because there isn't one."

[34] Schnackenburg (*Epistles*, 12–13) is doubtless correct when he said that the author "does not merely sail along without any particular plan."

Regarding the structure of 1 John, there is wide agreement only concerning the preface (1:1–4) and the epilogue (5:13–21).

The structural proposals for 1 John fall into three major categories: divisions into two, three, or multiple parts.[35] Among those who hold to a division into two parts, the main item of discussion is whether the break should be placed toward the end of chap. 2 or at 3:11. Among those who hold to a three-part structure, the debate centers on whether the first major break is at 2:17; 2:28; or 2:29, and whether the second major break is at 4:1 or 4:7. Among those who see multiple divisions, one finds a variety of proposals.[36]

The following outline for 1 John concurs with those who see a three-part structure to the book and specifically those who suggest the following major units: 1:5–2:27; 2:28–3:24; and 4:1–5:12. Within this overall structure, it is possible to discern interrelated paragraphs that provide a further breakdown of the flow of the argument of the letter. It is best to understand 1:5–2:27 as an extended overview of the rest of the letter, with 2:28–3:24 elaborating on the ethical and 4:1–5:12 on the doctrinal dimensions of believers' lives.[37]

OUTLINES

1 John

I. PROLOGUE (1:1–4)
II. OVERVIEW (1:5–2:27)
    A. True Believers Walk in the Light (1:5–2:2)
    B. True Believers Keep Jesus' Commandments (2:3–11)
    C. Grow in Christ and Do Not Love the World (2:12–17)
    D. Abiding and Departing (2:18–27)
III. ETHICS (2:28–3:24)
    A. Children of God Sanctify Themselves (2:28–3:10)
    B. Children of God Keep His Commandments (3:11–24)
IV. DOCTRINE (4:1–5:12)
    A. Test the Spirits (4:1–6)
    B. The Theological Basis of Brotherly Love (4:7–12)
    C. Confidence from Correct Doctrine (4:13–21)
    D. Testimony and Proof (5:1–12)
V. EPILOGUE (5:13–21)

2 John

I. INTRODUCTION (1–3)
II. BODY: "WALKING IN THE TRUTH" (4–11)
    A. "Walking in the Truth" Requires Brotherly Love (4–6)

---

[35] Brown, *Epistles of John*, 116–29.
[36] Ibid., 764; cf. L. Scott Kellum, "On the Semantic Structure of 1 John: A Modest Proposal," *Faith and Mission* 23 (2008): 36–38.
[37] For a thorough analysis of the structure of 1 John, see Kellum, "Semantic Structure of 1 John," 34–82.

B. "Walking in the Truth" Requires Guarding the Truth About the Son (7–11)
III. CONCLUSION (12–13)

3 John

I. INTRODUCTION (1–4)
II. BODY: COMMENDATION OF GAIUS AND DEMETRIUS, CONDEMNATION OF DIOTREPHES (5–12)
    A. Gaius's Godly Behavior Toward Other Believers (5–8)
    B. The Ungodly Behavior of Diotrephes (9–10)
    C. Commendation of Demetrius (11–12)
III. CONCLUSION (13–14)

UNIT-BY-UNIT DISCUSSIONS

1 JOHN

I. Prologue (1:1–4)

Like John's Gospel, 1 John begins with a prologue. The author claimed to be an eyewitness of Jesus and asserted that he was proclaiming to his recipients the message that he and the apostles had heard from Jesus.

II. Overview (1:5–2:27)

By way of introduction, this section features an ethical and doctrinal preview of the rest of the letter, sounding many major themes such as the need for believers to remain in Christ and the importance of brotherly love.[38]

A. True Believers Walk in the Light (1:5–2:2) The text is developed in terms of two implications of the principle that God is light (1:5), which may imply his holiness or the revelation provided by him or both. The first implication (1:6–7) is that if God is light, his children will "walk in the light," that is, conduct their lives in the sphere of righteousness. The second implication is that those who "walk in the light" confess their sins (1:9; cf. 2:1).[39]

B. True Believers Keep Jesus' Commandments (2:3–11) In 2:3 John elaborated on the previous unit.[40] Those who claim to be Christians either keep Jesus' commandments or they turn out to be liars. The principle described in 2:3–6 (those who remain in him keep his commandments) is illustrated in 2:7–11 by the failure of the secessionists to keep the most prominent of Jesus' commands, the "new commandment" of love (see John 13:34–35;

---

[38] Interestingly, the verb "to write" is used nine times in chaps. 1–2 and not again until the conclusion in 5:13. See Longacre, "Toward an Exegesis of 1 John," 276–77.

[39] Most likely, 2:2 concludes this section. For a detailed defense, see J. Callow, "Where Does 1 John 1 End?" in *Discourse Analysis and the New Testament*, 392–406.

[40] This is indicated by the continued subject matter, the walk of true Christians, and the continued use of the metaphor of walking in light and darkness in 2:9.

15:9–17). The present and the previous sections form the basis for the extended two-part appeal made in the next two units.

C. Grow in Christ and Do Not Love the World (2:12–17)   John proceeded to issue instructions to the shaken believers. The apostle did not doubt their salvation but sought to reassure them in light of the recent departure of the false teachers. John's comments to three groups at different levels of maturity move, somewhat curiously, from "little children" to "fathers" and then to "young men," whereby the instructions to young men are the most detailed.[41] Apparently, "little children" become "fathers" by following John's instructions for young men.

John then instructed the recipients of his letter not to love the world (2:15–17). This relates to the need for believers to remain in Christ, which constitutes the subject of the following section.[42] John reminded his readers that the things of this world will pass away, while those who do the will of God will remain forever.

D. Abiding and Departing (2:18–27)   John opened this section with a contrast between the secessionists who had left the church and the believers who had remained. The former (whom he called "antichrists") departed both theologically and physically, which demonstrated that they were not "of God." By contrast, true believers have an "anointing" from God and need no further instruction because the Holy Spirit is their teacher.[43] This contrast forms the foundation for the command in 2:24, "What you have heard from the beginning must remain in you" (see v. 27).

III. Ethics (2:28–3:24)

In the first major unit (1:5–2:27) John underscored the ethical and doctrinal necessities for believers. In the second major unit (2:28–3:24), he highlighted the first of these—the ethical dimension. His thesis seems to be that the children of God and the children of the devil are recognized by their deeds.

A. Children of God Sanctify Themselves (2:28–3:10)   In this section John elaborated on the differences between the children of God and the children of the devil. God's children, because Jesus was revealed to destroy sin, do not persist in a sinful lifestyle (i.e., they "do not [characteristically] sin"; see 3:6). John frankly acknowledged that Christians still sinned (2:1: "if anyone does sin"), but he made clear that, for believers, sin is not characteristic of, and compatible with, their true nature as God's children. Conversely, children of the devil are controlled by their sinful nature (3:8).

---

[41] For a striking parallel see Josh 1:8, where Joshua is told to be strong and to meditate on the word so he would have good success.

[42] The present passage is, in all probability, commenting on Gen 3:6, where the woman "saw that the tree was good for food and delightful to look at, and that it was desirable for obtaining wisdom."

[43] The phrase "you all have knowledge" (2:20) may constitute a thinly veiled polemic against an early gnostic element among John's opponents. The statement "you don't need anyone to teach you" (2:27) does not imply that believers are without need of instruction subsequent to salvation (see Eph 4:11; 1 Tim 2:7; 3:2; 4:11; 6:2; 2 Tim 1:11; 2:2) but merely warns the readers not to listen to the false teachers.

B. Children of God Keep His Commandments (3:11–24)   John transitioned from the negative (i.e., not practicing sin) to the positive (keeping God's commandments, especially the "new commandment" of love). John used the biblical illustration of Cain (the only OT character mentioned in the letter), who murdered his brother because Abel's works condemned his own. In essence, John's message is that words by themselves are empty; true love is expressed "in deed and truth" (3:18). The essence of remaining in Christ, therefore, is keeping his commands.

IV. Doctrine (4:1–5:12)

The issue of proper doctrine controls the present section. In 4:1–6, John cautioned Christians to be discerning about which spirits to believe. This judgment requires a correct Christology. Brotherly love, likewise, presupposes right doctrine (4:13–21). Finally, in 5:1–12 the author contended that only "the one who has the Son has life."

A. Test the Spirits (4:1–6)   John cautioned believers to exercise discernment. Since there were many false prophets, they should not "believe every spirit" (4:1) but should test the spirits to see if they are from God. This plainly echoes Jesus' warnings, especially in the Sermon on the Mount and the Olivet Discourse (Matt 7:15–20; 24:4–5,23–26 and parallels). Only the Spirit that confesses Jesus is the Spirit of God. The words "come in the flesh" may refer to a docetic error (denying the full humanity of Christ by arguing that Jesus only appeared to be human) but more likely pertain to the incarnation. If so, the issue at hand is that *Jesus* is the Messiah.[44] In either case, one's Christology identifies the spirit behind one's message. Those who receive the apostolic preaching regarding Jesus and remain in it can be victorious over the spirit of the world.

B. The Theological Basis of Brotherly Love (4:7–12)   Although it may appear that the command to love one another is a return to the ethics of the previous section, the basis for the command is not ethical (because this is morally right) but theological (because God is love). In fact, John made a theological point: believers love others because the God who is love indwells them. This is how "his love is perfected in us" (4:12).

C. Confidence from Correct Doctrine (4:13–21)   Possession of the Spirit is proof that a person is a believer (4:13), and confession of Jesus as the Son of God results in God's remaining in him or her (4:15). In 4:15–16 John took both elements of the previous sections and applied them to the believer: "Whoever confesses that Jesus is the Son of God—God remains in him and he in God. . . . God is love, and the one who remains in love remains in God, and God remains in him." God's love is manifested in believers so that they may have confidence on the day of judgment (4:17).

D. Testimony and Proof (5:1–12)   By restatement, John clarified the previous section's main points: "Everyone who believes that Jesus is the Messiah has been born of God, and everyone who loves the parent also loves his child" (5:1). John proceeded to note that

---

[44] This is the same emphasis as in John's Gospel. See the comments on John 20:31 in A. J. Köstenberger, *John*, BECNT (Grand Rapids: Baker, 2004), 582.

the essence of loving God is keeping his commandments, and this is not an impossible task because believers have been born of God. Thus faith in Jesus has overcome the world.

The evidence for John's confidence is stated in 5:6–12. The burden of proof (two or three witnesses) demanded in the OT is met by the testimony of the Spirit, the water, and the blood, a probable reference to Jesus' baptism, Jesus' death, and the inner testimony of the Spirit of God.[45] The content of the testimony is identified in 5:11: "God has given us eternal life, and this life is in his Son."

V. Epilogue (5:13–21)

The conclusion states the purpose of the letter: "I have written these things to you who believe in the name of the Son of God, so that you may know that you have eternal life" (5:13). John elaborated on this purpose in three ways, each of which includes the phrase "we know." First, 5:14–17 describes the confidence in prayer that believers possess when they ask according to God's will, including prayer for "those who commit sin that doesn't bring death" (5:16).[46] Second, those who belong to God do not practice sin (5:18). Third, believers know the truth and are in the truth (5:19–20). John's final comment, "Guard yourselves from idols," provides an abrupt and unconventional ending to the letter, but one that is appropriate for the occasion. It is a warning to believers to accept no substitute for God.

2 JOHN

I. Introduction (1–3)

John employed a standard prescript to this letter, including an identification of sender and recipients and a Christian "well-wish."

II. Body: "Walking in the Truth" (4–11)

The body of the letter consists of a sustained instruction to the church defining "walking in the truth." John instructed his readers to keep the "new commandment" and to guard themselves from antichrists.

---

[45] Many editions of the NT include what is known as the "Johannine Comma," which divides the witnesses between those in heaven and those on earth: "For there are three that testify *in heaven, the Father, the Word, and the Holy Spirit, and these three are One. And there are three who bear witness on earth:* the Spirit, the water, and the blood—and these three are in agreement" (5:7–8; the "Johannine Comma" is in italics). Today this is nearly universally understood to be a later addition. It appears in Erasmus's third edition of the NT (commonly known as the *Textus Receptus*), because a sixteenth-century Greek manuscript, the Codex Montfortianus (Britanicus), included it. This manuscript was produced for the purpose of getting Erasmus to include it in the text (see Brown, *Epistles*, 776, 780). Most rightly reject it on the grounds that it is impossibly late.

[46] There is no scholarly consensus on the exact identification of this sin. For a judicious discussion, see Stott, *Letters of John*, 189–93. Stott argued that John here used the term "brother" in a broad sense to refer to another person, not necessarily a fellow Christian (see 1 John 2:9,11; 3:16–17), and he identified the "sin unto death" as "a deliberate, open-eyed rejection of known truth" akin to the "blasphemy against the Holy Spirit" committed by the Pharisees, who ascribed Jesus' miracles, done in the power of the Holy Spirit, to Satan (Matt 12:28 and parallels). Other possibilities listed by Stott include a specific sin (a "mortal" sin) or apostasy.

A. "Walking in the Truth" Requires Brotherly Love (4–6)

The return of the group to the church (v. 4) provides the occasion for John to remind his readers to be diligent about "walking in the truth." This is defined as keeping the "new commandment" to love one another.

B. "Walking in the Truth" Requires Guarding the Truth about the Son (7–11)

John insisted that the church must guard itself against deceivers. This is done in two ways. First, believers must recognize imposters who do not abide by the apostolic teaching and thus have neither the Son nor the Father (v. 9). Second, once the false teachers have been identified, believers must not offer any help to them (v. 10).

III. Conclusion (12–13)

John concluded with a standard postscript that features plans to visit soon and greetings from mutual friends (the "elect sister" and "her children").

3 JOHN

I. Introduction (1–4)

Again, John employed a standard prescript, featuring sender, recipients, and a Christian well-wish. As in 2 John, it appears that the elder had received a delegation from the church led by Gaius, and he commended this group of believers for "walking in the truth."

II. Body: Commendation of Gaius and Demetrius, Condemnation of Diotrephes (5–12)

In the body of the letter, John requested support for Demetrius. Gaius is commended for his past exposure of the sin of Diotrephes, and the church is urged to support Demetrius.

A. Gaius's Godly Behavior Toward Other Believers (5–8) John began by commending Gaius's past behavior. Gaius displayed his faith by being hospitable to "the brothers," who most likely were emissaries from John. The apostle encouraged Gaius not only to receive this group but also to send them on with ample provisions. The future tense "you will do well" (v. 6) indicates that this implies support of Demetrius who is introduced later.

B. The Ungodly Behavior of Diotrephes (9–10) Verses 9–10 outline John's charges against Diotrephes, who did not recognize the authority of the elder and his emissaries and who slandered the apostolic group. What is more, he censored those who received them, all because he "love[d] to have first place among them," in blatant contradiction of Jesus' words that "whoever wants to be first among you must be your slave" (Matt 20:27).

C. The Commendation of Demetrius (11–12) The commendation of Demetrius is set in contrast with the reprehensible conduct of Diotrephes. John instructed Gaius not "to imitate what is evil" (i.e., Diotrephes). He concluded with a brief commendation of Demetrius, who had the respect of his peers, who spoke the truth itself (probably a commendation of his doctrine), and who had the respect of the apostle also (whom Gaius knew declared the truthful testimony).

III. Conclusion (13–14)

The conclusion (similar to 2 John) is a standard postscript that contains John's desire to meet Gaius face-to-face, a brief greeting from John's friends, and an instruction to "greet the friends by name."

THEOLOGY

Theological Themes

Christian Discipleship and Assurance of Salvation   The Johannine Letters give insight into the basic theological commitments of believers. Believers are not called on to develop a new theology but to cling to that which they received "from the beginning" (1 John 1:1). It turns out that there were "progressives" already then who, ironically, advanced in the wrong direction (2 John 9). Both 2 John and 3 John develop the appropriate Christian response to these individuals in further detail, calling on believers to reject aid to the "progressives" (2 John 9) and to provide aid to those associated with the apostle (3 John 6–8). Believers are challenged to love Christ and one another, not "in word or speech, but in deed and truth" (1 John 3:18), and to grow spiritually by remaining in his word (1 John 2:12–14).

But the major contribution comes from the grounds for assurance given in these letters.[47] The point of 1 John is to instill confidence in true believers that their salvation is assured, coupled with exhortations to persevere (see esp. 1 John 5:13). John wanted his Christian readers to be sure of their salvation, but he also wanted them to remain in Jesus and his word; by contrast, he was not satisfied with believers continuing in sin. Thus John painted a picture of the ideal believers: (1) they are confident of their standing in Christ because of the life-transforming regeneration they experienced through the Holy Spirit; (2) they are obedient because of their love for Christ; (3) they grow in maturity because of their steadfastness; (4) they love because of the nature of the God who changed their lives; and (5) they are victorious because of their faith in Christ.

Love   While not unique to the Johannine Letters, John's emphasis on love is pronounced. Marshall noted that "love is thematized in a way that is unparalleled elsewhere in the New Testament. . . . The indications are that for all the emphasis on right doctrine, the author's main concern is with the Christian behavior of his readers."[48] While the last phrase may be overstated (the author does not separate love from doctrine), it is beyond dispute that love (*agapē* and verbal cognates occur 48 times) is a major theme in 1 John. Marshall listed six dimensions of love in 1 John: (1) the source of love is God; (2) we love in response to God's love; (3) those who love demonstrate their birth from God; (4) love is expressed in

---

[47] For an excellent treatment of this topic in 1 John and the rest of the NT, see D. A. Carson, "Reflections on Christian Assurance," *WTJ* 54 (1992): 1–29.

[48] I. H. Marshall, *New Testament Theology: Many Witnesses, One Gospel* (Downers Grove: InterVarsity, 2004), 539.

obedience (especially the command to love one another); (5) it is possible for love to be only a claim; and (6) one can argue proof of our new birth from the presence or absence of love.[49]

POINTS OF APPLICATION

- Live in the light and not in moral darkness (1 John 1:5–7)
- Know that Jesus turned away God's wrath against sin and serves as our advocate with God the Father (1 John 2:1–2)
- Delight in the fact that God is love and that we are able to love others because he first loved us in Christ (1 John 3:1; 4:16, 19)
- If you are a genuine believer, be assured that you have eternal life (1 John 5:13)
- Don't support finally or otherwise those who are perpetrating false teaching (2 John)
- Don't be autocratic in your exercise of authority in the local church (3 John)

STUDY QUESTIONS

1. Which of these was probably written first: John's Gospel or the letters, and why?
2. Which major heresy is combated in 1 John?
3. What are two major purposes for John's writing of 1 John?
4. What are the purposes for John's writing of 2 John and 3 John?
5. Who is the "chosen lady"?
6. What is the "sin that brings death"?

FOR FURTHER STUDY

Akin, D. L. *1, 2, 3 John.* New American Commentary 38. Nashville: B&H, 2001.

Bruce, F. F. *The Epistles of John.* Grand Rapids: Eerdmans, 1979.

Hill, C. E. *The Johannine Corpus in the Early Church.* Oxford: University Press, 2004.

Kruse, C. G. *The Letters of John.* Pillar New Testament Commentary. Grand Rapids: Eerdmans, 2000.

Marshall, I. H. *The Epistles of John.* New International Commentary on the New Testament. Grand Rapids: Eerdmans, 1978.

Schnackenburg, R. *The Johannine Epistles: A Commentary.* 3 vols. New York: Crossroad, 1992.

Smalley, S. S. *1, 2, 3 John.* Word Biblical Commentary 51. Waco: Word, 1984.

Stott, J. R. W. *The Letters of John.* Tyndale New Testament Commentary. Rev. ed., Grand Rapids: Eerdmans, 1988.

Streett, D. R. *"They Went Out from Us": The Identity of the Opponents in First John.* Berlin: de Gruyter, 2011.

Thompson, M. M. *1–3 John.* IVP New Testament Commentary. Downers Grove: InterVarsity, 1992.

Yarbrough, R. W. *1–3 John.* Baker Exegetical Commentary on the New Testament. Grand Rapids: Baker, 2008.

---

[49] Ibid.

Chapter 20

The Book of Revelation

CORE KNOWLEDGE

Students should know the key facts of the book of Revelation. With regard to history, students should be able to identify the book's author, date, provenance, destination, and purpose. With regard to literature, they should be able to provide a basic outline of the book and identify core elements of the book's content found in the unit-by-unit discussion. With regard to theology, students should be able to identify the major theological themes in the book of Revelation.

KEY FACTS	
Author:	John
Date:	95–96
Provenance:	Patmos
Destination:	Ephesus, Smyrna, Pergamum, Thyatira, Sardis, Philadelphia, and Laodicea
Occasion:	Persecution of Christians in Asia Minor, John's visions
Purpose:	To encourage Christians to faithful endurance by depicting the final judgment and the establishment of Christ's kingdom on earth
Theme:	Jesus the slain and resurrected Lamb is coming again as the eschatological King and Judge
Key Verses:	1:7; 19:11–16

CONTRIBUTION TO THE CANON

- The worship of God and of Jesus Christ (e.g., chap. 4)
- The revelation of the future by the Lamb who was slain, the Lion of Judah (5:1–7)
- The need for uncompromising faithfulness to Christ through patient endurance (e.g., 14:12)
- The vindication of God's righteousness (theodicy) and of suffering believers for persecution by the hands of the unbelieving world (chaps. 6–18)
- The glorious return of Jesus as the supreme King and Lord (19:11–16)
- The millennial reign of Christ, the defeat of Satan, and the Great White Throne judgment (chap. 20)
- The restoration of all things in the new heaven and the new earth (chaps. 21–22)

INTRODUCTION

THROUGHOUT THE HISTORY of its interpretation, the book of Revelation has captured the imagination of many, producing a myriad of interpretations and theological schemas in an effort to understand the difficult yet fascinating teachings of the book.[1] Despite the multitude of challenges confronting the interpreter, interest in the book of Revelation continues unabated.[2]

HISTORY

Author

Since the author identified himself as "John," and since most scholars accept that the name was not a pseudonym, the focus of discussion has been on answering the question, *Which* John is the author of the book? Most scholars recognize three major candidates: (1) John the apostle and son of Zebedee;[3] (2) John the elder;[4] and (3) some other, unknown John who was a prophet.[5] In addition, John Mark[6] and John the Baptist[7] have been proposed as candidates but have failed to gain any serious support.

---

[1] On the history of interpretation of Revelation, see A. W. Wainwright, *Mysterious Apocalypse: Interpreting the Book of Revelation* (Nashville: Abingdon, 1993); J. Kovacs and C. Rowland, *Revelation: The Apocalypse of Jesus Christ*, BBC (Oxford: Blackwell, 2004).

[2] Important commentaries include D. E. Aune, *Revelation*, 3 vols., WBC 52 (Nashville: Nelson, 1997, 1998); G. K. Beale, *The Book of Revelation*, NIGTC (Grand Rapids: Eerdmans, 1999); and G. R. Osborne, *Revelation*, BECNT (Grand Rapids: Baker, 2002).

[3] Irenaeus, *Against Heresies* 4.20.11; Tertullian, *Against Marcion* 3.14.3; 3.24.4; Clement of Alexandria, *Paed.* 2.119; *Quis dives salvetur* 42; *Stromateis* 6.106; Hippolytus, *Antichrist* 36; Origen, *Commentary on the Gospel of John* 2.4.

[4] Eusebius, *Eccl. Hist.* 3.39.3–7. Apparently, Papias made a distinction between John the apostle and John the elder (see chap. 7 above). With reference to the two tombs of John in Ephesus, Eusebius conjectured that Papias attributed the Gospel to the apostle and Revelation to the elder.

[5] R. H. Charles, *The Revelation of St. John*, ICC (New York: Scribner's, 1920), 1.xxxviii.

[6] Eusebius, *Eccl. Hist.* 7.25.15. This was suggested but quickly dismissed by Dionysius of Alexandria (d. 265) as a possible alternative, since Mark's name also was John.

[7] J. M. Ford, *Revelation*, AB 38 (New York: Doubleday, 1975), 28–46.

Internal Evidence   Revelation is the only book in the Johannine corpus with an explicit declaration of authorship. The author identified himself as "John" three times at the beginning and once at the end (1:1,4,9; 22:8). The first-person references indicate that the author was an eyewitness and participant in the events narrated in the book.[8] At the very outset, the text says that John "testified" as an eyewitness to the veracity of the message directly handed down to him by God (1:2; see 1 John 1:1–3). In the other two opening self-references, it seems that John stated his name for the official record (1:4,9).[9] Hence he fulfilled the role of a witness to Christ and to the churches by submitting his testimony in writing.

The author referred to himself simply as "John," which suggests that he was a well-known figure in Asia Minor. Although he did not explicitly call himself a prophet, he did present himself as such. This is demonstrated by the simple self-designation "I, John" (1:9; 22:8), which conforms to the standard convention used in prophetic and apocalyptic writings.[10] He also designated his book as a "prophecy" (1:3; 22:7,11,18–19). The inaugural vision includes John's commission in a manner reminiscent of OT prophets (1:9–20).[11] Later in the book, John participates in the vision like a prophet when he eats a bittersweet scroll and is told that "it is necessary for [him] to prophesy again" (10:8–11, author's translation; see Ezek 3:1–3). He exhibited a special concern for Christian prophets (10:7; 11:10,18; 16:6; 18:20,24; 22:6,9) and condemned all false prophets (16:13; 19:20; 20:10). This suggests that John regarded himself as a prophet in the tradition of the OT prophets.

When John spoke of himself, he did so with humility, preferring to call himself a "servant" of God or Christ (1:1; see 2:20; 6:15; 7:3; etc.) and a "brother" (1:9). While John was an authoritative figure in the Christian community, he presented himself as one of the believers, a "joint participant" with his readers in hardships, the kingdom, and patient endurance (1:9; see 6:11; 12:10; 19:10; 22:9). What is more, linguistic and stylistic clues in the text strongly suggest that John was a Jewish Christian originally from Palestine.[12] In light of these observations there is good reason to believe that the author of Revelation was John the apostle, the son of Zebedee.

External Evidence   Early church tradition unanimously ascribes Revelation to John the apostle. Few other NT books enjoy such clear and unambiguous attribution

---

[8] F. Bovon, "John's Self-Presentation in Revelation 1:9–10," *CBQ* 62 (2000): 695.

[9] Beale, *Book of Revelation*, 1127–28.

[10] E.g., "I, Daniel" (Dan 7:15; 8:15,27; 9:2; 10:2,7; 12:5); "I, Baruch" (*2 Apoc. Bar.* 8:3; 9:1; 10:5; 11:1; 13:1; 32:8; 44:1); "I, Enoch" (*1 Enoch* 12:3); "I, Ezra" (*4 Ezra* 2:33). See also H. B. Swete, *Commentary on Revelation* (Grand Rapids: Kregel, 1977; repr. of 3rd ed. of *The Apocalypse of St. John* [1911]), 11; Aune, *Revelation 1–5*, 75.

[11] See esp. F. D. Mazzaferri, *The Genre of the Book of Revelation from a Source-critical Perspective*, BZNW 54 (Berlin: W. de Gruyter, 1989), 259–378. On the OT prophetic call narratives, see ibid., 88–102; D. E. Aune, *Prophecy in Early Christianity and the Ancient Mediterranean World* (Grand Rapids: Eerdmans, 1983), 97–103.

[12] This view is held by a majority of scholars, including Charles, *Revelation of St. John*, 1.xliv; Aune, *Revelation 1–5*, l; and G. R. Beasley-Murray, *Revelation*, NCBC (London: Oliphants, 1974), 35–37.

of authorship.[13] Explicit early and uncontested testimony asserting Johannine apostolic authorship is found in the writings of Justin Martyr (c. 100–165), Irenaeus (c. 130–200), Clement of Alexandria (c. 150–215), Hippolytus (c. 170–236), Origen (c. 185–254), and Tertullian (c. 160–225).[14] Justin Martyr in the second century (c. 100–165) provided the earliest extant evidence that John the apostle wrote Revelation (Justin, *Dialogue with Trypho* 81.4; see Eusebius, *Eccl. Hist.* 4.18.8).

This tradition was not only echoed and affirmed by later church fathers; there is absolutely no hint of any competing views to Johannine apostolic authorship. So strong is this evidence that Guthrie observes that those who deny Johannine apostolic authorship suppose that the early church fathers were simply ignorant of the true origins of the book and erroneously assumed that the author must have been the son of Zebedee.[15] Thus these early traditions make a solid case for John the son of Zebedee as the author of Revelation.

Date

Scholarly opinion concerning the date of Revelation's composition is divided between an early date (64–69) and a late date (95–96). Although certainty continues to be elusive, the late date, during the reign of Domitian, has considerably stronger support.

Internal Evidence The book of Revelation provides the following internal clues regarding its date of composition: (1) the persecution experienced by the churches of Asia Minor; (2) the spiritual condition of these churches; (3) the emperor cult; and (4) the references to "Babylon" in Revelation.

Type of Persecution One of the most common arguments for dating Revelation pertains to the notion that at the time of composition Christians were experiencing fierce persecution. Throughout church history Domitian has been viewed as a great persecutor of the church (Eusebius, *Eccl. Hist.* 4.26.9). But in recent decades this assumption has been increasingly questioned because of the paucity of evidence supporting an empire-wide persecution instigated by Domitian. Therefore, proponents of an early date contend that the persecution of Christians reflected in Revelation best corresponds to Nero's persecution.

The book of Revelation indicates various degrees of persecution and anticipates persecution on a much grander scale in the near future. John's banishment to Patmos came about because of hostility toward the exclusive claims of the gospel (1:9). The letters to the churches in Asia Minor also demonstrate local persecution, although the persecution experienced by Christians in Asia Minor did not result in death, except for one case (Antipas) in the city of Pergamum (2:13). These and other examples favor the time of Domitian. First, the persecution is not severe enough to be associated with Nero. Second, while

---

[13] See Charles, *Revelation of St. John*, 1.c; D. Guthrie, *New Testament Introduction*, rev. ed. (Downers Grove: InterVarsity, 1990), 933; D. A. Carson and D. J. Moo, *An Introduction to the New Testament*, 2nd ed. (Grand Rapids: Zondervan, 2005), 701.

[14] Irenaeus, *Against Heresies* 4.20.11; Clement of Alexandria, *Paed.* 2.119; *Quis div.* 42; *Stromateis* 6.106; Hippolytus, *Antichrist* 36; Origen, *Commentary on John* 2.4; Tertullian, *Against Marcion* 3.14.3; 3.24.4.

[15] Guthrie, *Introduction*, 935.

the notion that Domitian instituted an empirewide persecution has been exaggerated,[16] the fact that he did not systematically persecute Christians does not mean that he was favorably disposed toward them. To the contrary, believers were despised throughout the empire. Not all believers in Asia Minor faced the same level of antagonism; it seems that persecution was more intense in cities competing for Rome's favor. This also suggests the time of Domitian.

The State of the Churches in Asia Minor   Regarding the state of the churches in Asia Minor as described in Revelation, many of these churches were clearly in a deteriorated moral and spiritual condition. The Christians in Ephesus had forsaken their "first love" (2:4 KJV). The churches in Pergamum and Thyatira had permitted, and even succumbed to, false teaching (2:14–15,20–24). Believers in Sardis had become spiritually lethargic (3:1–2). The Laodiceans had indulged in "lukewarm" and arrogant self-sufficiency (3:15–17).[17] While it may be argued that developing this kind of spiritual apathy would have taken some time, thus supporting a late date, this piece of evidence is inconclusive by itself, especially since some of Paul's churches developed comparable problems already in the 50s and 60s.[18]

The Emperor Cult   The emperor cult is significant since many have suggested a Domitianic date because of the anti-imperial rhetoric in the book.[19] The phrase "our Lord and God" (4:11; see 19:6), in particular, parallels the Latin *dominus et deus noster*, a title applied to Domitian during his reign (Suetonius, *Dom.* 13.2). Faithfulness to the one true God in the midst of an idolatrous society is one of the major themes in the book. Evidence abounds from Domitian's critics and supporters that he arrogated titles of divinity beyond what was culturally acceptable. Aside from Caligula's excessive claims to divinity,[20] Domitian was the first Roman emperor to adopt and even mandate the title *deus*,[21] a claim his critics found repulsive.[22]

While the reference to "our Lord and God" in 4:11 does not conclusively pinpoint the emperor at the time of composition, of all the emperors Domitian is the most likely candidate. To be sure, all the emperors were afforded some measure of divinity, but this

---

[16] A. J. Bell, "The Date of John's Apocalypse: The Evidence of Some Roman Historians Reconsidered," *NTS* 25 (1978): 93–97; J. C. Wilson, "The Problem of the Domitianic Date of Revelation," *NTS* 39 (1993): 588–96; L. L. Thompson, *The Book of Revelation: Apocalypse and Empire* (New York: Oxford University Press, 1990), 116.

[17] Some also point to the reference to wealth in Laodicea as evidence for a later date since the city was destroyed by an earthquake c. 61 and rebuilt without the financial assistance of Rome (Tacitus, *Ann.* 14.27.1). If the city had been destroyed, one would naturally expect a much later date for the composition of the letter. See C. J. Hemer, *The Letters to the Seven Churches of Asia in Their Local Setting*, JSNTSup 11 (Sheffield: JSOT, 1986), 193–96; L. Morris, *The Revelation of St. John*, TNTC (Grand Rapids: Eerdmans, 1969), 37.

[18] See C. H. H. Scobie, "Local References in the Letters to the Seven Churches," *NTS* 39 (1993): 606–24.

[19] L. Mowry, "Revelation 4–5 and Early Christian Liturgical Usage," *JBL* 71 (1952): 80; Beale, *Book of Revelation*, 335; C. S. Keener, *Revelation*, NIVAC (Grand Rapids: Zondervan, 2000), 176; Osborne, *Revelation*, 240; Aune, *Revelation 1–5*, 310; id., "The Influence of Roman Imperial Court Ceremony on the Apocalypse of John," *BibRes* 28 (1983): 20–22.

[20] Philo, *Legat.* 353; J. S. McLaren, "Jews and the Imperial Cult: From Augustus to Domitian," *JSNT* 27 (2005): 266–69.

[21] T. B. Slater, "On the Social Setting of the Revelation to John," *NTS* 44 (1998): 236.

[22] Suetonius, *Dom.* 13.2; Dio Cassius, *Hist.* 67.4.7; 67.13.4; see Dio Chrysostom, *Def.* 45.1; Juvenal, *Sat.* 4.69–71. See also F. O. Parker, "'Our Lord and God' in Rev 4,11: Evidence for the Late Date of Revelation?," *Bib* 82 (2001): 209.

practice seems to have reached a new level under Domitian. What is more, in the accounts of Nero's conflict with Christians there is no evidence that Nero claimed to be divine. The same is true for all other emperors prior to Domitian. If 4:11 represents two competing claims for "our Lord and God," the evidence favors the time of Domitian for the date of the book.

The City "Babylon" The references to the city "Babylon" in the latter half of the book (14:8; 16:19; 17:5; 18:2,10,21) are intriguing. In 17:9, when explaining the vision of the prostitute riding atop a scarlet beast that has seven heads, the interpreting angel explains that "the seven heads are seven mountains on which the woman is seated." Since Rome was known throughout the ancient world as the city on seven hills, "Babylon" should be equated with Rome.[23] This represents a weighty piece of evidence supporting a post-70 date.[24] The reason "Babylon" became a fitting code name for Rome is that both empires destroyed the temple in Jerusalem. Two post-70 Jewish apocalypses use "Babylon" as a cipher for Rome (4 Ezra 3:1–2,28–31; 2 Bar 10:1–3; 11:1; 67:7; cf. *Sib. Or.* 5.143, 159–60).[25] This constitutes compelling evidence for identifying "Babylon" as Rome in Revelation, which suggests a post-70 date of composition.

External Evidence The earliest traditions located Revelation in the reigns of Claudius, Nero, Domitian, or Trajan. By far the bulk of early church tradition supports the time of Domitian.[26] Irenaeus's testimony constitutes the earliest available evidence regarding the date of the Apocalypse (c. 130–200).[27] Irenaeus, a native of Smyrna, may have received his information directly from Polycarp, a disciple of John (Irenaeus, *Against Heresies* 3.3.4), and his pronouncement gained broad acceptance in the early church.

Irenaeus's testimony was affirmed by Clement of Alexandria (c. 150–215), Origen (c. 185–254), Victorinus (died c. 304), Eusebius (c. 260–340), and Jerome (c. 354–420). Clement and Origen stated that John wrote from Patmos but did not name the emperor. Clement, writing around the end of the first century, remarked that John was released from exile on Patmos after the death of the "tyrant."[28] Although he did not provide the name, Eusebius assumed it was Domitian.[29] After Domitian died, Nerva promised a "new

---

[23] Virgil, *Georg.* 2.535; *Aen.* 6.738; Horace, *Carm.* 7; Cicero, *Att.* 6.5; Suetonius, *Dom.* 4; *Sib. Or.* 2.18; 13.45; 14.108; Keener, *Revelation*, 408n21.

[24] A. Y. Collins, *Crisis and Catharsis: The Power of the Apocalypse* (Philadelphia: Westminster, 1984), 57–58; J. N. Kraybill, *Imperial Cult and Commerce in John's Apocalypse*, JSNTSup 127 (Sheffield: Sheffield Academic Press, 1996), 142–47; S. J. Friesen, *Imperial Cults and the Apocalypse of John: Reading Revelation in the Ruins* (Oxford: University Press, 2001), 138–40.

[25] See J. J. Collins, *The Apocalyptic Imagination*, 2nd ed. (Grand Rapids: Eerdmans, 1998), 196.

[26] Irenaeus, *Against Heresies* 5.30.3; Clement of Alexandria, *Quis dives salvetur* 42; Origen, *Homily on Matthew* 16.6; Victorinus, *Apocalypse* 10.11; Eusebius, *Eccl. Hist.* 3.18; 3.20; Jerome, *De Viris illustribus* 9.

[27] Melito of Sardis (died c. 190) also supported a Domitianic dating as recorded by Eusebius (*Eccl. Hist.* 4.26.9). He wrote a commentary on Revelation and in his protest against Marcus Aurelius argued that Nero and Domitian unjustly persecuted Christians. See Charles, *Revelation of St. John*, 1.xcii.

[28] Clement, *Quis div. salv.* 42; cf. Eusebius, *Eccl. Hist.* 3.23.5–19.

[29] Eusebius, *Eccl. Hist.* 3.23.1; cf. Aune, *Revelation 1–5*, lix. On the release of those banished under Domitian, see Pliny, *Ep.* 1.5.10; 9.13.5; Dio Chrysostom, *Or.* 13.

era" of liberty and justice.[30] The tyrant in question could very well be Domitian, which would corroborate the date indicated by Irenaeus.

Eusebius accepted Irenaeus's testimony, asserting that Revelation was written in the fourteenth year of Domitian's reign (c. AD 95; *Eccl. Hist.* 3.18.1–3 citing Irenaeus, *Against Heresies* 5.30.3).[31] He depicted Domitian as a cruel tyrant, the successor of Nero, in his hostility toward God and his persecution of Christians.[32] He also affirmed the tradition that after John was released from Patmos, he took up residence in Ephesus subsequent to Domitian's death.[33] If his sources were in error and no such persecution took place, his dating becomes suspect. In any case, Eusebius's testimony preserved a tradition ascribing to Revelation a late date that was widely accepted in the early church.

Conclusion   The preponderance of the internal and external evidence suggests the mid-90s during the reign of Domitian as the most probable date of composition. The external testimony overwhelmingly favors the late date, which became the established tradition throughout church history. The internal testimony, while less than conclusive, also tends to support a later date. Although some passages may reflect historical circumstances prior to 70, most of the evidence seems to point to a later date. The book of Revelation was written around 95–96 by John in obedient submission to the vision he received while in exile on Patmos.

Provenance

John disclosed the location of where he received his vision as the little isle of Patmos in the Aegean Sea (1:9b).[34] Pliny and Strabo briefly mention Patmos as included among the Sporades islands.[35] It was situated about 40 miles west of Miletus and almost 60 miles southwest of Ephesus. This close proximity to the mainland of Asia Minor demonstrates its inclusion in the provincial boundaries. Patmos could have functioned as a place of exile, but no records exist identifying it as such. Although not uninhabited, Patmos's small rocky terrain made it an ideal spot for banishment. John indicated that the reason he was there was "the word of God and the testimony of Jesus," most likely indicating some form of persecution (see 6:9; 12:17; 20:4). This is supported by John's self-identification as a fellow participant with the churches in their hardships (1:9; see 2:9,10,22; 7:14). Therefore, John's presence on Patmos was most likely the result of official opposition to his message. According to Tertullian (c. 160–225), John was exiled to Patmos as an *insulam relegatur*.[36]

---

[30] Tacitus, *Agr.* 3; cf. Thompson, *Book of Revelation*, 110–11.

[31] Eusebius, *Chron.* PG 19.551–52; Aune, *Revelation 1–5*, lix.

[32] Eusebius, *Eccl. Hist.* 3.17.1; 3.18.4; he also (ibid., 3.20.7) cited Tertullian (*Apol.* 5) who stated, "Domitian also tried to do the same as he, for he was a Nero in cruelty, but, I believe, in as much as he had some sense, he stopped at once and recalled those whom he had banished."

[33] Eusebius, *Eccl. Hist.* 3.20.8–9; see Clement, *Quis div. salv.* 42; Jerome, *De Viris illustribus* 9.

[34] The island was about 30 miles in circumference according to Pliny the Elder, *Nat.* 4.12.23, 69; Strabo, *Geog.* 10.5.13; see Thucydides, *Peloponnesian War* 3.33.3.

[35] Pliny the Elder, *Nat.* 4.12.69; Strabo, *Geog.* 10.5.14.

[36] Tertullian, *Praescr.* 36; see Jerome, *De Viris illustribus* 9.

Thus it seems likely that John was banished from Ephesus in Asia Minor by a provincial governor.

Destination, Occasion, and Purpose

The book of Revelation is addressed to seven churches that existed at the end of the first century (95–96). John addressed Christians living in cities dotted along a postal route in the Roman province of Asia Minor.[37] The cities were Ephesus, Smyrna, Pergamum, Thyatira, Sardis, Philadelphia, and Laodicea. John explicitly stated several times that the occasion for writing was a direct command from the Lord (1:11,19; see 2:1, etc.).

John's vision arrived at a time when the churches of Asia Minor needed encouragement to remain faithful to Christ and to endure hardships as they swam against the currents of the surrounding culture (chaps. 2–3). The implicit occasion is that Christians in these cities stood at the crossroads between faith and culture, having to choose between compromise with the world system and their commitment to Christ.

The dominant culture was steeped in Greco-Roman paganism with its plethora of gods, goddesses, and temples. Christians represented a religious group that penetrated every level of society and consisted of both Jews and Gentiles. They were tenacious monotheists who refused to participate in local trade guilds or any other common pagan ritual, including the imperial cult. The imperial cult had existed as part of Asia Minor's religious climate ever since the time of Augustus. Pergamum hosted the very first temple dedicated to Augustus and the goddess Roma for the entire province of Asia beginning in 29 BC and remained active well past the reign of Hadrian.[38] During the reign of Tiberius, the cities of Sardis and Smyrna competed for the right to host a second provincial imperial cult in Asia, which was won by Smyrna in AD 26.[39] During the reign of Domitian, the city of Ephesus erected an unprecedented third imperial temple in Asia Minor (89/90).[40] Some estimates attest to more than 80 smaller localized imperial temples in more than 60 cities in Asia Minor.[41] The cult functioned politically to express just how grateful and loyal the provinces were to the emperor, using religious conventions for political purposes.[42] From its inception, the emperor, along with the goddess Roma, was worshipped and honored for his benevolence toward the provinces.

---

[37] The road connecting the cities formed a horseshoe-shaped circuit, and each city could be reached within a day or two by foot. See D. A. deSilva, *Introduction to the New Testament: Context, Methods, and Ministry Formation* (Downers Grove: InterVarsity, 2004), 895.

[38] S. J. Friesen, *Imperial Cults and the Apocalypse of John: Reading Revelation in the Ruins* (Oxford: Oxford University Press, 2001), 25, 27.

[39] Ibid., 36–38. So Tacitus, *Annals* 4.15.

[40] Friesen, *Imperial Cults*, 44–46.

[41] S. R. F. Price, *Rituals and Power: The Roman Imperial Cult in Asia Minor* (Cambridge: Cambridge University Press, 1998), 135. For an excellent map locating imperial temples in Asia Minor, see M. Wilson, *Charts on the Book of Revelation: Literary, Historical, and Theological Perspectives* (Grand Rapids: Kregel, 2007), 115.

[42] Price, *Rituals and Power*, 16, 29–31.

The imperial cult, however, was much more than a mere political tool; participants actually worshipped the emperor as divine. The use of the term *theos* ("god"), although rare, attests to the fact that worshippers esteemed emperors by elevating them to a status far above regular mortals. Conflict with the imperial cult in Revelation can hardly be ignored. There are what appear to be frequent references to the imperial cult in the latter half of the second vision (13:4,15–16; 14:9–11; 15:2; 16:2; see 20:4). John envisioned a time when worship of a ruler would escalate to a point of mandatory participation by all inhabitants of the earth.[43] Christians refusing to bow down in worship to the beast would incur his wrath and be summarily executed (13:15; see 6:9; 18:24; 20:4). Nevertheless, believers are exhorted to remain faithful and true to Christ even if this means death (2:10,13; 13:10; 14:12; 17:14).

While the local religious and political climate of each city varied, John, as one who experienced unjust exile, wrote to believers facing similar injustice. Believers might succumb to despair over the triumph of a corrupt justice system that condemns the innocent simply because of their Christian faith. But John's vision assuages these fears by depicting the eventual reversal of these travesties of justice. This concern for vindication is voiced by the martyred souls at the altar (6:9–11; 16:7). Revelation describes Jesus as wielding ultimate judicial authority and as the one who is worthy to unleash God's wrath upon impenitent humanity (1:12–20; 5:2–4; see John 5:17–29). No matter what fate Christians might have endured under unjust judges, they will one day reign with Christ and help execute the judgment of the nations (20:4).[44] Thus the intended purpose is to comfort the weary and oppressed, to fortify faithfulness and endurance, and to cleanse the churches from heresy and compromise by depicting the heavenly reality of Jesus as the glorified judge and all the events surrounding his return to establish his kingdom on earth.

LITERATURE

Genre

The very word *apocalypse* conjures up a myriad of images. Scholars typically distinguish between (1) "apocalypse"; (2) "apocalyptic"; and (3) "apocalypticism."[45] *Apocalypse* refers to a particular genre of literature written between approximately 200 BC and AD 200.[46] The adjective *apocalyptic* is used when describing either the literary genre or the worldview. *Apocalypticism* denotes a worldview, ideology, or theology merging the eschatological aims of particular groups into a cosmic and political arena.[47]

---

[43] See D. A. deSilva, "The 'Image of the Beast' and the Christians in Asia Minor: Escalation of Sectarian Tension in Revelation 13," *TrinJ* 12 (1991): 197–201.

[44] D. A. deSilva, "Honor Discourse and the Rhetorical Strategy of the Apocalypse of John," *JSNT* 71 (1998): 98.

[45] P. Hanson, *Dawn of Apocalyptic* (Philadelphia: Fortress, 1975), xi; Collins, *Apocalyptic Imagination*, 2.

[46] Collins, *Apocalyptic Imagination*, 21.

[47] K. Koch, *The Rediscovery of Apocalyptic*, trans. M. Kohl (Naperville: A. R. Allenson, 1972), 28–33.

J. J. Collins and other scholars developed the following classic definition:

> "Apocalypse" is a genre of revelatory literature with a narrative framework, in which a revelation is mediated by an otherworldly being to a human recipient, disclosing a transcendent reality which is both temporal, insofar as it envisages eschatological salvation, and spatial, insofar as it involves another, supernatural world.[48]

This definition emphasizes the form as a narrative framework involving an otherworldly mediator and the content as containing both temporal (eschatological salvation) and spatial (supernatural world) elements. But this definition lacks any reference to the *function* of an apocalypse. For this reason a subsequent study group added that an apocalypse is "intended to interpret present, earthly circumstances in light of the supernatural world and of the future, and to influence the understanding and behavior of the audience by means of divine authority."[49]

The book of Revelation constitutes one of the unique books of the Bible not only because it represents the pinnacle of inspired revelation but also because it is the only apocalyptic book in the NT. Revelation exhibits elements consistent with the genres of apocalyptic, prophecy, and letter. Some have maintained that the first word of the book, "revelation" (*apokalupsis*), suggests an immediate genre classification, especially given the use of apocalyptic language and imagery throughout Revelation. But a more accurate genre designation occurs in passages where John identified the book as a "prophecy" (1:3; 22:7,10,18–19; cf. 11:16; 19:10). This close association between apocalypse and prophecy is natural because the apocalyptic genre stems from and remained under the rubric of OT prophecy.[50] Apocalyptic writings derived from prophetic oracles, and therefore the lines of demarcation separating these genres, are somewhat fluid. What is more, Revelation is addressed to specific congregations and thus also has certain epistolary features.

Hence Revelation constitutes a mixed genre. The book falls into the overall genre of prophecy, but it corresponds to apocalyptic writings in many respects. G. E. Ladd correctly argued for the designation of "prophetic-apocalyptic."[51] Fiorenza also contended that the dichotomy between apocalyptic and prophecy cannot be sustained with regard to Revelation since the book blends both elements.[52] The best overall assessment regarding the genre of Revelation is that the book constitutes "a prophecy cast in an apocalyptic mold [which is] written down in a letter form."[53]

---

[48] J. J. Collins, "Introduction: Towards the Morphology of a Genre," *Sem* 14 (1979): 9.

[49] A. Y. Collins, "Introduction: Early Christian Apocalypticism," *Sem* 36 (1986): 7.

[50] Elisabeth Schüssler Fiorenza, *The Book of Revelation: Justice and Judgment*, 2nd ed. (Minneapolis: Fortress, 1998), 138.

[51] G. E. Ladd, "Why Not Prophetic-Apocalyptic?" *JBL* 76 (1957): 192–200.

[52] Fiorenza, *Book of Revelation*, 133–56.

[53] D. A. Carson, D. J. Moo, and L. Morris, *An Introduction to the New Testament* (Grand Rapids: Zondervan, 1992), 479.

Literary Plan

Like the turning of a kaleidoscope, scenes morph before the reader's eyes with a myriad of symbols, colors, numbers, and heavenly beings, leaving many mystified and confused regarding the literary plan of the book of Revelation.[54] The rapid shifts in scenery with various intercalations (i.e., insertions or interpolations), recapitulations, and asides have prompted some interpreters to conclude that the book consists of a patchwork of visions composed in various settings over extended periods of time.[55] But these source and compositional critics have failed to recognize that in its present form Revelation represents a literary unity.

The book of Revelation represents an intricately woven literary masterpiece intended to convey a unified message. Bauckham's seminal essay on the structure of Revelation convincingly demonstrates the intricate nature of its composition and literary unity.[56] What is more, narrative critical approaches not only presuppose this unity, but they also help to demonstrate how Revelation presents a unified literary composition.[57] As such, Revelation tells a story complete with characters, settings, plot, and climax.

Attempts at explaining Revelation's macrostructure are legion.[58] Although no formal consensus has emerged, scholars have successfully identified numerous structural features. Revelation has a clearly delineated prologue (1:1–8) and an epilogue (22:6–21). John divided the book into four visions marked by the phrase "in the Spirit" (1:10; 4:2; 17:3; 21:10). Although some scholars arrange the structure as a sevenfold series of sevens, there are only four instances of a clearly enumerated series of sevens (2:1–3:22; 6:1–8:1; 8:2–11:19; 15:1–16:21). John included materials that appear to interrupt or link aspects of the narrative, which have been labeled interludes, intercalations,[59] interlocking,[60] or interweaving.[61] Another commonly acknowledged structural feature is the intended contrast between the harlot city of Babylon (chaps. 17–18) and the bride city of the new Jerusalem (chaps. 21–22).

---

[54] See E. F. Scott, *The Book of Revelation* (New York: Charles Scribner's Sons, 1940), 44.

[55] Charles, *Revelation of St. John*, 1.lxxxvii–xci; Aune, *Revelation 1–5*, cx–cxxxiv; Ford, *Revelation*, 50–57.

[56] R. Bauckham, The *Climax of Prophecy: Studies on the Book of Revelation* (London: T&T Clark, 1993), 3–22.

[57] L. L. Thompson, "The Literary Unity of the Book of Revelation," in *Mappings of the Biblical Terrain: The Bible as Text*, ed. V. L. Tollers and J. Maier (Lewisburg: Bucknell University Press, 1990), 347–63; J. L. Resseguie, *Revelation Unsealed: A Narrative Critical Approach to John's Apocalypse*, Biblical Interpretation Series 32 (Leiden: Brill, 1998); D. Lee, *The Narrative Asides in the Book of Revelation* (Lanham: University Press of America, 2002); J. R. Michaels, "Revelation 1.19 and the Narrative Voices of the Apocalypse," *NTS* 37 (1991): 604–20.

[58] See D. L. Barr, *Tales of the End: A Narrative Commentary on the Book of Revelation* (Santa Rosa: Polebridge, 1998), 10; Beale, *Book of Revelation*, 108; Bauckham, *Climax of Prophecy*, 21.

[59] R. J. Loenertz, *The Apocalypse of Saint John*, trans. H. Carpenter (New York: Sheed & Ward, 1948), xiv–xix; Fiorenza, "Composition and Structure of the Book of Revelation," *CBQ* 39 (1977): 360–61.

[60] M. S. Hall, "The Hook Interlocking Structure of Revelation: The Most Important Verses in the Book and How They May Unify Its Structure," *NovT* 44 (2002): 278–96.

[61] Bauckham, *Climax of Prophecy*, 9.

As mentioned, Revelation consists of four separate interrelated visions introduced by the phrase "in the Spirit," all of which occur within a single day (1:10).[62] M. Tenney noted how "[e]ach occurrence of this phrase locates the seer in a different place."[63] The phrase indicates a shift of setting from Patmos (1:9) to the heavenly throne room (4:1–2) into a desert (17:3) and finally to a great high mountain (21:10). Moreover, the phrase "I will show you" occurs three times (4:1; 17:1; 21:9) in close proximity to "in the Spirit" (4:2; 17:3; 21:10), suggesting that these two phrases are used in conjunction with each other to signal major structural transitions.[64] Interestingly, 4:1–2 also contains one of the three occurrences of the phrase "what must take place" (1:1; 4:1; 22:6), which stresses the future prophetic nature of 4:1–22:6.[65]

OUTLINE

I. PROLOGUE (1:1–8)

II. VISION ONE (ON PATMOS): THE GLORIFIED CHRIST WHO INVESTIGATES HIS CHURCHES (1:9–3:22)
   A. The Inaugural Vision of Jesus Christ (1:9–20)
   B. The Messages to the Seven Churches of Asia Minor (2:1–3:22)

III. VISION TWO (IN HEAVEN): THE DIVINE COURT PROCEEDINGS AND THE TRIAL OF THE NATIONS (4:1–16:21)
   A. Transition from Patmos to Heaven (4:1–2)
   B. Worship Around the Throne (4:3–11)
   C. The Divine Courtroom (5:1–14)
   D. Preliminary Investigative Judgments (6:1–17)
   E. First Interlude: The Protective Sealing of God's People (7:1–17)
   F. Eschatological Investigative Judgments (8:1–9:21)
   G. Second Interlude: God's People as Prophetic Witnesses (10:1–11:19)
   H. Third Interlude: The Signs Narrative/God's People in Holy War (12:1–15:8)
   I. Final Investigative Judgments: The Seven Bowls (16:1–21)

IV. VISION THREE (IN THE DESERT): THE DESTRUCTION OF BABYLON AND THE RETURN OF CHRIST (17:1–21:8)
   A. Transition: "Come, I Will Show You the Judgment of the Notorious Prostitute" (17:1–2)
   B. The Prostitute City Babylon Described (17:3–6)
   C. The Prostitute City Babylon as Rome (17:7–18)
   D. The Trial and Sentencing of Babylon (18:1–24)
   E. Heavenly Celebration of Babylon's Destruction (19:1–10)
   F. The Divine Warrior and Final Tribunal (19:11–20:15)
   G. The Renewal of Creation and the Arrival of the New Jerusalem (21:1–8)

---

[62] Ibid., 3.

[63] M. C. Tenney, *Interpreting Revelation* (Grand Rapids: Eerdmans, 1957), 33. See also G. E. Ladd, *A Commentary on the Revelation of John* (Grand Rapids: Eerdmans, 1972), 14.

[64] Beale, *Book of Revelation*, 110.

[65] Ibid., 152–70; W. C. van Unnik, "A Formula Describing Prophecy," *NTS* 9 (1963): 92–94.

V. VISION FOUR (ON A MOUNTAIN): BELIEVERS' REWARD AND THE RENEWAL
   OF CREATION (21:9–22:5)
   A. Transition: "Come, I Will Show You the Bride" (21:9–10)
   B. The Description of the New Jerusalem Descending from Heaven (21:11–27)
   C. The Paradise of God: The Renewal of Creation (22:1–5)
VI. EPILOGUE (22:6–21)

UNIT-BY-UNIT DISCUSSION

I. Prologue (1:1–8)

The prologue informs the reader that this is a revelatory book containing a vision of
Jesus, which has his return as the content, John as the seer, and the churches as the recipients. God gave this revelation in order that all his servants may know what must happen in
the near future. The divine authority of this vision is expressed by a chain of intermediar-
ies: God°Jesus°angel°John°churches. John affirms the veracity of this vision by submitting
it as eyewitness testimony regarding everything he saw and heard.

After promising a blessing to the one who reads, hears, and obeys the vision (1:4–6),
John sent greetings from each member of the Trinity—the Father, the Son, and the Spirit
(symbolized by "the seven spirits"). Revelation 1:7 speaks of the visible and physical return
of Christ by fusing Dan 7:13 with Zech 12:10. The prologue ends with an assertion from
God the Father that he is the beginning and the end of history as the Eternal and Almighty
One.

II. Vision One (on Patmos): The Glorified Christ Who Investigates His Churches (1:9–3:22)

A. *The Inaugural Vision of Jesus Christ (1:9–20)* The first vision opens with an
account of John's call to prophesy and the inaugural vision of Jesus in his glory standing among his churches. John, while on Patmos, was in the Spirit on the Lord's Day and
heard a loud voice commanding him to write down the ensuing vision for seven churches
in Asia Minor. He turned to see the voice speaking to him, only to discover the glorified
Lord Jesus. The sight of him stretched the boundaries of John's language as he attempted
to describe Jesus using similes drawn from OT theophanies.

Overwhelmed, John fell at Jesus' feet as though dead. Christ responded by placing his
hand on John and announcing that he is the first and the last, the living Resurrected One,
and the one with authority over death and life. Jesus then explained that the seven lamp-
stands are the seven churches of Asia, and the seven stars in his hand are their angels. This
identification transitions from the inaugural vision of Christ to the messages intended for
the seven churches.

B. *The Messages to the Seven Churches of Asia Minor (2:1–3:22)* The messages
to the seven churches in chaps. 2–3 represent the most familiar portion of the book
of Revelation and provide the most practical instructions for believers. Although these

messages address situations historically and locally confined to those seven churches, they apply universally to all churches throughout all time. Because these letters diverge from the normal models of Greco-Roman epistolary writing, they are closer to the genre classification of a prophetic oracle.

The messages begin with an address to the angel of the particular church (cf. 1:20), a command to write, and a predication describing a characteristic of Christ drawn from the inaugural vision and relevant to that specific church (2:1,8,12,18; 3:1a, 7,14). The official body of the message begins with the "I know" speech that includes either commendations or accusations or both (2:2,9,13,19; 3:1,8b,15). Jesus then admonished the churches by either encouraging them to continue to persevere in a certain kind of conduct or by calling them to repent, accompanied by a warning of negative consequences in case of disobedience. The final two elements of these messages include a prophetic appeal to listen to what the Spirit says to the churches (2:7a,11a,17a,29; 3:6,13,22) and promise of deliverance for those who overcome (2:7b,11b,17b,26; 3:5,12,21).

III. Vision Two (in Heaven): The Divine Court Proceedings and the Trial of the Nations (4:1–16:21)

A. Transition from Patmos to Heaven (4:1–2)   John's entrance through the threshold of heaven signals a major transition into a new vision that also constitutes a thematic transition from a juridical investigation of the churches to an investigation of the nations (4:1–2).

B. Worship Around the Throne (4:3–11)   The scene radically transforms from the barren rocky isle of Patmos into the heavenly throne room. God's throne is in the center of a series of concentric circles, depicting his sovereignty over the cosmos. In describing his vision John drew from other prophetic visions involving God's throne (e.g., Ezek 1:5,10,18,22). John's vision of the heavenly throne room offers an apocalyptic perspective contrasting imperial pretensions of cosmic sovereignty with the true king and judge of the universe. The divine council convenes for the purpose of installing an eschatological judge worthy to prosecute God's judgment on the earth's inhabitants.

C. The Divine Courtroom (5:1–14)   The courtroom scene continues in chap. 5 with the introduction of the scroll and the Lamb. The scene depicts the installment of Christ as the Davidic King and his enthronement at the right hand of God as well as his commission as the eschatological judge who is the only one worthy to unleash God's judgment upon humanity. A sealed scroll is brought, and an angel announces the search for one worthy to break the seals and to open them. After an extensive search throughout the created order, only one is found (5:2–4). The Lamb, the conquering Lion of the tribe of Judah, is deemed worthy to take the scroll and to assume his role as king and judge (5:5–7). The remainder of the chapter is taken up with the adulation of the Lamb. This chapter sets the stage for the judgment of the nations.

D. Preliminary Investigative Judgments (6:1–17)   In the same way that Revelation 5 focuses on the worthiness of the Lamb to judge, chaps. 6–16 demonstrate the justness of his judgment on humanity. The scroll with seven seals rests securely in the hands of the Lamb who proceeds to break open the seals. Since the contents of the scroll cannot be read until all the seals are broken, the seals are best understood as preliminary judgments. The trials introduced by the seals represent the "birth pains" occurring prior to coming days of tribulation that will precede the return of Christ (see Mark 13:8,19).

The four horsemen constitute a pattern of conquest, war, famine, and death (6:1–8; see Matt 24:7). The martyred believers and their appeal for justice (6:9–11) indicate that during this time God's people will continue to endure persecution. The seals also represent a progressive intensification leading up to a time of cosmic upheaval as indicated by the breaking of the sixth seal. The seals initiate the preliminary judgments against the nations and include warnings directed to covenant violators in the respective churches. These judgments precede the seven trumpets that constitute the great tribulation.

E. First Interlude: The Protective Sealing of God's People (7:1–17)   Prior to the tribulation, the first of several interludes interwoven between the series of septets assures the believers of their protection from divine judgment and ultimate salvation (7:1–17). John placed the interlude between the breaking of the sixth and seventh seals (see 6:12; 8:1). The interlude is divided into two separate but related segments (7:1–8,9–17). The first unit pertains to the sealing of the 144,000 for protection prior to the tribulation (see 7:1,14; see Ezek 9:4–6). While some view the 144,000 as symbolic of the multitude of believers who have come out of the great tribulation, others take the reference literally as to the 12 tribes of Israel.

The second unit focuses on the salvation of God's people from every nation, tribe, people, and language (7:9–17). The fact that this group is standing before God's throne answers the question of who can stand during the day of his wrath (see 6:17). This interlude offers two perspectives regarding the same group of people. Most likely, the 144,000 represent the entire new covenant community of God's people *about to enter* the tribulation, while the multitude from many nations represents the multitude of the redeemed *coming out* of the tribulation. God's people are assured that God will protect them during this time of distress.

F. Eschatological Investigative Judgments (8:1–9:21)   After the protective sealing of the servants of God from the coming divine judgments, John returned to the series of septets with the breaking of the seventh seal in 8:1. He used the device of interlocking to transition from the seals to the trumpets, but he also intimately connected the succeeding trumpet judgments with the preceding seals. The breaking of the seventh seal results in immediate silence followed by the introduction of the seven angels and their trumpets. The first four trumpets impact all of life on earth: a third of the earth's vegetation burns up; a third of the saltwater turns to blood; a third of the freshwater turns bitter; and a third of the sun, moon, and stars turns dark.

The last three trumpets are directed specifically against the inhabitants of the earth. The fifth trumpet releases a horde of locust demons to scourge the inhabitants of the earth, and the sixth trumpet releases a demonic cavalry that inflicts even more terror. Believers are exempt from the last three judgments, as the locusts are commanded not to harm those with God's seal on their foreheads (9:4). Although each successive trumpet blast has dire consequences on the earth's inhabitants, they refuse to repent (9:20–21). The last trumpet comprises the consummation of God's wrath in that it contains the seven bowl judgments that destroy life on earth (see 16:1–21).

G. Second Interlude: God's People as Prophetic Witnesses (10:1–11:19) The second interlude appears between the sixth and seventh trumpet blasts (10:1–11:13). It depicts the role of the people of God on earth during the time of the corresponding trumpet judgments. The interlude divides into two separate but interrelated sections. The first unit contains John's second prophetic commission in which he receives a message pertaining to the nations (10:1–11). The second unit describes the ministry of the two prophetic witnesses before the nations (11:1–13). These sections are inextricably bound together because they pertain to the fulfillment of a prophetic ministry to the nations. John's prophetic commission is ultimately completed in the ministry of the faithful witnesses.

When the Spirit-inspired prophetic testimony of the witnesses reaches completion, they are murdered (11:7–10). John stated that the beast from the abyss will wage war against the two witnesses (11:7). This anticipates the war against believers instigated by the beast (13:1–18). The inhabitants of the earth revile these two witnesses to such an extent that a global celebration ensues once they have been violently murdered in the streets. That their corpses remain exposed where they lie indicates the level of umbrage and hatred expressed by humanity toward Christ's faithful representatives. After three and a half days, at a time corresponding with the seventh trumpet, God vindicates his witnesses through an awesome public display of resurrection and ascension (11:11–12). The time of testimony is completed, and the time for judgment has arrived.

H. Third Interlude: The Signs Narrative/God's People in Holy War (12:1–15:9) A third interlude appears between the sounding of the seventh trumpet (11:15–19) and the introduction of the seven bowls containing the final judgments (15:5–8). The narrative falls into three natural divisions of holy war in heaven (chap. 12); holy war on earth (chap. 13); and the vindication of the believers followed by the judgment of the wicked (chap. 14). Amid the scenes of this cosmic spiritual warfare, John made the purpose of this interlude explicit by interjecting calls for encouragement (12:10–12), patient endurance (13:9–10), and the ultimate vindication of the believers (14:6–13).

The dragon (Satan) enlists the aid of two beasts in order to execute his war against believers (13:1–18). The beast from the sea represents the brute force of the political and military power of Rome (13:1–8). The beast from the land represents the religious institution that enforces the worship of the first beast (i.e., the imperial cult; 13:11–17). Together these three form an unholy trio, whereby the dragon, the sea beast, and the land beast function in a capacity similar to the three persons of the Godhead. Thus 12:1–15:4 provides the basis and justification for the severity and finality of the judgments rendered upon the inhabitants of the earth.

The seventh trumpet, comprising the third woe, signals the final consummation of God's judgment (11:15–19) by introducing the angels with the seven bowls filled with his wrath (15:5–8).

I. Final Investigative Judgments: The Seven Bowls (16:1–21)   The seven bowls contain the wine of God's wrath poured out on the inhabitants of the earth. The objects of this wrath are specifically identified as everyone with the mark of the beast who worshipped his image (16:2). The seal judgments impacted a fourth of the earth and its population, the trumpets a third, but the bowls release the full fury of God's wrath in its entirety.

The first bowl inflicts all unbelievers (i.e., those with the mark of the beast) with ugly and painful sores. The second and third bowls transform all the oceans and freshwaters of the earth into putrid blood. The fourth bowl intensifies the power of the sun scorching all flesh. The fifth and sixth are direct assaults against the beast's kingdom with a plague of darkness and preparation for the final battle of Armageddon. When the last bowl empties, God's retribution is complete (16:19) as affirmed in the judgment doxology (16:5–7).

IV. Vision Three (in the Desert): The Destruction of Babylon and the Return of Christ (17:1–21:8)

A. Transition: "Come, I Will Show You the Judgment of the Notorious Prostitute" (17:1–2)   The last bowl completed the total outpouring of God's wrath, so that the third vision comprises an expanded and more detailed look at the final trial and sentencing of the prostitute city of Babylon. Thus the third vision represents a different perspective on the final events briefly described during the trumpets and bowls. John metaphorically presented Rome as a prostitute seducing kings and nations into committing fornication with her, and he contrasted the destiny of the prostitute city Babylon with the bride city of the new Jerusalem.

The third vision exhibits five distinct movements: (1) Babylon introduced (17:3–18); (2) Babylon judged as the eschatological judgment of the nations (18:1–19:10); (3) the return of Christ as a divine warrior (19:11–21); and (4) the first and second resurrections as the eschatological judgment of individuals (20:1–15). After the final judgment, (5) the believers are introduced to their eternal reward (21:1–8).

B. The Prostitute City Babylon Described (17:3–6)   John, once again, was carried away "in the Spirit" to a desert where he saw a great prostitute sitting astride the seven-headed beast and drunk on the blood of believers (17:3–6).

C. The Prostitute City Babylon as Rome (17:7–18)   The woman personifies the city of Rome with her military might, opulence, and allurement, and in a broader sense the world system represented by all great earthly civilizations. By depicting her on the back of the beast, John demonstrated her dependence on and relationship with Satan's kingdom.

He also underscored her political power, economic extravagance, and religious devotion. She enticed the earth's inhabitants to forsake truth, righteousness, and justice to indulge in her flagrant adulteries consisting of idolatry, greed, and murder. For all of this she deserves judgment.

D. *The Trial and Sentencing of Babylon (18:1–24)* Having identified Babylon with Rome, the tour of Babylon's judgment promised by the angel in 17:1 now comes into sharp focus. One salient feature of this entire scene is that John saturated this section with material drawn from OT prophetic oracles pertaining to the judgment of the historical Babylon. This interweaving of allusions creates the effect that Babylon's judgment represents the culmination of God's judgment against all pagan nations by way of military, political, and economic devastation. The verdict against Babylon is pronounced by an angel with great authority (18:1–3). The angel expresses the verdict in terms conveying the certainty of Babylon's destruction although the judgment is still a future event from John's vantage point.

God holds Babylon responsible for indulging in sins pertaining to wine, wealth, and political power, thereby leading the nations astray from the true God and obedience to his righteous decrees. Once the verdict is announced, another voice from heaven commences with Babylon's sentencing, which is characterized by a series of imperatives that God has decreed for Babylon based on her sins and crimes (18:6–7). God administers justice through rendering judgment warranted by the crimes committed.

As the angels announce heavenly judgment and its causes, the kings, merchants, and mariners express an earthly response. Although Babylon seemed so strong, wealthy, and powerful, God easily brought about her collapse with his judicial verdict. Babylon's sentencing concludes with a symbolic act depicting her complete destruction along with a final reassertion of her indictment (18:21–24).

E. *Heavenly Celebration of Babylon's Destruction (19:1–10)* Now that God has declared his verdict, believers duly acknowledge him with the appropriate praise for his avenging justice (19:1–10; see 6:10; Deut 32:43).

F. *The Divine Warrior and Final Tribunal (19:11–20:15)* In 19:11–21 Jesus returns to earth to prosecute the sentence against Babylon. He returns as the rightful king and divine warrior in this Christological culmination of the book. Accompanied by his army of redeemed believers whom he has made to be his kingdom (see 1:6), he comes as the divine warrior king to dispense justice through judgment and salvation as made explicit by the white horse, multiple diadems, a scepter of iron, his blazing eyes, and the sword protruding from his mouth. One of the most graphic images depicting Jesus as the divine warrior is his blood-soaked robe (19:13) from treading the winepress of the fury of God's wrath (19:15).

Jesus is, therefore, the full revelation of the divine warrior from the OT who executes judgment against all the enemies of God and his people. The great and final battle constitutes a slaughter that ends just as soon as it begins (19:17–21). Despite the boasts of the beast and the false prophet, they are quickly captured and tossed immediately into the lake of fire (19:20). The rest of the combatants die instantly at the spoken word of Christ (19:21). Christ effectively conquered all other kingdoms of the earth and subsumed them under his kingdom now established on earth.

The destruction of Babylon pertained to the judgment of the nations corporately as a political entity, but God will also judge all people individually. Having established his kingdom through a military victory (19:20–21), he orders the dragon bound and imprisoned for the duration of a thousand years (20:1–3). The entire scene in 20:4–6 corresponds to Dan 7:9–10 where the Ancient of Days holds court and books are opened for judgment, and Dan 7:22–27 where he renders a favorable verdict for believers by giving them the kingdom. The judicial verdict awarded to individual believers includes the right to reign with Christ, which includes judicial authority over the earth during this thousand-year period. At the end of this period, Satan will instigate one final and futile battle where unredeemed humanity stages a coup d'état against the Lord only to fail miserably.

The second resurrection (20:11–15) pertains to the individual judgment of all humanity. It constitutes the final judicial act of God before the complete renewal of the created order (i.e., the eschatological "age to come"). As the judge enters the courtroom, all the dead must rise to face the accounting of their deeds. Books are opened as the primary evidence consulted during the investigative trial of every individual human being all the way back to Adam. These books are the written records of each person's conduct.

G. The Renewal of Creation and the Arrival of the New Jerusalem (21:1–8) Each individual is judged according to his or her works. These works include attitudes of the heart such as cowardice, unbelief, and moral corruption, as well as external actions such as murder, sexual immorality, sorcery or witchcraft, idolatry, and lying (21:8). No one will escape the consequences of their guilt, and the lost will subsequently share the same fate as the dragon (Satan), the beast, and the false prophet in the lake of fire (20:14). The only hope for salvation is whether a person's name is written in the Lamb's book of life (20:14).

V. Vision Four (on a Mountain): Believers' Reward and the Renewal of Creation (21:9–22:4)

A. Transition: "Come, I Will Show You the Bride" (21:9–10) The final vision commences in 21:9–10 when another angel holding one of the seven bowls invites John to see the bride of the Lamb and he is carried away "in the Spirit" to a high mountain. It constitutes an expanded presentation of the new Jerusalem introduced in 21:1–8. This vision functions as the antithesis of the prostitute city Babylon and presents the glorified church as the bride city of the new Jerusalem. The purpose is to contrast the fate of Babylon with the glory of the new Jerusalem in which believers receive their ultimate vindication and eternal reward. This vision falls into two divisions that describe the Holy City as an eternal holy of holies (21:9–27) and then as a new Eden (22:1–5).

B. *The Description of the New Jerusalem Descending from Heaven (21:11–27)* The bride city descends from heaven shining with God's glory bedecked with precious stones. It has twelve gates named after the twelve patriarchs and twelve foundation stones named after the twelve apostles (21:12–14). The measurements indicate that it is a perfect cube of immense proportions. Thus the new Jerusalem resembles the holy of holies where God dwells with his people in absolute splendor and purity.

C. *The Paradise of God: The Renewal of Creation (22:1–5)* What is more, "the river of living water" flows from the throne of the Lamb and waters "the tree of life" lining the streets of the new Jerusalem. In the eternal and Eden-like paradise, God and humanity dwell together in perfect harmony, for the curse is no more.

VI. Epilogue (22:6–21)

The interpreting angel affirms the truthfulness of words of the prophecy because it has been authorized by God. John continued with a series of testimonies submitted as forensic verification for the churches. First, John testifies that he has presented an eyewitness account of what he has seen and heard (22:8–11). Second, Jesus testifies that he is coming soon to reward the righteous and punish the wicked (22:12–16). The third testimony comes from the Spirit and the bride (22:17), which probably refers to the Holy Spirit through the church as a prophetic witness (see 19:10). John solemnly warned against any tampering of his vision by invoking the legal consequences of altering a covenant document (22:18–19; see Deut 4:2). John concluded with a final testimony by Jesus who affirms that he is coming soon (22:20). These four testimonies constitute the strongest way possible to validate the truth of his vision by using legal categories.

THEOLOGY

Theological Themes

The Sovereignty of God The prominent depiction of God as the Creator of the universe sitting enthroned in heaven and reigning over all people, beings, events, and the cosmos makes his sovereignty a central theme of the book of Revelation. God's sovereignty over creation, events, and history is depicted in three distinct ways throughout the book: (1) designations of divine names, titles, and attributions; (2) depictions of the heavenly throne room and God's throne; and (3) displays of God's actions through decrees and judgments. The emphasis on God's sovereignty, a common characteristic of prophetic and apocalyptic writings, functions to remind the readers that God is in control of all their circumstances and that they may confidently trust him.

From the outset God is identified as the ultimate sovereign ruler of the universe (1:8). He is "the Alpha and Omega," "the One who is, who was, and who is coming," and "the Almighty."[66] "Alpha and Omega" stems from the first letter (alpha) and last letter (omega)

---

[66] R. Bauckham, *The Theology of the Book of Revelation* (Cambridge: Cambridge University Press, 1993), 25.

of the Greek alphabet and is equivalent to "I am the A to Z" in English. The title indicates that God is the origin and goal of all history because he precedes all creation and will bring everything to its eschatological fulfillment.[67]

God as "the one who is, who was, and who is coming" (1:4,8; 4:8; 11:17; 16:5) constitutes an interpreted expansion of the divine name YHWH (see Exod 3:14) and stresses his eternal presence in relationship to the world.[68] God is now; he has always been; and he will come in the future when he dramatically brings about the consummation of the ages (11:17; 16:5). The third designation for God as "the Almighty" (1:8; 4:8; 11:17; 15:3; 16:7,14; 19:6,15; 21:22) associates him with the "Lord of hosts" in the OT, emphasizing his omnipotent power and unrivaled authority.

The fourth designation asserting God's sovereignty is that he is addressed as "the One sitting on the throne" (4:9; 5:1,7,13; 6:16; 7:15; 21:5).[69] The sovereignty of God over creation, events, and history is also displayed through his decrees and acts of judgment. God as the Creator is the one who decrees the course and timing of all events while he governs from his throne in heaven. His activity is most apparent in the six scenes revolving around the heavenly throne room followed by ensuing judgments on the earth. The judgments produced on the earth by the seals, trumpets, and bowls represent a direct outworking of the proceedings in the divine courtroom.

God is the one who judges humanity (11:18; 18:8; 19:11; 20:12–13), and his judgment is swift, severe, and just (14:7; 16:7; 18:10; 19:2). God's activity is sometimes passive (as indicated by the frequent use of the divine passive verb "it was given").[70] He commissions some agents for the purpose of rendering judgments (e.g., the four horsemen and angels) and allows forces of evil to perform certain deeds (e.g., the beast). The fact that God is in control of everything, including the woes of both believers and unbelievers, powerfully reinforces the purpose of Revelation: encouraging believers in their faith in the midst of suffering.

Theodicy   Theodicy pertains to the justification of God concerning "the seeming triumph of the wicked and the suffering of the innocent."[71] The unfolding visions, therefore, illustrate the apocalyptic reality that while the righteous indeed suffer unjustly at the hands of the wicked, they will have their day in court when God's verdict results in a grand reversal of this present world order.

Theodicy represents an important theme in Revelation that conveys the justice and mercy of God.[72] The request of the martyrs directly addresses the question of justice: "O Lord, holy and true, how long until You judge and avenge our blood from those who

---

[67] Ibid. 27.

[68] Ibid., 28–30.

[69] Ibid., 31.

[70] Osborne, *Revelation*, 32.

[71] G. R. Osborne, "Theodicy in the Apocalypse," *TrinJ* 14 NS (1993): 63.

[72] Ibid., 77.

live on the earth?" (6:10). This request for vindication echoes the sentiments of generations of God's servants who suffered unjustly while the wicked appeared to remain unpunished.

The OT features the same inquiry as to when God will take judicial action vindicating the mistreatment of his people (e.g., Pss 79:5–10; 94:1–3).[73] The concern is not why evil exists in the world or why Christians suffer in general but specifically why they are suffering as a consequence of their faithfulness to Christ and their obedience to the righteous requirements of God's law. John's visions seek to answer this query by demonstrating that God will render true justice in a world filled with evil and injustice.

POINTS OF APPLICATION

- Remain faithful to Christ in persecution and endure until the end (2:2,3,19; 13:10; 14:12)
- Worship God and the Lord Jesus Christ, who alone are worthy to receive worship and praise (chaps. 4–5)
- Warn unbelievers of the wrath to come and urge them to repent (chaps. 6–18)
- Expectantly await Christ's return (19:11–16)
- Be encouraged that in heaven God will wipe away every tear and there will no longer be any death, grief, crying, or pain, and God will live with his people (21:3–4)

STUDY QUESTIONS

1. What are the two major alternatives for the time of composition of Revelation?
2. What were the occasion and purpose of the book of Revelation?
3. What is the definition of "Apocalypse," and what are some of its accompanying traits?
4. How many visions are recorded in Revelation, and what is the phrase indicating a new vision?
5. What are the respective locations of these visions, and what is the range of chapters for each vision in the book of Revelation?
6. What are the three primary theories of relating the seals, trumpets, and bowls in Revelation?

FOR FURTHER STUDY

Aune, D. E. *Revelation.* 3 vols. Word Biblical Commentary 52. Nashville: Thomas Nelson, 1997, 1998.
Bauckham, R. *The Climax of Prophecy: Studies on the Book of Revelation.* London: T&T Clark, 1993.
_____. *The Theology of the Book of Revelation.* New Testament Theology. Cambridge: Cambridge University Press, 1993.

---

[73] Cf. D. A. Carson, *How Long, O Lord? Reflections on Suffering and Evil*, 2nd ed. (Grand Rapids: Baker, 2006); J. N. Day, *Crying for Justice* (Grand Rapids: Kregel, 2005), 107; E. Nardoni, *Rise Up, O Judge: A Study of Justice in the Biblical World*, trans. S. C. Martin (Peabody, MA: Hendrickson, 2004), 123.

Beale, G. K. *The Book of Revelation*. New International Greek Testament Commentary. Grand Rapids: Eerdmans, 1999.

Ford, J. M. *Revelation*. Anchor Bible 38. New York: Doubleday, 1975.

Hemer, C. J. *The Letters to the Seven Churches of Asia in Their Local Setting*. Journal for the Study of the New Testament Supplement 11. Sheffield: JSOT, 1986.

Johnson, A. F. "Revelation." Pages 571–789 in *The Expositor's Bible Commentary*. Rev. ed. Vol. 13: *Hebrews-Revelation*. Grand Rapids: Zondervan, 2005.

Kovacs, J., and C. Rowland. *Revelation: The Apocalypse of Jesus Christ*. BBC. Oxford: Blackwell, 2004.

Ladd, G. E. *A Commentary on the Revelation of John*. Grand Rapids: Eerdmans, 1972.

Michaels, J. R. *Interpreting the Book of Revelation*. Guides to New Testament Exegesis. Grand Rapids: Baker, 1992.

_____. *Revelation*. IVP New Testament Commentary 20. Downers Grove: InterVarsity, 1997.

Mounce, R. H. *The Book of Revelation*. Rev. ed. New International Commentary on the New Testament. Grand Rapids: Eerdmans, 1997.

Osborne, G. R. *Revelation*. Baker Exegetical Commentary on the New Testament. Grand Rapids: Baker, 2002.

Wilson, M. *Charts on the Book of Revelation: Literary, Historical, and Theological Perspectives*. Grand Rapids: Kregel, 2007.

Glossary

agraphon (pl. *agrapha*)**:** words of Jesus not recorded in the canonical NT Gospels (e.g., Acts 20:35: "It is more blessed to give than to receive")

Agrippa I: grandson of Herod the Great (s.v.) and ruler of Judea (AD 37–44); called "Herod" in the book of Acts (see Acts 12:1–4,19–23); not to be confused with his son Agrippa II before whom Paul pleaded his case (see Acts 26)

Alexandrian text type: group of manuscripts that form the basis for the modern eclectic Greek text of the NT (e.g., Codex Sinaiticus)

Alexandrinus: s.v. Codex Alexandrinus

allegory: form of extended metaphor

allusion: indirect identifiable intentional reference to another text or statement

alogi: group of Christian heretics who flourished in Asia Minor around AD 170

amanuensis: scribe or secretary used by a biblical author to write down his message

amillennialism: belief that the biblical references to the thousand-year reign of Christ are symbolic in nature (s.v. millennium)

Annas: influential Jewish high priest (AD 6–15) and father-in-law of Caiaphas, high priest in the year of Jesus' crucifixion (see John 18:13–14)

Antichrist: end-time figure setting himself against God and the Lord Jesus Christ (e.g., 1 John 2:18; 2 John 7; s.v. man of lawlessness)

Anti-Marcionite Prologues: despite their name, these prefaces to Mark, Luke, and John (Matthew is lost) were most likely not written against Marcion and may date to the fourth century AD; except for the prologue to Luke (which may date to around AD 160–180), they only exist in Latin

antinomianism: an "antilaw" bias, frequently resulting in licentiousness

Antiochus Epiphanes IV (reigned 175–164 BC): Seleucid (Greek) ruler who sought to impose Greek culture onto the Jews, erecting the "abomination of desolation" in the

Jerusalem temple by setting up an altar to the supreme Greek god Zeus and sacrificing swine on it around 167 BC; in his opposition to God's people, he served as a precursor of the Antichrist (see Dan 9:27; 11:31; 12:11; 1 Macc 1:54; Matt 24:15; Mark 13:14)

Antipas: s.v. Herod Antipas

apocalypse: a literary work containing symbolic depictions of end-time events

Apocalypse of Peter: a gnostic document found in the Nag Hammadi library in Egypt

apocalyptic: a worldview that describes end-time events in symbolic terms

apocalypticism: the sociological phenomenon of a group steeped in an end-time perspective

Apocrypha: the OT Apocrypha, accepted as canonical by the Roman Catholic Church but not by those in the Protestant tradition, comprising writings such as 1 and 2 Esdras, 1, 2, 3, and 4 Maccabees, Tobit, Judith, and other writings produced subsequent to the OT prophetic period; the NT Apocrypha contains various Gospels, Acts, Epistles, and Apocalypses produced during the subapostolic period (s.v.) and are recognized by neither Roman Catholics nor Protestants as part of the NT canon

apocryphal: obscure or hidden; pertaining to the Apocrypha

aporia: apparent incongruity or literary seam indicating an author's use of written sources

apostle: in a narrow, technical sense, a member of the Twelve (see Matt 10:1–4 and parallels); slightly extended in the NT to include others also such as Paul and Barnabas; in a broader sense, also includes missionaries and other emissaries (e.g., Rom 16:7; 2 Cor 8:23; Phil 2:25)

apostolic eyewitness: the firsthand testimony of the Twelve recorded in the four canonical Gospels

Apostolic Fathers: group of writings produced during the early patristic period comprising *1 and 2 Clement*; The Letters of Ignatius; *The Letter of Polycarp to the Philippians* and *The Martyrdom of Polycarp*; *The Didache*; *The Epistle of Barnabas*; *The Shepherd of Hermas*; *The Epistle to Diognetus*; the Fragment of Quadratus; and Fragments of Papias

apostolic period: lifetime of those who were eyewitnesses of Jesus' ministry and had been specially appointed by him to serve as his messengers; normally viewed as ending with the writing of the last NT book, the book of Revelation (c. AD 95; s.v. also subapostolic period)

apostolicity: direct or indirect association of a given NT work with an apostle

Aquinas: s.v. Thomas Aquinas

Aramaic: ancient near Eastern language akin to Hebrew; in the OT, featured in portions of Daniel and Esther; also found in the Targums (s.v.); Jesus spoke Aramaic, and the NT Gospels preserve several authentic sayings of Jesus in Aramaic (e.g., Matt 27:46)

Armageddon: from Hb. *har megido* ("Mount Megiddo"); site of battle in OT times near the city of Meggido (2 Kgs 23:28–30; 2 Chr 35:20–25) and location of the final battle between the forces of God and Satan prior to the return of Christ (Rev 16:16)

asceticism: the suppression of bodily passions

Athanasius of Alexandria (c. AD 296–373): fourth-century AD bishop of Alexandria, best known for his Festal Letter in AD 367 listing all 27 canonical books of the NT

atonement: blood sacrifice rendered for sin

Augustine of Hippo (AD 354–430): North African church father and bishop of Hippo, son of the pious Monica and author of *Confessions* and *The City of God*

Augustinian view of the Synoptic Problem (s.v.): belief that the Gospels were written in the canonical order Matthew first, then Mark, and then Luke, with Mark using Matthew, and Luke using Matthew and Mark; some question whether Augustine actually held this view

Augustus: Roman emperor who ruled in 31/27 BC–AD 14

autographs: the original OT and NT manuscripts

"Babylon": code name for the Roman Empire (e.g., 1 Pet 5:13)

Babylonian Talmud: s.v. Talmud

Bar Kokhba revolt: Jewish rebellion against the Romans (AD 132–135)

Byzantine text type: also called the Majority Text, text form found in the majority of biblical manuscripts that also underlies the Textus Receptus translation (e.g., KJV)

Caesar: title of Roman emperors, harking back to Julius Caesar (born 100 BC and served as virtual dictator 46–44 BC, assassinated in 44 BC by Brutus and others in the Senate)

Caiaphas, Joseph: Jewish high priest (c. AD 18–36) in the year of Jesus' crucifixion

Caligula: Roman emperor (AD 37–41)

canon: from *kanōn* ("rule" or "standard"); collection of Christian Scriptures

canonicity: a book's status as to its inclusion in the collection of Christian Scriptures

catholic: universal; later used for the Roman Catholic Church

centurion: Roman military official, from Lat. meaning "commander of 100"

Cephas: Aramaic name for the Greek name Peter (both mean "rock"; see Matt 16:18; John 1:42)

Cerinthianism: early Christian heresy attributed to Cerinthus, a gnostic teacher who held that the "Christ spirit" descended on Jesus at his baptism and left him at the cross

Cerinthus: s.v. Cerinthianism

chain quotations: s.v. pearl stringing

Chaldean: Babylonian

chiasm: from name of Greek letter c; cross-wise arrangement of phrases in such a way that the second expression is in reverse order from the first (A B B′ A′)

chiliasm: the belief in the millennial (thousand-year) reign of Christ

Christophany: (preincarnate) appearance of Christ

Church Fathers: church leaders, writers, and theologians of the first few centuries of the Christian era (s.v. also patristic)

Claudius: Roman emperor (AD 41–54); s.v. also Edict of Claudius

Clement of Alexandria (c. AD 150–215): early church father and member of the Alexandrian school; author of *Stromateis* ("Miscellanies")

Clement of Rome: bishop of Rome and author of *1 Clement* (c. AD 96)

codex: the ancient equivalent of a book, consisting of sheets bound together

Codex Alexandrinus: fifth-century AD manuscript of the Greek Bible, containing most of the Septuagint and NT

Codex Sinaiticus: fourth-century AD manuscript containing the Christian Bible in Greek, including the complete NT

Codex Vaticanus: fourth-century AD Greek manuscript containing most of the Septuagint and NT

Council of Nicea: first ecumenical council convened by the Roman Emperor Constantine in Nicea, Bithynia, which is modern Turkey (AD 325)

covenant: (sacred) contract

Cynic philosophy: set of beliefs holding that a virtuous life was to be lived in accordance with nature and free from the bondage to material possessions

Day of Atonement: *Yom Kippur*, the most sacred holiday in the Jewish calendar (see Leviticus 16; s.v. atonement)

Day of the Lord: time of final divine judgment predicted by the OT prophets

deacon: from *diakonos* ("servant"); NT nonteaching, nongoverning church office (see 1 Tim 3:8–12)

deaconess: female deacon (s.v. deacon; see 1 Tim 3:11; Rom 16:1)

Dead Sea Scrolls (DSS): a body of Jewish sectarian literature found near the Dead Sea in the years following 1947, including the *Community Rule* (1QS), the *War Scroll* (1QM), and the *Damascus Document* (CD)

Decalogue: the Ten Commandments (see Exodus 20; Deuteronomy 5)

Decapolis: from *deka* ("ten") and *polis* ("city"), a group of 10 cities in the territory of Syria, Jordan, and Palestine bound together by a common location, language, and culture (including Gerasa, Gadara, Pella, Scythopolis, and Damascus)

Deism: belief that there is a God who created the universe but does not interfere with it

Delphi Inscription: inscription in the ancient Greek city of Delphi supposedly containing the maxims "know yourself" and "nothing in excess"

Deutero-Pauline: not authentically Pauline, that is, writing falsely or traditionally attributed to the apostle Paul

Diaspora: for "dispersion," the scattering of Jews beyond the region of Palestine subsequent to the Assyrian and Babylonian exiles

Diatessaron: Greek "through four," name for the first-known synopsis of the Gospels compiled by the church father Tatian (c. AD 150–160)

Didache: church manual from the late first or early second century AD providing information about early church practice regarding the administration of baptism, the Lord's Supper, etc.

Diocletian: Roman emperor (AD 284–305) who launched a major persecution against Christians (AD 302–3)

disciple Jesus loved, the: Johannine epithet for the disciple closest to Jesus during his earthly ministry (see John 13:23) who was also the author of John's Gospel (21:20,24); traditionally identified as John, the son of Zebedee

dispensationalism: theological system dividing salvation history into distinct periods (called "dispensations"); falling into classic, revised, and progressive dispensationalism

Dispersion: s.v. Diaspora

ditheism: belief in two gods

docetism: from *dokeō* ("to seem"); the teaching that Jesus only *appeared* to be human

Domitian: Roman emperor (AD 81–96)

doxology: from *doxa* ("glory") and *logos* ("word" or "saying"); a short statement or hymn in praise of God

early Catholicism: second-century AD formation of orthodox doctrine, ecclesiastical authority, and three-tiered church leadership structure

Ecclesiastical History: famous work by Eusebius (s.v.) in which he referred to many no longer extant works of early church fathers, such as Papias (s.v.)

ecclesiology: doctrine of the church

Edict of Claudius: decree by the Roman Emperor Claudius in AD 49 expelling the Jews from Rome; mentioned in Acts 18:2 (s.v. Claudius)

election: biblical doctrine that God chose certain individuals to salvation

emperor cult: worship of the Roman emperor as a god

end time: the period inaugurated by the coming of the Messiah, Jesus Christ, which will be consummated at his return or the Second Coming; also referred to as "the last days"

Enlightenment, the: an intellectual movement in the seventeenth and eighteenth centuries advocating the primacy of reason as the basis of authority

Epicureanism: philosophy based on the teachings of Epicurus (c. 341–c. 270 BC), a form of hedonism holding pleasure to be the supreme human good and teaching the pursuit of a virtuous and temperate life so one can enjoy life's simple pleasures

epiphany: revelation; from *epiphaneia* ("appearing"), one of the technical terms for the second coming of Christ (s.v. also *parousia*)

Epistle of Barnabas: s.v. Pseudo-Barnabas

Epistle to Diognetus: anonymous apologetic letter defending Christianity against its accusers dating to the second or third century AD

eschatology: doctrine of the end time

eschaton: Gk. term meaning "last"; usually refers to end-time events related to Christ's return

ethnarch: title of ancient ruler such as Archelaus, who was ethnarch of Judea, Samaria, and Edom (4 BC–AD 6)

Eusebius of Caesarea (c. AD 260–c. 340): fourth-century church father and emininent historian of the early church best known for his important work *Ecclesiastical History*

exile, the: the subjugation or deportation of the Jewish people by the Assyrians in 721 BC and the Babylonians in 605, 597, and 586 BC; also called "captivity"

experts in the Law: NT designation for Jewish scribes and Scripture scholars; often referred to as "scribes"

extant reference: passage available in an existing manuscript

external evidence: attestation of a given piece of writing by a source outside that document, such as by a patristic writer; in contrast with internal evidence (s.v.)

Felix: Roman procurator of Judea (AD 52–59; see Acts 24)

Festus, Porcius: Roman procurator of Judea (AD 60–62; see Acts 25)

formal equivalence: word-for-word approach to Bible translation (e.g., NASB)

fourfold Gospel: the notion that, properly understood, the four canonical Gospels constitute *one* gospel "according to" the four witnesses Matthew, Mark, Luke, and John

fulfillment quotations: statements by the authors of the four Gospels, especially Matthew and John, highlighting the fulfillment of various messianic passages in Jesus; introduced with a formula such as "that the words of the prophet might be fulfilled" (e.g., Matt 1:22; 2:5,15,17,23)

functional equivalence: phrase-by-phrase approach to Bible translation (e.g., NLT)

Gallio Inscription: inscription found in Delphi, Greece, that confirms that Gallio was the governor of Achaia when Paul was in Corinth in AD 51–52 (see Acts 18:12)

Gamaliel I the Elder, Rabbi: a preeminent first-century Jewish rabbi and teacher of Paul prior to the latter's conversion to Christianity (see Acts 22:3; cf. Acts 5:34–39; Phil 3:4–6)

gematria: numerical symbolism (e.g., Jesus' genealogy in Matt 1:1–17 in three groups of 14 generations since 14 is the total of the value of the three Hebrew letters in the name "David")

General Epistles: collective expression for a body of NT writings that contains Hebrews, James, 1–2 Peter, 1–3 John, and Jude; called "general" because they are addressed to a wide, varied, and often unspecified audience

Gnostic Gospels: body of literature produced by the adherents to an early Christian heresy called "Gnosticism" (s.v.) including the Gospel of Thomas, the so-called Gospel of Truth, and others

Gnosticism: from Greek *gnōsis* ("knowledge"), a second-century religion pitting spirit against matter, considering the former good and the latter evil; precursors may be attested in the later NT (e.g., 1 Tim 6:20–21)

God-fearer: Gentile (non-Jew) attracted to Jewish worship who participates in synagogue worship while not submitting to circumcision (s.v. also proselytes)

Gospel of Mary (Magdalene): second-century AD Gnostic Gospel falsely attributed to Mary Magdalene

Gospel of Peter: apocryphal Gospel falsely attributed to the apostle Peter, most likely dated to the second half of the second century AD

Gospel of Philip: apocryphal Gospel falsely attributed to the apostle Philip, most likely dated to the second half of the second century AD

Gospel of Thomas: late second-century AD Gnostic Gospel, falsely attributed to the apostle Thomas, found in the Nag Hammadi library in Egypt

Gospel tradition: oral and/or written material underlying the written Gospels (s.v. also Synoptic tradition)

Greco-Roman: pertaining to Greek and Roman culture

Greek: *lingua franca* of the first-century world and original language of the NT

Griesbach (or Two-Gospel) Hypothesis: the view, named after the German scholar J. J. Griesbach, that Matthew and Luke wrote first and Mark used both of these earlier Gospels

Hades: the abode of the dead awaiting final judgment

Hasmoneans: Jewish ruling dynasty established during the Maccabean period

Hebrew: ancient Near Eastern language spoken by the Jewish people and original language of the OT

Hellenism: Greek culture

Herod: this may refer to the head of the Herodian dynasty, Herod the Great (37–4 BC) or one of his descendants, such as his sons Archelaus (s.v. Herod Archelaus), Antipas (s.v. Herod Antipas), and Philip

Herod Antipas: tetrarch of Galilee and Perea (4 BC–AD 39)

Herod Archelaus: one of the sons of Herod the Great (s.v.) who was ethnarch of Judea, Samaria, and Idumea (4 BC–AD 6)

Herod the Great: s.v. Herod

historical Jesus: the product of scholarly research into the background of the person of Jesus Christ

history-of-religions school: approach that views history primarily in terms of the evolution of human religious consciousness and uses a comparative-religions approach seeking to understand Judaism and Christianity in relation to other ancient religions

Ignatius of Antioch (c. AD 35–110): bishop of Antioch and early church father who wrote letters to the Ephesians, Magnesians, Philadelphians, and others

imperial cult: s.v. emperor cult

inclusio: an ancient literary device bracketing a section by placing one and the same word or phrase at the beginning and at the end of that section

inclusio **of eyewitness testimony:** the literary practice of indicating the major eyewitness source of an account by featuring this person as the first and the last named character in the narrative

inerrancy: the doctrine affirming Scripture to be free from error

inspiration: the doctrine of God's determinative spiritual influence on the writers of Scripture resulting in an inerrant Bible

internal evidence: data derived from a given document itself (in contrast with external evidence, s.v.)

interpolation: insertion of text

ipsissima verba: exact words

ipsissima vox: exact voice, true sense

Irenaeus of Lyons (c. AD 130–200): bishop of Lyons, France, and early church father who wrote the important work *Against Heresies* refuting Gnosticism

Jerome (c. AD 345–420): fourth-century AD church father and translator of the Lat. Vulgate (s.v.)

Jerusalem Council: traditional designation for meeting of leaders in the early church in Jerusalem as narrated in Acts 15

"Jesus of faith": Jesus as the object of the early church's faith in distinction from Jesus during his earthly ministry (a distinction upheld by the German scholars M. Kähler, R. Bultmann, and others)

"Jesus of history": s.v. historical Jesus

Jewish War: usually refers to the first Jewish-Roman war (AD 66–73) during which Jerusalem and the temple were destroyed

Johannine: related to (the apostle) John (s.v. also Johannine corpus)

Johannine comma: embellishment of 1 John 5:7 not found in any Greek manuscript prior to the Reformation period

Johannine corpus: body of John's writings included in the Bible (i.e., Gospel of John, 1–3 John, Revelation)

Josephus (AD 37–100): Jewish historian; author of *Jewish Wars, Jewish Antiquities,* and *Against Apion*

Judaizers: first-century Jewish movement that wanted to require Gentiles to submit to circumcision as a condition for allowing them into the Christian church (see esp. Galatians)

Justin Martyr (c. AD 100–165): early Christian apologist; best known for his works *Dialogue with Trypho* and *First Apology*

lacuna **(pl.** *lacunae***):** gap in a manuscript, inscription, or text

Latinism: a Latin term or phrase

legalism: a pejorative term denoting the improper fixation on laws or codes of conduct

libertinism: indulgence of bodily passions, involving immoral behavior

lingua franca: universal language

Lord's Prayer, the: s.v. Model Prayer

Lost Gospels: general reference to apocryphal Gospels, that is, Gospels falsely attributed to an apostle or another figure mentioned in the NT (such as Mary Magdalene) that were written subsequent to the apostolic era; while referred to as "Lost Gospels," most of these documents are actually extant, though often in late copies and often fragmentary (s.v. also Gospel of Mary, Peter, Thomas, etc.)

LXX: s.v. Septuagint

Maccabean martyrs: Jews who lost their lives during the Maccabean uprising against the Seleucids in the second century BC (see 2 Maccabees)

Maccabees: a Jewish family that led the second-century BC revolt against the Seleucids issuing in a period of Jewish independence

"man of lawlessness": the Antichrist (see 2 Thess 2:1–12)

manuscript (ms.; pl. mss.): anything written by hand (a text or document)

manuscript tradition: history of the transmission of (biblical) manuscripts

Markan priority: the view that Mark wrote first and was used by the other two Synoptic writers (Matthew and Luke)

Masoretes: Jewish scribes responsible for the preservation of the OT text

Masoretic text (MT): s.v. Masoretes

Matthean priority: the view that Matthew was the first among the Synoptic Gospel writers to write his Gospel and that Mark and Luke used Matthew

Messiah: from Hb. *meshiach* ("anointed"); promised deliverer sent by God to save his people; identified in the NT as the Lord Jesus Christ (e.g., John 20:30–31)

messianic secret: term conventionally used to describe Jesus' reluctance to identify himself publicly as the Messiah, possibly due to the prevailing misunderstanding associated with the term (at least in part)

*midrash***:** ancient Jewish commentary, including interpretation of selected passages of Scripture, with a view toward pointing out their contemporary relevance

millennium: thousand-year reign of Christ (see Revelation 20)

minuscules: ancient manuscripts written in small cursive-like script

Mishnah: collection of Jewish rabbinic traditions compiled c. AD 200

Model Prayer: also called "The Lord's Prayer" (see Matt 6:9–11; Luke 11:2–4)

Monarchian Prologues: short introductions prefixed in many Vulgate (s.v.) mss. to the four Gospels, probably written in the fourth or fifth century AD

monotheism: belief in one God characteristic of Judaism, Christianity, and Islam

ms(s).: abbreviation for manuscript(s)

Muratorian Canon: an early canonical list probably dating to the later second century AD

mystery religions: Greco-Roman cults conceiving of religion primarily in terms of mystical union with the divine

mysticism: various approaches to spirituality focusing on human union with the divine, as in *merkabah* mysticism or mystery religions (s.v.)

myth: sacred story, particularly of human origins, that is of human fabrication rather than being rooted in actual history

Nag Hammadi Library: collection of gnostic writings found in Nag Hammadi in Upper Egypt in 1945

Nazarene: an inhabitant of Nazareth, the town where Jesus was raised; hence Jesus was called a "Nazarene" in fulfillment of prophecy (Matt 2:23)

Nero: Roman emperor (AD 54–68); responsible for the fire of Rome (AD 64) and the martyrdom of many Christians, including the apostles Peter and Paul (AD 65 or 66)

NT Apocrypha: various writings produced during the subapostolic period (s.v.) that imitate the canonical Gospels, Acts, Epistles, and Revelation (e.g., the Gospel of Thomas, the Acts of Thecla, or the Apocalypse of Peter)

Olivet Discourse: Jesus' teaching on the end time recorded in Matthew 24–25 with parallels in Mark 13 and Luke 21

oracle: vision

ordinance: church observance commanded by Christ, in particular baptism (Matt 28:18–20) and the Lord's Supper (1 Cor 11:23–26; see Matt 26:26–30 and parallels)

Origen (c. AD 185–c. 254): early church father, noted scholar, and member of the Alexandrian school of interpretation

orthodoxy: conformity of a given document with apostolic teaching (see Acts 2:42)

orthopraxy: right practice (s.v. also orthodoxy)

Ostian Way: a famous road that connected Rome with the port city of Ostia; traditional site of Paul's tomb

OT Apocrypha: body of literature included in the canon by Roman Catholics but not Protestants; contains 1 and 2 Esdras, Tobit, Judith, Additions to Esther, Wisdom of Solomon, Sirach, Baruch, Letter of Jeremiah, Prayer of Azariah and the Song of the Three Young Men, Susanna, Bel and the Dragon, Prayer of Manasseh, 1 and 2 Maccabees

Oxyrhynchus papyri: artifacts found at an archeological site in Egypt where a large collection of ancient papyri was discovered, including fragments of several Christian texts

paganism: a variety of animistic or other non-Christian religious beliefs and practices

Papias of Hierapolis (c. AD 60–130): church father whose *Expositions of the Lord's Sayings* are cited by Eusebius (s.v.) in his *Ecclesiastical History*

papyrus: ancient writing material or scroll on which some of the earliest NT manuscripts are found (e.g., $\mathfrak{P}^{52}$, a fragment of John's Gospel dating to c. AD 125)

Paraclete: from Gk. *paraklētos*; Jesus' title for the Holy Spirit ("Counselor," John 14:16,26; 15:26; 16:7); John used it for Jesus Christ ("advocate," 1 John 2:1)

parousia: from Gk. *parousia* ("presence"); technical term for Jesus' second coming

passion narrative: account of events surrounding Jesus' crucifixion in the four Gospels

passion, the: the events surrounding Jesus' crucifixion

Passover: Jewish religious festival instituted on the eve of Israel's exodus from Egypt (see Exodus 12)

Pastoral Epistles: conventional designation for Paul's letters to Timothy and Titus (1–2 Timothy, Titus)

Patmos, Isle of: place of exile where the apostle John received the visions recorded in the book of Revelation (see Rev 1:9)

patristic: related to the church fathers

Pauline: related to (the apostle) Paul (s.v. also Pauline circle, Pauline corpus)

Pauline circle: group of early Christians associated with the apostle Paul in his mission; includes coworkers such as Timothy, Titus, Luke, John Mark, Silas, Barnabas, and others

Pauline corpus: body of Paul's writings included in the Bible (i.e., his 13 letters)

pearl stringing: rabbinic practice of grouping together a series of related scriptural passages; imitated by Christian writers (e.g., Rom 3:10–18; Heb 1:5–14)

Pentateuch: from Gk. *penta* ("five"); the five books of Moses—Genesis, Exodus, Leviticus, Numbers, and Deuteronomy

Pentecost: from Gk. for "fiftieth"; Jewish festival described in Lev 23:5–21 and Deut 16:8–10; term used only in Acts 2:1; 20:16; 1 Cor 16:8

pesher: Jewish interpretive technique by which the contemporary application of a biblical reference is highlighted

Pharisees: influential Jewish sect known for its emphasis on the law; set itself in opposition to Jesus and, together with the Sadducees (s.v.), had him crucified

Philo (c. 20 BC–AD 50): Jewish thinker, author, and exegete from Alexandria, Egypt, who practiced an allegorical method of interpreting Scripture

plenary inspiration: the full or complete inspiration of every part of Scripture

Pliny the Elder: first-century AD Roman natural philosopher; author of *Natural History*

Pliny the Younger: son of Pliny the Elder and proconsul of the province of Bithynia in Asia Minor in the early second century AD

plural-to-singular device: shift from plural (group) to singular (individual) usage indicating eyewitness testimony (described by R. Bauckham in *Jesus and the Eyewitnesses*)

Plutarch: first-century AD Greek historian, biographer, and essayist; author of *Parallel Lives* and *Moralia*

pneumatic: from Greek *pneuma* ("Spirit" or "spirit"); related to spiritual matters, the human spirit, or the Holy Spirit

Polybius: second-century BC Greek historian; author of *The Histories*

Polycarp of Smyrna (c. AD 69–155): disciple of the apostle John, companion of Papias, bishop of Smyrna; author of *To the Philippians*; martyred by being burned at the stake

Pontius Pilate: Roman procurator of Judea (AD 26–36); together with the Jewish leaders, responsible for the crucifixion of Jesus as explained in all four Gospels

posttribulational rapture: belief that Christ will return at the end of the tribulation (s.v.)

prefect: Roman government official (e.g., Pontius Pilate)

premillennialism: Christian belief that the Lord Jesus Christ will return prior to ("pre") his thousand-year reign on earth; *millennium* is from Lat. *mille* ("thousand") and *annus* ("year")

pretribulational rapture: belief that Christ will return prior to the tribulation (s.v.)

Prison Epistles: conventional designation for Paul's four letters written from his first Roman imprisonment—Ephesians, Philippians, Colossians, and Philemon

procurator: Roman government official

proselyte: Gentile attracted to Jewish worship who submitted to circumcision and the keeping of Jewish Sabbath observances and food laws

provenance: place of writing

Pseudepigrapha: from Gk. meaning "false title"; a collective term for Jewish Second Temple literature not included in the Apocrypha

Pseudo-Barnabas: ancient letter falsely attributed to Barnabas (dated c. AD 135?)

pseudonymity: an author's attribution of a given piece of writing to someone other than the true author

"Q": a hypothetical source common to Matthew and Luke, possibly abbreviating the German word *Quelle* ("source")

Quest of (or for) the historical Jesus: modern waves of historical research into the background of the person of Jesus (distinguished as "first quest," "second quest," and "third quest")

Quirinius: governor of, or holder of administrative office in, Syria mentioned in Luke's birth narrative of Jesus in Luke 2:2

Qumran: region near the Dead Sea and site where the Qumran literature was found

Qumran literature: s.v. Dead Sea Scrolls

rabbinic literature: body of literature compiling the teachings of ancient Jewish rabbis, including the Mishnah (e.g., *m. Avot*), the Babylonian and Jerusalem Talmuds (e.g., *b. Sanh.*; *y. Yeb.*), and the Tosefta (*t. Zer.*)

rapture: from Lat. *raptura*, the Vulgate (s.v) rendering of "caught up" in 1 Thess 4:17; Christians' reunion with their Lord at the time of the Second Coming in connection with the tribulation (s.v.)

realized eschatology: aspects of the end time that have already been fulfilled in Christ and in the lives of believers (e.g., eternal life in John 5:24)

rhetoric: study and practice of effective communication; type of discourse

rhetorical criticism: a study of the rhetorical (communicative) features in a given document (such as the book of Romans)

rule of faith: orthodox apostolic teaching

sacrament: a religious rite believed by Roman Catholics to mediate grace, constituting a sacred mystery

Sadducees: Jewish aristocratic sect generally supportive of the political status quo in Palestine; together with the Pharisees (s.v.), they were responsible for Jesus' crucifixion

salvation history: the progressive unfolding of God's provision of salvation for humanity

Sanhedrin: Jewish ruling council made up of Sadducees and Pharisees that delivered Jesus to Pontius Pilate to be crucified

Saul of Tarsus: alternative name of the apostle Paul (Tarsus refers to his hometown)

Savior: religious deliverer; the NT claims that Jesus is the Savior of the world (John 4:42); the term was also used for emperors in the Greco-Roman world

secessionists: divisive heretics who left the congregation, suggesting they were never truly saved in the first place (see esp. 1 John 2:19)

Second Temple Judaism: the religion of the Jewish people during the Second Temple period (s.v. Second Temple period below)

Second Temple period: span between the reconstruction of the temple in 516 BC and the destruction of the temple by the Romans in AD 70

self-attestation of Scripture: the Bible's claims regarding its own nature

Semitic: Jewish, with reference to one of the sons of Noah, Shem (see Gen 6:10)

Semitism: also called Hebraism; a Jewish thought pattern or expression reflected in a Jewish writer's Greek document

Septuagint: Greek translation of the OT Hebrew Scriptures (abbreviated LXX)

sepulcher: type of tomb

Sermon on the Mount: body of Jesus' teaching presented in Matthew 5–7 (see Matt 5:1, "on the mountain")

Sermon on the Plain: Luke's equivalent to the Sermon on the Mount in Luke 6:17–49 (see Luke 6:17: "level place")

shekel: ancient Jewish coin

shekinah: the glorious presence of God, especially in the temple

Shema: from Hb. *shema* ("to hear" or "to listen"), the first word in Deut 6:4, "Listen, Israel: The Lord our God, the Lord is One"; the central Jewish affirmation of monotheism

Shepherd of Hermas: early second-century AD (?) Christian document

Sibylline Oracles: collection of oracles ascribed to a sibyl, a prophetess who uttered alleged divine revelation in a frenzied state

Sinaiticus: s.v. Codex Sinaiticus

Sirach: second-century BC OT apocryphal book also known as *The Wisdom of Ben Sira* or *Ecclesiasticus* (not the OT book of Ecclesiastes)

sons of Zebedee: the apostles John and James

subapostolic period: era subsequent to the apostolic era

substitutionary atonement: blood sacrifice on behalf of another

Suetonius (c. AD 70–130): Roman historian and author of *Lives of the Twelve Caesars*

Suffering Servant, the: figure in the second part of Isaiah (esp. 52:13–53:12) identified as Jesus the Messiah by the NT writers (e.g., 1 Pet 2:21–25)

syncretism: eclectic mix of religious beliefs and practices

Synoptic: pertaining to Matthew, Mark, and Luke

Synoptic Gospels: from Gk. *sunopsis* (lit. "seeing together"), technical designation for Matthew, Mark, and Luke because of their common viewpoint on Jesus' life

Synoptic parallels: related passages in the Synoptic Gospels

Synoptic problem: the nature of the relationship between the Gospels of Matthew, Mark, and Luke, deemed by some a "problem" due to alleged discrepancies in chronology and wording

Synoptic tradition: oral and/or written material underlying an account in the Gospels of Matthew, Mark, and/or Luke

Tacitus (born c. AD 56; died after AD 118): Roman historian and author of *The Annals* and *The Histories*

Talmud: compilation of Jewish writings in the Babylonian and Palestinian traditions

Targum (pl. Targums): Aramaic paraphrase of and commentary on the Hebrew Scriptures

Tatian: early church father and compiler of the synopsis of the Four Gospels called *The Diatessaron* (c. AD 150–160)

tax collectors: local residents in NT times who collected revenues for the Roman authorities and thus were despised by their fellow citizens as traitors

temple cult: religious rites and sacrifices offered in the Jerusalem sanctuary

temple, the: usually, shorthand for the Jerusalem temple, originally built by Solomon

Tertullian (c. AD 160–225): important early Christian apologist; author of *Against Marcion*, *Apology*, and *On Baptism*

testimonia: common OT messianic texts adduced by the early Christians to prove that Jesus was the Christ

Testimonium Flavianum: disputed portion in *Jewish Antiquities* by the Jewish historian Josephus that refers to Jesus, at least part of which is believed to be a later Christian interpolation

tetragrammaton: from Gk. meaning "four letters," referring to the OT name for God, "YHWH" (likely pronounced "Yahweh" but in most translations represented as "Lord")

tetrarch: "ruler of a quarter," title of governors such as Herod Antipas (s.v.)

text types: the four major Gk. manuscript text types of the NT books are commonly classified as Alexandrian, Caesarean, Byzantine, and Western

textual criticism: the science of adjudicating between variant manuscript readings through specific criteria such as dating, text type or geographic distribution, attested readings, and possible reasons for variants

textual witnesses: readings attested in particular manuscripts

Textus Receptus: Lat. for "received text," a form of the Byzantine text type also attested in the Majority Text, which constituted the textual base for the translations by Wycliffe and Luther and for the KJV

theodicy: from Gk. *theos* ("God") and *dikaios* ("righteous"); an attempt at justifying God's actions (e.g., see Job, Romans, and Revelation)

theophany: from Gk. *theos* ("God") and *phainō* ("appear"); an appearance of God to humans

Tiberius: Roman emperor (AD 14–37)

Torah: translation of Hebrew word for "doctrine" or "teaching"; broadly, the Jewish law encompassing both oral and written teachings; narrowly, the five books of Moses (the Pentateuch)

Tosefta: from Aram. *tosefta* ("addition, supplement"); additional teaching supplementing the Mishnah

Trajan: Roman emperor (AD 98–117)

transfiguration: event at which Jesus' outward appearance was transformed in anticipation of his heavenly glory (see Matt 17:1–8 and parallels)

transmission: the process of copying and preserving a text (Scripture)

tribulation: a period of great suffering and affliction in relation to the return of Christ

triumphal entry: Jesus' arrival in Jerusalem and his popular acclaim as Messiah during Passion week (Palm Sunday; see Matt 21:1–11 and parallels)

Two-Document Hypothesis: s.v. Two-Source Theory

Two-Gospel Hypothesis: s.v. Griesbach Hypothesis

Two-Source Theory: hypothesis that Matthew and Luke both independently used two written sources, Mark and "Q" (s.v.)

typology: biblical pattern of correspondence along salvation-historical lines (e.g., John 3:14, where Jesus elaborated on the relationship between the serpent lifted up by Moses in the wilderness and Jesus being lifted up at the crucifixion, in both cases giving life to the one who looks in faith)

uncial: ancient manuscript written in all capital letters without spaces or punctuation

universalism: erroneous belief that all eventually will be saved

Vaticanus: s.v. Codex Vaticanus

verbal inspiration: the divine nature of the very words of Scripture

Vespasian: Roman emperor (AD 69–79)

Vulgate: Jerome's fourth-century AD Lat. translation of the Bible

"we" passages: portions of narrative in the book of Acts written in the first person plural, in all likelihood indicating that the author of Acts participated in the travels narrated in those portions of his account (Acts 16:10–17; 20:5–15; 21:1–18; 27:1–28:16)

Yahweh: approximate transliteration from the Hebrew consonants *yhwh* (s.v. tetragrammaton); OT name for God based on the divine self-reference in Exod 3:14 to Moses, "I AM WHO I AM"

YHWH: tetragrammaton (s.v.); Yahweh

Zion: holy mountain in Jerusalem (e.g., 2 Sam 5:7; Ps 2:6; Isa 28:16)

Name Index

Achtemeier, P. J.   *293, 328, 364*
A. J.Köstenberger   *106,–9, 111,*
   113, 116–20
Akin, D. L.   *362, 373*
Aland, B.   *7, 18*
Aland, K.   *7, 18, 45*
Alexander, L. C. A.   *236*
Allen, D.   *290, 293*
Allison, D. C., Jr.   *48, 56, 75*
Archer, G. L., Jr.   *18*
Arnold, C. E.   *243–44, 271,*
   285
Aune, D. E.   *375–76, 378–80,*
   383–84, 395

Barclay, J. M. G.   *140*
Barnett, P. W.   *137,148, 206*
Barr, D. L.   *384*
Barrett, C. K.   *25, 27, 36, 120,*
   148, 178, 180, 206, 210
Bartchy, S. S.   *263*
Barth, M.   *243*
Bartholomew, C. G.   *104*
Barton, G. A.   *292*
Barton, J.   *3*
Bateman, H. W.   *307, 308*
Bauckham, R.   *7, 9, 16, 51, 55,*
   77, 79, 88, 107, 109–10,
   137, 270, 311, 313, 323,
   338–39, 343, 345–49,
   351, 354, 384, 393–95
Baugh, S. M.   *285*
Baur, F. C.   *259*
Beale, G. K.   *14, 173–74,*
   375–76, 378, 384–85,
   396
Beare, G. W.   *234*
Beasley-Murray, G. R.   *120, 376*
Beckwith, R.   *17*
Behm, J.   *7*
Bell, A. A.   *378*
Belleville, L. L.   *187, 205*
Bernheim, P.-A.   *310*
Best, E.   *47, 164, 243*
Betz, H. D.   *155*
Bevere, A. R.   *258*

Black, D. A.   *289*
Blomberg, C. L.   *18, 51, 75, 92,*
   103, 120, 127, 137, 206
Bock, D. L.   *48, 51, 91, 95,*
   104, 181
Bockmuehl, M.   *234, 238, 264*
Borchert, G. L.   *106*
Bovon, F.   *376*
Bowley, J. E.   *28*
Bowman, R.   *51*
Boyd, G. A.   *51*
Brand, C. O.   *282*
Brooke, A. E.   *359, 363*
Brooks, J. A.   *78, 86*
Brown, R. E.   *241, 292, 358,*
   363, 366, 370
Bruce, F. F.   *17, 18, 89, 127,*
   137, 141, 148, 153, 160,
   173–74, 187, 229, 234,
   243, 264, 297, 303, 308,
   373
Burge, G. M.   *36*
Burridge, R. A.   *51*

Caird, G. B.   *379*
Callow, J.   *367*
Calvin, J.   *357*
Caragounis, C. C.   *65, 249*
Carson, D. A.   *xiv, 6, 14, 43,*
   48, 54, 57, 75, 78–79,
   88–91, 108–10, 120,
   184, 187, 234, 236–37,
   242–44, 258, 260–61,
   263–64, 269, 271, 285,
   292, 360, 363–64, 372,
   377, 383, 395
Chapell, B.   *285*
Chapman, D. W.   *36*
Charles, J. D.   *354*
Charles, R. H.   *375–77, 379,*
   384
Charlesworth, J. H.   *36*
Chester, A.   *314, 322*
Chilton, B. D.   *32, 310, 323*
Church, F. F.   *261*
Cohick, L. H.   *36*

Cole, A.   *152, 156*
Collins, A. Y.   *379, 383–84*
Collins, J. J.   *379, 382–83*
Collins, R. F.   *268*
Cousar, C. B.   *151*
Cowan, S. B.   *282*
Cranfield, C. E. B.   *217*
Croteau, D. A.   *108*

Dandamayev, M. A.   *263*
Davids, P. H.   *323, 329,*
   338–39, 341, 354
Davies, W. D.   *48, 56*
Day, J. N.   *395*
Deissmann, A.   *315*
deSilva, D. A.   *29, 313, 260,*
   381–82
De Witt Burton, E.   *152*
Dibelius, M.   *88, 315*
Dillon, J. M.   *32*
Dockery, D.   *17*
Dodd, C. H.   *209*
Donahue, J. R.   *83–84*
Donaldson, T. L.   *61*
Donfried, K. P.   *166*
Doty, W. G.   *268*
Duff, J.   *270*
Duncan, G.   *151*
Dunn, J. D. G.   *51, 160,*
   212–14, 251–52, 260,
   325, 347

Eddy, P. R.   *51*
Edson, C.   *166*
Ehrman, B. D.   *10, 18*
Eisenman, R.   *310*
Ellingworth, P.   *308*
Elliott, J. H.   *325, 328, 354*
Elliott, J. K.   *7*
Ellis, E. E.   *140, 229, 268–69,*
   271, 273, 285, 325
Evans, C. A.   *36, 51, 85–86,*
   310, 323, 351

Fant, C. F.   *181*

Fee, G. D.   *178, 180, 206, 234, 236, 238, 264, 267, 274–75*
Fein, P.   *7*
Ferguson, E.   *33, 36*
Finegan, J.   *210*
Fiorenza, E. S.   *383–84*
Fitzmyer, J. A.   *90–91,209, 211–12, 217*
Ford, J. M.   *375, 384, 396*
France, R. T.   *52, 54, 75, 86, 308*
Francis, F. O.   *315*
Friesen, S. J.   *379, 381*
Fung, R. Y. K.   *160*
Furnish, V. P.   *178, 211*

Gamble, H. Y.   *17–18*
Garland, D. E.   *82, 86, 178, 182, 206, 264*
Gasque, W. W.   *17*
Gaston, L.   *291*
Geisler, N. L.   *5, 17*
Gempf, C.   *137*
George, T.   *160*
Giles, K.   *276*
Gill, D. W. J.   *25, 137*
Gombis, T. G.   *248*
Gorday, J.   *285*
Gordon, T. D.   *277*
Goulder, M. D.   *57*
Gowan, D. E.   *36*
Grabbe, L. L.   *23, 26*
Grayston, K.   *359*
Green, E. M. B.   *355*
Green, G. L.   *36, 174, 355*
Green, J. B.   *52, 104, 293, 364*
Green, M.   *337, 347, 355*
Griffin, H. P., Jr.   *275, 285*
Griffith, T.   *361*
Grudem, W. A.   *xiv, 15, 328–29, 355*
Guelich, R. A.   *77–78, 80, 86*
Gundry, R.   *55–57, 80, 86, 187, 361*
Guthrie, D.   *28, 164, 184, 187, 267, 269, 271, 275, 285, 311, 323, 358, 377*
Guthrie, G.   *291, 294, 305, 307–8*

Hafemann, S. J.   *205–6*

Hagner, D. A.   *58, 75, 229, 290, 308, 348*
Hahn, F.   *82*
Hall, M. S.   *384*
Hansen, G. W.   *151–52, 160*
Hanson, P.   *382*
Harris, M. J.   *178, 180, 187, 206*
Harris, R. L.   *17*
Harris, W. H., III   *247*
Harrison, E. F.   *229*
Hartin, P. J.   *313*
Hawthorne, G. F.   *148, 234–36*
Head, P. M.   *50*
Heil, J. P.   *248*
Helyer, L. R.   *25, 36*
Hemer, C. J.   *90, 125, 142, 164, 378, 396*
Hendriksen, W.   *78–80*
Hengel, M.   *52, 54, 313, 320*
Hennecke, E.   *146*
Henry, C. F. H.   *17*
Herrick, G. J.   *51*
Hewitt, T.   *290*
Hill, C. E.   *358, 373*
Hodge, C.   *209*
Hoehner, H. W.   *27, 40–43, 51, 241, 242, 243, 247, 248, 249*
Holmes, M. W.   *4, 174, 179, 186*
Hoppins, R.   *290*
Huffman, D. S.   *92*
Hughes, F. W.   *168*
Hughes, P. E.   *205, 293, 308*
Hughes, R. K.   *285*
Humphreys, C. J.   *44*
Hurst, L. D.   *289, 291*
Jervell, J.   *104*
Jewett, R.   *164, 168, 174*
Jobes, K. H.   *329, 331–32, 355*
Johnson, A. F.   *396*
Johnson, L. T.   *90, 267–68, 273, 285, 289, 292, 296, 308, 311, 313–14, 323*
Jones, P.   *205*
Juel, D.   *83*

Kaiser, W. C, Jr.   *18*
Karris, R. J.   *274–75*
Käsemann, E.   *325*

Keener, C. S.   *48, 75, 110, 120, 378, 379*
Kelber, W.   *83*
Kellum, L. S.   *366*
Kelly, J. N. D.   *285, 327, 336, 343, 346, 355*
Kennedy, G.   *168*
Kent, H. A., Jr.   *127*
Kent, J. H.   *211*
Kim, S.   *140, 148*
Klein, W. W.   *264*
Kline, M. G.   *9*
Knight, G. W.   *267, 269, 285*
Knox, J.   *151, 259*
Koch, K.   *382*
Kohlenberger, J. R. III   *11*
Komoszewski, J. E.   *51*
Köstenberger, A. J.   *xiv, xv, 14–15, 18, 41–43, 74, 80, 137, 140, 147, 149, 201, 227, 248, 267, 273, 275–77, 282–83, 285, 369*
Köstenberger, M. E.   *51, 86*
Kovacs, J.   *375, 396*
Kruger, M. J.   *337, 355*
Kruse, C. G.   *206*
Kruse, J.   *363, 365, 373*
Kümmel, W.   *234*
Kümmel, W. G.   *7*
Kupp, D. D.   *59*

Ladd, G. E.   *34, 383, 385, 396*
Lane, W. L.   *78–79, 81, 86, 291–92, 295–98, 304–5, 308*
Laniak, T. S.   *285*
Larkin, W. J., Jr.   *127, 137, 181*
Lea, T. D.   *275, 285*
Lee, D.   *384*
Levinskaya, I.   *137*
Liefeld, W. L.   *104*
Lierman, J.   *109*
Lightfoot, J. B.   *152, 156, 252*
Lightfoot, N. R.   *10, 17*
Lincoln, A. T.   *120, 248*
Lindars, B.   *289, 292, 308*
Loenertz, R. J.   *384*
Lohse, E.   *257*
Longacre, R.   *367*
Longenecker, B. W.   *161*

Longenecker, R. N.   *14, 137,
      152, 156, 161, 271*
Luther, M.   *208, 290, 310, 357*

MacGregor, K. R.   *197*
Maier, P. L.   *28, 41*
Marcus, J.   *78*
Marshall, I. H.   *52, 91, 104,
      127, 137, 173–74,
      268–70, 277, 327, 329,
      355, 363, 365, 372–73*
Martin, D. M.   *174*
Martin, R. P.   *86, 148, 314,
      323, 350, 355*
Martyn, J. L.   *160*
Mason, S.   *35, 210*
Matil, A. J.   *124*
Mazzaferri, F. D.   *376, 385*
McDonald, L. M.   *3, 6, 17,
      235, 252*
McGrath, A. E.   *18*
McKnight, S.   *51–52*
McLaren, J. S.   *378*
McRay, J.   *142*
McRay, W.   *181–82*
Meier, J. P.   *43*
Melick, R. R., Jr.   *264*
Merkle, B. L.   *282, 285*
Metzger, B. M.   *3, 10, 17–18,
      215, 243, 260, 270*
Michaels, J. R.   *326, 329, 332,
      355, 384, 396*
Mikolaski, S. J.   *12*
Milligan, G.   *164*
Milns, R. D.   *24*
Mitton, C. L.   *242*
Moffatt, J.   *290*
Moloney, F. J.   *110*
Moo, D. J.   *6, 43, 54, 57, 79,
      88–91, 184, 187, 212,
      214, 227, 229, 234, 237,
      242–44, 258, 260–61,
      263, 265, 271, 292, 323,
      325, 339–40, 347, 355,
      360, 363–64, 377, 383*
Moreland, J. P.   *51*
Morgan, C. W.   *289*
Morris, L.   *14, 54, 75, 89–91,
      104, 120, 151, 161, 174,
      187, 206, 210, 230, 378,
      383*
Mounce, R. H.   *378, 384, 396*

Mounce, W. D.   *15, 268–70,
      273–74, 276, 285*
Mowry, L.   *378*
Murphy-OConnor, J.   *181–82,
      211*

Nardoni, E.   *395*
Neusner, J.   *310*
Nickelsburg, G. W. E.   *36*
Nix, W. E.   *5, 17*
Nolland, J.   *75, 104*
Nordling, J. G.   *261*
Norman, R. S.   *282*

Oakes, P.   *240*
O'Brien, P. T.   *74, 80, 137, 140,
      147, 149, 167, 234, 236,
      242–44, 248, 249, 252,
      259, 262, 265*
Olsson, B.   *365*
Osborne, G. R.   *9, 18, 375,
      378, 394, 396*

Pache, R.   *17*
Painter, J.   *310, 358*
Pao, D. W.   *104*
Patterson, R. D.   *xv, 18*
Patzia, A. G.   *17, 258, 261*
Penner, T. C.   *313*
Peterson, D.   *137*
Peterson, R. A.   *289*
Picirilli, R. E.   *337*
Pines, S.   *39*
Piper, J.   *201*
Plummer, R. L.   *141*
Polhill, J. B.   *137, 143, 149*
Pollard, T. E.   *106*
Porter, S. E.   *7–8, 52, 175, 358,
      365*
Porton, G. G.   *35*
Price, S. R. F.   *381*
Prigent   *384*
Prior, M.   *270*
Pryor, J. W.   *120*

Quinn, J. D.   *268, 285*

Ramsay, W.   *290*
Rapske, B.   *137*
Reasoner, M.   *212*
Reddish, M. G.   *181*
Reed, J. T.   *236*

Reese, R. A.   *355*
Reid, D. G.   *148*
Reid, M. L.   *212*
Reinhard, D. R.   *249*
Renan, E.   *88*
Resseguie, J. L.   *384*
Rhoads, D. M.   *81, 86*
Richardson, K.   *323*
Ridderbos, H. N.   *110, 117,
      120, 149*
Riesner, R.   *149*
Riggenbach, E.   *290*
Robbins, M. M.   *290*
Roberts, M. D.   *52*
Robinson, J. A.   *244*
Robinson, J. A. T.   *313–14,
      327, 338, 348*
Roller, O.   *209*
Ropes, J. H.   *320*
Rowland, C.   *375, 396*
Rowston, D. J.   *345*
Ryken, L.   *18*

Sanders, J. A.   *17*
Sanders, J. N.   *106*
Sandy, D. B.   *25*
Schelkle, K. H.   *347*
Schlatter, A.   *16–17, 51, 108,
      137, 230*
Schnabel, E. J.   *137, 140, 145,
      149*
Schnackenburg, R.   *241, 361,
      363, 365, 373*
Schneemelcher, W.   *146*
Schreiner, T. R.   *149, 212, 214,
      216, 227, 230, 277, 283,
      285, 326, 328–29, 332,
      334, 339–40, 355*
Schürer, E.   *35–36*
Scobie, C. H. H.   *378*
Scorgie, G. G.   *11, 18*
Scott, J. J., Jr.   *23, 36*
Sellin, G.   *349*
Selwyn, E. G.   *327*
Senior, D. P.   *82–85, 355*
Shanks, H.   *310*
Silva, M.   *161, 234, 237–38,
      265*
Skarsaune, O.   *274*
Slater, T. B.   *378*
Smalley, S. S.   *373*
Smith, I. K.   *253*

Spicq, C. *293*
Stanton, G. N. *7*
Stein, R. *46–47, 50–52*
Stemberger, G. *36*
Stibbe, M. W. G. *117*
Stott, J. R. W. *127, 137, 363, 370, 373*
Stowers, S. *315*
Stowers, S. K. *236, 261*
Strack, H. L. *36*
Strauss, M. *103–4*
Strauss, M. L. *18*
Streeter, B. H. *358–59*
Stuhlmacher, P. *214*
Stuhlmueller, C. *82–85*
Swain, S. R. *32, 119–20*
Swete, H. B. *376*

Tasker, R. V. G. *54*
Telford, W. *82, 84*
Tenney, M. C. *385*
Theissen, G. *349*
Thielman, F. *136, 149, 161, 234, 240, 244, 249, 265*
Thiselton, A. *104, 206*
Thompson, L. L. *378, 380, 384*

Thompson, M. M. *293, 364, 373*
Tomasino, A. J. *24*
Towner, P. H. *270, 274*
Trobisch, D. *358*
Trotter, A. H., Jr. *308*
Turner, D. L. *75*

van Staden, P. J. *365*
van Unnik, W. C. *385*
Van Voorst, R. E. *51*
Verheyden, J. *89*
Vermes, G. *36*
Vielhauer, P. *138*
von Harnack, A. *290*

Wacker, W. C. *285*
Waddington, W. G. *44*
Wainwright, A. W. *375*
Wallace, D. B. *248*
Wanamaker, C. *166, 168, 173, 175*
Warfield, B. B. *17*
Watson, D. F. *337, 351*
Webb, R. L. *346, 348, 351*
Wegner, P. D. *18*

Weima, J. A. D. *175, 365*
Weiss, J. *347*
Wenham, D. *139, 148–49*
Westcott, B. A. *17*
Westfall, C. L. *300, 304*
White, J. L. *365*
Wilder, T. L. *269, 285*
Wilkins, M. J. *51, 75*
Williams, J. F. *81, 85*
Williams, M. C. *50*
Wilson, A. N. *123*
Wilson, J. C. *378*
Wilson, M. *381, 396*
Windisch, H. *346–47*
Witherington, B., III *36, 161, 180, 206, 310, 236*
Wrede, W. *86*
Wright, N. T. *230, 265*

Yamauchi, E. *32*
Yarbrough, R. W. *373*
Yoder Neufeld, T. R. *266*
Young, F. M. *273*

Zahn, T. *290–92*

Subject Index

A

Acts   *122*
  author   *123*
  date   *124*
  destination   *125*
  genre   *126*
  literary plan   *127*
  outline   *127*
  provenance   *124*
  purpose   *125*
  unit-by-unit discussion   *128*
Alexander the Great   *24*
allusions to Jesus in Pauls
        Letters   *139*
antiquity   *6*
Apocrypha   *29*
apostolicity   *6*
Augustinian view   *49*
autographs   *10*

B

Babylonian period   *23*
beginning of Jesus' ministry   *41*
birth of Jesus   *40*

C

canonicity, criteria of   *5*
canonization, stimuli for   *5*
chronology
  of Jesus' ministry   *40*
church fathers
  witness of   *4*
Colossian heresy, the   *253*
Colossians, letter to the   *250*
  author   *251*
  date   *251*
  destination   *252*
  literary plan   *254*
  occasion   *253*
  outline   *254*
  provenance   *251*
  purpose   *253*
  unit-by-unit discussion   *254*

contribution to the Canon
  Acts   *122*
  Corinthians   *177*
  Galatians   *150*
  Hebrews   *288*
  Johannine Epistles   *357*
  John   *105*
  Jude   *325*
  Luke   *87*
  Mark   *76*
  Matthew   *53, 75, 85, 103,
      120, 136, 160, 174, 205,
      229, 264, 284, 308, 322,
      354, 373, 395*
  Pastoral Epistles   *267*
  Petrine Epistles   *325*
  Philemon   *232*
  Revelation   *375*
  Romans   *207*
  Thessalonians   *163*
Corinthians, 1–2   *176*
  author   *178*
  date and provenance   *179*
  destination   *180*
  literary plan   *188*
  occasion   *183*
  outlines   *188*
  purpose   *186*
  sequence of visits and
        letters   *179*
  unit-by-unit discussion   *190*

D

Dead Sea Scrolls   *30*
death of Jesus   *43*
duration of Jesus' ministry   *42*
dynamic or functional
        equivalence   *11*

E

early church's use of
        Scripture   *14*
ecclesiastical usage   *6*
emperor worship   *31, 378*

Ephesians, letter to the   *241*
  author   *242*
  date   *242*
  destination   *243*
  literary plan   *244*
  occasion   *243*
  outline   *245*
  provenance   *243*
  purpose   *244*
  unit-by-unit discussion   *245*
Epiphanes   *25*

F

formal equivalence   *11*
Fourfold Gospel, the   *6*
fulfillment
  of Old Testament festival   *114*
  of OT prophecy   *74*

G

Galatians, letter to the   *150*
  author   *151*
  date   *154*
  destination   *152*
  literary plan   *155*
  occasion and purpose   *154*
  outline   *156*
  provenance   *152*
  unit-by-unit discussion   *156*
Gnosticism   *31, 361*
Gospel according to John   *105*
  date   *108*
  destination   *109*
  literary plan   *110*
  occasion   *109*
  outline   *112*
  provenance   *109*
  purpose   *110*
  unit-by-unit discussion   *112*
Gospel according to Luke   *87*
  author   *88*
  date   *90*
  destination   *91*
  literary plan   *92*

outline   93
provenance   91
purpose   92
unit-by-unit discussion   94
Gospel according to Mark   76
   author   77
   date   78
   destination   79
   literary plan   80
   outline   81
   provenance   78
   purpose   80
   unit-by-unit discussion   82
Gospel according to
      Matthew   53
   author   54
   date   55
   five discourses   59
   literary plan   57
   provenance and
         destination   56
   purpose   57
   unit-by-unit discussion   59
Great Commission   74
Greek period   24
Greek philosophy   32

H

Hasmoneans, the   26
Hebrews, letter to the   288
   author   289
   date   291
   destination   293
   genre   296
   literary plan   297
   outline   297
   provenance   292
   purpose and occasion   295
   unit-by-unit discussion   297
"hermeneutical triad"   xiv
Herodian dynasty   27

I

"I Am" sayings   111
inerrancy, definition of   12
Inerrancy of Scripture   16
inspiration of Scripture   3, 12

J

James, letter to   309

author   311
date   313
destination   314
genre   315
literary plan   315
occasion   315
outline   316
provenance   314
unit-by-unit discussion   316
Jerusalem Council   133, 144
Jesus
   and the Gospels   37
   use of Scripture   13
Jewish sects   35
Jewish self-rule   25
Jewish theology   34
John, 1–3
   author   357
   date   359
   destination   360
   genre   364
   introductory matters unique to
         2 and 3 John   363
   literary plan   365
   occasion   361
   outlines   366
   provenance   360
   purpose   363
   unit-by-unit discussion   367
John the Baptist
   beginning of ministry   41
Judaism   32
Jude, letter of   345
   author   346
   date   347
   destination   349
   genre   350
   literary plan   351
   occasion and purpose   349
   outline   352
   provenance   348
   unit-by-unit discussion   352
justification   219

L

Latinisms   79
literary independence   48
literary interdependence   48

M

man of lawlessness   172
Messianism   34
monotheism   32
Muratorian Canon   5
mystery religions   31

N

new covenant documents   9
new creation   160

O

Olivet Discourse   71
order of New Testament
      books   8
orthodoxy   6

P

paganism   31
parables of Jesus   66–68
parables of the kingdom   65,
      68, 71
Pastoral Epistles, the   266
   genre   277
   pseudonymity   269
Paul
   appearance   145
   conversion   143
   early life and training   141
   final years   145
   follower of Jesus or founder of
         Christianity   138
   gospel   147
   life of   140
   name   141
   Rabbinic training   142
   Roman citizenship   141
   the man and the message   138
Pauline letter collection, the   7
Paul's missionary travels   144
   early travels   144
   first missionary journey   132,
         144
   second missionary
         journey   133, 145
   third missionary journey   134,
         145
people of the land   35
Persian period   23

Peter, First   *324*
    author   *326*
    date   *327*
    destination   *328*
    literary plan   *329*
    occasion   *329*
    outline   *330*
    provenance   *328*
    purpose   *329*
    unit-by-unit discussion   *330*
Peter, Second   *336*
    author   *336*
    date   *338*
    destination   *338*
    literary plan   *339*
    occasion and purpose   *339*
    outline   *340*
    provenance   *338*
    unit-by-unit discussion   *340*
Pharisees   *35*
Philemon, letter to   *258*
    author   *259*
    date   *259*
    destination   *259*
    literary plan   *261*
    occasion   *260*
    outline   *261*
    provenance   *260*
    unit-by-unit discussion   *262*
Philippians, letter to the   *232*
    author   *233*
    date   *233*
    destination   *235*
    literary plan   *236*
    occasion   *235*
    outline   *237*
    provenance   *234*
    purpose   *236*
    unit-by-unit discussion   *237*
political and religious
            background of the New
            Testament   *19*
proselytes and God-fearers   *33*
Pseudepigrapha   *30*
Ptolemaic period   *25*

R

Rabbinic schools   *33*
rapture   *171*
references to Jesus outside the
        Gospels   *38*

relationships between the
        Gospels   *45*
religious calendar   *33–34*
resurrection appearances of
        Jesus   *102*
Revelation, book of   *374*
    author   *375*
    date   *377*
    genre   *382*
    literary plan   *384*
    occasion, destination and
            purpose   *381*
    outline   *385*
    provenance   *380*
    unit-by-unit discussion   *386*
rhetoric   *167*
Roman period   *26*
Romans, letter to the   *207*
    author   *209*
    date   *210*
    destination   *212*
    literary plan   *216*
    occasion   *214*
    outline   *217*
    provenance   *211*
    purpose   *214*
    unit-by-unit discussion   *218*
rule of faith   *6*

S

Sadducees   *35*
Sanhedrin   *35*
Scripture   *4, 15*
Scripture's self-witness   *12*
Second Temple literature   *29*
Second Temple period   *20*
Seleucid or Syrian period   *25*
Sermon on the Mount, the   *61*
seven words of Jesus at the
        Cross   *118*
signs of Jesus   *115*
superstition and syncretism   *31*
synagogue, the   *32*

T

temple, the   *33*
theological theme in Jude   *353*
    contending for the faith   *353*
theological themes in
        1 Peter   *334*

Christian suffering and the end
        time   *334*
    identity of believers and
            their witness to the
            world   *335*
theological themes in
        2 Peter   *343*
    apostolic eyewitness versus
            heresy   *344*
    pursuit of Christian virtues
            in light of the end
            time   *343*
theological themes in Acts   *135*
    Holy Spirit   *135*
    resurrection and ascension of
            Jesus   *136*
theological themes in
        Colossians   *256*
    proper Christian
            conduce   *257*
    the supremacy of Christ   *256*
theological themes in
        Corinthians   *204*
    nature of the resurrection
            body   *204*
    new versus old covenant   *205*
theological theme in Ephesians
    the church   *249*
theological themes in
        Galatians   *159*
    justification by faith verses
            works of the law   *159*
    transformation of the
            believer   *159*
theological themes in
        Hebrews   *306*
    perseverance and Christian
            assurance   *307*
    superiority of the person and
            work of Christ and His
            high priesthood   *306*
theological themes in
        James   *320*
    faith and works   *320*
    wisdom and ethics   *321*
theological themes in Johannine
        Epistles   *372*
    discipleship and assurance of
            salvation   *372*
    love   *372*
theological themes in John   *119*
    Jesus as the Word, the Lamb of

God, and the Messianic
  Son of God *119*
the signs *119*
theological themes in Luke *101*
  Jesus' concern for the
    lowly *102*
  salvation history *101*
theological themes in Mark *84*
  Jesus the Son of God *84*
  nature of discipleship *85*
theological themes in
  Matthew *73*
  Great Commission and
    inclusion of Gentiles *74*
  Jesus the Messiah *73*
theological themes in
  Philemon *263*
  Christian approach to
    slavery and other social
    issues *263*
  mutual love and brotherhood
    in the body of
    Christ *263*
theological themes in
  Philippians *240*
  Christian suffering *240*
  Christian unity *240*
  joy in Christ *240*

theological themes in
  Revelation *393*
  sovereignty of God *393*
  theodicy *394*
theological themes in
  Romans *227*
  the gospel *227*
  the righteousness of God *228*
theological themes in the
  Pastorals *282*
  preservation of believers *283*
  qualifications of church
    leaders *282*
theological themes in
  Thessalonians *173*
  Christian work ethic *173*
  Second Coming *173*
Thessalonians, 1–2 *162*
  author *163*
  date *164*
  destination *165*
  literary plan *167*
  occasion *166*
  outline *168*
  provenance *165*
  purpose *167*
  unit-by-unit discussion *169*
Timothy, 1–2 *266*

  author *268*
  date and provenance *273*
  destination *271*
  occasion *274*
  outline *279*
  purpose *275*
  unit-by-unit discussion *279*
Titus, letter to
  date and provenance *273*
  destination *272*
  occasion *274*
  outline *281*
  purpose *276*
  unit-by-discussion *281*
translation of the New
  Testament *11*
transmission of the New
  Testament *10*
travel narrative, Lukan *93*
trial of Jesus *100*

W

We passages in Acts *124*

Z

Zealots *35*

Scripture Index

Genesis

1:1 *112*
1:28 *298*
2:2 *299*
3:6 *95, 368*
6–9 *339*
8:8–12 *60*
11:1–9 *129*
12:1–3 *59*
12:3 *224*
14:18–20 *307*
15:1–18 *303*
15:6 *151, 208, 218, 220–21,*
  318, 321
18:12 *336*
22 *318*
28:12 *113*
42:17–18 *43*

Exodus

1–2 *60*
2:15 *82*
3:14 *394*
12:1–4 *114*
12:1–14 *34*
12:15–20 *34, 114*
12:48 *332*
13:3–10 *34*
16:9 *332*
17:14 *12*
18 *35*
19:3 *61*
19:5–6 *332*
20:2–6 *32*
20:4 *195*
23:15 *34*
23:16 *34*
23:20 *48*
24:7 *9*
24:12 *199*
24:13 *61*
24:18 *61*
25–30 *289*

29:9 *300*
29:18 *199*
29:33 *300*
31:18 *199*
32:15 *199*
34:1 *199*
34:18 *34*
34:22 *34*
34:29–35 *68, 205*
35–40 *289*

Leviticus

9:7–8 *332*
10:4–5 *332*
11:44–45 *329*
16 *34*
19:2 *330*
19:18 *160, 318*
19:28 *238*
20:7 *330*
21:5 *238*
23 *33*
23:4–5 *114*
23:5 *34*
23:6–8 *34, 114*
23:9–14 *34, 114*
23:15–21 *34*
23:15–22 *114*
23:23–25 *34*
23:23–35 *114*
23:26–32 *34, 114*
23:33–36 *34*
23:34–43 *114*
23:39–43 *34*
23:44–46 *114*

Numbers

9:1–14 *34*
12:7 *299*
13–14 *289, 299, 307*
15:27–31 *304*
15:30 *304*
23:19 *13*

27:17 *63*
28:16 *34*
28:17–25 *34*
28:26–31 *34*
29:1–6 *34*
29:1–11 *114*
29:7–11 *34*
29:12–34 *34*

Deuteronomy

4:2 *13, 393*
4:20 *332*
5:6–10 *32*
6:4 *32, 194*
6:13 *74*
6:16 *74*
7:6 *332*
8:3 *74*
9:10 *199*
14:1 *238*
16:1–7 *34*
16:3–4 *34*
16:8 *34*
16:9–12 *34*
16:13–15 *34*
17:7 *192*
21:23 *143, 327*
25:4 *4*
27:26 *159*
28:58–59 *12*
29:20 *9*
31:9 *9*
31:26 *9*
31–33 *116*
32:21 *225*
32:43 *298, 391*
33:29 *61*

Joshua

1:8 *368*
1:18 *12*
2 *318*
8:32 *12*

1 Samuel

15:29   *13*
23:14   *82*
30:12–13   *43*

2 Samuel

7:14   *298*

1 Kings

5:5   *332*
5–8   *33*
18:28   *238*
19:3–4   *82*

2 Kings

4:42–44   *82*
22:8   *12*
22:13   *12*
23:2   *9*
23:21   *9*
24:12   *23*
24–25   *23*
25:3   *23*

2 Chronicles

10:5   *43*
10:12   *43*
20:20   *12*
34:14   *12*
34:30   *9*
36:5–21   *23*

Ezra

1:1–4   *24*
3   *33*

Nehemiah

8:1   *12*

Esther

1:1   *24*
4:16–5:1   *43*
9:18–32   *34*

Psalms

2:7   *60, 298*

8:4–6   *298*
22:1   *74*
22:7–8   *74*
22:18   *74*
32:1–2   *221, 228*
34:5   *332*
34:8   *331*
34:12–16   *333*
45:6   *298*
66:10   *333*
68:8   *247*
69:21   *74*
78:2   *74*
79:5–10   *395*
89:35   *13*
94:1–3   *395*
95   *299, 307*
95:7–11   *299–300*
102:25–27   *298*
104:4   *298*
110:1   *72, 74, 298, 307*
110:1–4   *303*
110:4   *300, 307*
118:22   *331*
118:22–23   *74, 99*
118:26   *74, 99*
151   *30*

Proverbs

3:34   *322*
8:8   *13*
10:12   *320*
11:31   *334*
26:11   *342*
30:5–6   *13*

Isaiah

4:2   *60*
5:1–2   *74*
6:9–10   *74, 126, 135*
7:14   *13, 59, 74*
8:8   *74*
8:10   *74*
8:14   *224, 332*
9:1–2   *74*
11:1   *60, 74*
15:2   *238*
22:13   *32*
28:11–12   *196*
28:16   *224–25, 331*

28:18   *90*
29:13   *74*
35:5   *90*
35:5–6   *62, 74*
40:3   *30, 74, 82, 113*
40:6–8   *331*
42:1   *60*
42:1–4   *74– 75*
42:18   *74*
43:21   *332*
44:6   *394*
44:28–45:13   *24*
52:7   *225*
52:13–53:12   *34*
53   *56, 327*
53:1   *225*
53:2   *74*
53:4   *62, 74*
53:12   *229*
55:10–11   *119*
55:11   *119*
56:7   *69, 74, 83, 332*
57:20   *350*
61:1   *74, 90*
61:1–2   *92, 95, 129*
62:11   *74*
65:1   *225*
65:25   *143*

Jeremiah

1:9   *13*
7:11   *74*
12:7   *74*
22:5   *74*
23:5   *60*
29   *315*
29:4–13   *365*
31:15   *60, 74*
31:31–34   *295, 302*
32:6–9   *74*
33:15   *60*
34:18–20   *303*
36:28   *13*
39:2   *23*

Ezekiel

1:5   *387*
1:10   *106, 387*
1:18   *387*
1:22   *387*

3:1–3   *376*
9:4–6   *388*
11:19   *200*
11:19–20   *160*
34   *349*
34:5   *63*
36:26–27   *160, 200*
43:11   *13*

Daniel

6:23   *143*
7:9–10   *392*
7:13   *34, 72, 386*
7:15   *376*
7:22–27   *392*
8:8   *25*
8:15   *376*
8:27   *376*
9:2   *376*
9:27   *21*
10:2   *376*
10:7   *376*
11:31   *21*
12:5   *376*
12:11   *21*

Hosea

7:14   *238*
11:1   *74*

Joel

2:28   *136*
2:28–32   *129*
2:32   *218*
9:11   *133*

Amos

5:18–20   *173*

Obadiah

15   *173*

Jonah

1:17   *74*
5:2   *74*
6:8   *322*
7:6   *74*

Micah

5:2   *34*

Habakkuk

2:2   *13*
2:4   *207, 218–20, 228*

Zephaniah

1:2–18   *173*
3:5   *13*

Haggai

1–2   *33*

Zechariah

4   *33*
9:9   *69, 99*
11:12   *74*
11:12–13   *74*
12:10   *386*
13:7   *74*
14:16–19   *34*

Malachi

3:1   *48, 74, 82, 90*
3:1–4   *333*

Matthew

1:1   *74*
1:1–2:23   *59*
1:1–17   *53, 59, 75, 86, 94,*
     104, 120, 136, 160, 174,
     205, 229, 264, 284, 308,
     322, 354
1:1–18   *73*
1–4   *53, 73*
1:18–2:12   *21*
1:18–25   *53, 59*
1:22   *13*
1:22–23   *59, 74*
2   *27*
2:1   *40*
2:1–12   *59*
2:5   *13*
2:5–6   *34, 74*
2:13–18   *60*
2:13–20   *44*

2:15   *13, 74*
2:16   *41*
2:17   *13*
2:18   *60, 74*
2:19–23   *60*
2:21–23   *22*
2:23   *13, 74*
3:1–4–25   *60*
3:1–6   *60*
3:2   *61*
3:3   *13, 74, 113*
3:7–12   *60*
3:13–17   *60*
3:15   *61*
4:1–11   *14, 61, 74*
4:1–12   *65*
4:4   *13*
4:10   *56*
4:11–25   *61*
4:12–16   *61*
4:12–18:35   *61*
4:14   *13*
4:15–16   *74*
4:17   *61*
4:18   *63*
4:18–22   *61*
4:21   *63*
4:23   *47*
4:23–25   *61*
4:24–25   *47*
5:3   *220, 312*
5:5   *312*
5:6   *61*
5–7   *53, 58, 61, 73*
5:8   *312*
5:10–11   *333*
5:11–12   *312*
5:13–16   *61*
5:14–15   *66*
5:17–20   *61*
5:18   *14*
5:21–48   *61*
5:22   *312*
5:33–37   *312, 320*
5:38–42   *139*
5:48   *312*
6:1–18   *62*
6:19–21   *312*
6:19–34   *62*
6:24   *312*
7:1   *312*
7:1–16   *62*

7:7–11 *312*
7:7–14 *62*
7:9–11 *66*
7:13–14 *66*
7:15–20 *369*
7:15–23 *62*
7:16–18 *312*
7:16–20 *66, 318*
7:21 *310*
7:24 *312*
7:24–27 *66*
7:24–29 *62*
7:26 *312*
7:28 *58*
8:1–4 *47*
8:5–13 *33*
8:14–15 *47*
8:16–17 *47*
8:17 *62, 64, 74*
9:1–8 *47, 62*
9:9 *55*
9:9–13 *47, 63*
9:13 *4*
9:14–17 *47*
9:15 *66*
9:16 *66*
9:17 *66*
9:35–38 *63*
10:1–4 *47*
10:2–3 *6*
10:3 *63*
10:4 *35, 63*
10:5–6 *66, 83*
10:5–42 *58*
10:10 *139*
10:22 *307, 312*
10:35–36 *74*
11:1 *58*
11:1–19 *64*
11:5 *74*
11:10 *48, 74*
11:20–24 *64*
11:25–30 *64*
12:1–8 *47*
12:1–14 *64*
12:3 *48*
12:4 *332*
12:5 *13, 48*
12:9–14 *47*
12:15–16 *47*
12:15–21 *64*
12:17–21 *74*

12:22–37 *64*
12:28 *370*
12:29–30 *66*
12:30 *43*
12:33–37 *318*
12:38–45 *64*
12:40 *43, 74*
12:46–50 *64*
13 *53, 73*
13:1–9 *66*
13:1–23 *65*
13:1–52 *58*
13:14–15 *74*
13:18–23 *66*
13:24–30 *65–66*
13:27–28 *65*
13:31–32 *66*
13:31–35 *65*
13:33 *66*
13:35 *74*
13:36–39 *65*
13:36–43 *65–66*
13:44 *66*
13:44–46 *65*
13:45–46 *66*
13:47–50 *66*
13:47–51 *65*
13:52 *65–66*
13:53 *58*
13:53–58 *65*
13:55 *6, 346*
14:3–12 *22*
14:13–21 *65*
14:22–36 *65*
15:1–20 *65*
15:6 *13*
15:7–9 *74*
15:10–20 *139*
15:21–28 *65*
15:24 *66*
15:26 *66*
15:29–39 *67*
16:1–12 *67*
16:13 *312*
16:13–17 *63*
16:13–20 *67*
16:16–19 *118*
16:18 *55, 68*
16:21 *43*
16:21–23 *34, 45–46*
17:1–13 *68*
17:5 *344*

17:20 *139*
17:23 *43*
17:24–27 *56, 68*
18 *53*
18:1–9 *68*
18:1–35 *58*
18:10–14 *68*
18:12–14 *66*
18:15 *312*
18:15–20 *68*
18:21–35 *68*
18:23–35 *66*
19:1 *58*
19:1–12 *68, 139*
19:4 *48*
19:13–15 *68*
19:16–30 *68*
20:1–16 *66, 68–69*
20:17–19 *69*
20:19 *43*
20:20–28 *69*
20:27 *371*
21:1–11 *69*
21:5 *74*
21:9 *74*
21:12–17 *69*
21:13 *74, 332*
21:16 *48*
21:18–22 *69*
21:23–27 *69*
21:28–32 *66, 69*
21:33 *74*
21:33–46 *66, 69*
21:42 *13, 48, 74*
22:1–14 *70*
22:15–22 *55, 70*
22:23–33 *70*
22:29 *13*
22:31 *48*
22:34–40 *70*
22:36–40 *312*
22:37–40 *139*
22:40 *13*
22:41–45 *70, 307*
22:44 *74*
22:46 *70*
23:1–7 *33*
23:1–39 *70*
23:12 *312*
23:15 *142*
23:23 *13*
23–25 *53, 58*

23:38–39 *74*
24 *139*
24:1–2 *22*
24:2 *55*
24:4–5 *369*
24:7 *388*
24:13 *312*
24:15 *21*
24:15–18 *47*
24:23–26 *369*
24–25 *173*
24:29–31 *173*
24:30–31 *173*
24:31 *114*
24:32–36 *66*
24:42–44 *67*
24:43–44 *139*
24:45–51 *67, 139*
25:1–13 *67, 71, 139*
25:6 *173*
25:14–30 *67, 71*
25:31–46 *67, 71*
25:34–35 *312*
26:1 *58*
26:1–2 *71*
26:3–5 *71*
26:6–16 *71*
26:14–16 *63*
26:15 *74*
26:17–25 *71*
26:20 *44, 107*
26:26–30 *71, 139*
26:31 *74*
26:31–35 *71*
26:36–46 *71*
26:47–56 *71*
26:54 *74*
26:56 *74*
26:57–68 *72, 100*
26:69–75 *72*
27:1–6 *28*
27:1–10 *72*
27:1–25 *100*
27:3–10 *63*
27:9–10 *74*
27:11–26 *72*
27:27–50 *72*
27:34–35 *74*
27:39 *74*
27:43 *74*
27:46 *74, 118*
27:48 *74*

27:51–56 *72*
27:54 *75*
27:57–66 *73*
27:62 *43*
27:64 *43*
28:1–10 *73*
28:8–10 *102*
28:11–15 *73*
28:16–20 *53, 73, 102*
28:19–20 *75*

Mark

1:1 *76, 77, 80, 82, 85*
1:1–8:26 *81–82*
1:1–13 *82*
1:2 *48*
1:3 *113*
1:11 *76, 80–82, 85*
1:14 *83*
1:14–3:35 *82*
1:14–15 *77, 82*
1:16 *77*
1:16–20 *82*
1:21–22 *47*
1:21–28 *82*
1:23–28 *47*
1:25 *80*
1:29–31 *47*
1:32–34 *47*
1:34 *82–83*
1:35–38 *47*
1:38–39 *83*
1:39 *47*
1:40–45 *46–47*
1:44–45 *83*
1:45 *83*
2:1–12 *47, 80*
2:13–17 *47, 82*
2:14 *55*
2:17 *4*
2:18 *63*
2:18–22 *47*
2:19–20 *66*
2:21 *66*
2:22 *66*
2:23 *43*
2:23–28 *47*
2:26 *332*
3:1–6 *47*
3:7–12 *47*

3:11 *81, 85*
3:11–12 *80*
3:12 *83*
3:13–19 *47, 82*
3:14 *83*
3:17 *63, 79*
3:18 *63*
3:22–27 *66*
3:31–35 *82*
4:1–8:26 *82*
4:1–9 *66*
4:11–13 *85*
4:13–20 *66*
4:21–25 *66*
4:26–29 *66*
4:30–32 *66*
4:33–34 *85*
4:35–5:43 *76, 80*
4:40 *76, 85*
5:1–20 *80, 82*
5:7 *76, 80–81, 85*
5:20 *83*
5:41 *79*
5:43 *83*
6:1–6 *82*
6:3 *6, 346*
6:6–13 *82–83*
6:12 *83*
6:12–13 *82*
6:14–29 *27, 83*
6:17–29 *22*
6:30–52 *83*
6:39 *43*
6:41 *83*
6:48 *79*
6:51–52 *76, 85*
7:3–5 *79*
7:11 *79*
7:17–23 *139*
7:19 *79*
7:24–30 *82–83*
7:26 *83*
7:31–8:12 *83*
7:34 *79*
7:36 *83*
7:36–37 *83*
8:1–10 *82*
8:4 *85*
8:14–21 *85*
8:15 *82*
8:16–21 *76*
8:22–26 *85*

8:26 *83*
8:27–9:1 *83*
8:27–9:32 *83*
8:27–16:8 *81, 83*
8:27–30 *81*
8:29 *84*
8:29–30 *83*
8:31 *80*
8:31–33 *45–46*
8:33 *76, 85*
8:34 *83, 85*
8:35 *77*
9:2 *63*
9:7 *76, 80–81, 85*
9:9 *83*
9:14–21 *85*
9:18–19 *76*
9:30 *83*
9:30–41 *83*
9:31 *80*
9:33 *83*
10:1 *83*
10:1–12 *139*
10:17 *83*
10:29 *77*
10:32 *83*
10:32–45 *83*
10:33–34 *80*
10:45 *76*
10:46 *83*
10:46–52 *85*
10:52 *83*
11:1–13:37 *83*
11:12–14 *84*
11:17 *83*
11:20–26 *84*
12:1–2 *84*
12:1–12 *66*
12:6 *80–81*
12:9 *84*
12:10 *13, 48*
12:13 *82*
12:24 *13*
12:26 *48*
12:42 *79*
13 *139, 173*
13:8 *388*
13:10 *77*
13:14–16 *47*
13:19 *388*
13:28–31 *84*
13:28–32 *66*

13:32 *81, 85*
13:34–37 *66*
13:35 *79*
14:1–16:8 *84*
14:12 *79*
14–15 *85*
14:17 *44, 107–8*
14:19 *77*
14:22–26 *139*
14:28 *84*
14:33 *63*
14:36 *79, 139*
14:53–65 *84, 100*
14:61 *80–81, 85*
14:66–72 *76*
15:1–15 *100*
15:2 *84*
15:16 *79*
15:21 *79*
15:34 *79, 118*
15:39 *76, 79, 81, 84–85*
15:42 *43, 79*
16:7 *77, 84*
16:8 *76*

Luke

1:1 *101*
1:1–4 *88–89, 91, 94*
1:2 *123*
1:3 *89, 91, 125*
1:4 *91–92, 125*
1:5 *40*
1:5–2:52 *94*
1:5–4:13 *94*
1:9 *90*
1:16 *94*
1:31–33 *101*
1:32 *94*
1:46–55 *103*
1:47 *101*
1:48–49 *103*
1:68–71 *101*
1:69 *101*
1:71 *101*
1:77 *94, 101*
2:1 *22, 88*
2:1–2 *40*
2:1–20 *21*
2:10 *103*
2:11 *94, 101*
2:16 *22*

2:17 *103*
2:23–24 *13*
2:27 *103*
2:30–32 *94*
2:32 *103*
2:36–38 *94*
2:40 *103*
2:49 *94*
3:1 *28, 44, 88*
3:1–2 *22, 41*
3:1–4:13 *94*
3:4 *113*
3:21 *22*
3:23 *42*
3:23–28 *92*
3:23–38 *94*
3:37 *87*
4:1–11 *94*
4:1–13 *14, 92, 94*
4:14–7:50 *95*
4:14–9:50 *95*
4:14–30 *95*
4:16–30 *32*
4:17 *13*
4:18 *95, 103*
4:18–19 *87, 129*
4:18–21 *14*
4:21 *4*
4:25–27 *103*
4:31–32 *47*
4:31–41 *95, 103*
4:33–37 *47*
4:38–39 *47*
4:40–41 *47*
4:42–43 *47*
4:43 *95*
4:44 *47*
5:1–11 *47, 95*
5:3 *88*
5–7 *95*
5:12–16 *47*
5:12–26 *103*
5:17–26 *47*
5:27 *55*
5:27–32 *47, 95, 103*
5:30 *103*
5:31–32 *87*
5:32 *103*
5:33–39 *47, 66*
5:36 *66*
5:37–39 *66*
6:1–5 *47*

6:1–11   95
6:6–11   47, 103
6:12–16   47, 95
6:15   63
6:16   63, 346
6:17–19   47, 103
6:17–49   95
6:20   312
6:20–23   103
6:23   312
6:29–30   139
6:43–44   312
6:47–49   66
7:1–10   95
7:9   103
7:11–17   93, 95
7:18–35   95
7:20   90
7:22   103
7:27   48, 90
7:28   103
7:30   103
7:34   88, 103
7:36–50   95, 103
7:41–50   67
7:50   101
8:1–3   93, 95, 103
8:1–39   95
8:2–3   88, 103
8:4–8   66
8:11–15   66
8:12   101
8:15   95
8:16–18   66, 95
8:21   13, 95
8:22–25   96
8:22–39   95
8:25   96
8:26–9:2   103
8:26–39   96
8:40–9:50   96
8:40–42   96
8:43–48   96
8:48   103
8:49–56   96
9:1–6   96
9:7–9   96
9:10   96
9:10–17   96
9:18–20   93
9:18–27   96
9:21–22   46

9:21–27   93
9:21–44   90
9:22   45
9:28–36   96
9:31   96
9:37–43   103
9:41   96
9:46–48   96, 103
9:49–50   96
9:51   93, 101
9:51–9:27   93
9:51–19:27   96
9:51–24:51   96
9:52–56   96
9:57–62   97
10:1–20   97
10:7   4, 139
10:21–22   103
10:25–28   312
10:25–37   67, 93, 97
10:26   48
10:30–37   103
10:38–42   97, 103
10:42   96
11:1–4   97
11:1–13:21   97
11:5–8   67
11:5–13   97
11:11–13   66
11:14–26   97
11:19–13   312
11:21–23   66
11:27–28   97
11:28   13
11:29–36   97
11:32   97
11:37–54   97
11:51   332
11:54   97
12:1–12   97
12:13–21   67, 103
12:13–34   97–98
12:33–34   312
12:34   97
12:35–38   66
12:36–38   139
12:39–40   67
12:42–46   67
12:42–48   139
12:49   97
12:49–59   97
13:1–9   97

13:6–9   67
13:10–17   97, 103
13:18–19   66
13:20–21   66
13:23   101
13:23–27   66
13:24–30   97
13:32   22
13:35   97
14:7–14   67
14:11   98, 312
14:13   103
14:16–24   67
14:21–24   103
14:23   103
14:28–30   67
14:31–33   67
15:1–2   103
15:1–7   66–67
15:2   98
15:8–10   67
15:11–32   67, 93
16:1–8   67
16:9   98
16:14   98
16:16   101
16:17   14
16:19–31   67, 103
16:29   13, 47
16:31   13, 47
17:1–10   98
17:1–17   103
17:2   103
17:7–10   67
17:11–19   98, 103
17:16   103
17:21   34
18:1–8   67, 98
18:8   98
18:9–14   67, 98
18:14   98, 312
18:15–17   98, 103
18:18–23   98
18:29–30   98
18:31–33   90
18:31–34   98
18:35   98
18:35–43   103
19:1–10   98
19:7   103
19:9   101
19:10   87–88, 93, 101

19:11–27   *67, 99*
19:28–22:38   *99*
19:28–44   *99*
19:38   *99*
19:39–40   *99*
19:41–48   *99*
19:45–48   *99*
19:48   *99*
20:1–8   *99*
20:9–19   *66, 99*
20:19–25   *102*
20:20–40   *99*
20:41–47   *99*
21   *139*
21:1–4   *103*
21:1–36   *99*
21:19   *99*
21:20–22   *47*
21:20–24   *99*
21:29–33   *66, 99*
21:34–36   *99*
22:1–6   *100*
22:7–38   *100*
22:8   *107*
22:14   *44, 108*
22:14–23   *139*
22:39–24:51   *100*
22:39–46   *100*
22:53   *100*
22:54–62   *63*
22:55–62   *100*
22:63–71   *100*
23:1–6   *100*
23:1–7   *100*
23:7–11   *100*
23:7–12   *22*
23:12–25   *100*
23:15   *100*
23:24–33   *100*
23:34   *118*
23:43   *118*
23:44–46   *101*
23:46   *118*
23:47–48   *101*
23:49   *93*
23:54   *43*
23:55–24:10   *103*
24:1–8   *101*
24:1–12   *103*
24:6   *90*
24:13–32   *102*
24:13–33   *101*

24:13–35   *93*
24:25   *13*
24:26   *101*
24:27   *13*
24:34–49   *101*
24:36–49   *139*
24:44–49   *102*
24:46–49   *93*
24:49   *129*
24:50–51   *101*
24:52–53   *101*
24:53   *90*

John

1:1   *105, 110, 112, 117, 119, 359*
1:1–3   *110*
1:1–18   *110, 112, 120*
1:6–8   *113*
1:6–9   *113*
1:10–11   *112–13*
1–12   *119*
1:12–13   *112*
1:14   *105–6, 108, 109–10, 112, 114, 359*
1:15   *113*
1:18   *105, 112, 117*
1:19–12:50   *110–11, 113, 115*
1:19–28   *113*
1:19–34   *110*
1:19–36   *113*
1:23   *13, 113*
1:29   *105, 110–11, 113, 119*
1:29–36   *114*
1:31   *113*
1:34   *110*
1:35–39   *63*
1:36   *105, 111, 113, 119*
1:40   *63*
1:41   *110–11*
1:42   *55*
1:43–48   *63*
1:43–49   *63*
1:49   *34*
1:50–51   *113*
2:1–4:54   *110*
2:1–11   *113, 115*
2:11   *106, 108, 110, 113*
2:13   *23, 114*
2:13–22   *113, 115*

2:14–16   *33*
2:16   *332*
2:18–22   *109*
2:20   *42, 44, 113*
2:23   *43*
2:23–25   *113*
2:24–25   *113*
3:1–21   *113*
3:16   *34, 105*
3:18   *105*
4:1–42   *113*
4:6–7   *119*
4:21–24   *109*
4:25   *111*
4:43–54   *113*
4:46–54   *33, 113, 115*
4:54   *110*
5:1–10:42   *110*
5:1–15   *113, 115*
5:16   *113*
5:17–29   *382*
5:17–47   *113*
5:25   *173*
5:39   *13*
6:1   *108, 118*
6:1–15   *113, 115*
6:4   *43, 114*
6:5–7   *63*
6:8   *63*
6:10   *43*
6:14   *34*
6:23   *118*
6:30–59   *32*
6:31–59   *119*
6:35   *111*
6:48   *111*
6:48–58   *111*
6:51   *111*
6:70–71   *63*
7:19   *13*
7:23   *13*
7:27   *34, 111*
7:31   *111*
7:35   *35, 314*
7:38–39   *114*
7:41–42   *34*
7:49   *13*
7:51   *13*
7:52   *111*
8:12   *111, 114*
8:17   *13*
8:24   *119*

8:34   *119*
8:58   *119*
9:1   *119*
9:1–41   *113, 115*
9:5   *114*
9:5   *111*
10:7   *111*
10:10   *34*
10:11   *111*
10:14   *111*
10:15   *111*
10:17–18   *111*
10:22   *21*
10:24   *111*
10:34   *13*
10:35–36   *13*
10:40–41   *110*
11:1–44   *113, 115*
11–12   *110*
11:16   *63*
11:25   *111*
11:27   *111*
11:33   *119*
11:35   *119*
11:39   *119*
11:45–57   *115*
11:54   *115*
11:55   *43, 114*
12:1   *43, 114*
12:1–8   *115*
12:4–6   *63*
12:12–13   *34*
12:12–19   *115*
12:20–36   *115*
12:21–22   *63*
12:22   *34, 63*
12:34   *34, 111*
12:36–40   *120*
12:36–41   *115, 119*
12:37–40   *111*
12:37–41   *117*
12:37–50   *115*
12:38   *13*
12:41   *119*
13:1   *43, 111*
13:1–3   *117, 119*
13:1–17   *116*
13:1–20:31   *110*
13:1–30   *111, 116*
13:2   *44, 107*
13:6–9   *107*
13:18   *13*

13:18–30   *116*
13–20   *115*
13:21–30   *63*
13:23   *63, 106–8, 118*
13:23–24   *107*
13:26–27   *107*
13:31–16:33   *111, 116*
13:34–35   *360, 367*
14:2   *116*
14:5   *63, 107*
14:6   *14, 111, 116*
14:8–9   *107*
14:12–18   *105*
14:17   *14, 116*
14:22   *63, 107*
14:26   *14*
15:1   *111, 116*
15:5   *116*
15:9–17   *368*
15:18–16:33   *116*
15:25   *13*
15:26   *14*
16:13   *14*
16:28   *119*
16:33   *116*
17:1–5   *116*
17:1–26   *116*
17:5   *119*
17:6–19   *116*
17:12   *13, 63*
17:17   *13–14*
17:20–26   *116*
18:4   *116–17*
18:15–16   *107*
18:15–18   *116, 118*
18:18:25–27   *116*
18:19–23   *100*
18:19–24   *116*
18:20   *32*
18:24–28   *100*
18:25–27   *118*
18:28   *43*
18:28–19:16   *116–17*
18:29–19:6   *100*
18:31   *13*
18:31–32   *108*
18:36   *84*
18:37–38   *108*
18:39   *43*
19:7   *13*
19:14   *43–44*
19:16–42   *117*

19:24   *13*
19:26   *106*
19:26–27   *118*
19:28   *13, 118–19*
19:30   *118*
19:31   *43–44*
19:34   *360*
19:35   *108*
19:36   *13*
19:37   *13*
19:42   *43*
20:1–10   *117*
20:2   *106*
20:2–9   *107*
20:9   *13*
20:11–18   *102, 117*
20:19–23   *117*
20:19–29   *139*
20:21   *117*
20:21–23   *111*
20:22   *117*
20:23   *117*
20:24–29   *63, 117*
20:26–29   *102*
20:28   *31, 117, 119*
20:30–31   *84, 105, 111, 115,*
         117, 119–20, 361, 363
20:31   *110, 369*
21:1   *108*
21:1–14   *118, 139*
21:1–23   *102*
21:2   *63*
21:2   *107*
21:4   *118*
21:7   *106–7*
21:15–19   *63, 118*
21:18–19   *118*
21;20   *106, 118*
21:20–23   *107*
21:20–25   *118*
21:23   *118*
21:24   *106, 118*
21:25   *106, 119*

Acts

1:1   *8, 89–90, 125, 135*
1:1–2   *127*
1:1–2:41   *128*
1:1–3   *91*
1:1–5   *128*
1:1–6:7   *127*

1–2 *146*
1:2 *136*
1:3–8 *102*
1:4 *135*
1:4–8 *135*
1:6–26 *128*
1:8 *122, 125, 129–31, 135*
1:8–9 *129*
1–12 *118*
1:12 *125*
1:13 *63, 107, 346*
1:14 *346*
1:15–26 *128*
1:16–20 *63*
1:19 *125*
2 *196*
2:1 *125*
2:1–4 *135*
2:1–13 *128*
2:1–40 *114*
2:1–47 *128*
2:10 *213*
2:14–21 *129*
2:14–40 *129*
2:16–21 *136*
2:21 *333*
2:22–36 *129*
2:23 *327*
2:33 *135, 327*
2:36 *327*
2:37–40 *129*
2:38 *136, 327*
2:41–47 *129*
2:42 *6, 122*
3:1–4:23 *107*
3:1–4:31 *129*
3:1–6:7 *129*
3:1–10 *129*
3:13–26 *129*
3:15 *136*
4:1–4 *129*
4:5–22 *130*
4:12 *333*
4:23 *136*
4:26 *132*
4:31 *130*
4:32–6:7 *130*
4:32–37 *130*
4:33 *136*
4:36 *125*
5:1–11 *130*
5:12–16 *130*

5:17 *344*
5:20 *130, 136*
5:29 *130, 327*
5:33–39 *142*
5:34–39 *142*
5:40 *130*
6:1–6 *283*
6:1–7 *130*
6:5 *131*
6–7 *295*
6:7 *130, 293*
6:8–7:60 *130*
6:8–9:31 *130*
6:8–15 *130*
6:9–9:31 *127*
7:21 *142*
7:56 *135*
8:1–3 *130*
8:1–9:31 *130*
8:4–8 *131*
8:4–25 *63*
8:9–25 *131*
8:14–25 *107*
8:26–38 *131*
8:26–40 *63*
8:29 *136*
8:39 *136*
8:39–40 *131*
9:1–9 *6*
9:1–18 *135*
9:1–19 *146*
9:1–31 *131*
9:2 *333*
9:3–6 *102*
9:3–28:31 *127*
9:15 *131, 143*
9:16 *109*
9:26–30 *144, 154*
9:32–11:18 *131*
9:32–12:24 *131*
9:32–43 *131*
9:36 *125*
10 *33*
10:2 *33*
10:9–16 *33*
10:9–29 *131*
10:14 *125*
10:19–20 *136*
10:22 *33*
10:24–48 *131*
10:34–43 *77, 80*
10:35 *33*

10:39 *327*
10:42 *327*
11:1–18 *131, 313*
11:16 *15*
11:19 *315*
11:19–26 *131*
11:26 *333*
11:27–12:24 *132*
11:27–30 *132, 144*
11:28 *90*
11:28–30 *313*
11:30 *154, 273*
12:1–3 *22*
12:1–4 *313–14, 316*
12:1–5 *63*
12:1–23 *132*
12:2 *107*
12:4 *125*
12:12 *78*
12:17 *312–13*
12:25 *78, 132*
13:1–14:28 *132*
13:1–16:5 *132*
13:2 *136*
13:4 *132, 136*
13:4–14:28 *154*
13:6 *33*
13:7 *142*
13:8 *125, 132*
13:13 *78*
13:13–52 *32*
13–14 *146, 154*
13:15 *295*
13:16–41 *132*
13:26 *33*
13:28–39 *136*
13:38–39 *154*
13:43 *33*
13:45 *155*
13:48 *154*
13:50 *33*
14:1–7 *132*
14:3 *155*
14:4 *154*
14:8–20 *132, 271*
14:11–13 *31*
14:21 *154*
14:21–23 *272*
14:23 *273*
15 *146, 150, 311*
15:1 *133, 144, 155*
15:1–20 *154*

15:1–21 *313*
15:1–29 *126*
15:1–30 *154*
15:1–35 *133*
15:2 *273*
15:5 *133, 313, 344*
15:13 *311*
15:14 *311, 337*
15:16–17 *14*
15:19 *311*
15:20 *133*
15:23 *311*
15:23–29 *133, 315, 365*
15:29 *311*
15:36 *133*
15:36–16:5 *133*
15:37–39 *78*
15:37–40 *78*
15:38 *145*
16:1 *179, 272*
16:1–2 *271*
16:2 *271*
16:6 *153*
16:6–10 *136*
16:6–19:20 *133*
16:6::40 *235*
16:8–17 *123*
16:10 *133*
16:14 *33, 235*
16:15 *235*
16–18 *146*
17 *165–66, 170*
17:1–10 *166*
17:2 *133*
17:3 *134, 166*
17:4 *33*
17:5 *166*
17:5–10 *164*
17:10 *169*
17:13–14 *164*
17:14–15 *271*
17:14–16 *165*
17:16–18:17 *180*
17:17 *33*
17:18 *32, 134*
17:23 *134*
17:34 *134*
18 *180*
18:1–22 *183*
18:2 *22, 227, 294*
18:3 *141*
18:4 *182*

18:5 *165, 271*
18:7 *33*
18:8 *182*
18:11 *146*
18:12 *146*
18:17 *179, 182*
18:21 *134*
18:23 *153*
18:23–19:20 *134*
18:23–20:1 *183*
18:24–19:7 *134*
19:8 *243, 271*
19:10 *146, 243*
19:11–20 *134*
19–21 *146*
19:21 *210, 214*
19:21–21:16 *134*
19:21–28:31 *134*
19:22 *211, 271*
19:23–20:1 *185*
19:28–41 *271*
19:29 *211, 364*
20 *91, 210*
20:1–2 *146*
20:1–3 *210*
20:1–6 *180, 272*
20:2 *180*
20:3 *211, 214*
20:4 *153, 211, 364*
20:16 *125*
20:17 *273*
20:22–23 *136*
20:25 *91*
20:28 *136, 273*
20:28–31 *273–74*
20:31 *146, 243, 271*
21:1–16 *135*
21:4 *136*
21:10–14 *90*
21:15–17 *154*
21:17–23:35 *135*
21:18 *273*
21:18–25 *312*
21–23 *146*
21:27–40 *146*
21–28 *227*
21:38 *210*
21:39 *141*
22:3 *141–42*
23:6 *142*
23:8 *35*
23:11 *134–35*

23:16 *311*
23:26 *91, 125*
24:1–26:32 *135*
24:1–27 *135*
24:3 *91, 125*
24:5 *344*
24:14 *333*
24:15 *136*
24–27 *146*
25:1–12 *135*
25:13–27 *135*
25:19 *136*
25–26 *22*
26:1–32 *135*
26:5 *142, 344*
26:9–11 *143*
26:14 *143*
26:22 *136*
26:23 *136*
26:25 *91, 125*
26:28 *333*
27 *123, 146*
27:1–28:31 *135*
27:2 *252*
27:7–13 *272*
27:27–40 *146*
28 *147, 273*
28:15 *173*
28:16 *234*
28:20 *136*
28:23–28 *123*
28:25–27 *126*
28:28 *126*
28:30–31 *90, 234*

Romans

1:1 *218*
1:1–2 *220*
1:1–4 *207*
1:1–4:25 *228*
1:1–7 *216–18*
1:1–15 *218*
1:2 *147, 218, 229*
1:3–4 *147*
1:4 *218*
1:5 *190*
1:5–6 *213*
1:7 *212*
1–8 *223*
1:8–10 *219*
1:8–15 *217, 219*

1:10–15 *216*
1:13 *109*
1:15 *212–13*
1:16 *147, 218*
1:16–4:25 *216*
1:16–11:36 *216*
1:16–17 *207, 216, 219–20*
1:17 *14, 208, 218–19, 228*
1:18 *147, 219*
1:18–3:20 *208, 217, 219, 227*
1:18–4:25 *219*
1:18–32 *147, 215*
1:26–27 *219*
2 *213*
2:1 *220*
2:4 *220*
2:5 *220*
2:5–16 *147*
2:9 *215*
2:25 *220*
2:27 *220*
2:28–29 *220*
3:1–4 *220*
3:7–8 *220*
3:9 *215, 220*
3:9–20 *147*
3:10–18 *14*
3:19–20 *220*
3:21–4:20 *228*
3:21–4:25 *217, 220*
3:21–5:2 *208*
3:21–22 *228*
3:21–23 *220*
3:21–25 *114*
3:21–26 *207, 219*
3:22 *216, 221*
3:23 *208, 215*
3:25 *221*
3:28 *320*
3:28–30 *216*
3:31 *221, 321*
4:1 *213*
4:3 *14, 178, 208, 221, 228, 321*
4:9 *208*
4:10 *221*
4:13–15 *221*
4:18 *221*
4:19 *221*
4:22–23 *208*
4:25 *218, 229*

5:1 *178, 221*
5:1–5 *221*
5:1–8:39 *216, 221, 228*
5:1–11 *217, 221*
5:6 *221*
5:6–8 *147*
5:8 *208*
5:9 *148*
5:9–11 *222*
5:10 *147*
5:12 *222*
5:12–21 *217, 222*
5:13 *222*
5:15 *222*
5:20 *222*
5:21 *217, 222*
6:1–2 *222*
6:1–7:6 *148*
6:1–8:39 *216*
6:1–23 *217, 222*
6:3 *222*
6–8 *208*
6:11–14 *222*
6:14 *213*
6:18 *222*
6:23 *147, 208, 217*
7:1 *213, 222*
7:1–25 *217, 222*
7:4 *213, 222*
7:7 *222*
7:13 *223*
7:14–25 *223*
7:23 *217*
8:1–4 *148, 228*
8:1–17 *217, 223*
8:2 *223*
8:3 *147, 224*
8:5 *224*
8:9 *223, 350*
8:15 *139*
8:15–17 *148*
8:17 *223*
8:18 *223*
8:18–39 *217, 223*
8:28 *223*
8:29–30 *223*
8:39 *217*
9:1–5 *217, 223*
9:1–11:36 *223*
9:2 *178*
9:6 *224–25*
9:6–18 *14*

9:6–29 *217, 224*
9–11 *208, 214–16, 223, 225, 228*
9:12–19 *147*
9:14–18 *224*
9:19–21 *224*
9:30–10:21 *217, 224*
9:30–32 *224*
9:33 *224*
10:1–4 *224*
10:4 *221, 223*
10:9 *148, 208, 218, 225*
10:13 *218, 225, 333*
10:14–21 *225*
10:19 *225*
10:20 *225*
11 *225*
11:1–10 *217, 225*
11:11–12 *225*
11:11–32 *217, 225*
11:13 *213*
11:17–21 *225*
11:31 *213*
11:33–36 *217, 225*
12:1 *225*
12:1–2 *217, 225*
12:1–15:13 *216, 225, 228*
12:2 *226*
12:3–8 *226*
12:3–21 *217, 226*
12:9–21 *226*
12:14 *139*
13:1 *336*
13:1–7 *215, 218, 226*
13:5 *336*
13:8–10 *139*
13:8–14 *218, 226*
13:13–14 *208*
14:1–8 *226*
14:1–15:6 *215*
14:1–15:13 *213, 216, 218, 226*
14:14 *139*
14–15 *214*
14:19 *226*
15 *210*
15:14–16 *215*
15:14–16:27 *226*
15:14–33 *216, 218, 226*
15:19 *210, 216*
15:20 *214, 227*
15:21 *216*

15:23   *210*
15:23–29   *145*
15:24   *210, 226, 234*
15:25   *210*
15:25–29   *214*
15:26   *210, 214*
15:28   *210*
16   *211*
16:1–2   *146, 211, 227, 283*
16:1–16   *218, 226–27*
16:1–23   *216*
16:3–5   *227*
16:5   *213*
16:13   *79*
16:14   *213*
16:15   *213*
16:17–18   *218, 227*
16:17–20   *215*
16:19–24   *218, 227*
16:21   *272*
16:22   *209*
16:23   *146, 182, 364*
16:25–27   *216, 218, 227*

1 Corinthians

1:1   *179, 182*
1:1–3   *188, 190*
1:1–9   *190*
1:2   *180*
1:2–3   *190*
1–4   *177*
1:4–9   *188, 190*
1:7–10   *190*
1:10–4:7   *350*
1:10–4:20   *188, 191*
1:10–4:21   *186*
1:10–17   *178, 191*
1:11   *184, 186*
1:12   *186*
1:14   *211, 364*
1:18–25   *191*
1:19   *275*
1:26–31   *191*
2:1–5   *191*
2:6–16   *191*
2:14   *350*
3:1–3   *331*
3:1–9   *191*
3:10–17   *191*
3:18–23   *192*
4   *102*

4:1–20   *192*
4:6–8   *182*
4:10–13   *182*
4:12   *141*
4:17   *271*
4:21   *184*
5   *177*
5:1–13   *186, 188, 192*
5:9   *146, 180, 183, 270*
5:10–13   *183*
5:11   *146, 180*
5:13   *192*
6:1–11   *189, 192*
6:12–20   *186, 189, 193*
7   *177*
7:1   *167, 186, 188*
7:1–5   *204*
7:1–7   *193, 274*
7:1–16:4   *193*
7:1–40   *189, 193*
7:8   *193*
7:10–11   *139*
7:10–16   *193*
7:17–24   *193*
7:21–23   *182*
7:25   *167, 188*
7:25–40   *193*
7:37   *188*
8:1   *167, 188*
8:1–11:1   *189, 193*
8:1–13   *182, 194*
9   *177*
9:1–18   *141*
9:1–27   *194*
9:5   *346, 349*
9:14   *139*
10:1–13   *194*
10:1–22   *182*
10:14–22   *195*
10:23–11:1   *195*
10:25–11:1   *182*
11:2–6   *204*
11:2–16   *195*
11:2–34   *189, 195*
11:8–9   *257*
11:17–22   *195*
11:17–24   *215*
11:17–34   *195*
11:19   *344*
11:23   *44*
11:23–26   *139*
11:27–34   *195*

12:1   *188*
12:1–3   *195*
12:1–14:40   *189, 195*
12:4–11   *195*
12:12–31   *196*
12:13   *33*
12–14   *177*
13   *178*
13:1   *204*
13:1–3   *176*
13:1–13   *196*
13:2   *139*
13:12   *xviii*
14:1–6   *196*
14:6–12   *196*
14:8–10   *196*
14:13–19   *196*
14:20–25   *196*
14:21   *196*
14:26–33   *196*
14:33–36   *197*
14:37–40   *197*
15   *177, 204*
15:1–2   *197*
15:1–58   *189, 197*
15:2   *321*
15:3–4   *197*
15:3–5   *139*
15:5   *102*
15:5–8   *197*
15:6   *102*
15:7   *102, 313, 346*
15:8   *102, 290*
15:9–11   *197*
15:12   *274*
15:12–19   *197*
15:12–57   *148*
15:14   *218*
15:17   *218*
15:20   *114, 218*
15:20–28   *197*
15:23   *204*
15:27–28   *336*
15:32   *32*
15:34   *274*
15:35–49   *197*
15:35–57   *139*
15:50–58   *197*
15:51–52   *114*
15:52   *173*
16   *201*
16:1   *153, 188*

16:1–4   *177, 189, 198*
16:5–11   *184*
16:5–12   *189, 198*
16:5–24   *198*
16:8   *179–80*
16:9   *185*
16:10   *272*
16:10–11   *184*
16:12   *188*
16:13–18   *189, 198*
16:15–18   *184*
16:16   *336*
16:19   *271*
16:19–24   *189, 198*

2 Corinthians

1:1   *179–80, 201*
1:1–2   *189, 198*
1:2   *190*
1:3–7   *189, 198*
1:3–11   *177*
1:8–11   *189, 198*
1:12   *178*
1:12–14   *189, 198*
1:15–22   *189, 199*
1:15–24   *184*
1:23–2:4   *189, 199*
2:1   *180, 184*
2:2–4   *184*
2:3–9   *185*
2:4   *146, 180, 184, 270*
2:5   *178*
2:5–11   *177, 189, 199*
2:8   *275*
2:12   *185*
2:12–13   *272*
2:12–17   *189–90, 199*
2:13   *185*
3   *205*
3:1–3   *189, 199*
3:4–6   *189, 200*
3:7–18   *189, 200*
4:1–6   *200*
4:4   *257*
4:7–18   *177, 200*
4:14   *178*
5:1–10   *200*
5:10   *178*
5:11–6:2   *200*
5:16–21   *177*
5:17   *148, 178*

5:20   *201*
5:21   *147, 221*
6:3–13   *201*
6:4–7:1   *182*
6:5   *141*
6:7   *178*
6:14–7:1   *201*
6:16   *178*
7:2–16   *201*
7:5   *180*
7:5–6   *272*
7:8   *146, 180, 270*
7:8–12   *185*
7:10   *185*
7:13–14   *272*
8:1   *180*
8:1–4   *185*
8:1–7   *182, 201*
8:2   *185*
8:6   *272*
8:8–15   *201*
8:13–15   *182*
8:16   *272*
8:16–24   *202*
8:23   *272*
9   *177*
9:1–5   *202*
9:2   *180, 185*
9:6–15   *202*
10:1–11   *202*
10:3–6   *242*
10:12–18   *202*
11:1–4   *185*
11:1–5   *202*
11:7–11   *165*
11:9–10   *178*
11:16–33   *203*
11:23   *141*
11:23–29   *145*
11:27   *141*
11:32–33   *144*
12:1–10   *177, 203*
12:11   *185*
12:11–13   *203*
12:14–3:4   *203*
12:16   *178*
12:18   *272*
13:1–2   *146*
13:5–12   *203*
13:13   *203*

Galatians

1:1   *152*
1:1–5   *156*
1:1–9   *156*
1:2   *152*
1:3   *190*
1:6–2:21   *157*
1:6–9   *150, 155*
1:8   *153*
1:10–2:21   *156*
1:10–6:10   *156*
1:11–12   *157*
1:11–16   *290*
1:13   *143*
1:14   *142*
1:16   *155*
1:17   *144*
1:18   *144, 154*
1:19   *312, 346*
1:21   *155*
1:23   *348*
2:1   *153*
2:1–3   *272*
2:1–5   *272*
2:1–10   *144, 154*
2:2   *155*
2:3–5   *272*
2:5   *155*
2:9   *107, 153, 321, 346*
2:10   *155*
2:11–13   *313*
2:11–14   *150, 157*
2:11–21   *33*
2:13   *153*
2:15   *151*
2:15–16   *159, 320*
2:19   *153*
3:1   *152*
3:1–4:7   *151*
3:1–4:11   *158*
3:1–5   *158*
3:1–5:1   *156*
3:2   *159*
3:5   *159*
3:6   *151, 221, 321*
3:6–9   *158*
3:6–14   *159*
3:10–14   *143, 147, 150, 159*
3:11   *219*
3:13   *157, 327*

3:15–16 *158*
3:16–26 *28*
3:19–26 *158*
3:22 *14*
3:24 *151*
3:27–4:7 *158*
3:28 *33, 150*
4:4 *28*
4:5–7 *28*
4:6 *139*
4:8–11 *158*
4:11–15 *153*
4:12–6:10 *158*
4:12–16 *145*
4:12–20 *158*
4:13 *154*
4:13–16 *154*
4:19 *153*
4:21–31 *158*
4:22 *14*
4:30 *14*
5:1–15 *151*
5:2–6:10 *156*
5:3 *155*
5:11 *142*
5:13–15 *160*
5:14 *139*
5:15–26 *158*
5:16–26 *151*
5:20 *344*
5:22 *159*
5:22–23 *248*
5:22–24 *148*
6:11 *146, 152, 270*
6:11–18 *156, 159*
6:15 *150, 160*
6:16 *160*

Ephesians

1:1 *248*
1:1–2 *245*
1:2 *190, 248*
1:3 *245, 249*
1:3–3:21 *245*
1:3–6:20 *245*
1:3–14 *245, 248*
1:4–5 *245*
1:4–14 *249*
1:5 *148*
1:6 *245*
1:7–12 *245*

1:9–10 *241*
1:10 *148, 232, 241, 245, 249*
1:12 *245*
1:13 *245, 248*
1:13–14 *241*
1:14 *245*
1:15 *248*
1:15–3:21 *245*
1:15–23 *245*
1:17 *249*
1:19 *248*
1:19–22 *249*
1:20 *246, 249*
1:20–23 *232, 246*
1:21 *247*
1:22 *148, 336*
2:1–10 *245, 246*
2:4–5 *148, 246*
2:5 *248*
2:6 *246, 249*
2:7 *246*
2:8 *246, 248*
2:8–9 *246, 320–21*
2:8–10 *147, 321*
2:10 *246*
2:11–12 *246*
2:11–20 *246*
2:11–22 *232, 245–46, 249*
2:13–22 *249*
2:14–18 *248*
2:15 *246*
2:16 *249*
2:18 *249*
2:19 *249*
2:19–20 *275*
2:21–22 *246*
2:22 *249*
3:1–13 *232, 245, 247*
3:2 *243*
3:4–5 *249*
3:5–6 *247*
3:6 *248*
3:8–9 *247*
3:10 *247, 249*
3:12 *248*
3:14–17 *249*
3:14–19 *249*
3:14–21 *245, 247*
3:15 *249*
3:17 *248*
3:18–19 *247*
3:20–21 *247*

3:21 *148, 246*
4:1 *247, 275*
4:1–6 *232, 247*
4:1–6:9 *232*
4:1–6:20 *245, 247*
4:1–13 *247*
4:1–16 *247*
4:3 *248, 250*
4:4–6 *249–50*
4:5 *248*
4:7–10 *247*
4:7–13 *247*
4:8 *247*
4:9 *249*
4:11 *368*
4:11–12 *247*
4:12–13 *247*
4:13 *247–48, 250*
4:14 *247, 350*
4:15 *248*
4:15–16 *247*
4:17–19 *247*
4:17–32 *247*
4:21 *243, 248*
4:24 *248*
4:24–25 *248*
5:1–6 *247*
5:2 *247*
5:6–7 *247*
5:6–14 *247*
5:7–14 *247*
5:8 *247*
5:8–10 *247*
5:9 *248*
5:11–14 *247*
5:15 *247*
5:15–6:9 *247*
5:15–17 *247*
5:18 *248*
5:18–20 *249*
5:19 *248*
5:20 *248*
5:21 *248, 336*
5:22 *248*
5:22–6:9 *232, 248*
5:23 *248*
5:24 *336*
5:26 *248*
5:28 *248*
6:1 *248*
6:3 *249*
6:4 *248*

6:5–9 *336*
6:9 *248*
6:10–13 *248*
6:10–17 *247*
6:10–18 *232, 242*
6:10–20 *247–48*
6:11 *247–48*
6:12 *249*
6:13 *247–48*
6:14 *247–48*
6:14–17 *248*
6:18 *248*
6:18–20 *247–48*
6:19–20 *248*
6:21 *232*
6:21–22 *249*
6:21–24 *249*
6:22 *249*
6:23 *249*
6:24 *249*

Philippians

1:1 *235, 237, 272*
1:1–2 *237*
1:2 *190, 237*
1:3–4:20 *237*
1:3–11 *237*
1:5 *232, 235, 237*
1:5–6 *240*
1:6 *147, 237*
1:7 *234, 237*
1:8 *237*
1:9–11 *237*
1:12–2:30 *238*
1:12–4:9 *238*
1:12–13 *240*
1:12–14 *233*
1:12–20 *232*
1:12–26 *238*
1:13 *234–35*
1:14 *234*
1:15–17 *238*
1:17 *234*
1:19 *235*
1:20–24 *238*
1:21 *233*
1:21–25 *231*
1:21–26 *233*
1:27 *236, 240*
1:27–30 *232*
1:28 *238, 240*

1:29 *238*
2:2 *178*
2:3–4 *240*
2:5–11 *238, 240*
2:5–12 *232*
2:7–8 *147*
2:8 *240*
2:9–10 *333*
2:9–11 *147*
2:10–11 *233*
2:12–13 *240*
2:19–22 *272*
2:19–23 *236*
2:19–24 *238*
2:20 *271*
2:22 *272*
2:24 *234, 236*
2:25–30 *236, 238*
2:27 *238, 240*
2:30 *238*
3:1–3 *238*
3:1–4:9 *238*
3:2 *240*
3:4–6 *238*
3:5 *141*
3:5–6 *142*
3:7 *238*
3:8 *238*
3:9 *239*
3:10 *239*
3:11 *239–40*
3:12 *239*
3:12–14 *xviii, 239*
3:15 *239*
3:16 *239*
3:17 *238*
3:17–19 *239*
3:19 *239*
3:20 *239*
3:20–21 *148, 239*
3:21 *139, 336*
4 *239*
4:1 *239*
4:2 *235, 239–40*
4:3 *239–40*
4:4 *232–33, 239*
4:6 *239*
4:7 *239*
4:8 *239*
4:9 *238–39*
4:10 *239*
4:10–20 *239*

4:10–23 *315*
4:11 *239*
4:12 *239*
4:13 *233, 239–40*
4:14 *239*
4:15–16 *236, 239*
4:16 *166*
4:18 *239*
4:19 *239*
4:20 *148, 239*
4:21–23 *239*
4:22 *234–35, 239*
4:23 *239*

Colossians

1:1 *251, 259, 272*
1:1–2 *254*
1:1–8 *254*
1–2 *257*
1:2 *190*
1:3–8 *254*
1:4–5 *254*
1:5–6 *254*
1:6 *254*
1:7 *254, 259*
1:9 *254*
1:9–2:23 *254*
1:9–4:6 *254*
1:9–12 *232*
1:10–12 *254*
1:12–13 *255*
1:14 *255*
1:15 *147, 255, 257*
1:15–17 *255*
1:15–20 *232, 253, 255–56*
1:16 *257*
1:17 *232, 257*
1:18 *255, 257*
1:18–20 *255*
1:19 *255*
1:20 *255*
1:21 *147*
1:21–22 *255*
1:21–23 *255*
1:23 *251, 255*
1:24 *255*
1:24–2:3 *232*
1:24–2:5 *255*
1:25 *255*
1:26 *255*
1:27 *255*

1:28 255
1:29 255
2:1 255
2:2 255
2:3 255
2:4 255
2:4–23 32
2:5 255
2:6–7 232, 255
2:6–10 250
2:6–23 255
2:8 253, 274
2:9 147, 253, 255
2:10 253, 255
2:11 253
2:11–12 255
2:13 253–56
2:14 256
2:15 256
2:16 253
2:16–17 256, 274
2:16–23 274
2:18 253
2:18–19 256
2:18–23 274
2:20–21 253
2:20–23 256
2:21 253
2:23 253
3:1–2 253, 257
3:1–4 148, 256
3:1–4:1 232
3:1–4:6 256
3:1–17 157
3:5 257
3:5–8 256
3:8 331
3:9 257
3:9–10 148
3:9–11 256
3:10 257
3:12–17 232, 256
3:17 232, 258
3:18 336
3:18–4:1 232, 256, 258
3:19 332
4:1 263
4:2 232
4:2–4 256
4:5–6 256
4:7 232
4:7–9 256

4:7–18 256
4:9 232, 259–60
4:10 78, 259
4:10–14 256
4:12 232
4:14 88, 91, 259
4:15–17 256
4:16 270
4:17 259
4:18 251, 256

1 Thessalonians

1:1 169, 190
1:2–3:13 169
1:2–4 169
1:2–10 169
1:4 163
1:5 166
1:5–7 169
1:8–10 169
1:9 166
2:1–4 169
2:1–12 169
2:5–9 169
2:9 141, 166
2:10–12 169
2:13–16 169
2:17–3:10 170
2:17–20 170
3:1–5 170
3:1–10 165
3:2 272
3:6–10 170
3:11–13 170
3:12 170
3:13 170
4:1 275
4:1–2 170
4:1–5:11 139
4:1–5:22 170
4:1–8 170
4:2 170
4:3 170
4:3–8 170
4:7 171
4:8 170
4:9 167, 170
4:9–12 170
4:10 170
4:10–12 174
4:11 170

4:12 170
4:13 171
4:13–5:11 170, 215
4:13–18 162–63, 170, 173
4:14–16 171
4:16–17 114
4:17 148, 171
5:1 167
5:1–8 171
5:1–11 171, 173
5:1–22 163
5:9–11 171
5:12–14 163
5:12–18 171
5:12–22 171
5:14 170, 173
5:19–22 171
5:23 163
5:23–28 171
5:24 171
5:27 5

2 Thessalonians

1:1 164
1:1–2 171
1:2 190
1:3–4 171
1:5–7 171
1:5–10 148
1:7–10 171
1:11–12 171
2:1–2 171
2:1–3 173
2:1–12 139
2:2 270
2:2–3 164
2:3 172
2:3–4 163
2:3–12 172
2:3–19 172
2:4 172
2:5–8 172
2:7 163
2:8 171, 270
2:9–12 172
2:13–15 163, 172
2:13–17 172
2:16–17 172
3:1–5 172
3:1–15 172
3:3–5 172

3:6   *172*
3:6–13   *163*
3:6–15   *172–73*
3:7–13   *172*
3:8   *141*
3:11   *167, 174*
3:16–18   *172*
3:17   *164, 270*

1 Timothy

1:1   *269, 275*
1:1–2   *279*
1:2   *271*
1:3   *91, 271, 273–74*
1:3–4   *275, 278*
1:3–11   *279*
1:3–20   *279*
1:4   *274, 344*
1:6   *274–75, 284*
1:7   *274*
1:12–17   *278–79*
1:15   *284*
1:18–20   *279*
1:19   *284*
1:19–20   *274*
1:20   *274, 278, 283, 339*
2:1   *275, 278*
2:1–3:16   *278–79*
2:1–8   *278, 279*
2:3–4   *267*
2:7   *368*
2:8–15   *279*
2:9–15   *267, 278, 283*
2:11–15   *276*
2:14–15   *283*
2:15   *32*
3:1   *284*
3:1–7   *280, 282*
3:1–12   *267, 276*
3:2   *368*
3:3   *274*
3:6   *283*
3:7   *283*
3:8–10   *283*
3:8–12   *282*
3:8–13   *280, 283*
3:13   *283*
3:14–15   *277–78*
3:14–16   *280*
3:15   *276*
3:16   *275, 278, 362*

4:1   *276, 278*
4:1–3   *274, 283*
4:1–5   *32, 274, 280*
4:1–6:2   *280*
4:3   *274*
4:6–16   *280*
4:7   *274–75, 344*
4:7–8   *32*
4:8–9   *284*
4:10   *267*
4:11   *368*
4:11–16   *267, 278*
4:12   *272*
4:13   *5*
4:16   *267, 284*
5:1–2   *280, 282*
5:1–16   *283*
5:3–16   *276, 278, 280*
5:13   *284*
5:14–15   *283*
5:15   *284*
5:17–25   *276, 278, 280, 283*
5:18   *4, 9, 15–16, 139*
5:19–20   *272*
6:1–2   *278, 280*
6:2   *274, 368*
6:2–10   *280, 283*
6:2–21   *280*
6:3–10   *278*
6:4   *274*
6:5   *274*
6:6   *267*
6:7   *268*
6:9   *284*
6:9–10   *283*
6:10   *268, 284*
6:11   *284*
6:11–16   *278*
6:12   *284*
6:15–16   *280*
6:17–19   *278, 280, 283*
6:20   *31, 274–75, 283*
6:20–21   *268, 278, 280*
6:21   *284, 348*

2 Timothy

1:1   *269, 275*
1:1–2   *280*
1:1–7   *278*
1:2   *271*
1:3–7   *280*

1:3–18   *280*
1:5   *271*
1:8   *276*
1:8–12   *278*
1:8–14   *280*
1:9–10   *276*
1:10   *267*
1:11   *368*
1:12   *276, 284*
1:14   *276, 284*
1:15–18   *280*
2:1–7   *278, 280*
2:1–26   *280*
2:2   *368*
2:11–13   *284*
2:14   *274*
2:14–26   *278, 281*
2:15   *xiii*
2:15   *16*
2:16   *274*
2:16–19   *204*
2:17–18   *274, 339, 349*
2:18–13   *281*
2:19   *276*
2:22   *267, 274, 284*
2:23   *274–75*
2:26   *283–84*
3:1–4:8   *281*
3:1–9   *281*
3:2   *274*
3:3–4   *274*
3:4   *274*
3:6–9   *274*
3:10–11   *271*
3:10–17   *281*
3:15   *xvii, 271*
3:16   *4, 12, 16*
3:16–17   *xiii, xiv*
3:16–17   *15*
3:17   *16*
4:1–2   *266, 276*
4:1–8   *281*
4:2   *274*
4:4   *274, 344*
4:6–8   *276*
4:7   *284*
4:9–18   *281*
4:10   *272–73*
4:11   *6, 78, 88, 124*
4:14   *339*
4:15   *284*
4:18   *284*

4:19–22 *281*
4:20 *180, 211*

Titus

1:1 *269, 275*
1:1–4 *281*
1:4 *190, 272*
1:5 *272–73, 276,
    278*
1:5–9 *281*
1:5–16 *281*
1:6–9 *276, 282–83*
1:7 *273*
1:10 *272, 274*
1:10–13 *274*
1:10–16 *281*
1:11 *274*
1:12 *272*
1:13 *274*
1:14 *274, 344*
1:15 *274*
2:1–2 *282*
2:1–15 *282*
2:3–5 *282*
2:5 *336*
2:9 *336*
2:9–10 *282*
2:10 *278*
2:11–14 *282*
2:15 *282*
3:1 *279, 336*
3:1–2 *282*
3:1–15 *282*
3:3–11 *282*
3:4–7 *276*
3:4–8 *284*
3:9 *274–75*
3:10 *274*
3:12 *273*
3:12–15 *279*

Philemon

1 *259, 262, 272*
1–3 *262*
1–7 *262*
2 *256, 259–60, 262*
3 *190, 262*
4 *262*
4–7 *262*
5 *259, 262*

6 *262*
7 *259, 262–63*
8–9 *262*
8–11 *262*
8–20 *262*
10 *232, 262–63,
    275*
11 *262*
12 *263*
12–16 *262*
13 *262*
14 *262*
15–16 *262*
17 *262*
17–20 *258, 262*
18–19 *262*
19 *259, 263*
20 *263*
21 *233, 262*
21–25 *261–62*
22 *231, 260, 263*
23 *232, 259, 261*
23–24 *263*
24 *78, 88, 259*
25 *263*

Hebrews

1:1–2 *12, 15*
1:1–3:2 *297*
1:1–4 *288, 297*
1:1–4:16 *297*
1:2 *305*
1:4 *297–98, 333*
1:5 *297*
1:5–6 *298*
1:5–14 *298*
1:5–18 *298*
1:7–12 *298*
1:13–14 *298*
2:1–4 *288, 298,
    307*
2:3 *15, 290–94*
2:5 *296*
2:5–9 *298*
2:9 *298*
2:11 *298*
2:12–13 *298*
2:14–15 *298*
2:16–18 *298*
2:17 *300*
3:1 *300*

3:1–2 *299*
3:1–4:13 *299*
3:1–6 *299*
3:3–4 *299*
3:6 *299*
3:7–4:11 *292*
3:7–4:13 *307*
3:7–19 *299*
3:12 *308*
3:14 *301, 307*
4:1–13 *299*
4:2 *307*
4:8 *299*
4:11 *299–300*
4:11–6:3 *300*
4:11–10:25 *300*
4:11–16 *299–300*
4:12 *17*
4:13 *300*
4:14 *296, 300*
4:14–5:10 *289*
4:14–16 *300, 304*
4:16 *300*
5:1–10 *300*
5:5–6 *300*
5:7–8 *300*
5:8 *300*
5:10 *296*
5:11 *296*
5:11–6:3 *294*
5:11–6:8 *295*
5:11–6:12 *307*
5:12–14 *331*
6:1 *295*
6:1–2 *301*
6:1–7:3 *301*
6:4–6 *301*
6:4–12 *301*
6:6 *301*
6:7–8 *301*
6:8 *308*
6:9 *296, 307*
6:9–10 *301*
6:10 *294*
6:13–7:3 *301*
7:1 *296*
7:1–3 *301*
7:1–9:28 *296*
7:1–28 *289*
7:4–10 *302*
7:4–10:25 *301*
7:4–28 *301*

7:11–19 *302*
7:17 *302*
7:20–25 *302*
7:25 *307*
7:26 *302*
7:27 *288*
8:1 *296*
8:1–6 *302*
8:1–9:25 *289*
8:1–10:18 *302*
8:6 *302*
8:7–13 *302*
8:8 *302*
8:8–13 *295*
8:26 *288*
9:1–10 *302*
9:1–14 *302*
9:5 *296*
9:6–10 *292*
9:8 *303*
9:11–14 *303*
9:11–28 *114*
9:15–28 *303*
10:1–4 *303*
10:5–10 *303*
10:11–14 *303*
10:19–11:40 *304*
10:19–13:16 *304*
10:19–25 *295, 302,
    304*
10:19–39 *307*
10:22 *295*
10:23 *295*
10:24 *296, 304*
10:25 *294*
10:26–31 *304*
10:26–39 *304*
10:29 *304*
10:32 *292, 294*
10:32–39 *304*
10:34 *294*
10:39 *305, 307*
11:1 *305*
11:1–3 *305*
11:4–12 *305*
11:7 *321*
11:12 *221*
11:13–16 *305*
11:17–31 *305*
11:19 *221*
11:31 *318*
11:32 *291, 296*

11:32–40 *305*
12:1–2 *288, 296, 305*
12:1–13 *305*
12:1–40 *305*
12:3–13 *294*
12:4 *292, 294*
12:4–10 *305*
12:11 *305*
12:12–13 *305*
12:14 *305*
12:14–17 *305*
12:14–29 *307*
12:15 *305*
12:18–24 *306*
12:25–29 *306*
13:1–4 *306*
13:1–16 *306*
13:5–6 *306*
13:5–16 *306*
13:7 *294*
13:7–8 *306*
13:9–15 *306*
13:12–14 *294*
13:13 *294*
13:16 *306*
13:17 *294, 306, 336*
13:17–25 *306*
13:18–19 *306*
13:19–23 *290*
13:20–25 *306, 320*
13:22 *289, 295–96*
13:23 *272, 291–92*
13:24 *292, 294*

James

1:1 *6, 309, 311, 314–16, 346*
1:2 *312*
1:2–4 *316*
1:2–12 *316*
1:2–18 *316, 321*
1:2–27 *316*
1:4 *312*
1:5 *310, 312*
1:5–8 *316*
1:6 *314*
1:9–11 *310, 316*
1:10 *311*
1:11 *311, 314*
1:12 *312*
1:16 *317*
1:17 *312, 316*

1:18 *317*
1:19 *317*
1:19–20 *317*
1:19–21 *317*
1:19–27 *317, 321*
1:20 *312*
1:21 *317*
1:22 *317*
1:22–23 *312*
1:22–27 *317*
1:26 *318*
1:26–27 *317*
1:27 *311*
2:1 *317, 322*
2:1–7 *317*
2:1–13 *310, 317, 321*
2:1–26 *316–17*
2:2 *314*
2:4 *318*
2:5 *311–12, 318*
2:7 *311*
2:8 *14, 311*
2:8–13 *317–18*
2:10–12 *312*
2:11 *311*
2:11–5:11 *317*
2:13 *312*
2:14–16 *312*
2:14–26 *310, 317, 320–21*
2:15–17 *318*
2:17 *321*
2:18 *321*
2:19 *318*
2:21 *311, 314, 318*
2:21–22 *309*
2:23 *311, 321*
2:24 *318, 321*
2:25 *311, 318*
2:26 *318*
3:1 *318*
3:1–4:10 *316–19*
3:1–12 *310, 317–18, 321*
3:3–5 *318*
3:6 *314, 318*
3:8 *318*
3:9 *311*
3:12 *312, 314*
3:13 *318*
3:13–18 *310, 322*
3:14 *318, 350*
3:15 *350*
3:17 *317, 319*

3:17–18 *318–19*
4:1–5 *317*
4:1–10 *319*
4:1–17 *322*
4:2 *319*
4:2–3 *312*
4:3 *319*
4:4 *312, 319, 322*
4:5 *350*
4:6 *311, 319*
4:8 *312*
4:11–5:11 *316–17, 319*
4:11–12 *319*
4:13 *314*
4:13–17 *310*
4:16–17 *319*
4:52 *14*
5:1–3 *312*
5:1–6 *310, 316*
5:2 *311*
5:5 *319*
5:7 *314*
5:7–11 *319*
5:10 *312*
5:11 *310–11, 319*
5:12 *312, 320*
5:12–20 *320*
5:13–18 *320*
5:14–16 *320*
5:17 *310–11*
5:18 *311*
5:19 *311*
5:19–20 *312, 320*
5:20 *320*

1 Peter

1:1 *314, 325, 328, 330, 334–35, 338, 359*
1:1–2 *329–30*
1:1–2:10 *329*
1:2 *327, 330*
1:3 *334*
1:3–2:10 *331*
1:3–6 *331*
1:3–7 *321*
1:3–12 *329, 331*
1:5 *334*
1:5–6 *329*
1:6 *329*
1:6–7 *335*
1:7–9 *331*

1:10–12 *331*
1:11 *327*
1:12 *327*
1:12–13 *336*
1:13 *334*
1:13–16 *331*
1:13–25 *331*
1:16 *14, 330*
1:17 *314, 330–31, 335*
1:17–21 *331*
1:18 *328*
1:20 *327*
1:20–21 *334*
1:22–25 *331*
2:1 *331*
2:1–3 *331*
2:1–10 *325, 331*
2:2 *331*
2:3 *331*
2:4 *327, 331–32*
2:4–10 *331*
2:5 *327, 331–32*
2:6 *331*
2:7 *331*
2:7–8 *331*
2:8 *331*
2:9 *335*
2:9–10 *332*
2:11 *314, 329–30, 335*
2:11–3:12 *332*
2:11–4:11 *329, 332*
2:11–12 *332*
2:12 *344*
2:13 *332, 336*
2:13–3:7 *325*
2:13–15 *332*
2:13–17 *330, 332, 336*
2:16–17 *332*
2:17 *336*
2:18 *332, 336*
2:18–25 *330, 332*
2:19 *329*
2:21–25 *325, 332, 335*
2:24 *327*
3:1 *336*
3:1–6 *332*
3:1–7 *330, 332, 336*
3:5 *336*
3:7 *332*
3:8 *336*
3:8–4:11 *330*
3:8–12 *332*

3:10–12 *333*
3:13 *333*
3:13–4:6 *332–33*
3:13–17 *332*
3:13–18 *325*
3:14 *327*
3:15 *336*
3:15–17 *324*
3:16 *329, 333*
3:18–22 *332*
3:19–20 *333*
3:22 *327, 333, 335–36*
4:1 *327, 333*
4:1–2 *335*
4:1–6 *332*
4:2 *327*
4:3 *328*
4:5 *333*
4:6 *333*
4:7 *330, 335*
4:7–11 *332–33, 335*
4:8 *320*
4:11 *329*
4:12 *327, 329–30*
4:12–5:11 *333*
4:12–5:14 *329*
4:12–19 *333*
4:13 *329*
4:14 *329*
4:16 *333, 336*
4:19 *329, 334*
5:1 *328, 334–35*
5:1–4 *333*
5:1–7 *330, 334*
5:1–11 *334*
5:2–3 *334*
5:4 *334–35*
5:5 *334, 336*
5:6–7 *333–34, 336*
5:8–9 *334*
5:8–11 *330, 333*
5:9 *336*
5:10–11 *334–35*
5:12 *334*
5:12–14 *329–30, 334*
5:13 *6, 78, 328, 338*
5:14 *334*

2 Peter

1:1 *337*
1:1–2 *339–40*

1:2 *341*
1:3 *343–44*
1:3–3:13 *339*
1:3–7 *343*
1:3–11 *325, 340–41, 343*
1:3–21 *340–41*
1:4 *343*
1:5–7 *344*
1:6–7 *343*
1:6–21 *341*
1:8–11 *341*
1:11 *343–44*
1:12 *339, 341*
1:12–15 *340–41*
1:12–21 *340, 343*
1:14 *341*
1:14–15 *338*
1:15 *339, 341*
1:16 *334, 339–40, 342, 344*
1:16–18 *341*
1:16–21 *340*
1:17 *334*
1:17–18 *344*
1:19 *341, 344*
1:19–21 *16, 344*
1:20 *4*
1:20–21 *341, 344*
1:21 *12, 325*
2:1 *339, 344*
2:1–3 *342, 344*
2:1–3:10 *343*
2:1–22 *339, 341*
2:2 *339, 343*
2:4 *342*
2:4–9 *340*
2:4–10 *342*
2:5 *347*
2:5–6 *342*
2:7–9 *347*
2:10–12 *342*
2:10–16 *342*
2:13 *339*
2:15 *343*
2:15–16 *342, 347*
2:17–22 *342*
2:18–19 *339*
2:22 *342*
3:1 *326, 338*
3:1–13 *325, 339–40, 342*
3:2 *15*
3:3–4 *339, 343*
3:4 *339, 344*

3:6 *343*
3:7 *343*
3:8–9 *343*
3:11 *343*
3:11–13 *343*
3:12 *344*
3:14 *344*
3:14–18 *339, 343*
3:15 *338*
3:15–16 *4*
3:16 *9, 15*
3:17–18 *324, 339*
3:18 *341*

1 John

1:1 *359, 372*
1:1–3 *376*
1:1–4 *344, 363, 367*
1:1–5 *15, 362*
1:5–2:2 *367*
1:5–2:27 *366–68*
1:6–7 *367*
1:6–10 *362*
1:9 *367*
2 *361*
2:1 *363, 367–68*
2:2 *357*
2:3 *367*
2:3–6 *367*
2:3–11 *367*
2:4–5 *363*
2:7–8 *360*
2:7–11 *367*
2:9 *370*
2:9–10 *361*
2:11 *370*
2:12–14 *359, 363, 372*
2:12–15 *363*
2:12–17 *368*
2:15–17 *368*
2:17 *366*
2:18 *361*
2:18–27 *368*
2:24 *363, 368*
2:26 *361–62*
2:27 *368*
2:27–28 *363*
2:28 *366*
2:28–3:10 *368*
2:28–3:24 *366, 368*
2:29 *366*

3:6 *368*
3:8 *368*
3:10 *361*
3:10–15 *362*
3:11 *366*
3:11–24 *369*
3:14 *363*
3:16–17 *370*
3:17 *363*
3:18 *369, 372*
4:1 *366, 369*
4:1–5:12 *366, 369*
4:1–6 *369*
4:2 *362*
4:2–3 *362*
4:7 *361, 366*
4:7–12 *369*
4:12 *369*
4:13 *363, 369*
4:13–21 *369*
4:15 *362, 369*
4:15–16 *369*
4:16 *357*
4:17 *369*
5:1 *362, 369*
5:1–12 *369*
5:5 *362*
5:6 *360, 362*
5:6–12 *370*
5:11 *370*
5:11–12 *356*
5:11–13 *357*
5:13 *363, 370, 372*
5:13–21 *370*
5:14–17 *370*
5:16 *370*
5:18 *370*
5:19–20 *370*

2 John

1 *363*
1–3 *370*
4 *371*
4–6 *371*
4–11 *370*
7 *361–62*
7–8 *358*
7–11 *371*
8–9 *362*
8–11 *364*
9 *363, 371–72*

9–11 *356*
10 *349, 371*
12–13 *371*
13 *363*

3 John

1 *211, 363*
1–4 *371*
4 *356*
5–8 *371*
5–10 *349*
5–12 *371*
6 *371*
6–8 *372*
9–10 *371*
11–12 *371*
12 *364*
13–14 *372*

Jude

1 *6, 354*
1–2 *352*
1–4 *350*
3 *325, 345, 349–51, 353*
3–4 *352*
4 *349*
5–7 *352*
5–19 *350–53*
6 *350*
7 *349*
8 *349*
8–16 *352*
9–10 *349*
10 *349*
11 *350*
11–13 *349*
12 *349*
12–13 *350*
14 *348*
15 *350*
16 *350*
17–19 *352*
18 *350*
19 *349–50*
20–21 *350*
20–23 *350–51, 353*
21 *348*
22–23 *350*
23 *349–50*
24 *348*
24–25 *345, 351, 353*

Revelation

1:1   *376, 385*
1:1–8   *384, 386*
1:3   *376, 383*
1:4   *376, 394*
1:4–6   *386*
1:6   *391*
1:7   *374, 386*
1:8   *393–94*
1:9   *376, 380, 385*
1:9–3:22   *386*
1:9–20   *376, 386*
1:10   *384–85*
1:11   *381*
1:12–20   *382*
1:19   *381*
2:1   *381, 387*
2:1–3:22   *384, 386*
2:2   *387*
2–3   *365, 381*
2:4   *378*
2:7   *387*
2:9   *380, 387*
2:10   *380, 382*
2:11   *387*
2:12   *387*
2:13   *377, 382, 387*
2:14–15   *378*
2:17   *387*
2:18   *387*
2:19   *387*
2:20   *376*
2:20–24   *378*
2:22   *380*
2:29   *387*
3:1   *387*
3:1–2   *378*
3:5   *387*
3:6   *387*
3:7   *387*
3:8   *387*
3:12   *387*
3:13   *387*
3:14   *387*
3:14–22   *252*
3:15   *387*
3:15–17   *378*
3:21   *387*
3:22   *387*
4:1   *385*
4:1–2   *385, 387*

4:1–16:21   *387*
4:2   *384–85*
4:3–11   *387*
4:6–15   *106*
4:8   *394*
4:9   *394*
4:11   *378*
5:1   *394*
5:1–7   *375*
5:1–14   *387*
5:2–4   *382, 387*
5:5–7   *387*
5:7   *394*
5:13   *394*
6:1–8   *388*
6:1–8:1   *384*
6:1–17   *388*
6:9–11   *382, 388*
6:10   *391, 395*
6:11   *376*
6:12   *388*
6:15   *376*
6–16   *388*
6:16   *394*
6:17   *388*
6–18   *375*
7:1   *388*
7:1–8   *388*
7:1–17   *388*
7:3   *376*
7:9–17   *388*
7:14   *380, 388*
7:15   *394*
8:1   *388*
8:1–9:21   *388*
8:2–11:19   *384*
9:4   *389*
9:20–21   *389*
10:1–11   *389*
10:1–11:13   *389*
10:1–11:19   *389*
10:7   *376*
10:8–11   *376*
11:1–13   *389*
11:7   *389*
11:7–10   *389*
11:10   *376*
11:11–12   *389*
11:15–19   *389–90*
11:16   *383*
11:17   *394*
11:18   *376, 394*

12   *389*
12:1–15:1   *389*
12:1–15:4   *390*
12:10   *376*
12:10–12   *389*
13   *389*
13:1–18   *389*
13:4   *382*
13:9–10   *389*
13:10   *382*
13:11–17   *389*
13:15   *382*
13:15–16   *382*
14   *389*
14:6–13   *389*
14:7   *394*
14:8   *379*
14:9–11   *382*
14:12   *375, 382*
15:1–16:21   *384*
15:2   *382*
15:3   *394*
15:5–8   *389–90*
16:1–21   *389–90*
16:2   *382, 390*
16:5   *394*
16:5–7   *390*
16:6   *376*
16:7   *382, 394*
16:13   *376*
16:14   *394*
16:19   *379*
17:1   *385, 391*
17:1–2   *390*
17:1–21:8   *390*
17:3   *384–85*
17:3–6   *390*
17:3–18   *390*
17:5   *379*
17:7–18   *390*
17:9   *379*
17:14   *382*
17–18   *384*
18:1–3   *391*
18:1–19:10   *390*
18:1–24   *391*
18:2   *379*
18:6–7   *391*
18:8   *394*
18:10   *379, 394*
18:20   *376*
18:21   *379*

18:21–24 *391*
18:24 *376*
19:1–10 *391*
19:2 *394*
19:6 *394*
19:10 *376, 383, 393*
19:11 *394*
19:11–16 *374–75*
19:11–20:15 *391*
19:11–21 *390*
19:13 *391*
19:15 *391, 394*
19:17–21 *391*
19:20 *376, 392*
19:20–21 *392*
19:21 *392*
20 *375*

20:1–3 *392*
20:1–15 *390*
20:4 *382*
20:4–6 *392*
20:10 *376*
20:11–15 *392*
20:12 *394*
20:14 *392*
21:1–8 *390, 392*
21:5 *394*
21:8 *387, 392*
21:9 *385*
21:9–10 *392*
21:9–22:4 *392*
21:9–27 *392*
21:10 *384–85*
21:11–27 *393*

21:12–14 *393*
21–22 *375, 384*
21:22 *394*
22:1–5 *9, 392–93*
22:6 *376, 385*
22:6–21 *384, 393*
22:7 *376, 383*
22:8 *376*
22:8–11 *393*
22:9 *376*
22:10 *383*
22:11 *376*
22:12–16 *393*
22:18–19 *376, 383, 393*
22:20 *393*

JEWISH EXPANSION UNDER THE HASMONEAN DYNASTY

- • City
- ○ City (uncertain location)
- ▲ Mountain peak
- Judea before the Maccabean revolt
- Conquests of Jonathan
- Conquests of Simon
- Conquests of Hyrcanus I
- Conquests of Aristobulus I
- Conquests of Alexander Jannaeus

Aristobulus completes the conquest of Upper Galilee by defeating the Itureans (104 B.C.)

Jannaeus subdues the attack of Demetrius III and executes 800 Pharisees in reprisal (88 B.C.)

Hyrcanus I destroys Samaritan temple (128 B.C.)

Simon is murdered in a palace coup (135 B.C.)

John Hyrcanus attacks and conquers Medeba in 129 B.C.

COELE-SYRIA

Sidon
Damascus
Abana R.

Litani R.
Mt. Hermon ▲
ITUREA
Tyre
Panias
Pharpar R.

PHOENICIA

Cadasa (Kedesh)
Gischala (Gush Halav)
Asor (Hazor)
Seleucia

Ptolemais (Acco)
Gennesaret
Bethsaida
Dathema
Jotapata
Taricheae (Magdala)
Sea of Galilee
Gamala
Asochis (Hannathon)
Cana
Arbela
Hippos
Sepphoris
GALILEE
Abila
Mt. Carmel ▲
Geba
Mt. Tabor ▲ Philoteria (Beth-Yerah)
Yarmuk R.
Gadara

Dora
Legio (Megiddo)

MEDITERRANEAN SEA

Strato's Tower
Scythopolis (Beth-shan)
Pella
Dion
Narbata
SAMARIA
Samaria
Gerasa (Jerash)
Mt. Ebal ▲
Apollonia
Pegae (Aphek)
Mt. Gerizim ▲ Shechem
Amathus
Yarkon R.
Pharathon
Acrabeta
Coreae
Joppa
Arimathea
Lebonah
Alexandrium
Zeredah
Gophna
Gedor (Gadara)
Tabbok R.
Gilead
Adida
Jazer
Lydda
Ber-zetha
Apherema
PEREA
Tyrus
Philadelphia (Amman)
Modein
Bethel
Jamina
Gazara (Gezer)
Mizpah
Doc
Abila
Beth-horon
Adasa
Michmash
Jericho
Esbus (Heshbon)
Azotus (Ashdod)
Kidron
Emmaus
JUDEA
Beth-ramatha
Samaga
Accaron (Ekron)
Beth-haccherem
Jerusalem
Mt. Nebo ▲
Medeba
Ascalon (Ashkelon)
Adullam
Bethlehem
Hyrcania
Marisa (Mareshah)
Keilah
Beth-basi
Herodium
Nezib
Beth-zur
Tekoa
Lachish
Asphar
Lemba
Anthedon
Adora (Adoraim)
Hebron
Machaerus
Gaza
IDUMEA
En-gedi
DEAD SEA
Gerar
Orda
Masada
Eglaim
Raphia
Beersheba
Malatha
Kir-Moab
Arnon R.
Rhinocorura
Oronaim (Horonaim)
NABATEA
W. el-Arish
Elusa
Gabalis
Zoar
Zered R.

Arabah
Sela

0 10 20 30 40 50 Miles
0 10 20 30 40 50 Kilometers

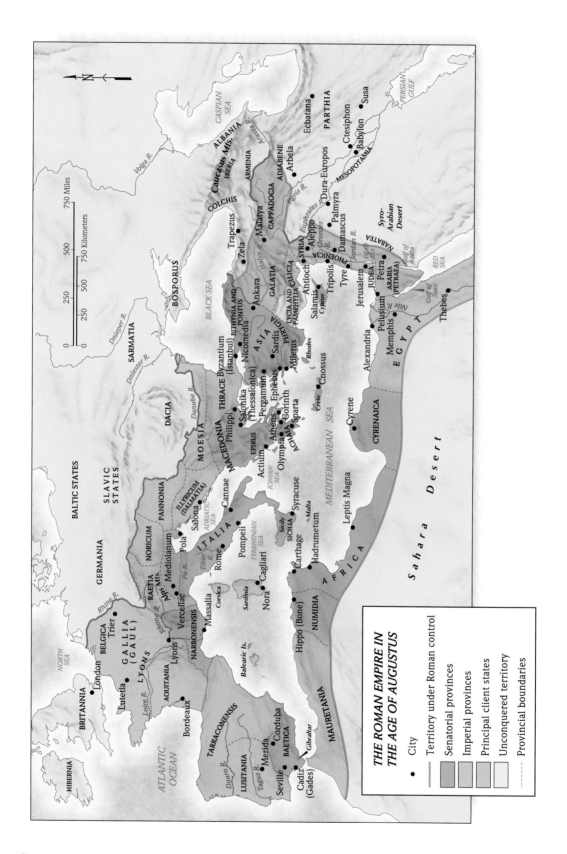

THE ROMAN EMPIRE IN
THE AGE OF AUGUSTUS

- City

Territory under Roman control
- Senatorial provinces
- Imperial provinces
- Principal client states
- Unconquered territory
- Provincial boundaries

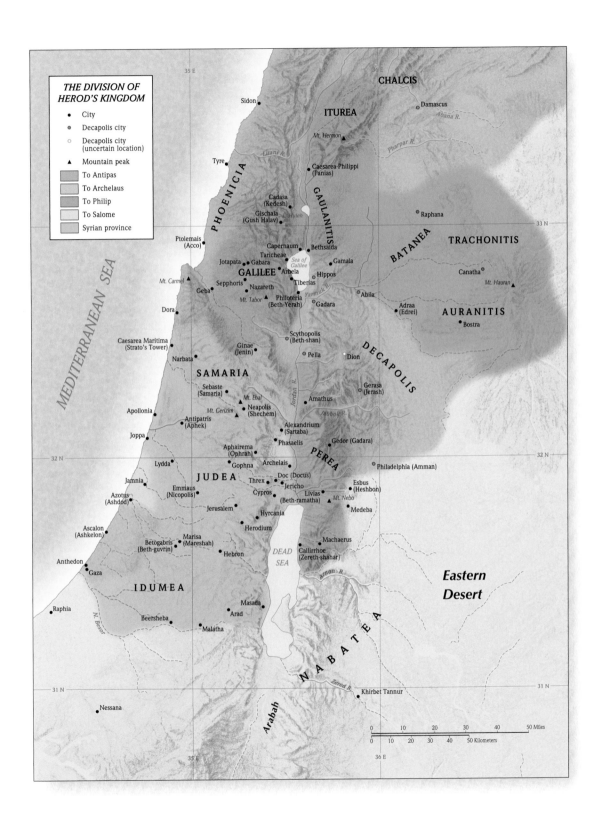

THE DIVISION OF
HEROD'S KINGDOM

- • City
- • Decapolis city
- ○ Decapolis city (uncertain location)
- ▲ Mountain peak
- To Antipas
- To Archelaus
- To Philip
- To Salome
- Syrian province

MEDITERRANEAN SEA

CHALCIS

ITUREA

Damascus

Abana R.

Sidon

Mt. Hermon ▲

Litani R.

Pharpar R.

Tyre

PHOENICIA

GAULANITIS

Caesarea-Philippi (Panias)

Cadasa (Kedesh)
Gischala (Gush Halav)

Huleh

BATANEA

TRACHONITIS

Raphana

33 N

Ptolemais (Acco)

Capernaum
Bethsaida

Taricheae

Jotapata Gabara
Sea of Galilee

Gamala

GALILEE
Arbela
Hippos

Canatha

Mt. Carmel ▲

Geba
Sepphoris
Nazareth
Tiberias

Mt. Hauran ▲

Philoteria (Beth-Yerah)

Mt. Tabor ▲

Yarmuk R.

Gadara

Abila

AURANITIS

Dora

Adraa (Edrei)

Bostra

Caesarea Maritima (Strato's Tower)

Narbata

Ginae (Jenin)

Scythopolis (Beth-shan)

Jordan R.

Pella

Dion

DECAPOLIS

SAMARIA

Sebaste (Samaria)

Mt. Ebal ▲
Mt. Gerizim ▲
Neapolis (Shechem)

Amathus

Gerasa (Jerash)

Apollonia

Antipatris (Aphek)

Jabbok R.

Joppa

Alexandrium (Sartaba)

Phasaelis

32 N

Aphairema (Ophrah)

Gedor (Gadara)

PEREA

Philadelphia (Amman)

Lydda

Gophna

Archelais

JUDEA

Threx
Doc (Docus)
Jericho

Jamnia

Emmaus (Nicopolis)

Cypros
Livias (Beth-ramatha)

Esbus (Heshbon)

Azotus (Ashdod)

Jerusalem

Mt. Nebo ▲

Medeba

Ascalon (Ashkelon)

Hyrcania

Herodium

Betogabris (Beth-guvrin)

Marisa (Mareshah)

Hebron

Machaerus

Anthedon

Gaza

Callirrhoe (Zereth-shahar)

DEAD SEA

Arnon R.

IDUMEA

Eastern Desert

Raphia

Masada

Arad

Beersheba

Malatha

N. Besor

N A B A T E A

31 N

Nessana

Arabah

Zered R.

Khirbet Tannur

0   10   20   30   40   50 Miles

0 10 20 30 40 50 Kilometers

35 E

36 E

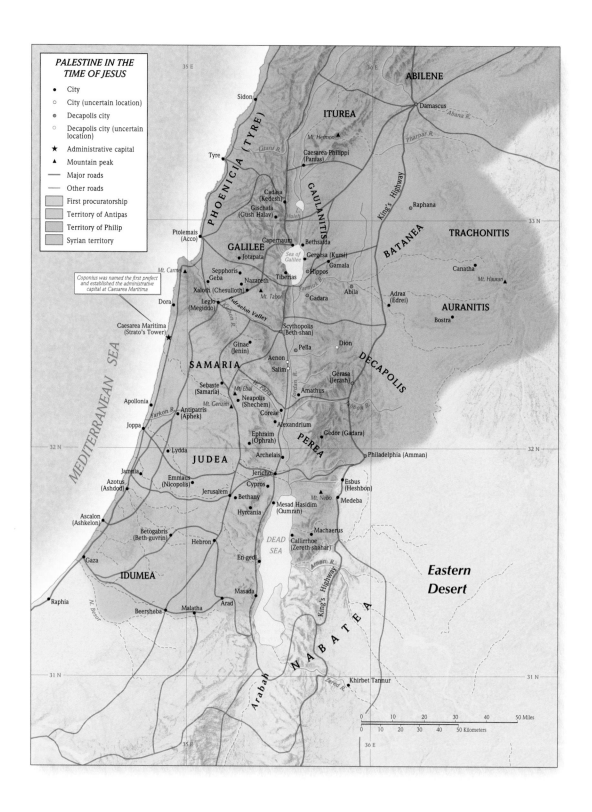

PALESTINE IN THE TIME OF JESUS

- • City
- ○ City (uncertain location)
- ● Decapolis city
- ○ Decapolis city (uncertain location)
- ★ Administrative capital
- ▲ Mountain peak
- — Major roads
- — Other roads
- First procuratorship
- Territory of Antipas
- Territory of Philip
- Syrian territory

Coponius was named the first prefect and established the administrative capital at Caesarea Maritima

ABILENE

Sidon

ITUREA

Damascus

Abana R.

PHOENICIA (TYRE)

Litani R.

Mt. Hermon ▲

Tyre

Caesarea-Philippi (Panias)

Pharpar R.

King's Highway

Cadasa (Kedesh)

Gischala (Gush Halav)

GAULANITIS

Huleh

Raphana

33 N

BATANEA

TRACHONITIS

Ptolemais (Acco)

GALILEE

Capernaum

Bethsaida

Sea of Galilee

Gergesa (Kursi)

Gamala

Canatha

Mt. Carmel ▲

Sepphoris

Jotapata

Geba

Nazareth

Tiberias

Hippos

Adraa (Edrei)

Mt. Hauran ▲

Xaloth (Chesulloth)

Mt. Tabor ▲

Gadara

Abila

AURANITIS

Dora

Leglo (Megiddo)

Esdraelon Valley

Kison R.

Scythopolis (Beth-shan)

Yarmuk R.

Bostra

Caesarea Maritima (Strato's Tower) ★

Ginae (Jenin)

Pella

Dion

DECAPOLIS

MEDITERRANEAN SEA

SAMARIA

Aenon

Salim

Jordan R.

Gerasa (Jerash)

Sebaste (Samaria)

Mt. Ebal ▲

Neapolis (Shechem)

Mt. Gerizim ▲

Amathus

Apollonia

Coreae

Jabbok R.

Antipatris (Aphek)

Yarkon R.

Joppa

Ephraim (Ophrah)

Alexandrium

Gedor (Gadara)

PEREA

32 N

Lydda

Archelais

Philadelphia (Amman)

32 N

JUDEA

Jericho

Jamnia

Azotus (Ashdod)

Emmaus (Nicopolis)

Cypros

Esbus (Heshbon)

Jerusalem

Bethany

Medeba

Ascalon (Ashkelon)

Hyrcania

Mt. Nebo ▲

Mesad Hasidim (Qumran)

Betogabris (Beth-guvrin)

Hebron

Machaerus

DEAD SEA

Callirrhoe (Zereth-shahar)

Gaza

En-gedi

Arnon R.

IDUMEA

Masada

Eastern Desert

Raphia

N. Besor

Beersheba

Malatha

Arad

King's Highway

NABATEA

31 N

Arabah

Zered R.

Khirbet Tannur

31 N

0 10 20 30 40 50 Miles

0 10 20 30 40 50 Kilometers

35 E

36 E

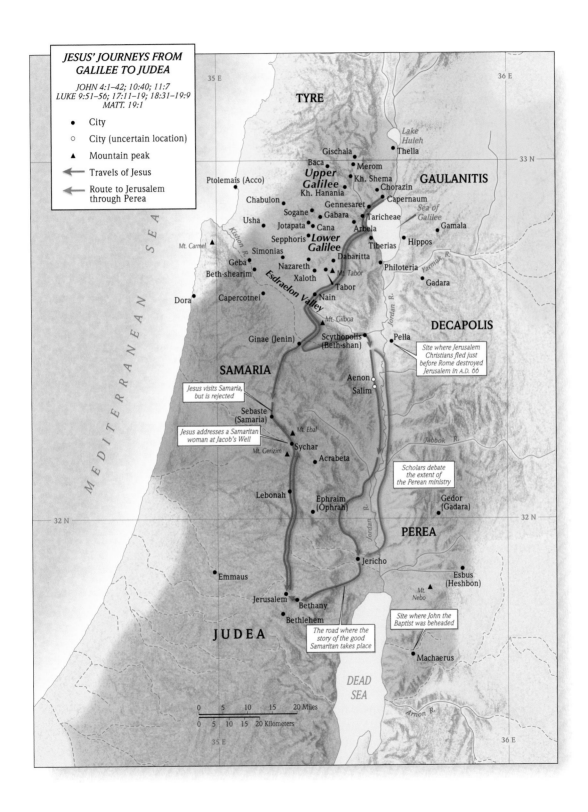

JESUS' JOURNEYS FROM
GALILEE TO JUDEA

JOHN 4:1–42; 10:40; 11:7
LUKE 9:51–56; 17:11–19; 18:31–19:9
MATT. 19:1

● City
○ City (uncertain location)
▲ Mountain peak
← Travels of Jesus
← Route to Jerusalem
  through Perea

TYRE

Lake
Huleh

Thella

GAULANITIS

Gischala

Baca
Merom
Kh. Shema
Upper
Galilee
Chorazin
Kh. Hanania
Ptolemais (Acco)
Capernaum
Chabulon
Gennesaret
Sea of
Galilee
Usha
Sogane
Gabara
Taricheae
Gamala
Jotapata
Cana
Arbela
Sepphoris
Lower
Galilee
Tiberias
Hippos
Mt. Carmel
Simonias
Dabaritta
Geba
Nazareth
Mt. Tabor
Philoteria
Beth-shearim
Xaloth
Tabor
Gadara
Dora
Capercotnei
Nain

Esdraelon Valley

Mt. Gilboa

DECAPOLIS

Ginae (Jenin)
Scythopolis
(Beth-shan)
Pella

Site where Jerusalem
Christians fled just
before Rome destroyed
Jerusalem in A.D. 66

SAMARIA

Aenon
Salim

Jesus visits Samaria,
but is rejected

Sebaste
(Samaria)

Mt. Ebal
Jesus addresses a Samaritan
woman at Jacob's Well
Sychar
Mt. Gerizim
Acrabeta

Scholars debate
the extent of
the Perean ministry

Lebonah
Ephraim
(Ophrah)
Jabbok R.
Gedor
(Gadara)

Jordan R.

PEREA

Jericho

Emmaus

Esbus
(Heshbon)
Mt.
Nebo

Jerusalem
Bethany
Bethlehem

The road where the
story of the good
Samaritan takes place

Site where John the
Baptist was beheaded

JUDEA

Machaerus

DEAD
SEA

Arnon R.

0   5   10   15   20 Miles
0   5   10   15   20 Kilometers

MEDITERRANEAN SEA

Kishon R.

Yarmuk R.

35 E
36 E
33 N
32 N
35 E
36 E

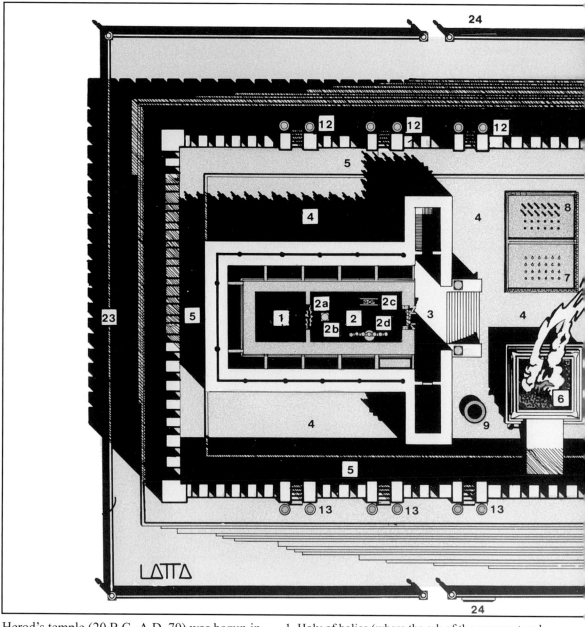

Herod's temple (20 B.C.-A.D. 70) was begun in the 18th year of King Herod the Great's reign (37-4B.C.).According to Josephus, the first-century Jewish historian, Herod's temple was constructed after removing the old foundations. The old edifice, Zerubbabel's temple, was a modest restoration of the temple of Solomon destroyed by the Babylonian conquest. The central building was completed in just two years—without any interruption of the temple services. The surrounding buildings and spacious courts, considerably enlarged, were not completed until A.D. 64. The Temple was destroyed by the Romans under the command of Titus during the second Jewish revolt in A.D.70.

1. Holy of holies (where the ark of the covenant and the giant cherubim were once enshrined).

2. Holy place.

2a. Veil (actually two giant tapestries hung before the entrance of the holy of holies to allow the high priest entry between them with exposing the sacred shrine. It was this veil that was "split in two:" upon the death of Jesus).

2b. Altar of Incense.

2c.Table of Shewbread.

2d. Seven-branched Lampstand (Great Menorah).

3. Temple porch.

4. Court of priests.

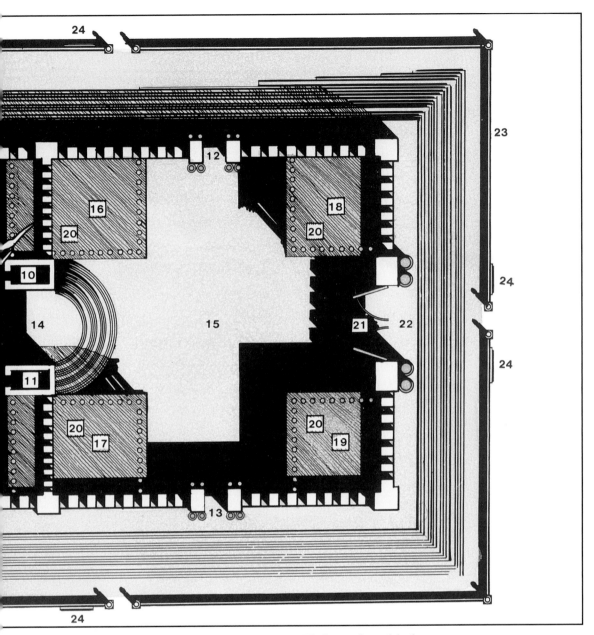

5. Court of Israel (men).

6. Altar of burnt offerings.

7. Animal tethering area.

8. Slaughtering and skinning area.

9. Laver.

10. Chamber of Phineas (storage of vestments).

11. Chamber of the bread maker.

12. North gates of the inner courts.

13. South gates of the inner courts.

14. East (Nicanor) Gate.

15. Court of women.

16. Court of Nazirites.

17. Court of woodshed.

18. Lepers' Chamber.

19. Shemanyah (possible meaning "oil of Yah").

20. Women's Balconies (for viewing Temple activities).

21. Gate Beautiful (?).

22. Terrace.

23. Soreg (three-cubit high partition).

24. Warning Inscriptions to Gentiles.

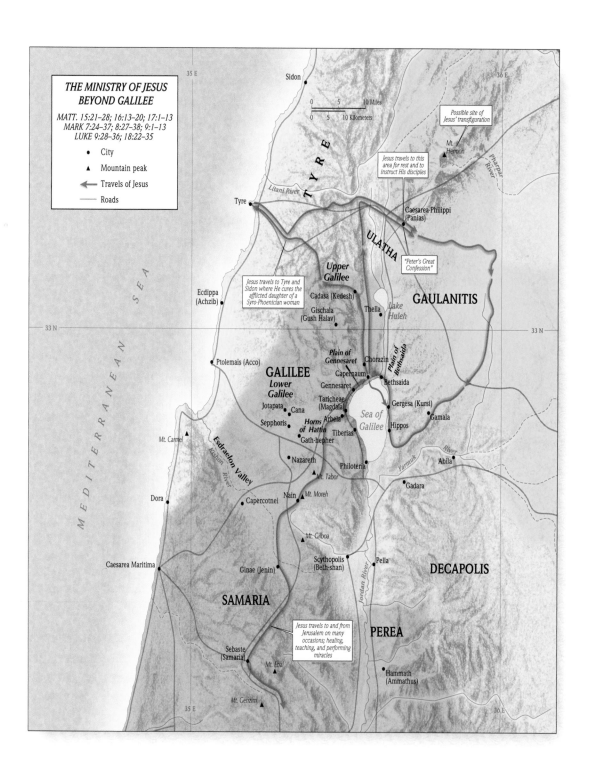

THE MINISTRY OF JESUS BEYOND GALILEE

MATT. 15:21–28; 16:13–20; 17:1–13
MARK 7:24–37; 8:27–38; 9:1–13
LUKE 9:28–36; 18:22–35

- City
▲ Mountain peak
← Travels of Jesus
— Roads

Possible site of
Jesus' transfiguration

Jesus travels to this
area for rest and to
instruct His disciples

Jesus travels to Tyre and
Sidon where He cures the
afflicted daughter of a
Syro-Phoenician woman

"Peter's Great
Confession"

Jesus travels to and from
Jerusalem on many
occasions; healing,
teaching, and performing
miracles

Sidon

Mt. Hermon

Pharpar River

Tyre

Caesarea-Philippi
(Panias)

ULATHA

Litani River

GAULANITIS

Ecdippa
(Achzib)

Upper
Galilee

Cadasa (Kedesh)

Thella

Lake
Huleh

Gischala
(Gush Halav)

33 N

33 N

Ptolemais (Acco)

Plain of
Gennesaret

Chorazin

Plain of
Bethsaida

GALILEE

Capernaum

Lower
Galilee

Gennesaret

Bethsaida

Taricheae
(Magdala)

Jotapata

Cana

Arbela

Gergesa (Kursi)

Sepphoris

Horns
of Hattin

Tiberias

Sea of
Galilee

Hippos

Gamala

Gath-hepher

MEDITERRANEAN SEA

Mt. Carmel

Esdraelon Valley

Kishon River

Nazareth

Philoteria

Yarmuk River

Abila

Mt. Tabor

Dora

Nain

Mt. Moreh

Gadara

Capercotnei

Mt. Gilboa

Caesarea Maritima

Ginae (Jenin)

Scythopolis
(Beth-shan)

Pella

DECAPOLIS

SAMARIA

Jordan River

PEREA

Sebaste
(Samaria)

Mt. Ebal

Hammath
(Ammathus)

Mt. Gerizim

35 E

36 E

0   5   10 Miles
0   5   10 Kilometers

35 E

36 E

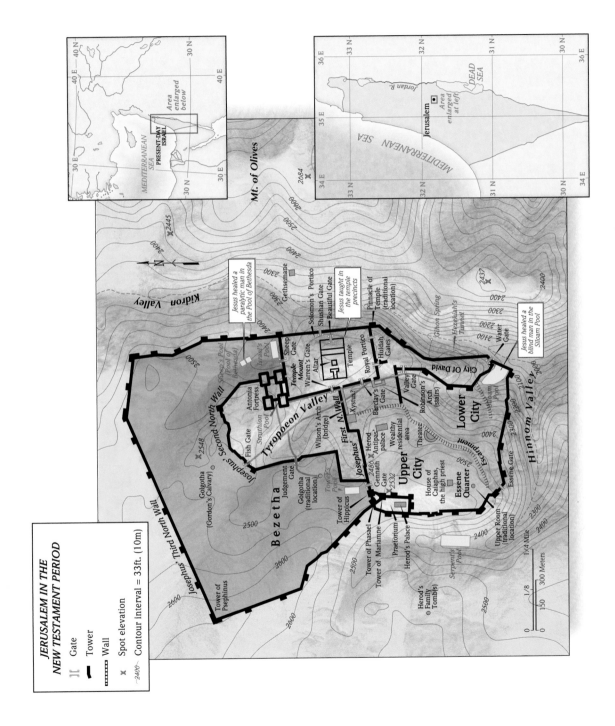

JERUSALEM IN THE
NEW TESTAMENT PERIOD

⌐L Gate

⌐ Tower

▬▬ Wall

✕ Spot elevation

~2400~ Contour interval = 33ft. (10m)

MEDITERRANEAN SEA

40 N
30 N
40 E
30 E

PRESENT-DAY ISRAEL

Area enlarged below

36 N
33 N
32 N
31 N
30 N
36 E
35 E
34 E
33 E
32 E
31 E
30 E

MEDITERRANEAN SEA

DEAD SEA

Jordan R.

Jerusalem

Area enlarged at left

Mt. of Olives

Kidron Valley

✕ 2445

✕ 2684

✕ 2437

Gethsemane

Jesus healed a paralytic man in the Pool of Bethesda

Solomon's Portico

Shushan Gate

Beautiful Gate

Jesus taught in the temple precincts

Pinnacle of Temple (traditional location)

Sheep Gate

Warren's Gate

Temple Mount

Altar

Temple

Royal Portico

Huldah Gates

Fish Gate

Antonia Fortress

Israel's Pool

Sheep's Pool (Pool of Bethesda)

Struthion Pool

Josephus' Second North Wall

Tyropoeon Valley

Wilson's Arch (bridge)

First N. Wall

Xystus?

Barclay's Gate

Robinson's Arch (stairs)

Valley Gate

City Of David

Gihon Spring

Hezekiah's Tunnel

Water Gate

Jesus healed a blind man in the Siloam Pool

Siloam Pool

Lower City

Hinnom Valley

✕ 2548

Golgotha (Gordon's Calvary)

Bezetha

Judgement Gate

Golgotha (traditional location)

Tower of Hippicus

✕ 2480

✕ 2532

Josephus'

Herod Antipas' palace

Gennath Gate

Pool?

Wealthy residential area

Theater

Upper City

House of Caiaphas, the high priest

Essene Quarter

Escarpment

Essene Gate

Josephus' Third North Wall

Tower of Psephinus

Tower of Phasael

Tower of Mariamne

Praetorium

Herod's Palace

Herod's Family Tomb(s)

Serpent's Pool

Upper Room (traditional location)

0   150   300 Meters

0   1/8   1/4 Mile

N

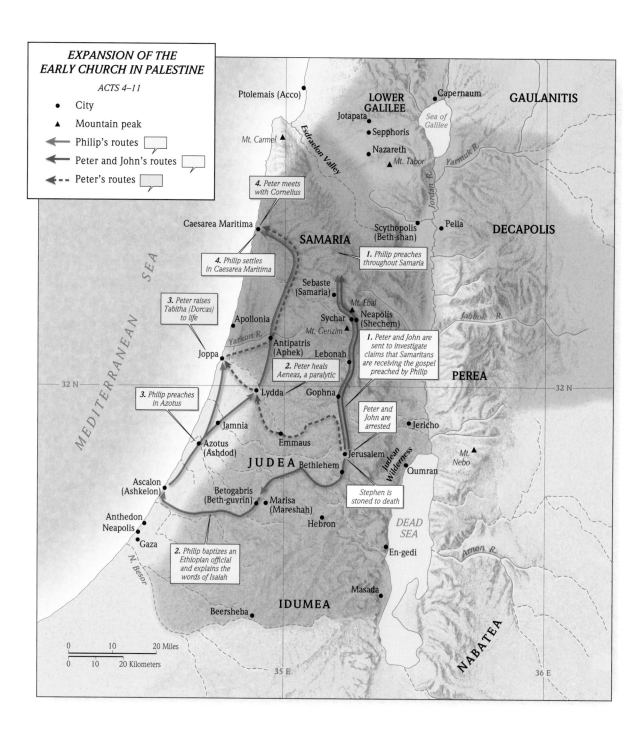

EXPANSION OF THE EARLY CHURCH IN PALESTINE

ACTS 4–11

- • City
- ▲ Mountain peak
- ⟵ Philip's routes
- ⟵ Peter and John's routes
- ⟵--- Peter's routes

4. Peter meets with Cornelius

4. Philip settles in Caesarea Maritima

3. Peter raises Tabitha (Dorcas) to life

1. Philip preaches throughout Samaria

1. Peter and John are sent to investigate claims that Samaritans are receiving the gospel preached by Philip

2. Peter heals Aeneas, a paralytic

3. Philip preaches in Azotus

Peter and John are arrested

Stephen is stoned to death

2. Philip baptizes an Ethiopian official and explains the words of Isaiah

Ptolemais (Acco)

LOWER GALILEE

Capernaum

GAULANITIS

Jotapata

Sepphoris

Sea of Galilee

Mt. Carmel

Nazareth

Mt. Tabor

Jordan R.

Yarmuk R.

Caesarea Maritima

SAMARIA

Scythopolis (Beth-shan)

Pella

DECAPOLIS

Sebaste (Samaria)

Mt. Ebal

Neapolis (Shechem)

Sychar

Mt. Gerizim

Jabbok R.

Apollonia

Yarkon R.

Antipatris (Aphek)

Lebonah

PEREA

Joppa

Lydda

Gophna

MEDITERRANEAN SEA

32 N

32 N

Jamnia

Emmaus

Jericho

Mt. Nebo

Azotus (Ashdod)

JUDEA

Bethlehem

Jerusalem

Judean Wilderness

Qumran

Ascalon (Ashkelon)

Betogabris (Beth-guvrin)

Marisa (Mareshah)

Hebron

DEAD SEA

Anthedon Neapolis

Gaza

N. Besor

En-gedi

Arnon R.

IDUMEA

Masada

Beersheba

NABATEA

0   10   20 Miles

0   10   20 Kilometers

35 E

36 E

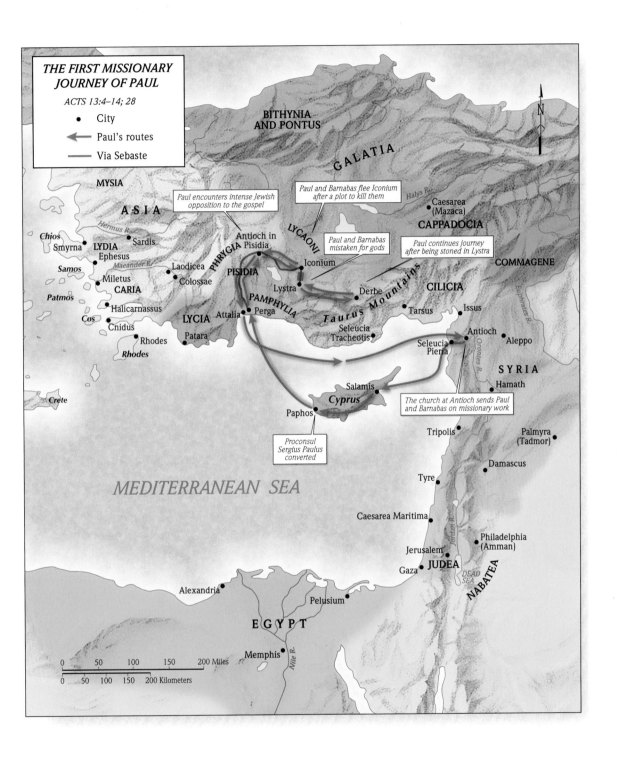

THE FIRST MISSIONARY JOURNEY OF PAUL

ACTS 13:4–14; 28

- • City
- ← Paul's routes
- Via Sebaste

BITHYNIA AND PONTUS

GALATIA

MYSIA

ASIA

Hermus R.

Chios

Smyrna LYDIA Sardis

Ephesus

Samos

Maeander R. Laodicea

Miletus Colossae

CARIA

Patmos

Halicarnassus

Cos

Cnidus

Rhodes

Rhodes Patara

Crete

PHRYGIA

PISIDIA

Antioch in Pisidia

LYCAONI

Iconium

Lystra

Derbe

Paul encounters intense Jewish opposition to the gospel

Paul and Barnabas flee Iconium after a plot to kill them

Paul and Barnabas mistaken for gods

Paul continues journey after being stoned in Lystra

Halys R.

Caesarea (Mazaca)

CAPPADOCIA

COMMAGENE

Euphrates R.

Taurus Mountains

CILICIA

Tarsus

Issus

Antioch

Aleppo

SYRIA

Hamath

PAMPHYLIA

Attalia Perga

LYCIA

Seleucia Tracheotis

Seleucia Pieria

Orontes R.

Salamis

Cyprus

Paphos

The church at Antioch sends Paul and Barnabas on missionary work

Proconsul Sergius Paulus converted

MEDITERRANEAN SEA

Tripolis

Palmyra (Tadmor)

Damascus

Tyre

Caesarea Maritima

Jordan R.

Philadelphia (Amman)

Jerusalem

Gaza JUDEA

DEAD SEA

NABATEA

Alexandria

Pelusium

EGYPT

Memphis

Nile R.

| 0 | 50 | 100 | 150 | 200 Miles |

| 0 | 50 | 100 | 150 | 200 Kilometers |

N

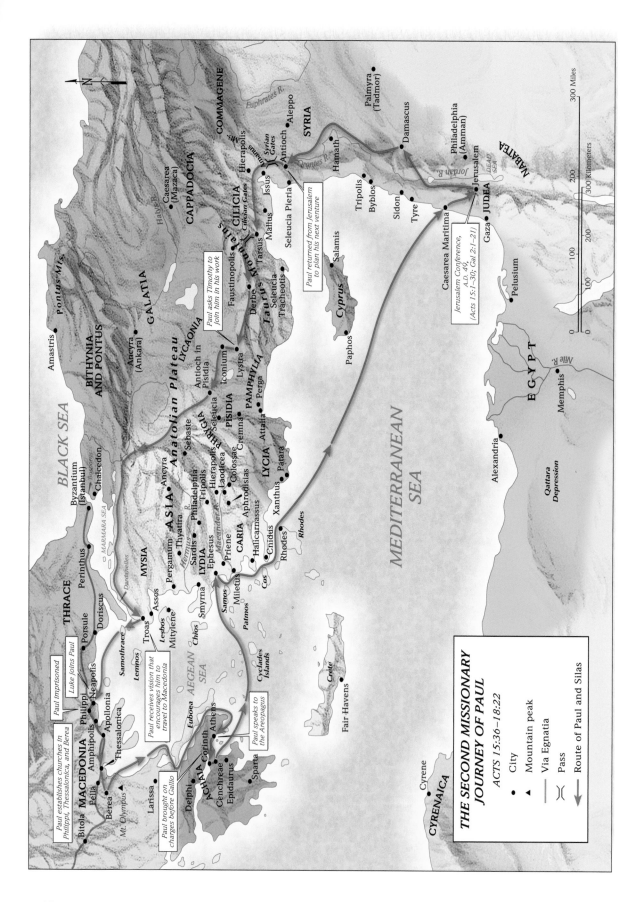

THE SECOND MISSIONARY JOURNEY OF PAUL

ACTS 15:36–18:22

- ● City
- ▲ Mountain peak
- Via Egnatia
-)—(Pass
- → Route of Paul and Silas

Paul asks Timothy to join him in his work

Paul returned from Jerusalem to plan his next venture

Jerusalem Conference, A.D. 49, (Acts 15:1–30; Gal 2:1–21)

Paul imprisoned

Luke joins Paul

Paul establishes churches in Philippi, Thessalonica, and Berea

Paul receives vision that encourages him to travel to Macedonia

Paul speaks to the Areopagus

Paul brought on charges before Gallio

BLACK SEA

MEDITERRANEAN SEA

AEGEAN SEA

MARMARA SEA

DEAD SEA

300 Miles

300 Kilometers

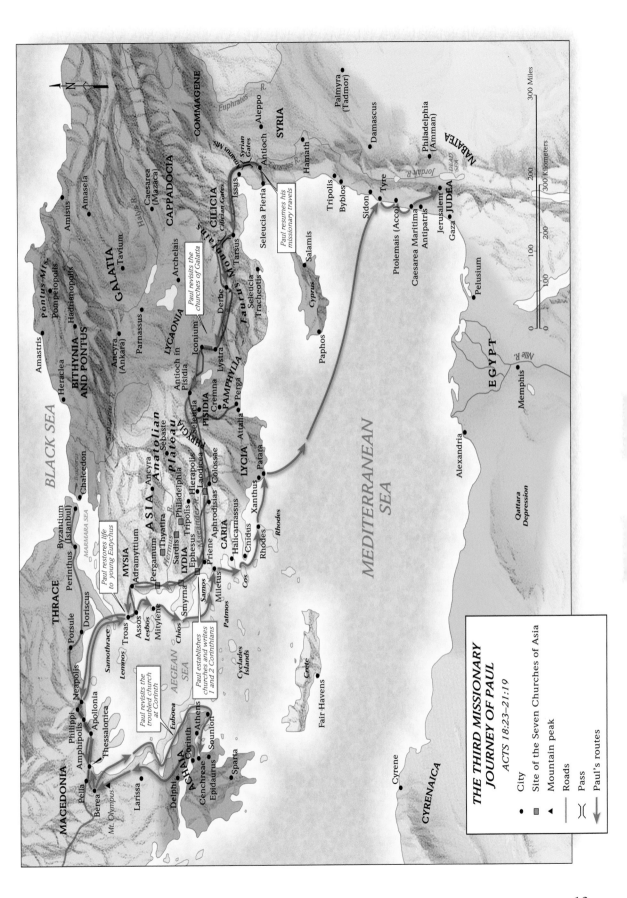

THE THIRD MISSIONARY
JOURNEY OF PAUL
ACTS 18:23–21:19

• City
▪ Site of the Seven Churches of Asia
▲ Mountain peak
) (Pass
↓ Paul's routes
— Roads

Paul revisits the churches of Galatia

Paul resumes his missionary travels

Paul restores life to young Eutychus

Paul establishes churches and writes 1 and 2 Corinthians

Paul revisits the troubled church at Corinth

300 Miles
300 Kilometers

13

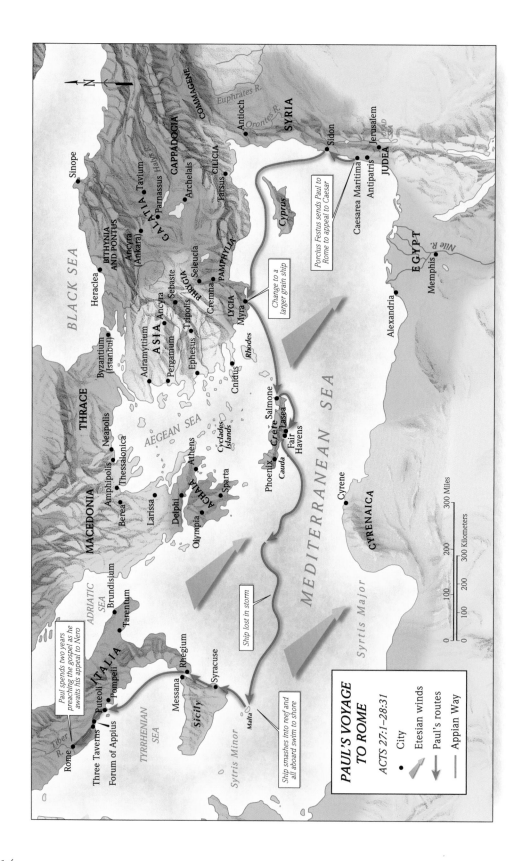

PAUL'S VOYAGE TO ROME

ACTS 27:1–28:31

- Etesian winds
- Paul's routes
- Appian Way
- City

Paul spends two years preaching the gospel as he awaits his appeal to Nero

Ship smashes into reef and all aboard swim to shore

Ship lost in storm

Porcius Festus sends Paul to Rome to appeal to Caesar

Change to a larger grain ship

BLACK SEA

Sinope

Heraclea

Byzantium (Istanbul)

THRACE

Neapolis

Amphipolis

Thessalonica

Berea

Larissa

Delphi

Olympia

ACHAIA

Athens

Sparta

MACEDONIA

AEGEAN SEA

Cyclades Islands

ASIA

Adramyttium

Pergamum

Ephesus

Ancyra

Cnidus

BITHYNIA AND PONTIUS

Ancyra (Ankara)

GALATIA

Tavium

Parnassus Halys

CAPPADOCIA

Archelais

COMMAGENE

Euphrates R.

Antioch

Orontes R.

SYRIA

Sidon

Caesarea Maritima

Antipatris

Jerusalem

DEAD SEA

JUDEA

Tarsus

CILICIA

Sebaste

Tripolis

Seleucia

PHRYGIA

Cremna

PAMPHYLIA

LYCIA

Myra

Rhodes

Cyprus

Salmone

Lasea

Crete

Fair Havens

Phoenix

Cauda

MEDITERRANEAN SEA

Cyrene

CYRENAICA

Syrtis Major

Syrtis Minor

EGYPT

Nile R.

Memphis

Alexandria

Malta

Syracuse

Messana

Sicily

Rhegium

ITALIA

Pompeii

Puteoli

Tarentum

Brundisium

ADRIATIC SEA

TYRRHENIAN SEA

Rome

Tiber R.

Three Taverns

Forum of Appius

300 Miles

300 Kilometers

0   100   200

0   100   200   300

N

14

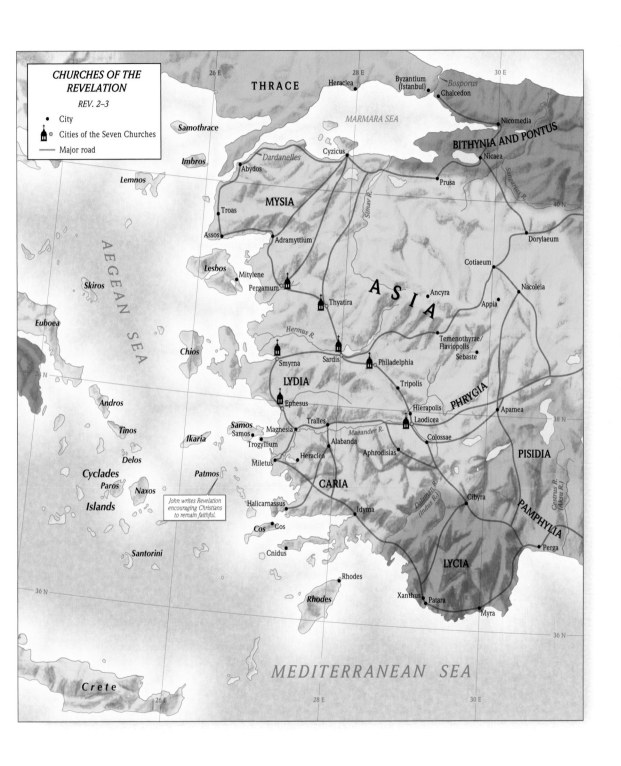

CHURCHES OF THE
REVELATION

REV. 2–3

• City

🏛 Cities of the Seven Churches

— Major road

THRACE

Heraclea

Byzantium
(Istanbul)

Bosporus

Chalcedon

MARMARA SEA

Nicomedia

BITHYNIA AND PONTUS

Samothrace

Nicaea

Imbros

Dardanelles

Cyzicus

Prusa

Sangarius R.

Abydos

Lemnos

Troas

MYSIA

Simav R.

40 N

Dorylaeum

Assos

Adramyttium

Cotiaeum

Lesbos

Mitylene

Nacoleia

AEGEAN SEA

Skiros

Pergamum

ASIA

Ancyra

Appia

Thyatira

Temenothyrae/
Flaviopolis

Sebaste

Euboea

Chios

Hermus R.

Smyrna

Sardis

Philadelphia

38 N

LYDIA

Tripolis

PHRYGIA

Andros

Ephesus

Hierapolis

Apamea

Tinos

Samos

Magnesia

Tralles

Laodicea

38 N

Ikaria

Samos

Maeander R.

Trogyllium

Alabanda

Colossae

Delos

Miletus

Heraclea

Aphrodisias

PISIDIA

Cyclades

Paros

Patmos

CARIA

Naxos

Islands

Santorini

John writes Revelation
encouraging Christians
to remain faithful.

Halicarnassus

Idyma

*Dalaman R.
(Indus R.)*

Cibyra

PAMPHYLIA

*Cestrus R.
(Aksu R.)*

Cos

Cos

Perga

Cnidus

LYCIA

Rhodes

36 N

Rhodes

Xanthus

Patara

Myra

36 N

MEDITERRANEAN SEA

Crete

26 E

28 E

30 E

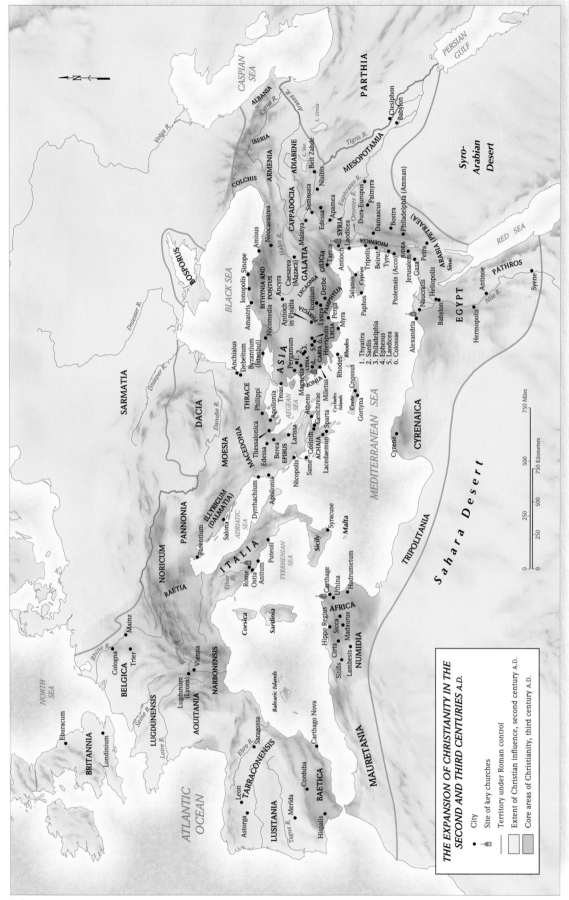

THE EXPANSION OF CHRISTIANITY IN THE
SECOND AND THIRD CENTURIES A.D.

- • City
- ⌂ Site of key churches
- ── Territory under Roman control
- ── Extent of Christian influence, second century A.D.
- ── Core areas of Christianity, third century A.D.

1. Thyatira
2. Sardis
3. Philadelphia
4. Ephesus
5. Laodicea
6. Colossae

0   250   500   750 Miles
0   250   500   750 Kilometers